THE SODDYSSEY

and other
**TALES of
SUPERNATURAL
LAW**

by **BATTON LASH**

EXHIBIT
A
PRESS

SAN DIEGO, CALIFORNIA

Writer/artist: Batton Lash
Editor/letterer: Jackie Estrada
Technical consultant: Mitch Berger, Esq.
Art and production assistant: Melissa Uran (including art for
   "The Returns of Roger Rizzoli")
Art assists: Derek Ozawa
Staff 'n stuff: S. Derma

Dedicated to Mitch Berger

Acknowledgments

"The * Files" originally appeared in *Wolff & Byrd, Counselors of the Macabre* issue 9; "I'm Carrying Satan's Baby" originally appeared in *Wolff & Byrd, Counselors of the Macabre* issue 10; the stories included in "Strange Bedfellows" originally appeared in *Wolff & Byrd, Counselors of the Macabre* issue 11; "Guardian Angels and Personal Injuries" originally appeared in *Wolff & Byrd, Counselors of the Macabre* issue 12; "Triskaidekaphobia" originally appeared in *Wolff & Byrd, Counselors of the Macabre* issue 13; "Bad Blood" originally appeared in *Wolff & Byrd, Counselors of the Macabre* issue 14; "The Statue of Limitations," "The Returns of Roger Rizzoli," and "The Littlest Loup Garou" originally appeared in *Wolff & Byrd, Counselors of the Macabre* issue 15; "Sodd, We Hardly Knew Ye" originally appeared in *Wolff & Byrd, Counselors of the Macabre* issue 16. All stories have been "remastered" for this collection: Most have been completely relettered, and many have been retoned; in some cases art has been redrawn.

Special thanks go to the following artists who contributed to the final chapter of "The Soddyssey": Steve Bissette, Jeff Smith, Bernie Wrightson, Phil Hester, Charles Vess, and Shawn McManus. Also, a tip of the barrister's wig to Michael T. Gilbert for editing and John Clark for lettering on "The Littlest Loup Garou."

A note about the title: Several of the stories in this collection focus on Sodd, The Thing Called It, a "walking plant" represented by the law firm of Wolff & Byrd, Counselors of the Macabre. Sodd's saga concludes with the final story in this volume.

10 9 8 7 6 5 4 3 2 1

Printed in the United States of America

ISBN: 0-9815519-0-4
ISBN 13: 978-0-9815519-0-6

Contents

Introduction

I don't like lawyers.

With good reason. Since 1996 I've been sued three times for no cause. In each case those suits eventually resulted in a summary judgment dismissing all claims with prejudice (which means that's the end of it—they can't be reopened).

Notice I said "eventually." Before each of those dismissals I had to plod through years of interrogatories and depositions. And even though the cases were all proven to be without merit, my malpractice premiums went up.

The plaintiffs' attorneys had cast wide nets and didn't give a damn who they hauled in. It cost them next to nothing to send out extra subpoenas. Like buying extra lottery tickets. Hey, who knows? Maybe one will pay off. And in the end I had no recourse against them, so they went their merry ways, free to do the same again and again.

So I repeat: I don't like lawyers.

But I do like Wolff and Byrd.

I like the stories, mainly because they're *stories*—they start, go someplace, and then end in a way that's relevant and adds symmetry to what has gone before. You don't see that enough in comics these days. Hardly at all. They've become soap operas. Sure, *W&B* has some longer arcs and recurring clients, but they act as bridges between the stories without *becoming* the stories.

Another joy of the series is its use of the English language. Batton Lash does not write down to his readers. His love of language is evident on every page. And that's fitting. Alanna and Jeff are lawyers; their weapons are words, so we expect them to use them well. And they do. Their aim is true. Their repartee is bright, clever, and witty. Wordplay abounds. ("The Laws of Gravidity" . . . "The Statue of Limitations" . . . ha!) I don't know about you, but I love whimsical wordplay, and even a bad pun is better than no pun.

But I take special pleasure in the cultural references peppered throughout the stories. (Dennis Miller, eat your heart out.) I'm not talking about the inspiration for "The * Files"— that'd be obvious; no, I mean the origin of the names of the two FBI agents, and the town of Ft. Charles, NJ. Doesn't that judge in "I'm Carrying Satan's Baby!" look familiar? Did you have any doubt who Dr. Skratzsch might be when you heard his name and saw the acronym for Doctor's In-utero Services? (Keeping up here?) And consider the cast of "Personal Injuries and Guardian Angels"—the characterizations are spot on, although I do miss a certain raspy-voiced valet.

Wolff and Byrd's relationship rings true. They're rounded characters with distinct personalities and lives outside the plots; they care about each other both personally and professionally.

But I like Wolff and Byrd most of all because they tend to do the right thing. They take on the system on behalf of the outcasts, the "different" ones, the rejects . . . the *monsters*, if you will. They defend the sanctity of the individual and (as long as he, she, or it doesn't initiate force) the right to be different.

Yeah. Wolff and Byrd . . . they could almost make me like lawyers.

Almost.

F. Paul Wilson
author, *The Keep*,
"Repairman Jack" series

v

THE SODDYSSEY

and other
**TALES of
SUPERNATURAL
LAW**

Part One

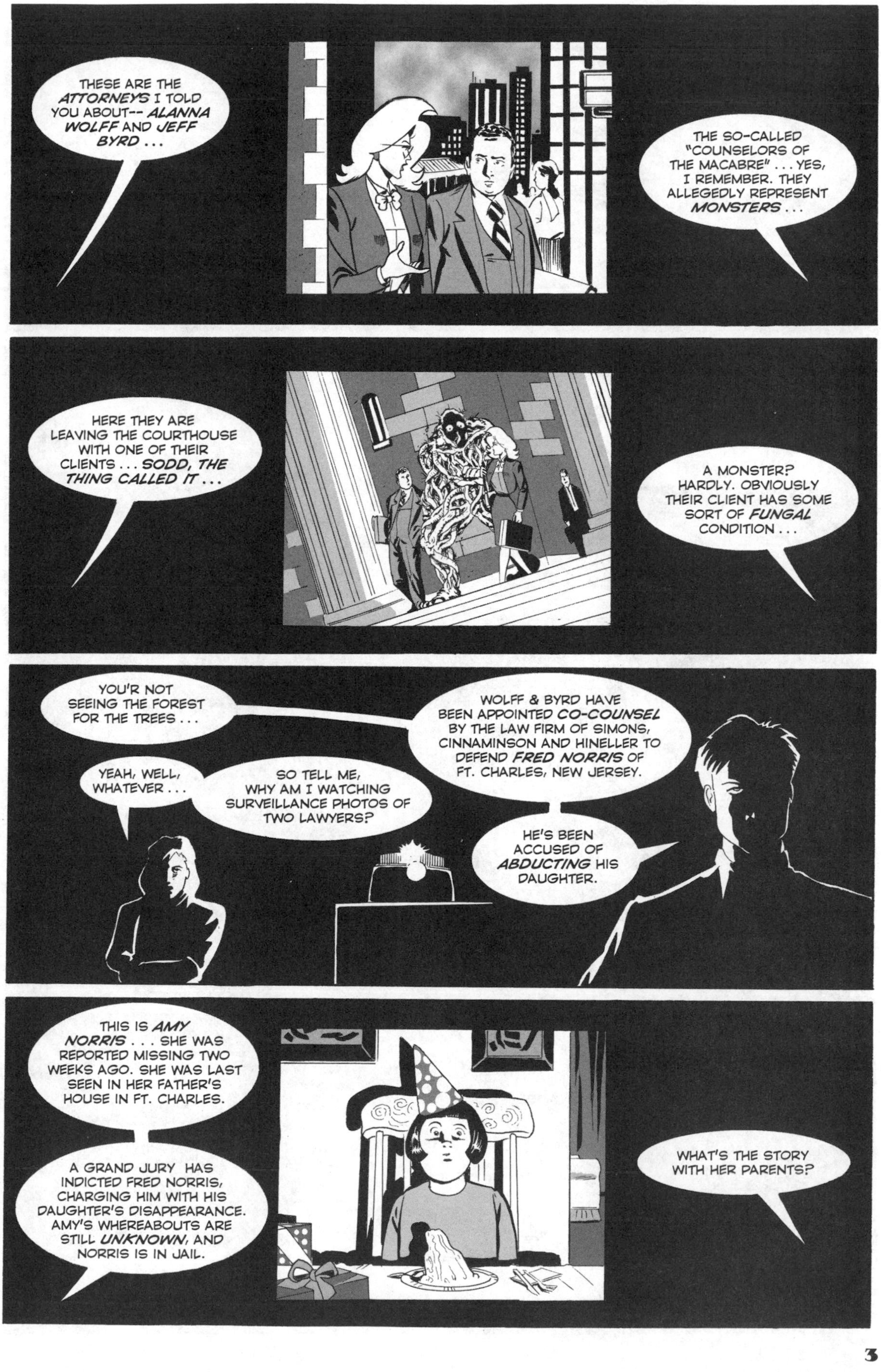
THESE ARE THE ATTORNEYS I TOLD YOU ABOUT-- ALANNA WOLFF AND JEFF BYRD . . .
THE SO-CALLED "COUNSELORS OF THE MACABRE" . . . YES, I REMEMBER. THEY ALLEGEDLY REPRESENT MONSTERS . . .
HERE THEY ARE LEAVING THE COURTHOUSE WITH ONE OF THEIR CLIENTS . . . SODD, THE THING CALLED IT . . .
A MONSTER? HARDLY. OBVIOUSLY THEIR CLIENT HAS SOME SORT OF FUNGAL CONDITION . . .
YOU'R NOT SEEING THE FOREST FOR THE TREES . . .
WOLFF & BYRD HAVE BEEN APPOINTED CO-COUNSEL BY THE LAW FIRM OF SIMONS, CINNAMINSON AND HINELLER TO DEFEND FRED NORRIS OF FT. CHARLES, NEW JERSEY.
YEAH, WELL, WHATEVER . . .
SO TELL ME, WHY AM I WATCHING SURVEILLANCE PHOTOS OF TWO LAWYERS?
HE'S BEEN ACCUSED OF ABDUCTING HIS DAUGHTER.
THIS IS AMY NORRIS . . . SHE WAS REPORTED MISSING TWO WEEKS AGO. SHE WAS LAST SEEN IN HER FATHER'S HOUSE IN FT. CHARLES.
A GRAND JURY HAS INDICTED FRED NORRIS, CHARGING HIM WITH HIS DAUGHTER'S DISAPPEARANCE. AMY'S WHEREABOUTS ARE STILL UNKNOWN, AND NORRIS IS IN JAIL.
WHAT'S THE STORY WITH HER PARENTS?

THE PARENTS ARE *DIVORCED*-- AMY'S MOTHER, *ALLISON,* IS AN ACTRESS. SHE WON CUSTODY OF THE CHILD. FRED GETS HIS DAUGHTER ON ALTERNATING WEEKENDS.

HERE ARE FRED AND ALLISON IN HAPPIER TIMES . . .

LOOKS LIKE A MATCH MADE IN HEAVEN. WHAT BROUGHT THESE STAR-CROSSED LOVERS TOGETHER?

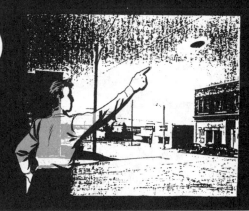

WHAT ELSE? THE *STARS* THEMSELVES. FRED AND ALLISON MET AT A NEW AGE CONVENTION. ALLISON WAS THERE TO PICK UP SOME NEW CRYSTALS . . .

FRED IS HEAVILY INTO *EXTRATERRESTRIAL STUDIES.* SHE MET HIM AT HIS SLIDE SHOW OF PHOTOS HE'D TAKEN OF *UFOs.*

OH, BOY, HERE WE GO . . .

SO WHAT ARE YOU SAYING? THAT FRED THINKS A *UFO* ABDUCTED HIS DAUGHTER?

NORRIS THINKS THE UFO WAS COMING FOR *HIM*-- HE CLAIMS HE WAS IN RADIO CONTACT WITH THE SPACECRAFT SHORTLY BEFORE AMY DIS-APPEARED . . .

WHAT SPACECRAFT? YOU DON'T MEAN THAT *SMUDGE,* DO YOU?

THAT'S *NO* SMUDGE. LOOK *CLOSER*-- YOU CAN MAKE OUT THE SAUCER SHAPE--

YOU'RE NOT LOOKING HARD ENOUGH!

IT LOOKS EVEN *BLURRIER* UP CLOSE

I CAN'T SEE SOMETHING THAT'S NOT THERE

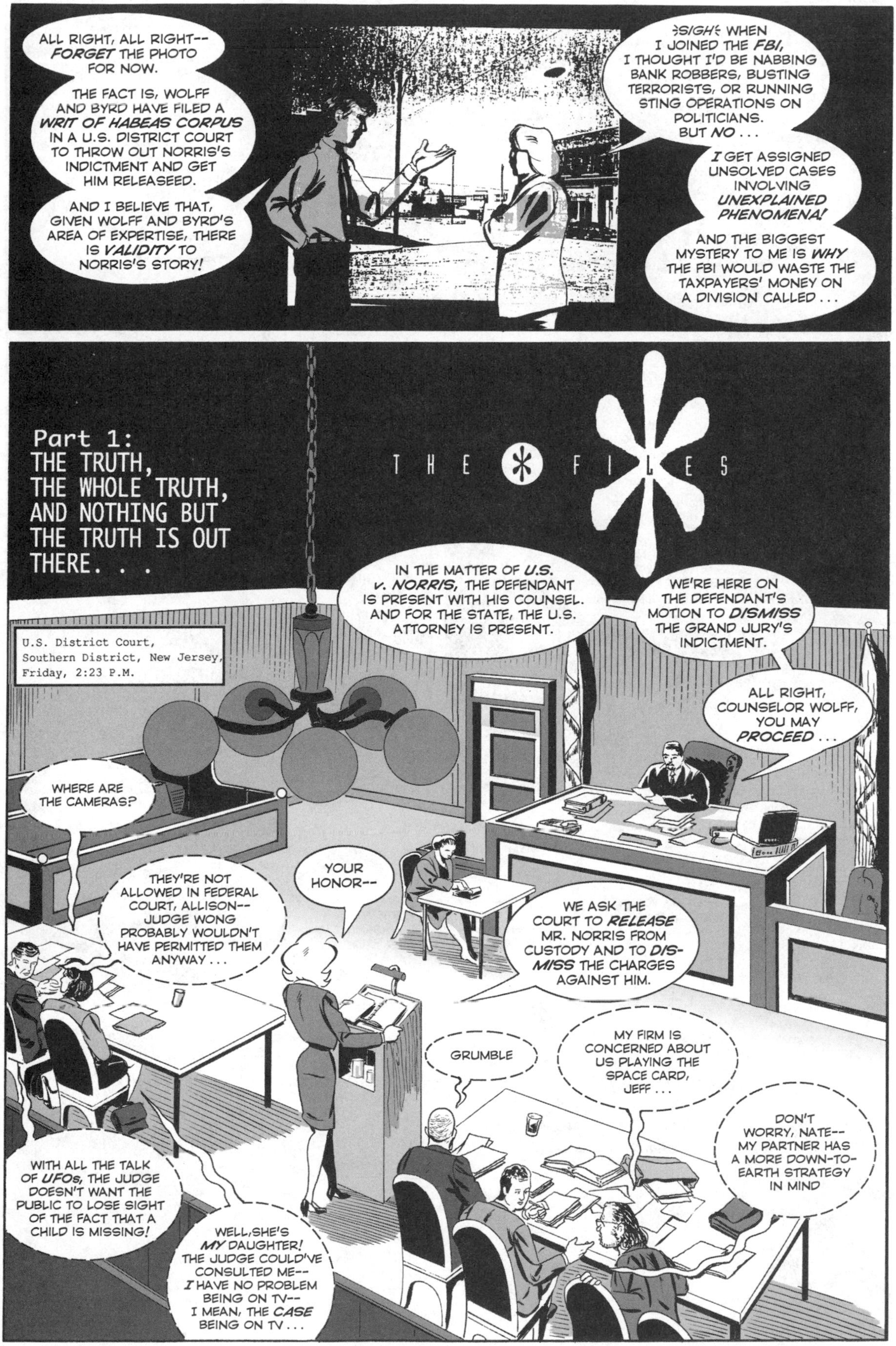
ALL RIGHT, ALL RIGHT-- *FORGET* THE PHOTO FOR NOW.
THE FACT IS, WOLFF AND BYRD HAVE FILED A *WRIT OF HABEAS CORPUS* IN A U.S. DISTRICT COURT TO THROW OUT NORRIS'S INDICTMENT AND GET HIM RELEASEED.
AND I BELIEVE THAT, GIVEN WOLFF AND BYRD'S AREA OF EXPERTISE, THERE IS *VALIDITY* TO NORRIS'S STORY!
SIGH WHEN I JOINED THE *FBI*, I THOUGHT I'D BE NABBING BANK ROBBERS, BUSTING TERRORISTS, OR RUNNING STING OPERATIONS ON POLITICIANS. BUT *NO* . . .
I GET ASSIGNED UNSOLVED CASES INVOLVING *UNEXPLAINED PHENOMENA!*
AND THE BIGGEST MYSTERY TO ME IS *WHY* THE FBI WOULD WASTE THE TAXPAYERS' MONEY ON A DIVISION CALLED . . .
Part 1:
THE TRUTH, THE WHOLE TRUTH, AND NOTHING BUT THE TRUTH IS OUT THERE. . .
THE * FILES
U.S. District Court, Southern District, New Jersey, Friday, 2:23 P.M.
IN THE MATTER OF *U.S. v. NORRIS,* THE DEFENDANT IS PRESENT WITH HIS COUNSEL. AND FOR THE STATE, THE U.S. ATTORNEY IS PRESENT.
WE'RE HERE ON THE DEFENDANT'S MOTION TO *DISMISS* THE GRAND JURY'S INDICTMENT.
ALL RIGHT, COUNSELOR WOLFF, YOU MAY *PROCEED* . . .
WHERE ARE THE CAMERAS?
THEY'RE NOT ALLOWED IN FEDERAL COURT, ALLISON-- JUDGE WONG PROBABLY WOULDN'T HAVE PERMITTED THEM ANYWAY . . .
YOUR HONOR--
WE ASK THE COURT TO *RELEASE* MR. NORRIS FROM CUSTODY AND TO *DISMISS* THE CHARGES AGAINST HIM.
GRUMBLE
MY FIRM IS CONCERNED ABOUT US PLAYING THE SPACE CARD, JEFF . . .
DON'T WORRY, NATE-- MY PARTNER HAS A MORE DOWN-TO-EARTH STRATEGY IN MIND
WITH ALL THE TALK OF *UFOs*, THE JUDGE DOESN'T WANT THE PUBLIC TO LOSE SIGHT OF THE FACT THAT A CHILD IS MISSING!
WELL, SHE'S *MY* DAUGHTER! THE JUDGE COULD'VE CONSULTED ME-- *I* HAVE NO PROBLEM BEING ON TV-- I MEAN, THE *CASE* BEING ON TV . . .

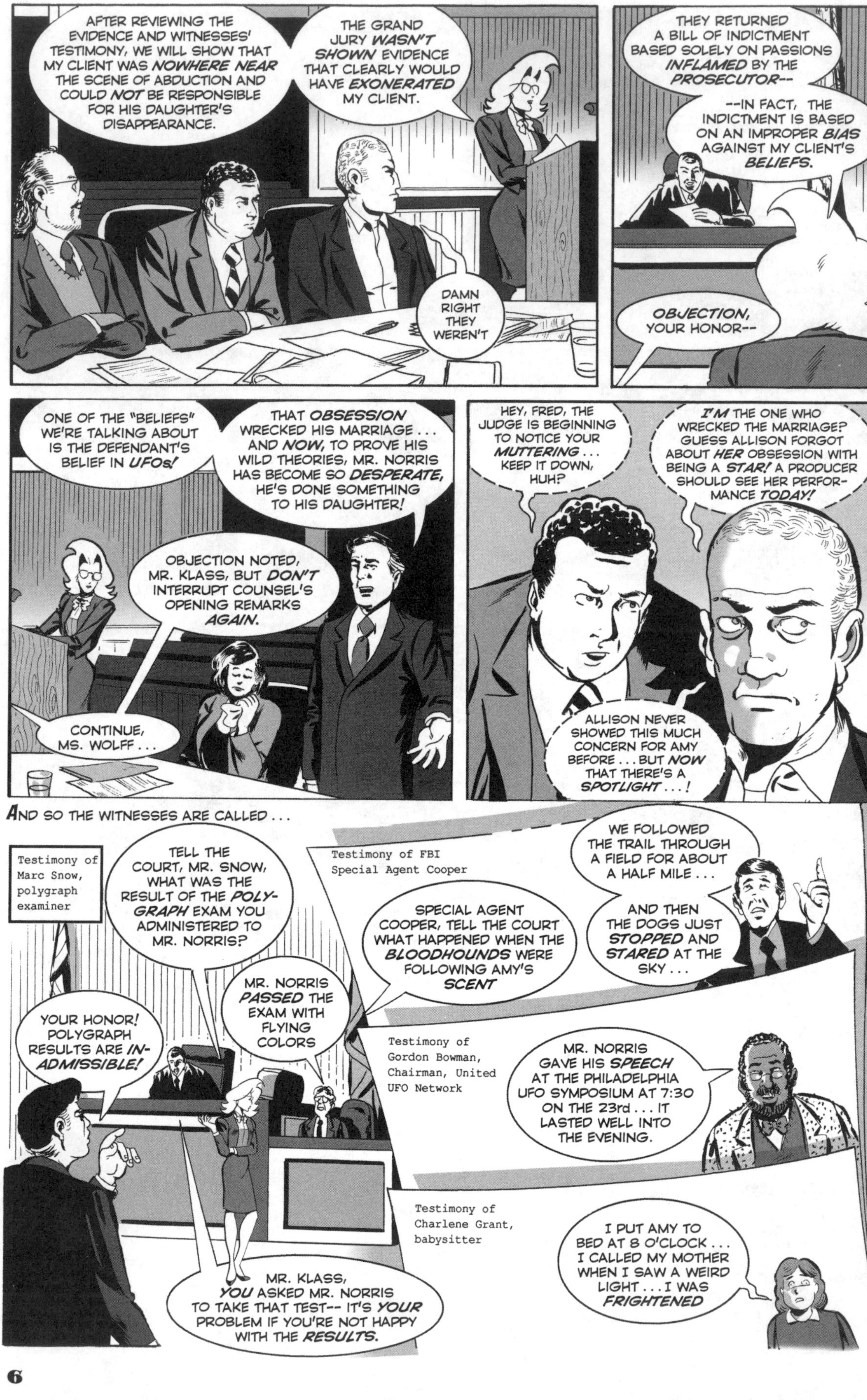
AFTER REVIEWING THE EVIDENCE AND WITNESSES' TESTIMONY, WE WILL SHOW THAT MY CLIENT WAS NOWHERE NEAR THE SCENE OF ABDUCTION AND COULD NOT BE RESPONSIBLE FOR HIS DAUGHTER'S DISAPPEARANCE.
THE GRAND JURY WASN'T SHOWN EVIDENCE THAT CLEARLY WOULD HAVE EXONERATED MY CLIENT.
DAMN RIGHT THEY WEREN'T
THEY RETURNED A BILL OF INDICTMENT BASED SOLELY ON PASSIONS INFLAMED BY THE PROSECUTOR--
--IN FACT, THE INDICTMENT IS BASED ON AN IMPROPER BIAS AGAINST MY CLIENT'S BELIEFS.
OBJECTION, YOUR HONOR--
ONE OF THE "BELIEFS" WE'RE TALKING ABOUT IS THE DEFENDANT'S BELIEF IN UFOs!
THAT OBSESSION WRECKED HIS MARRIAGE . . . AND NOW, TO PROVE HIS WILD THEORIES, MR. NORRIS HAS BECOME SO DESPERATE, HE'S DONE SOMETHING TO HIS DAUGHTER!
OBJECTION NOTED, MR. KLASS, BUT DON'T INTERRUPT COUNSEL'S OPENING REMARKS AGAIN.
CONTINUE, MS. WOLFF . . .
HEY, FRED, THE JUDGE IS BEGINNING TO NOTICE YOUR MUTTERING . . . KEEP IT DOWN, HUH?
I'M THE ONE WHO WRECKED THE MARRIAGE? GUESS ALLISON FORGOT ABOUT HER OBSESSION WITH BEING A STAR! A PRODUCER SHOULD SEE HER PERFORMANCE TODAY!
ALLISON NEVER SHOWED THIS MUCH CONCERN FOR AMY BEFORE . . . BUT NOW THAT THERE'S A SPOTLIGHT . . . !
AND SO THE WITNESSES ARE CALLED . . .
Testimony of Marc Snow, polygraph examiner
TELL THE COURT, MR. SNOW, WHAT WAS THE RESULT OF THE POLYGRAPH EXAM YOU ADMINISTERED TO MR. NORRIS?
MR. NORRIS PASSED THE EXAM WITH FLYING COLORS
YOUR HONOR! POLYGRAPH RESULTS ARE INADMISSIBLE!
MR. KLASS, YOU ASKED MR. NORRIS TO TAKE THAT TEST-- IT'S YOUR PROBLEM IF YOU'RE NOT HAPPY WITH THE RESULTS.
Testimony of FBI Special Agent Cooper
SPECIAL AGENT COOPER, TELL THE COURT WHAT HAPPENED WHEN THE BLOODHOUNDS WERE FOLLOWING AMY'S SCENT
WE FOLLOWED THE TRAIL THROUGH A FIELD FOR ABOUT A HALF MILE . . .
AND THEN THE DOGS JUST STOPPED AND STARED AT THE SKY . . .
Testimony of Gordon Bowman, Chairman, United UFO Network
MR. NORRIS GAVE HIS SPEECH AT THE PHILADELPHIA UFO SYMPOSIUM AT 7:30 ON THE 23rd . . . IT LASTED WELL INTO THE EVENING.
Testimony of Charlene Grant, babysitter
I PUT AMY TO BED AT 8 O'CLOCK . . . I CALLED MY MOTHER WHEN I SAW A WEIRD LIGHT . . . I WAS FRIGHTENED

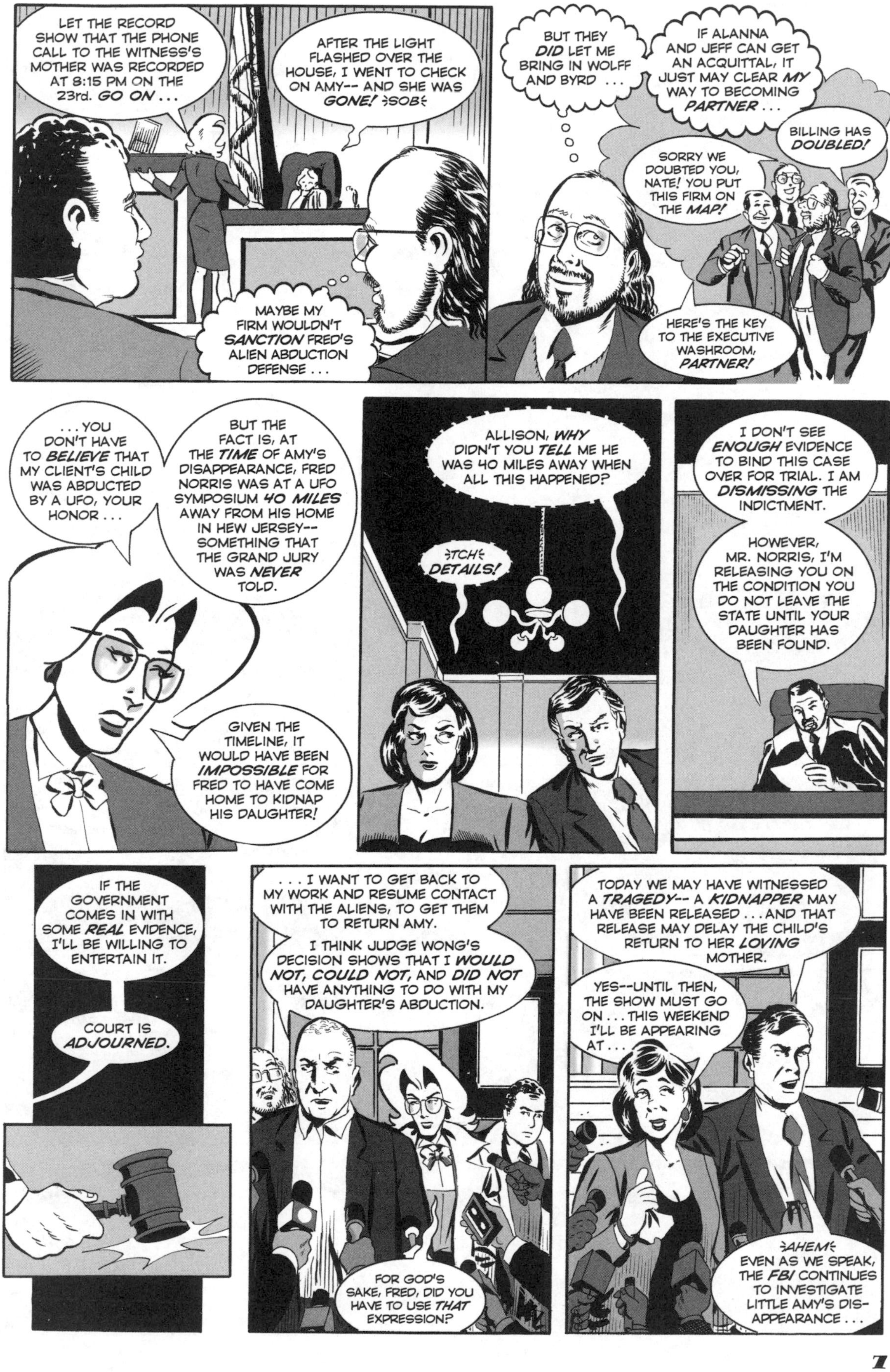
LET THE RECORD SHOW THAT THE PHONE CALL TO THE WITNESS'S MOTHER WAS RECORDED AT 8:15 PM ON THE 23rd. GO ON . . .
AFTER THE LIGHT FLASHED OVER THE HOUSE, I WENT TO CHECK ON AMY-- AND SHE WAS GONE! SOB
MAYBE MY FIRM WOULDN'T SANCTION FRED'S ALIEN ABDUCTION DEFENSE . . .
BUT THEY DID LET ME BRING IN WOLFF AND BYRD . . .
IF ALANNA AND JEFF CAN GET AN ACQUITTAL, IT JUST MAY CLEAR MY WAY TO BECOMING PARTNER . . .
BILLING HAS DOUBLED!
SORRY WE DOUBTED YOU, NATE! YOU PUT THIS FIRM ON THE MAP!
HERE'S THE KEY TO THE EXECUTIVE WASHROOM, PARTNER!
. . . YOU DON'T HAVE TO BELIEVE THAT MY CLIENT'S CHILD WAS ABDUCTED BY A UFO, YOUR HONOR . . .
BUT THE FACT IS, AT THE TIME OF AMY'S DISAPPEARANCE, FRED NORRIS WAS AT A UFO SYMPOSIUM 40 MILES AWAY FROM HIS HOME IN HEW JERSEY-- SOMETHING THAT THE GRAND JURY WAS NEVER TOLD.
GIVEN THE TIMELINE, IT WOULD HAVE BEEN IMPOSSIBLE FOR FRED TO HAVE COME HOME TO KIDNAP HIS DAUGHTER!
ALLISON, WHY DIDN'T YOU TELL ME HE WAS 40 MILES AWAY WHEN ALL THIS HAPPENED?
TCH DETAILS!
I DON'T SEE ENOUGH EVIDENCE TO BIND THIS CASE OVER FOR TRIAL. I AM DISMISSING THE INDICTMENT.
HOWEVER, MR. NORRIS, I'M RELEASING YOU ON THE CONDITION YOU DO NOT LEAVE THE STATE UNTIL YOUR DAUGHTER HAS BEEN FOUND.
IF THE GOVERNMENT COMES IN WITH SOME REAL EVIDENCE, I'LL BE WILLING TO ENTERTAIN IT.
COURT IS ADJOURNED.
. . . I WANT TO GET BACK TO MY WORK AND RESUME CONTACT WITH THE ALIENS, TO GET THEM TO RETURN AMY.
I THINK JUDGE WONG'S DECISION SHOWS THAT I WOULD NOT, COULD NOT, AND DID NOT HAVE ANYTHING TO DO WITH MY DAUGHTER'S ABDUCTION.
FOR GOD'S SAKE, FRED, DID YOU HAVE TO USE THAT EXPRESSION?
TODAY WE MAY HAVE WITNESSED A TRAGEDY-- A KIDNAPPER MAY HAVE BEEN RELEASED . . . AND THAT RELEASE MAY DELAY THE CHILD'S RETURN TO HER LOVING MOTHER.
YES--UNTIL THEN, THE SHOW MUST GO ON . . . THIS WEEKEND I'LL BE APPEARING AT . . .
AHEM
EVEN AS WE SPEAK, THE FBI CONTINUES TO INVESTIGATE LITTLE AMY'S DIS-APPEARANCE . . .

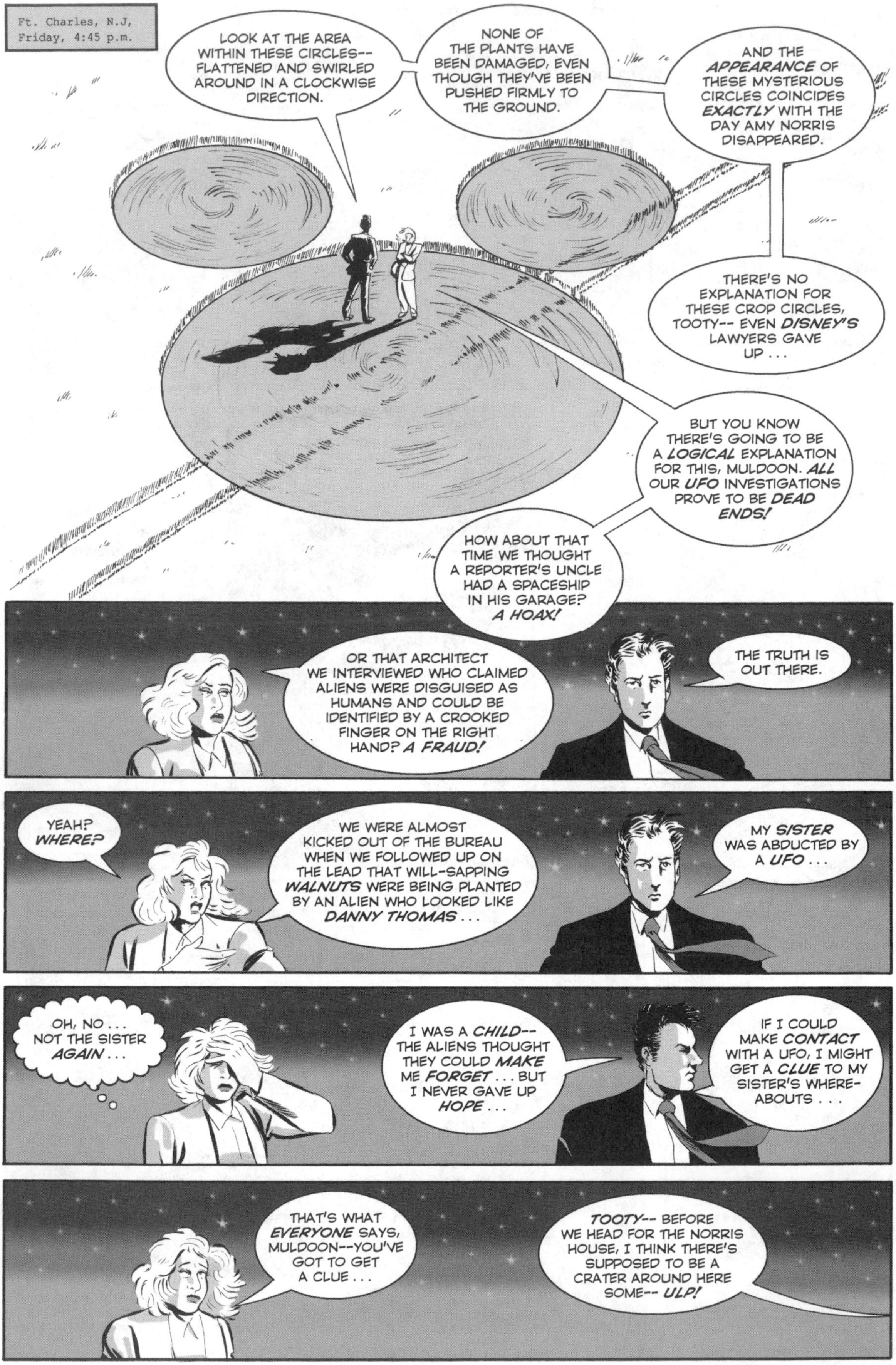
Ft. Charles, N.J, Friday, 4:45 p.m.
LOOK AT THE AREA WITHIN THESE CIRCLES-- FLATTENED AND SWIRLED AROUND IN A CLOCKWISE DIRECTION.
NONE OF THE PLANTS HAVE BEEN DAMAGED, EVEN THOUGH THEY'VE BEEN PUSHED FIRMLY TO THE GROUND.
AND THE APPEARANCE OF THESE MYSTERIOUS CIRCLES COINCIDES EXACTLY WITH THE DAY AMY NORRIS DISAPPEARED.
THERE'S NO EXPLANATION FOR THESE CROP CIRCLES, TOOTY-- EVEN DISNEY'S LAWYERS GAVE UP . . .
BUT YOU KNOW THERE'S GOING TO BE A LOGICAL EXPLANATION FOR THIS, MULDOON. ALL OUR UFO INVESTIGATIONS PROVE TO BE DEAD ENDS!
HOW ABOUT THAT TIME WE THOUGHT A REPORTER'S UNCLE HAD A SPACESHIP IN HIS GARAGE? A HOAX!
OR THAT ARCHITECT WE INTERVIEWED WHO CLAIMED ALIENS WERE DISGUISED AS HUMANS AND COULD BE IDENTIFIED BY A CROOKED FINGER ON THE RIGHT HAND? A FRAUD!
THE TRUTH IS OUT THERE.
YEAH? WHERE?
WE WERE ALMOST KICKED OUT OF THE BUREAU WHEN WE FOLLOWED UP ON THE LEAD THAT WILL-SAPPING WALNUTS WERE BEING PLANTED BY AN ALIEN WHO LOOKED LIKE DANNY THOMAS . . .
MY SISTER WAS ABDUCTED BY A UFO . . .
OH, NO . . . NOT THE SISTER AGAIN . . .
I WAS A CHILD-- THE ALIENS THOUGHT THEY COULD MAKE ME FORGET . . . BUT I NEVER GAVE UP HOPE . . .
IF I COULD MAKE CONTACT WITH A UFO, I MIGHT GET A CLUE TO MY SISTER'S WHERE-ABOUTS . . .
THAT'S WHAT EVERYONE SAYS, MULDOON--YOU'VE GOT TO GET A CLUE . . .
TOOTY-- BEFORE WE HEAD FOR THE NORRIS HOUSE, I THINK THERE'S SUPPOSED TO BE A CRATER AROUND HERE SOME-- ULP!

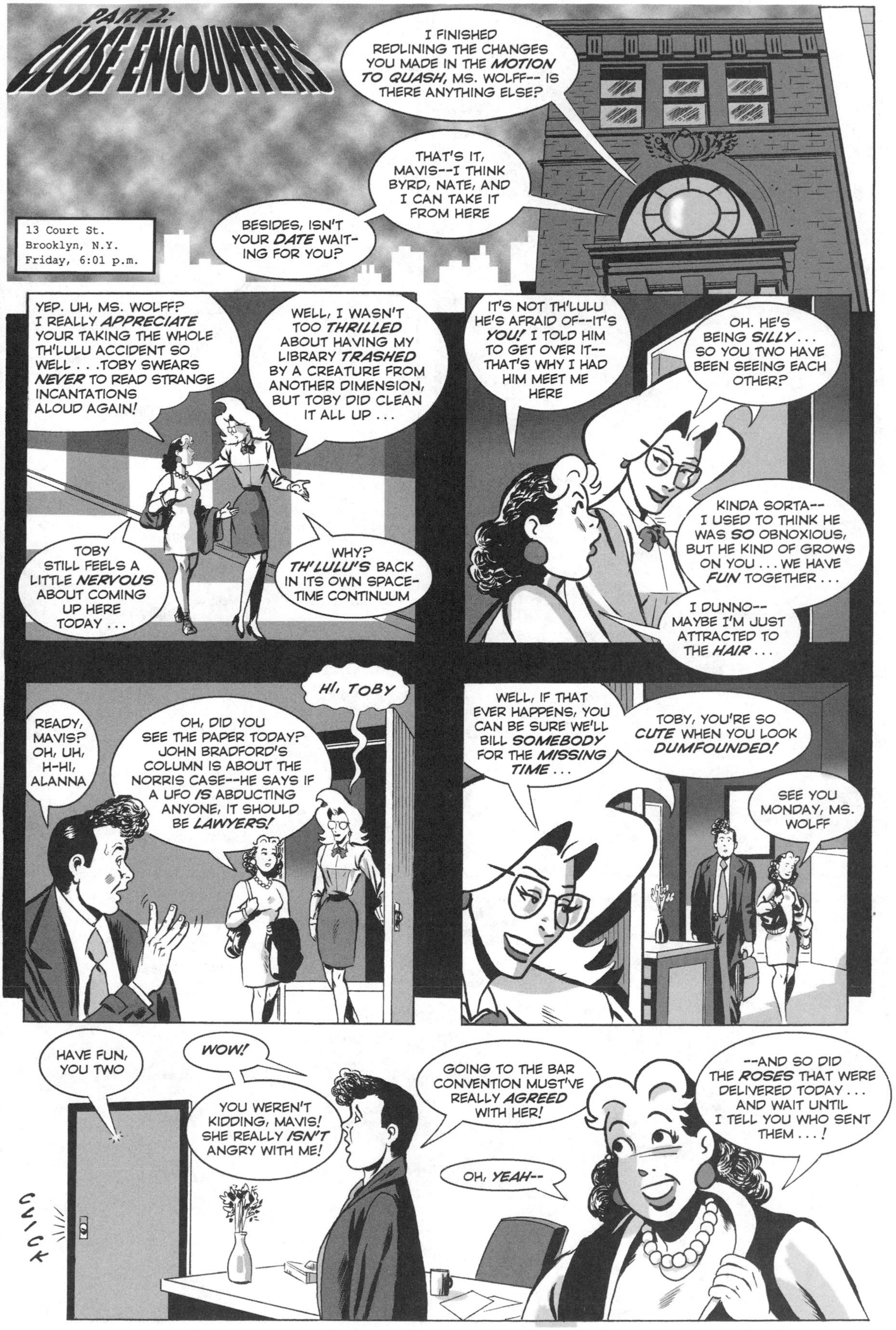
PART 2:
CLOSE ENCOUNTERS
I FINISHED REDLINING THE CHANGES YOU MADE IN THE MOTION TO QUASH, MS. WOLFF-- IS THERE ANYTHING ELSE?
THAT'S IT, MAVIS--I THINK BYRD, NATE, AND I CAN TAKE IT FROM HERE
BESIDES, ISN'T YOUR DATE WAITING FOR YOU?
13 Court St.
Brooklyn, N.Y.
Friday, 6:01 p.m.
YEP. UH, MS. WOLFF? I REALLY APPRECIATE YOUR TAKING THE WHOLE TH'LULU ACCIDENT SO WELL . . . TOBY SWEARS NEVER TO READ STRANGE INCANTATIONS ALOUD AGAIN!
WELL, I WASN'T TOO THRILLED ABOUT HAVING MY LIBRARY TRASHED BY A CREATURE FROM ANOTHER DIMENSION, BUT TOBY DID CLEAN IT ALL UP . . .
TOBY STILL FEELS A LITTLE NERVOUS ABOUT COMING UP HERE TODAY . . .
WHY? TH'LULU'S BACK IN ITS OWN SPACE-TIME CONTINUUM
IT'S NOT TH'LULU HE'S AFRAID OF--IT'S YOU! I TOLD HIM TO GET OVER IT--THAT'S WHY I HAD HIM MEET ME HERE
OH. HE'S BEING SILLY . . . SO YOU TWO HAVE BEEN SEEING EACH OTHER?
KINDA SORTA-- I USED TO THINK HE WAS SO OBNOXIOUS, BUT HE KIND OF GROWS ON YOU . . . WE HAVE FUN TOGETHER . . .
I DUNNO-- MAYBE I'M JUST ATTRACTED TO THE HAIR . . .
READY, MAVIS? OH, UH, H-HI, ALANNA
HI, TOBY
OH, DID YOU SEE THE PAPER TODAY? JOHN BRADFORD'S COLUMN IS ABOUT THE NORRIS CASE--HE SAYS IF A UFO IS ABDUCTING ANYONE, IT SHOULD BE LAWYERS!
WELL, IF THAT EVER HAPPENS, YOU CAN BE SURE WE'LL BILL SOMEBODY FOR THE MISSING TIME . . .
TOBY, YOU'RE SO CUTE WHEN YOU LOOK DUMFOUNDED!
SEE YOU MONDAY, MS. WOLFF
HAVE FUN, YOU TWO
CLICK
WOW!
YOU WEREN'T KIDDING, MAVIS! SHE REALLY ISN'T ANGRY WITH ME!
GOING TO THE BAR CONVENTION MUST'VE REALLY AGREED WITH HER!
OH, YEAH--
--AND SO DID THE ROSES THAT WERE DELIVERED TODAY . . . AND WAIT UNTIL I TELL YOU WHO SENT THEM . . . !

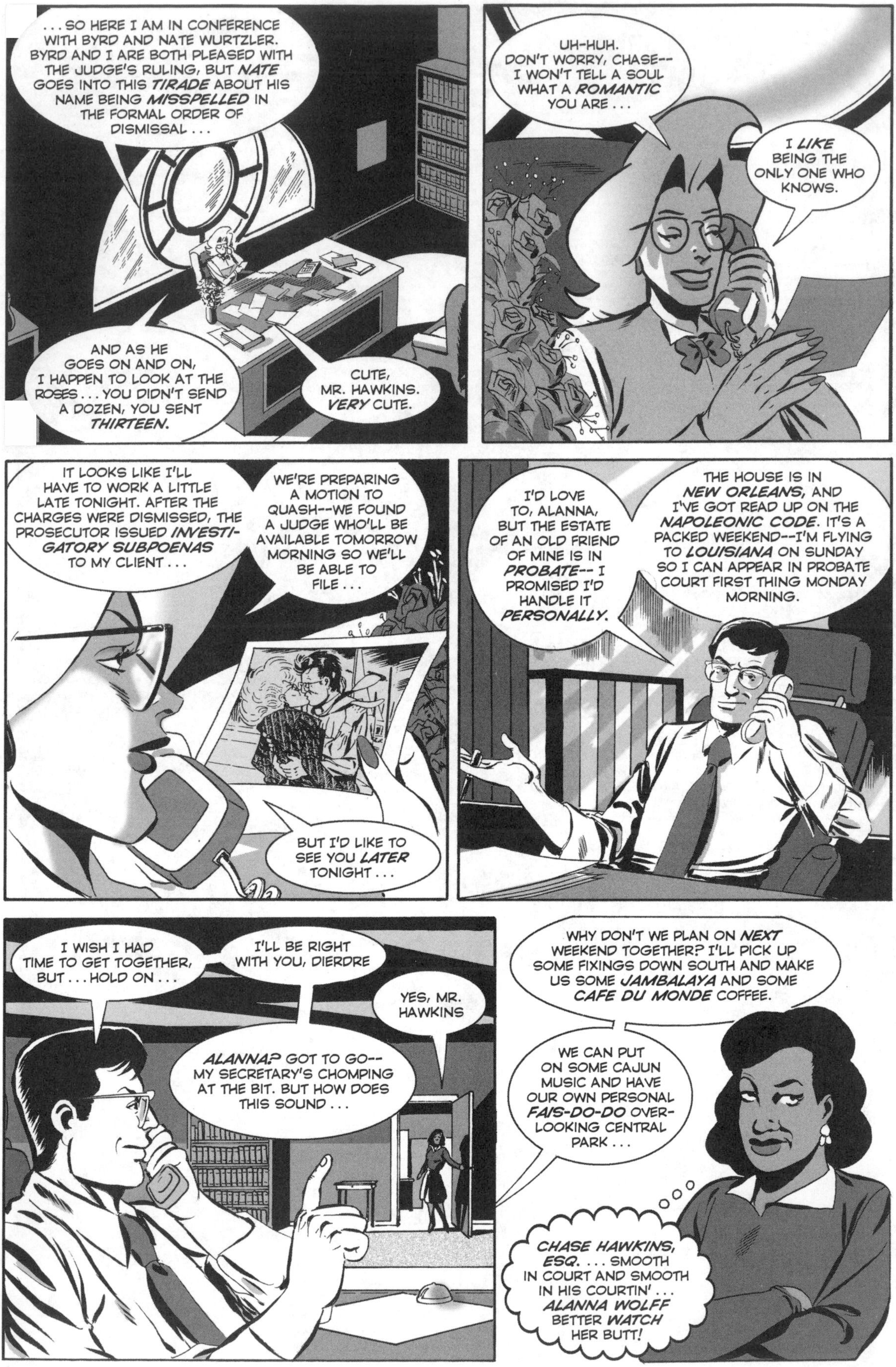
. . . SO HERE I AM IN CONFERENCE WITH BYRD AND NATE WURTZLER. BYRD AND I ARE BOTH PLEASED WITH THE JUDGE'S RULING, BUT NATE GOES INTO THIS TIRADE ABOUT HIS NAME BEING MISSPELLED IN THE FORMAL ORDER OF DISMISSAL . . .
AND AS HE GOES ON AND ON, I HAPPEN TO LOOK AT THE ROSES . . . YOU DIDN'T SEND A DOZEN, YOU SENT THIRTEEN.
CUTE, MR. HAWKINS. VERY CUTE.
UH-HUH. DON'T WORRY, CHASE-- I WON'T TELL A SOUL WHAT A ROMANTIC YOU ARE . . .
I LIKE BEING THE ONLY ONE WHO KNOWS.
IT LOOKS LIKE I'LL HAVE TO WORK A LITTLE LATE TONIGHT. AFTER THE CHARGES WERE DISMISSED, THE PROSECUTOR ISSUED INVESTIGATORY SUBPOENAS TO MY CLIENT . . .
WE'RE PREPARING A MOTION TO QUASH--WE FOUND A JUDGE WHO'LL BE AVAILABLE TOMORROW MORNING SO WE'LL BE ABLE TO FILE . . .
BUT I'D LIKE TO SEE YOU LATER TONIGHT . . .
I'D LOVE TO, ALANNA, BUT THE ESTATE OF AN OLD FRIEND OF MINE IS IN PROBATE-- I PROMISED I'D HANDLE IT PERSONALLY.
THE HOUSE IS IN NEW ORLEANS, AND I'VE GOT READ UP ON THE NAPOLEONIC CODE. IT'S A PACKED WEEKEND--I'M FLYING TO LOUISIANA ON SUNDAY SO I CAN APPEAR IN PROBATE COURT FIRST THING MONDAY MORNING.
I WISH I HAD TIME TO GET TOGETHER, BUT . . . HOLD ON . . .
I'LL BE RIGHT WITH YOU, DIERDRE
YES, MR. HAWKINS
ALANNA? GOT TO GO-- MY SECRETARY'S CHOMPING AT THE BIT. BUT HOW DOES THIS SOUND . . .
WHY DON'T WE PLAN ON NEXT WEEKEND TOGETHER? I'LL PICK UP SOME FIXINGS DOWN SOUTH AND MAKE US SOME JAMBALAYA AND SOME CAFE DU MONDE COFFEE.
WE CAN PUT ON SOME CAJUN MUSIC AND HAVE OUR OWN PERSONAL FAIS-DO-DO OVERLOOKING CENTRAL PARK . . .
CHASE HAWKINS, ESQ. . . . SMOOTH IN COURT AND SMOOTH IN HIS COURTIN' . . . ALANNA WOLFF BETTER WATCH HER BUTT!

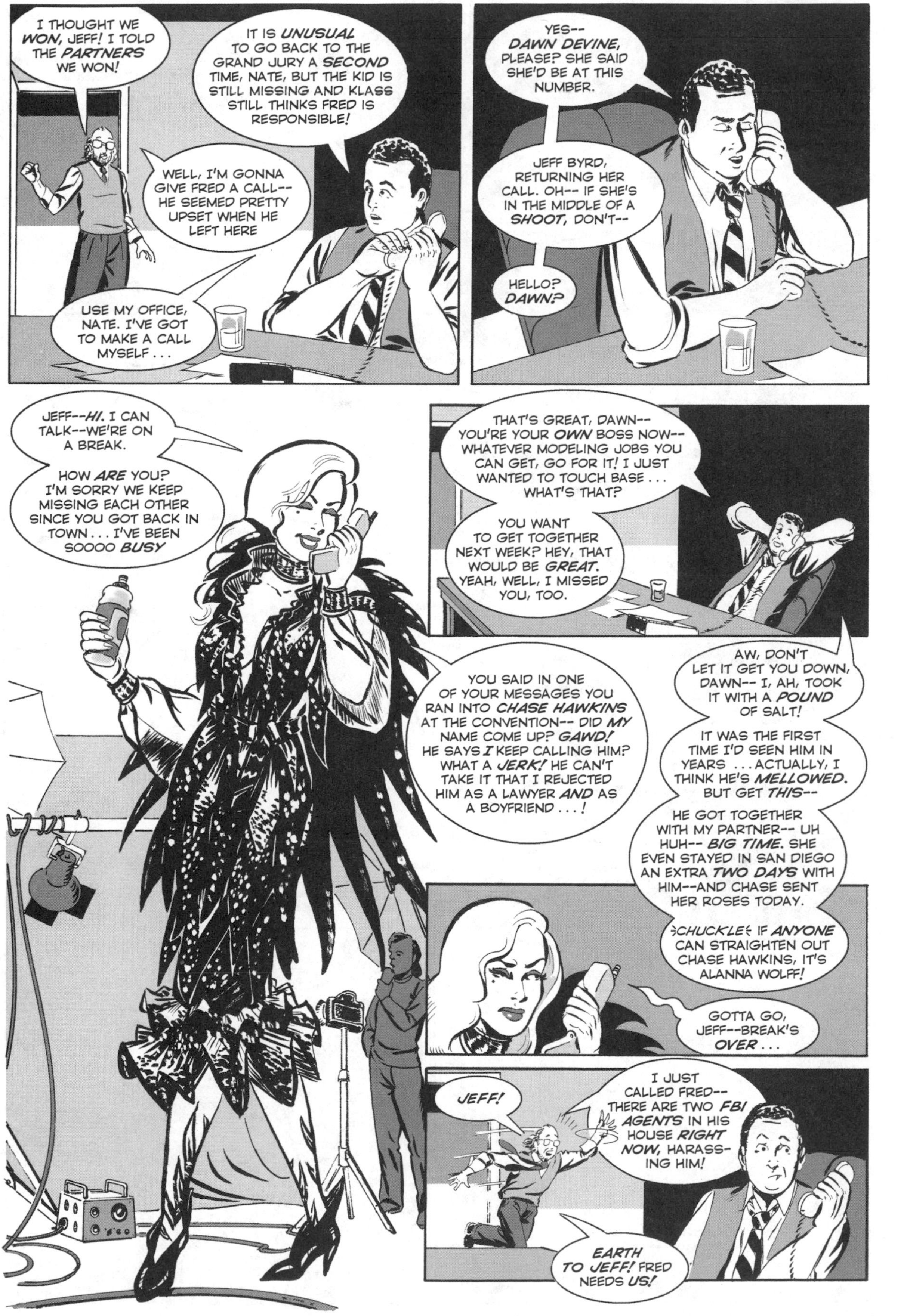
I THOUGHT WE WON, JEFF! I TOLD THE PARTNERS WE WON!
IT IS UNUSUAL TO GO BACK TO THE GRAND JURY A SECOND TIME, NATE, BUT THE KID IS STILL MISSING AND KLASS STILL THINKS FRED IS RESPONSIBLE!
WELL, I'M GONNA GIVE FRED A CALL-- HE SEEMED PRETTY UPSET WHEN HE LEFT HERE
USE MY OFFICE, NATE. I'VE GOT TO MAKE A CALL MYSELF . . .
YES-- DAWN DEVINE, PLEASE? SHE SAID SHE'D BE AT THIS NUMBER.
JEFF BYRD, RETURNING HER CALL. OH-- IF SHE'S IN THE MIDDLE OF A SHOOT, DON'T--
HELLO? DAWN?
JEFF--HI. I CAN TALK--WE'RE ON A BREAK.
HOW ARE YOU? I'M SORRY WE KEEP MISSING EACH OTHER SINCE YOU GOT BACK IN TOWN . . . I'VE BEEN SOOOO BUSY
THAT'S GREAT, DAWN-- YOU'RE YOUR OWN BOSS NOW-- WHATEVER MODELING JOBS YOU CAN GET, GO FOR IT! I JUST WANTED TO TOUCH BASE . . . WHAT'S THAT?
YOU WANT TO GET TOGETHER NEXT WEEK? HEY, THAT WOULD BE GREAT. YEAH, WELL, I MISSED YOU, TOO.
YOU SAID IN ONE OF YOUR MESSAGES YOU RAN INTO CHASE HAWKINS AT THE CONVENTION-- DID MY NAME COME UP? GAWD! HE SAYS I KEEP CALLING HIM? WHAT A JERK! HE CAN'T TAKE IT THAT I REJECTED HIM AS A LAWYER AND AS A BOYFRIEND . . . !
AW, DON'T LET IT GET YOU DOWN, DAWN-- I, AH, TOOK IT WITH A POUND OF SALT!
IT WAS THE FIRST TIME I'D SEEN HIM IN YEARS . . . ACTUALLY, I THINK HE'S MELLOWED. BUT GET THIS--
HE GOT TOGETHER WITH MY PARTNER-- UH HUH-- BIG TIME. SHE EVEN STAYED IN SAN DIEGO AN EXTRA TWO DAYS WITH HIM--AND CHASE SENT HER ROSES TODAY.
CHUCKLE IF ANYONE CAN STRAIGHTEN OUT CHASE HAWKINS, IT'S ALANNA WOLFF!
GOTTA GO, JEFF--BREAK'S OVER . . .
JEFF!
I JUST CALLED FRED-- THERE ARE TWO FBI AGENTS IN HIS HOUSE RIGHT NOW, HARASS-ING HIM!
EARTH TO JEFF! FRED NEEDS US!

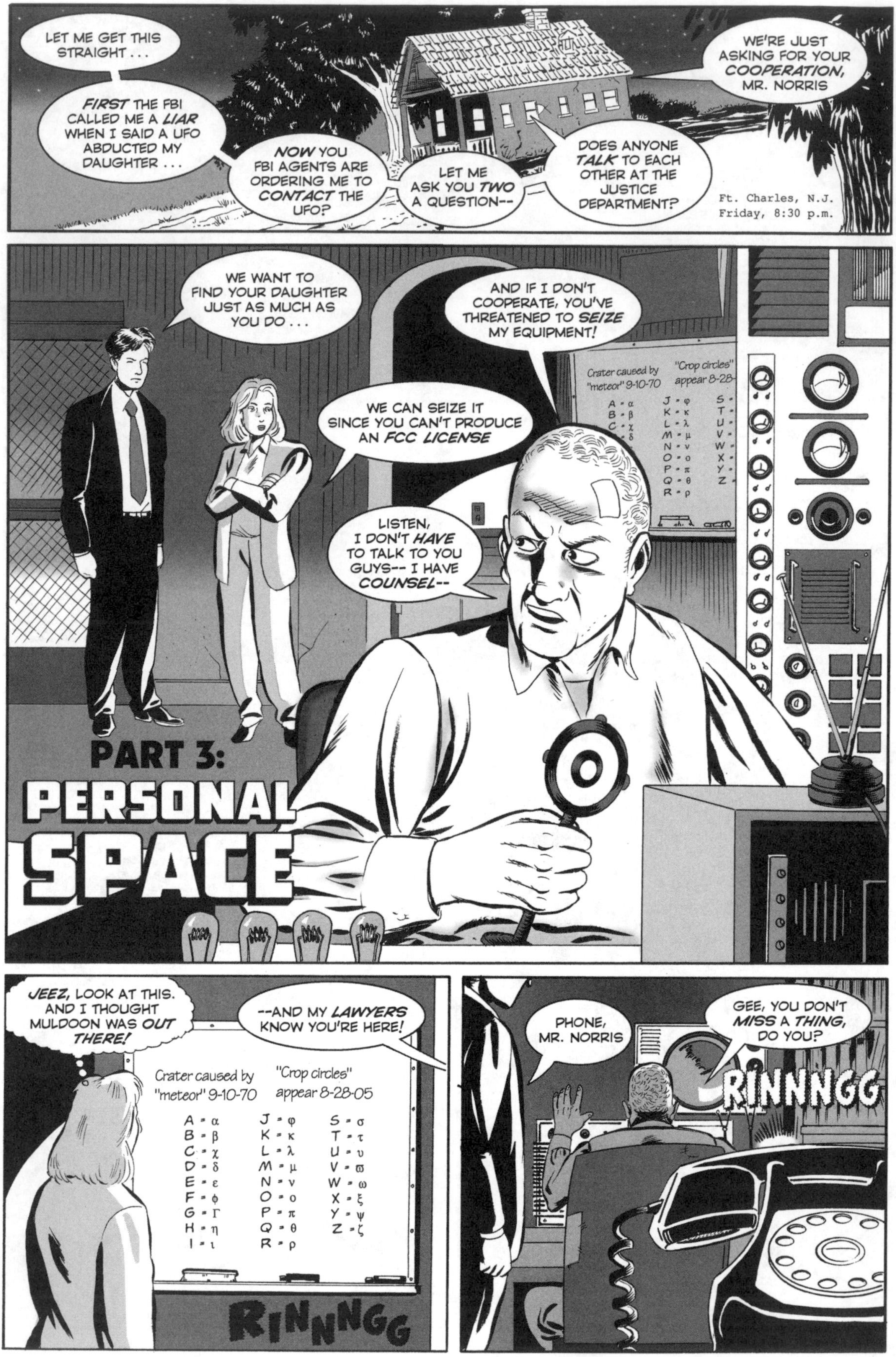
LET ME GET THIS STRAIGHT . . .
FIRST THE FBI CALLED ME A LIAR WHEN I SAID A UFO ABDUCTED MY DAUGHTER . . .
NOW YOU FBI AGENTS ARE ORDERING ME TO CONTACT THE UFO?
LET ME ASK YOU TWO A QUESTION--
DOES ANYONE TALK TO EACH OTHER AT THE JUSTICE DEPARTMENT?
WE'RE JUST ASKING FOR YOUR COOPERATION, MR. NORRIS
Ft. Charles, N.J.
Friday, 8:30 p.m.
WE WANT TO FIND YOUR DAUGHTER JUST AS MUCH AS YOU DO . . .
AND IF I DON'T COOPERATE, YOU'VE THREATENED TO SEIZE MY EQUIPMENT!
WE CAN SEIZE IT SINCE YOU CAN'T PRODUCE AN FCC LICENSE
LISTEN, I DON'T HAVE TO TALK TO YOU GUYS-- I HAVE COUNSEL--
PART 3:
PERSONAL SPACE
JEEZ, LOOK AT THIS. AND I THOUGHT MULDOON WAS OUT THERE!
--AND MY LAWYERS KNOW YOU'RE HERE!
Crater caused by "meteor" 9-10-70
"Crop circles" appear 8-28-05
A = α B = β C = χ D = δ E = ε F = ϕ G = Γ H = η I = ι
J = φ K = κ L = λ M = μ N = ν O = ο P = π Q = θ R = ρ
S = σ T = τ U = υ V = ϖ W = ω X = ξ Y = ψ Z = ζ
RINNNGG
PHONE, MR. NORRIS
GEE, YOU DON'T MISS A THING, DO YOU?
RINNNGG

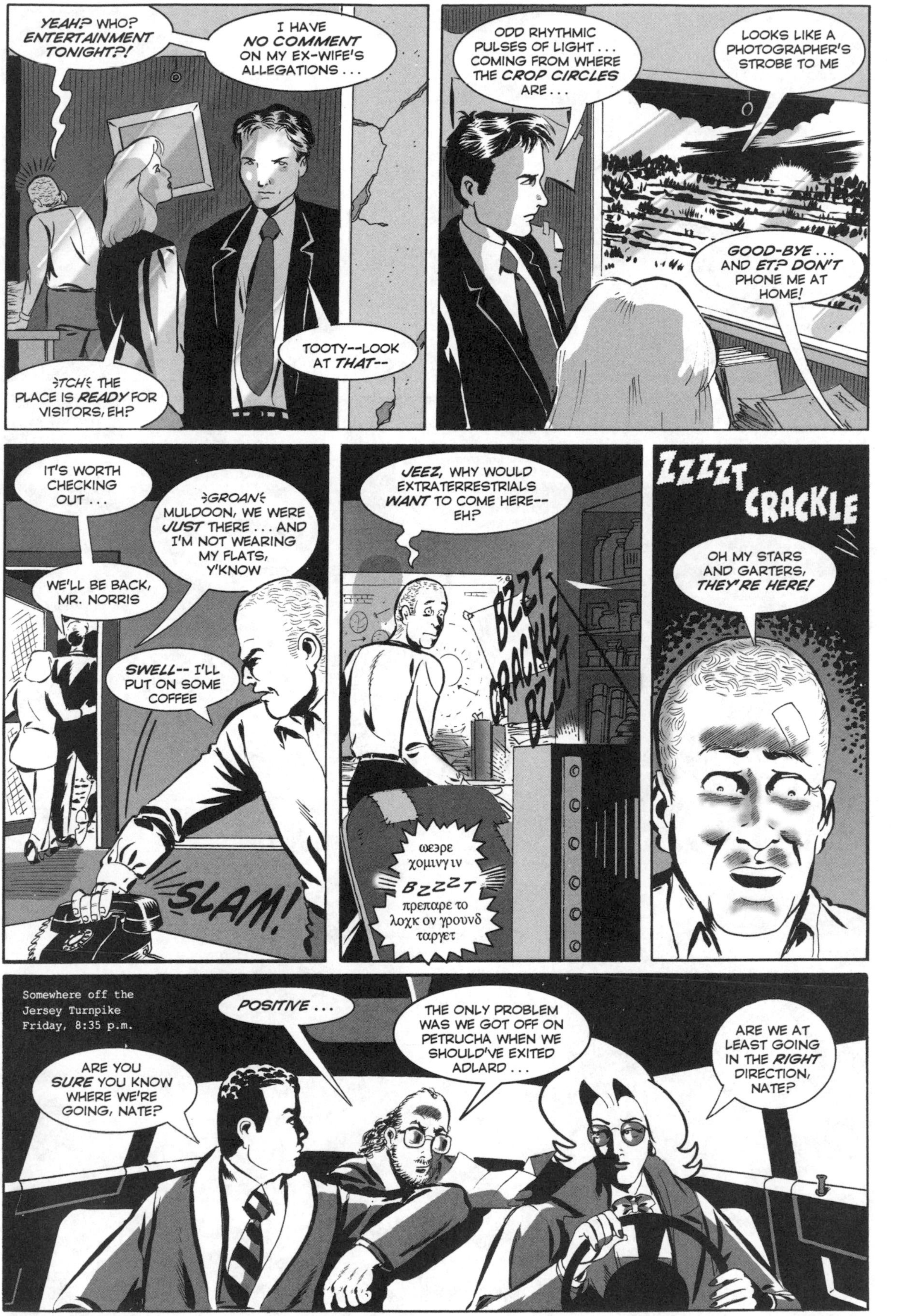
YEAH? WHO? ENTERTAINMENT TONIGHT?!
I HAVE NO COMMENT ON MY EX-WIFE'S ALLEGATIONS . . .
TCH THE PLACE IS READY FOR VISITORS, EH?
TOOTY--LOOK AT THAT--
ODD RHYTHMIC PULSES OF LIGHT . . . COMING FROM WHERE THE CROP CIRCLES ARE . . .
LOOKS LIKE A PHOTOGRAPHER'S STROBE TO ME
GOOD-BYE . . . AND ET? DON'T PHONE ME AT HOME!
IT'S WORTH CHECKING OUT . . .
GROAN MULDOON, WE WERE JUST THERE . . . AND I'M NOT WEARING MY FLATS, Y'KNOW
WE'LL BE BACK, MR. NORRIS
SWELL-- I'LL PUT ON SOME COFFEE
SLAM!
JEEZ, WHY WOULD EXTRATERRESTRIALS WANT TO COME HERE-- EH?
BZZT CRACKLE BZZT
ωεэρε χομινγ ιν BZZZT πρεπαρε το λοχκ ον γρουνδ ταργετ
ZZZZT CRACKLE
OH MY STARS AND GARTERS, THEY'RE HERE!
Somewhere off the Jersey Turnpike Friday, 8:35 p.m.
ARE YOU SURE YOU KNOW WHERE WE'RE GOING, NATE?
POSITIVE . . .
THE ONLY PROBLEM WAS WE GOT OFF ON PETRUCHA WHEN WE SHOULD'VE EXITED ADLARD . . .
ARE WE AT LEAST GOING IN THE RIGHT DIRECTION, NATE?

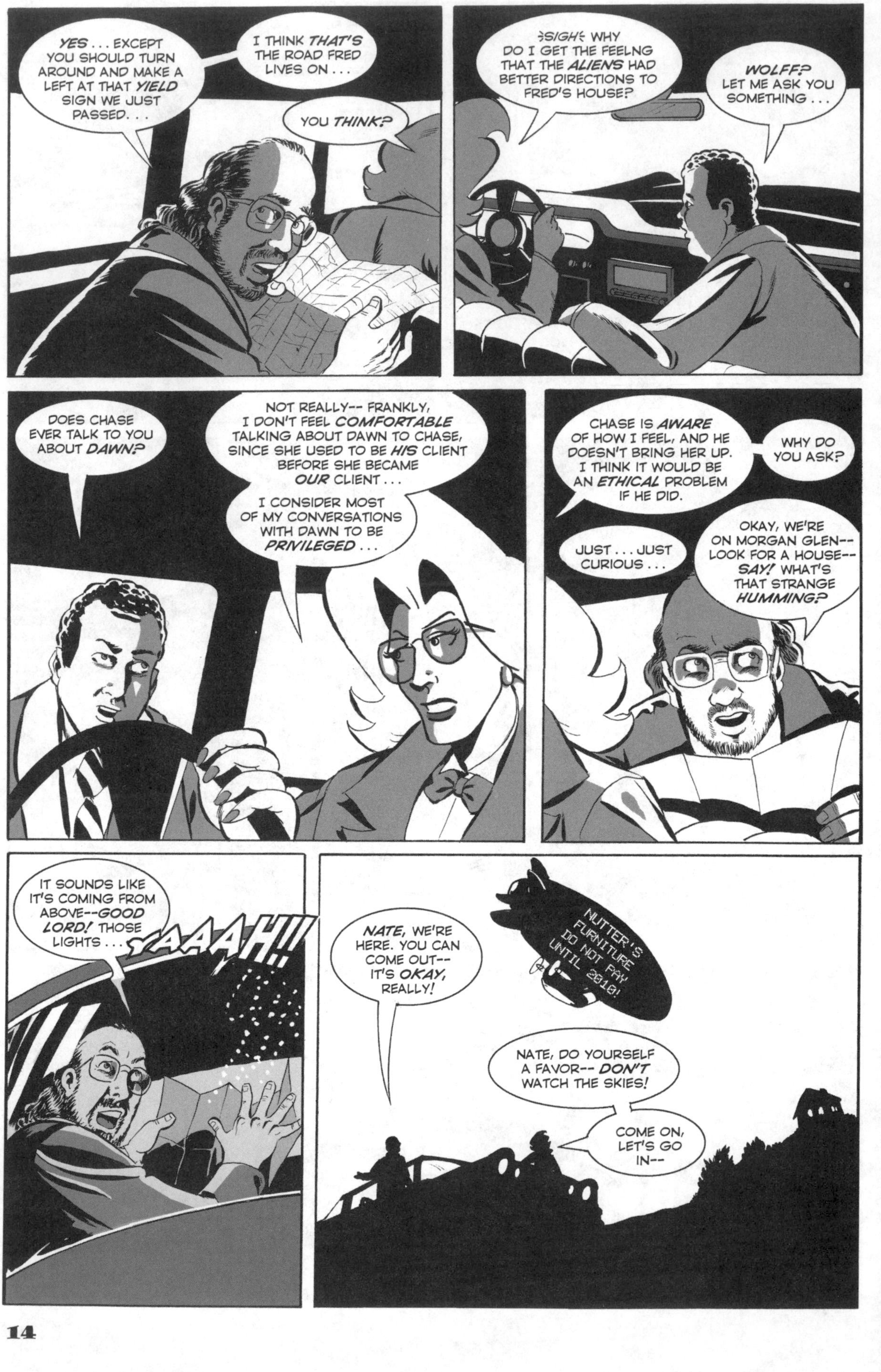
YES . . . EXCEPT YOU SHOULD TURN AROUND AND MAKE A LEFT AT THAT YIELD SIGN WE JUST PASSED. . .
I THINK THAT'S THE ROAD FRED LIVES ON . . .
YOU THINK?
SIGH WHY DO I GET THE FEELNG THAT THE ALIENS HAD BETTER DIRECTIONS TO FRED'S HOUSE?
WOLFF? LET ME ASK YOU SOMETHING . . .
DOES CHASE EVER TALK TO YOU ABOUT DAWN?
NOT REALLY-- FRANKLY, I DON'T FEEL COMFORTABLE TALKING ABOUT DAWN TO CHASE, SINCE SHE USED TO BE HIS CLIENT BEFORE SHE BECAME OUR CLIENT . . .
I CONSIDER MOST OF MY CONVERSATIONS WITH DAWN TO BE PRIVILEGED . . .
CHASE IS AWARE OF HOW I FEEL, AND HE DOESN'T BRING HER UP. I THINK IT WOULD BE AN ETHICAL PROBLEM IF HE DID.
WHY DO YOU ASK?
JUST . . . JUST CURIOUS . . .
OKAY, WE'RE ON MORGAN GLEN-- LOOK FOR A HOUSE-- SAY! WHAT'S THAT STRANGE HUMMING?
IT SOUNDS LIKE IT'S COMING FROM ABOVE--GOOD LORD! THOSE LIGHTS . . .
YAAAH!!
NATE, WE'RE HERE. YOU CAN COME OUT-- IT'S OKAY, REALLY!
NUTTER'S FURNITURE DO NOT PAY UNTIL 2010!
NATE, DO YOURSELF A FAVOR-- DON'T WATCH THE SKIES!
COME ON, LET'S GO IN--

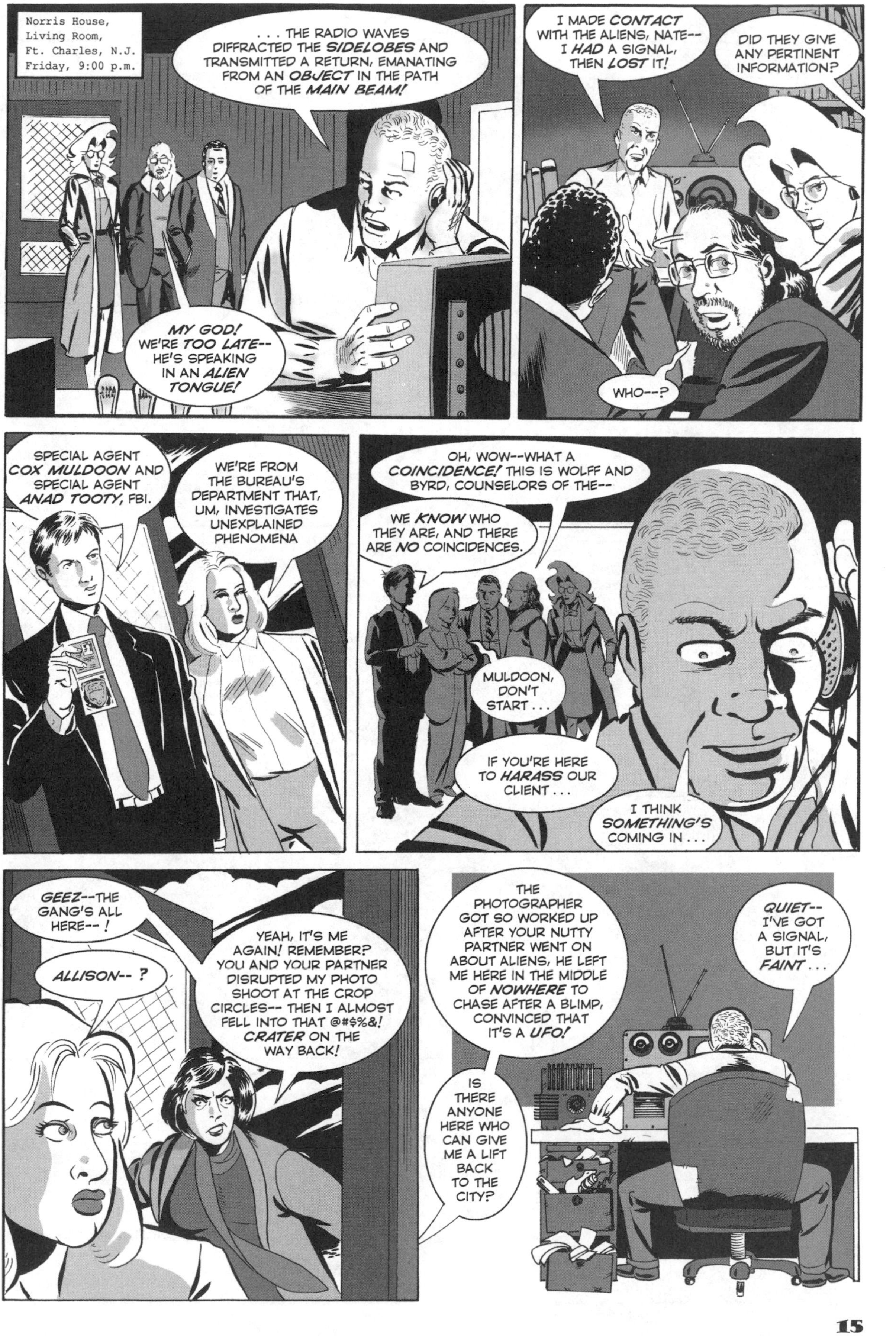
Norris House, Living Room, Ft. Charles, N.J. Friday, 9:00 p.m.
. . . THE RADIO WAVES DIFFRACTED THE SIDELOBES AND TRANSMITTED A RETURN, EMANATING FROM AN OBJECT IN THE PATH OF THE MAIN BEAM!
MY GOD! WE'RE TOO LATE-- HE'S SPEAKING IN AN ALIEN TONGUE!
I MADE CONTACT WITH THE ALIENS, NATE-- I HAD A SIGNAL, THEN LOST IT!
DID THEY GIVE ANY PERTINENT INFORMATION?
WHO--?
SPECIAL AGENT COX MULDOON AND SPECIAL AGENT ANAD TOOTY, FBI.
WE'RE FROM THE BUREAU'S DEPARTMENT THAT, UM, INVESTIGATES UNEXPLAINED PHENOMENA
OH, WOW--WHAT A COINCIDENCE! THIS IS WOLFF AND BYRD, COUNSELORS OF THE--
WE KNOW WHO THEY ARE, AND THERE ARE NO COINCIDENCES.
MULDOON, DON'T START . . .
IF YOU'RE HERE TO HARASS OUR CLIENT . . .
I THINK SOMETHING'S COMING IN . . .
GEEZ--THE GANG'S ALL HERE-- !
ALLISON-- ?
YEAH, IT'S ME AGAIN! REMEMBER? YOU AND YOUR PARTNER DISRUPTED MY PHOTO SHOOT AT THE CROP CIRCLES-- THEN I ALMOST FELL INTO THAT @#$%&! CRATER ON THE WAY BACK!
THE PHOTOGRAPHER GOT SO WORKED UP AFTER YOUR NUTTY PARTNER WENT ON ABOUT ALIENS, HE LEFT ME HERE IN THE MIDDLE OF NOWHERE TO CHASE AFTER A BLIMP, CONVINCED THAT IT'S A UFO!
IS THERE ANYONE HERE WHO CAN GIVE ME A LIFT BACK TO THE CITY?
QUIET-- I'VE GOT A SIGNAL, BUT IT'S FAINT . . .

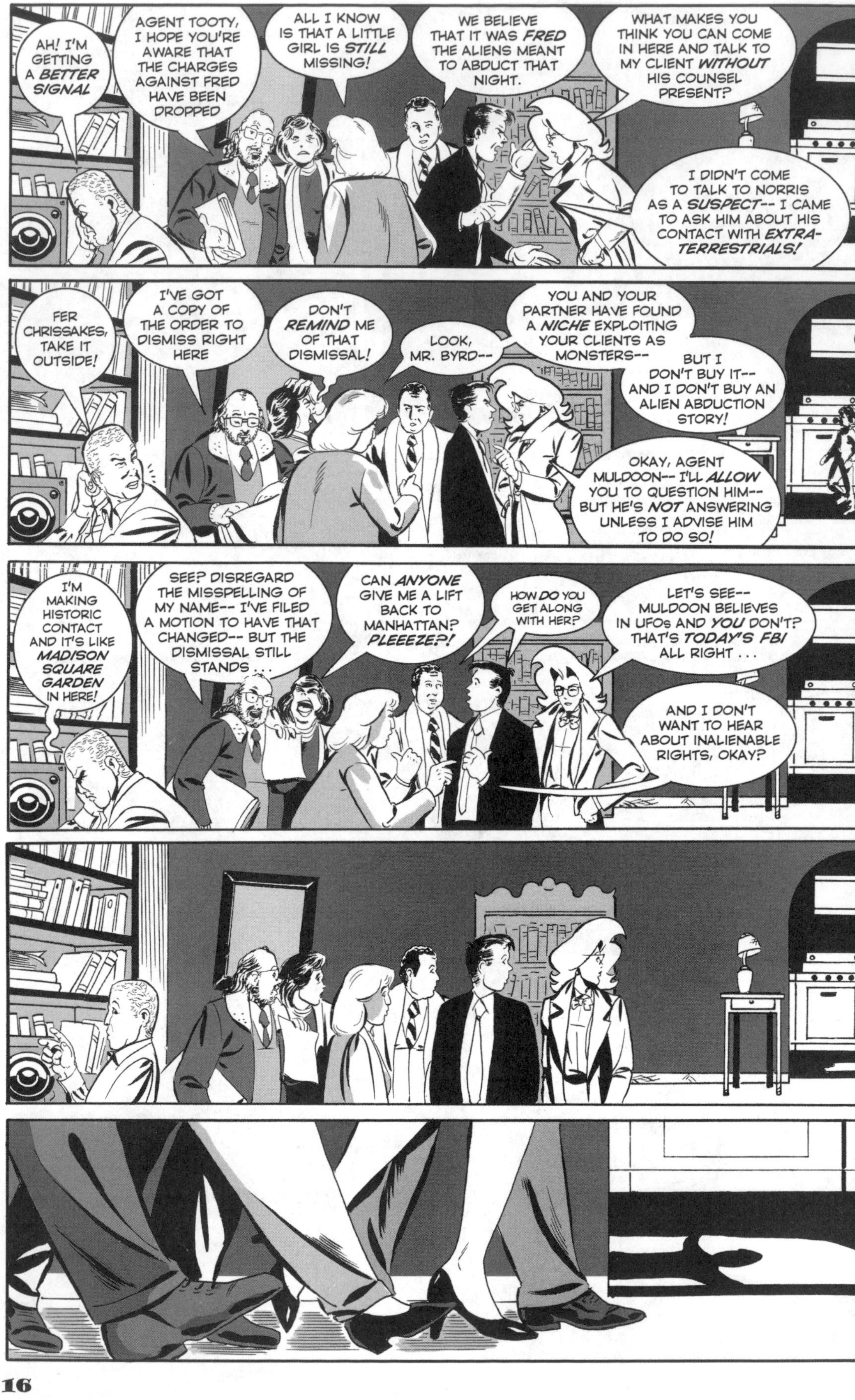
AH! I'M GETTING A BETTER SIGNAL
AGENT TOOTY, I HOPE YOU'RE AWARE THAT THE CHARGES AGAINST FRED HAVE BEEN DROPPED
ALL I KNOW IS THAT A LITTLE GIRL IS STILL MISSING!
WE BELIEVE THAT IT WAS FRED THE ALIENS MEANT TO ABDUCT THAT NIGHT.
WHAT MAKES YOU THINK YOU CAN COME IN HERE AND TALK TO MY CLIENT WITHOUT HIS COUNSEL PRESENT?
I DIDN'T COME TO TALK TO NORRIS AS A SUSPECT-- I CAME TO ASK HIM ABOUT HIS CONTACT WITH EXTRA-TERRESTRIALS!
FER CHRISSAKES, TAKE IT OUTSIDE!
I'VE GOT A COPY OF THE ORDER TO DISMISS RIGHT HERE
DON'T REMIND ME OF THAT DISMISSAL!
LOOK, MR. BYRD--
YOU AND YOUR PARTNER HAVE FOUND A NICHE EXPLOITING YOUR CLIENTS AS MONSTERS--
BUT I DON'T BUY IT-- AND I DON'T BUY AN ALIEN ABDUCTION STORY!
OKAY, AGENT MULDOON-- I'LL ALLOW YOU TO QUESTION HIM-- BUT HE'S NOT ANSWERING UNLESS I ADVISE HIM TO DO SO!
I'M MAKING HISTORIC CONTACT AND IT'S LIKE MADISON SQUARE GARDEN IN HERE!
SEE? DISREGARD THE MISSPELLING OF MY NAME-- I'VE FILED A MOTION TO HAVE THAT CHANGED-- BUT THE DISMISSAL STILL STANDS . . .
CAN ANYONE GIVE ME A LIFT BACK TO MANHATTAN? PLEEEZE?!
HOW DO YOU GET ALONG WITH HER?
LET'S SEE-- MULDOON BELIEVES IN UFOs AND YOU DON'T? THAT'S TODAY'S FBI ALL RIGHT . . .
AND I DON'T WANT TO HEAR ABOUT INALIENABLE RIGHTS, OKAY?

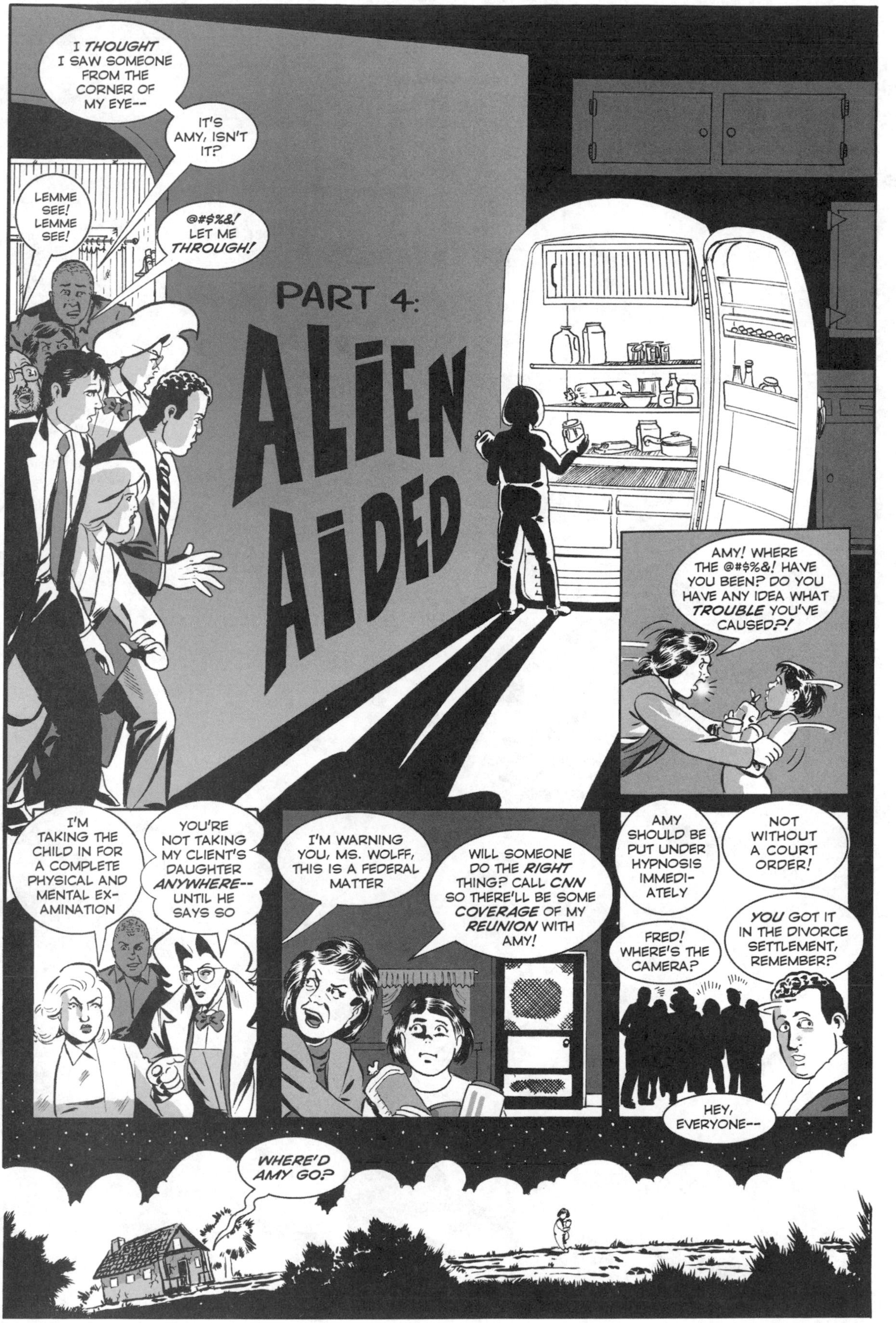
I THOUGHT I SAW SOMEONE FROM THE CORNER OF MY EYE--
IT'S AMY, ISN'T IT?
LEMME SEE! LEMME SEE!
@#$%&! LET ME THROUGH!
PART 4:
ALIEN AIDED
AMY! WHERE THE @#$%&! HAVE YOU BEEN? DO YOU HAVE ANY IDEA WHAT TROUBLE YOU'VE CAUSED?!
I'M TAKING THE CHILD IN FOR A COMPLETE PHYSICAL AND MENTAL EXAMINATION
YOU'RE NOT TAKING MY CLIENT'S DAUGHTER ANYWHERE-- UNTIL HE SAYS SO
I'M WARNING YOU, MS. WOLFF, THIS IS A FEDERAL MATTER
WILL SOMEONE DO THE RIGHT THING? CALL CNN SO THERE'LL BE SOME COVERAGE OF MY REUNION WITH AMY!
AMY SHOULD BE PUT UNDER HYPNOSIS IMMEDI-ATELY
NOT WITHOUT A COURT ORDER!
FRED! WHERE'S THE CAMERA?
YOU GOT IT IN THE DIVORCE SETTLEMENT, REMEMBER?
HEY, EVERYONE--
WHERE'D AMY GO?

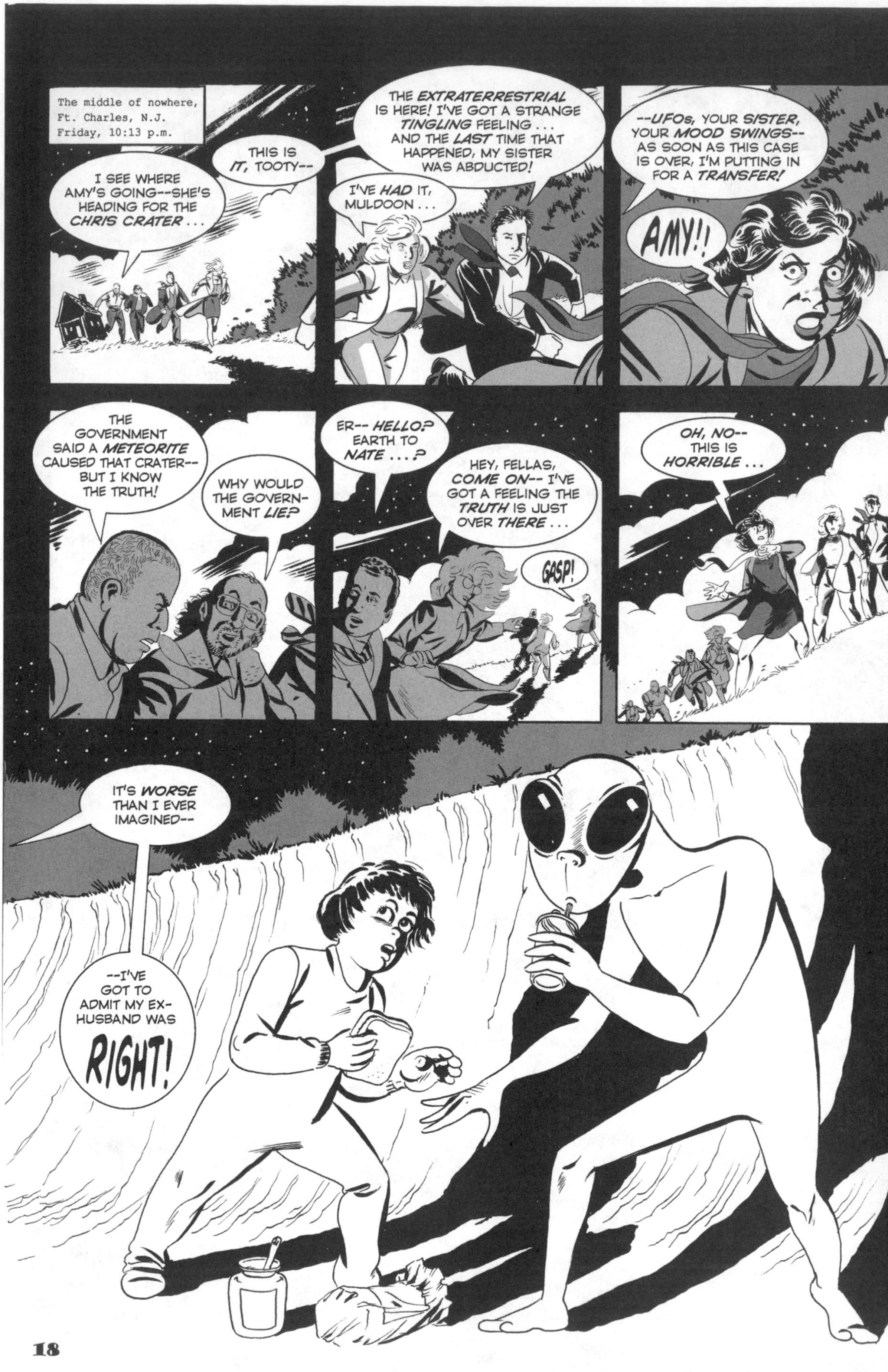
The middle of nowhere,
Ft. Charles, N.J.
Friday, 10:13 p.m.
I SEE WHERE AMY'S GOING--SHE'S HEADING FOR THE CHRIS CRATER...
THIS IS IT, TOOTY--
THE EXTRATERRESTRIAL IS HERE! I'VE GOT A STRANGE TINGLING FEELING... AND THE LAST TIME THAT HAPPENED, MY SISTER WAS ABDUCTED!
I'VE HAD IT, MULDOON...
--UFOs, YOUR SISTER, YOUR MOOD SWINGS-- AS SOON AS THIS CASE IS OVER, I'M PUTTING IN FOR A TRANSFER!
AMY!!
THE GOVERNMENT SAID A METEORITE CAUSED THAT CRATER-- BUT I KNOW THE TRUTH!
WHY WOULD THE GOVERNMENT LIE?
ER-- HELLO? EARTH TO NATE...?
HEY, FELLAS, COME ON-- I'VE GOT A FEELING THE TRUTH IS JUST OVER THERE...
GASP!
OH, NO-- THIS IS HORRIBLE...
IT'S WORSE THAN I EVER IMAGINED--
--I'VE GOT TO ADMIT MY EX-HUSBAND WAS RIGHT!

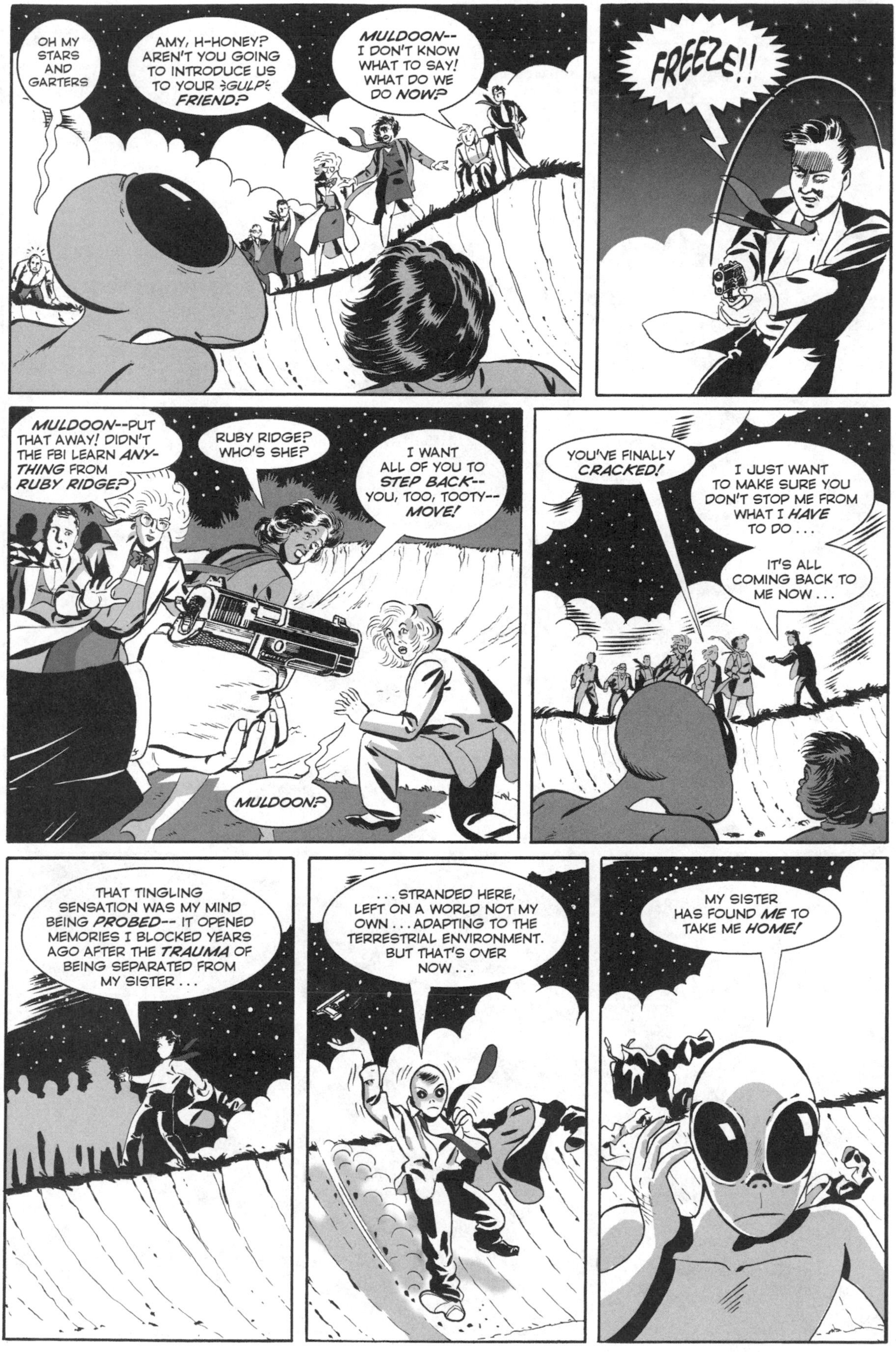
OH MY STARS AND GARTERS
AMY, H-HONEY? AREN'T YOU GOING TO INTRODUCE US TO YOUR *GULP* FRIEND?
MULDOON-- I DON'T KNOW WHAT TO SAY! WHAT DO WE DO NOW?
FREEZE!!
MULDOON--PUT THAT AWAY! DIDN'T THE FBI LEARN ANYTHING FROM RUBY RIDGE?
RUBY RIDGE? WHO'S SHE?
I WANT ALL OF YOU TO STEP BACK-- YOU, TOO, TOOTY-- MOVE!
MULDOON?
YOU'VE FINALLY CRACKED!
I JUST WANT TO MAKE SURE YOU DON'T STOP ME FROM WHAT I HAVE TO DO . . .
IT'S ALL COMING BACK TO ME NOW . . .
THAT TINGLING SENSATION WAS MY MIND BEING PROBED-- IT OPENED MEMORIES I BLOCKED YEARS AGO AFTER THE TRAUMA OF BEING SEPARATED FROM MY SISTER . . .
. . . STRANDED HERE, LEFT ON A WORLD NOT MY OWN . . . ADAPTING TO THE TERRESTRIAL ENVIRONMENT. BUT THAT'S OVER NOW . . .
MY SISTER HAS FOUND ME TO TAKE ME HOME!

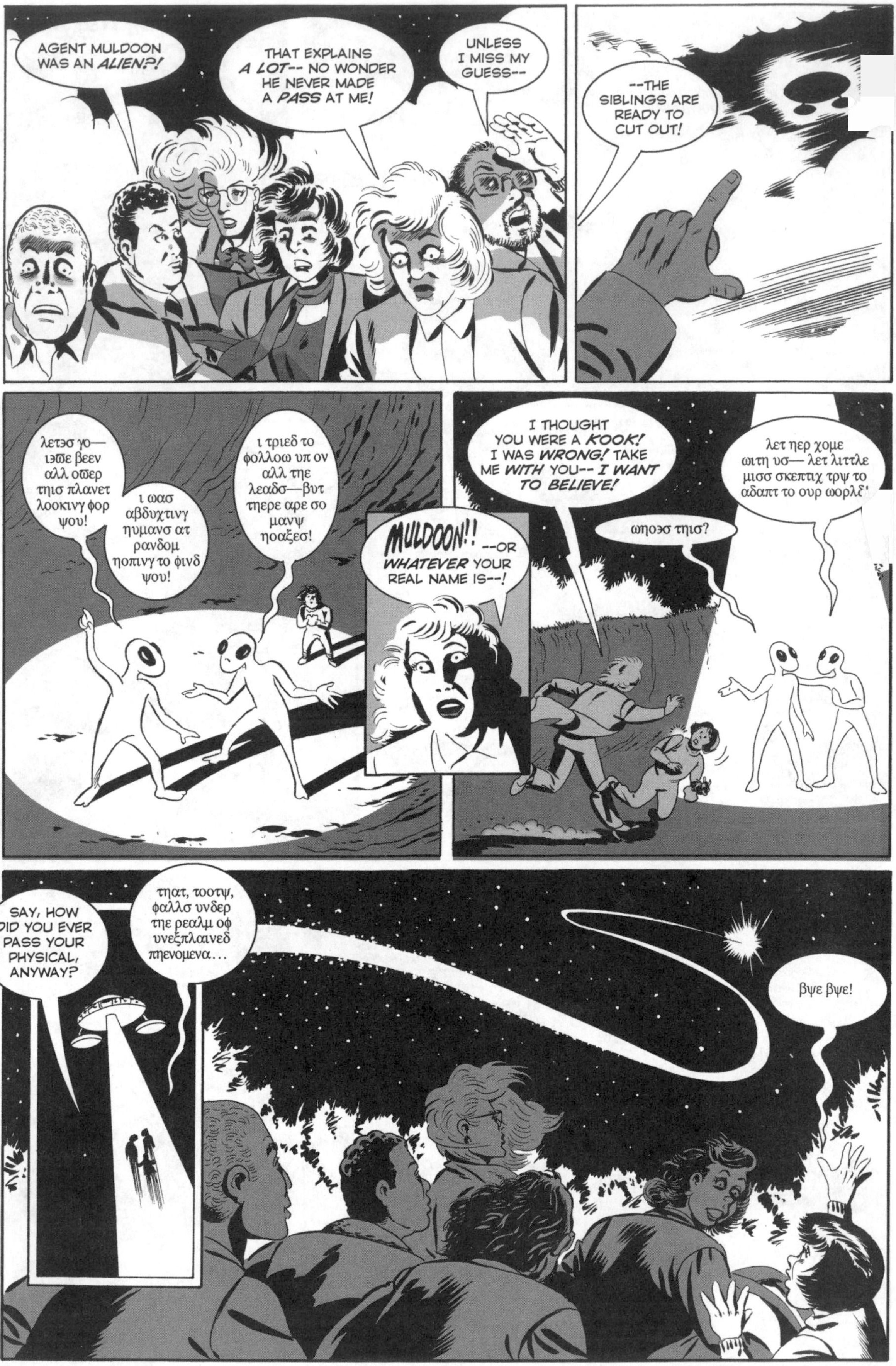
AGENT MULDOON WAS AN *ALIEN?!*
THAT EXPLAINS *A LOT*-- NO WONDER HE NEVER MADE A *PASS* AT ME!
UNLESS I MISS MY GUESS--
--THE SIBLINGS ARE READY TO CUT OUT!
λετэσ γο— ιэϖε βεεν αλλ οϖερ τηισ πλανετ λοοκινγ φορ ψου!
ι ωασ αβδυχτινγ ηυμανσ ατ ρανδομ ηοπινγ το φινδ ψου!
ι τριεδ το φολλοω υπ ον αλλ τηε λεαδσ—βυτ τηερε αρε σο μανψ ηοαξεσ!
MULDOON!! --OR *WHATEVER* YOUR REAL NAME IS--!
I THOUGHT YOU WERE A *KOOK!* I WAS *WRONG!* TAKE ME *WITH* YOU-- *I WANT TO BELIEVE!*
λετ ηερ χομε ωιτη υσ— λετ λιττλε μισσ σκεπτιχ τρψ το αδαπτ το ουρ ωορλδ
ωηοэσ τηισ?
SAY, HOW DID YOU EVER PASS YOUR PHYSICAL, ANYWAY?
τηατ, τοοτψ, φαλλσ υνδερ τηε ρεαλμ οφ υνεξπλαινεδ πηενομενα...
βψε βψε!

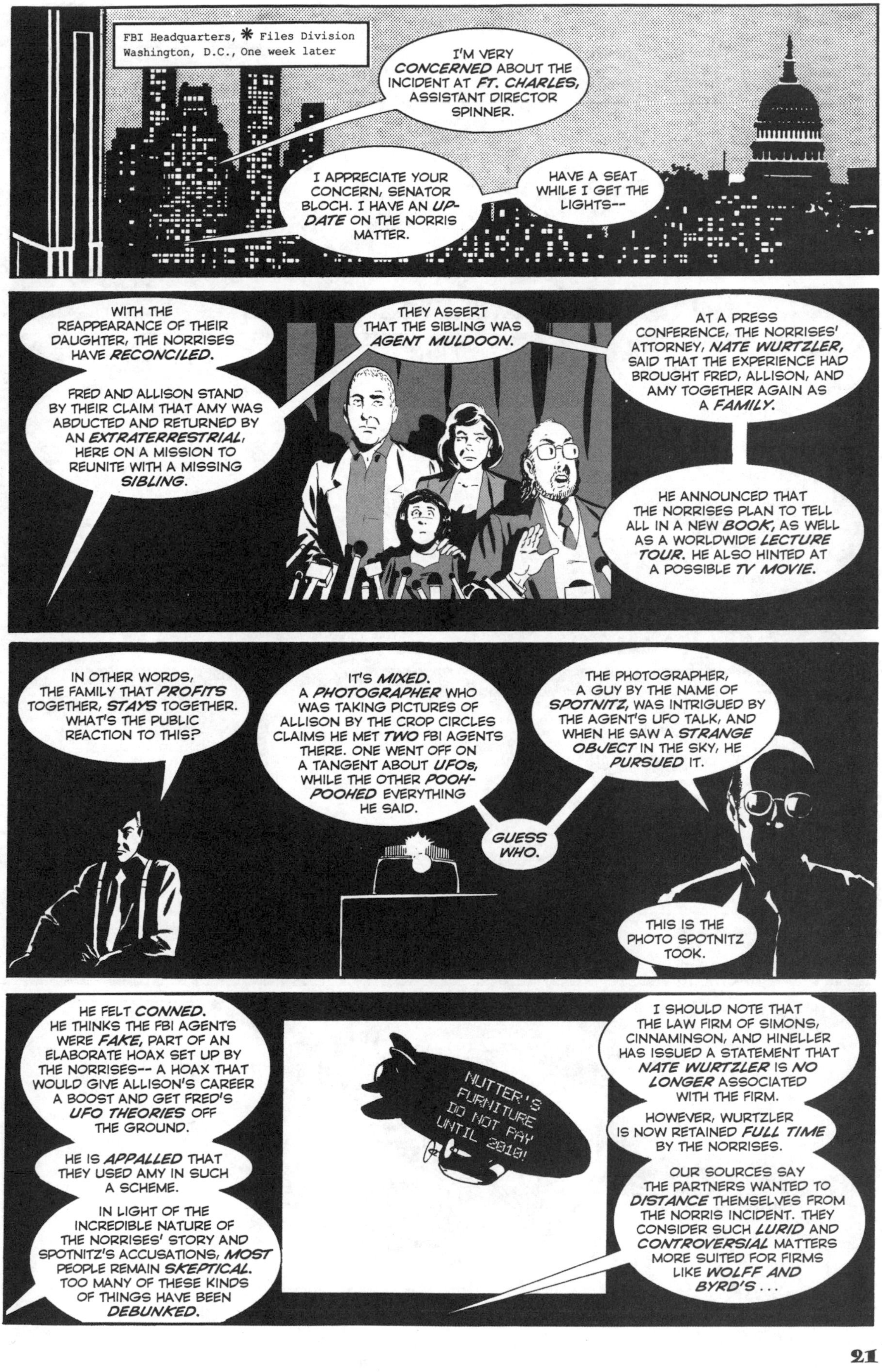
FBI Headquarters, ✱ Files Division
Washington, D.C., One week later
I'M VERY CONCERNED ABOUT THE INCIDENT AT FT. CHARLES, ASSISTANT DIRECTOR SPINNER.
I APPRECIATE YOUR CONCERN, SENATOR BLOCH. I HAVE AN UP-DATE ON THE NORRIS MATTER.
HAVE A SEAT WHILE I GET THE LIGHTS--
WITH THE REAPPEARANCE OF THEIR DAUGHTER, THE NORRISES HAVE RECONCILED.
FRED AND ALLISON STAND BY THEIR CLAIM THAT AMY WAS ABDUCTED AND RETURNED BY AN EXTRATERRESTRIAL, HERE ON A MISSION TO REUNITE WITH A MISSING SIBLING.
THEY ASSERT THAT THE SIBLING WAS AGENT MULDOON.
AT A PRESS CONFERENCE, THE NORRISES' ATTORNEY, NATE WURTZLER, SAID THAT THE EXPERIENCE HAD BROUGHT FRED, ALLISON, AND AMY TOGETHER AGAIN AS A FAMILY.
HE ANNOUNCED THAT THE NORRISES PLAN TO TELL ALL IN A NEW BOOK, AS WELL AS A WORLDWIDE LECTURE TOUR. HE ALSO HINTED AT A POSSIBLE TV MOVIE.
IN OTHER WORDS, THE FAMILY THAT PROFITS TOGETHER, STAYS TOGETHER. WHAT'S THE PUBLIC REACTION TO THIS?
IT'S MIXED. A PHOTOGRAPHER WHO WAS TAKING PICTURES OF ALLISON BY THE CROP CIRCLES CLAIMS HE MET TWO FBI AGENTS THERE. ONE WENT OFF ON A TANGENT ABOUT UFOs, WHILE THE OTHER POOH-POOHED EVERYTHING HE SAID.
GUESS WHO.
THE PHOTOGRAPHER, A GUY BY THE NAME OF SPOTNITZ, WAS INTRIGUED BY THE AGENT'S UFO TALK, AND WHEN HE SAW A STRANGE OBJECT IN THE SKY, HE PURSUED IT.
THIS IS THE PHOTO SPOTNITZ TOOK.
HE FELT CONNED. HE THINKS THE FBI AGENTS WERE FAKE, PART OF AN ELABORATE HOAX SET UP BY THE NORRISES-- A HOAX THAT WOULD GIVE ALLISON'S CAREER A BOOST AND GET FRED'S UFO THEORIES OFF THE GROUND.
HE IS APPALLED THAT THEY USED AMY IN SUCH A SCHEME.
IN LIGHT OF THE INCREDIBLE NATURE OF THE NORRISES' STORY AND SPOTNITZ'S ACCUSATIONS, MOST PEOPLE REMAIN SKEPTICAL. TOO MANY OF THESE KINDS OF THINGS HAVE BEEN DEBUNKED.
NUTTER'S FURNITURE DO NOT PAY UNTIL 2010!
I SHOULD NOTE THAT THE LAW FIRM OF SIMONS, CINNAMINSON, AND HINELLER HAS ISSUED A STATEMENT THAT NATE WURTZLER IS NO LONGER ASSOCIATED WITH THE FIRM.
HOWEVER, WURTZLER IS NOW RETAINED FULL TIME BY THE NORRISES.
OUR SOURCES SAY THE PARTNERS WANTED TO DISTANCE THEMSELVES FROM THE NORRIS INCIDENT. THEY CONSIDER SUCH LURID AND CONTROVERSIAL MATTERS MORE SUITED FOR FIRMS LIKE WOLFF AND BYRD'S . . .

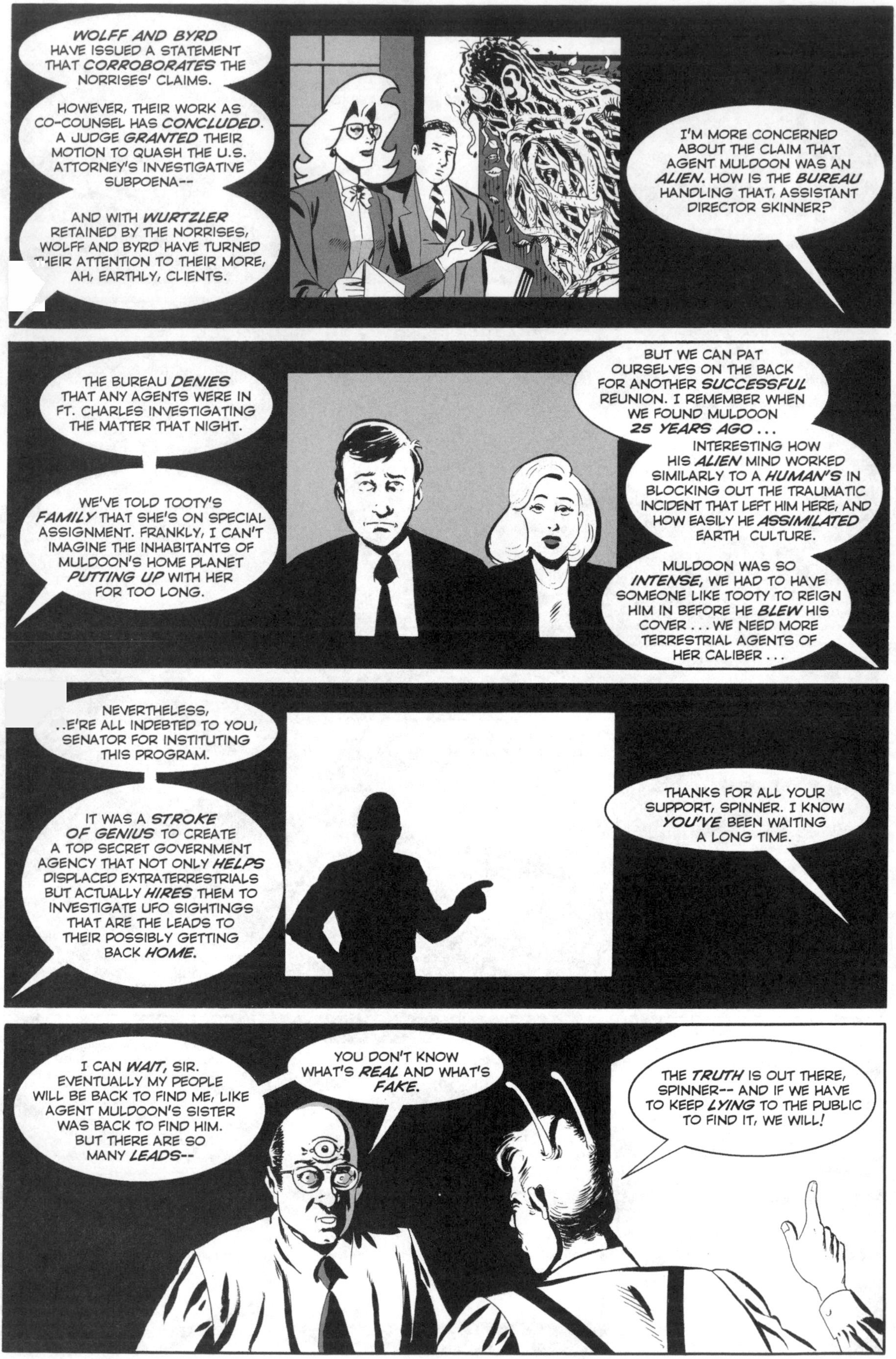
WOLFF AND BYRD HAVE ISSUED A STATEMENT THAT CORROBORATES THE NORRISES' CLAIMS.
HOWEVER, THEIR WORK AS CO-COUNSEL HAS CONCLUDED. A JUDGE GRANTED THEIR MOTION TO QUASH THE U.S. ATTORNEY'S INVESTIGATIVE SUBPOENA--
AND WITH WURTZLER RETAINED BY THE NORRISES, WOLFF AND BYRD HAVE TURNED THEIR ATTENTION TO THEIR MORE, AH, EARTHLY, CLIENTS.
I'M MORE CONCERNED ABOUT THE CLAIM THAT AGENT MULDOON WAS AN ALIEN. HOW IS THE BUREAU HANDLING THAT, ASSISTANT DIRECTOR SKINNER?
THE BUREAU DENIES THAT ANY AGENTS WERE IN FT. CHARLES INVESTIGATING THE MATTER THAT NIGHT.
WE'VE TOLD TOOTY'S FAMILY THAT SHE'S ON SPECIAL ASSIGNMENT. FRANKLY, I CAN'T IMAGINE THE INHABITANTS OF MULDOON'S HOME PLANET PUTTING UP WITH HER FOR TOO LONG.
BUT WE CAN PAT OURSELVES ON THE BACK FOR ANOTHER SUCCESSFUL REUNION. I REMEMBER WHEN WE FOUND MULDOON 25 YEARS AGO . . .
INTERESTING HOW HIS ALIEN MIND WORKED SIMILARLY TO A HUMAN'S IN BLOCKING OUT THE TRAUMATIC INCIDENT THAT LEFT HIM HERE, AND HOW EASILY HE ASSIMILATED EARTH CULTURE.
MULDOON WAS SO INTENSE, WE HAD TO HAVE SOMEONE LIKE TOOTY TO REIGN HIM IN BEFORE HE BLEW HIS COVER . . . WE NEED MORE TERRESTRIAL AGENTS OF HER CALIBER . . .
NEVERTHELESS, ..E'RE ALL INDEBTED TO YOU, SENATOR FOR INSTITUTING THIS PROGRAM.
IT WAS A STROKE OF GENIUS TO CREATE A TOP SECRET GOVERNMENT AGENCY THAT NOT ONLY HELPS DISPLACED EXTRATERRESTRIALS BUT ACTUALLY HIRES THEM TO INVESTIGATE UFO SIGHTINGS THAT ARE THE LEADS TO THEIR POSSIBLY GETTING BACK HOME.
THANKS FOR ALL YOUR SUPPORT, SPINNER. I KNOW YOU'VE BEEN WAITING A LONG TIME.
I CAN WAIT, SIR. EVENTUALLY MY PEOPLE WILL BE BACK TO FIND ME, LIKE AGENT MULDOON'S SISTER WAS BACK TO FIND HIM. BUT THERE ARE SO MANY LEADS--
YOU DON'T KNOW WHAT'S REAL AND WHAT'S FAKE.
THE TRUTH IS OUT THERE, SPINNER-- AND IF WE HAVE TO KEEP LYING TO THE PUBLIC TO FIND IT, WE WILL!

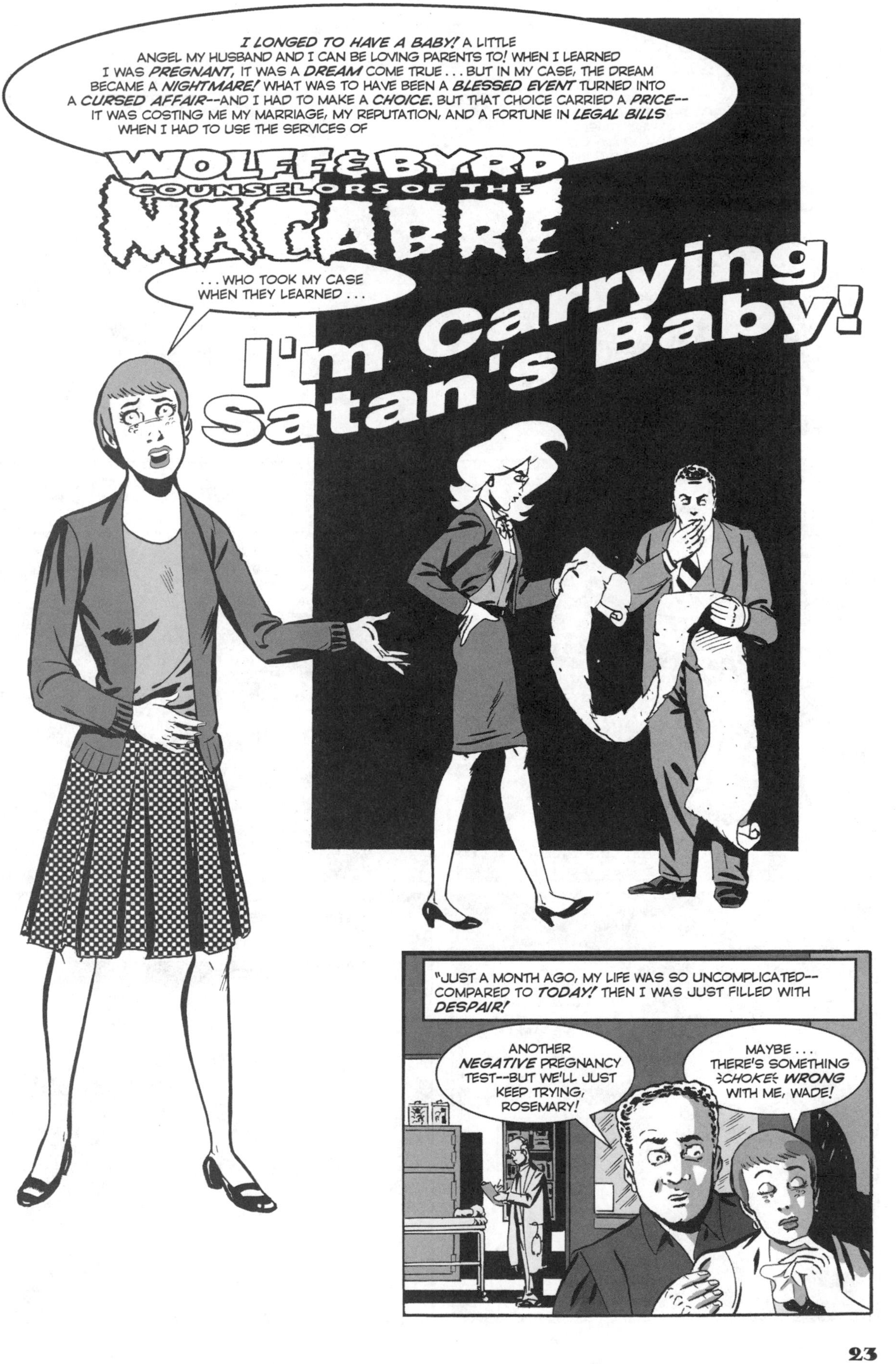

I LONGED TO HAVE A BABY! A LITTLE ANGEL MY HUSBAND AND I CAN BE LOVING PARENTS TO! WHEN I LEARNED I WAS PREGNANT, IT WAS A DREAM COME TRUE . . . BUT IN MY CASE, THE DREAM BECAME A NIGHTMARE! WHAT WAS TO HAVE BEEN A BLESSED EVENT TURNED INTO A CURSED AFFAIR--AND I HAD TO MAKE A CHOICE. BUT THAT CHOICE CARRIED A PRICE--IT WAS COSTING ME MY MARRIAGE, MY REPUTATION, AND A FORTUNE IN LEGAL BILLS WHEN I HAD TO USE THE SERVICES OF
WOLFF & BYRD
COUNSELORS OF THE
MACABRE
. . . WHO TOOK MY CASE WHEN THEY LEARNED . . .
I'm Carrying Satan's Baby!
"JUST A MONTH AGO, MY LIFE WAS SO UNCOMPLICATED--COMPARED TO TODAY! THEN I WAS JUST FILLED WITH DESPAIR!
ANOTHER NEGATIVE PREGNANCY TEST--BUT WE'LL JUST KEEP TRYING, ROSEMARY!
MAYBE . . . THERE'S SOMETHING ƐCHOKEƎ WRONG WITH ME, WADE!

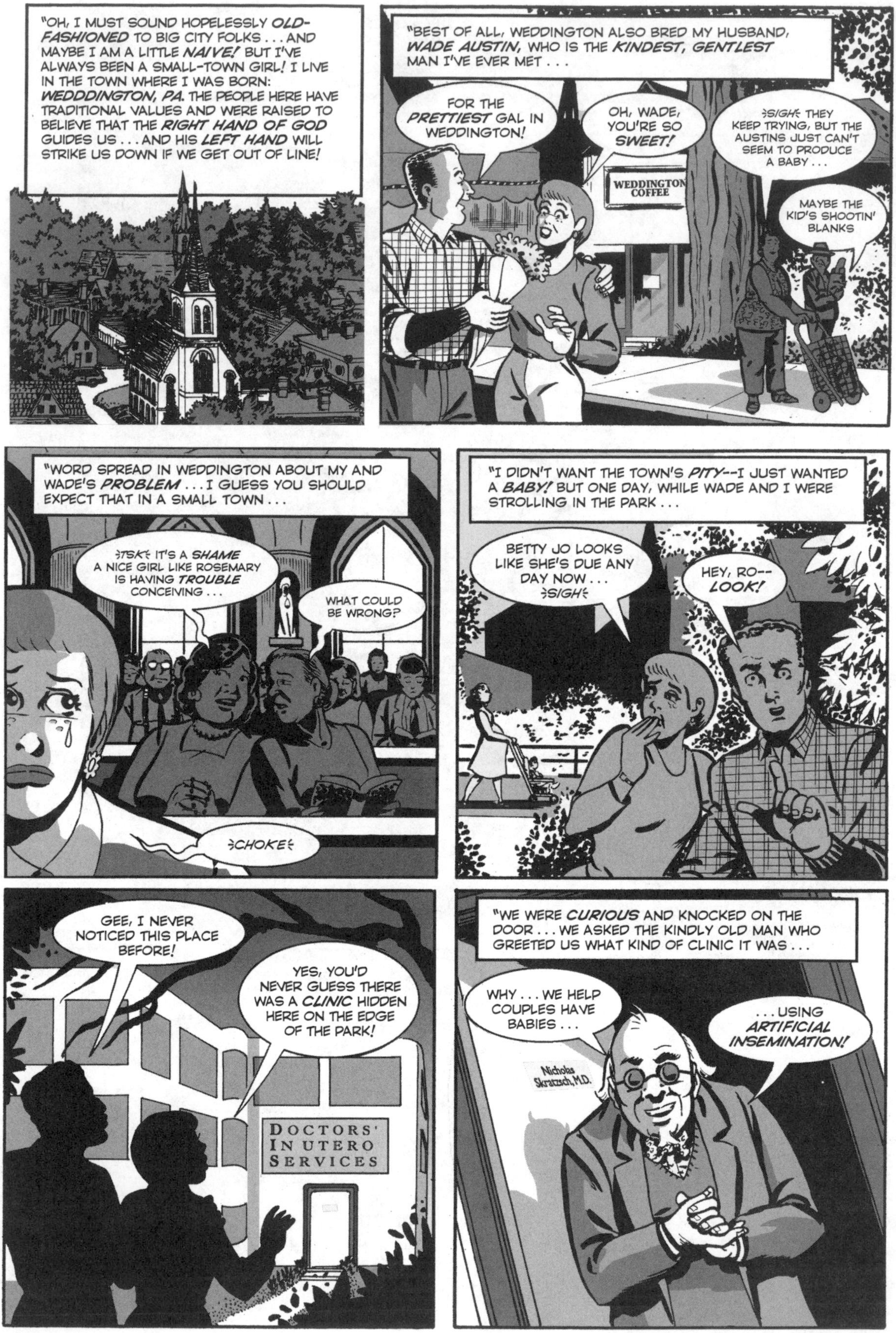
"OH, I MUST SOUND HOPELESSLY OLD-FASHIONED TO BIG CITY FOLKS . . . AND MAYBE I AM A LITTLE NAIVE! BUT I'VE ALWAYS BEEN A SMALL-TOWN GIRL! I LIVE IN THE TOWN WHERE I WAS BORN: WEDDDINGTON, PA. THE PEOPLE HERE HAVE TRADITIONAL VALUES AND WERE RAISED TO BELIEVE THAT THE RIGHT HAND OF GOD GUIDES US . . . AND HIS LEFT HAND WILL STRIKE US DOWN IF WE GET OUT OF LINE!
"BEST OF ALL, WEDDINGTON ALSO BRED MY HUSBAND, WADE AUSTIN, WHO IS THE KINDEST, GENTLEST MAN I'VE EVER MET . . .
FOR THE PRETTIEST GAL IN WEDDINGTON!
OH, WADE, YOU'RE SO SWEET!
WEDDINGTON COFFEE
SIGH THEY KEEP TRYING, BUT THE AUSTINS JUST CAN'T SEEM TO PRODUCE A BABY . . .
MAYBE THE KID'S SHOOTIN' BLANKS
"WORD SPREAD IN WEDDINGTON ABOUT MY AND WADE'S PROBLEM . . . I GUESS YOU SHOULD EXPECT THAT IN A SMALL TOWN . . .
TSK IT'S A SHAME A NICE GIRL LIKE ROSEMARY IS HAVING TROUBLE CONCEIVING . . .
WHAT COULD BE WRONG?
CHOKE
"I DIDN'T WANT THE TOWN'S PITY--I JUST WANTED A BABY! BUT ONE DAY, WHILE WADE AND I WERE STROLLING IN THE PARK . . .
BETTY JO LOOKS LIKE SHE'S DUE ANY DAY NOW . . . SIGH
HEY, RO-- LOOK!
GEE, I NEVER NOTICED THIS PLACE BEFORE!
YES, YOU'D NEVER GUESS THERE WAS A CLINIC HIDDEN HERE ON THE EDGE OF THE PARK!
DOCTORS' IN UTERO SERVICES
"WE WERE CURIOUS AND KNOCKED ON THE DOOR . . . WE ASKED THE KINDLY OLD MAN WHO GREETED US WHAT KIND OF CLINIC IT WAS . . .
WHY . . . WE HELP COUPLES HAVE BABIES . . .
. . . USING ARTIFICIAL INSEMINATION!
Nicholas Skratzsch, M.D.

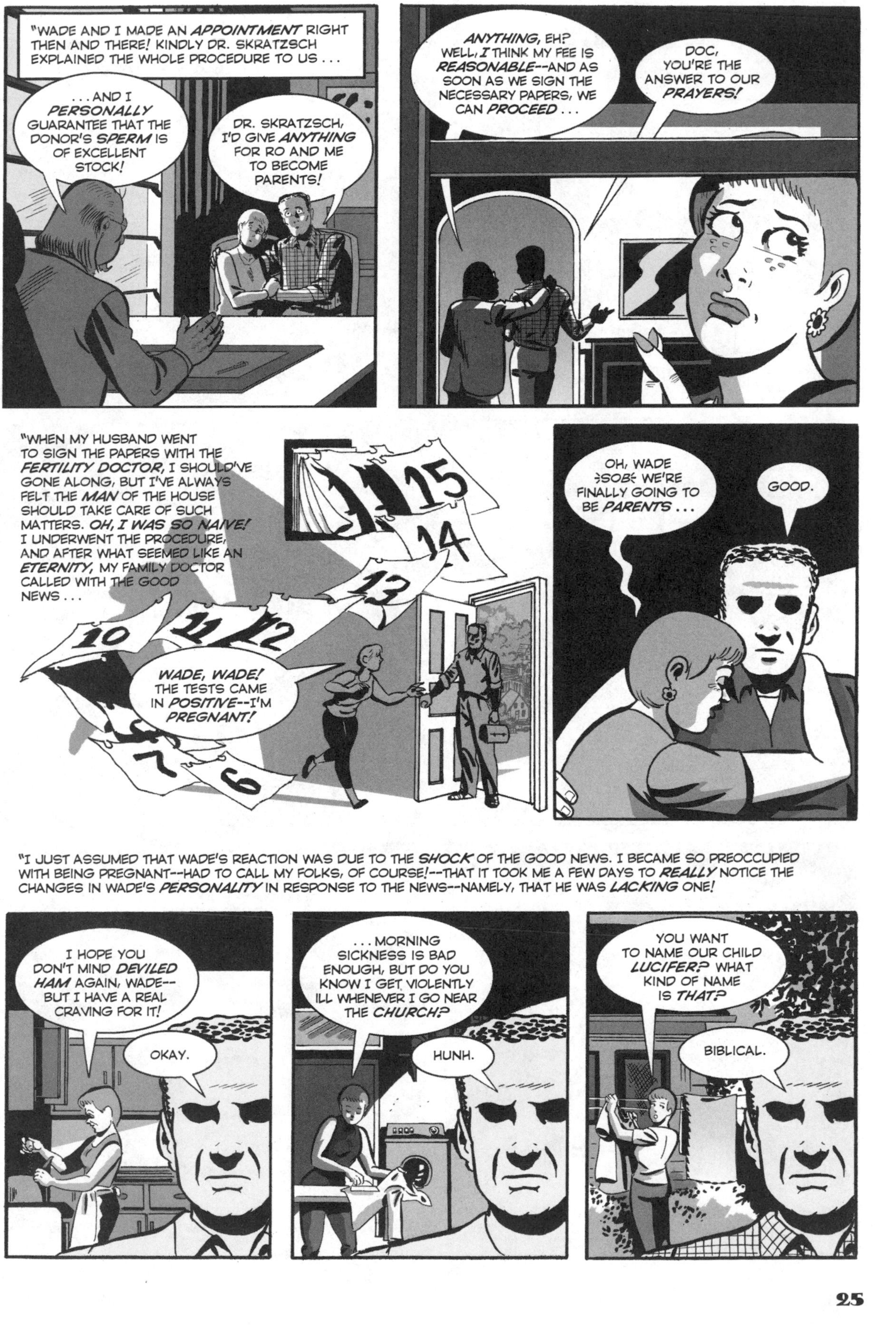
"WADE AND I MADE AN APPOINTMENT RIGHT THEN AND THERE! KINDLY DR. SKRATZSCH EXPLAINED THE WHOLE PROCEDURE TO US . . .
. . . AND I PERSONALLY GUARANTEE THAT THE DONOR'S SPERM IS OF EXCELLENT STOCK!
DR. SKRATZSCH, I'D GIVE ANYTHING FOR RO AND ME TO BECOME PARENTS!
ANYTHING, EH? WELL, I THINK MY FEE IS REASONABLE--AND AS SOON AS WE SIGN THE NECESSARY PAPERS, WE CAN PROCEED . . .
DOC, YOU'RE THE ANSWER TO OUR PRAYERS!
"WHEN MY HUSBAND WENT TO SIGN THE PAPERS WITH THE FERTILITY DOCTOR, I SHOULD'VE GONE ALONG, BUT I'VE ALWAYS FELT THE MAN OF THE HOUSE SHOULD TAKE CARE OF SUCH MATTERS. OH, I WAS SO NAIVE! I UNDERWENT THE PROCEDURE, AND AFTER WHAT SEEMED LIKE AN ETERNITY, MY FAMILY DOCTOR CALLED WITH THE GOOD NEWS . . .
15
14
13
10
11
12
7
6
WADE, WADE! THE TESTS CAME IN POSITIVE--I'M PREGNANT!
OH, WADE *SOB* WE'RE FINALLY GOING TO BE PARENTS . . .
GOOD.
"I JUST ASSUMED THAT WADE'S REACTION WAS DUE TO THE SHOCK OF THE GOOD NEWS. I BECAME SO PREOCCUPIED WITH BEING PREGNANT--HAD TO CALL MY FOLKS, OF COURSE!--THAT IT TOOK ME A FEW DAYS TO REALLY NOTICE THE CHANGES IN WADE'S PERSONALITY IN RESPONSE TO THE NEWS--NAMELY, THAT HE WAS LACKING ONE!
I HOPE YOU DON'T MIND DEVILED HAM AGAIN, WADE--BUT I HAVE A REAL CRAVING FOR IT!
OKAY.
. . . MORNING SICKNESS IS BAD ENOUGH, BUT DO YOU KNOW I GET VIOLENTLY ILL WHENEVER I GO NEAR THE CHURCH?
HUNH.
YOU WANT TO NAME OUR CHILD LUCIFER? WHAT KIND OF NAME IS THAT?
BIBLICAL.

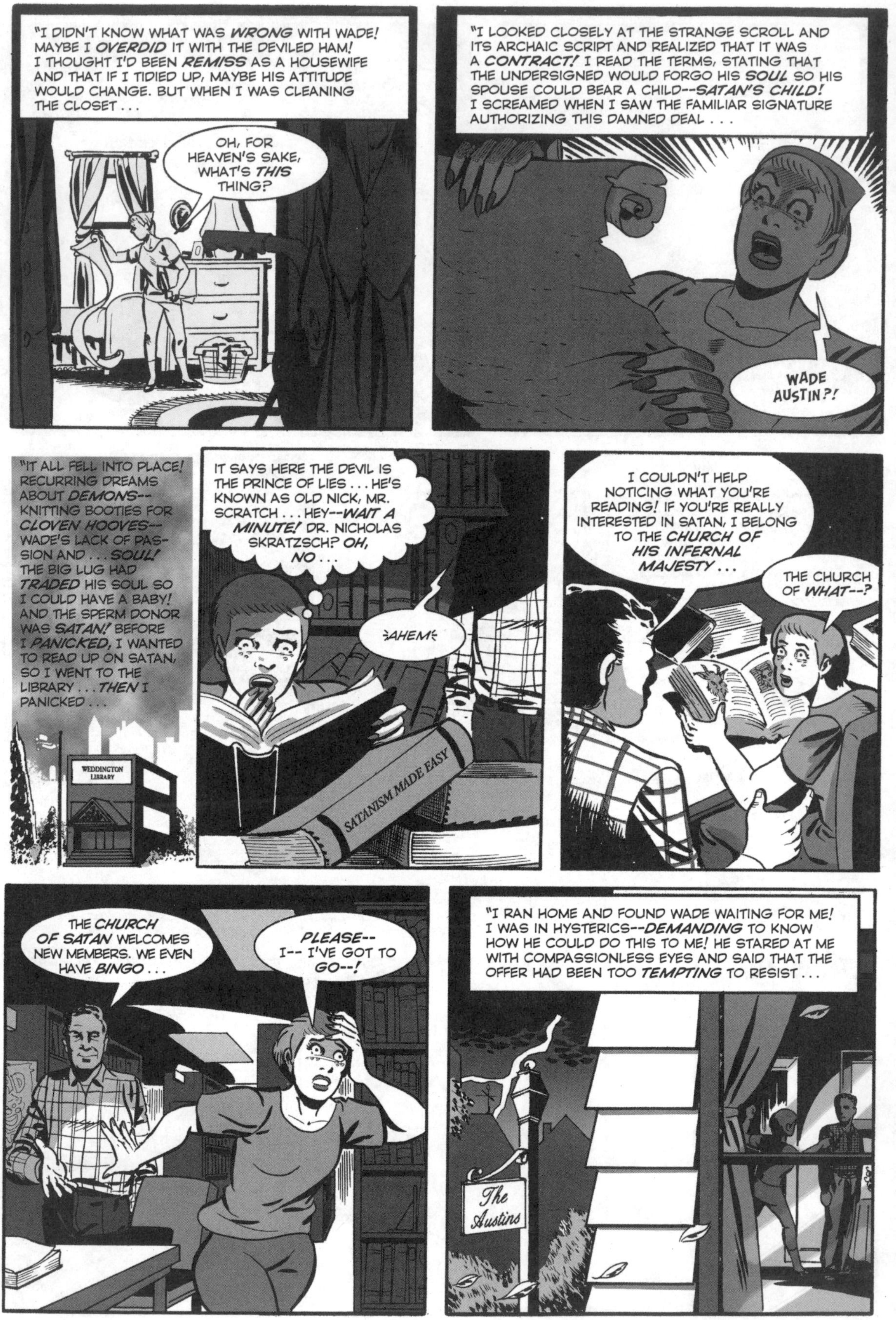
"I DIDN'T KNOW WHAT WAS WRONG WITH WADE! MAYBE I OVERDID IT WITH THE DEVILED HAM! I THOUGHT I'D BEEN REMISS AS A HOUSEWIFE AND THAT IF I TIDIED UP, MAYBE HIS ATTITUDE WOULD CHANGE. BUT WHEN I WAS CLEANING THE CLOSET . . .
OH, FOR HEAVEN'S SAKE, WHAT'S THIS THING?
"I LOOKED CLOSELY AT THE STRANGE SCROLL AND ITS ARCHAIC SCRIPT AND REALIZED THAT IT WAS A CONTRACT! I READ THE TERMS, STATING THAT THE UNDERSIGNED WOULD FORGO HIS SOUL SO HIS SPOUSE COULD BEAR A CHILD--SATAN'S CHILD! I SCREAMED WHEN I SAW THE FAMILIAR SIGNATURE AUTHORIZING THIS DAMNED DEAL . . .
WADE AUSTIN?!
"IT ALL FELL INTO PLACE! RECURRING DREAMS ABOUT DEMONS-- KNITTING BOOTIES FOR CLOVEN HOOVES-- WADE'S LACK OF PASSION AND . . . SOUL! THE BIG LUG HAD TRADED HIS SOUL SO I COULD HAVE A BABY! AND THE SPERM DONOR WAS SATAN! BEFORE I PANICKED, I WANTED TO READ UP ON SATAN, SO I WENT TO THE LIBRARY . . . THEN I PANICKED . . .
WEDDINGTON LIBRARY
IT SAYS HERE THE DEVIL IS THE PRINCE OF LIES . . . HE'S KNOWN AS OLD NICK, MR. SCRATCH . . . HEY--WAIT A MINUTE! DR. NICHOLAS SKRATZSCH? OH, NO . . .
AHEM
SATANISM MADE EASY
I COULDN'T HELP NOTICING WHAT YOU'RE READING! IF YOU'RE REALLY INTERESTED IN SATAN, I BELONG TO THE CHURCH OF HIS INFERNAL MAJESTY . . .
THE CHURCH OF WHAT--?
THE CHURCH OF SATAN WELCOMES NEW MEMBERS. WE EVEN HAVE BINGO . . .
PLEASE-- I-- I'VE GOT TO GO--!
"I RAN HOME AND FOUND WADE WAITING FOR ME! I WAS IN HYSTERICS--DEMANDING TO KNOW HOW HE COULD DO THIS TO ME! HE STARED AT ME WITH COMPASSIONLESS EYES AND SAID THAT THE OFFER HAD BEEN TOO TEMPTING TO RESIST . . .
The Austins

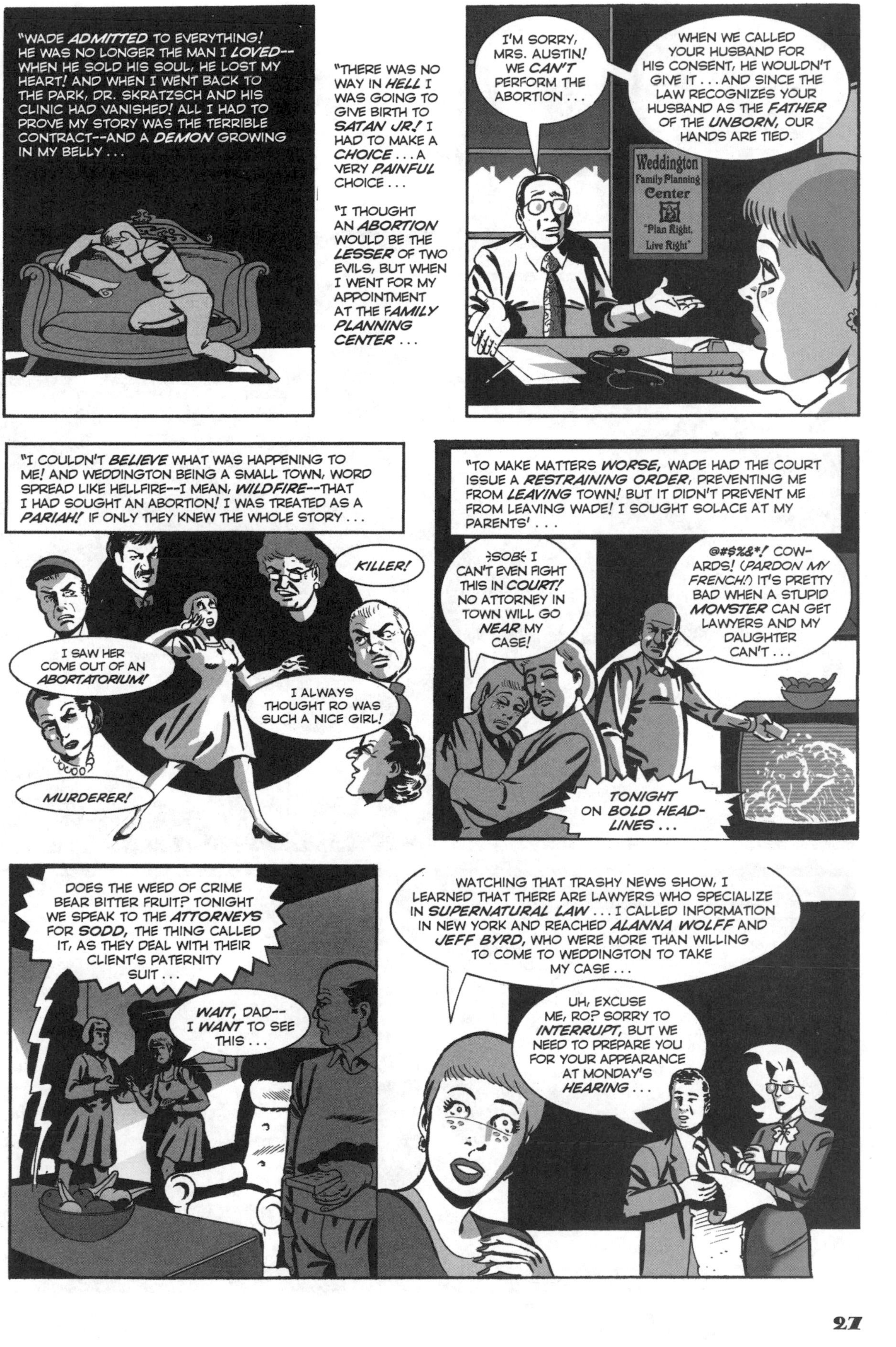
"WADE ADMITTED TO EVERYTHING! HE WAS NO LONGER THE MAN I LOVED-- WHEN HE SOLD HIS SOUL, HE LOST MY HEART! AND WHEN I WENT BACK TO THE PARK, DR. SKRATZSCH AND HIS CLINIC HAD VANISHED! ALL I HAD TO PROVE MY STORY WAS THE TERRIBLE CONTRACT--AND A DEMON GROWING IN MY BELLY . . .
"THERE WAS NO WAY IN HELL I WAS GOING TO GIVE BIRTH TO SATAN JR.! I HAD TO MAKE A CHOICE . . . A VERY PAINFUL CHOICE . . .
"I THOUGHT AN ABORTION WOULD BE THE LESSER OF TWO EVILS, BUT WHEN I WENT FOR MY APPOINTMENT AT THE FAMILY PLANNING CENTER . . .
I'M SORRY, MRS. AUSTIN! WE CAN'T PERFORM THE ABORTION . . .
WHEN WE CALLED YOUR HUSBAND FOR HIS CONSENT, HE WOULDN'T GIVE IT . . . AND SINCE THE LAW RECOGNIZES YOUR HUSBAND AS THE FATHER OF THE UNBORN, OUR HANDS ARE TIED.
Weddington Family Planning Center "Plan Right, Live Right"
"I COULDN'T BELIEVE WHAT WAS HAPPENING TO ME! AND WEDDINGTON BEING A SMALL TOWN, WORD SPREAD LIKE HELLFIRE--I MEAN, WILDFIRE--THAT I HAD SOUGHT AN ABORTION! I WAS TREATED AS A PARIAH! IF ONLY THEY KNEW THE WHOLE STORY . . .
KILLER!
I SAW HER COME OUT OF AN ABORTATORIUM!
I ALWAYS THOUGHT RO WAS SUCH A NICE GIRL!
MURDERER!
"TO MAKE MATTERS WORSE, WADE HAD THE COURT ISSUE A RESTRAINING ORDER, PREVENTING ME FROM LEAVING TOWN! BUT IT DIDN'T PREVENT ME FROM LEAVING WADE! I SOUGHT SOLACE AT MY PARENTS' . . .
SOB I CAN'T EVEN FIGHT THIS IN COURT! NO ATTORNEY IN TOWN WILL GO NEAR MY CASE!
@#$%&*! COW-ARDS! (PARDON MY FRENCH!) IT'S PRETTY BAD WHEN A STUPID MONSTER CAN GET LAWYERS AND MY DAUGHTER CAN'T . . .
TONIGHT ON BOLD HEAD-LINES . . .
DOES THE WEED OF CRIME BEAR BITTER FRUIT? TONIGHT WE SPEAK TO THE ATTORNEYS FOR SODD, THE THING CALLED IT, AS THEY DEAL WITH THEIR CLIENT'S PATERNITY SUIT . . .
WAIT, DAD-- I WANT TO SEE THIS . . .
WATCHING THAT TRASHY NEWS SHOW, I LEARNED THAT THERE ARE LAWYERS WHO SPECIALIZE IN SUPERNATURAL LAW . . . I CALLED INFORMATION IN NEW YORK AND REACHED ALANNA WOLFF AND JEFF BYRD, WHO WERE MORE THAN WILLING TO COME TO WEDDINGTON TO TAKE MY CASE . . .
UH, EXCUSE ME, RO? SORRY TO INTERRUPT, BUT WE NEED TO PREPARE YOU FOR YOUR APPEARANCE AT MONDAY'S HEARING . . .

THE LAWS OF GRAVIDITY!

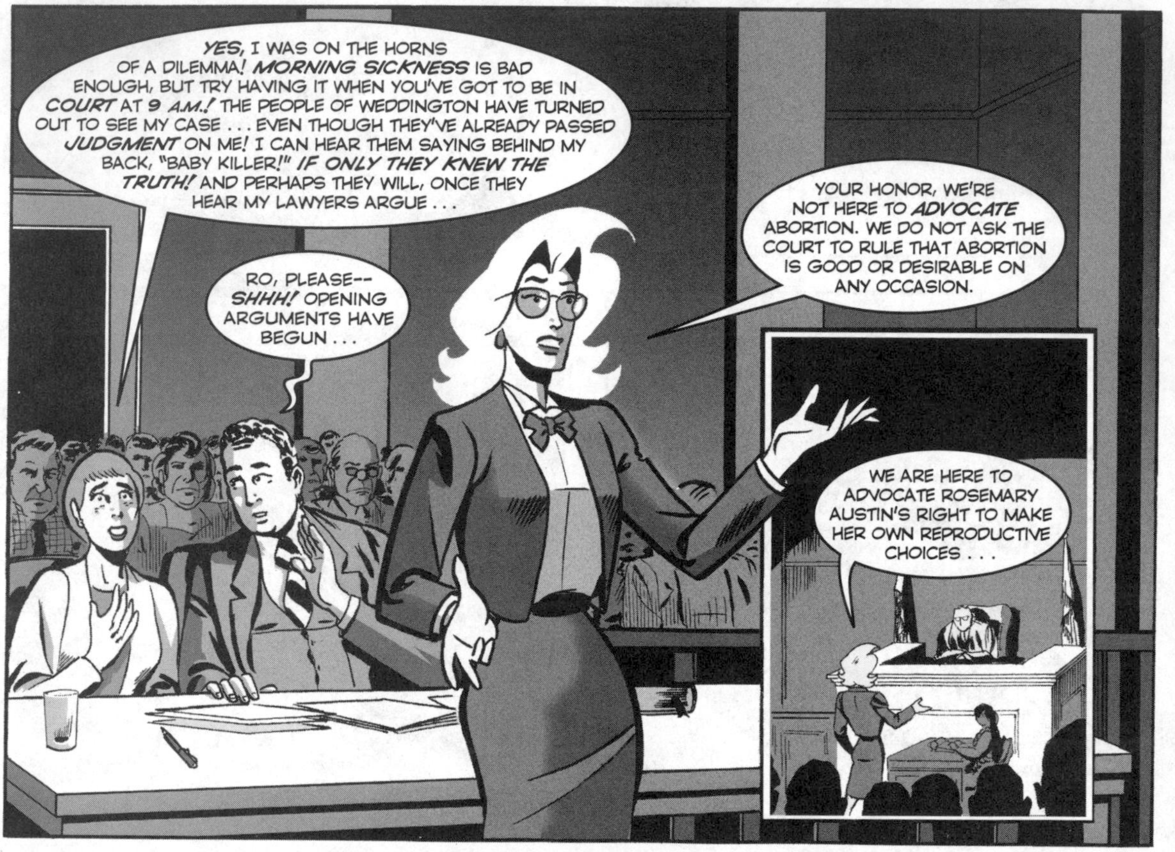
YES, I WAS ON THE HORNS OF A DILEMMA! MORNING SICKNESS IS BAD ENOUGH, BUT TRY HAVING IT WHEN YOU'VE GOT TO BE IN COURT AT 9 A.M.! THE PEOPLE OF WEDDINGTON HAVE TURNED OUT TO SEE MY CASE . . . EVEN THOUGH THEY'VE ALREADY PASSED JUDGMENT ON ME! I CAN HEAR THEM SAYING BEHIND MY BACK, "BABY KILLER!" IF ONLY THEY KNEW THE TRUTH! AND PERHAPS THEY WILL, ONCE THEY HEAR MY LAWYERS ARGUE . . .
RO, PLEASE-- SHHH! OPENING ARGUMENTS HAVE BEGUN . . .
YOUR HONOR, WE'RE NOT HERE TO ADVOCATE ABORTION. WE DO NOT ASK THE COURT TO RULE THAT ABORTION IS GOOD OR DESIRABLE ON ANY OCCASION.
WE ARE HERE TO ADVOCATE ROSEMARY AUSTIN'S RIGHT TO MAKE HER OWN REPRODUCTIVE CHOICES . . .

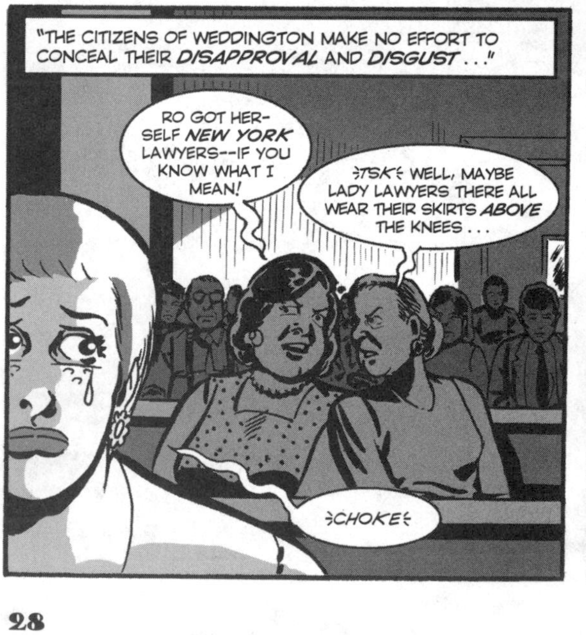
"THE CITIZENS OF WEDDINGTON MAKE NO EFFORT TO CONCEAL THEIR DISAPPROVAL AND DISGUST . . ."
RO GOT HER-SELF NEW YORK LAWYERS--IF YOU KNOW WHAT I MEAN!
TSK WELL, MAYBE LADY LAWYERS THERE ALL WEAR THEIR SKIRTS ABOVE THE KNEES . . .
CHOKE

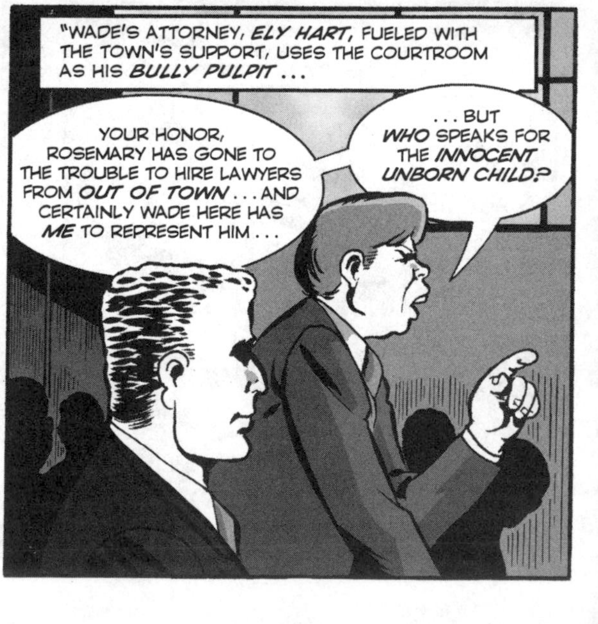
"WADE'S ATTORNEY, ELY HART, FUELED WITH THE TOWN'S SUPPORT, USES THE COURTROOM AS HIS BULLY PULPIT . . .
YOUR HONOR, ROSEMARY HAS GONE TO THE TROUBLE TO HIRE LAWYERS FROM OUT OF TOWN . . . AND CERTAINLY WADE HERE HAS ME TO REPRESENT HIM . . .
. . . BUT WHO SPEAKS FOR THE INNOCENT UNBORN CHILD?

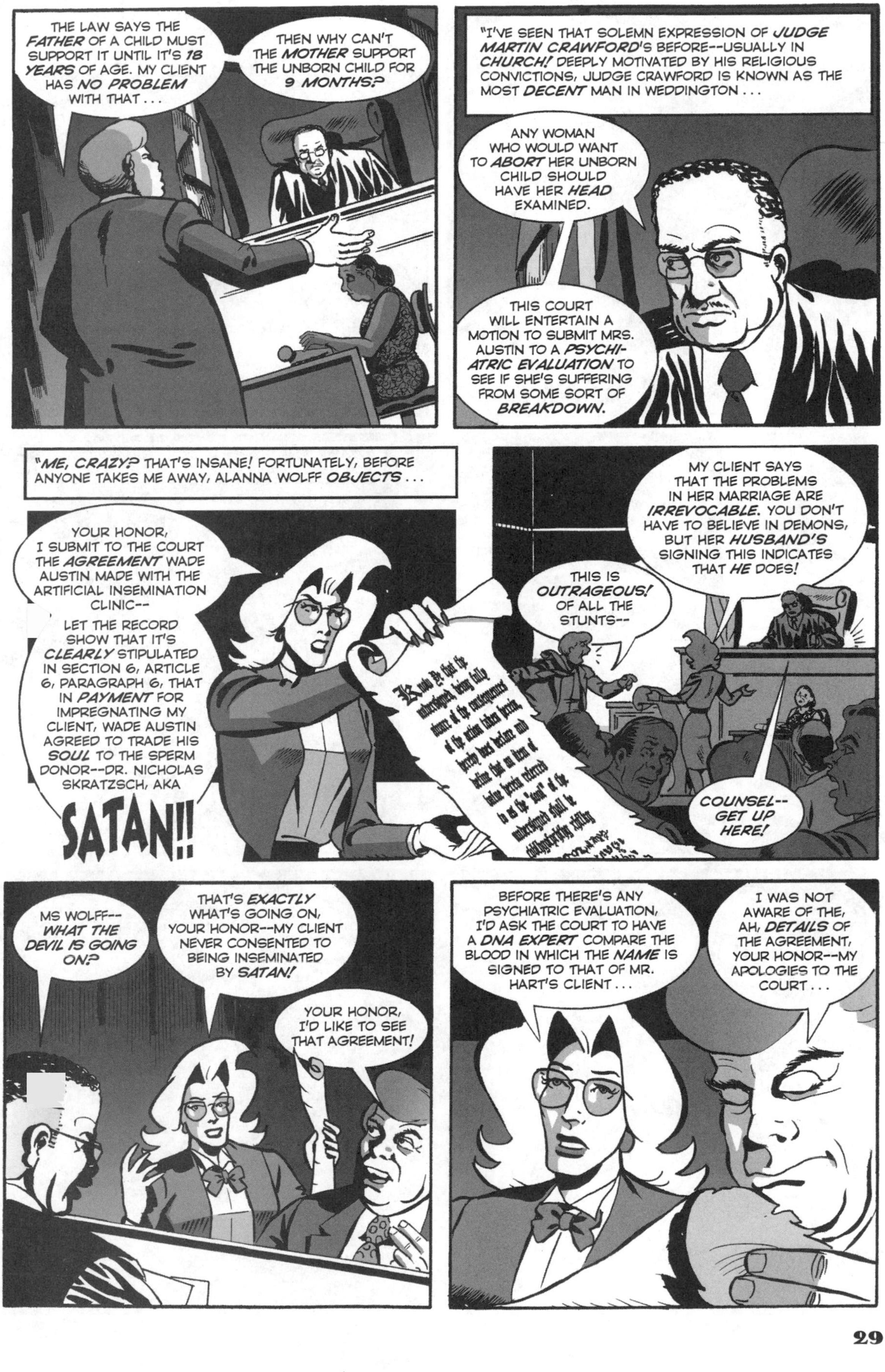
THE LAW SAYS THE FATHER OF A CHILD MUST SUPPORT IT UNTIL IT'S 18 YEARS OF AGE. MY CLIENT HAS NO PROBLEM WITH THAT . . .
THEN WHY CAN'T THE MOTHER SUPPORT THE UNBORN CHILD FOR 9 MONTHS?
"I'VE SEEN THAT SOLEMN EXPRESSION OF JUDGE MARTIN CRAWFORD'S BEFORE--USUALLY IN CHURCH! DEEPLY MOTIVATED BY HIS RELIGIOUS CONVICTIONS, JUDGE CRAWFORD IS KNOWN AS THE MOST DECENT MAN IN WEDDINGTON . . .
ANY WOMAN WHO WOULD WANT TO ABORT HER UNBORN CHILD SHOULD HAVE HER HEAD EXAMINED.
THIS COURT WILL ENTERTAIN A MOTION TO SUBMIT MRS. AUSTIN TO A PSYCHIATRIC EVALUATION TO SEE IF SHE'S SUFFERING FROM SOME SORT OF BREAKDOWN.
"ME, CRAZY? THAT'S INSANE! FORTUNATELY, BEFORE ANYONE TAKES ME AWAY, ALANNA WOLFF OBJECTS . . .
YOUR HONOR, I SUBMIT TO THE COURT THE AGREEMENT WADE AUSTIN MADE WITH THE ARTIFICIAL INSEMINATION CLINIC--
LET THE RECORD SHOW THAT IT'S CLEARLY STIPULATED IN SECTION 6, ARTICLE 6, PARAGRAPH 6, THAT IN PAYMENT FOR IMPREGNATING MY CLIENT, WADE AUSTIN AGREED TO TRADE HIS SOUL TO THE SPERM DONOR--DR. NICHOLAS SKRATZSCH, AKA
SATAN!!
THIS IS OUTRAGEOUS! OF ALL THE STUNTS--
MY CLIENT SAYS THAT THE PROBLEMS IN HER MARRIAGE ARE IRREVOCABLE. YOU DON'T HAVE TO BELIEVE IN DEMONS, BUT HER HUSBAND'S SIGNING THIS INDICATES THAT HE DOES!
COUNSEL-- GET UP HERE!
MS WOLFF-- WHAT THE DEVIL IS GOING ON?
THAT'S EXACTLY WHAT'S GOING ON, YOUR HONOR--MY CLIENT NEVER CONSENTED TO BEING INSEMINATED BY SATAN!
YOUR HONOR, I'D LIKE TO SEE THAT AGREEMENT!
BEFORE THERE'S ANY PSYCHIATRIC EVALUATION, I'D ASK THE COURT TO HAVE A DNA EXPERT COMPARE THE BLOOD IN WHICH THE NAME IS SIGNED TO THAT OF MR. HART'S CLIENT . . .
I WAS NOT AWARE OF THE, AH, DETAILS OF THE AGREEMENT, YOUR HONOR--MY APOLOGIES TO THE COURT . . .

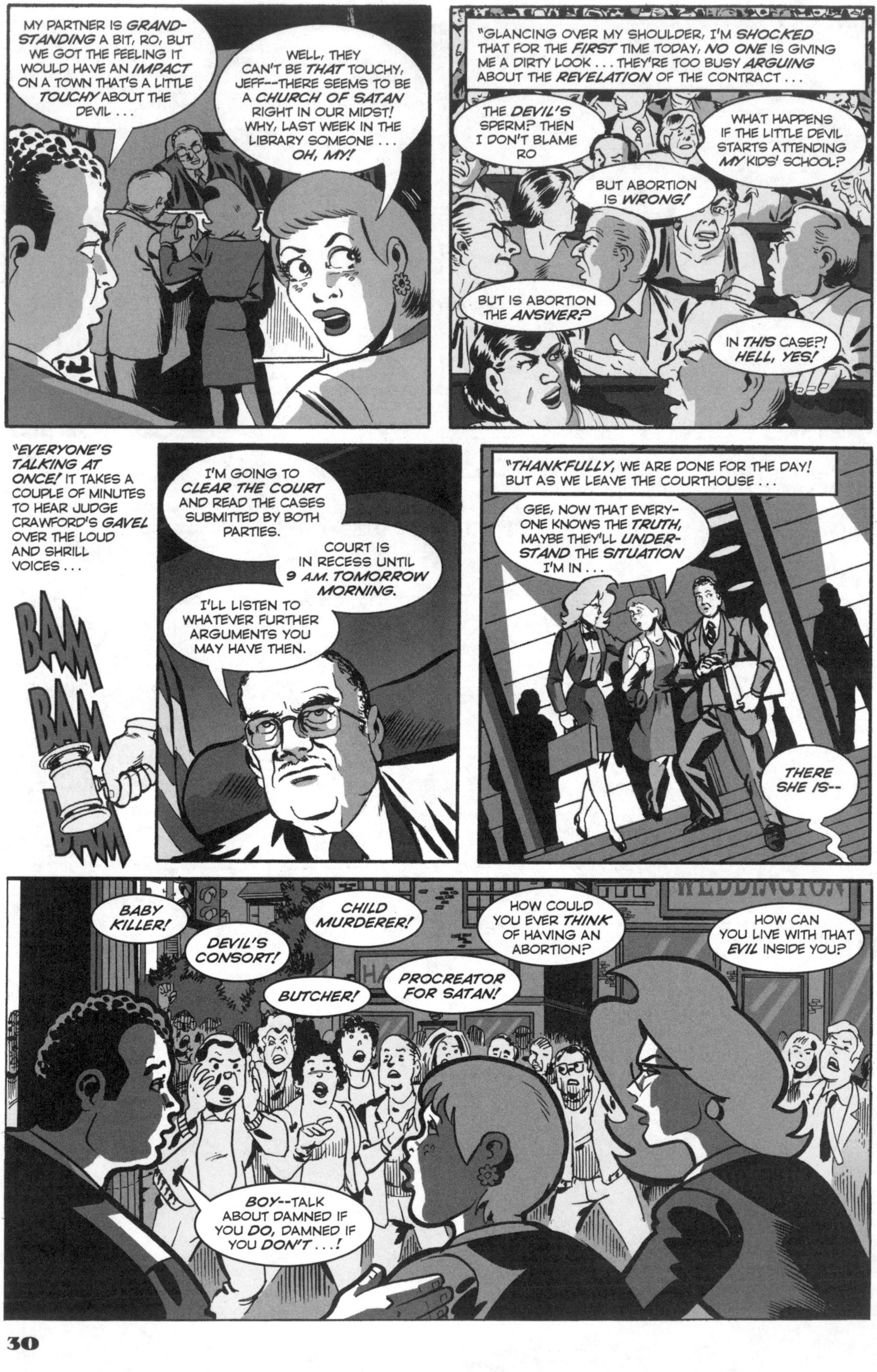
MY PARTNER IS GRAND-STANDING A BIT, RO, BUT WE GOT THE FEELING IT WOULD HAVE AN IMPACT ON A TOWN THAT'S A LITTLE TOUCHY ABOUT THE DEVIL . . .
WELL, THEY CAN'T BE THAT TOUCHY, JEFF--THERE SEEMS TO BE A CHURCH OF SATAN RIGHT IN OUR MIDST! WHY, LAST WEEK IN THE LIBRARY SOMEONE . . . OH, MY!
"GLANCING OVER MY SHOULDER, I'M SHOCKED THAT FOR THE FIRST TIME TODAY, NO ONE IS GIVING ME A DIRTY LOOK . . . THEY'RE TOO BUSY ARGUING ABOUT THE REVELATION OF THE CONTRACT . . .
THE DEVIL'S SPERM? THEN I DON'T BLAME RO
WHAT HAPPENS IF THE LITTLE DEVIL STARTS ATTENDING MY KIDS' SCHOOL?
BUT ABORTION IS WRONG!
BUT IS ABORTION THE ANSWER?
IN THIS CASE?! HELL, YES!
"EVERYONE'S TALKING AT ONCE! IT TAKES A COUPLE OF MINUTES TO HEAR JUDGE CRAWFORD'S GAVEL OVER THE LOUD AND SHRILL VOICES . . .
BAM
BAM
BAM
I'M GOING TO CLEAR THE COURT AND READ THE CASES SUBMITTED BY BOTH PARTIES.
COURT IS IN RECESS UNTIL 9 A.M. TOMORROW MORNING.
I'LL LISTEN TO WHATEVER FURTHER ARGUMENTS YOU MAY HAVE THEN.
"THANKFULLY, WE ARE DONE FOR THE DAY! BUT AS WE LEAVE THE COURTHOUSE . . .
GEE, NOW THAT EVERY-ONE KNOWS THE TRUTH, MAYBE THEY'LL UNDER-STAND THE SITUATION I'M IN . . .
THERE SHE IS--
WEDDINGTON
BABY KILLER!
DEVIL'S CONSORT!
CHILD MURDERER!
BUTCHER!
PROCREATOR FOR SATAN!
HOW COULD YOU EVER THINK OF HAVING AN ABORTION?
HOW CAN YOU LIVE WITH THAT EVIL INSIDE YOU?
BOY--TALK ABOUT DAMNED IF YOU DO, DAMNED IF YOU DON'T . . .!

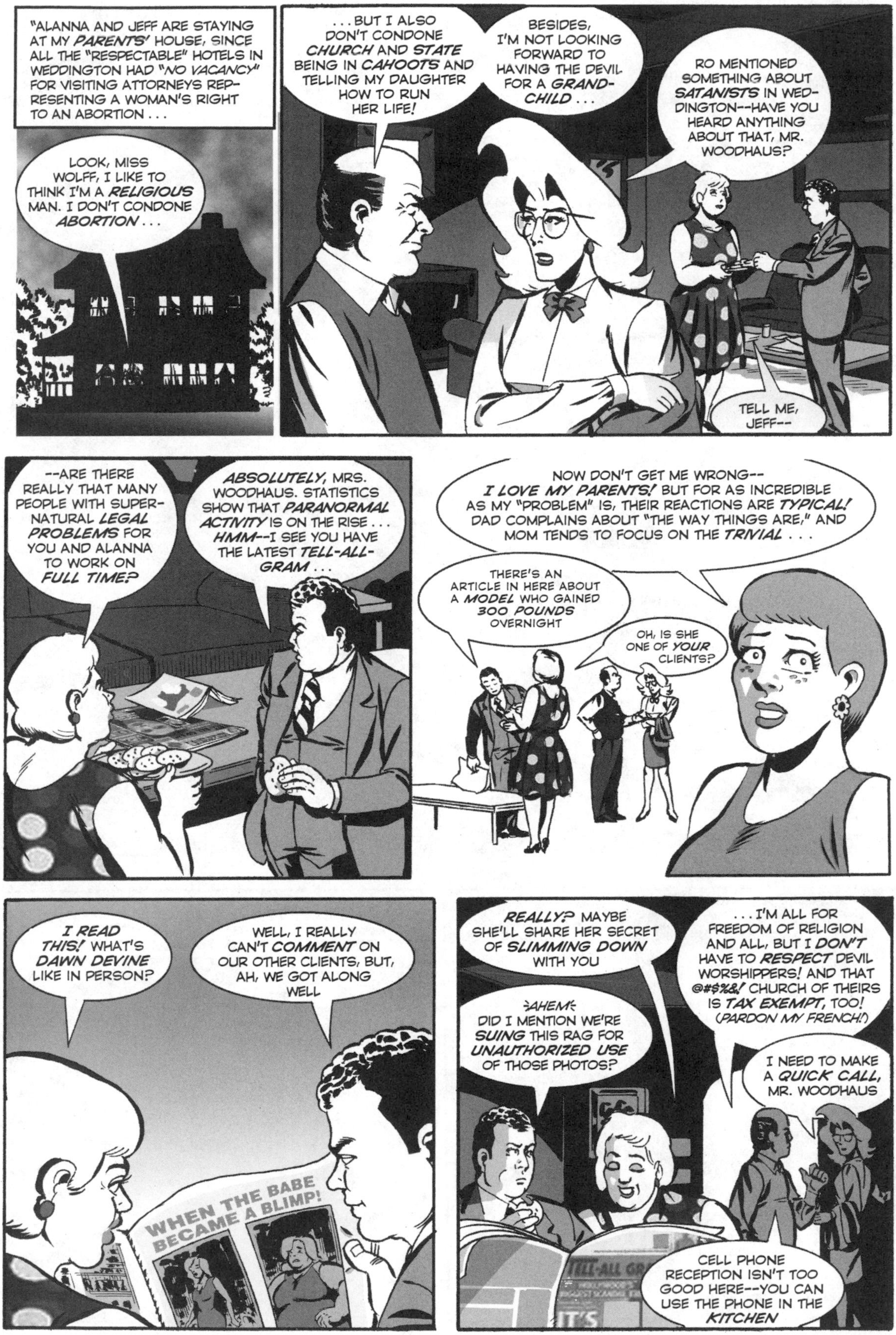

"ALANNA AND JEFF ARE STAYING AT MY PARENTS' HOUSE, SINCE ALL THE "RESPECTABLE" HOTELS IN WEDDINGTON HAD "NO VACANCY" FOR VISITING ATTORNEYS REPRESENTING A WOMAN'S RIGHT TO AN ABORTION . . .
LOOK, MISS WOLFF, I LIKE TO THINK I'M A RELIGIOUS MAN. I DON'T CONDONE ABORTION . . .
. . . BUT I ALSO DON'T CONDONE CHURCH AND STATE BEING IN CAHOOTS AND TELLING MY DAUGHTER HOW TO RUN HER LIFE!
BESIDES, I'M NOT LOOKING FORWARD TO HAVING THE DEVIL FOR A GRAND-CHILD . . .
RO MENTIONED SOMETHING ABOUT SATANISTS IN WEDDINGTON--HAVE YOU HEARD ANYTHING ABOUT THAT, MR. WOODHAUS?
TELL ME, JEFF--
--ARE THERE REALLY THAT MANY PEOPLE WITH SUPERNATURAL LEGAL PROBLEMS FOR YOU AND ALANNA TO WORK ON FULL TIME?
ABSOLUTELY, MRS. WOODHAUS. STATISTICS SHOW THAT PARANORMAL ACTIVITY IS ON THE RISE . . . HMM--I SEE YOU HAVE THE LATEST TELL-ALL-GRAM . . .
NOW DON'T GET ME WRONG-- I LOVE MY PARENTS! BUT FOR AS INCREDIBLE AS MY "PROBLEM" IS, THEIR REACTIONS ARE TYPICAL! DAD COMPLAINS ABOUT "THE WAY THINGS ARE," AND MOM TENDS TO FOCUS ON THE TRIVIAL . . .
THERE'S AN ARTICLE IN HERE ABOUT A MODEL WHO GAINED 300 POUNDS OVERNIGHT
OH, IS SHE ONE OF YOUR CLIENTS?
I READ THIS! WHAT'S DAWN DEVINE LIKE IN PERSON?
WELL, I REALLY CAN'T COMMENT ON OUR OTHER CLIENTS, BUT, AH, WE GOT ALONG WELL
WHEN THE BABE BECAME A BLIMP!
REALLY? MAYBE SHE'LL SHARE HER SECRET OF SLIMMING DOWN WITH YOU
AHEM
DID I MENTION WE'RE SUING THIS RAG FOR UNAUTHORIZED USE OF THOSE PHOTOS?
. . . I'M ALL FOR FREEDOM OF RELIGION AND ALL, BUT I DON'T HAVE TO RESPECT DEVIL WORSHIPPERS! AND THAT @#$%&! CHURCH OF THEIRS IS TAX EXEMPT, TOO! (PARDON MY FRENCH!)
I NEED TO MAKE A QUICK CALL, MR. WOODHAUS
CELL PHONE RECEPTION ISN'T TOO GOOD HERE--YOU CAN USE THE PHONE IN THE KITCHEN
IT'S

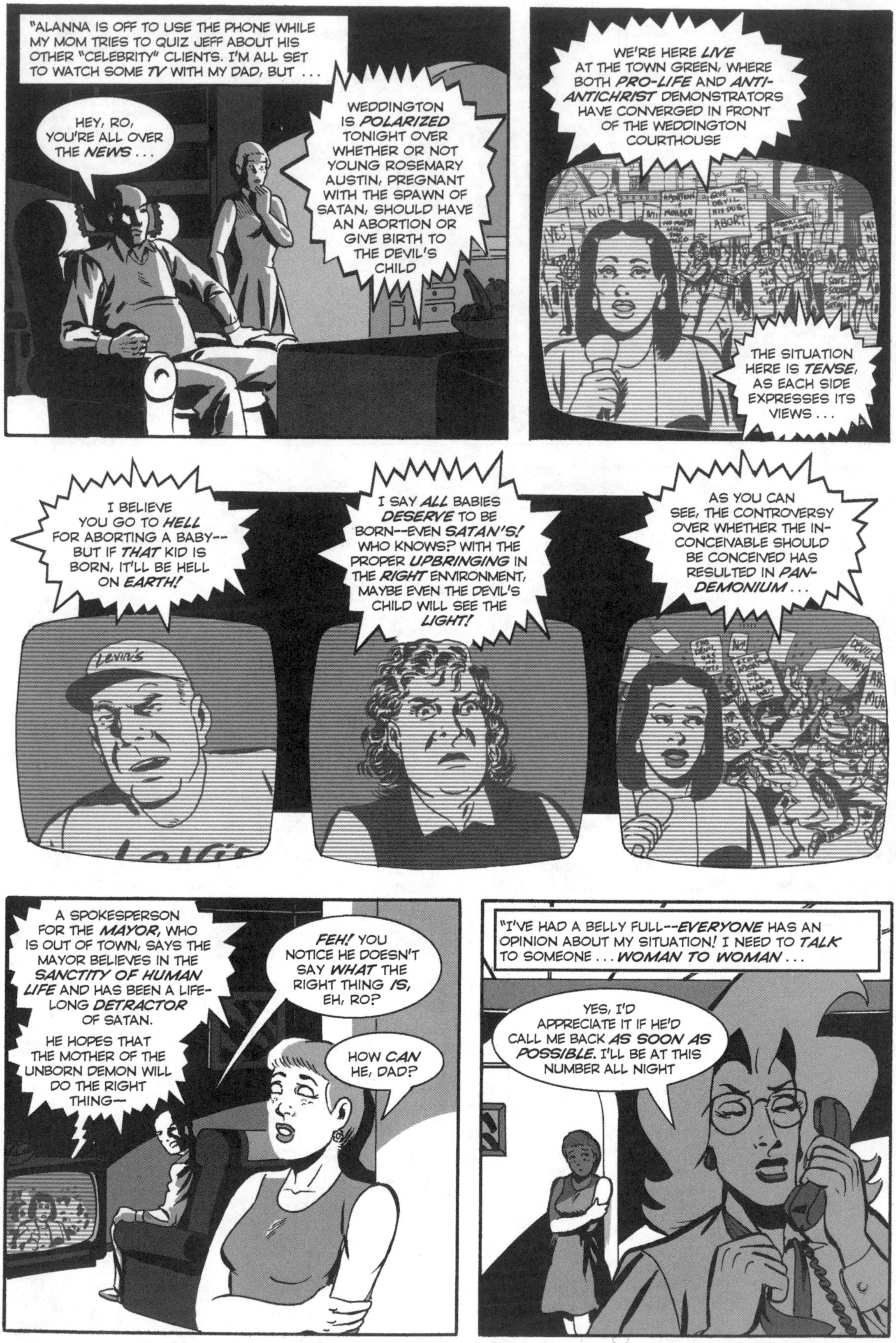
"ALANNA IS OFF TO USE THE PHONE WHILE MY MOM TRIES TO QUIZ JEFF ABOUT HIS OTHER "CELEBRITY" CLIENTS. I'M ALL SET TO WATCH SOME TV WITH MY DAD, BUT . . .
HEY, RO, YOU'RE ALL OVER THE NEWS . . .
WEDDINGTON IS POLARIZED TONIGHT OVER WHETHER OR NOT YOUNG ROSEMARY AUSTIN, PREGNANT WITH THE SPAWN OF SATAN, SHOULD HAVE AN ABORTION OR GIVE BIRTH TO THE DEVIL'S CHILD
WE'RE HERE LIVE AT THE TOWN GREEN, WHERE BOTH PRO-LIFE AND ANTI-ANTICHRIST DEMONSTRATORS HAVE CONVERGED IN FRONT OF THE WEDDINGTON COURTHOUSE
THE SITUATION HERE IS TENSE, AS EACH SIDE EXPRESSES ITS VIEWS . . .
I BELIEVE YOU GO TO HELL FOR ABORTING A BABY--BUT IF THAT KID IS BORN, IT'LL BE HELL ON EARTH!
I SAY ALL BABIES DESERVE TO BE BORN--EVEN SATAN'S! WHO KNOWS? WITH THE PROPER UPBRINGING IN THE RIGHT ENVIRONMENT, MAYBE EVEN THE DEVIL'S CHILD WILL SEE THE LIGHT!
AS YOU CAN SEE, THE CONTROVERSY OVER WHETHER THE IN-CONCEIVABLE SHOULD BE CONCEIVED HAS RESULTED IN PAN-DEMONIUM . . .
A SPOKESPERSON FOR THE MAYOR, WHO IS OUT OF TOWN, SAYS THE MAYOR BELIEVES IN THE SANCTITY OF HUMAN LIFE AND HAS BEEN A LIFE-LONG DETRACTOR OF SATAN.
HE HOPES THAT THE MOTHER OF THE UNBORN DEMON WILL DO THE RIGHT THING--
FEH! YOU NOTICE HE DOESN'T SAY WHAT THE RIGHT THING IS, EH, RO?
HOW CAN HE, DAD?
"I'VE HAD A BELLY FULL--EVERYONE HAS AN OPINION ABOUT MY SITUATION! I NEED TO TALK TO SOMEONE . . . WOMAN TO WOMAN . . .
YES, I'D APPRECIATE IT IF HE'D CALL ME BACK AS SOON AS POSSIBLE. I'LL BE AT THIS NUMBER ALL NIGHT

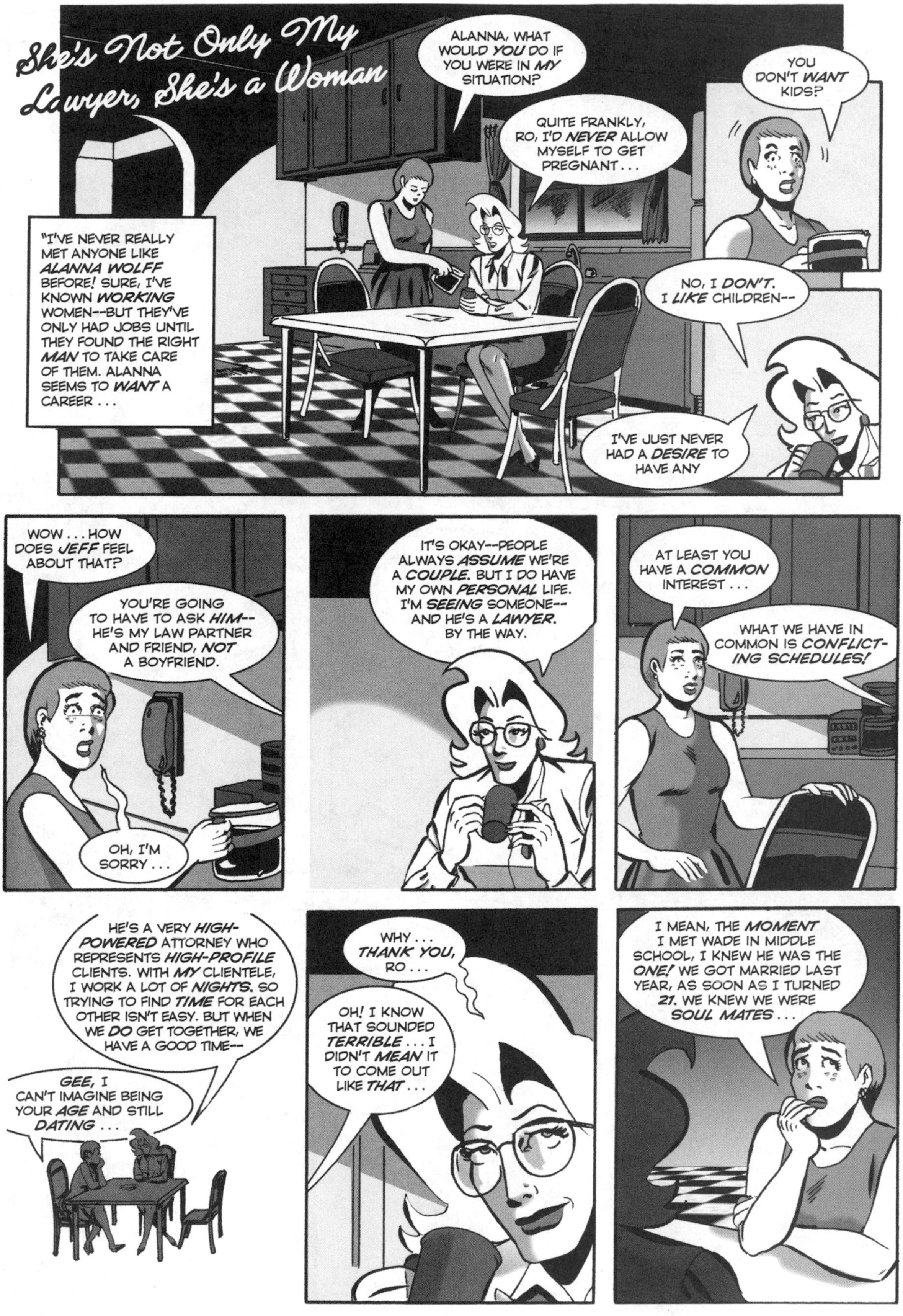
She's Not Only My Lawyer, She's a Woman
ALANNA, WHAT WOULD YOU DO IF YOU WERE IN MY SITUATION?
QUITE FRANKLY, RO, I'D NEVER ALLOW MYSELF TO GET PREGNANT . . .
YOU DON'T WANT KIDS?
"I'VE NEVER REALLY MET ANYONE LIKE ALANNA WOLFF BEFORE! SURE, I'VE KNOWN WORKING WOMEN--BUT THEY'VE ONLY HAD JOBS UNTIL THEY FOUND THE RIGHT MAN TO TAKE CARE OF THEM. ALANNA SEEMS TO WANT A CAREER . . .
NO, I DON'T. I LIKE CHILDREN--
I'VE JUST NEVER HAD A DESIRE TO HAVE ANY
WOW . . . HOW DOES JEFF FEEL ABOUT THAT?
YOU'RE GOING TO HAVE TO ASK HIM--HE'S MY LAW PARTNER AND FRIEND, NOT A BOYFRIEND.
OH, I'M SORRY . . .
IT'S OKAY--PEOPLE ALWAYS ASSUME WE'RE A COUPLE. BUT I DO HAVE MY OWN PERSONAL LIFE. I'M SEEING SOMEONE--AND HE'S A LAWYER, BY THE WAY.
AT LEAST YOU HAVE A COMMON INTEREST . . .
WHAT WE HAVE IN COMMON IS CONFLICTING SCHEDULES!
HE'S A VERY HIGH-POWERED ATTORNEY WHO REPRESENTS HIGH-PROFILE CLIENTS. WITH MY CLIENTELE, I WORK A LOT OF NIGHTS, SO TRYING TO FIND TIME FOR EACH OTHER ISN'T EASY. BUT WHEN WE DO GET TOGETHER, WE HAVE A GOOD TIME--
GEE, I CAN'T IMAGINE BEING YOUR AGE AND STILL DATING . . .
WHY . . . THANK YOU, RO . . .
OH! I KNOW THAT SOUNDED TERRIBLE . . . I DIDN'T MEAN IT TO COME OUT LIKE THAT . . .
I MEAN, THE MOMENT I MET WADE IN MIDDLE SCHOOL, I KNEW HE WAS THE ONE! WE GOT MARRIED LAST YEAR, AS SOON AS I TURNED 21. WE KNEW WE WERE SOUL MATES . . .

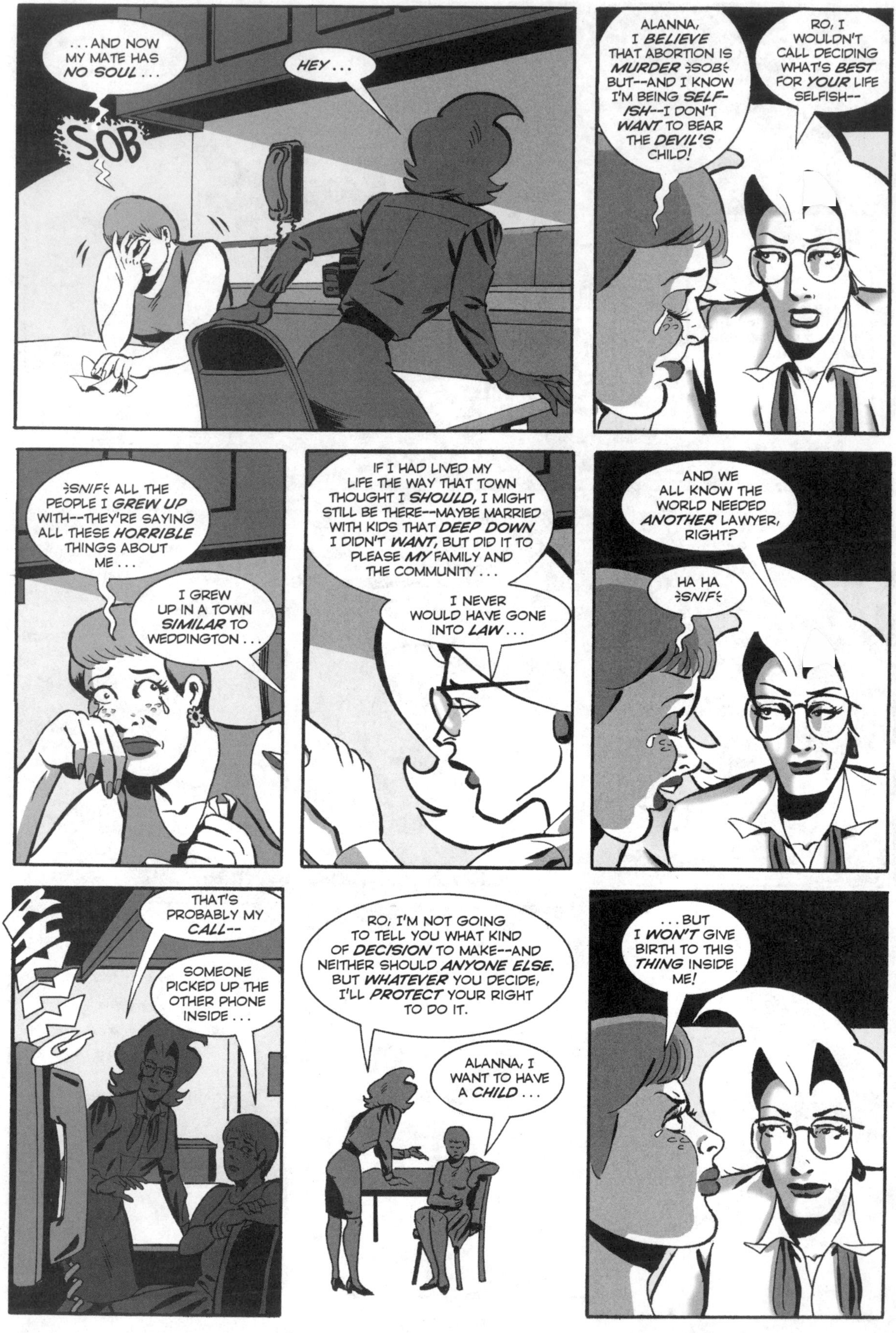
...AND NOW MY MATE HAS NO SOUL...
SOB
HEY...
ALANNA, I BELIEVE THAT ABORTION IS MURDER SOB BUT--AND I KNOW I'M BEING SELF-ISH--I DON'T WANT TO BEAR THE DEVIL'S CHILD!
RO, I WOULDN'T CALL DECIDING WHAT'S BEST FOR YOUR LIFE SELFISH--
SNIF ALL THE PEOPLE I GREW UP WITH--THEY'RE SAYING ALL THESE HORRIBLE THINGS ABOUT ME...
I GREW UP IN A TOWN SIMILAR TO WEDDINGTON...
IF I HAD LIVED MY LIFE THE WAY THAT TOWN THOUGHT I SHOULD, I MIGHT STILL BE THERE--MAYBE MARRIED WITH KIDS THAT DEEP DOWN I DIDN'T WANT, BUT DID IT TO PLEASE MY FAMILY AND THE COMMUNITY...
I NEVER WOULD HAVE GONE INTO LAW...
AND WE ALL KNOW THE WORLD NEEDED ANOTHER LAWYER, RIGHT?
HA HA SNIF
THAT'S PROBABLY MY CALL--
SOMEONE PICKED UP THE OTHER PHONE INSIDE...
RO, I'M NOT GOING TO TELL YOU WHAT KIND OF DECISION TO MAKE--AND NEITHER SHOULD ANYONE ELSE. BUT WHATEVER YOU DECIDE, I'LL PROTECT YOUR RIGHT TO DO IT.
ALANNA, I WANT TO HAVE A CHILD...
...BUT I WON'T GIVE BIRTH TO THIS THING INSIDE ME!

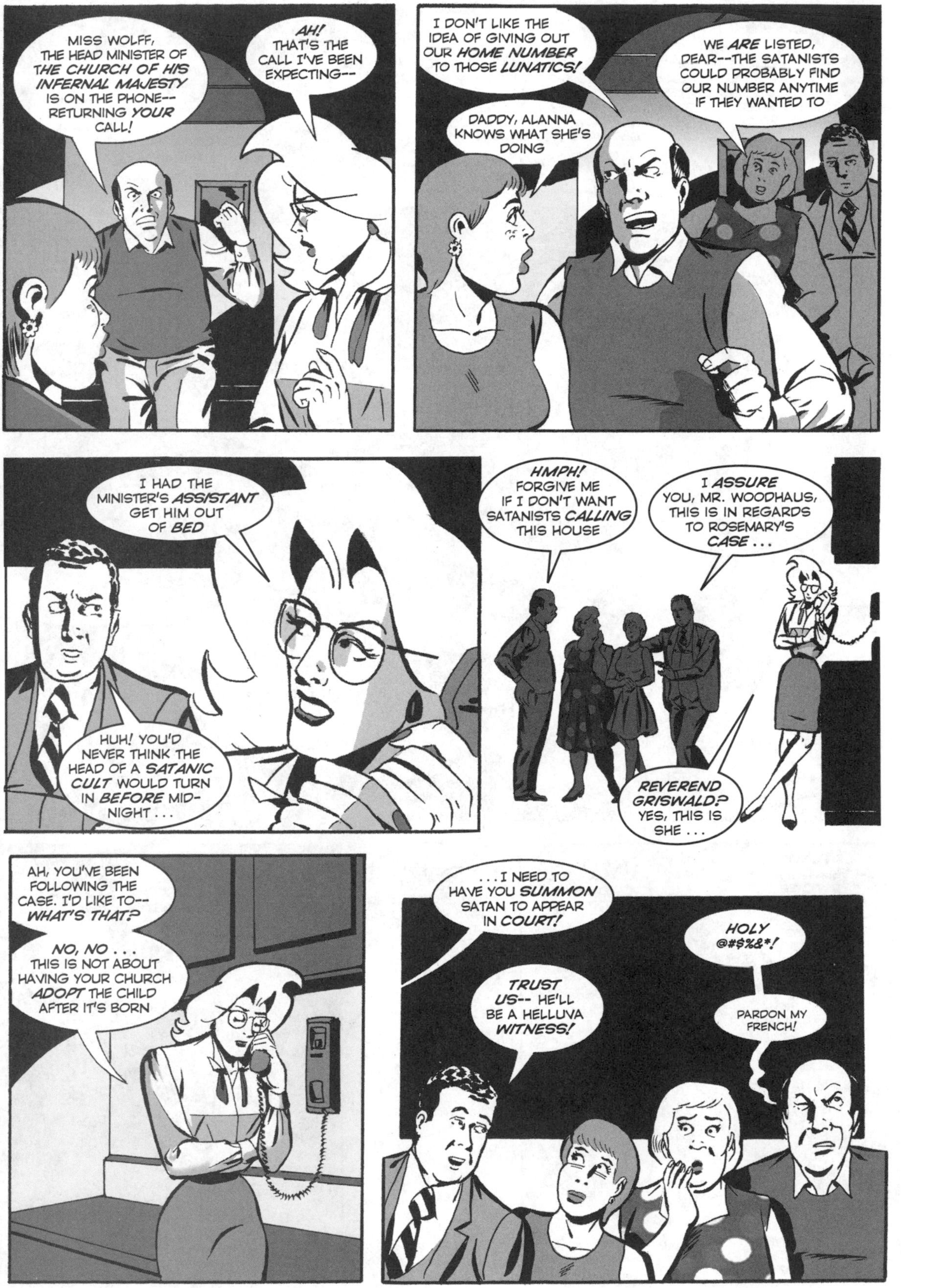
MISS WOLFF, THE HEAD MINISTER OF THE CHURCH OF HIS INFERNAL MAJESTY IS ON THE PHONE-- RETURNING YOUR CALL!
AH! THAT'S THE CALL I'VE BEEN EXPECTING--
I DON'T LIKE THE IDEA OF GIVING OUT OUR HOME NUMBER TO THOSE LUNATICS!
WE ARE LISTED, DEAR--THE SATANISTS COULD PROBABLY FIND OUR NUMBER ANYTIME IF THEY WANTED TO
DADDY, ALANNA KNOWS WHAT SHE'S DOING
I HAD THE MINISTER'S ASSISTANT GET HIM OUT OF BED
HUH! YOU'D NEVER THINK THE HEAD OF A SATANIC CULT WOULD TURN IN BEFORE MID-NIGHT . . .
HMPH! FORGIVE ME IF I DON'T WANT SATANISTS CALLING THIS HOUSE
I ASSURE YOU, MR. WOODHAUS, THIS IS IN REGARDS TO ROSEMARY'S CASE . . .
REVEREND GRISWALD? YES, THIS IS SHE . . .
AH, YOU'VE BEEN FOLLOWING THE CASE. I'D LIKE TO-- WHAT'S THAT?
NO, NO . . . THIS IS NOT ABOUT HAVING YOUR CHURCH ADOPT THE CHILD AFTER IT'S BORN
. . . I NEED TO HAVE YOU SUMMON SATAN TO APPEAR IN COURT!
HOLY @#$%&*!
TRUST US-- HE'LL BE A HELLUVA WITNESS!
PARDON MY FRENCH!

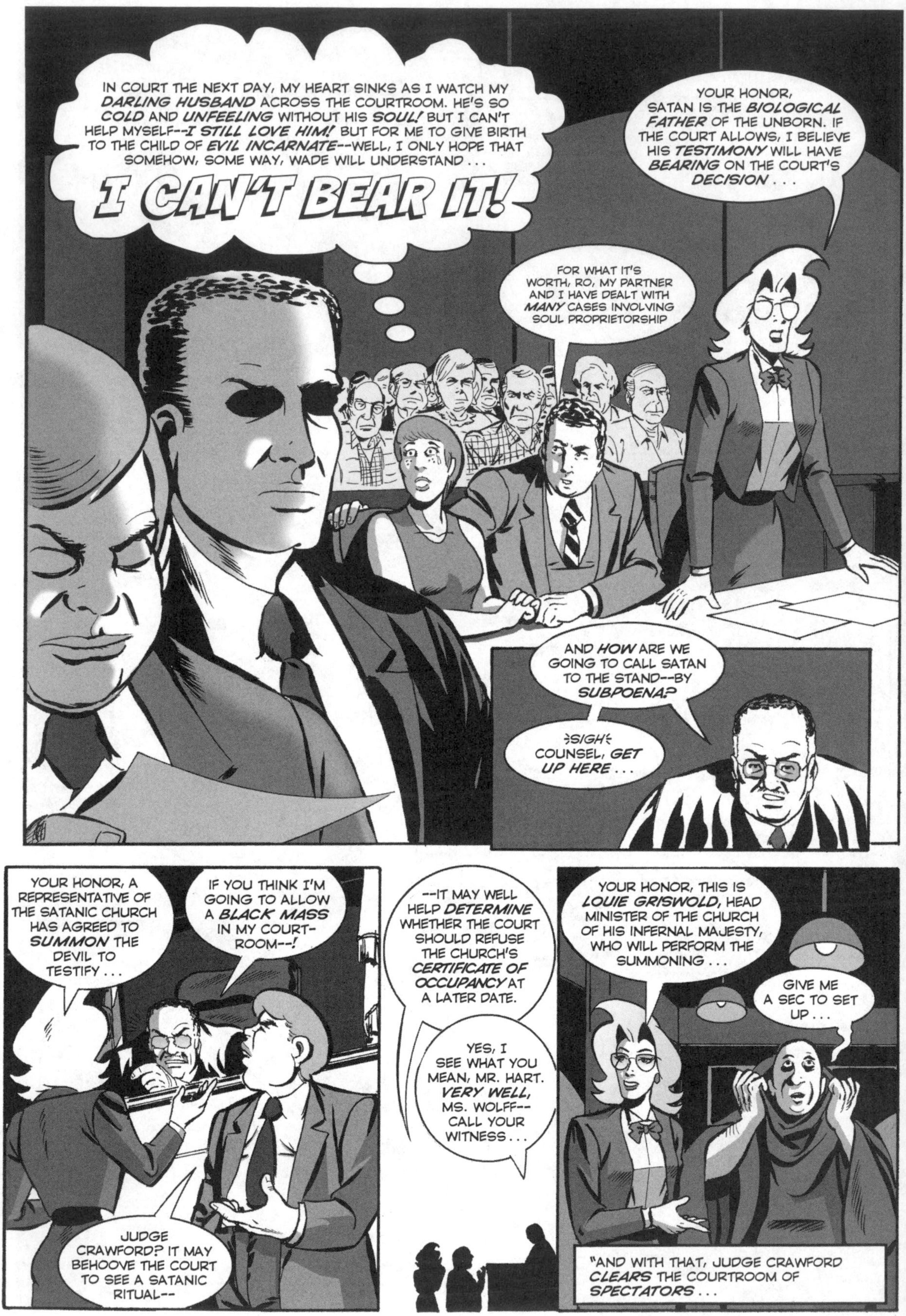

IN COURT THE NEXT DAY, MY HEART SINKS AS I WATCH MY DARLING HUSBAND ACROSS THE COURTROOM. HE'S SO COLD AND UNFEELING WITHOUT HIS SOUL! BUT I CAN'T HELP MYSELF--I STILL LOVE HIM! BUT FOR ME TO GIVE BIRTH TO THE CHILD OF EVIL INCARNATE--WELL, I ONLY HOPE THAT SOMEHOW, SOME WAY, WADE WILL UNDERSTAND . . .
I CAN'T BEAR IT!
YOUR HONOR, SATAN IS THE BIOLOGICAL FATHER OF THE UNBORN. IF THE COURT ALLOWS, I BELIEVE HIS TESTIMONY WILL HAVE BEARING ON THE COURT'S DECISION . . .
FOR WHAT IT'S WORTH, RO, MY PARTNER AND I HAVE DEALT WITH MANY CASES INVOLVING SOUL PROPRIETORSHIP
AND HOW ARE WE GOING TO CALL SATAN TO THE STAND--BY SUBPOENA?
SIGH COUNSEL, GET UP HERE . . .
YOUR HONOR, A REPRESENTATIVE OF THE SATANIC CHURCH HAS AGREED TO SUMMON THE DEVIL TO TESTIFY . . .
IF YOU THINK I'M GOING TO ALLOW A BLACK MASS IN MY COURT-ROOM--!
JUDGE CRAWFORD? IT MAY BEHOOVE THE COURT TO SEE A SATANIC RITUAL--
--IT MAY WELL HELP DETERMINE WHETHER THE COURT SHOULD REFUSE THE CHURCH'S CERTIFICATE OF OCCUPANCY AT A LATER DATE.
YES, I SEE WHAT YOU MEAN, MR. HART. VERY WELL, MS. WOLFF--CALL YOUR WITNESS . . .
YOUR HONOR, THIS IS LOUIE GRISWOLD, HEAD MINISTER OF THE CHURCH OF HIS INFERNAL MAJESTY, WHO WILL PERFORM THE SUMMONING . . .
GIVE ME A SEC TO SET UP . . .
"AND WITH THAT, JUDGE CRAWFORD CLEARS THE COURTROOM OF SPECTATORS . . .

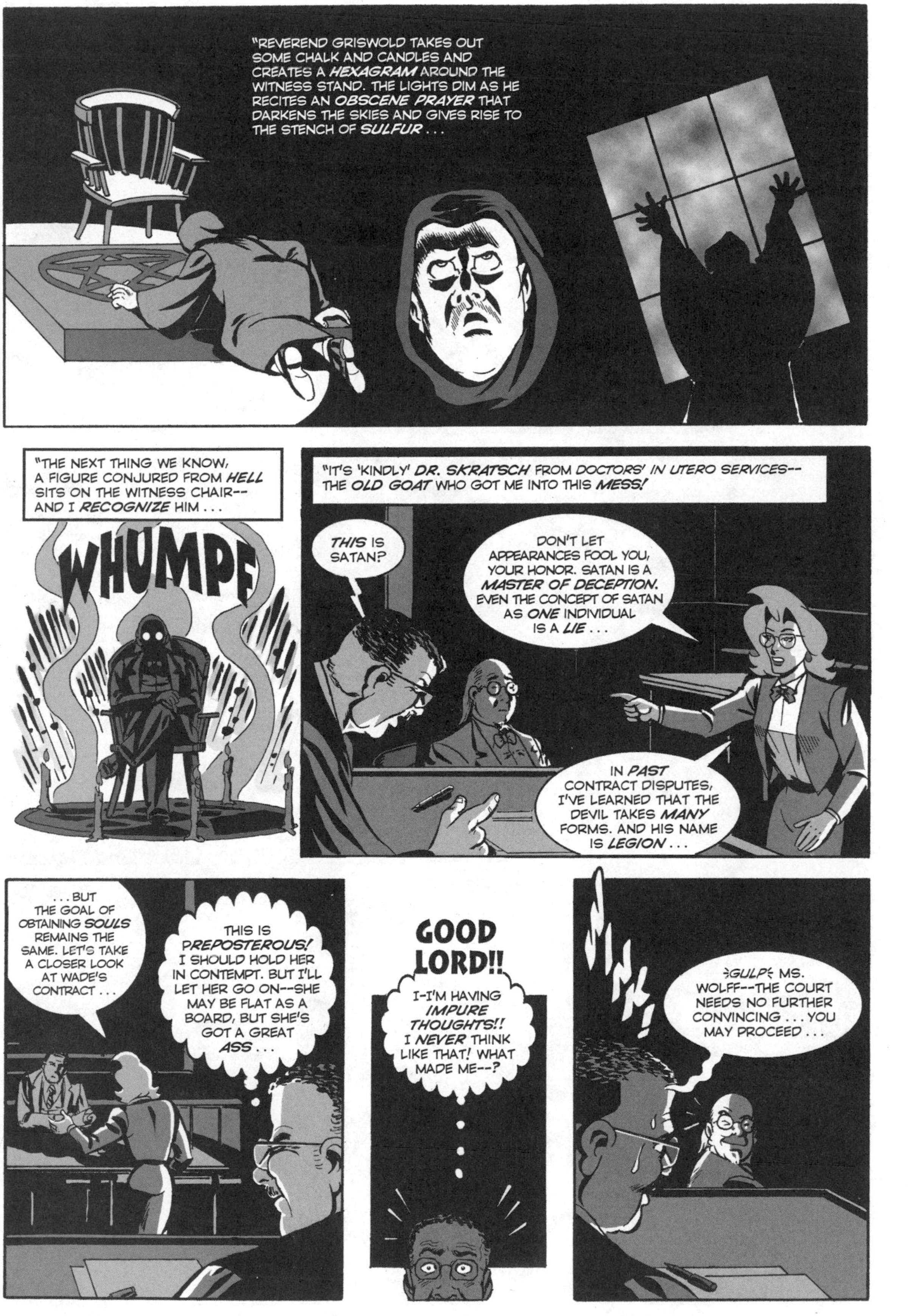
"REVEREND GRISWOLD TAKES OUT SOME CHALK AND CANDLES AND CREATES A HEXAGRAM AROUND THE WITNESS STAND. THE LIGHTS DIM AS HE RECITES AN OBSCENE PRAYER THAT DARKENS THE SKIES AND GIVES RISE TO THE STENCH OF SULFUR . . .
"THE NEXT THING WE KNOW, A FIGURE CONJURED FROM HELL SITS ON THE WITNESS CHAIR-- AND I RECOGNIZE HIM . . .
WHUMPF
"IT'S 'KINDLY' DR. SKRATSCH FROM DOCTORS' IN UTERO SERVICES-- THE OLD GOAT WHO GOT ME INTO THIS MESS!
THIS IS SATAN?
DON'T LET APPEARANCES FOOL YOU, YOUR HONOR. SATAN IS A MASTER OF DECEPTION. EVEN THE CONCEPT OF SATAN AS ONE INDIVIDUAL IS A LIE . . .
IN PAST CONTRACT DISPUTES, I'VE LEARNED THAT THE DEVIL TAKES MANY FORMS. AND HIS NAME IS LEGION . . .
. . . BUT THE GOAL OF OBTAINING SOULS REMAINS THE SAME. LET'S TAKE A CLOSER LOOK AT WADE'S CONTRACT . . .
THIS IS PREPOSTEROUS! I SHOULD HOLD HER IN CONTEMPT. BUT I'LL LET HER GO ON--SHE MAY BE FLAT AS A BOARD, BUT SHE'S GOT A GREAT ASS . . .
GOOD LORD!!
I-I'M HAVING IMPURE THOUGHTS!! I NEVER THINK LIKE THAT! WHAT MADE ME--?
WINK!
GULP MS. WOLFF--THE COURT NEEDS NO FURTHER CONVINCING . . . YOU MAY PROCEED . . .

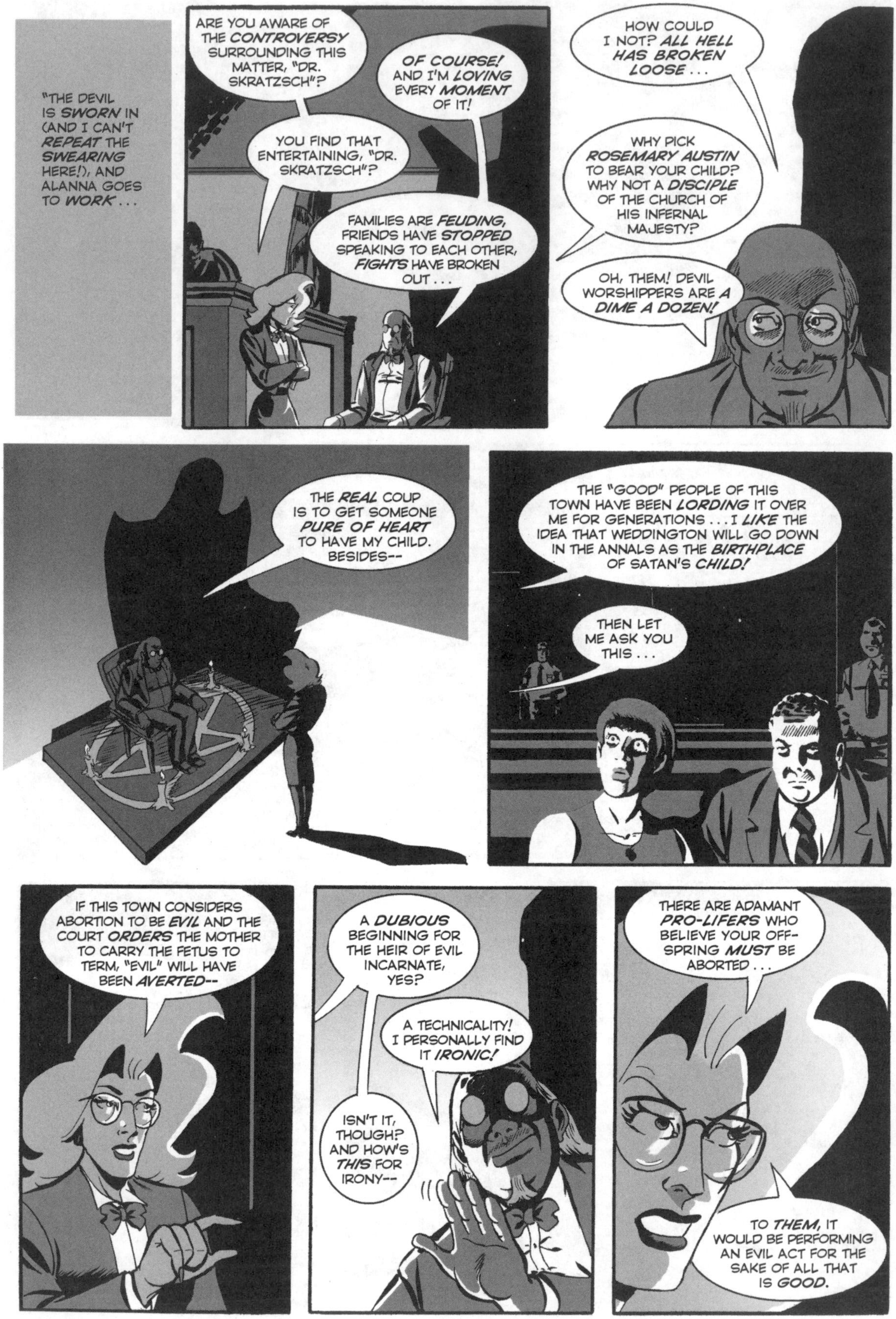
"THE DEVIL IS SWORN IN (AND I CAN'T REPEAT THE SWEARING HERE!), AND ALANNA GOES TO WORK . . .
ARE YOU AWARE OF THE CONTROVERSY SURROUNDING THIS MATTER, "DR. SKRATZSCH"?
OF COURSE! AND I'M LOVING EVERY MOMENT OF IT!
YOU FIND THAT ENTERTAINING, "DR. SKRATZSCH"?
FAMILIES ARE FEUDING, FRIENDS HAVE STOPPED SPEAKING TO EACH OTHER, FIGHTS HAVE BROKEN OUT . . .
HOW COULD I NOT? ALL HELL HAS BROKEN LOOSE . . .
WHY PICK ROSEMARY AUSTIN TO BEAR YOUR CHILD? WHY NOT A DISCIPLE OF THE CHURCH OF HIS INFERNAL MAJESTY?
OH, THEM! DEVIL WORSHIPPERS ARE A DIME A DOZEN!
THE REAL COUP IS TO GET SOMEONE PURE OF HEART TO HAVE MY CHILD. BESIDES--
THE "GOOD" PEOPLE OF THIS TOWN HAVE BEEN LORDING IT OVER ME FOR GENERATIONS . . . I LIKE THE IDEA THAT WEDDINGTON WILL GO DOWN IN THE ANNALS AS THE BIRTHPLACE OF SATAN'S CHILD!
THEN LET ME ASK YOU THIS . . .
IF THIS TOWN CONSIDERS ABORTION TO BE EVIL AND THE COURT ORDERS THE MOTHER TO CARRY THE FETUS TO TERM, "EVIL" WILL HAVE BEEN AVERTED--
A DUBIOUS BEGINNING FOR THE HEIR OF EVIL INCARNATE, YES?
A TECHNICALITY! I PERSONALLY FIND IT IRONIC!
ISN'T IT, THOUGH? AND HOW'S THIS FOR IRONY--
THERE ARE ADAMANT PRO-LIFERS WHO BELIEVE YOUR OFF-SPRING MUST BE ABORTED . . .
TO THEM, IT WOULD BE PERFORMING AN EVIL ACT FOR THE SAKE OF ALL THAT IS GOOD.

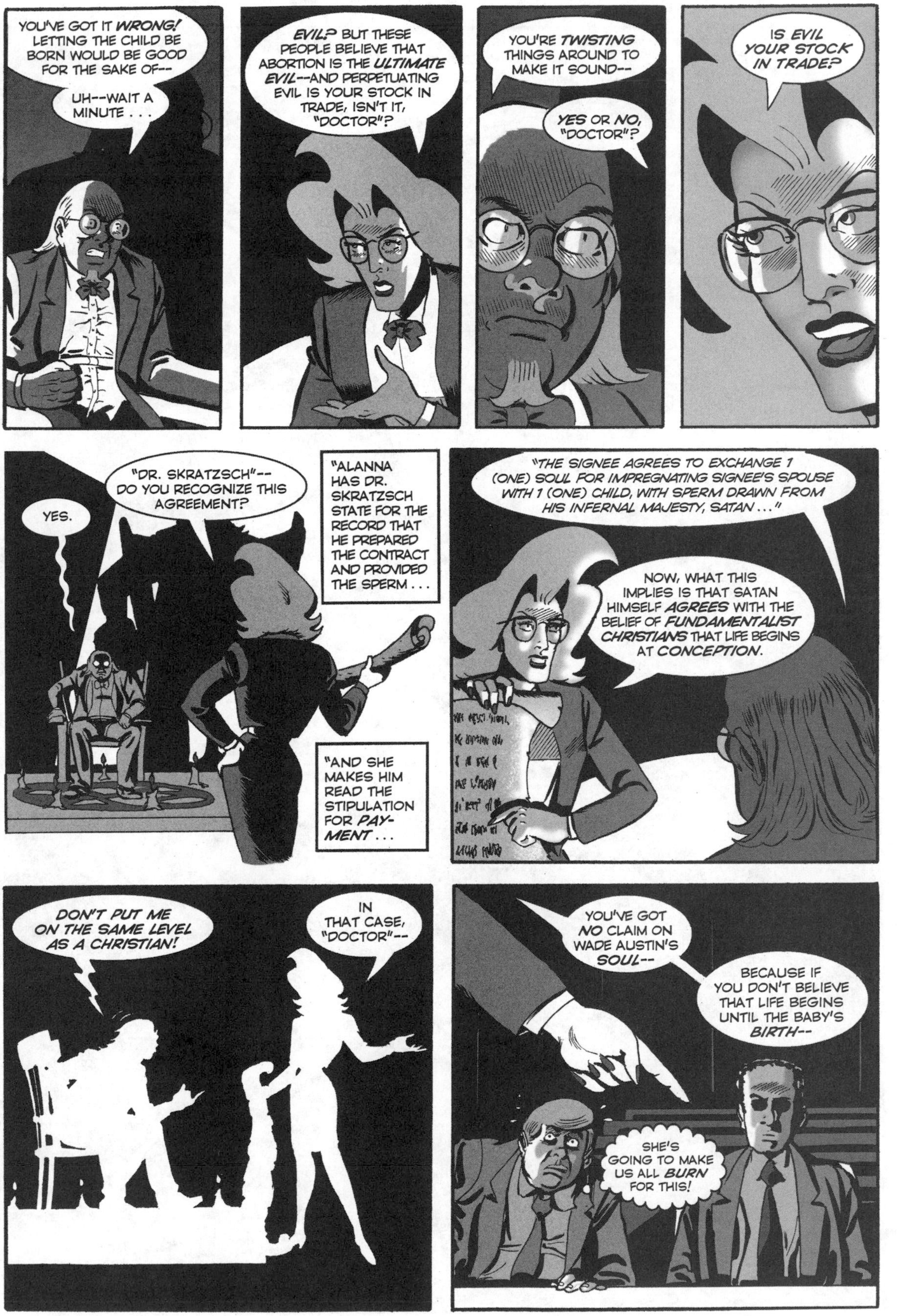
YOU'VE GOT IT WRONG! LETTING THE CHILD BE BORN WOULD BE GOOD FOR THE SAKE OF--
UH--WAIT A MINUTE . . .
EVIL? BUT THESE PEOPLE BELIEVE THAT ABORTION IS THE ULTIMATE EVIL--AND PERPETUATING EVIL IS YOUR STOCK IN TRADE, ISN'T IT, "DOCTOR"?
YOU'RE TWISTING THINGS AROUND TO MAKE IT SOUND--
YES OR NO, "DOCTOR"?
IS EVIL YOUR STOCK IN TRADE?
"DR. SKRATZSCH"--DO YOU RECOGNIZE THIS AGREEMENT?
YES.
"ALANNA HAS DR. SKRATZSCH STATE FOR THE RECORD THAT HE PREPARED THE CONTRACT AND PROVIDED THE SPERM . . .
"AND SHE MAKES HIM READ THE STIPULATION FOR PAY-MENT . . .
"THE SIGNEE AGREES TO EXCHANGE 1 (ONE) SOUL FOR IMPREGNATING SIGNEE'S SPOUSE WITH 1 (ONE) CHILD, WITH SPERM DRAWN FROM HIS INFERNAL MAJESTY, SATAN . . ."
NOW, WHAT THIS IMPLIES IS THAT SATAN HIMSELF AGREES WITH THE BELIEF OF FUNDAMENTALIST CHRISTIANS THAT LIFE BEGINS AT CONCEPTION.
DON'T PUT ME ON THE SAME LEVEL AS A CHRISTIAN!
IN THAT CASE, "DOCTOR"--
YOU'VE GOT NO CLAIM ON WADE AUSTIN'S SOUL--
BECAUSE IF YOU DON'T BELIEVE THAT LIFE BEGINS UNTIL THE BABY'S BIRTH--
SHE'S GOING TO MAKE US ALL BURN FOR THIS!

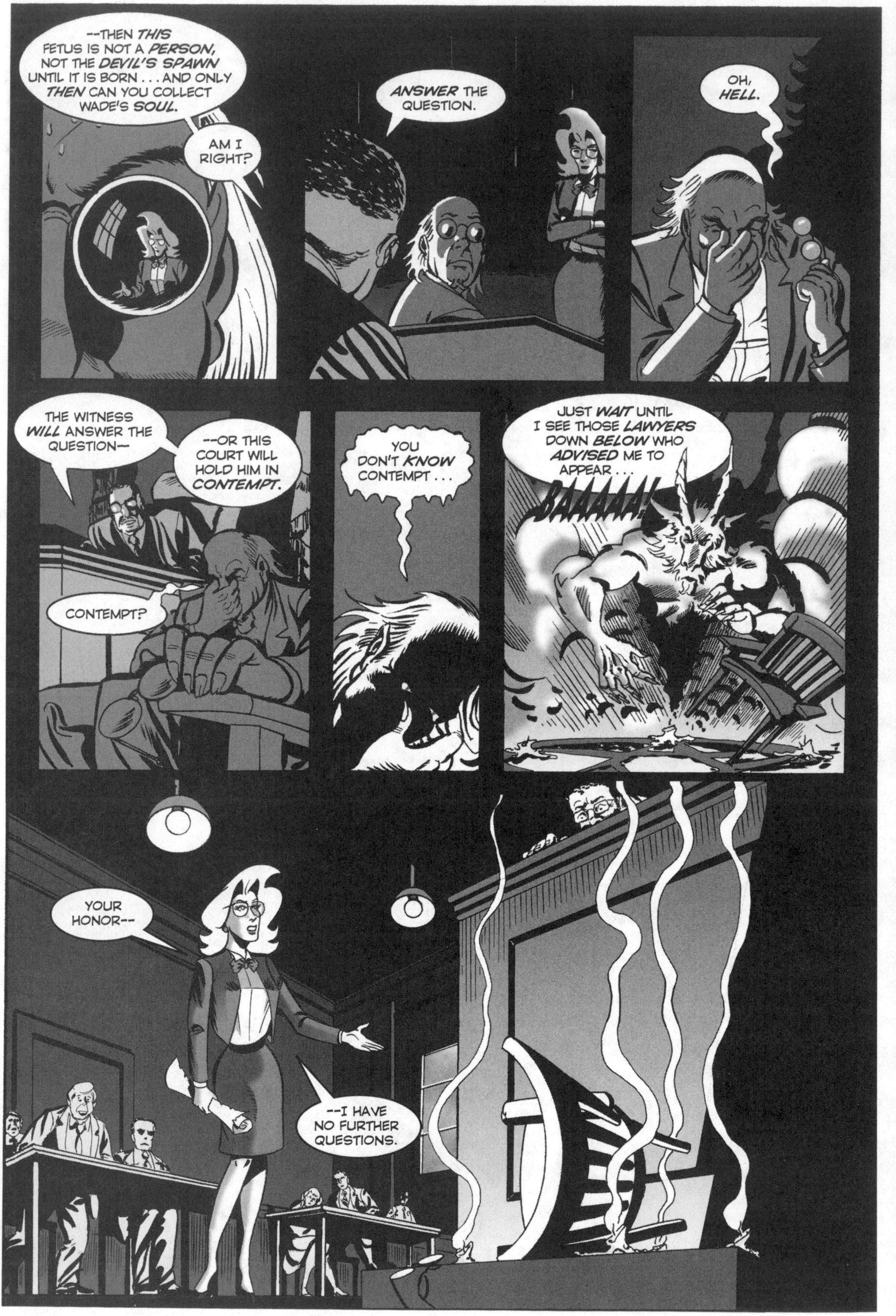
--THEN THIS FETUS IS NOT A PERSON, NOT THE DEVIL'S SPAWN UNTIL IT IS BORN . . . AND ONLY THEN CAN YOU COLLECT WADE'S SOUL.
AM I RIGHT?
ANSWER THE QUESTION.
OH, HELL.
THE WITNESS WILL ANSWER THE QUESTION--
--OR THIS COURT WILL HOLD HIM IN CONTEMPT.
CONTEMPT?
YOU DON'T KNOW CONTEMPT . . .
JUST WAIT UNTIL I SEE THOSE LAWYERS DOWN BELOW WHO ADVISED ME TO APPEAR . . .
BAAAAA!
YOUR HONOR--
--I HAVE NO FURTHER QUESTIONS.

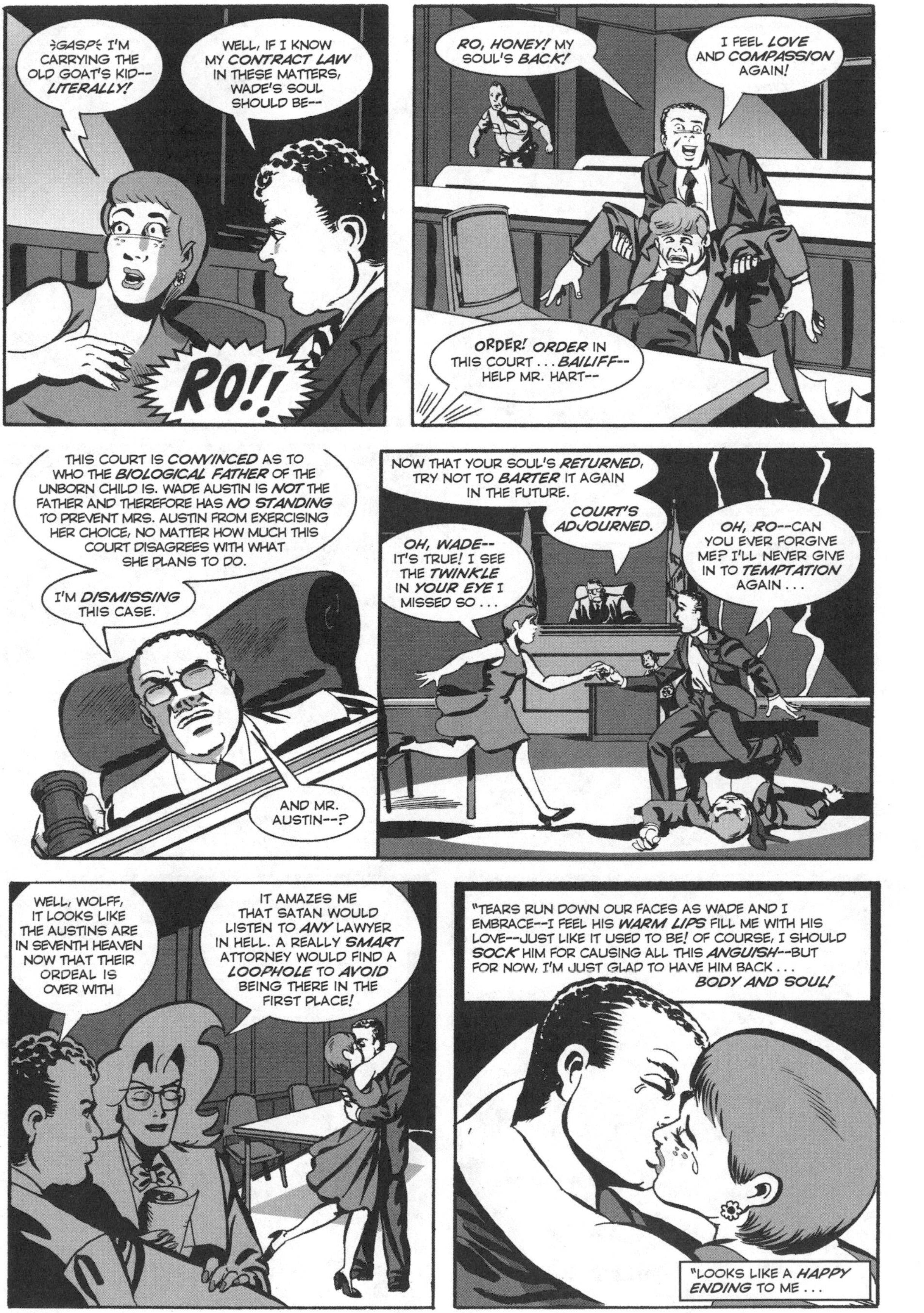

GASP I'M CARRYING THE OLD GOAT'S KID-- LITERALLY!
WELL, IF I KNOW MY CONTRACT LAW IN THESE MATTERS, WADE'S SOUL SHOULD BE--
RO!!
RO, HONEY! MY SOUL'S BACK!
I FEEL LOVE AND COMPASSION AGAIN!
ORDER! ORDER IN THIS COURT . . . BAILIFF-- HELP MR. HART--
THIS COURT IS CONVINCED AS TO WHO THE BIOLOGICAL FATHER OF THE UNBORN CHILD IS. WADE AUSTIN IS NOT THE FATHER AND THEREFORE HAS NO STANDING TO PREVENT MRS. AUSTIN FROM EXERCISING HER CHOICE, NO MATTER HOW MUCH THIS COURT DISAGREES WITH WHAT SHE PLANS TO DO.
I'M DISMISSING THIS CASE.
AND MR. AUSTIN--?
NOW THAT YOUR SOUL'S RETURNED, TRY NOT TO BARTER IT AGAIN IN THE FUTURE.
COURT'S ADJOURNED.
OH, WADE-- IT'S TRUE! I SEE THE TWINKLE IN YOUR EYE I MISSED SO . . .
OH, RO--CAN YOU EVER FORGIVE ME? I'LL NEVER GIVE IN TO TEMPTATION AGAIN . . .
WELL, WOLFF, IT LOOKS LIKE THE AUSTINS ARE IN SEVENTH HEAVEN NOW THAT THEIR ORDEAL IS OVER WITH
IT AMAZES ME THAT SATAN WOULD LISTEN TO ANY LAWYER IN HELL. A REALLY SMART ATTORNEY WOULD FIND A LOOPHOLE TO AVOID BEING THERE IN THE FIRST PLACE!
"TEARS RUN DOWN OUR FACES AS WADE AND I EMBRACE--I FEEL HIS WARM LIPS FILL ME WITH HIS LOVE--JUST LIKE IT USED TO BE! OF COURSE, I SHOULD SOCK HIM FOR CAUSING ALL THIS ANGUISH--BUT FOR NOW, I'M JUST GLAD TO HAVE HIM BACK . . . BODY AND SOUL!
"LOOKS LIKE A HAPPY ENDING TO ME . . .

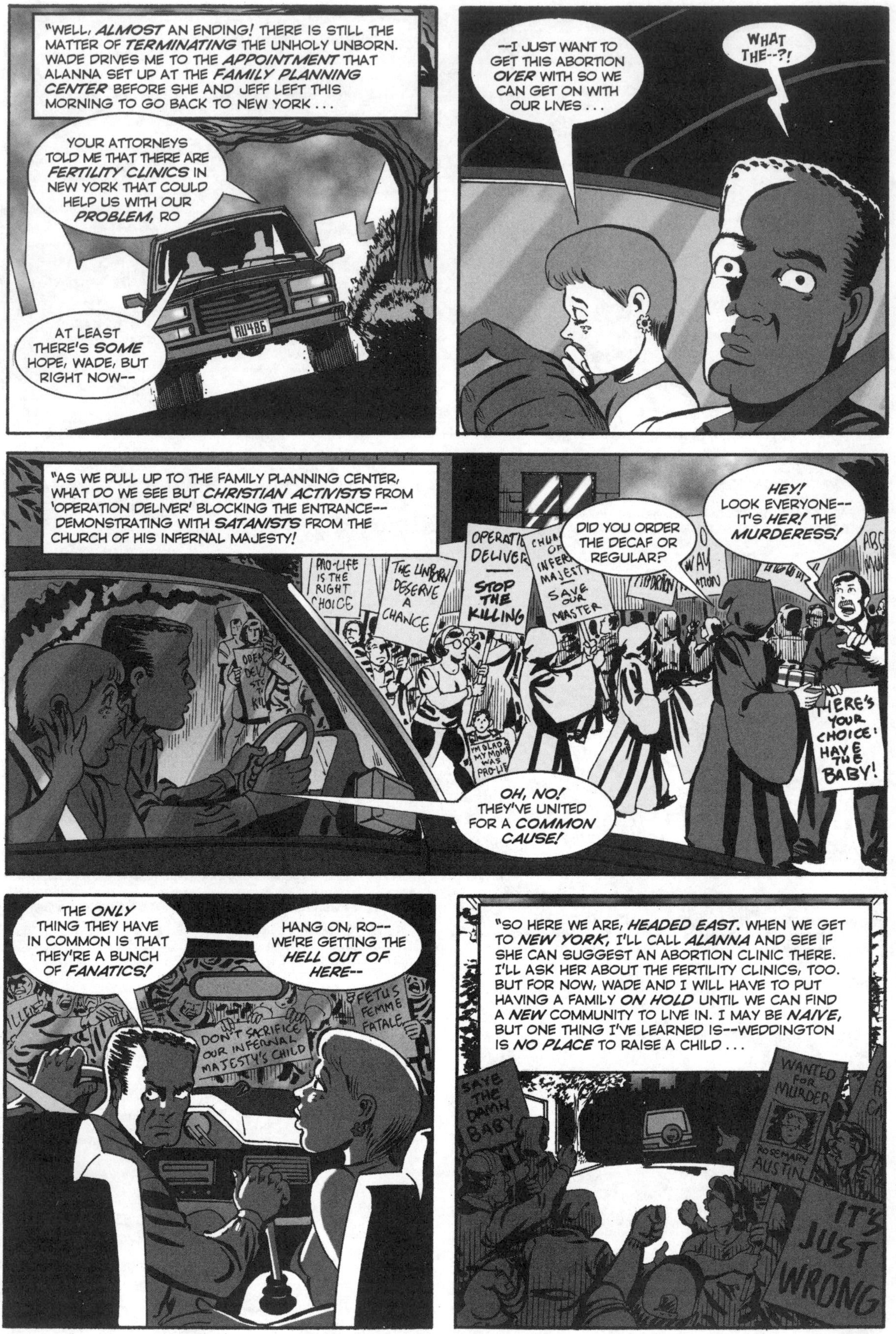
"WELL, ALMOST AN ENDING! THERE IS STILL THE MATTER OF TERMINATING THE UNHOLY UNBORN. WADE DRIVES ME TO THE APPOINTMENT THAT ALANNA SET UP AT THE FAMILY PLANNING CENTER BEFORE SHE AND JEFF LEFT THIS MORNING TO GO BACK TO NEW YORK . . .
YOUR ATTORNEYS TOLD ME THAT THERE ARE FERTILITY CLINICS IN NEW YORK THAT COULD HELP US WITH OUR PROBLEM, RO
AT LEAST THERE'S SOME HOPE, WADE, BUT RIGHT NOW--
RU486
--I JUST WANT TO GET THIS ABORTION OVER WITH SO WE CAN GET ON WITH OUR LIVES . . .
WHAT THE--?!
"AS WE PULL UP TO THE FAMILY PLANNING CENTER, WHAT DO WE SEE BUT CHRISTIAN ACTIVISTS FROM 'OPERATION DELIVER' BLOCKING THE ENTRANCE-- DEMONSTRATING WITH SATANISTS FROM THE CHURCH OF HIS INFERNAL MAJESTY!
PRO-LIFE IS THE RIGHT CHOICE
THE UNBORN DESERVE A CHANCE
OPERATION DELIVER
STOP THE KILLING
SAVE OUR MASTER
DID YOU ORDER THE DECAF OR REGULAR?
HEY! LOOK EVERYONE-- IT'S HER! THE MURDERESS!
I'M GLAD MY MOM WAS PRO-LIFE
HERE'S YOUR CHOICE: HAVE THE BABY!
OH, NO! THEY'VE UNITED FOR A COMMON CAUSE!
THE ONLY THING THEY HAVE IN COMMON IS THAT THEY'RE A BUNCH OF FANATICS!
HANG ON, RO-- WE'RE GETTING THE HELL OUT OF HERE--
FETUS FEMME FATALE
DON'T SACRIFICE OUR INFERNAL MAJESTY'S CHILD
"SO HERE WE ARE, HEADED EAST. WHEN WE GET TO NEW YORK, I'LL CALL ALANNA AND SEE IF SHE CAN SUGGEST AN ABORTION CLINIC THERE. I'LL ASK HER ABOUT THE FERTILITY CLINICS, TOO. BUT FOR NOW, WADE AND I WILL HAVE TO PUT HAVING A FAMILY ON HOLD UNTIL WE CAN FIND A NEW COMMUNITY TO LIVE IN. I MAY BE NAIVE, BUT ONE THING I'VE LEARNED IS--WEDDINGTON IS NO PLACE TO RAISE A CHILD . . .
SAVE THE DAMN BABY
WANTED FOR MURDER
ROSEMARY AUSTIN
IT'S JUST WRONG

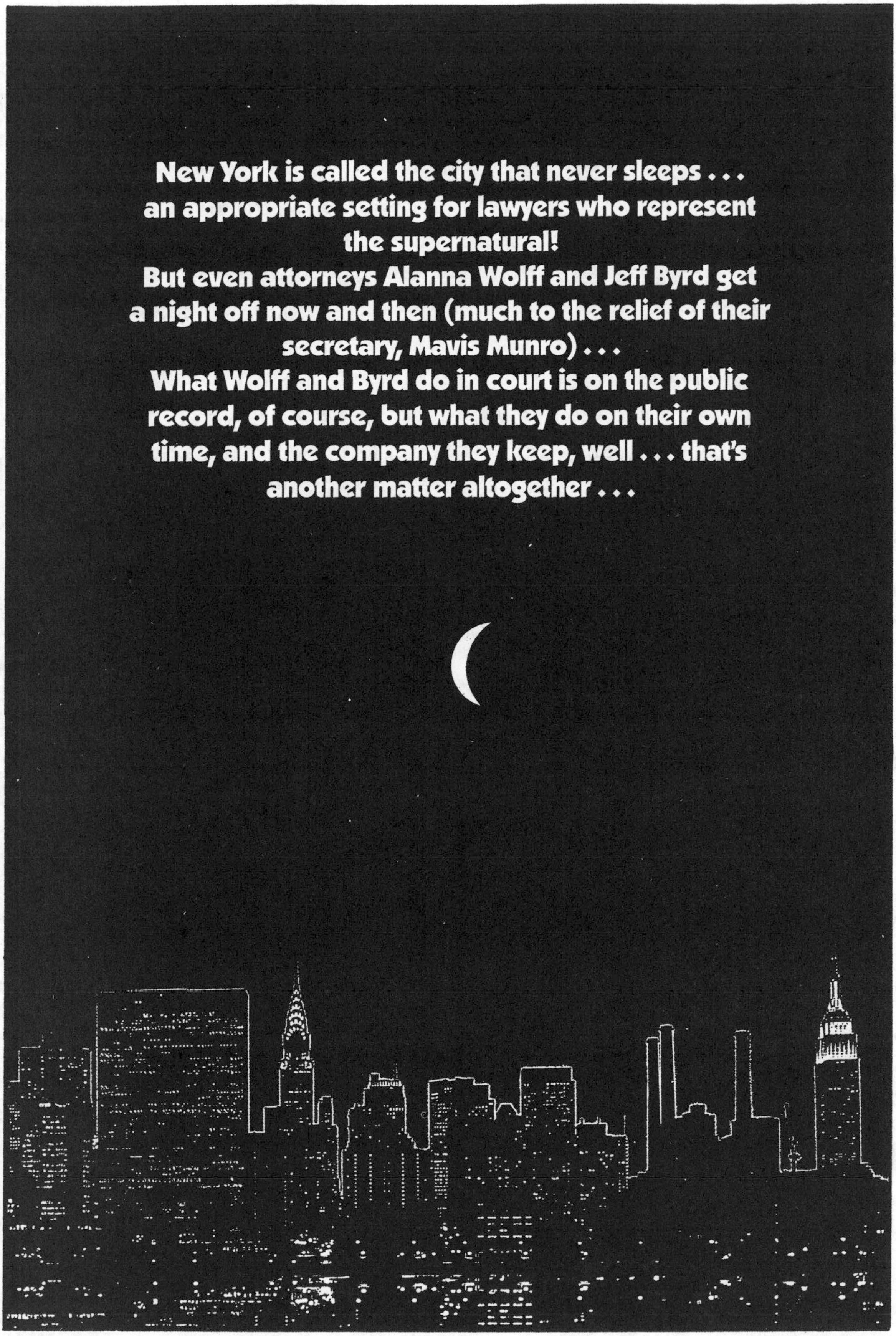
New York is called the city that never sleeps . . .
an appropriate setting for lawyers who represent
the supernatural!
But even attorneys Alanna Wolff and Jeff Byrd get
a night off now and then (much to the relief of their
secretary, Mavis Munro) . . .
What Wolff and Byrd do in court is on the public
record, of course, but what they do on their own
time, and the company they keep, well . . . that's
another matter altogether . . .

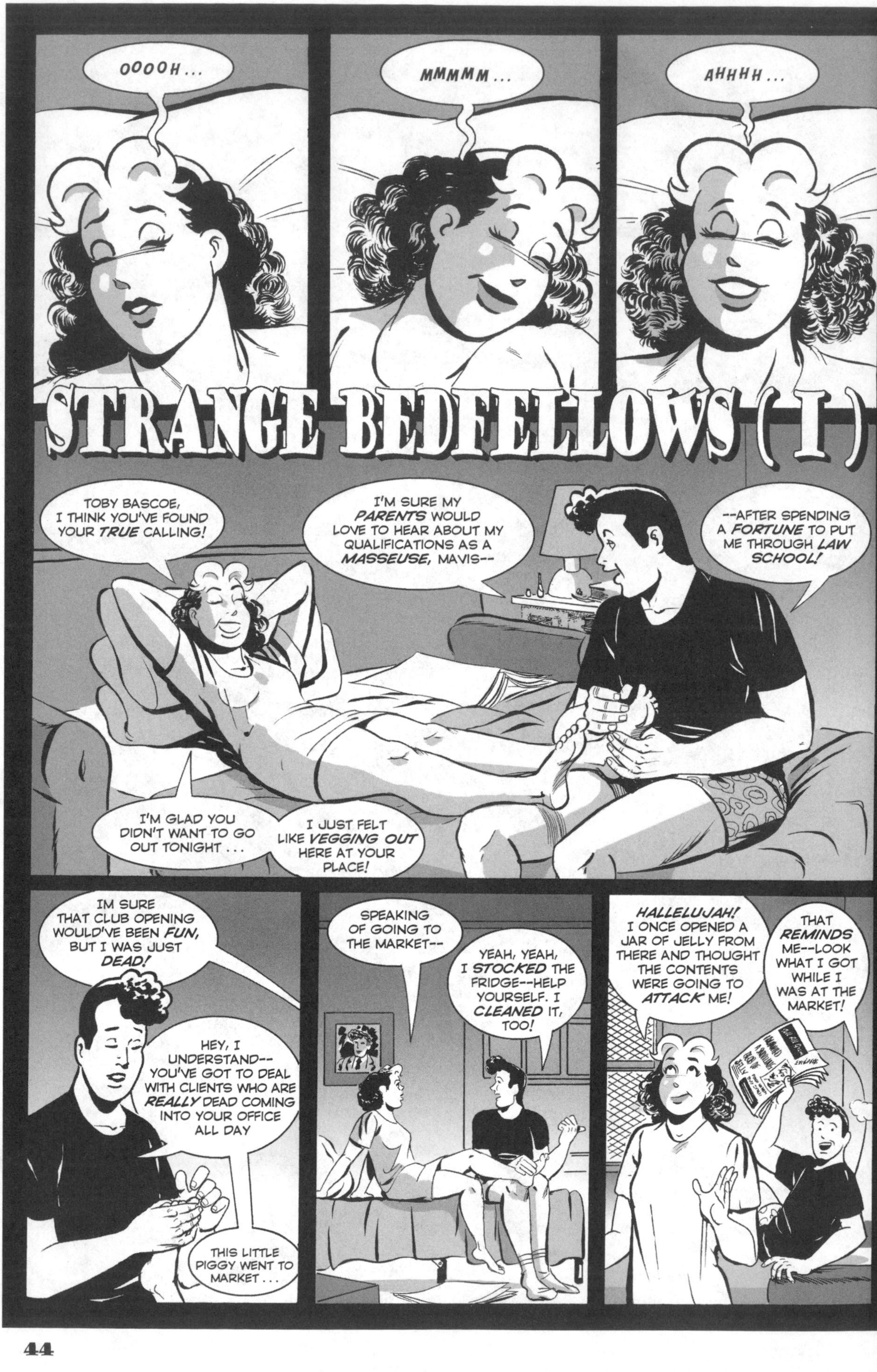
OOOOH . . .
MMMMM . . .
AHHHH . . .
STRANGE BEDFELLOWS (I)
TOBY BASCOE, I THINK YOU'VE FOUND YOUR TRUE CALLING!
I'M SURE MY PARENTS WOULD LOVE TO HEAR ABOUT MY QUALIFICATIONS AS A MASSEUSE, MAVIS--
--AFTER SPENDING A FORTUNE TO PUT ME THROUGH LAW SCHOOL!
I'M GLAD YOU DIDN'T WANT TO GO OUT TONIGHT . . .
I JUST FELT LIKE VEGGING OUT HERE AT YOUR PLACE!
IM SURE THAT CLUB OPENING WOULD'VE BEEN FUN, BUT I WAS JUST DEAD!
HEY, I UNDERSTAND-- YOU'VE GOT TO DEAL WITH CLIENTS WHO ARE REALLY DEAD COMING INTO YOUR OFFICE ALL DAY
THIS LITTLE PIGGY WENT TO MARKET . . .
SPEAKING OF GOING TO THE MARKET--
YEAH, YEAH, I STOCKED THE FRIDGE--HELP YOURSELF. I CLEANED IT, TOO!
HALLELUJAH! I ONCE OPENED A JAR OF JELLY FROM THERE AND THOUGHT THE CONTENTS WERE GOING TO ATTACK ME!
THAT REMINDS ME--LOOK WHAT I GOT WHILE I WAS AT THE MARKET!

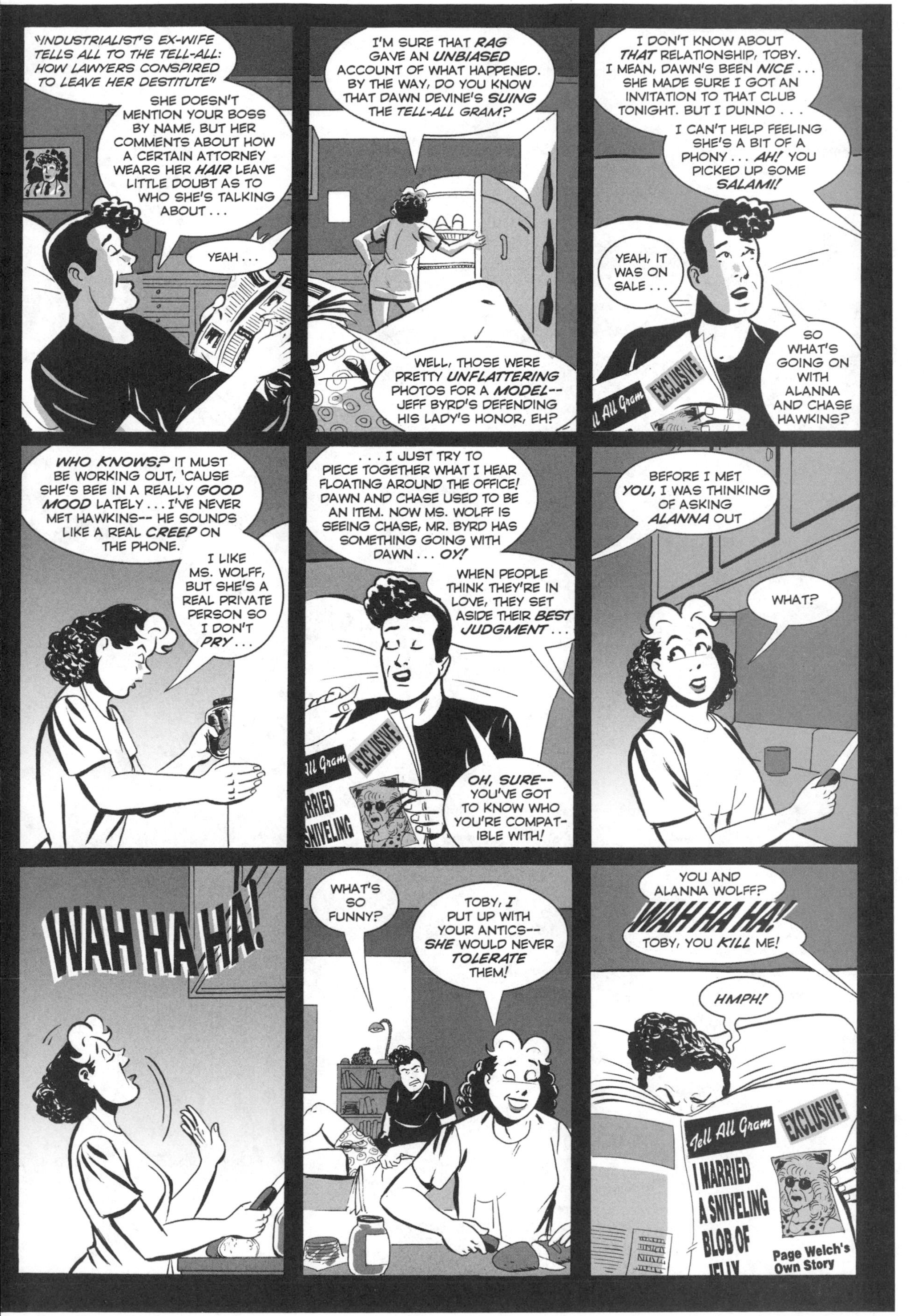

"INDUSTRIALIST'S EX-WIFE TELLS ALL TO THE TELL-ALL: HOW LAWYERS CONSPIRED TO LEAVE HER DESTITUTE"
SHE DOESN'T MENTION YOUR BOSS BY NAME, BUT HER COMMENTS ABOUT HOW A CERTAIN ATTORNEY WEARS HER HAIR LEAVE LITTLE DOUBT AS TO WHO SHE'S TALKING ABOUT . . .
YEAH . . .
I'M SURE THAT RAG GAVE AN UNBIASED ACCOUNT OF WHAT HAPPENED. BY THE WAY, DO YOU KNOW THAT DAWN DEVINE'S SUING THE TELL-ALL GRAM?
WELL, THOSE WERE PRETTY UNFLATTERING PHOTOS FOR A MODEL-- JEFF BYRD'S DEFENDING HIS LADY'S HONOR, EH?
I DON'T KNOW ABOUT THAT RELATIONSHIP, TOBY. I MEAN, DAWN'S BEEN NICE . . . SHE MADE SURE I GOT AN INVITATION TO THAT CLUB TONIGHT. BUT I DUNNO . . .
I CAN'T HELP FEELING SHE'S A BIT OF A PHONY . . . AH! YOU PICKED UP SOME SALAMI!
YEAH, IT WAS ON SALE . . .
SO WHAT'S GOING ON WITH ALANNA AND CHASE HAWKINS?
EXCLUSIVE
WHO KNOWS? IT MUST BE WORKING OUT, 'CAUSE SHE'S BEE IN A REALLY GOOD MOOD LATELY . . . I'VE NEVER MET HAWKINS-- HE SOUNDS LIKE A REAL CREEP ON THE PHONE.
I LIKE MS. WOLFF, BUT SHE'S A REAL PRIVATE PERSON SO I DON'T PRY . . .
. . . I JUST TRY TO PIECE TOGETHER WHAT I HEAR FLOATING AROUND THE OFFICE! DAWN AND CHASE USED TO BE AN ITEM. NOW MS. WOLFF IS SEEING CHASE, MR. BYRD HAS SOMETHING GOING WITH DAWN . . . OY!
WHEN PEOPLE THINK THEY'RE IN LOVE, THEY SET ASIDE THEIR BEST JUDGMENT . . .
OH, SURE-- YOU'VE GOT TO KNOW WHO YOU'RE COMPATIBLE WITH!
EXCLUSIVE
BEFORE I MET YOU, I WAS THINKING OF ASKING ALANNA OUT
WHAT?
WAH HA HA!
WHAT'S SO FUNNY?
TOBY, I PUT UP WITH YOUR ANTICS-- SHE WOULD NEVER TOLERATE THEM!
YOU AND ALANNA WOLFF?
WAH HA HA!
TOBY, YOU KILL ME!
HMPH!
Tell All Gram
EXCLUSIVE
I MARRIED A SNIVELING BLOB OF JELLY
Page Welch's Own Story

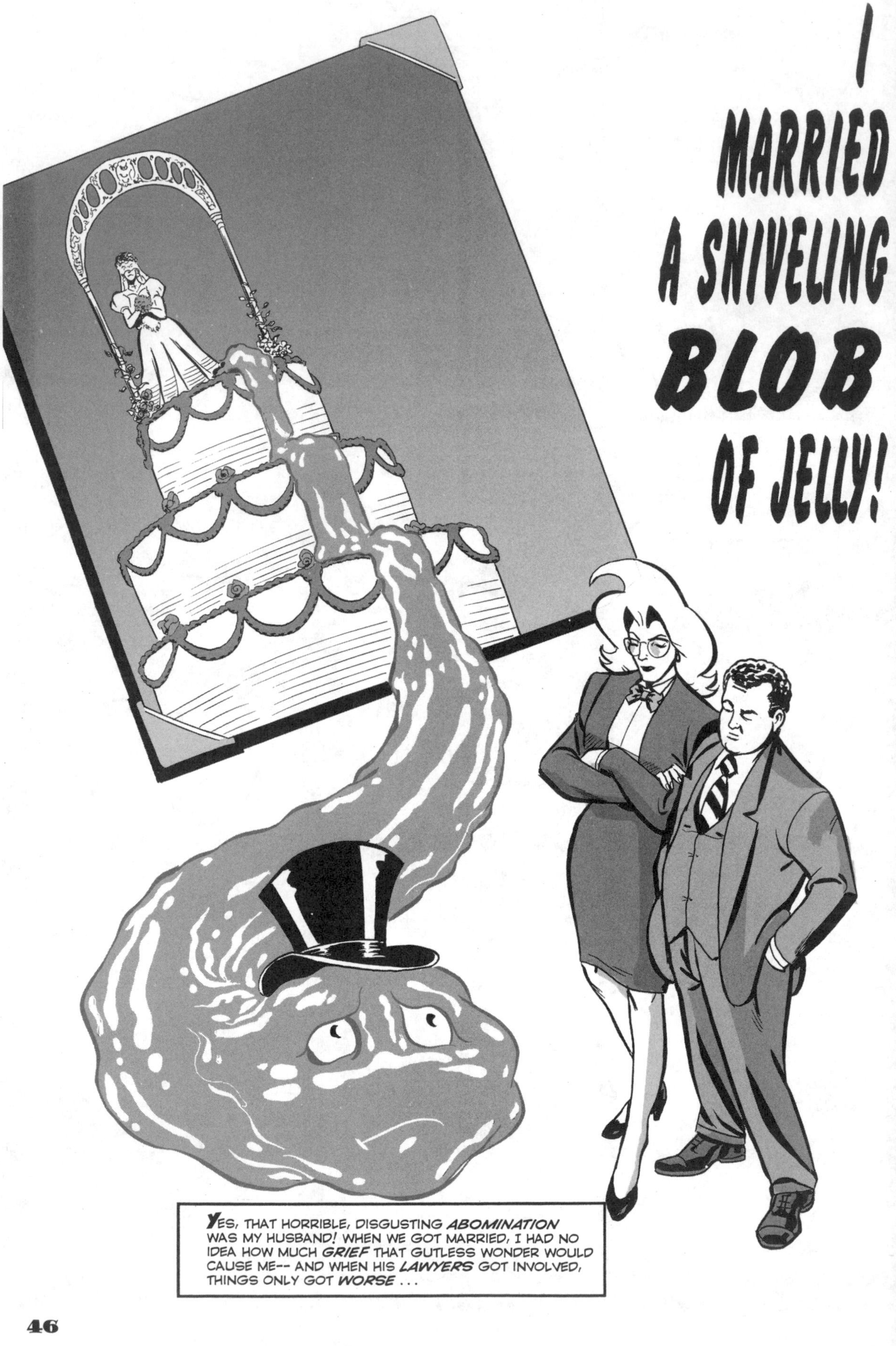
I MARRIED A SNIVELING BLOB OF JELLY!
YES, THAT HORRIBLE, DISGUSTING ABOMINATION WAS MY HUSBAND! WHEN WE GOT MARRIED, I HAD NO IDEA HOW MUCH GRIEF THAT GUTLESS WONDER WOULD CAUSE ME-- AND WHEN HIS LAWYERS GOT INVOLVED, THINGS ONLY GOT WORSE . . .

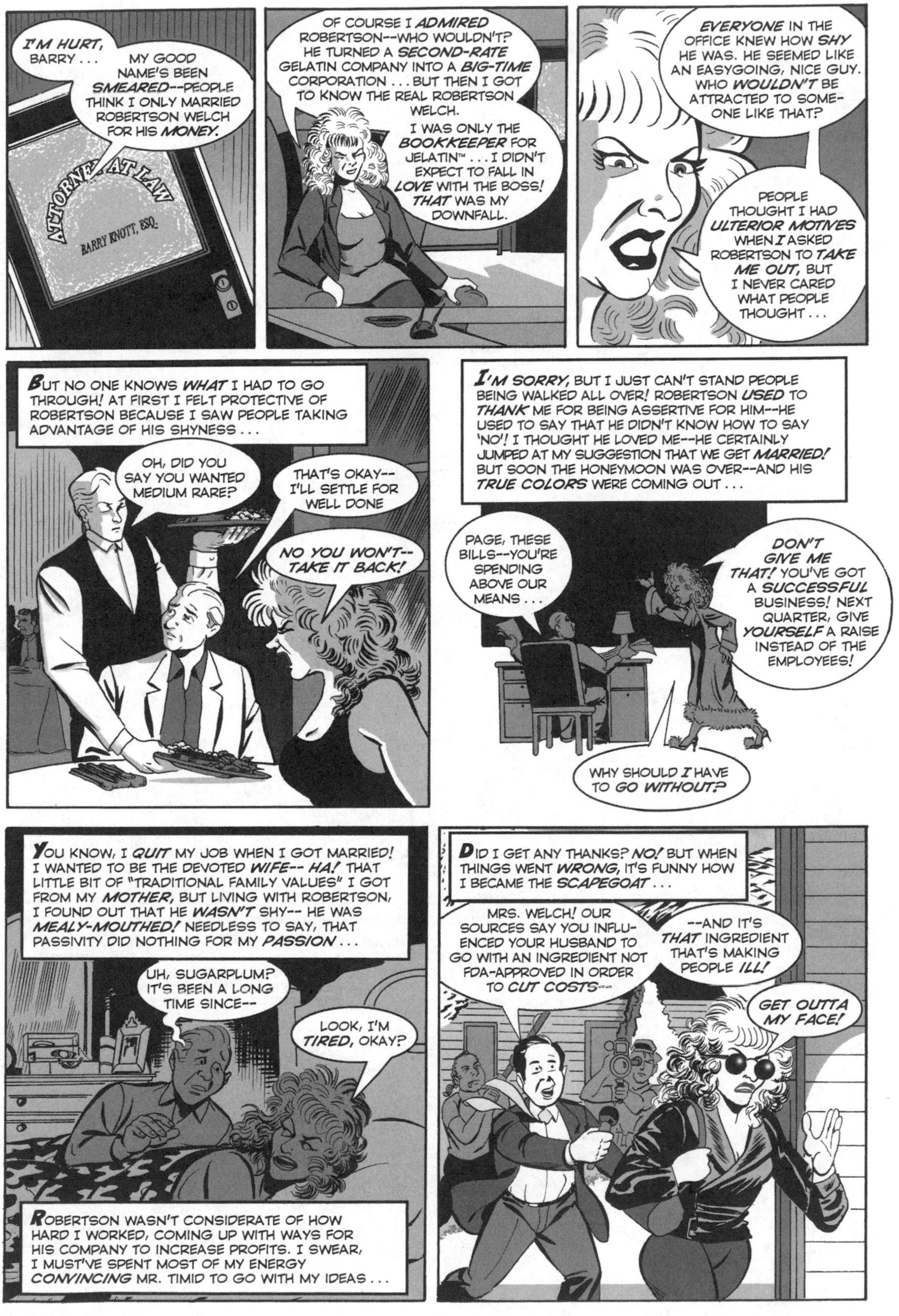
I'M HURT, BARRY . . .
MY GOOD NAME'S BEEN SMEARED--PEOPLE THINK I ONLY MARRIED ROBERTSON WELCH FOR HIS MONEY.
ATTORNEY AT LAW
BARRY KNOTT, ESQ.
OF COURSE I ADMIRED ROBERTSON--WHO WOULDN'T? HE TURNED A SECOND-RATE GELATIN COMPANY INTO A BIG-TIME CORPORATION . . . BUT THEN I GOT TO KNOW THE REAL ROBERTSON WELCH.
I WAS ONLY THE BOOKKEEPER FOR JELATIN™ . . . I DIDN'T EXPECT TO FALL IN LOVE WITH THE BOSS! THAT WAS MY DOWNFALL.
EVERYONE IN THE OFFICE KNEW HOW SHY HE WAS. HE SEEMED LIKE AN EASYGOING, NICE GUY. WHO WOULDN'T BE ATTRACTED TO SOMEONE LIKE THAT?
PEOPLE THOUGHT I HAD ULTERIOR MOTIVES WHEN I ASKED ROBERTSON TO TAKE ME OUT, BUT I NEVER CARED WHAT PEOPLE THOUGHT . . .
BUT NO ONE KNOWS WHAT I HAD TO GO THROUGH! AT FIRST I FELT PROTECTIVE OF ROBERTSON BECAUSE I SAW PEOPLE TAKING ADVANTAGE OF HIS SHYNESS . . .
OH, DID YOU SAY YOU WANTED MEDIUM RARE?
THAT'S OKAY-- I'LL SETTLE FOR WELL DONE
NO YOU WON'T-- TAKE IT BACK!
I'M SORRY, BUT I JUST CAN'T STAND PEOPLE BEING WALKED ALL OVER! ROBERTSON USED TO THANK ME FOR BEING ASSERTIVE FOR HIM--HE USED TO SAY THAT HE DIDN'T KNOW HOW TO SAY 'NO'! I THOUGHT HE LOVED ME--HE CERTAINLY JUMPED AT MY SUGGESTION THAT WE GET MARRIED! BUT SOON THE HONEYMOON WAS OVER--AND HIS TRUE COLORS WERE COMING OUT . . .
PAGE, THESE BILLS--YOU'RE SPENDING ABOVE OUR MEANS . . .
DON'T GIVE ME THAT! YOU'VE GOT A SUCCESSFUL BUSINESS! NEXT QUARTER, GIVE YOURSELF A RAISE INSTEAD OF THE EMPLOYEES!
WHY SHOULD I HAVE TO GO WITHOUT?
YOU KNOW, I QUIT MY JOB WHEN I GOT MARRIED! I WANTED TO BE THE DEVOTED WIFE-- HA! THAT LITTLE BIT OF "TRADITIONAL FAMILY VALUES" I GOT FROM MY MOTHER, BUT LIVING WITH ROBERTSON, I FOUND OUT THAT HE WASN'T SHY-- HE WAS MEALY-MOUTHED! NEEDLESS TO SAY, THAT PASSIVITY DID NOTHING FOR MY PASSION . . .
UH, SUGARPLUM? IT'S BEEN A LONG TIME SINCE--
LOOK, I'M TIRED, OKAY?
ROBERTSON WASN'T CONSIDERATE OF HOW HARD I WORKED, COMING UP WITH WAYS FOR HIS COMPANY TO INCREASE PROFITS. I SWEAR, I MUST'VE SPENT MOST OF MY ENERGY CONVINCING MR. TIMID TO GO WITH MY IDEAS . . .
DID I GET ANY THANKS? NO! BUT WHEN THINGS WENT WRONG, IT'S FUNNY HOW I BECAME THE SCAPEGOAT . . .
MRS. WELCH! OUR SOURCES SAY YOU INFLUENCED YOUR HUSBAND TO GO WITH AN INGREDIENT NOT FDA-APPROVED IN ORDER TO CUT COSTS--
--AND IT'S THAT INGREDIENT THAT'S MAKING PEOPLE ILL!
GET OUTTA MY FACE!

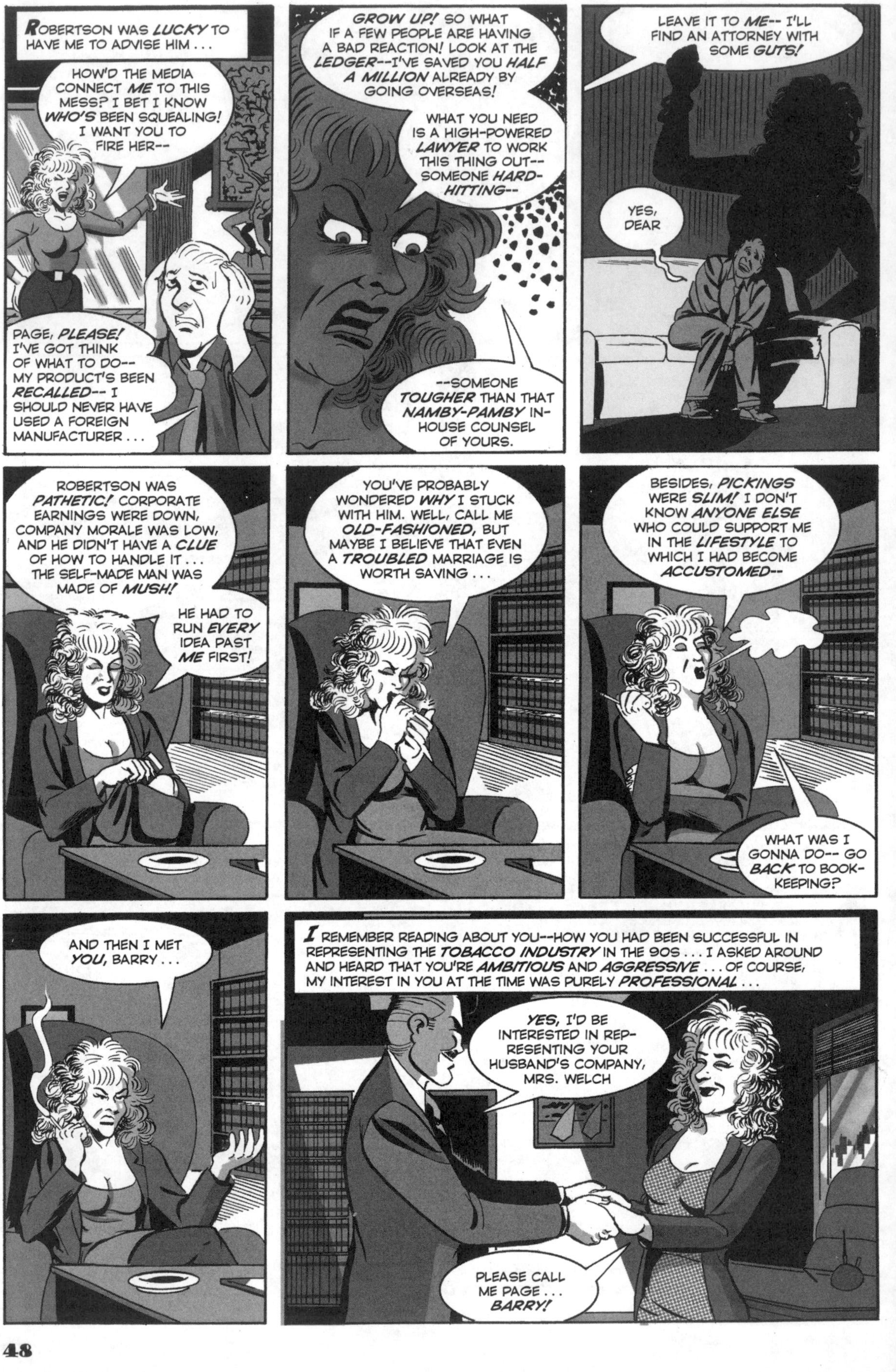
ROBERTSON WAS LUCKY TO HAVE ME TO ADVISE HIM . . .
HOW'D THE MEDIA CONNECT ME TO THIS MESS? I BET I KNOW WHO'S BEEN SQUEALING! I WANT YOU TO FIRE HER--
PAGE, PLEASE! I'VE GOT THINK OF WHAT TO DO-- MY PRODUCT'S BEEN RECALLED-- I SHOULD NEVER HAVE USED A FOREIGN MANUFACTURER . . .
GROW UP! SO WHAT IF A FEW PEOPLE ARE HAVING A BAD REACTION! LOOK AT THE LEDGER--I'VE SAVED YOU HALF A MILLION ALREADY BY GOING OVERSEAS!
WHAT YOU NEED IS A HIGH-POWERED LAWYER TO WORK THIS THING OUT-- SOMEONE HARD-HITTING--
--SOMEONE TOUGHER THAN THAT NAMBY-PAMBY IN-HOUSE COUNSEL OF YOURS.
LEAVE IT TO ME-- I'LL FIND AN ATTORNEY WITH SOME GUTS!
YES, DEAR
ROBERTSON WAS PATHETIC! CORPORATE EARNINGS WERE DOWN, COMPANY MORALE WAS LOW, AND HE DIDN'T HAVE A CLUE OF HOW TO HANDLE IT . . . THE SELF-MADE MAN WAS MADE OF MUSH!
HE HAD TO RUN EVERY IDEA PAST ME FIRST!
YOU'VE PROBABLY WONDERED WHY I STUCK WITH HIM. WELL, CALL ME OLD-FASHIONED, BUT MAYBE I BELIEVE THAT EVEN A TROUBLED MARRIAGE IS WORTH SAVING . . .
BESIDES, PICKINGS WERE SLIM! I DON'T KNOW ANYONE ELSE WHO COULD SUPPORT ME IN THE LIFESTYLE TO WHICH I HAD BECOME ACCUSTOMED--
WHAT WAS I GONNA DO-- GO BACK TO BOOK-KEEPING?
AND THEN I MET YOU, BARRY . . .
I REMEMBER READING ABOUT YOU--HOW YOU HAD BEEN SUCCESSFUL IN REPRESENTING THE TOBACCO INDUSTRY IN THE 90S . . . I ASKED AROUND AND HEARD THAT YOU'RE AMBITIOUS AND AGGRESSIVE . . . OF COURSE, MY INTEREST IN YOU AT THE TIME WAS PURELY PROFESSIONAL . . .
YES, I'D BE INTERESTED IN REPRESENTING YOUR HUSBAND'S COMPANY, MRS. WELCH
PLEASE CALL ME PAGE . . . BARRY!

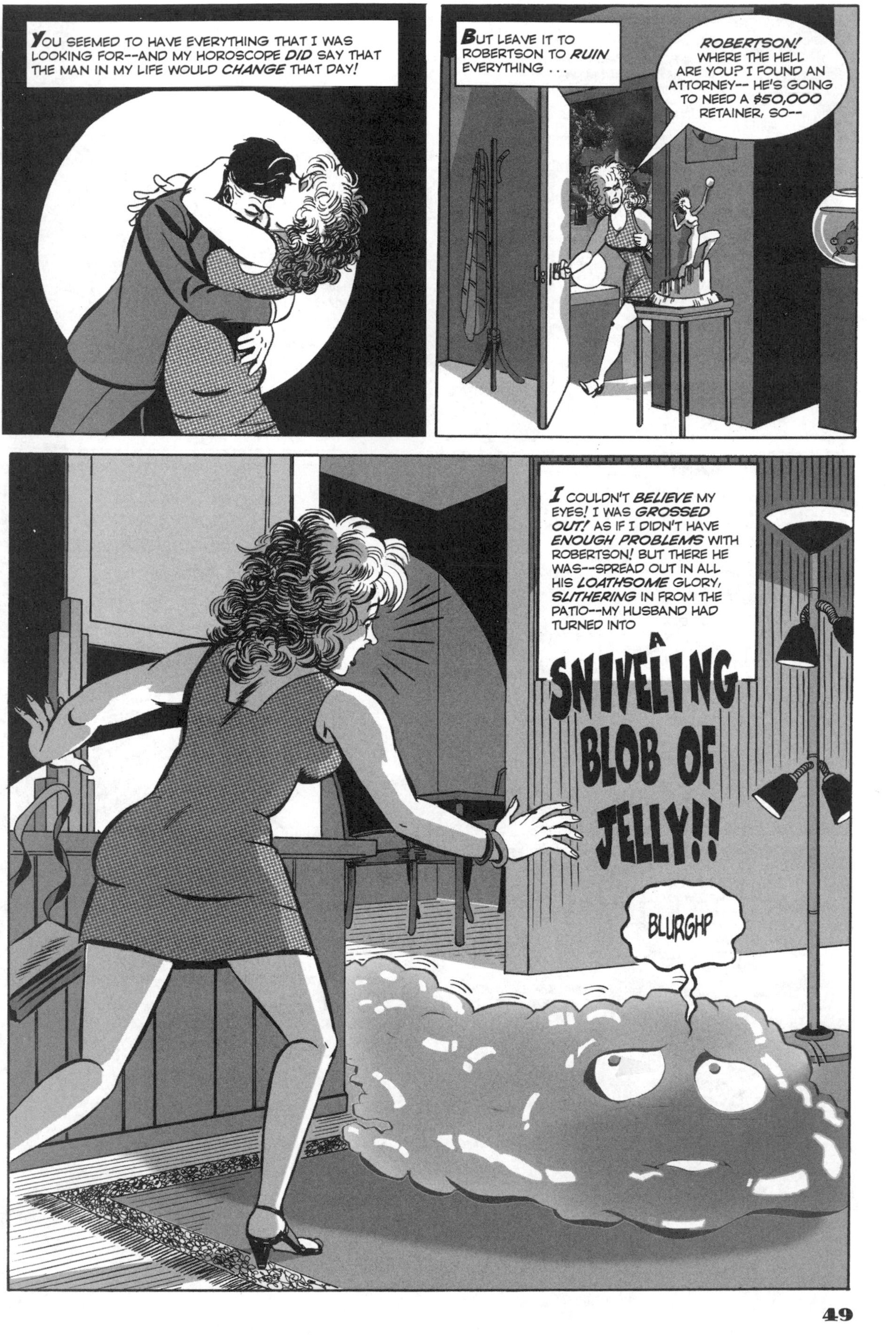
YOU SEEMED TO HAVE EVERYTHING THAT I WAS LOOKING FOR--AND MY HOROSCOPE DID SAY THAT THE MAN IN MY LIFE WOULD CHANGE THAT DAY!
BUT LEAVE IT TO ROBERTSON TO RUIN EVERYTHING . . .
ROBERTSON! WHERE THE HELL ARE YOU? I FOUND AN ATTORNEY-- HE'S GOING TO NEED A $50,000 RETAINER, SO--
I COULDN'T BELIEVE MY EYES! I WAS GROSSED OUT! AS IF I DIDN'T HAVE ENOUGH PROBLEMS WITH ROBERTSON! BUT THERE HE WAS--SPREAD OUT IN ALL HIS LOATHSOME GLORY, SLITHERING IN FROM THE PATIO--MY HUSBAND HAD TURNED INTO
A SNIVELING BLOB OF JELLY!!
BLURGHP

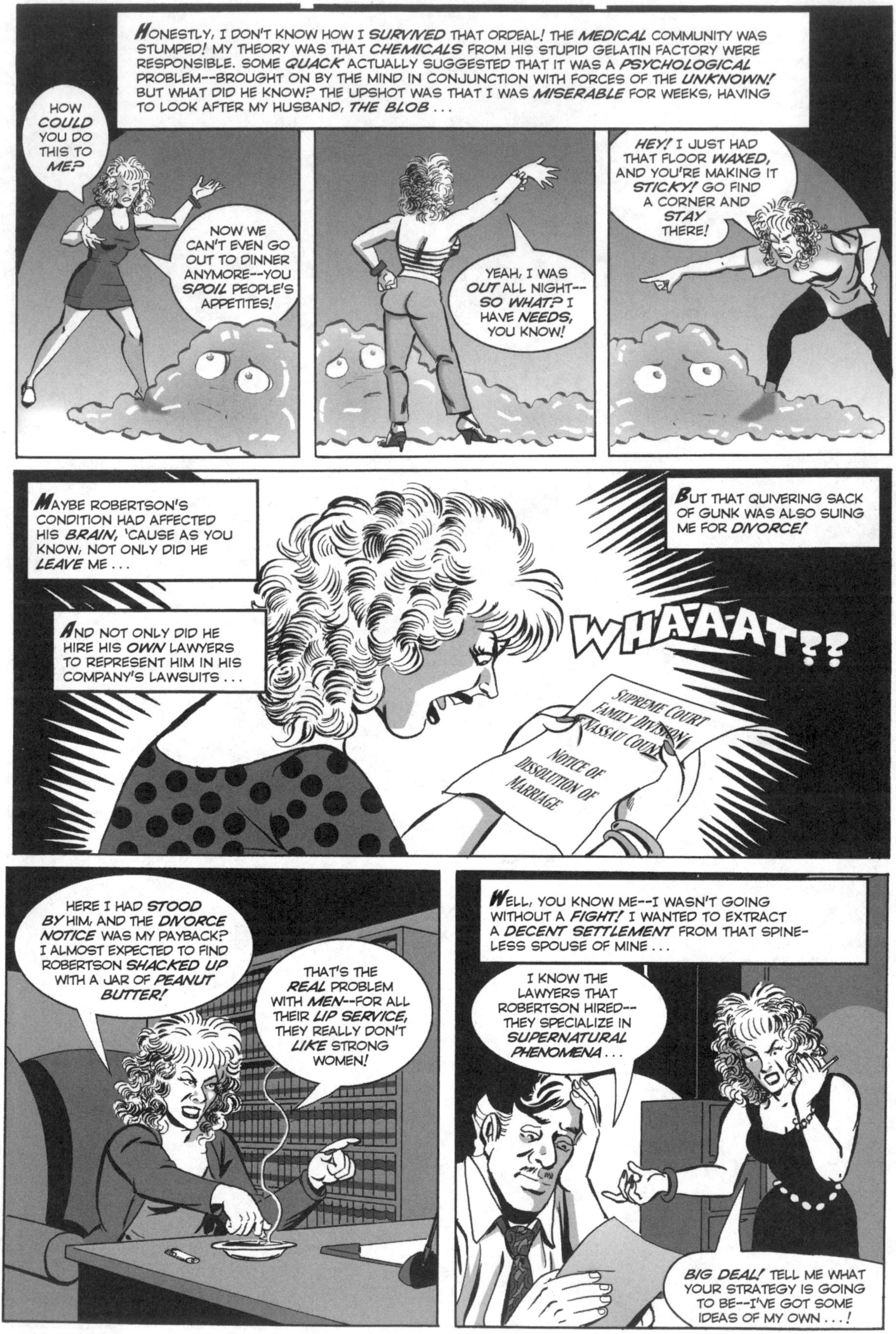
HONESTLY, I DON'T KNOW HOW I SURVIVED THAT ORDEAL! THE MEDICAL COMMUNITY WAS STUMPED! MY THEORY WAS THAT CHEMICALS FROM HIS STUPID GELATIN FACTORY WERE RESPONSIBLE. SOME QUACK ACTUALLY SUGGESTED THAT IT WAS A PSYCHOLOGICAL PROBLEM--BROUGHT ON BY THE MIND IN CONJUNCTION WITH FORCES OF THE UNKNOWN! BUT WHAT DID HE KNOW? THE UPSHOT WAS THAT I WAS MISERABLE FOR WEEKS, HAVING TO LOOK AFTER MY HUSBAND, THE BLOB . . .
HOW COULD YOU DO THIS TO ME?
NOW WE CAN'T EVEN GO OUT TO DINNER ANYMORE--YOU SPOIL PEOPLE'S APPETITES!
YEAH, I WAS OUT ALL NIGHT-- SO WHAT? I HAVE NEEDS, YOU KNOW!
HEY! I JUST HAD THAT FLOOR WAXED, AND YOU'RE MAKING IT STICKY! GO FIND A CORNER AND STAY THERE!
MAYBE ROBERTSON'S CONDITION HAD AFFECTED HIS BRAIN, 'CAUSE AS YOU KNOW, NOT ONLY DID HE LEAVE ME . . .
AND NOT ONLY DID HE HIRE HIS OWN LAWYERS TO REPRESENT HIM IN HIS COMPANY'S LAWSUITS . . .
BUT THAT QUIVERING SACK OF GUNK WAS ALSO SUING ME FOR DIVORCE!
WHA-A-AT??
SUPREME COURT FAMILY DIVISION NASSAU COUN
NOTICE OF DISSOLUTION OF MARRIAGE
HERE I HAD STOOD BY HIM, AND THE DIVORCE NOTICE WAS MY PAYBACK? I ALMOST EXPECTED TO FIND ROBERTSON SHACKED UP WITH A JAR OF PEANUT BUTTER!
THAT'S THE REAL PROBLEM WITH MEN--FOR ALL THEIR LIP SERVICE, THEY REALLY DON'T LIKE STRONG WOMEN!
WELL, YOU KNOW ME--I WASN'T GOING WITHOUT A FIGHT! I WANTED TO EXTRACT A DECENT SETTLEMENT FROM THAT SPINE-LESS SPOUSE OF MINE . . .
I KNOW THE LAWYERS THAT ROBERTSON HIRED-- THEY SPECIALIZE IN SUPERNATURAL PHENOMENA . . .
BIG DEAL! TELL ME WHAT YOUR STRATEGY IS GOING TO BE--I'VE GOT SOME IDEAS OF MY OWN . . . !

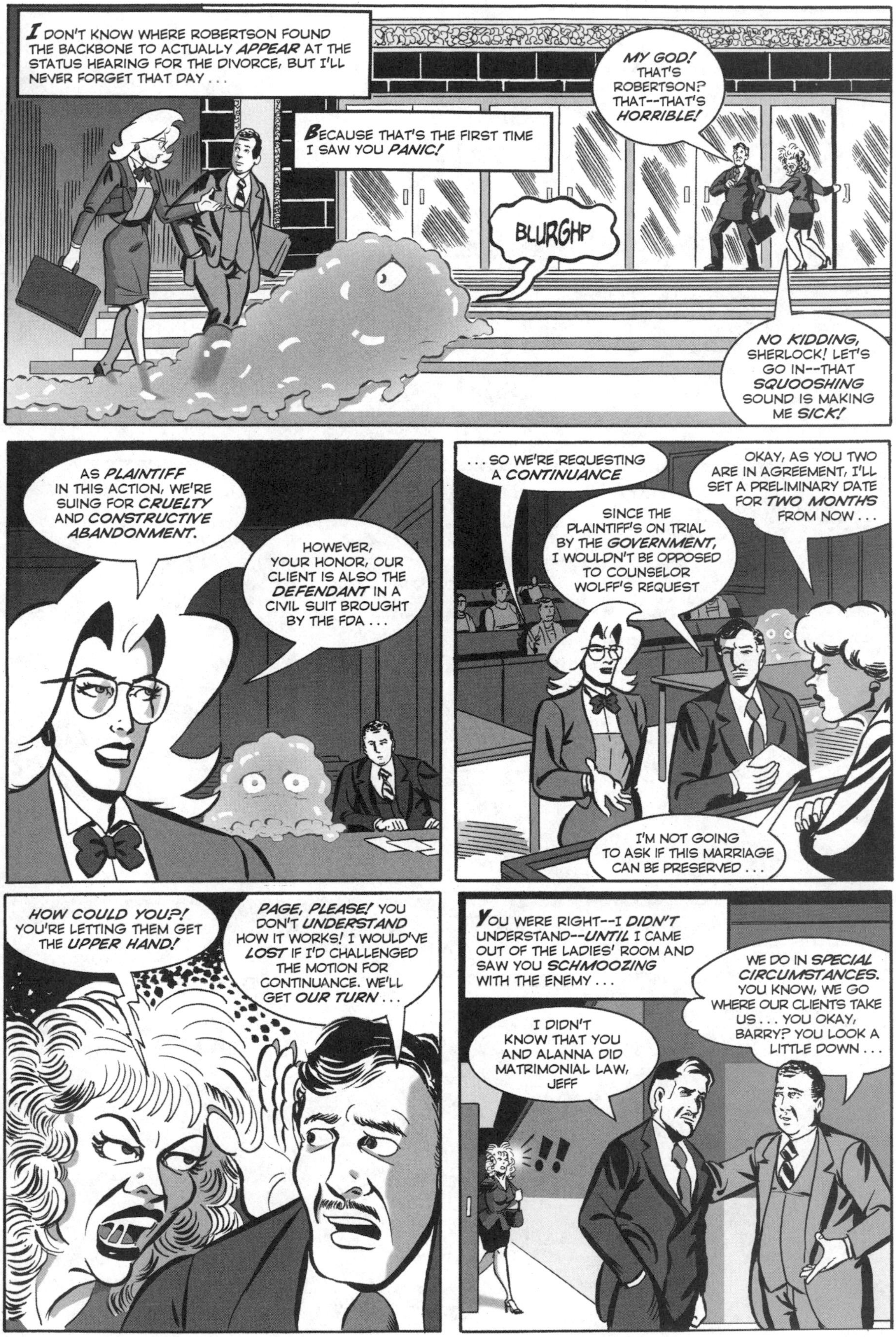
I DON'T KNOW WHERE ROBERTSON FOUND THE BACKBONE TO ACTUALLY APPEAR AT THE STATUS HEARING FOR THE DIVORCE, BUT I'LL NEVER FORGET THAT DAY . . .
BECAUSE THAT'S THE FIRST TIME I SAW YOU PANIC!
MY GOD! THAT'S ROBERTSON? THAT--THAT'S HORRIBLE!
BLURGHP
NO KIDDING, SHERLOCK! LET'S GO IN--THAT SQUOOSHING SOUND IS MAKING ME SICK!
AS PLAINTIFF IN THIS ACTION, WE'RE SUING FOR CRUELTY AND CONSTRUCTIVE ABANDONMENT.
HOWEVER, YOUR HONOR, OUR CLIENT IS ALSO THE DEFENDANT IN A CIVIL SUIT BROUGHT BY THE FDA . . .
. . . SO WE'RE REQUESTING A CONTINUANCE
SINCE THE PLAINTIFF'S ON TRIAL BY THE GOVERNMENT, I WOULDN'T BE OPPOSED TO COUNSELOR WOLFF'S REQUEST
OKAY, AS YOU TWO ARE IN AGREEMENT, I'LL SET A PRELIMINARY DATE FOR TWO MONTHS FROM NOW . . .
I'M NOT GOING TO ASK IF THIS MARRIAGE CAN BE PRESERVED . . .
HOW COULD YOU?! YOU'RE LETTING THEM GET THE UPPER HAND!
PAGE, PLEASE! YOU DON'T UNDERSTAND HOW IT WORKS! I WOULD'VE LOST IF I'D CHALLENGED THE MOTION FOR CONTINUANCE. WE'LL GET OUR TURN . . .
YOU WERE RIGHT--I DIDN'T UNDERSTAND--UNTIL I CAME OUT OF THE LADIES' ROOM AND SAW YOU SCHMOOZING WITH THE ENEMY . . .
I DIDN'T KNOW THAT YOU AND ALANNA DID MATRIMONIAL LAW, JEFF
WE DO IN SPECIAL CIRCUMSTANCES. YOU KNOW, WE GO WHERE OUR CLIENTS TAKE US . . . YOU OKAY, BARRY? YOU LOOK A LITTLE DOWN . . .
!!

SO THIS IS HOW IT *WORKS*, EH? THE *FRATERNITY OF LAWYERS* BUYING TIME FOR *EACH OTHER* ON THE CLIENT'S *DIME!*

PAGE, DON'T BE *RIDICULOUS!* WE'RE JUST TALKING *SHOP!*

EXCUSE ME, JEFF . . .

I DON'T KNOW ABOUT *YOU*, BYRD-- BUT IT SOUNDS TO *ME* LIKE THAT RELATIONSHIP IS MORE THAN JUST *PROFESSIONAL* . . .

IF BARRY'S HAVING AN AFFAIR WITH *THAT* CLIENT, HE'S PAYING A *HEAVIER PRICE* THAN ANY COURT COULD IMPOSE!

NEXT TIME YOU WANT TO TALK SHOP, TALK TO ME

YES, DEAR

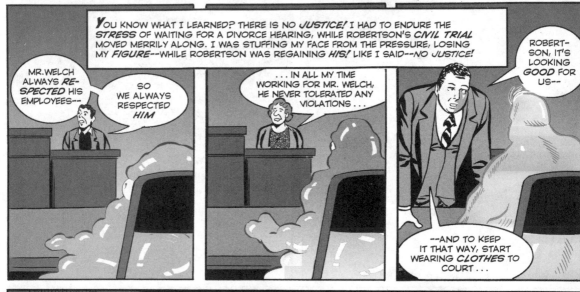

*Y*OU KNOW WHAT I LEARNED? THERE IS NO *JUSTICE!* I HAD TO ENDURE THE *STRESS* OF WAITING FOR A DIVORCE HEARING, WHILE ROBERTSON'S *CIVIL TRIAL* MOVED MERRILY ALONG. I WAS STUFFING MY FACE FROM THE PRESSURE, LOSING MY *FIGURE*--WHILE ROBERTSON WAS REGAINING *HIS!* LIKE I SAID--*NO JUSTICE!*

MR. WELCH ALWAYS *RE-SPECTED* HIS EMPLOYEES--

SO WE ALWAYS RESPECTED *HIM*

. . . IN ALL MY TIME WORKING FOR MR. WELCH, HE NEVER TOLERATED ANY VIOLATIONS . . .

ROBERT-SON, IT'S LOOKING *GOOD* FOR US--

--AND TO KEEP IT THAT WAY, START WEARING *CLOTHES* TO COURT . . .

*A*ND WHEN THE DIVORCE HEARING FINALLY ROLLED AROUND, I COUNTED ON YOU, BARRY, TO MAKE EVERYTHING GEL . . .

IF SHE HANDLES THE *LAW* THE WAY SHE DOES HER *HAIR*, I'D SAY WE HAVE *NOTHING* TO WORRY ABOUT-- RIGHT, BARRY?

IT'S GOING TO BE A *LONG* DAY, ROBERTSON-- AFTER THIS HEARING WE GO TO FEDERAL COURT--THE JUDGE IN THE FDA SUIT IS EXPECTED TO MAKE A *DECISION*--

--BUT GIVEN THE *STRONG* EVIDENCE ON YOUR BEHALF, I THINK THE JUDGE WILL RULE IN YOUR FAVOR . . . I THINK YOU'RE IN GREAT SHAPE!

PAGE, JUST GIVE ME A MINUTE TO GET EVERYTHING IN ORDER HERE . . .

REALLY? IT MUST BE THE ISO-METRIC EXERCISES

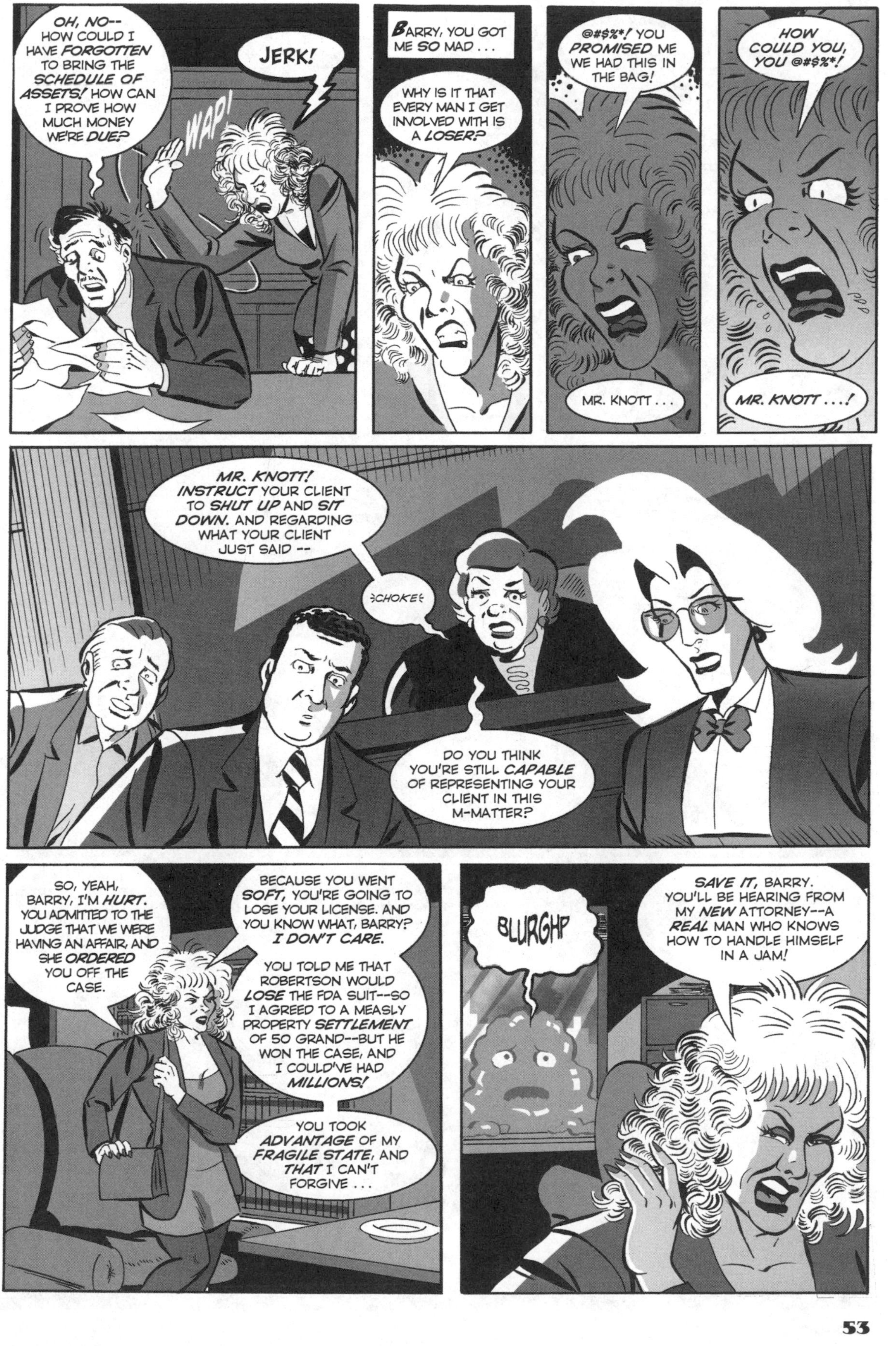

OH, NO-- HOW COULD I HAVE FORGOTTEN TO BRING THE SCHEDULE OF ASSETS! HOW CAN I PROVE HOW MUCH MONEY WE'RE DUE?
JERK!
WAP!
BARRY, YOU GOT ME SO MAD . . .
WHY IS IT THAT EVERY MAN I GET INVOLVED WITH IS A LOSER?
@#$%*! YOU PROMISED ME WE HAD THIS IN THE BAG!
MR. KNOTT . . .
HOW COULD YOU, YOU @#$%*!
MR. KNOTT . . . !
MR. KNOTT! INSTRUCT YOUR CLIENT TO SHUT UP AND SIT DOWN. AND REGARDING WHAT YOUR CLIENT JUST SAID --
CHOKE
DO YOU THINK YOU'RE STILL CAPABLE OF REPRESENTING YOUR CLIENT IN THIS M-MATTER?
SO, YEAH, BARRY, I'M HURT. YOU ADMITTED TO THE JUDGE THAT WE WERE HAVING AN AFFAIR, AND SHE ORDERED YOU OFF THE CASE.
BECAUSE YOU WENT SOFT, YOU'RE GOING TO LOSE YOUR LICENSE. AND YOU KNOW WHAT, BARRY? I DON'T CARE.
YOU TOLD ME THAT ROBERTSON WOULD LOSE THE FDA SUIT--SO I AGREED TO A MEASLY PROPERTY SETTLEMENT OF 50 GRAND--BUT HE WON THE CASE, AND I COULD'VE HAD MILLIONS!
YOU TOOK ADVANTAGE OF MY FRAGILE STATE, AND THAT I CAN'T FORGIVE . . .
BLURGHP
SAVE IT, BARRY. YOU'LL BE HEARING FROM MY NEW ATTORNEY--A REAL MAN WHO KNOWS HOW TO HANDLE HIMSELF IN A JAM!

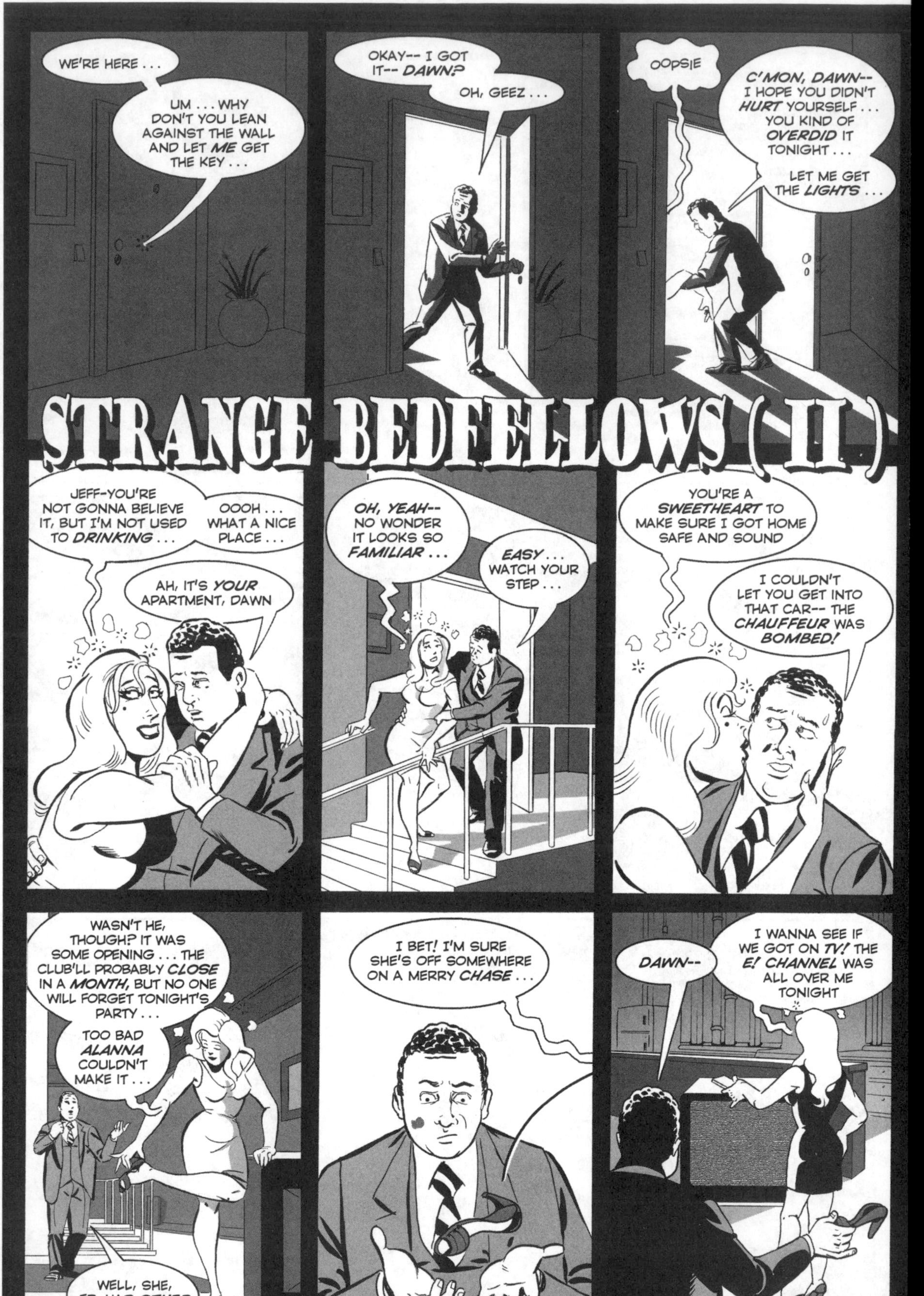
WE'RE HERE . . .
UM . . . WHY DON'T YOU LEAN AGAINST THE WALL AND LET ME GET THE KEY . . .
OKAY-- I GOT IT-- DAWN?
OH, GEEZ . . .
OOPSIE
C'MON, DAWN-- I HOPE YOU DIDN'T HURT YOURSELF . . . YOU KIND OF OVERDID IT TONIGHT . . .
LET ME GET THE LIGHTS . . .
STRANGE BEDFELLOWS (II)
JEFF-YOU'RE NOT GONNA BELIEVE IT, BUT I'M NOT USED TO DRINKING . . .
OOOH . . . WHAT A NICE PLACE . . .
AH, IT'S YOUR APARTMENT, DAWN
OH, YEAH-- NO WONDER IT LOOKS SO FAMILIAR . . .
EASY . . . WATCH YOUR STEP . . .
YOU'RE A SWEETHEART TO MAKE SURE I GOT HOME SAFE AND SOUND
I COULDN'T LET YOU GET INTO THAT CAR-- THE CHAUFFEUR WAS BOMBED!
WASN'T HE, THOUGH? IT WAS SOME OPENING . . . THE CLUB'LL PROBABLY CLOSE IN A MONTH, BUT NO ONE WILL FORGET TONIGHT'S PARTY . . .
TOO BAD ALANNA COULDN'T MAKE IT . . .
WELL, SHE, ER, HAD OTHER PLANS . . .
I BET! I'M SURE SHE'S OFF SOMEWHERE ON A MERRY CHASE . . .
DAWN--
I WANNA SEE IF WE GOT ON TV! THE E! CHANNEL WAS ALL OVER ME TONIGHT

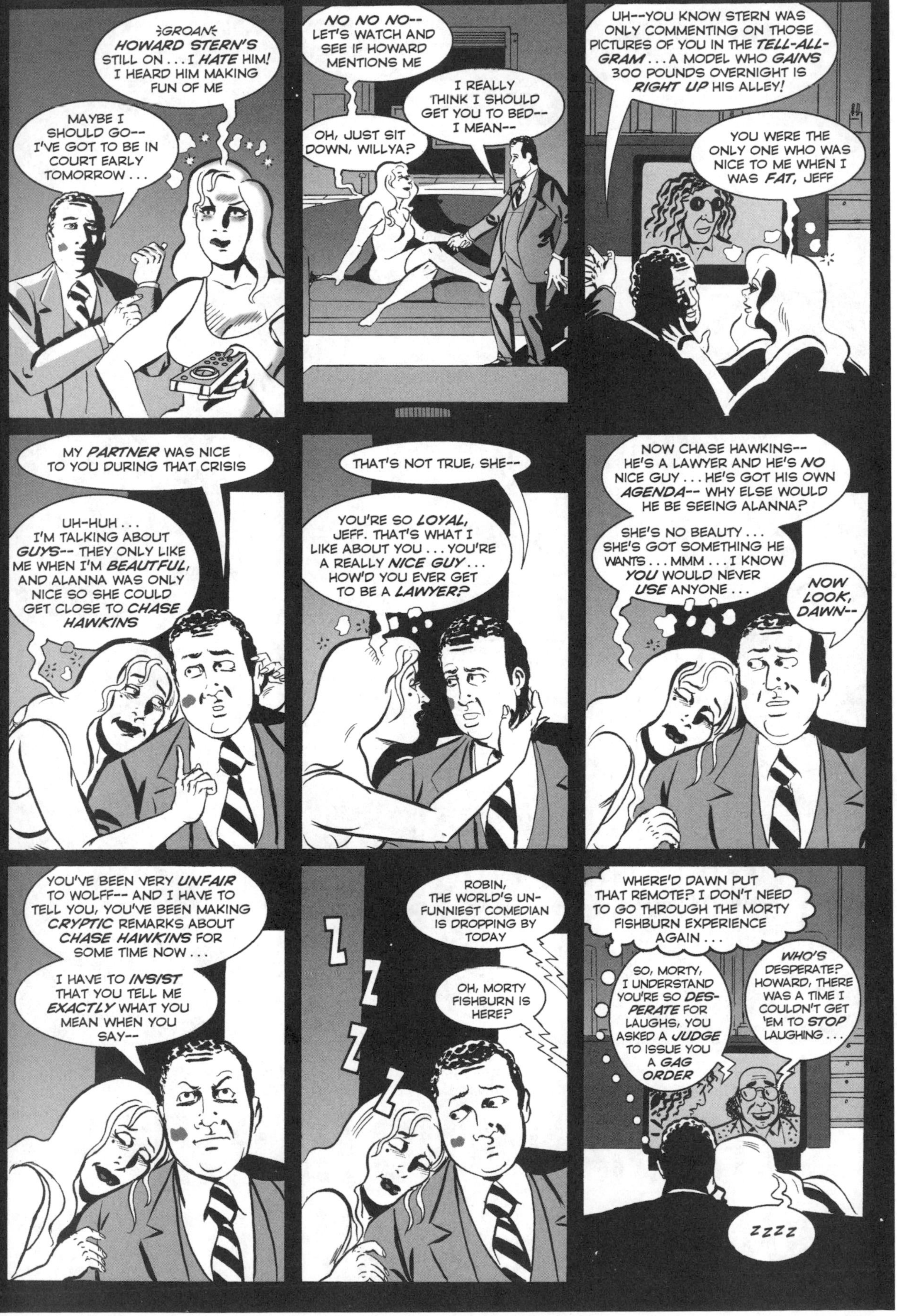
GROAN
HOWARD STERN'S STILL ON . . . I HATE HIM! I HEARD HIM MAKING FUN OF ME
MAYBE I SHOULD GO-- I'VE GOT TO BE IN COURT EARLY TOMORROW . . .
NO NO NO-- LET'S WATCH AND SEE IF HOWARD MENTIONS ME
I REALLY THINK I SHOULD GET YOU TO BED-- I MEAN--
OH, JUST SIT DOWN, WILLYA?
UH--YOU KNOW STERN WAS ONLY COMMENTING ON THOSE PICTURES OF YOU IN THE TELL-ALL-GRAM . . . A MODEL WHO GAINS 300 POUNDS OVERNIGHT IS RIGHT UP HIS ALLEY!
YOU WERE THE ONLY ONE WHO WAS NICE TO ME WHEN I WAS FAT, JEFF
MY PARTNER WAS NICE TO YOU DURING THAT CRISIS
UH-HUH . . . I'M TALKING ABOUT GUYS-- THEY ONLY LIKE ME WHEN I'M BEAUTFUL, AND ALANNA WAS ONLY NICE SO SHE COULD GET CLOSE TO CHASE HAWKINS
THAT'S NOT TRUE, SHE--
YOU'RE SO LOYAL, JEFF. THAT'S WHAT I LIKE ABOUT YOU . . . YOU'RE A REALLY NICE GUY . . . HOW'D YOU EVER GET TO BE A LAWYER?
NOW CHASE HAWKINS-- HE'S A LAWYER AND HE'S NO NICE GUY . . . HE'S GOT HIS OWN AGENDA-- WHY ELSE WOULD HE BE SEEING ALANNA?
SHE'S NO BEAUTY . . . SHE'S GOT SOMETHING HE WANTS . . . MMM . . . I KNOW YOU WOULD NEVER USE ANYONE . . .
NOW LOOK, DAWN--
YOU'VE BEEN VERY UNFAIR TO WOLFF-- AND I HAVE TO TELL YOU, YOU'VE BEEN MAKING CRYPTIC REMARKS ABOUT CHASE HAWKINS FOR SOME TIME NOW . . .
I HAVE TO INSIST THAT YOU TELL ME EXACTLY WHAT YOU MEAN WHEN YOU SAY--
Z
Z
Z
Z
ROBIN, THE WORLD'S UN-FUNNIEST COMEDIAN IS DROPPING BY TODAY
OH, MORTY FISHBURN IS HERE?
WHERE'D DAWN PUT THAT REMOTE? I DON'T NEED TO GO THROUGH THE MORTY FISHBURN EXPERIENCE AGAIN . . .
SO, MORTY, I UNDERSTAND YOU'RE SO DES-PERATE FOR LAUGHS, YOU ASKED A JUDGE TO ISSUE YOU A GAG ORDER
WHO'S DESPERATE? HOWARD, THERE WAS A TIME I COULDN'T GET 'EM TO STOP LAUGHING . . .
ZZZZ

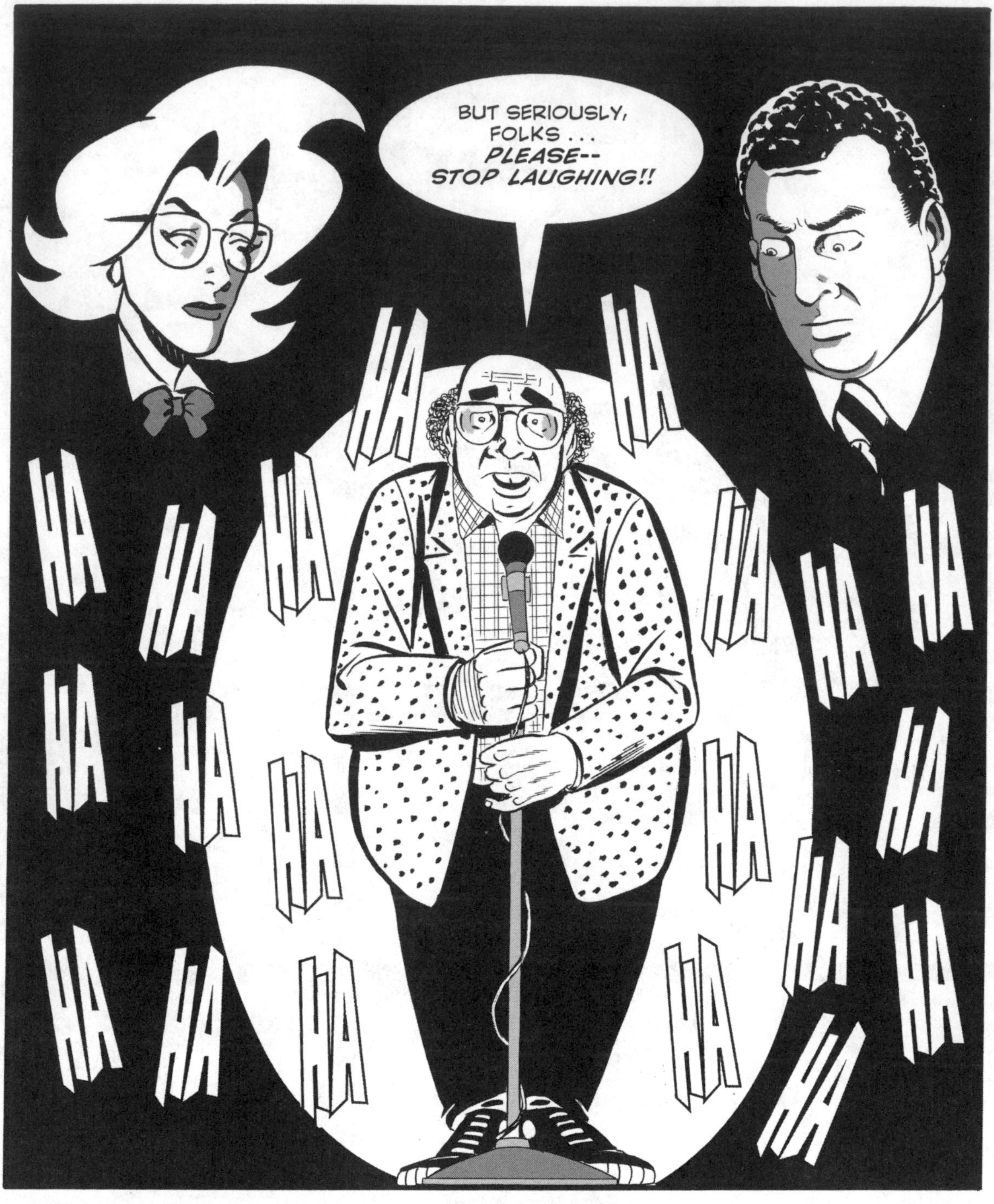
BUT SERIOUSLY, FOLKS ... PLEASE-- STOP LAUGHING!!
HA HA HA HA HA HA HA HA HA HA HA HA HA HA HA HA HA HA HA HA HA HA HA HA

WHAT COMEDIAN WOULDN'T WANT TO HEAR *ENDLESS* PEALS OF LAUGHTER, GUFFAWS, AND CHORTLES FROM *EVERYTHING* HE SAID? WELL, DIDJA EVER HEAR THE ONE ABOUT . . .

THE MAN WHO HAD HIS OWN PERSONAL LAUGHTRACK!

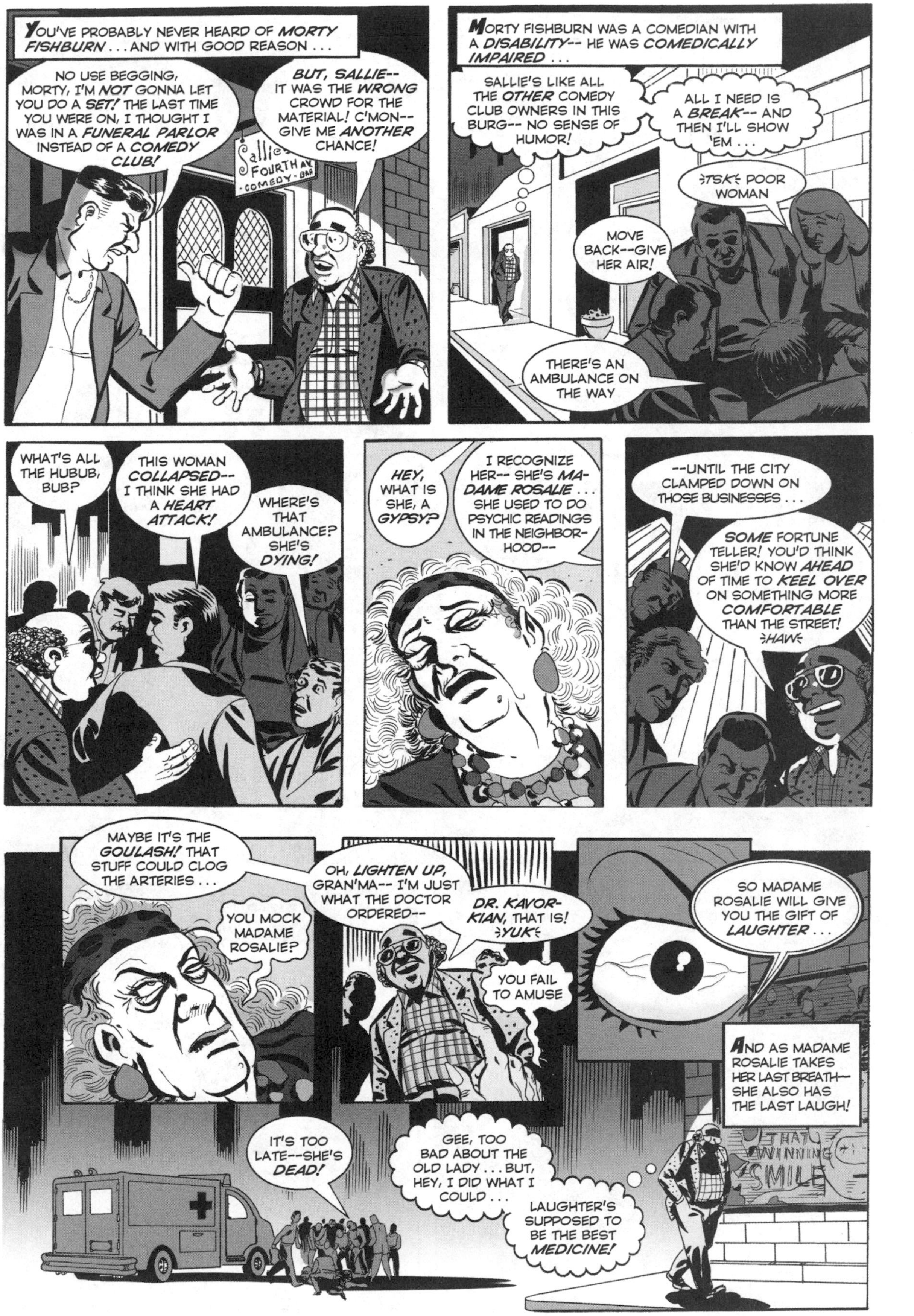
YOU'VE PROBABLY NEVER HEARD OF MORTY FISHBURN . . . AND WITH GOOD REASON . . .
NO USE BEGGING, MORTY, I'M NOT GONNA LET YOU DO A SET! THE LAST TIME YOU WERE ON, I THOUGHT I WAS IN A FUNERAL PARLOR INSTEAD OF A COMEDY CLUB!
BUT, SALLIE-- IT WAS THE WRONG CROWD FOR THE MATERIAL! C'MON-- GIVE ME ANOTHER CHANCE!
FOURTH AV. COMEDY · BAR
MORTY FISHBURN WAS A COMEDIAN WITH A DISABILITY-- HE WAS COMEDICALLY IMPAIRED . . .
SALLIE'S LIKE ALL THE OTHER COMEDY CLUB OWNERS IN THIS BURG-- NO SENSE OF HUMOR!
ALL I NEED IS A BREAK-- AND THEN I'LL SHOW 'EM . . .
TSK POOR WOMAN
MOVE BACK--GIVE HER AIR!
THERE'S AN AMBULANCE ON THE WAY
WHAT'S ALL THE HUBUB, BUB?
THIS WOMAN COLLAPSED-- I THINK SHE HAD A HEART ATTACK!
WHERE'S THAT AMBULANCE? SHE'S DYING!
HEY, WHAT IS SHE, A GYPSY?
I RECOGNIZE HER-- SHE'S MADAME ROSALIE . . . SHE USED TO DO PSYCHIC READINGS IN THE NEIGHBORHOOD--
--UNTIL THE CITY CLAMPED DOWN ON THOSE BUSINESSES . . .
SOME FORTUNE TELLER! YOU'D THINK SHE'D KNOW AHEAD OF TIME TO KEEL OVER ON SOMETHING MORE COMFORTABLE THAN THE STREET! HAW
MAYBE IT'S THE GOULASH! THAT STUFF COULD CLOG THE ARTERIES . . .
YOU MOCK MADAME ROSALIE?
OH, LIGHTEN UP, GRAN'MA-- I'M JUST WHAT THE DOCTOR ORDERED--
DR. KAVORKIAN, THAT IS! YUK
YOU FAIL TO AMUSE
SO MADAME ROSALIE WILL GIVE YOU THE GIFT OF LAUGHTER . . .
AND AS MADAME ROSALIE TAKES HER LAST BREATH-- SHE ALSO HAS THE LAST LAUGH!
IT'S TOO LATE--SHE'S DEAD!
GEE, TOO BAD ABOUT THE OLD LADY . . . BUT, HEY, I DID WHAT I COULD . . .
LAUGHTER'S SUPPOSED TO BE THE BEST MEDICINE!
THAT WINNING SMILE

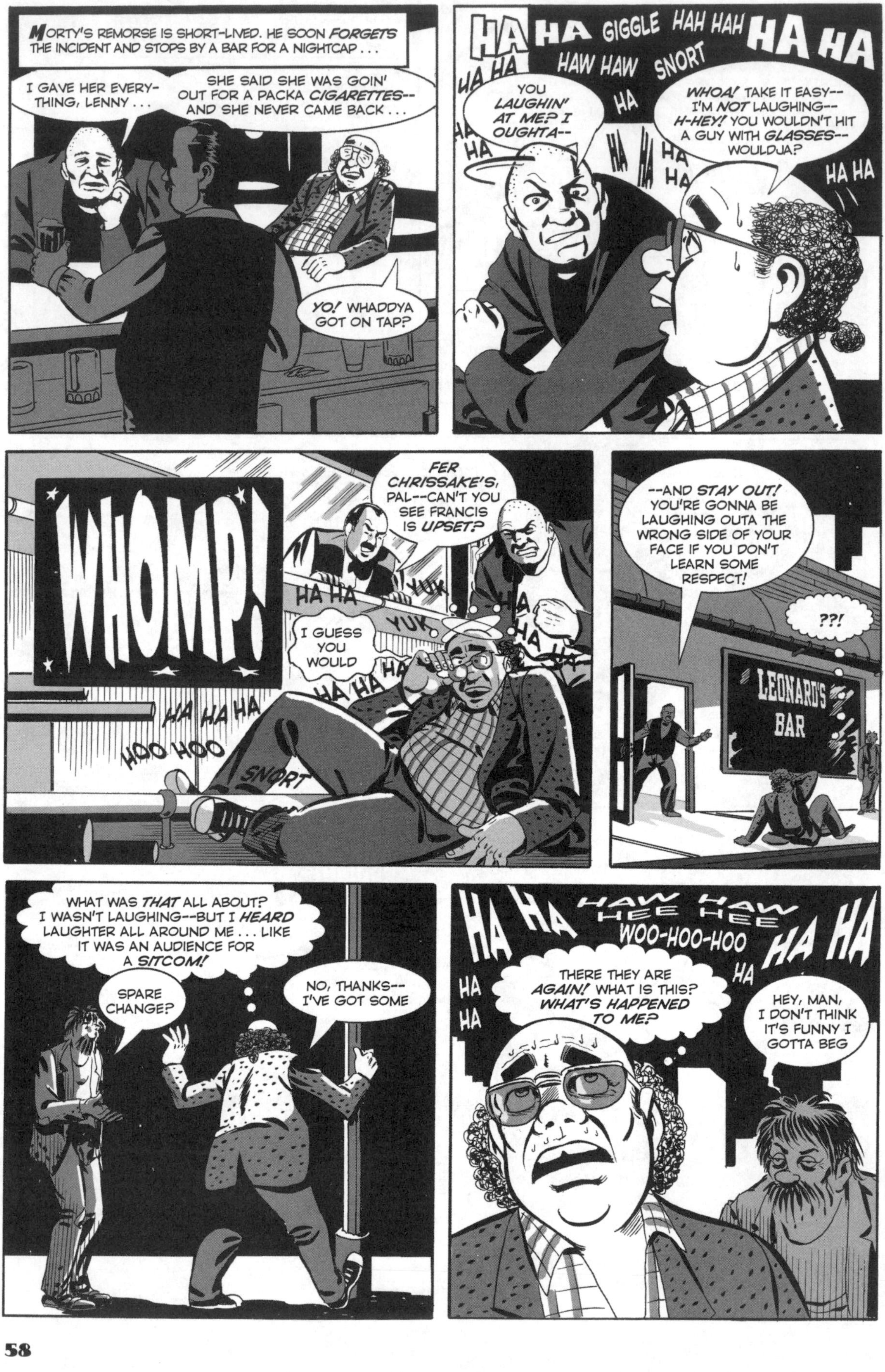
MORTY'S REMORSE IS SHORT-LIVED. HE SOON FORGETS THE INCIDENT AND STOPS BY A BAR FOR A NIGHTCAP . . .
I GAVE HER EVERY-THING, LENNY . . .
SHE SAID SHE WAS GOIN' OUT FOR A PACKA CIGARETTES-- AND SHE NEVER CAME BACK . . .
YO! WHADDYA GOT ON TAP?
HA HA GIGGLE HAH HAH HA HA
HA HA HAW HAW SNORT
YOU LAUGHIN' AT ME? I OUGHTA--
HA
WHOA! TAKE IT EASY-- I'M NOT LAUGHING-- H-HEY! YOU WOULDN'T HIT A GUY WITH GLASSES-- WOULDJA?
HA HA HA HA
HA HA
WHOMP!
FER CHRISSAKE'S, PAL--CAN'T YOU SEE FRANCIS IS UPSET?
HA HA YUK
YUK
I GUESS YOU WOULD
HA HA HA
HA HA HA
HA HA HA
HOO HOO
SNORT
--AND STAY OUT! YOU'RE GONNA BE LAUGHING OUTA THE WRONG SIDE OF YOUR FACE IF YOU DON'T LEARN SOME RESPECT!
??!
LEONARD'S BAR
WHAT WAS THAT ALL ABOUT? I WASN'T LAUGHING--BUT I HEARD LAUGHTER ALL AROUND ME . . . LIKE IT WAS AN AUDIENCE FOR A SITCOM!
SPARE CHANGE?
NO, THANKS-- I'VE GOT SOME
HA HA HAW HAW HEE HEE WOO-HOO-HOO HA HA
HA HA HA
THERE THEY ARE AGAIN! WHAT IS THIS? WHAT'S HAPPENED TO ME?
HEY, MAN, I DON'T THINK IT'S FUNNY I GOTTA BEG

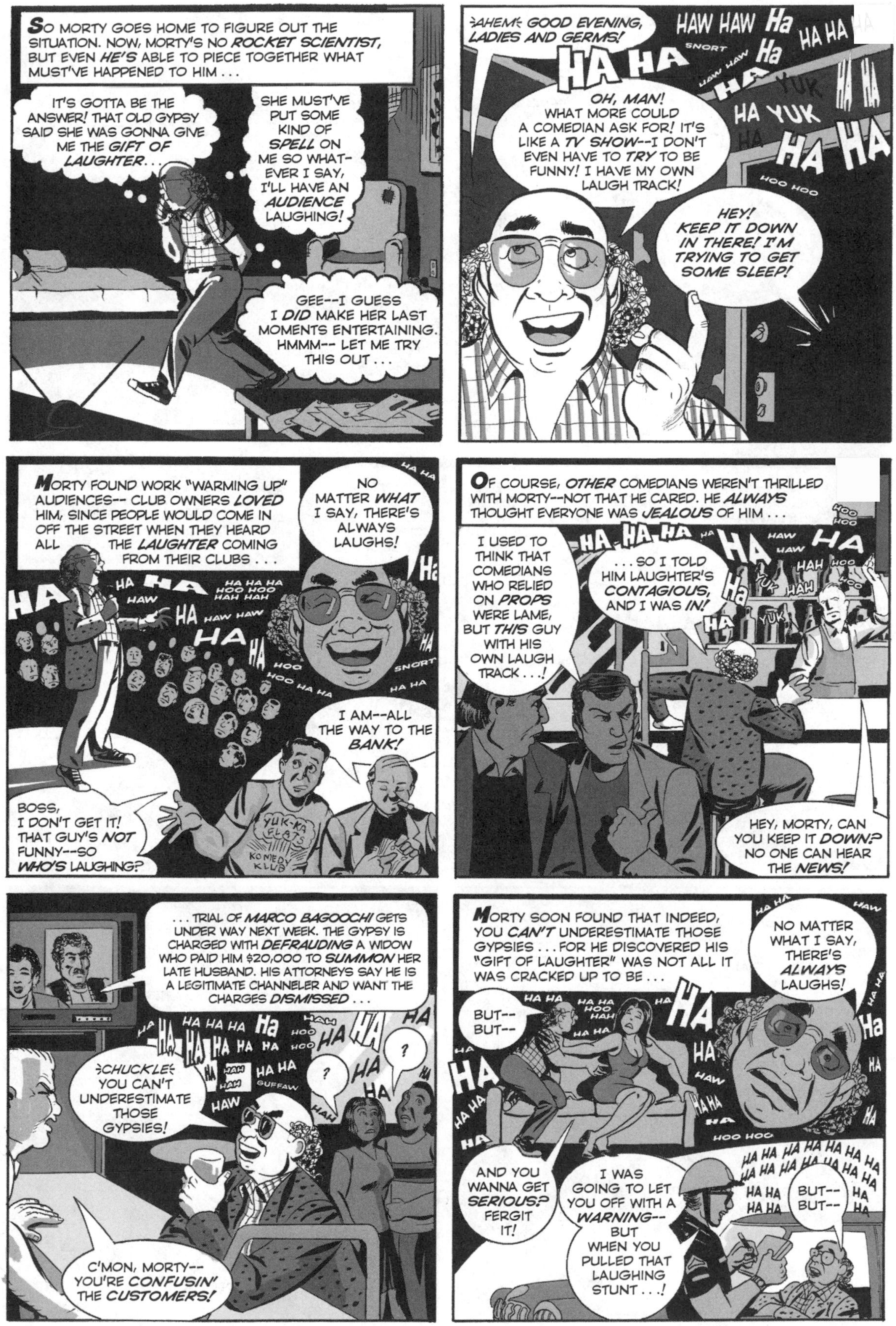
SO MORTY GOES HOME TO FIGURE OUT THE SITUATION. NOW, MORTY'S NO ROCKET SCIENTIST, BUT EVEN HE'S ABLE TO PIECE TOGETHER WHAT MUST'VE HAPPENED TO HIM . . .
IT'S GOTTA BE THE ANSWER! THAT OLD GYPSY SAID SHE WAS GONNA GIVE ME THE GIFT OF LAUGHTER . . .
SHE MUST'VE PUT SOME KIND OF SPELL ON ME SO WHATEVER I SAY, I'LL HAVE AN AUDIENCE LAUGHING!
GEE--I GUESS I DID MAKE HER LAST MOMENTS ENTERTAINING. HMMM-- LET ME TRY THIS OUT . . .
AHEM GOOD EVENING, LADIES AND GERMS!
HAW HAW Ha HA HA HA HA SNORT HAW HAW Ha HA YUK HA HA HA YUK HA HA HA HOO HOO
OH, MAN! WHAT MORE COULD A COMEDIAN ASK FOR! IT'S LIKE A TV SHOW--I DON'T EVEN HAVE TO TRY TO BE FUNNY! I HAVE MY OWN LAUGH TRACK!
HEY! KEEP IT DOWN IN THERE! I'M TRYING TO GET SOME SLEEP!
MORTY FOUND WORK "WARMING UP" AUDIENCES-- CLUB OWNERS LOVED HIM, SINCE PEOPLE WOULD COME IN OFF THE STREET WHEN THEY HEARD ALL THE LAUGHTER COMING FROM THEIR CLUBS . . .
NO MATTER WHAT I SAY, THERE'S ALWAYS LAUGHS!
HA HA HA HA HA HAW HA HA HA HOO HOO HAH HAH HA HAW HAW HA HA HOO HOO HA HA SNORT HA HA Ha HA
I AM--ALL THE WAY TO THE BANK!
BOSS, I DON'T GET IT! THAT GUY'S NOT FUNNY--SO WHO'S LAUGHING?
YUK-KA FLATS KOMEDY KLUB
OF COURSE, OTHER COMEDIANS WEREN'T THRILLED WITH MORTY--NOT THAT HE CARED. HE ALWAYS THOUGHT EVERYONE WAS JEALOUS OF HIM . . .
I USED TO THINK THAT COMEDIANS WHO RELIED ON PROPS WERE LAME, BUT THIS GUY WITH HIS OWN LAUGH TRACK . . .!
. . . SO I TOLD HIM LAUGHTER'S CONTAGIOUS, AND I WAS IN!
HA HA HA HA HA HAW HAW HA HAH HOO YUK HAH Ha HOO HA YUK HOO HOO
HEY, MORTY, CAN YOU KEEP IT DOWN? NO ONE CAN HEAR THE NEWS!
. . . TRIAL OF MARCO BAGOOCHI GETS UNDER WAY NEXT WEEK. THE GYPSY IS CHARGED WITH DEFRAUDING A WIDOW WHO PAID HIM $20,000 TO SUMMON HER LATE HUSBAND. HIS ATTORNEYS SAY HE IS A LEGITIMATE CHANNELER AND WANT THE CHARGES DISMISSED . . .
HA HA HA HA HA Ha HAH HOO HA HA HA HA HA HA HA HOO HA HA HA HAH HAH HA HA GUFFAW HAW HA HA HAH
CHUCKLE YOU CAN'T UNDERESTIMATE THOSE GYPSIES!
?
?
C'MON, MORTY-- YOU'RE CONFUSIN' THE CUSTOMERS!
MORTY SOON FOUND THAT INDEED, YOU CAN'T UNDERESTIMATE THOSE GYPSIES . . . FOR HE DISCOVERED HIS "GIFT OF LAUGHTER" WAS NOT ALL IT WAS CRACKED UP TO BE . . .
NO MATTER WHAT I SAY, THERE'S ALWAYS LAUGHS!
BUT-- BUT--
HA HA HA HA HOO HAH HA HA HAW HA Ha HA HA HA HAW HA HA HA HA HOO HOO HA
AND YOU WANNA GET SERIOUS? FERGIT IT!
I WAS GOING TO LET YOU OFF WITH A WARNING-- BUT WHEN YOU PULLED THAT LAUGHING STUNT . . .!
HA HA HA HA HA HA HA HA HA HA HA HA HA HA HA HA HA HA HA HA
BUT-- BUT--

ALTHOUGH MORTY *TRIED* TO BE CAREFUL, THERE WAS NO WAY TO GET AROUND THE FACT THAT WHENEVER HE OPENED HIS MOUTH, *UPROARIOUS LAUGHTER* WOULD FOLLOW . . .

HA HA HA HA HA HOO HOO HAH HAH YUK YUK HAW HAW *GIGGLE TEE HEE SNORT HAW HAW* HOO HOO HA HA

WHA-- WHO--? JEEZ . . . I MUSTA BEEN TALKING IN MY *SLEEP* AGAIN!

HA HAH HAH HA HAW HAW HOO HOO SNORT HAW HAW TEE HEE HAW HAW Ha Ha Ha Ha GIGGLE YUK YUK

OH, MAN-- I CAN'T GO ON LIKE THIS! IT *WAS* A GYPSY *CURSE* AFTER ALL! WHAT AM I GONNA DO?

WAITAMINNIT-- THAT GYPSY WHO'S ON TRIAL-- MAYBE *HE* WOULD KNOW HOW TO GET THESE *LAUGHING IDIOTS* UNDER CONTROL!

LAST TIME I'M WARNING YOU, FISHBURN! EVERY NIGHT YOU'VE GOT A PARTY IN THERE, AND I CAN'T SLEEP!

*S*O THE NEXT MORNING, MORTY HEADS DOWNTOWN TO *FOLEY SQUARE* . . .

*M*AKING SURE HE DOESN'T UTTER A *WORD* (HE DOESN'T WANT TO GET *THROWN OUT* OF THE COURTHOUSE), MORTY SEEKS OUT THE COURTROOM WHERE *HILLSDALE V. BAGOOCHI* IS IN SESSION . . .

. . . IN RESPONSE TO THE ALLEGATION, MY CLIENT LEGITIMATELY TRIED TO CONTACT THE LATE MR. HILLSDALE--

MR. BAGOOCHI IS A PRACTITIONER OF THE SCIENCE OF *BLACK MAGIC*, WHICH IS AS *UNPREDICTABLE* AS IT IS *DANGEROUS*

MY CLIENT GAVE THE PLAINTIFF NO *GUARANTEE* THAT HE WOULD BE SUCCESSFUL IN CHANNELING MRS. HILLSDALE'S HUSBAND . . . AND SHE *KNEW* THAT!

MS. WOLFF WOULD HAVE US *BELIEVE* THAT MR. BAGOOCHI IS WELL VERSED IN THE OCCULT . . . DURING THIS TRIAL, THE JURY WILL SEE THAT THE DEFENDANT'S AREA OF EXPERTISE IS THE OLD *CONFIDENCE GAME!*

MR. BAGOOCHI CLAIMED HE COULD *SUMMON* MY CLIENT'S BELOVED HUSBAND . . . BUT HE PRODUCED *NO* RESULTS, AND NOW SHE'S OUT $20,000!

MR. BYRD--I FEEL THE *SPIRITS!* I SENSE THE DENIZENS OF THE *BEYOND*-- I CANNOT *HEAR* THEM . . . BUT THEY'RE *HERE!*

MR. BAGOOCHI, IF YOU CAN CONTACT THEM, TELL THEM TO HANG AROUND FOR THE AFTERNOON SESSION-- I THINK THE JUDGE IS GOING TO CALL A *RECESS* . . .

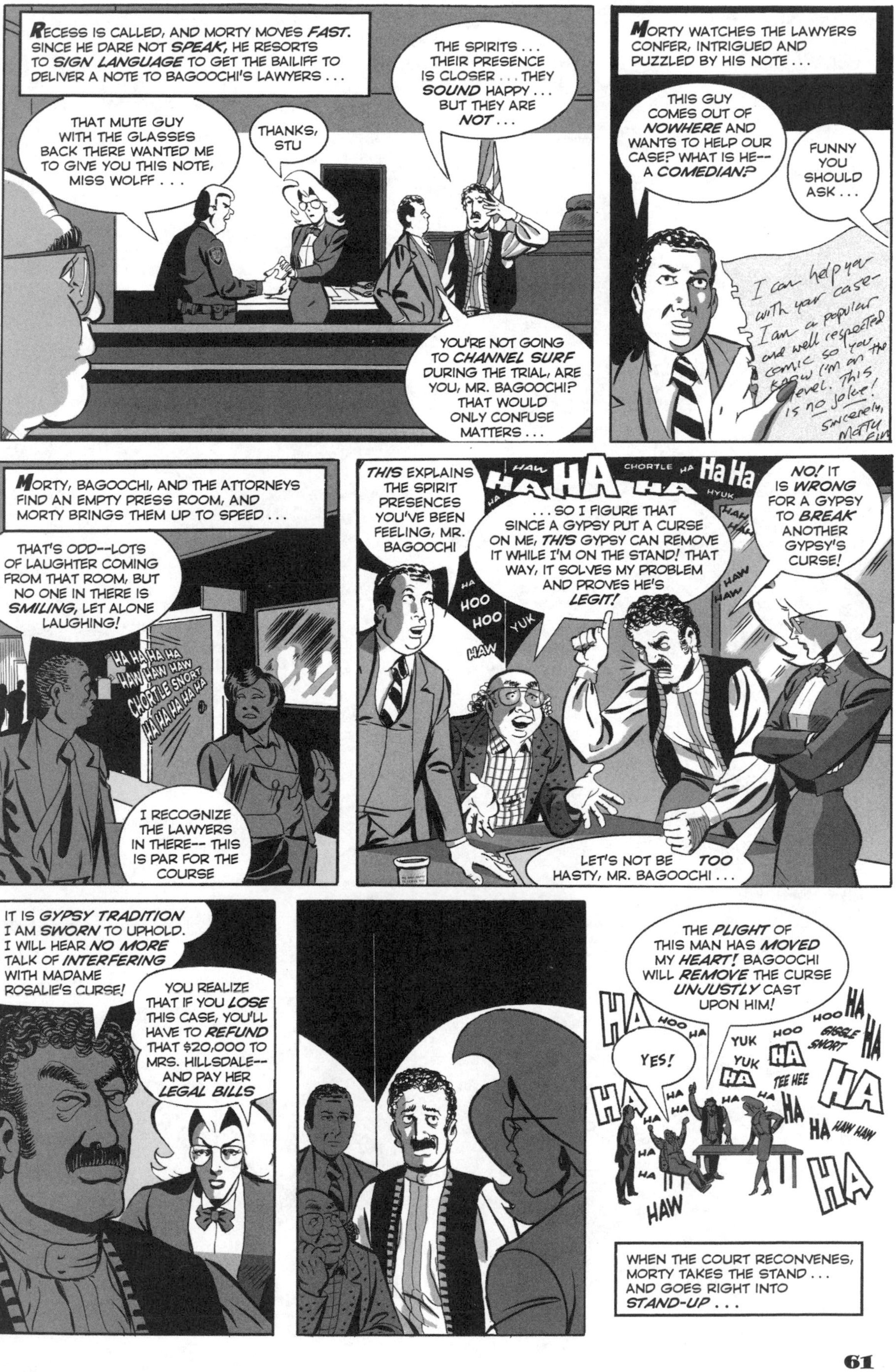
RECESS IS CALLED, AND MORTY MOVES FAST. SINCE HE DARE NOT SPEAK, HE RESORTS TO SIGN LANGUAGE TO GET THE BAILIFF TO DELIVER A NOTE TO BAGOOCHI'S LAWYERS . . .
THAT MUTE GUY WITH THE GLASSES BACK THERE WANTED ME TO GIVE YOU THIS NOTE, MISS WOLFF . . .
THANKS, STU
THE SPIRITS . . . THEIR PRESENCE IS CLOSER . . . THEY SOUND HAPPY . . . BUT THEY ARE NOT . . .
YOU'RE NOT GOING TO CHANNEL SURF DURING THE TRIAL, ARE YOU, MR. BAGOOCHI? THAT WOULD ONLY CONFUSE MATTERS . . .
MORTY WATCHES THE LAWYERS CONFER, INTRIGUED AND PUZZLED BY HIS NOTE . . .
THIS GUY COMES OUT OF NOWHERE AND WANTS TO HELP OUR CASE? WHAT IS HE-- A COMEDIAN?
FUNNY YOU SHOULD ASK . . .
I can help you with your case- I am a popular and well respected comic so you know I'm on the level. This is no joke! Sincerely, Morty
MORTY, BAGOOCHI, AND THE ATTORNEYS FIND AN EMPTY PRESS ROOM, AND MORTY BRINGS THEM UP TO SPEED . . .
THAT'S ODD--LOTS OF LAUGHTER COMING FROM THAT ROOM, BUT NO ONE IN THERE IS SMILING, LET ALONE LAUGHING!
HA HA HA HA HAW HAW HAW CHORTLE SNORT HA HA HA HA HA HA
I RECOGNIZE THE LAWYERS IN THERE-- THIS IS PAR FOR THE COURSE
THIS EXPLAINS THE SPIRIT PRESENCES YOU'VE BEEN FEELING, MR. BAGOOCHI
HAW HA HA HA CHORTLE HA Ha Ha HYUK
. . . SO I FIGURE THAT SINCE A GYPSY PUT A CURSE ON ME, THIS GYPSY CAN REMOVE IT WHILE I'M ON THE STAND! THAT WAY, IT SOLVES MY PROBLEM AND PROVES HE'S LEGIT!
HA HOO HOO YUK HAW
NO! IT IS WRONG FOR A GYPSY TO BREAK ANOTHER GYPSY'S CURSE!
HAW HAW
LET'S NOT BE TOO HASTY, MR. BAGOOCHI . . .
IT IS GYPSY TRADITION I AM SWORN TO UPHOLD. I WILL HEAR NO MORE TALK OF INTERFERING WITH MADAME ROSALIE'S CURSE!
YOU REALIZE THAT IF YOU LOSE THIS CASE, YOU'LL HAVE TO REFUND THAT $20,000 TO MRS. HILLSDALE-- AND PAY HER LEGAL BILLS
THE PLIGHT OF THIS MAN HAS MOVED MY HEART! BAGOOCHI WILL REMOVE THE CURSE UNJUSTLY CAST UPON HIM!
YES!
HA HOO HA YUK HOO HOO HA GIGGLE SNORT HA YUK HA HA TEE HEE HA HA HA HA HA HA HA HAW HAW HA HA HAW HA
WHEN THE COURT RECONVENES, MORTY TAKES THE STAND . . . AND GOES RIGHT INTO STAND-UP . . .

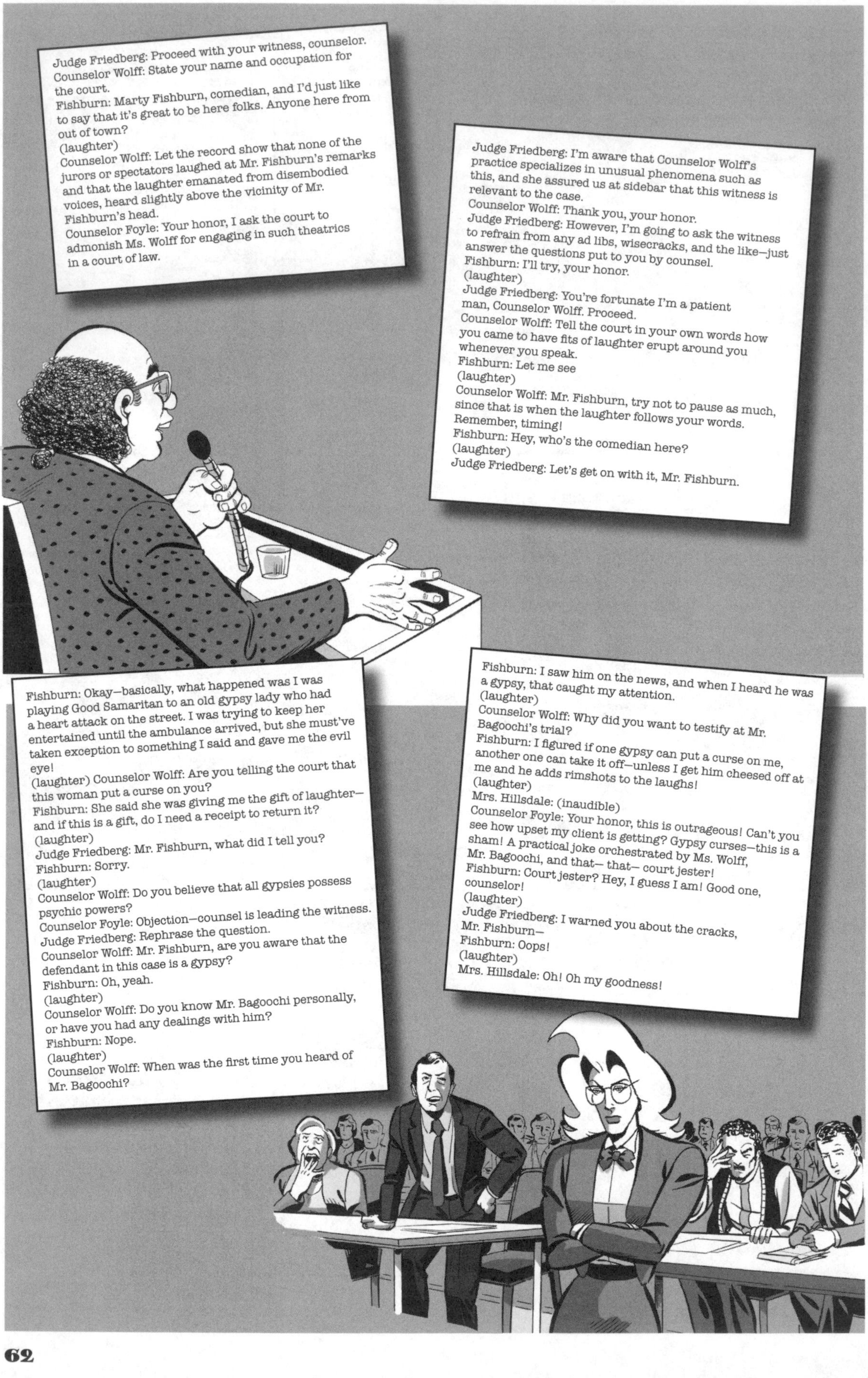

Judge Friedberg: Proceed with your witness, counselor.
Counselor Wolff: State your name and occupation for the court.
Fishburn: Marty Fishburn, comedian, and I'd just like to say that it's great to be here folks. Anyone here from out of town?
(laughter)
Counselor Wolff: Let the record show that none of the jurors or spectators laughed at Mr. Fishburn's remarks and that the laughter emanated from disembodied voices, heard slightly above the vicinity of Mr. Fishburn's head.
Counselor Foyle: Your honor, I ask the court to admonish Ms. Wolff for engaging in such theatrics in a court of law.
Judge Friedberg: I'm aware that Counselor Wolff's practice specializes in unusual phenomena such as this, and she assured us at sidebar that this witness is relevant to the case.
Counselor Wolff: Thank you, your honor.
Judge Friedberg: However, I'm going to ask the witness to refrain from any ad libs, wisecracks, and the like—just answer the questions put to you by counsel.
Fishburn: I'll try, your honor.
(laughter)
Judge Friedberg: You're fortunate I'm a patient man, Counselor Wolff. Proceed.
Counselor Wolff: Tell the court in your own words how you came to have fits of laughter erupt around you whenever you speak.
Fishburn: Let me see
(laughter)
Counselor Wolff: Mr. Fishburn, try not to pause as much, since that is when the laughter follows your words. Remember, timing!
Fishburn: Hey, who's the comedian here?
(laughter)
Judge Friedberg: Let's get on with it, Mr. Fishburn.
Fishburn: Okay—basically, what happened was I was playing Good Samaritan to an old gypsy lady who had a heart attack on the street. I was trying to keep her entertained until the ambulance arrived, but she must've taken exception to something I said and gave me the evil eye!
(laughter) Counselor Wolff: Are you telling the court that this woman put a curse on you?
Fishburn: She said she was giving me the gift of laughter—and if this is a gift, do I need a receipt to return it?
(laughter)
Judge Friedberg: Mr. Fishburn, what did I tell you?
Fishburn: Sorry.
(laughter)
Counselor Wolff: Do you believe that all gypsies possess psychic powers?
Counselor Foyle: Objection—counsel is leading the witness.
Judge Friedberg: Rephrase the question.
Counselor Wolff: Mr. Fishburn, are you aware that the defendant in this case is a gypsy?
Fishburn: Oh, yeah.
(laughter)
Counselor Wolff: Do you know Mr. Bagoochi personally, or have you had any dealings with him?
Fishburn: Nope.
(laughter)
Counselor Wolff: When was the first time you heard of Mr. Bagoochi?
Fishburn: I saw him on the news, and when I heard he was a gypsy, that caught my attention.
(laughter)
Counselor Wolff: Why did you want to testify at Mr. Bagoochi's trial?
Fishburn: I figured if one gypsy can put a curse on me, another one can take it off—unless I get him cheesed off at me and he adds rimshots to the laughs!
(laughter)
Mrs. Hillsdale: (inaudible)
Counselor Foyle: Your honor, this is outrageous! Can't you see how upset my client is getting? Gypsy curses—this is a sham! A practical joke orchestrated by Ms. Wolff, Mr. Bagoochi, and that— that— court jester!
Fishburn: Court jester? Hey, I guess I am! Good one, counselor!
(laughter)
Judge Friedberg: I warned you about the cracks, Mr. Fishburn—
Fishburn: Oops!
(laughter)
Mrs. Hillsdale: Oh! Oh my goodness!

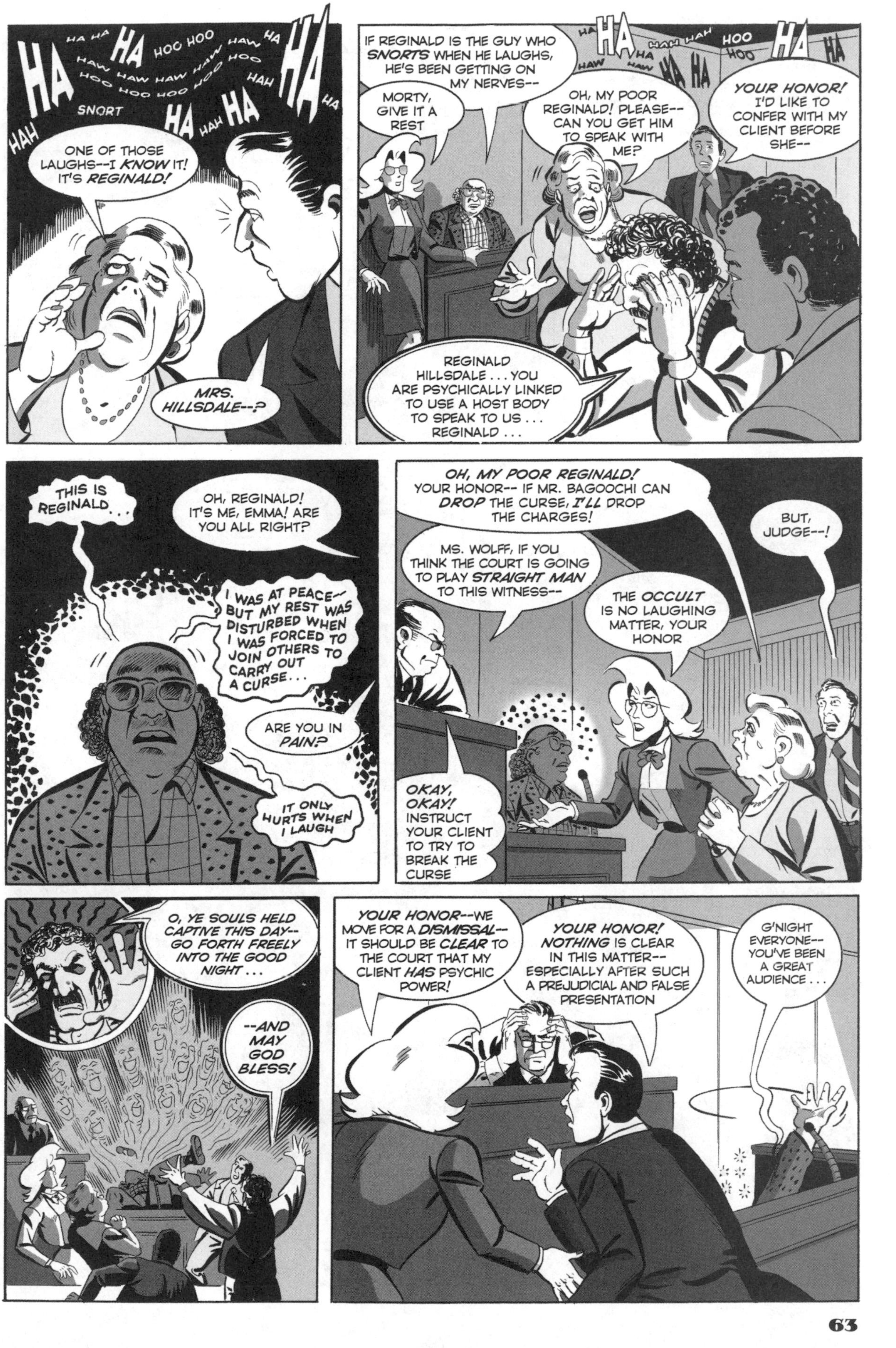
HA HA HA HA HOO HOO HAW HAW HAW HAW HAW HAW HOO HOO HOO HOO HOO HOO HAH HA HAH SNORT HA HAH HA HA HA
ONE OF THOSE LAUGHS--I KNOW IT! IT'S REGINALD!
MRS. HILLSDALE--?
IF REGINALD IS THE GUY WHO SNORTS WHEN HE LAUGHS, HE'S BEEN GETTING ON MY NERVES--
MORTY, GIVE IT A REST
HA HA HAW HAW HAH HAH HA HA HA HOO HOO HA HA
OH, MY POOR REGINALD! PLEASE-- CAN YOU GET HIM TO SPEAK WITH ME?
YOUR HONOR! I'D LIKE TO CONFER WITH MY CLIENT BEFORE SHE--
REGINALD HILLSDALE . . . YOU ARE PSYCHICALLY LINKED TO USE A HOST BODY TO SPEAK TO US . . . REGINALD . . .
THIS IS REGINALD . . .
OH, REGINALD! IT'S ME, EMMA! ARE YOU ALL RIGHT?
I WAS AT PEACE-- BUT MY REST WAS DISTURBED WHEN I WAS FORCED TO JOIN OTHERS TO CARRY OUT A CURSE . . .
ARE YOU IN PAIN?
IT ONLY HURTS WHEN I LAUGH
OH, MY POOR REGINALD! YOUR HONOR-- IF MR. BAGOOCHI CAN DROP THE CURSE, I'LL DROP THE CHARGES!
BUT, JUDGE--!
MS. WOLFF, IF YOU THINK THE COURT IS GOING TO PLAY STRAIGHT MAN TO THIS WITNESS--
THE OCCULT IS NO LAUGHING MATTER, YOUR HONOR
OKAY, OKAY! INSTRUCT YOUR CLIENT TO TRY TO BREAK THE CURSE
O, YE SOULS HELD CAPTIVE THIS DAY-- GO FORTH FREELY INTO THE GOOD NIGHT . . .
--AND MAY GOD BLESS!
YOUR HONOR--WE MOVE FOR A DISMISSAL-- IT SHOULD BE CLEAR TO THE COURT THAT MY CLIENT HAS PSYCHIC POWER!
YOUR HONOR! NOTHING IS CLEAR IN THIS MATTER-- ESPECIALLY AFTER SUCH A PREJUDICIAL AND FALSE PRESENTATION
G'NIGHT EVERYONE-- YOU'VE BEEN A GREAT AUDIENCE . . .

WHEN THE DUST HAD FINALLY SETTLED...

BAGOOCHI HAS BEEN *VINDICATED!* NOW THE *WORLD* WILL KNOW THAT IT WAS PROVEN IN *COURT* THAT I HAVE PSYCHIC ABILITIES!

NOT NECESSARILY, MR. BAGOOCHI

THE JUDGE *DISMISSED* THE CASE BECAUSE MRS. HILLSDALE *DROPPED* THE CHARGES ... THERE'S *NOTHING* ON THE RECORD SAYING THE COURT IS CONVINCED OF YOUR POWERS

BAH! BAGOOCHI KNOWS THE *TRUTH!*

HEY-- *BAGOOCHI!* YOU OWE ME!

MORTY-- WATCH WHAT YOU SAY ...

YEAH--YOU *KNOW* THE POWER OF A GYPSY'S CURSE-- DON'T KID AROUND

I DID YOU A *SOLID*-- IN RETURN, HOW ABOUT *SUMMONING* SOME OF THOSE GHOSTS AND INSTRUCTING THEM ONLY TO *LAUGH* WHEN I TELL A *JOKE!*

I *CANNOT!* I HAVE TAKEN GREAT *RISK* CANCELING *ANOTHER* GYPSY'S CURSE-- MY *DEBT* TO *YOU* HAS BEEN PAID!

SPARE ME THE SPOOKY SCHTICK, OKAY? WE'RE BOTH IN *SHOW BIZ,* SO I KNOW WHERE YER COMIN' FROM! NOW LET'S TALK ABOUT THE *GHOSTS*--OR IS THE GYPSY OUT TO *GYP* ME?

YOU *MOCK* MARCO BAGOOCHI ...

P.S. A WEEK LATER, MORTY WOUND UP IN BAGOOCHI'S LAWYERS' OFFICE ...

MS. WOLFF, YOU GOTTA PUT ME IN TOUCH WITH *BAGOOCHI!* HE *MISUNDERSTOOD* WHAT I WANTED!

MORTY, GYPSIES MOVE IN MYSTERIOUS WAYS ... WE DON'T HAVE ANY IDEA WHERE HE IS NOW!

WHEN WE HEAR FROM HIM, WE'LL LET HIM KNOW YOU MADE A *MISTAKE* ...

WE TRIED TO *WARN* YOU-- BUT YOU *BADGERED* BAGOOCHI FOR *GHOSTS,* AND HE *GAVE* THEM TO YOU!

BUT *LISTEN* TO THEM--!!

BOO BOOOO BOOOO BOOO BOO BOO BOO BOOOOOOOO BOO BOO BOOOOOOO BOO BOO BOO BOO BOO BOO BOOO BOO BOOO BOOO

I *CAN'T* DO STAND-UP WITH *THEM* AROUND ... THEY'RE THE *ULTIMATE HECKLERS!*

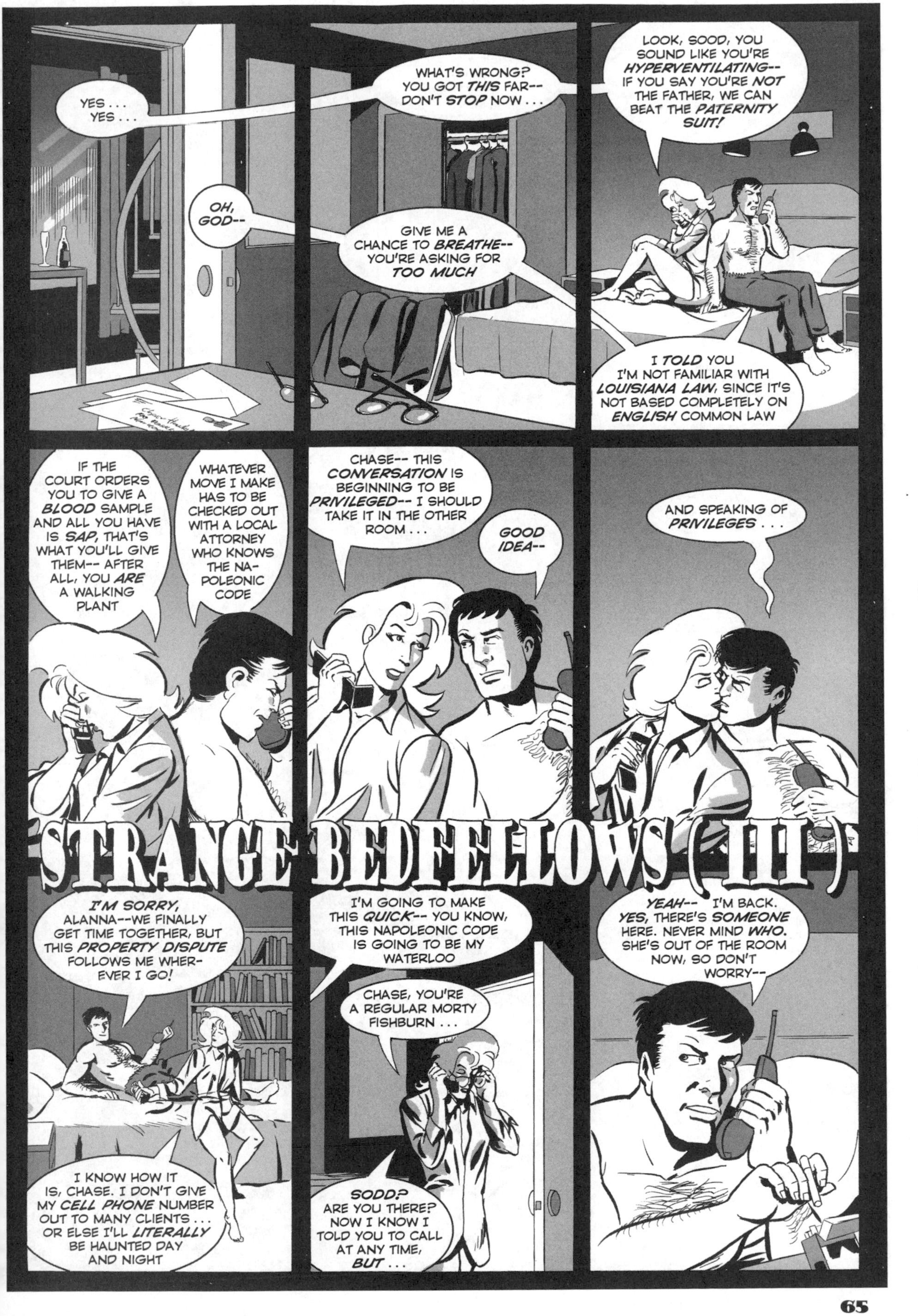

YES . . . YES . . .
WHAT'S WRONG? YOU GOT THIS FAR-- DON'T STOP NOW . . .
LOOK, SOOD, YOU SOUND LIKE YOU'RE HYPERVENTILATING-- IF YOU SAY YOU'RE NOT THE FATHER, WE CAN BEAT THE PATERNITY SUIT!
OH, GOD--
GIVE ME A CHANCE TO BREATHE-- YOU'RE ASKING FOR TOO MUCH
I TOLD YOU I'M NOT FAMILIAR WITH LOUISIANA LAW, SINCE IT'S NOT BASED COMPLETELY ON ENGLISH COMMON LAW
IF THE COURT ORDERS YOU TO GIVE A BLOOD SAMPLE AND ALL YOU HAVE IS SAP, THAT'S WHAT YOU'LL GIVE THEM-- AFTER ALL, YOU ARE A WALKING PLANT
WHATEVER MOVE I MAKE HAS TO BE CHECKED OUT WITH A LOCAL ATTORNEY WHO KNOWS THE NA-POLEONIC CODE
CHASE-- THIS CONVERSATION IS BEGINNING TO BE PRIVILEGED-- I SHOULD TAKE IT IN THE OTHER ROOM . . .
GOOD IDEA--
AND SPEAKING OF PRIVILEGES . . .
STRANGE BEDFELLOWS (III)
I'M SORRY, ALANNA--WE FINALLY GET TIME TOGETHER, BUT THIS PROPERTY DISPUTE FOLLOWS ME WHER-EVER I GO!
I KNOW HOW IT IS, CHASE. I DON'T GIVE MY CELL PHONE NUMBER OUT TO MANY CLIENTS . . . OR ELSE I'LL LITERALLY BE HAUNTED DAY AND NIGHT
I'M GOING TO MAKE THIS QUICK-- YOU KNOW, THIS NAPOLEONIC CODE IS GOING TO BE MY WATERLOO
CHASE, YOU'RE A REGULAR MORTY FISHBURN . . .
SODD? ARE YOU THERE? NOW I KNOW I TOLD YOU TO CALL AT ANY TIME, BUT . . .
YEAH-- I'M BACK. YES, THERE'S SOMEONE HERE. NEVER MIND WHO. SHE'S OUT OF THE ROOM NOW, SO DON'T WORRY--

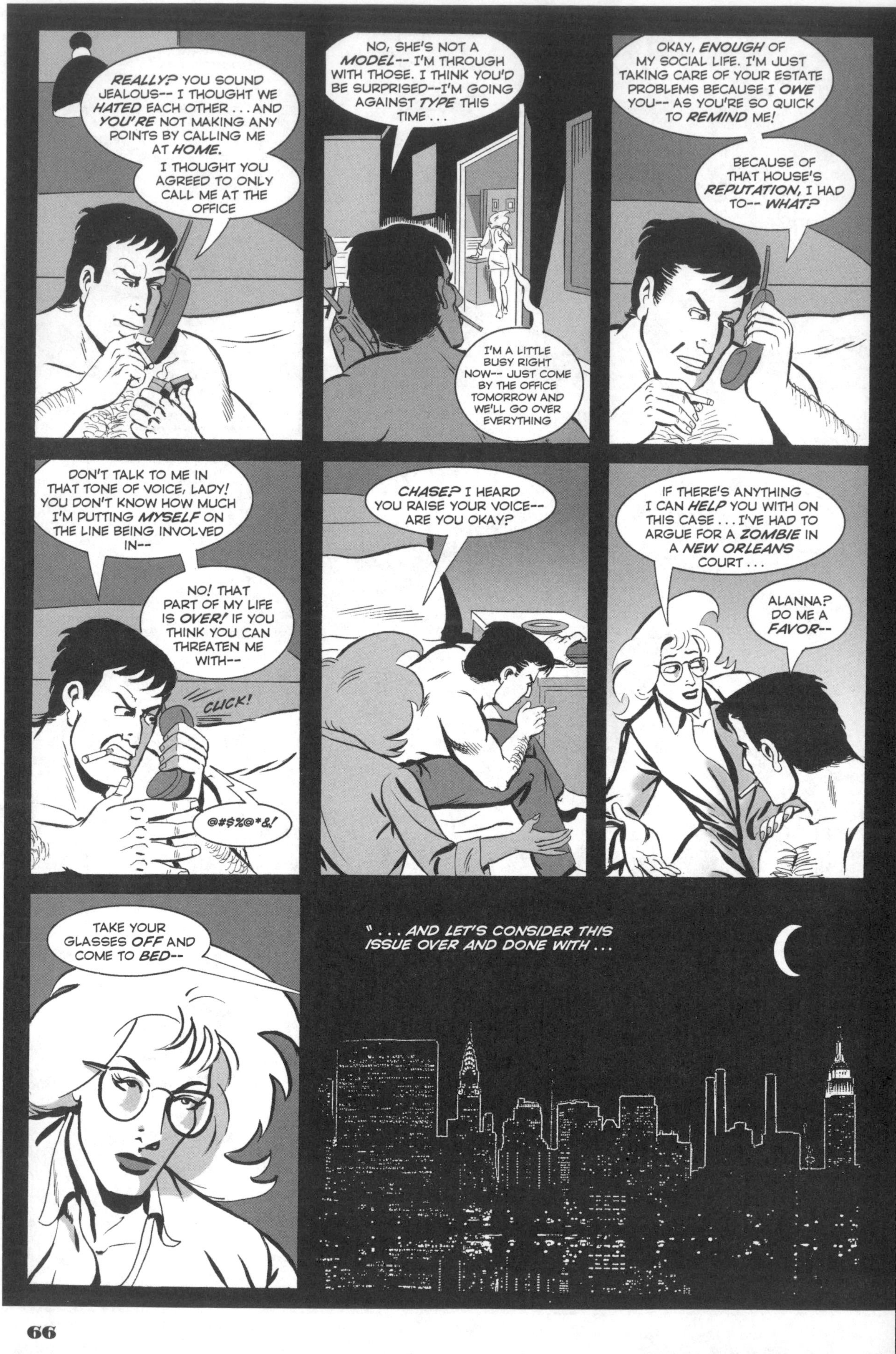
REALLY? YOU SOUND JEALOUS-- I THOUGHT WE HATED EACH OTHER . . . AND YOU'RE NOT MAKING ANY POINTS BY CALLING ME AT HOME.
I THOUGHT YOU AGREED TO ONLY CALL ME AT THE OFFICE
NO, SHE'S NOT A MODEL-- I'M THROUGH WITH THOSE. I THINK YOU'D BE SURPRISED--I'M GOING AGAINST TYPE THIS TIME . . .
I'M A LITTLE BUSY RIGHT NOW-- JUST COME BY THE OFFICE TOMORROW AND WE'LL GO OVER EVERYTHING
OKAY, ENOUGH OF MY SOCIAL LIFE. I'M JUST TAKING CARE OF YOUR ESTATE PROBLEMS BECAUSE I OWE YOU-- AS YOU'RE SO QUICK TO REMIND ME!
BECAUSE OF THAT HOUSE'S REPUTATION, I HAD TO-- WHAT?
DON'T TALK TO ME IN THAT TONE OF VOICE, LADY! YOU DON'T KNOW HOW MUCH I'M PUTTING MYSELF ON THE LINE BEING INVOLVED IN--
NO! THAT PART OF MY LIFE IS OVER! IF YOU THINK YOU CAN THREATEN ME WITH--
CLICK!
@#$%@*&!
CHASE? I HEARD YOU RAISE YOUR VOICE-- ARE YOU OKAY?
IF THERE'S ANYTHING I CAN HELP YOU WITH ON THIS CASE . . . I'VE HAD TO ARGUE FOR A ZOMBIE IN A NEW ORLEANS COURT . . .
ALANNA? DO ME A FAVOR--
TAKE YOUR GLASSES OFF AND COME TO BED--
" . . . AND LET'S CONSIDER THIS ISSUE OVER AND DONE WITH . . .

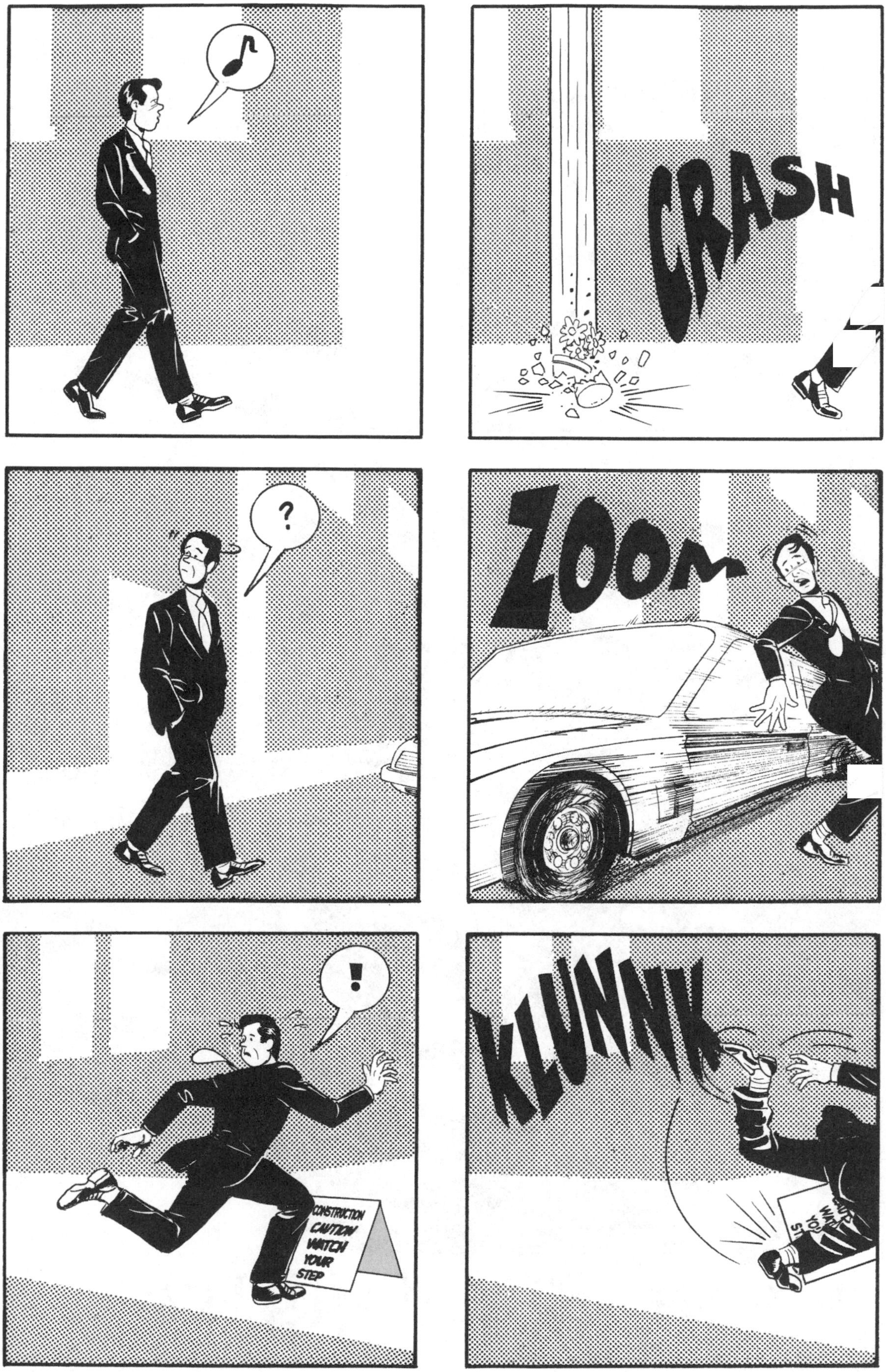
♪
CRASH
?
ZOOM
!
CONSTRUCTION
CAUTION
WATCH
YOUR
STEP
KLUNNK

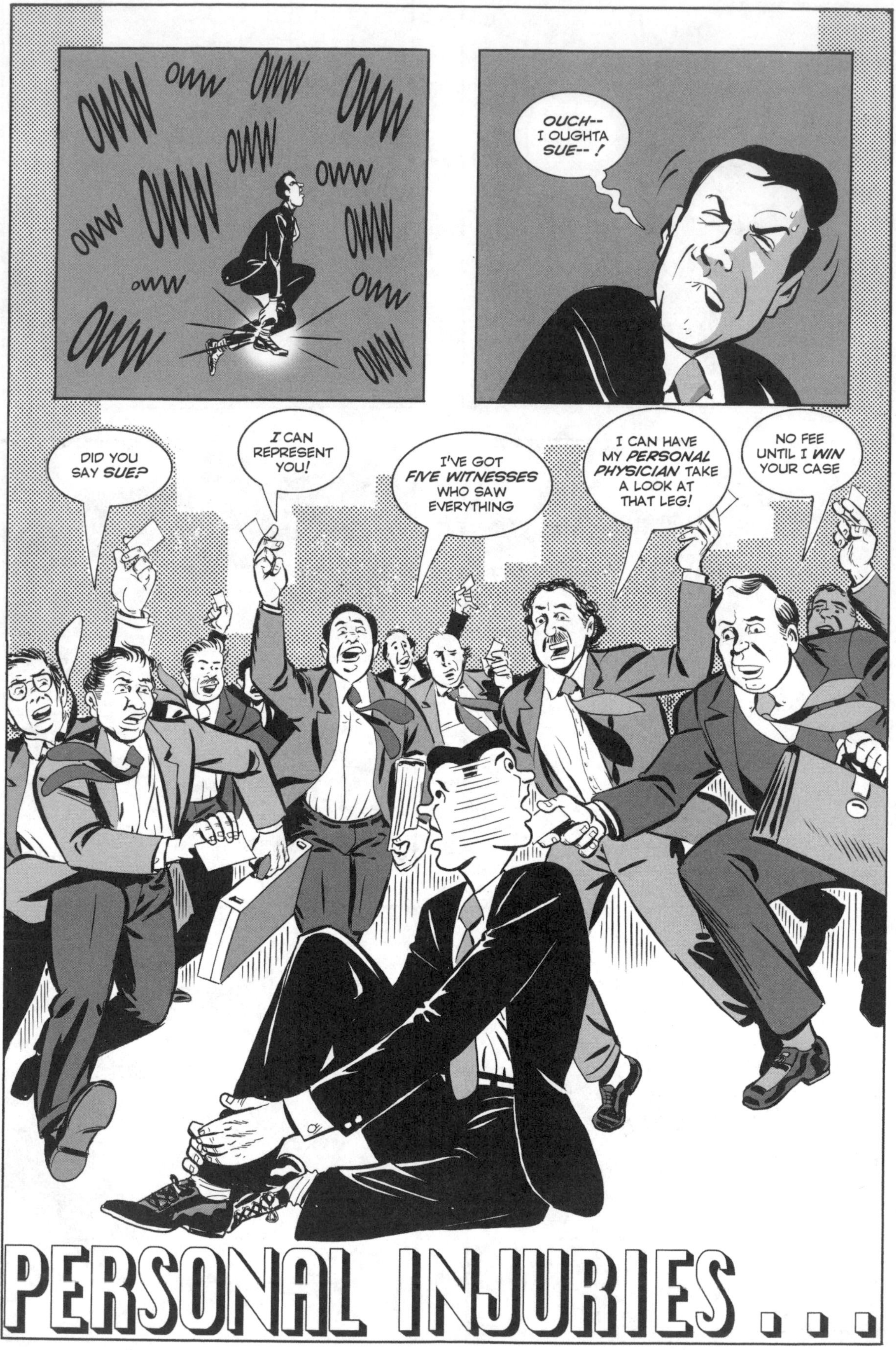

OWW OWW OWW OWW OWW OWW OWW OWW OWW OWW OWW OWW OWW
OUCH-- I OUGHTA SUE-- !
DID YOU SAY SUE?
I CAN REPRESENT YOU!
I'VE GOT FIVE WITNESSES WHO SAW EVERYTHING
I CAN HAVE MY PERSONAL PHYSICIAN TAKE A LOOK AT THAT LEG!
NO FEE UNTIL I WIN YOUR CASE
PERSONAL INJURIES . . .

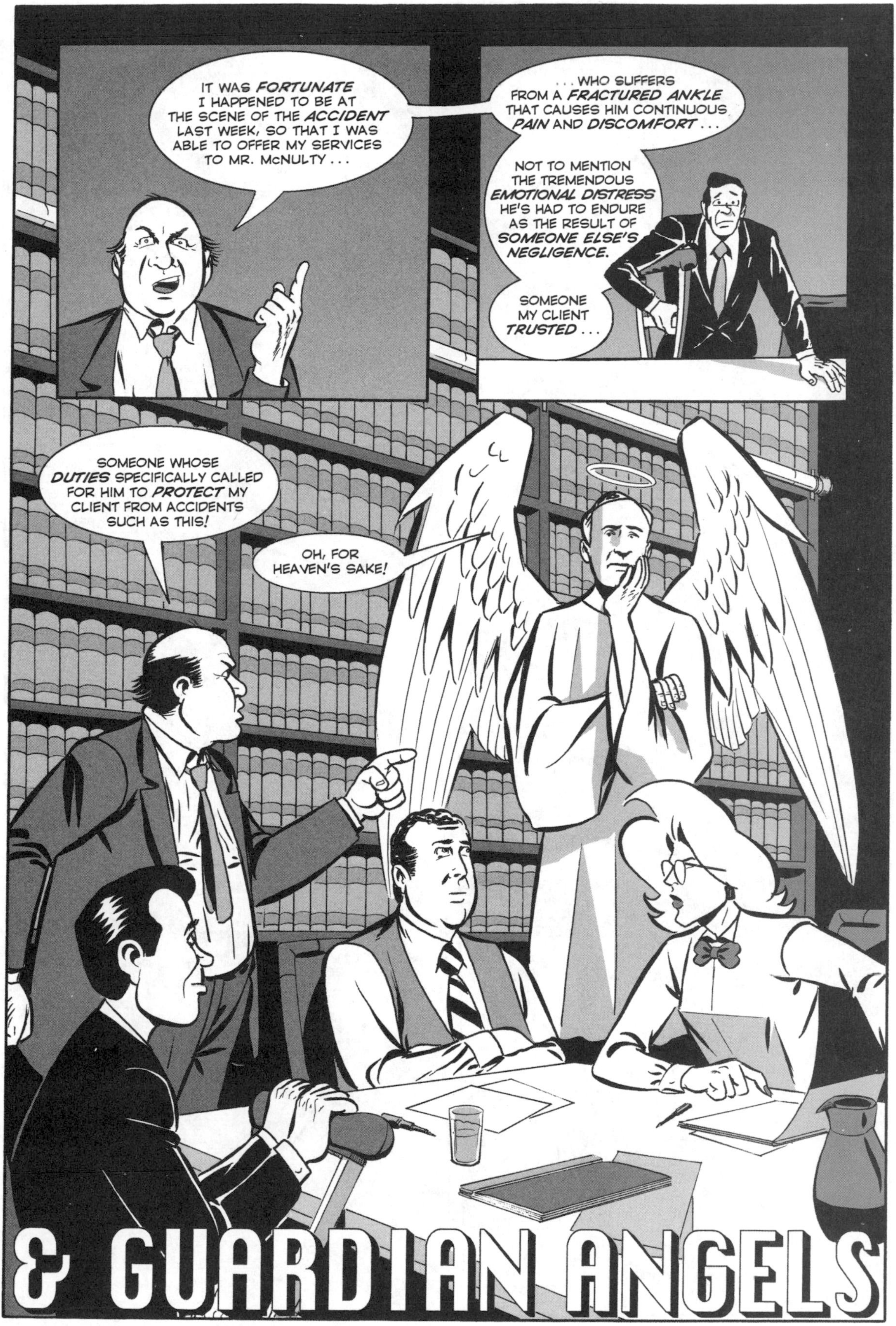

IT WAS FORTUNATE I HAPPENED TO BE AT THE SCENE OF THE ACCIDENT LAST WEEK, SO THAT I WAS ABLE TO OFFER MY SERVICES TO MR. McNULTY . . .
. . . WHO SUFFERS FROM A FRACTURED ANKLE THAT CAUSES HIM CONTINUOUS PAIN AND DISCOMFORT . . .
NOT TO MENTION THE TREMENDOUS EMOTIONAL DISTRESS HE'S HAD TO ENDURE AS THE RESULT OF SOMEONE ELSE'S NEGLIGENCE.
SOMEONE MY CLIENT TRUSTED . . .
SOMEONE WHOSE DUTIES SPECIFICALLY CALLED FOR HIM TO PROTECT MY CLIENT FROM ACCIDENTS SUCH AS THIS!
OH, FOR HEAVEN'S SAKE!
& GUARDIAN ANGELS

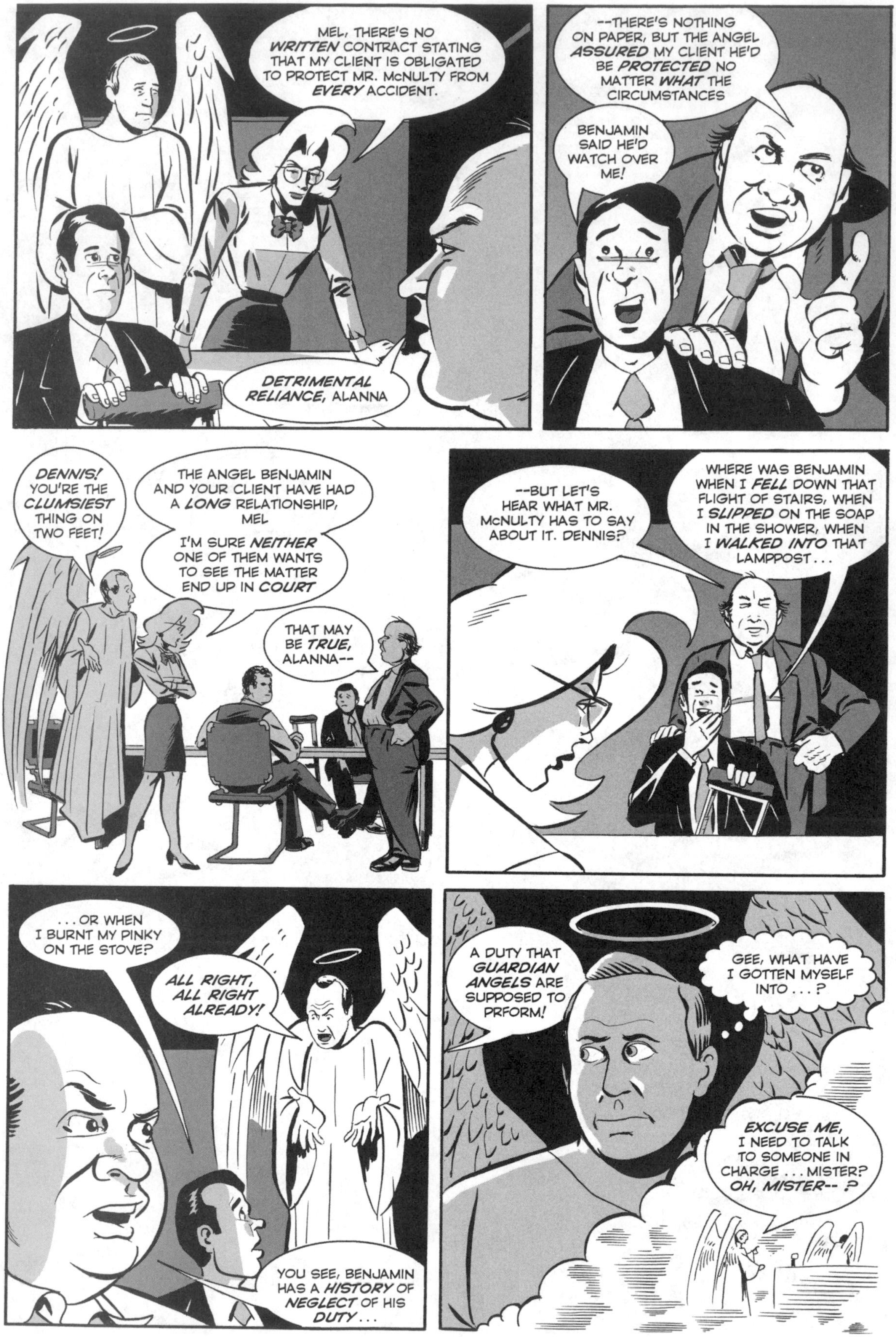
MEL, THERE'S NO WRITTEN CONTRACT STATING THAT MY CLIENT IS OBLIGATED TO PROTECT MR. McNULTY FROM EVERY ACCIDENT.
DETRIMENTAL RELIANCE, ALANNA
--THERE'S NOTHING ON PAPER, BUT THE ANGEL ASSURED MY CLIENT HE'D BE PROTECTED NO MATTER WHAT THE CIRCUMSTANCES
BENJAMIN SAID HE'D WATCH OVER ME!
DENNIS! YOU'RE THE CLUMSIEST THING ON TWO FEET!
THE ANGEL BENJAMIN AND YOUR CLIENT HAVE HAD A LONG RELATIONSHIP, MEL
I'M SURE NEITHER ONE OF THEM WANTS TO SEE THE MATTER END UP IN COURT
THAT MAY BE TRUE, ALANNA--
--BUT LET'S HEAR WHAT MR. McNULTY HAS TO SAY ABOUT IT. DENNIS?
WHERE WAS BENJAMIN WHEN I FELL DOWN THAT FLIGHT OF STAIRS, WHEN I SLIPPED ON THE SOAP IN THE SHOWER, WHEN I WALKED INTO THAT LAMPPOST...
...OR WHEN I BURNT MY PINKY ON THE STOVE?
ALL RIGHT, ALL RIGHT ALREADY!
YOU SEE, BENJAMIN HAS A HISTORY OF NEGLECT OF HIS DUTY...
A DUTY THAT GUARDIAN ANGELS ARE SUPPOSED TO PRFORM!
GEE, WHAT HAVE I GOTTEN MYSELF INTO...?
EXCUSE ME, I NEED TO TALK TO SOMEONE IN CHARGE...MISTER? OH, MISTER--?

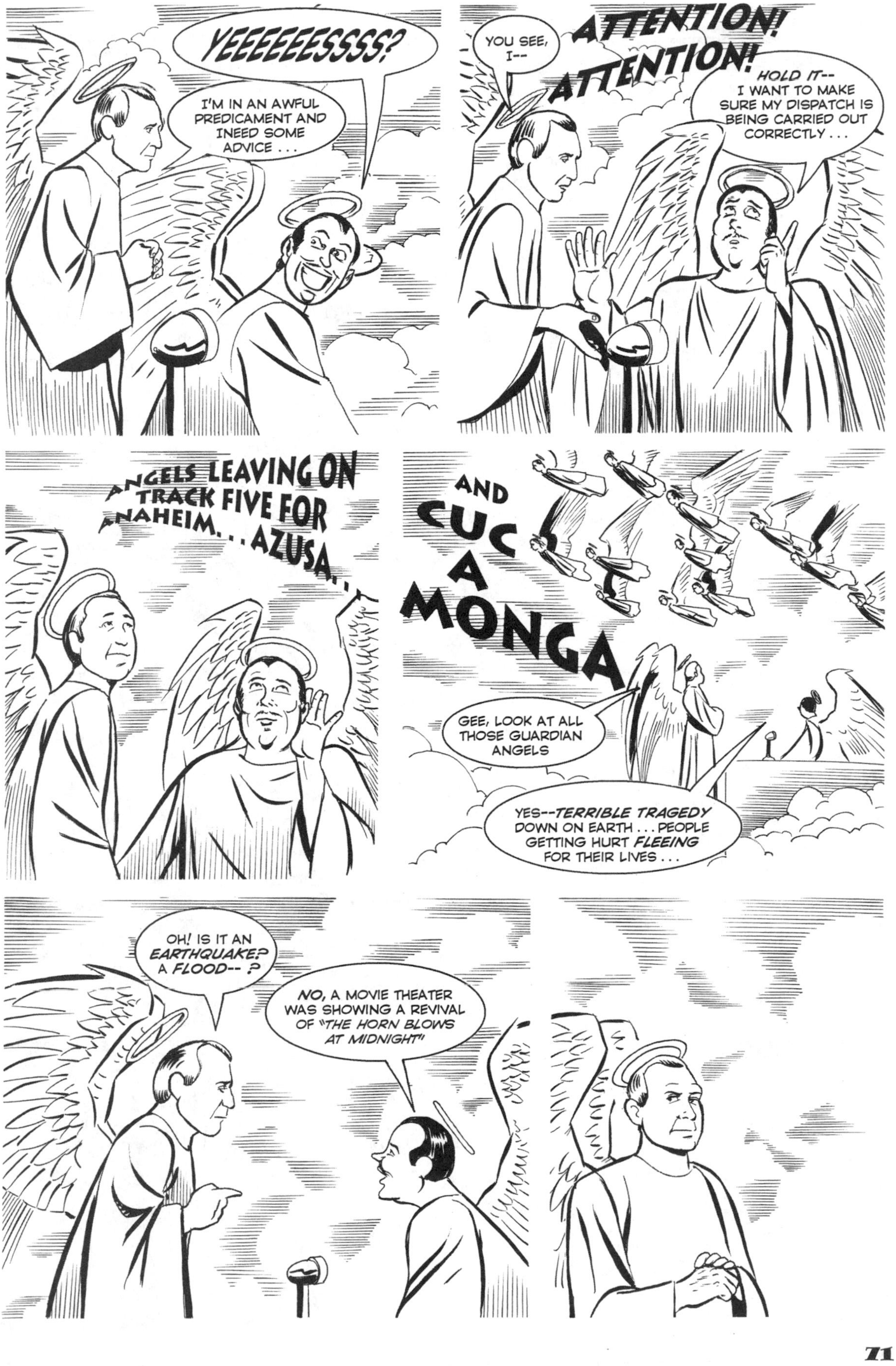
YEEEEEEESSSS?
I'M IN AN AWFUL PREDICAMENT AND INEED SOME ADVICE . . .
YOU SEE, I--
ATTENTION! ATTENTION!
HOLD IT-- I WANT TO MAKE SURE MY DISPATCH IS BEING CARRIED OUT CORRECTLY . . .
ANGELS LEAVING ON TRACK FIVE FOR ANAHEIM. . . AZUSA. . .
AND CUC A MONGA
GEE, LOOK AT ALL THOSE GUARDIAN ANGELS
YES--TERRIBLE TRAGEDY DOWN ON EARTH . . . PEOPLE GETTING HURT FLEEING FOR THEIR LIVES . . .
OH! IS IT AN EARTHQUAKE? A FLOOD-- ?
NO, A MOVIE THEATER WAS SHOWING A REVIVAL OF "THE HORN BLOWS AT MIDNIGHT"

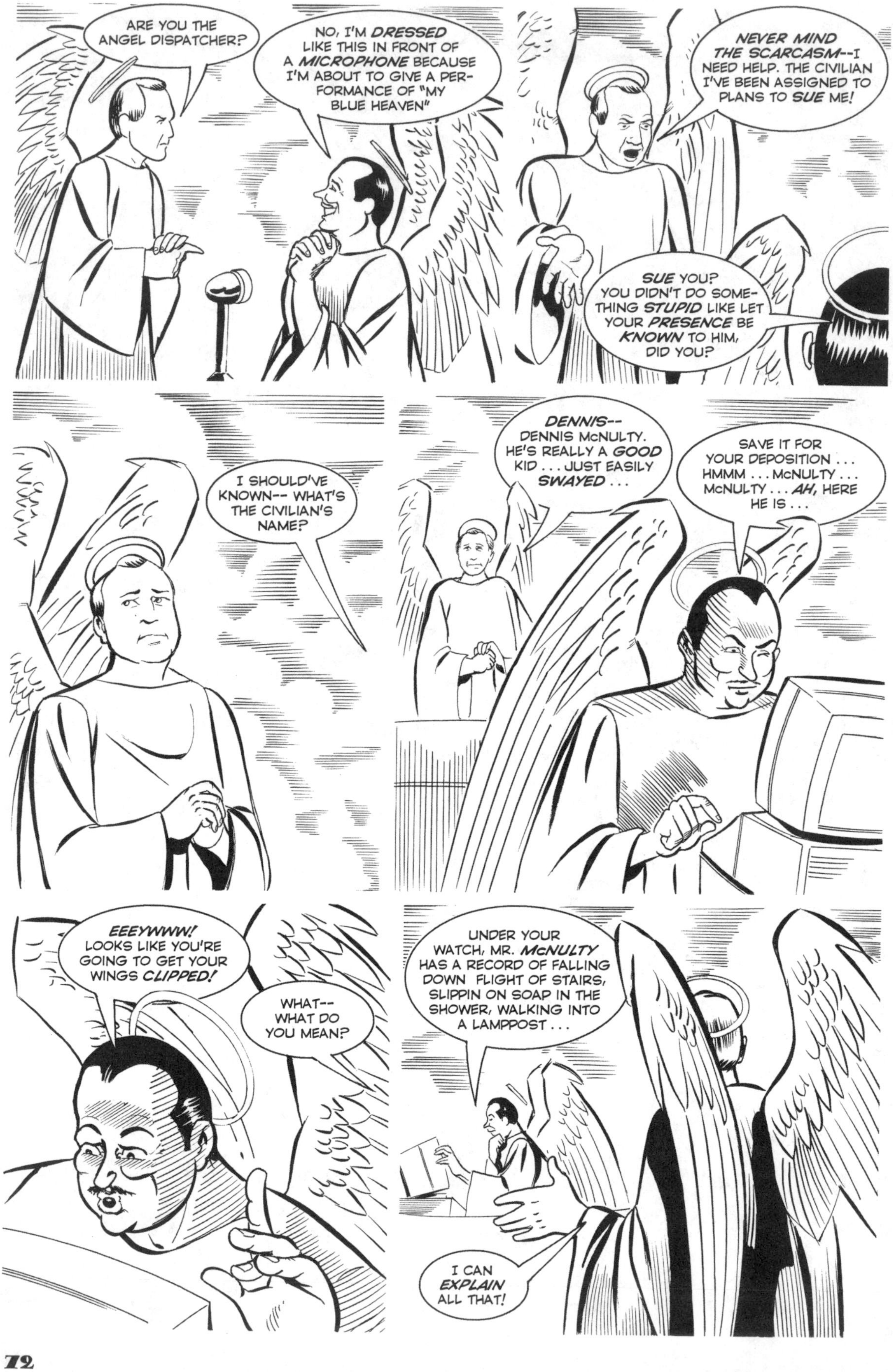
ARE YOU THE ANGEL DISPATCHER?
NO, I'M *DRESSED* LIKE THIS IN FRONT OF A *MICROPHONE* BECAUSE I'M ABOUT TO GIVE A PERFORMANCE OF "MY BLUE HEAVEN"
NEVER MIND THE SCARCASM--I NEED HELP. THE CIVILIAN I'VE BEEN ASSIGNED TO PLANS TO *SUE* ME!
SUE YOU? YOU DIDN'T DO SOMETHING *STUPID* LIKE LET YOUR *PRESENCE* BE *KNOWN* TO HIM, DID YOU?
I SHOULD'VE KNOWN-- WHAT'S THE CIVILIAN'S NAME?
DENNIS-- DENNIS McNULTY. HE'S REALLY A *GOOD* KID . . . JUST EASILY *SWAYED* . . .
SAVE IT FOR YOUR DEPOSITION . . . HMMM . . . McNULTY . . . McNULTY . . . *AH,* HERE HE IS . . .
EEEYWWW! LOOKS LIKE YOU'RE GOING TO GET YOUR WINGS *CLIPPED!*
WHAT-- WHAT DO YOU MEAN?
UNDER YOUR WATCH, MR. *McNULTY* HAS A RECORD OF FALLING DOWN FLIGHT OF STAIRS, SLIPPIN ON SOAP IN THE SHOWER, WALKING INTO A LAMPPOST . . .
I CAN *EXPLAIN* ALL THAT!

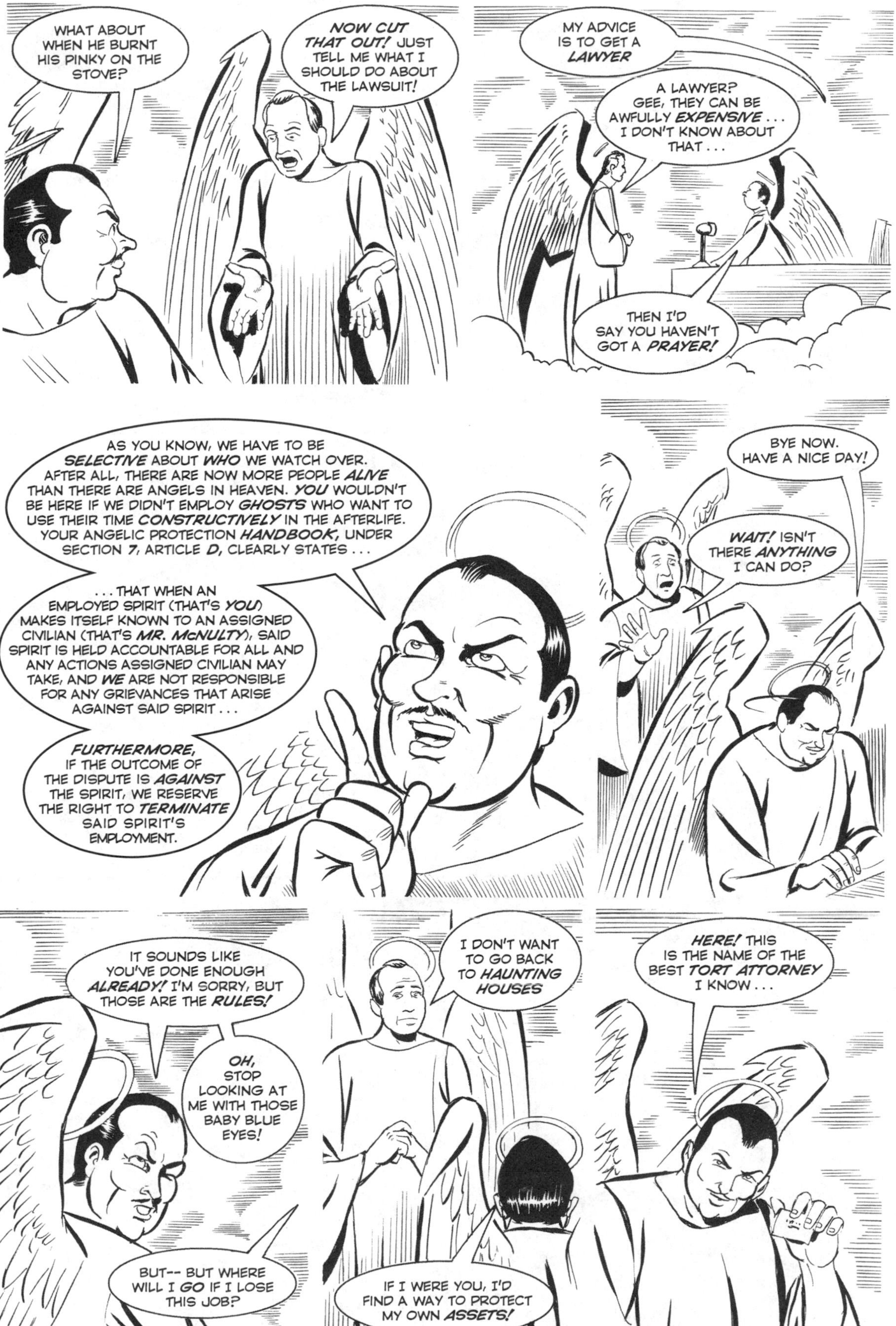
WHAT ABOUT WHEN HE BURNT HIS PINKY ON THE STOVE?
NOW CUT THAT OUT! JUST TELL ME WHAT I SHOULD DO ABOUT THE LAWSUIT!
MY ADVICE IS TO GET A LAWYER
A LAWYER? GEE, THEY CAN BE AWFULLY EXPENSIVE . . . I DON'T KNOW ABOUT THAT . . .
THEN I'D SAY YOU HAVEN'T GOT A PRAYER!
AS YOU KNOW, WE HAVE TO BE SELECTIVE ABOUT WHO WE WATCH OVER. AFTER ALL, THERE ARE NOW MORE PEOPLE ALIVE THAN THERE ARE ANGELS IN HEAVEN. YOU WOULDN'T BE HERE IF WE DIDN'T EMPLOY GHOSTS WHO WANT TO USE THEIR TIME CONSTRUCTIVELY IN THE AFTERLIFE. YOUR ANGELIC PROTECTION HANDBOOK, UNDER SECTION 7, ARTICLE D, CLEARLY STATES . . .
. . . THAT WHEN AN EMPLOYED SPIRIT (THAT'S YOU) MAKES ITSELF KNOWN TO AN ASSIGNED CIVILIAN (THAT'S MR. McNULTY), SAID SPIRIT IS HELD ACCOUNTABLE FOR ALL AND ANY ACTIONS ASSIGNED CIVILIAN MAY TAKE, AND WE ARE NOT RESPONSIBLE FOR ANY GRIEVANCES THAT ARISE AGAINST SAID SPIRIT . . .
FURTHERMORE, IF THE OUTCOME OF THE DISPUTE IS AGAINST THE SPIRIT, WE RESERVE THE RIGHT TO TERMINATE SAID SPIRIT'S EMPLOYMENT.
BYE NOW. HAVE A NICE DAY!
WAIT! ISN'T THERE ANYTHING I CAN DO?
IT SOUNDS LIKE YOU'VE DONE ENOUGH ALREADY! I'M SORRY, BUT THOSE ARE THE RULES!
OH, STOP LOOKING AT ME WITH THOSE BABY BLUE EYES!
BUT-- BUT WHERE WILL I GO IF I LOSE THIS JOB?
I DON'T WANT TO GO BACK TO HAUNTING HOUSES
IF I WERE YOU, I'D FIND A WAY TO PROTECT MY OWN ASSETS!
HERE! THIS IS THE NAME OF THE BEST TORT ATTORNEY I KNOW . . .

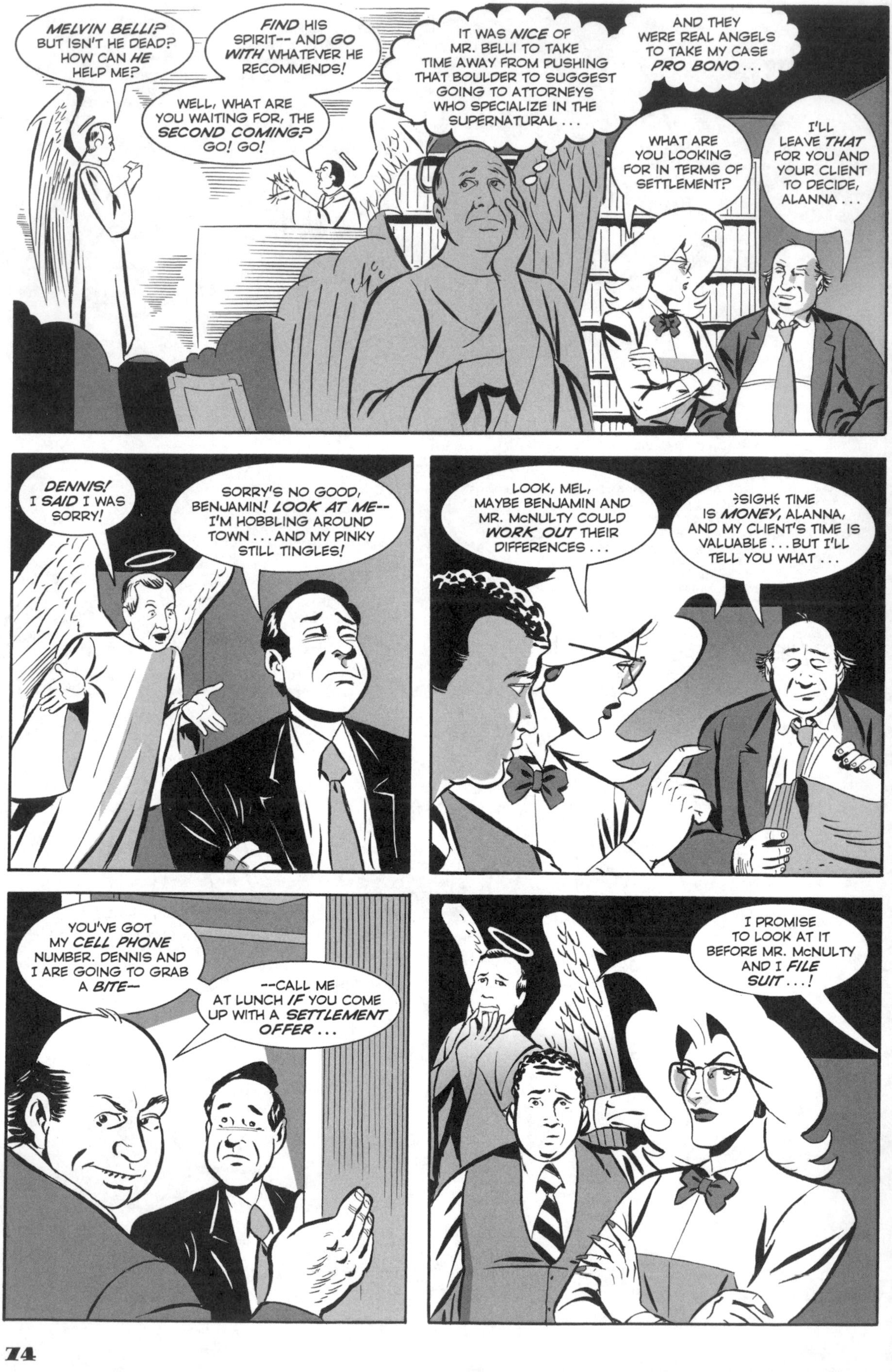
MELVIN BELLI? BUT ISN'T HE DEAD? HOW CAN HE HELP ME?
FIND HIS SPIRIT-- AND GO WITH WHATEVER HE RECOMMENDS!
WELL, WHAT ARE YOU WAITING FOR, THE SECOND COMING? GO! GO!
IT WAS NICE OF MR. BELLI TO TAKE TIME AWAY FROM PUSHING THAT BOULDER TO SUGGEST GOING TO ATTORNEYS WHO SPECIALIZE IN THE SUPERNATURAL . . .
AND THEY WERE REAL ANGELS TO TAKE MY CASE PRO BONO . . .
WHAT ARE YOU LOOKING FOR IN TERMS OF SETTLEMENT?
I'LL LEAVE THAT FOR YOU AND YOUR CLIENT TO DECIDE, ALANNA . . .
DENNIS! I SAID I WAS SORRY!
SORRY'S NO GOOD, BENJAMIN! LOOK AT ME-- I'M HOBBLING AROUND TOWN . . . AND MY PINKY STILL TINGLES!
LOOK, MEL, MAYBE BENJAMIN AND MR. McNULTY COULD WORK OUT THEIR DIFFERENCES . . .
SIGH TIME IS MONEY, ALANNA, AND MY CLIENT'S TIME IS VALUABLE . . . BUT I'LL TELL YOU WHAT . . .
YOU'VE GOT MY CELL PHONE NUMBER. DENNIS AND I ARE GOING TO GRAB A BITE--
--CALL ME AT LUNCH IF YOU COME UP WITH A SETTLEMENT OFFER . . .
I PROMISE TO LOOK AT IT BEFORE MR. McNULTY AND I FILE SUIT . . .!

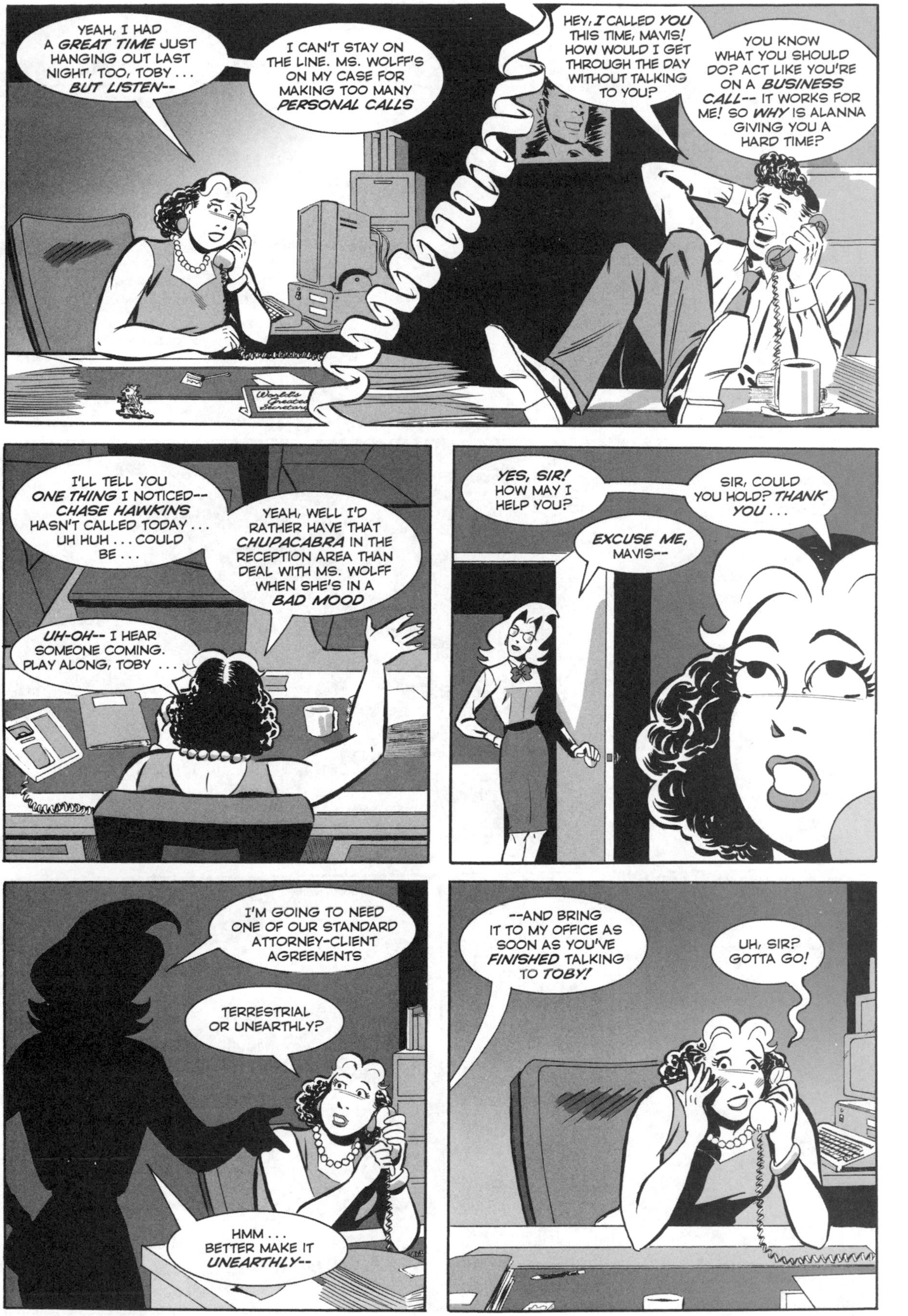
YEAH, I HAD A GREAT TIME JUST HANGING OUT LAST NIGHT, TOO, TOBY . . . BUT LISTEN--
I CAN'T STAY ON THE LINE. MS. WOLFF'S ON MY CASE FOR MAKING TOO MANY PERSONAL CALLS
HEY, I CALLED YOU THIS TIME, MAVIS! HOW WOULD I GET THROUGH THE DAY WITHOUT TALKING TO YOU?
YOU KNOW WHAT YOU SHOULD DO? ACT LIKE YOU'RE ON A BUSINESS CALL-- IT WORKS FOR ME! SO WHY IS ALANNA GIVING YOU A HARD TIME?
World's Greatest Secretary
I'LL TELL YOU ONE THING I NOTICED-- CHASE HAWKINS HASN'T CALLED TODAY . . . UH HUH . . . COULD BE . . .
YEAH, WELL I'D RATHER HAVE THAT CHUPACABRA IN THE RECEPTION AREA THAN DEAL WITH MS. WOLFF WHEN SHE'S IN A BAD MOOD
UH-OH-- I HEAR SOMEONE COMING. PLAY ALONG, TOBY . . .
YES, SIR! HOW MAY I HELP YOU?
SIR, COULD YOU HOLD? THANK YOU . . .
EXCUSE ME, MAVIS--
I'M GOING TO NEED ONE OF OUR STANDARD ATTORNEY-CLIENT AGREEMENTS
TERRESTRIAL OR UNEARTHLY?
HMM . . . BETTER MAKE IT UNEARTHLY--
--AND BRING IT TO MY OFFICE AS SOON AS YOU'VE FINISHED TALKING TO TOBY!
UH, SIR? GOTTA GO!

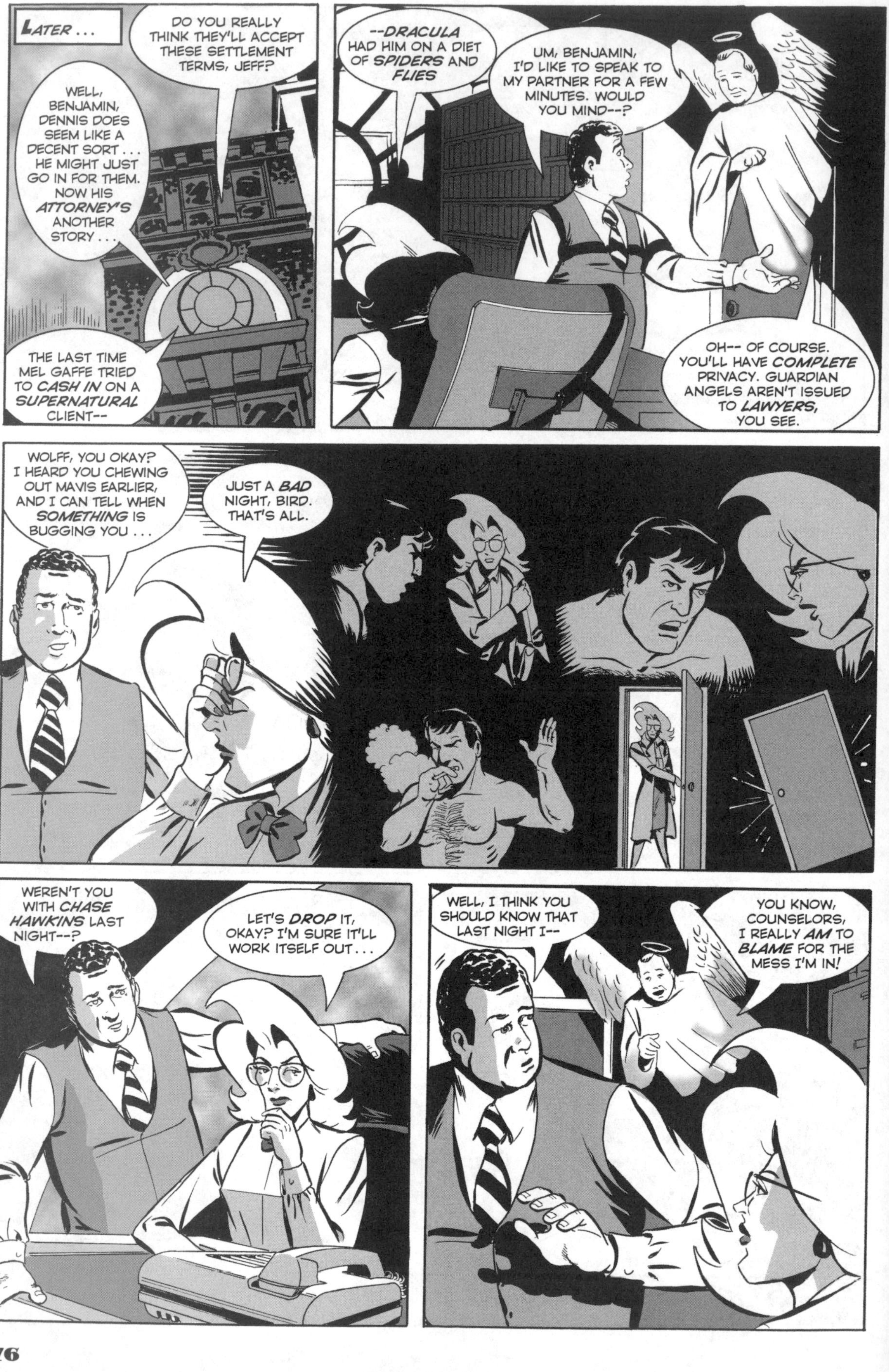
LATER . . .
DO YOU REALLY THINK THEY'LL ACCEPT THESE SETTLEMENT TERMS, JEFF?
WELL, BENJAMIN, DENNIS DOES SEEM LIKE A DECENT SORT . . . HE MIGHT JUST GO IN FOR THEM. NOW HIS ATTORNEY'S ANOTHER STORY . . .
THE LAST TIME MEL GAFFE TRIED TO CASH IN ON A SUPERNATURAL CLIENT--
--DRACULA HAD HIM ON A DIET OF SPIDERS AND FLIES
UM, BENJAMIN, I'D LIKE TO SPEAK TO MY PARTNER FOR A FEW MINUTES. WOULD YOU MIND--?
OH-- OF COURSE. YOU'LL HAVE COMPLETE PRIVACY. GUARDIAN ANGELS AREN'T ISSUED TO LAWYERS, YOU SEE.
WOLFF, YOU OKAY? I HEARD YOU CHEWING OUT MAVIS EARLIER, AND I CAN TELL WHEN SOMETHING IS BUGGING YOU . . .
JUST A BAD NIGHT, BIRD. THAT'S ALL.
WEREN'T YOU WITH CHASE HAWKINS LAST NIGHT--?
LET'S DROP IT, OKAY? I'M SURE IT'LL WORK ITSELF OUT . . .
WELL, I THINK YOU SHOULD KNOW THAT LAST NIGHT I--
YOU KNOW, COUNSELORS, I REALLY AM TO BLAME FOR THE MESS I'M IN!

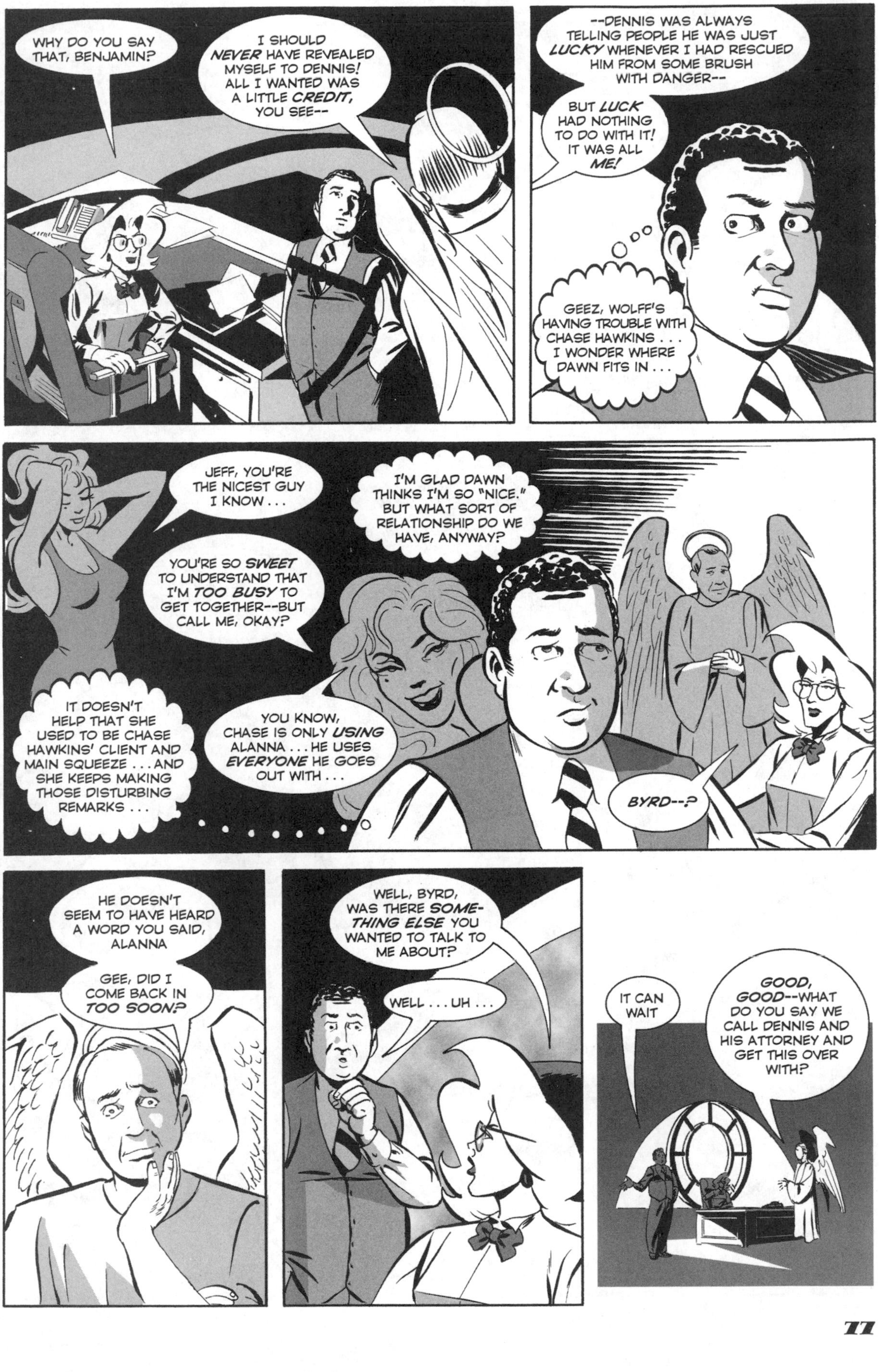
WHY DO YOU SAY THAT, BENJAMIN?
I SHOULD NEVER HAVE REVEALED MYSELF TO DENNIS! ALL I WANTED WAS A LITTLE CREDIT, YOU SEE--
--DENNIS WAS ALWAYS TELLING PEOPLE HE WAS JUST LUCKY WHENEVER I HAD RESCUED HIM FROM SOME BRUSH WITH DANGER--
BUT LUCK HAD NOTHING TO DO WITH IT! IT WAS ALL ME!
GEEZ, WOLFF'S HAVING TROUBLE WITH CHASE HAWKINS . . . I WONDER WHERE DAWN FITS IN . . .
JEFF, YOU'RE THE NICEST GUY I KNOW . . .
YOU'RE SO SWEET TO UNDERSTAND THAT I'M TOO BUSY TO GET TOGETHER--BUT CALL ME, OKAY?
I'M GLAD DAWN THINKS I'M SO "NICE." BUT WHAT SORT OF RELATIONSHIP DO WE HAVE, ANYWAY?
IT DOESN'T HELP THAT SHE USED TO BE CHASE HAWKINS' CLIENT AND MAIN SQUEEZE . . . AND SHE KEEPS MAKING THOSE DISTURBING REMARKS . . .
YOU KNOW, CHASE IS ONLY USING ALANNA . . . HE USES EVERYONE HE GOES OUT WITH . . .
BYRD--?
HE DOESN'T SEEM TO HAVE HEARD A WORD YOU SAID, ALANNA
GEE, DID I COME BACK IN TOO SOON?
WELL, BYRD, WAS THERE SOMETHING ELSE YOU WANTED TO TALK TO ME ABOUT?
WELL . . . UH . . .
IT CAN WAIT
GOOD, GOOD--WHAT DO YOU SAY WE CALL DENNIS AND HIS ATTORNEY AND GET THIS OVER WITH?

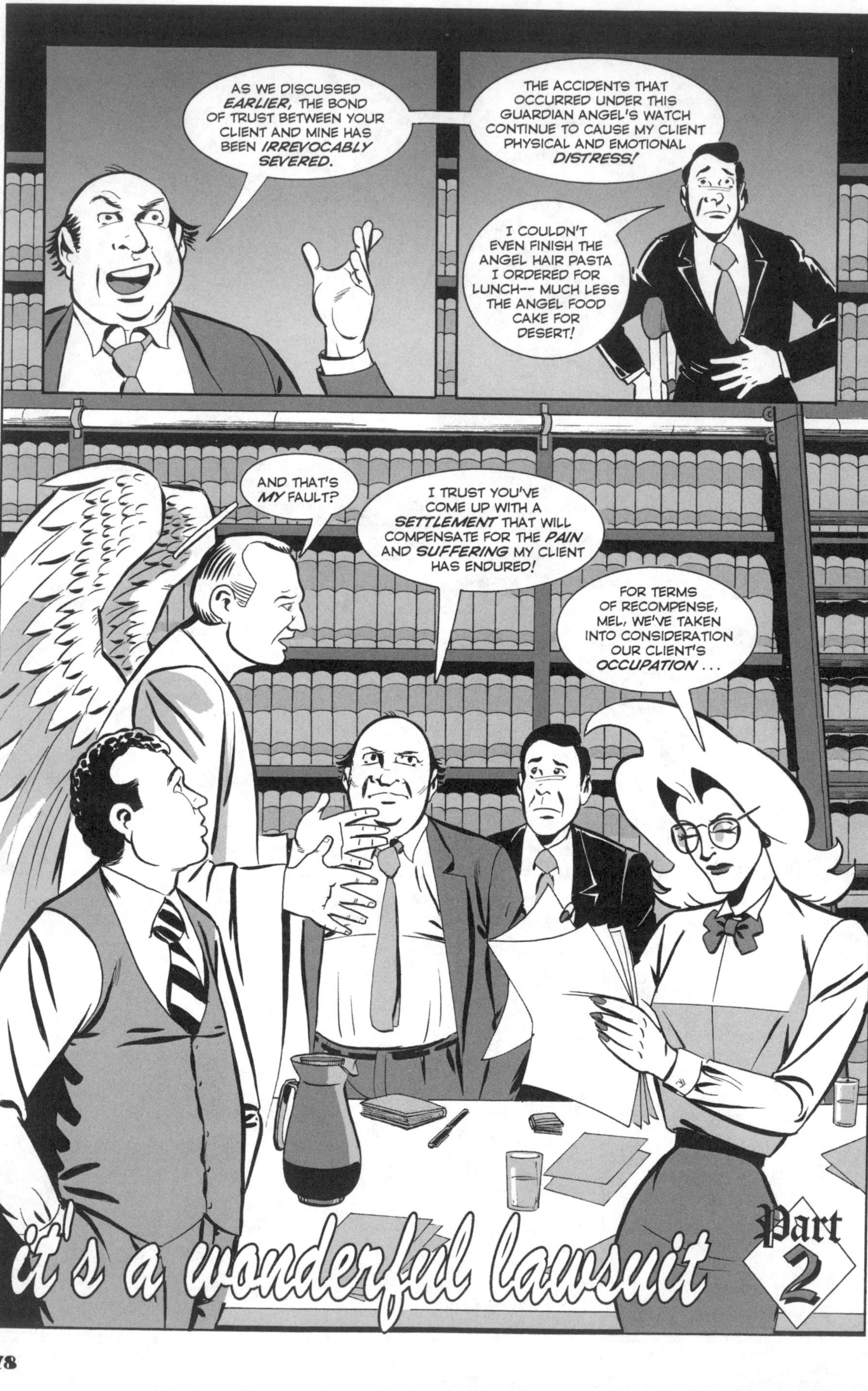
AS WE DISCUSSED EARLIER, THE BOND OF TRUST BETWEEN YOUR CLIENT AND MINE HAS BEEN IRREVOCABLY SEVERED.
THE ACCIDENTS THAT OCCURRED UNDER THIS GUARDIAN ANGEL'S WATCH CONTINUE TO CAUSE MY CLIENT PHYSICAL AND EMOTIONAL DISTRESS!
I COULDN'T EVEN FINISH THE ANGEL HAIR PASTA I ORDERED FOR LUNCH-- MUCH LESS THE ANGEL FOOD CAKE FOR DESERT!
AND THAT'S MY FAULT?
I TRUST YOU'VE COME UP WITH A SETTLEMENT THAT WILL COMPENSATE FOR THE PAIN AND SUFFERING MY CLIENT HAS ENDURED!
FOR TERMS OF RECOMPENSE, MEL, WE'VE TAKEN INTO CONSIDERATION OUR CLIENT'S OCCUPATION . . .
it's a wonderful lawsuit
Part 2

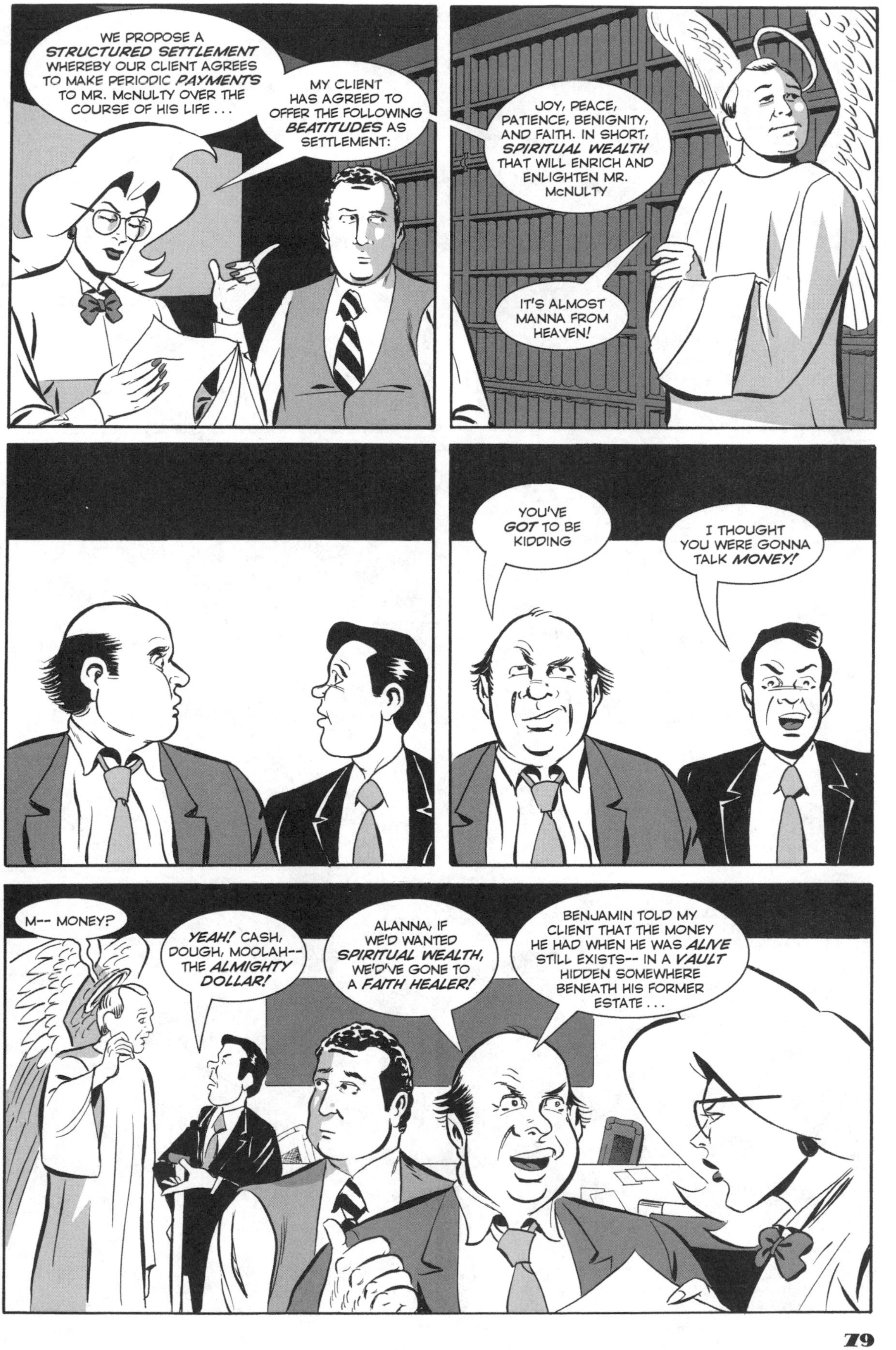

WE PROPOSE A STRUCTURED SETTLEMENT WHEREBY OUR CLIENT AGREES TO MAKE PERIODIC PAYMENTS TO MR. McNULTY OVER THE COURSE OF HIS LIFE . . .
MY CLIENT HAS AGREED TO OFFER THE FOLLOWING BEATITUDES AS SETTLEMENT:
JOY, PEACE, PATIENCE, BENIGNITY, AND FAITH. IN SHORT, SPIRITUAL WEALTH THAT WILL ENRICH AND ENLIGHTEN MR. McNULTY
IT'S ALMOST MANNA FROM HEAVEN!
YOU'VE GOT TO BE KIDDING
I THOUGHT YOU WERE GONNA TALK MONEY!
M-- MONEY?
YEAH! CASH, DOUGH, MOOLAH-- THE ALMIGHTY DOLLAR!
ALANNA, IF WE'D WANTED SPIRITUAL WEALTH, WE'D'VE GONE TO A FAITH HEALER!
BENJAMIN TOLD MY CLIENT THAT THE MONEY HE HAD WHEN HE WAS ALIVE STILL EXISTS-- IN A VAULT HIDDEN SOMEWHERE BENEATH HIS FORMER ESTATE . . .

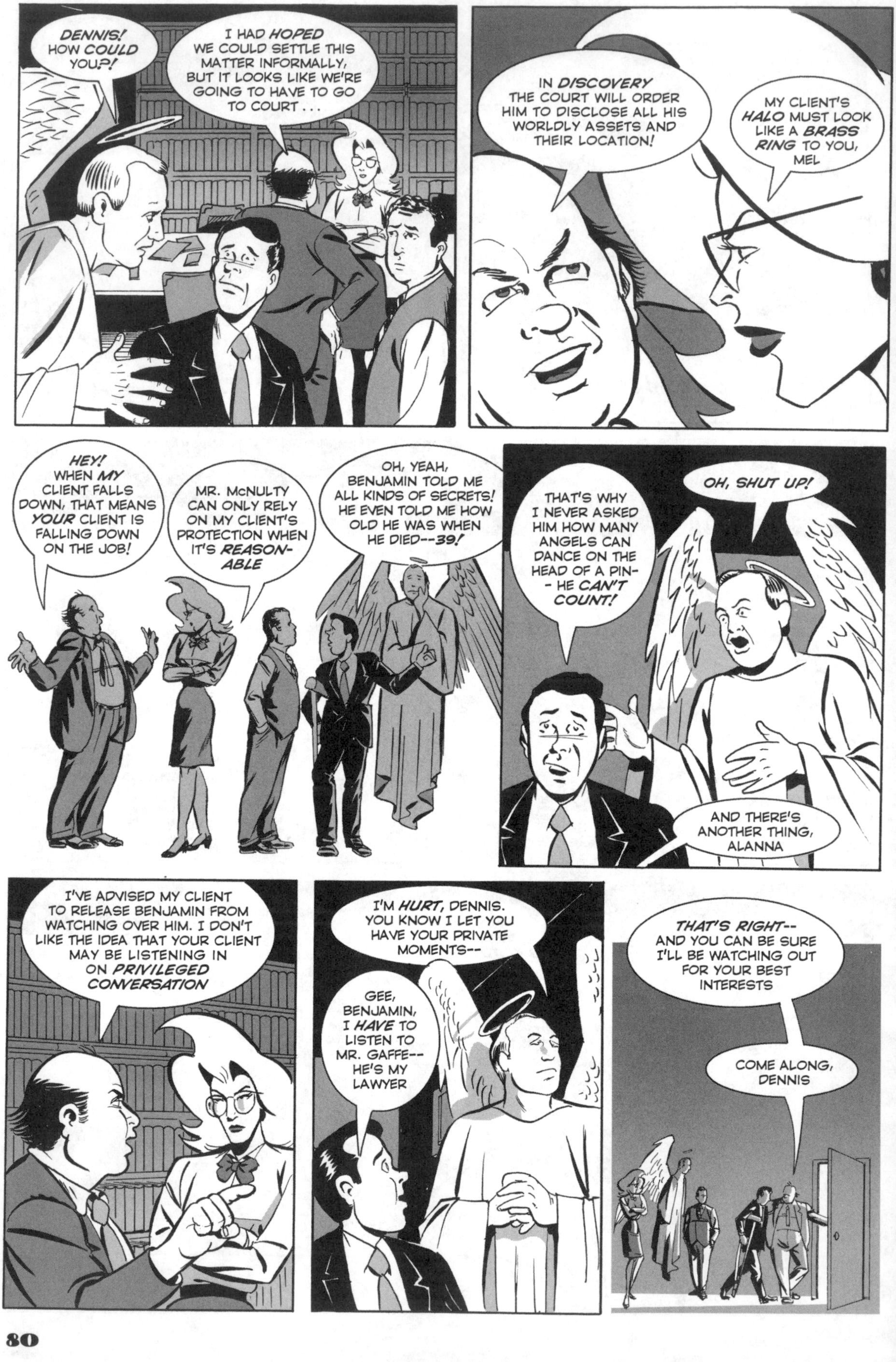
DENNIS! HOW COULD YOU?!
I HAD HOPED WE COULD SETTLE THIS MATTER INFORMALLY, BUT IT LOOKS LIKE WE'RE GOING TO HAVE TO GO TO COURT . . .
IN DISCOVERY THE COURT WILL ORDER HIM TO DISCLOSE ALL HIS WORLDLY ASSETS AND THEIR LOCATION!
MY CLIENT'S HALO MUST LOOK LIKE A BRASS RING TO YOU, MEL
HEY! WHEN MY CLIENT FALLS DOWN, THAT MEANS YOUR CLIENT IS FALLING DOWN ON THE JOB!
MR. McNULTY CAN ONLY RELY ON MY CLIENT'S PROTECTION WHEN IT'S REASON-ABLE
OH, YEAH, BENJAMIN TOLD ME ALL KINDS OF SECRETS! HE EVEN TOLD ME HOW OLD HE WAS WHEN HE DIED--39!
THAT'S WHY I NEVER ASKED HIM HOW MANY ANGELS CAN DANCE ON THE HEAD OF A PIN- - HE CAN'T COUNT!
OH, SHUT UP!
AND THERE'S ANOTHER THING, ALANNA
I'VE ADVISED MY CLIENT TO RELEASE BENJAMIN FROM WATCHING OVER HIM. I DON'T LIKE THE IDEA THAT YOUR CLIENT MAY BE LISTENING IN ON PRIVILEGED CONVERSATION
I'M HURT, DENNIS. YOU KNOW I LET YOU HAVE YOUR PRIVATE MOMENTS--
GEE, BENJAMIN, I HAVE TO LISTEN TO MR. GAFFE-- HE'S MY LAWYER
THAT'S RIGHT-- AND YOU CAN BE SURE I'LL BE WATCHING OUT FOR YOUR BEST INTERESTS
COME ALONG, DENNIS

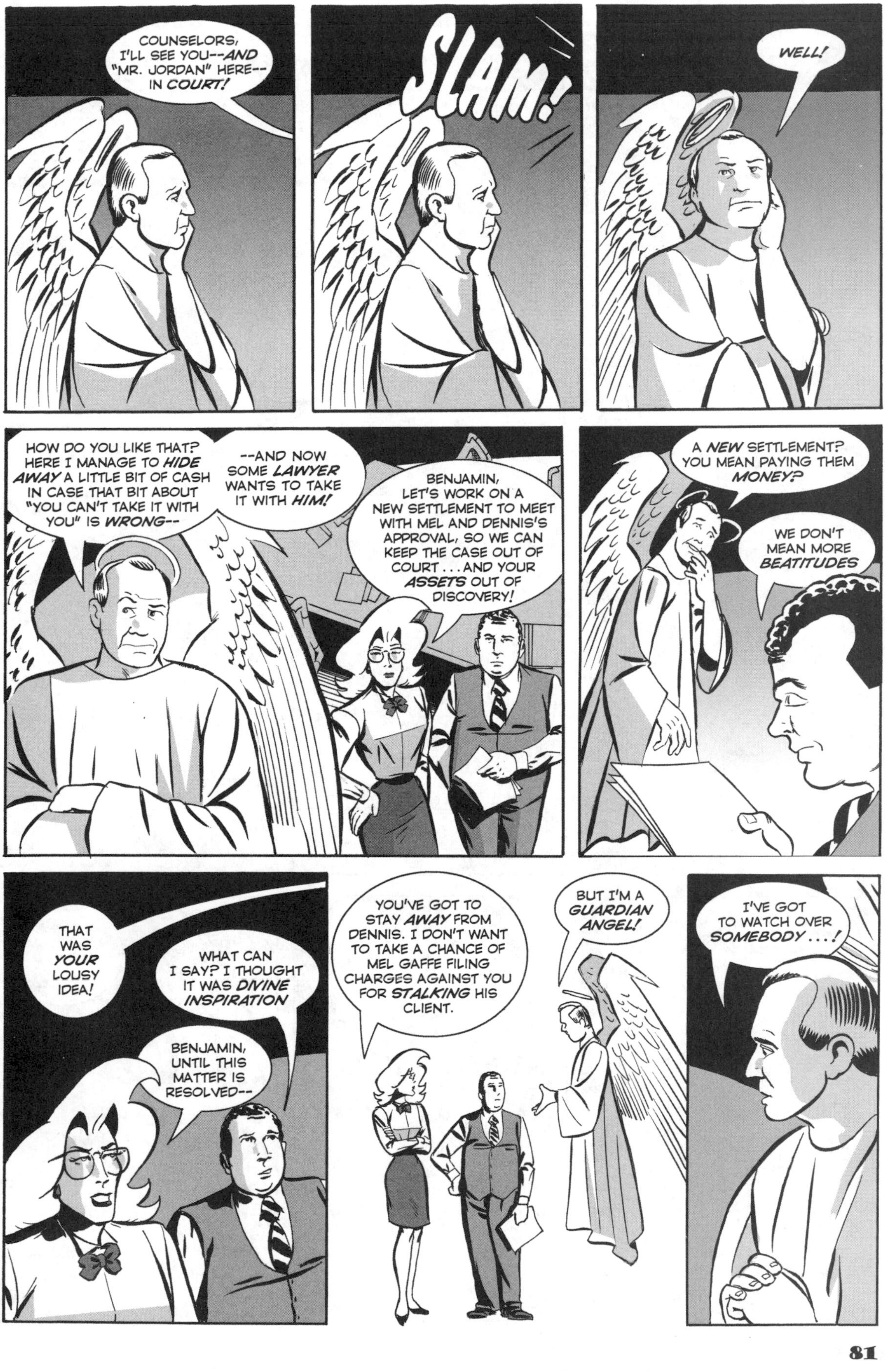
COUNSELORS, I'LL SEE YOU--AND "MR. JORDAN" HERE--IN COURT!
SLAM!
WELL!
HOW DO YOU LIKE THAT? HERE I MANAGE TO HIDE AWAY A LITTLE BIT OF CASH IN CASE THAT BIT ABOUT "YOU CAN'T TAKE IT WITH YOU" IS WRONG--
--AND NOW SOME LAWYER WANTS TO TAKE IT WITH HIM!
BENJAMIN, LET'S WORK ON A NEW SETTLEMENT TO MEET WITH MEL AND DENNIS'S APPROVAL, SO WE CAN KEEP THE CASE OUT OF COURT... AND YOUR ASSETS OUT OF DISCOVERY!
A NEW SETTLEMENT? YOU MEAN PAYING THEM MONEY?
WE DON'T MEAN MORE BEATITUDES
THAT WAS YOUR LOUSY IDEA!
WHAT CAN I SAY? I THOUGHT IT WAS DIVINE INSPIRATION
BENJAMIN, UNTIL THIS MATTER IS RESOLVED--
YOU'VE GOT TO STAY AWAY FROM DENNIS. I DON'T WANT TO TAKE A CHANCE OF MEL GAFFE FILING CHARGES AGAINST YOU FOR STALKING HIS CLIENT.
BUT I'M A GUARDIAN ANGEL!
I'VE GOT TO WATCH OVER SOMEBODY...!

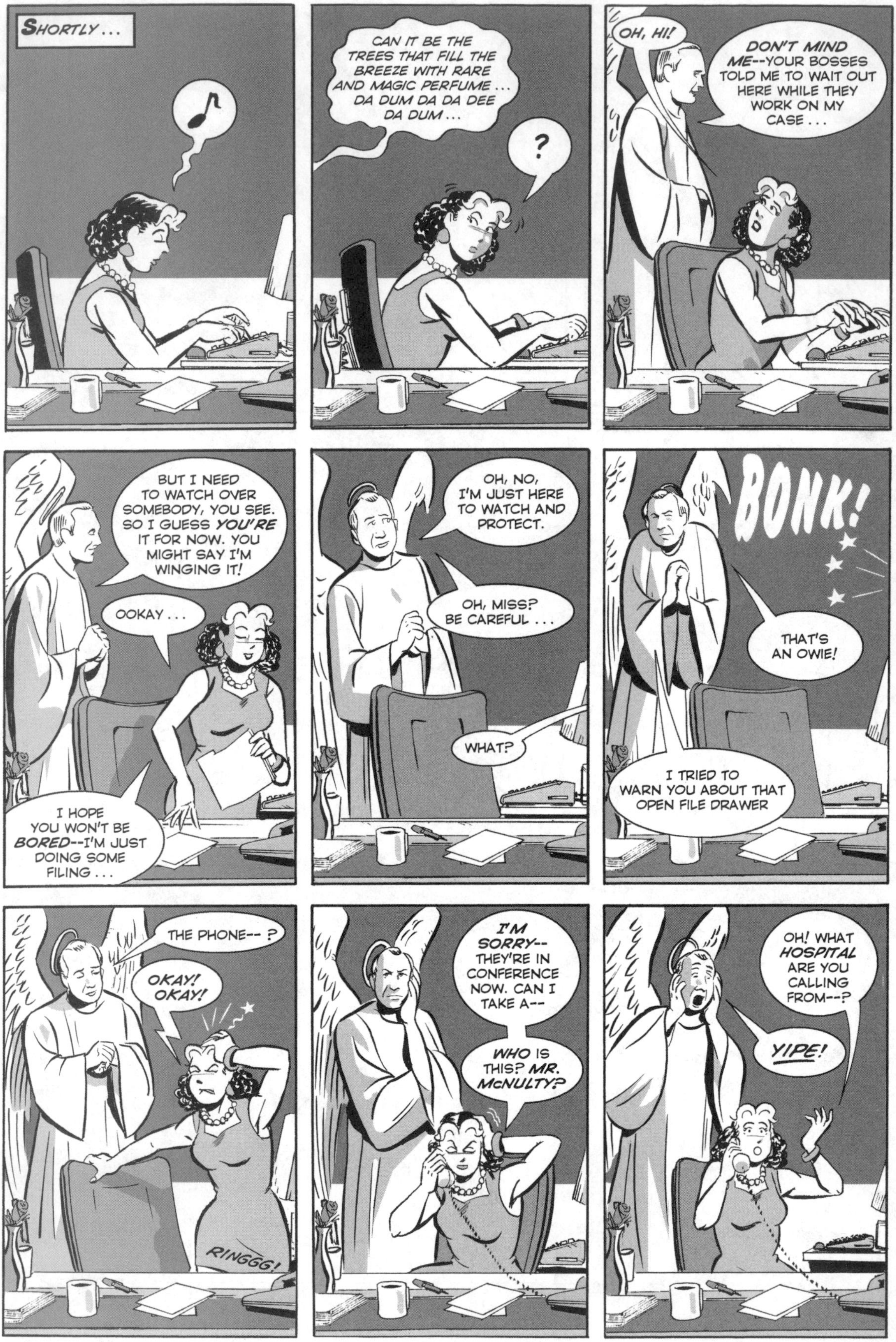

SHORTLY . . .
CAN IT BE THE TREES THAT FILL THE BREEZE WITH RARE AND MAGIC PERFUME . . . DA DUM DA DA DEE DA DUM . . .
?
OH, HI!
DON'T MIND ME--YOUR BOSSES TOLD ME TO WAIT OUT HERE WHILE THEY WORK ON MY CASE . . .
BUT I NEED TO WATCH OVER SOMEBODY, YOU SEE. SO I GUESS YOU'RE IT FOR NOW. YOU MIGHT SAY I'M WINGING IT!
OOKAY . . .
I HOPE YOU WON'T BE BORED--I'M JUST DOING SOME FILING . . .
OH, NO, I'M JUST HERE TO WATCH AND PROTECT.
OH, MISS? BE CAREFUL . . .
WHAT?
BONK!
THAT'S AN OWIE!
I TRIED TO WARN YOU ABOUT THAT OPEN FILE DRAWER
THE PHONE-- ?
OKAY! OKAY!
RINGGG!
I'M SORRY-- THEY'RE IN CONFERENCE NOW. CAN I TAKE A--
WHO IS THIS? MR. McNULTY?
OH! WHAT HOSPITAL ARE YOU CALLING FROM--?
YIPE!

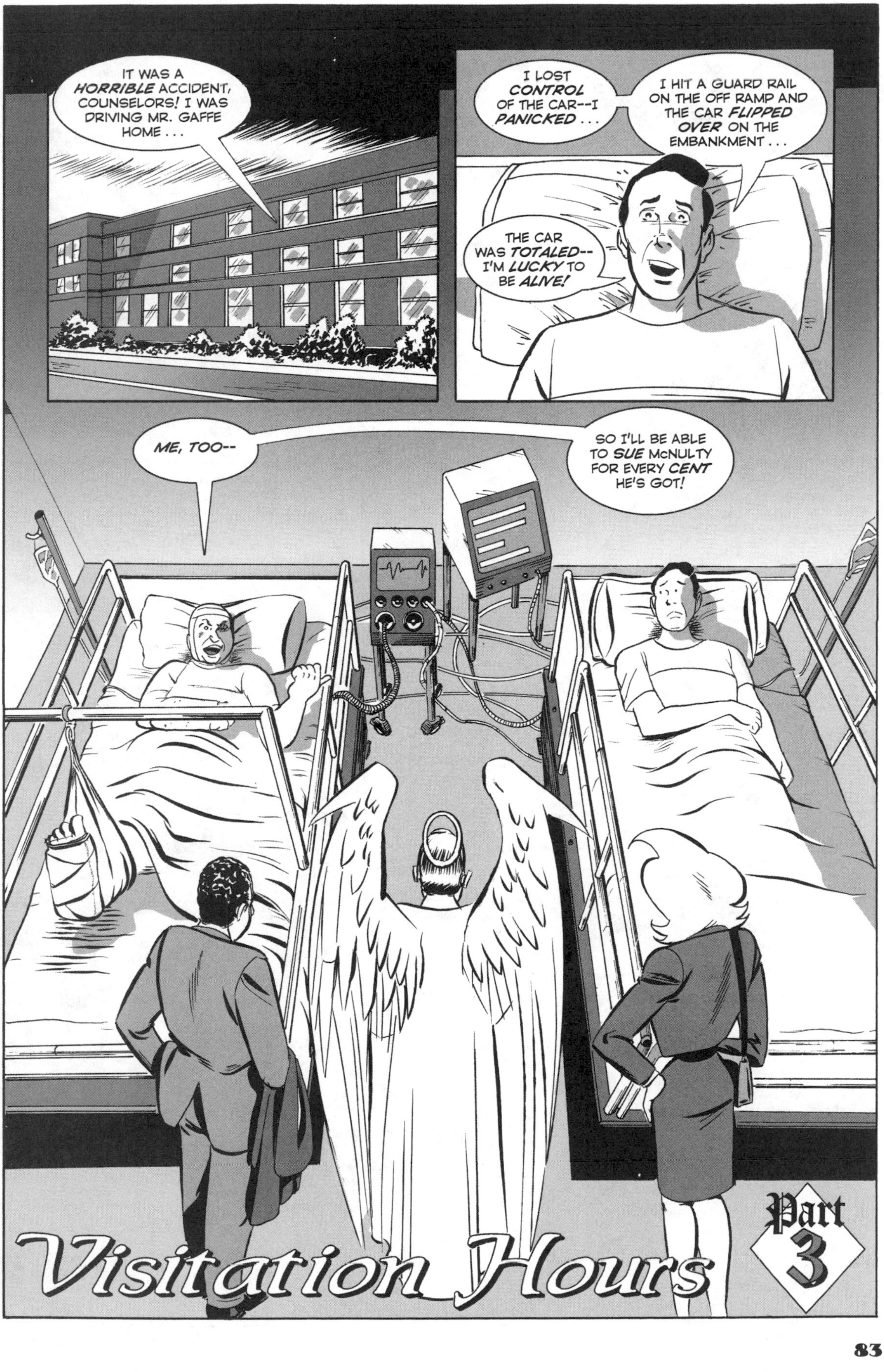
IT WAS A HORRIBLE ACCIDENT, COUNSELORS! I WAS DRIVING MR. GAFFE HOME . . .
I LOST CONTROL OF THE CAR--I PANICKED . . .
I HIT A GUARD RAIL ON THE OFF RAMP AND THE CAR FLIPPED OVER ON THE EMBANKMENT . . .
THE CAR WAS TOTALED-- I'M LUCKY TO BE ALIVE!
ME, TOO--
SO I'LL BE ABLE TO SUE McNULTY FOR EVERY CENT HE'S GOT!
Visitation Hours
Part 3

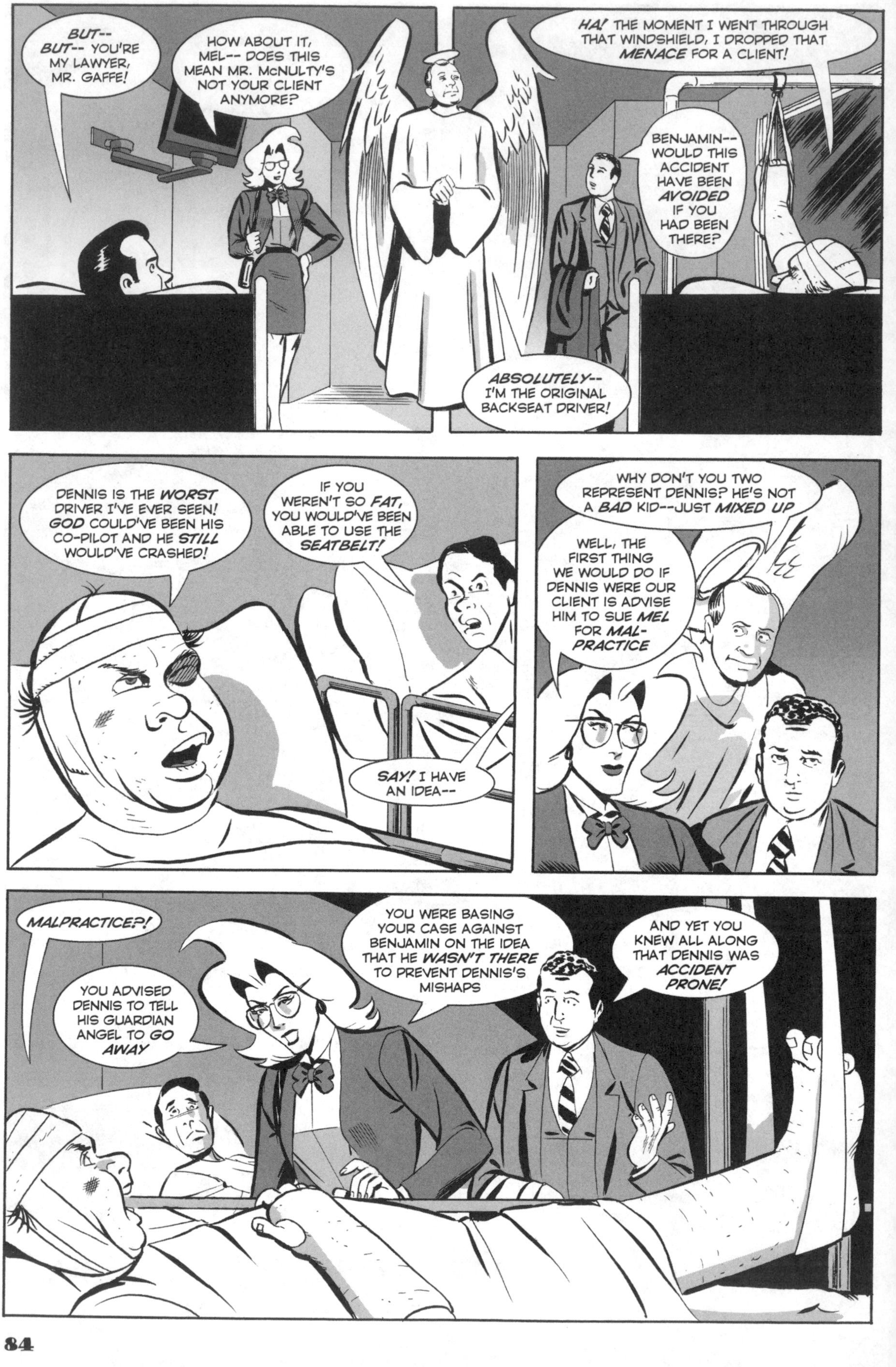
BUT-- BUT-- YOU'RE MY LAWYER, MR. GAFFE!
HOW ABOUT IT, MEL-- DOES THIS MEAN MR. McNULTY'S NOT YOUR CLIENT ANYMORE?
HA! THE MOMENT I WENT THROUGH THAT WINDSHIELD, I DROPPED THAT MENACE FOR A CLIENT!
BENJAMIN-- WOULD THIS ACCIDENT HAVE BEEN AVOIDED IF YOU HAD BEEN THERE?
ABSOLUTELY-- I'M THE ORIGINAL BACKSEAT DRIVER!
DENNIS IS THE WORST DRIVER I'VE EVER SEEN! GOD COULD'VE BEEN HIS CO-PILOT AND HE STILL WOULD'VE CRASHED!
IF YOU WEREN'T SO FAT, YOU WOULD'VE BEEN ABLE TO USE THE SEATBELT!
SAY! I HAVE AN IDEA--
WHY DON'T YOU TWO REPRESENT DENNIS? HE'S NOT A BAD KID--JUST MIXED UP
WELL, THE FIRST THING WE WOULD DO IF DENNIS WERE OUR CLIENT IS ADVISE HIM TO SUE MEL FOR MAL-PRACTICE
MALPRACTICE?!
YOU ADVISED DENNIS TO TELL HIS GUARDIAN ANGEL TO GO AWAY
YOU WERE BASING YOUR CASE AGAINST BENJAMIN ON THE IDEA THAT HE WASN'T THERE TO PREVENT DENNIS'S MISHAPS
AND YET YOU KNEW ALL ALONG THAT DENNIS WAS ACCIDENT PRONE!

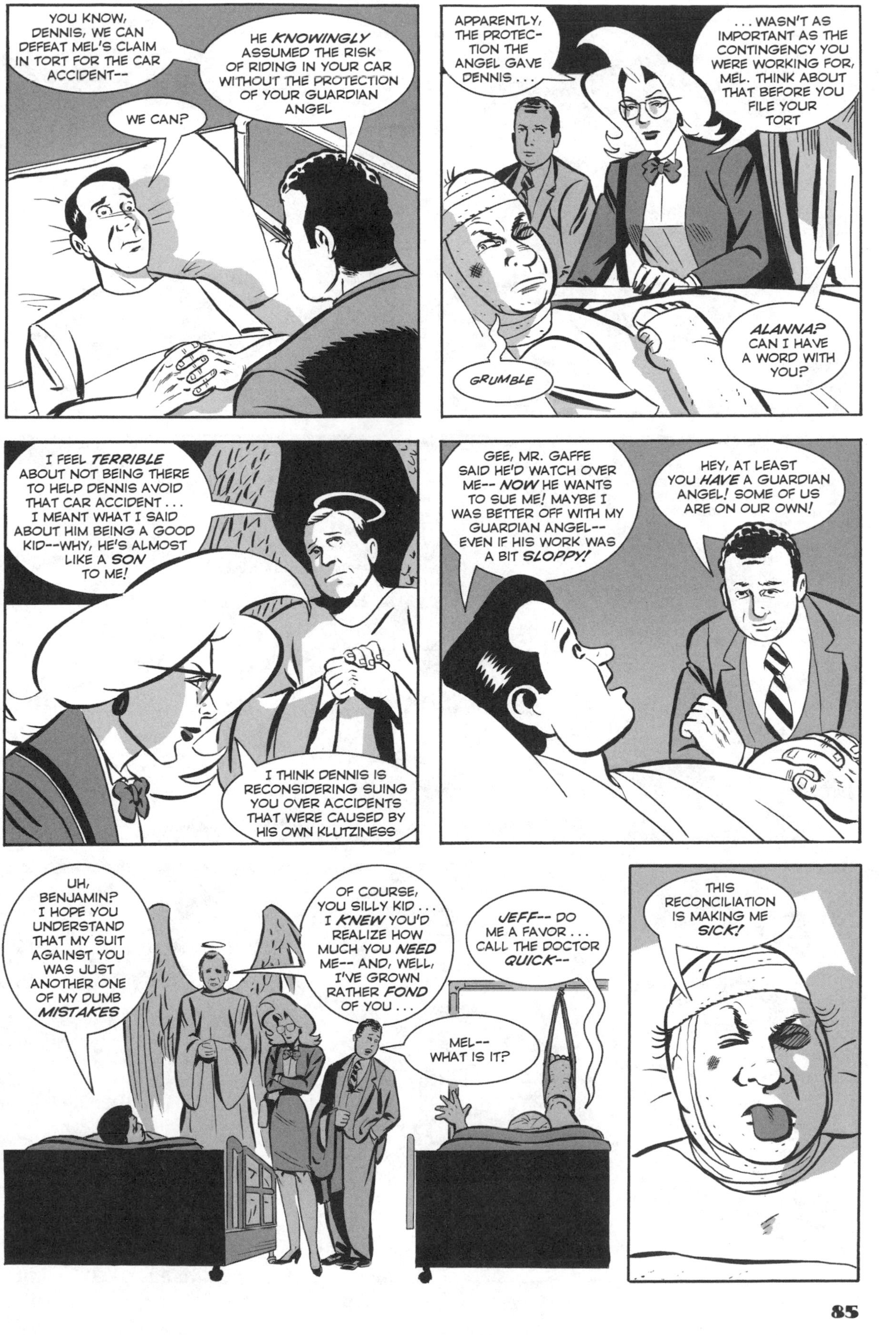
YOU KNOW, DENNIS, WE CAN DEFEAT MEL'S CLAIM IN TORT FOR THE CAR ACCIDENT--
HE *KNOWINGLY* ASSUMED THE RISK OF RIDING IN YOUR CAR WITHOUT THE PROTECTION OF YOUR GUARDIAN ANGEL
WE CAN?
APPARENTLY, THE PROTECTION THE ANGEL GAVE DENNIS . . .
. . . WASN'T AS IMPORTANT AS THE CONTINGENCY YOU WERE WORKING FOR, MEL. THINK ABOUT THAT BEFORE YOU FILE YOUR TORT
ALANNA? CAN I HAVE A WORD WITH YOU?
GRUMBLE
I FEEL *TERRIBLE* ABOUT NOT BEING THERE TO HELP DENNIS AVOID THAT CAR ACCIDENT . . . I MEANT WHAT I SAID ABOUT HIM BEING A GOOD KID--WHY, HE'S ALMOST LIKE A *SON* TO ME!
I THINK DENNIS IS RECONSIDERING SUING YOU OVER ACCIDENTS THAT WERE CAUSED BY HIS OWN KLUTZINESS
GEE, MR. GAFFE SAID HE'D WATCH OVER ME-- *NOW* HE WANTS TO SUE ME! MAYBE I WAS BETTER OFF WITH MY GUARDIAN ANGEL-- EVEN IF HIS WORK WAS A BIT *SLOPPY!*
HEY, AT LEAST YOU *HAVE* A GUARDIAN ANGEL! SOME OF US ARE ON OUR OWN!
UH, BENJAMIN? I HOPE YOU UNDERSTAND THAT MY SUIT AGAINST YOU WAS JUST ANOTHER ONE OF MY DUMB *MISTAKES*
OF COURSE, YOU SILLY KID . . . I *KNEW* YOU'D REALIZE HOW MUCH YOU *NEED* ME-- AND, WELL, I'VE GROWN RATHER *FOND* OF YOU . . .
JEFF-- DO ME A FAVOR . . . CALL THE DOCTOR *QUICK*--
MEL-- WHAT IS IT?
THIS RECONCILIATION IS MAKING ME *SICK!*

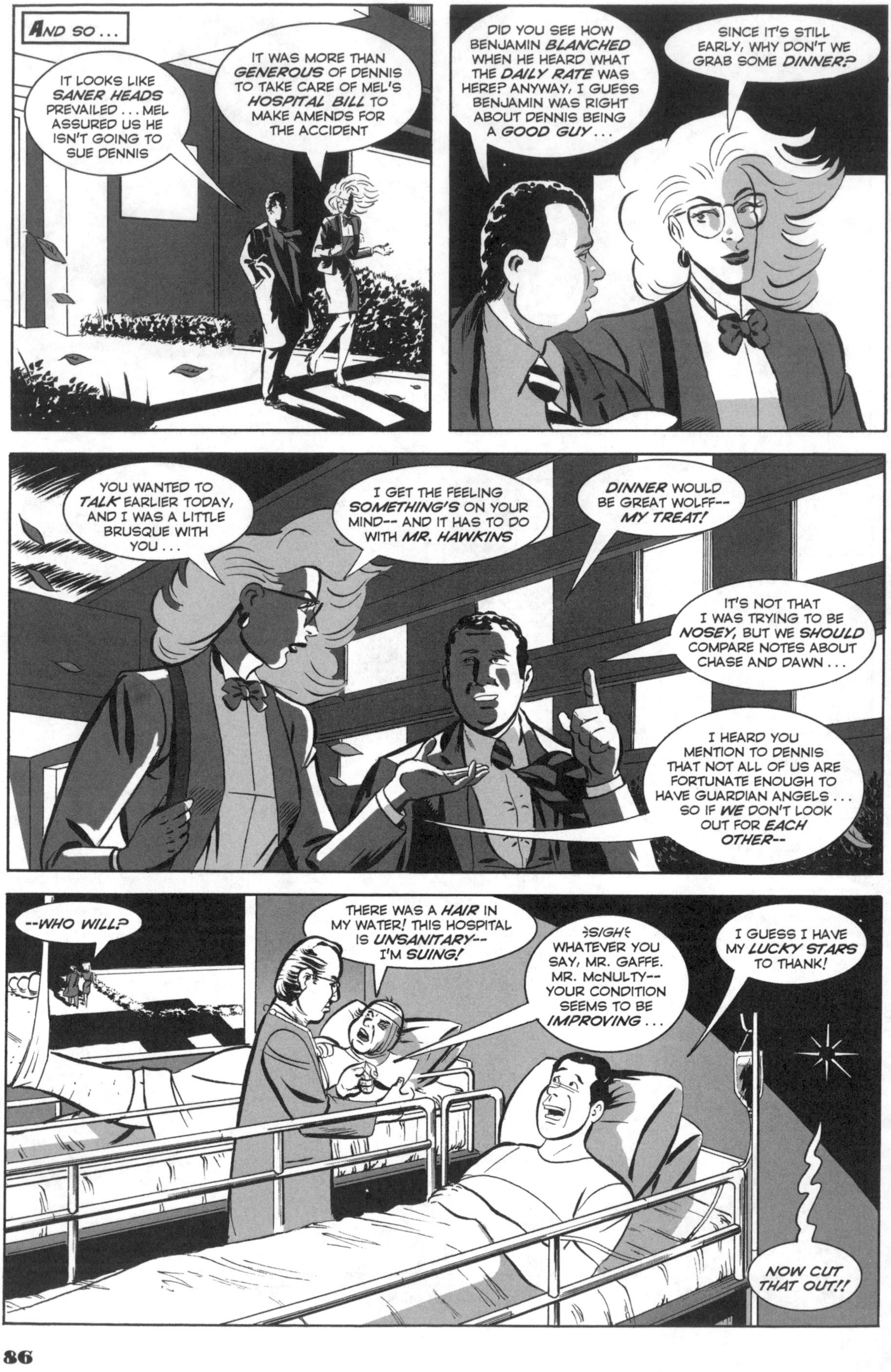
AND SO . . .
IT LOOKS LIKE SANER HEADS PREVAILED . . . MEL ASSURED US HE ISN'T GOING TO SUE DENNIS
IT WAS MORE THAN GENEROUS OF DENNIS TO TAKE CARE OF MEL'S HOSPITAL BILL TO MAKE AMENDS FOR THE ACCIDENT
DID YOU SEE HOW BENJAMIN BLANCHED WHEN HE HEARD WHAT THE DAILY RATE WAS HERE? ANYWAY, I GUESS BENJAMIN WAS RIGHT ABOUT DENNIS BEING A GOOD GUY . . .
SINCE IT'S STILL EARLY, WHY DON'T WE GRAB SOME DINNER?
YOU WANTED TO TALK EARLIER TODAY, AND I WAS A LITTLE BRUSQUE WITH YOU . . .
I GET THE FEELING SOMETHING'S ON YOUR MIND-- AND IT HAS TO DO WITH MR. HAWKINS
DINNER WOULD BE GREAT WOLFF-- MY TREAT!
IT'S NOT THAT I WAS TRYING TO BE NOSEY, BUT WE SHOULD COMPARE NOTES ABOUT CHASE AND DAWN . . .
I HEARD YOU MENTION TO DENNIS THAT NOT ALL OF US ARE FORTUNATE ENOUGH TO HAVE GUARDIAN ANGELS . . . SO IF WE DON'T LOOK OUT FOR EACH OTHER--
--WHO WILL?
THERE WAS A HAIR IN MY WATER! THIS HOSPITAL IS UNSANITARY-- I'M SUING!
SIGH WHATEVER YOU SAY, MR. GAFFE. MR. McNULTY-- YOUR CONDITION SEEMS TO BE IMPROVING . . .
I GUESS I HAVE MY LUCKY STARS TO THANK!
NOW CUT THAT OUT!!

Part 2

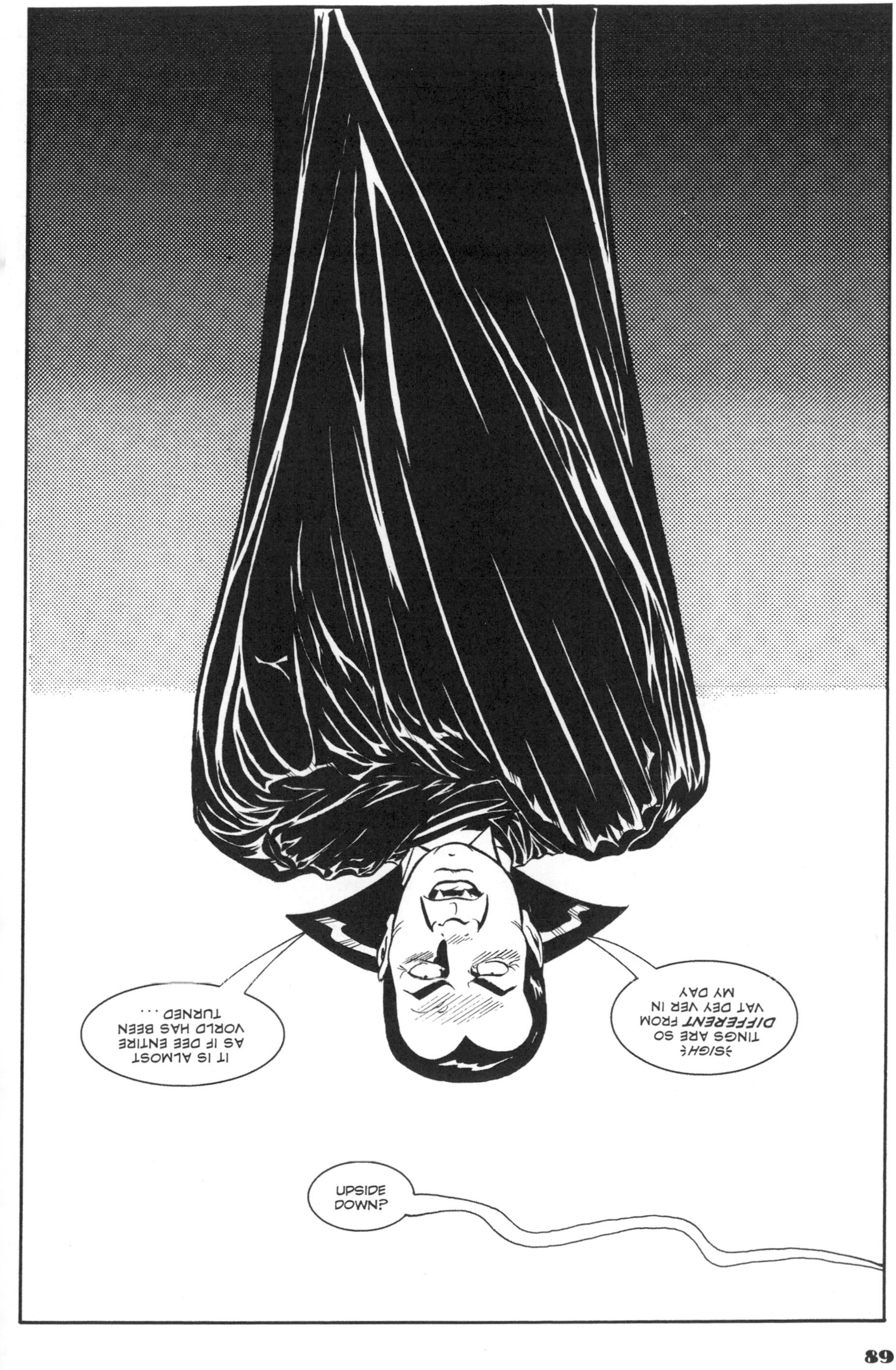
SIGH TINGS ARE SO **DIFFERENT** FROM VAT DEY VER IN MY DAY
IT IS ALMOST AS IF DEE ENTIRE VORLD HAS BEEN TURNED . . .
UPSIDE DOWN?

Wednesday the 11th

YEAH, WELL-- IT'S A *COMPLICATED* WORLD, COUNT--YOU GOTTA KEEP UP WITH THE TIMES

YES, YOU *UNDERSTAND,* DOT IS *RARE* FOR A *YOUNG* PERSON SUCH AS YOURSELF...

IT IS NOT VAT IT VAS LIKE IN DEE OLD *DAYS*--TAKE MY VORD FOR IT...

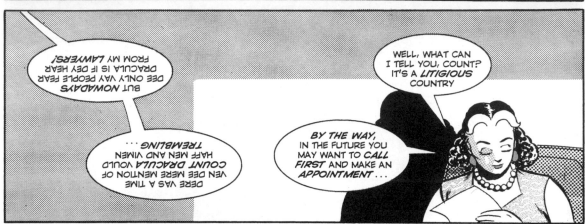

WELL, WHAT CAN I TELL YOU, COUNT? IT'S A *LITIGIOUS* COUNTRY

BY THE WAY, IN THE FUTURE YOU MAY WANT TO *CALL FIRST* AND MAKE AN *APPOINTMENT*...

BUT *NOWADAYS* DEE ONLY VAY PEOPLE FEAR DRACULA IS IF DEY HEAR FROM MY *LAWYERS!*

DERE VAS A TIME VEN DEE MERE MENTION OF *COUNT DRACULA* VOULD HAFF MEN AND VIMEN *TREMBLING*...

MS. WOLFF AND MR. BYRD HAD A READING OF A *WILL* IN CONNECTICUT THIS EVENING--

IF THEY HAD *KNOWN* YOU WERE COMING BY, AT LEAST *ONE* OF THEM WOULD'VE STAYED HERE TO MEET WITH YOU

I HAFF HEARD FROM DEE *NEW BREED* OF VAMPIRE... DOT *MY* DAY HASS PASSED... DOT MY VAYS ARE DOSE OF DEE OLD VORLD

RRRRRNG

THAT MIGHT BE DEM, I MEAN *THEM,* NOW...

OH, MAN, TIMES MUST BE *TOUGH*-- DRACULA'S GETTING *WISTFUL*...

BUT DOSE DAYS VER FILLED VIT *PLEASURES* AND *POWER* DOT DEE NEW BREED HAFF NEFFER DREAMED UFF...

I KNOW, FOR I VAS DERE, AND I REMEMBER

SIGH

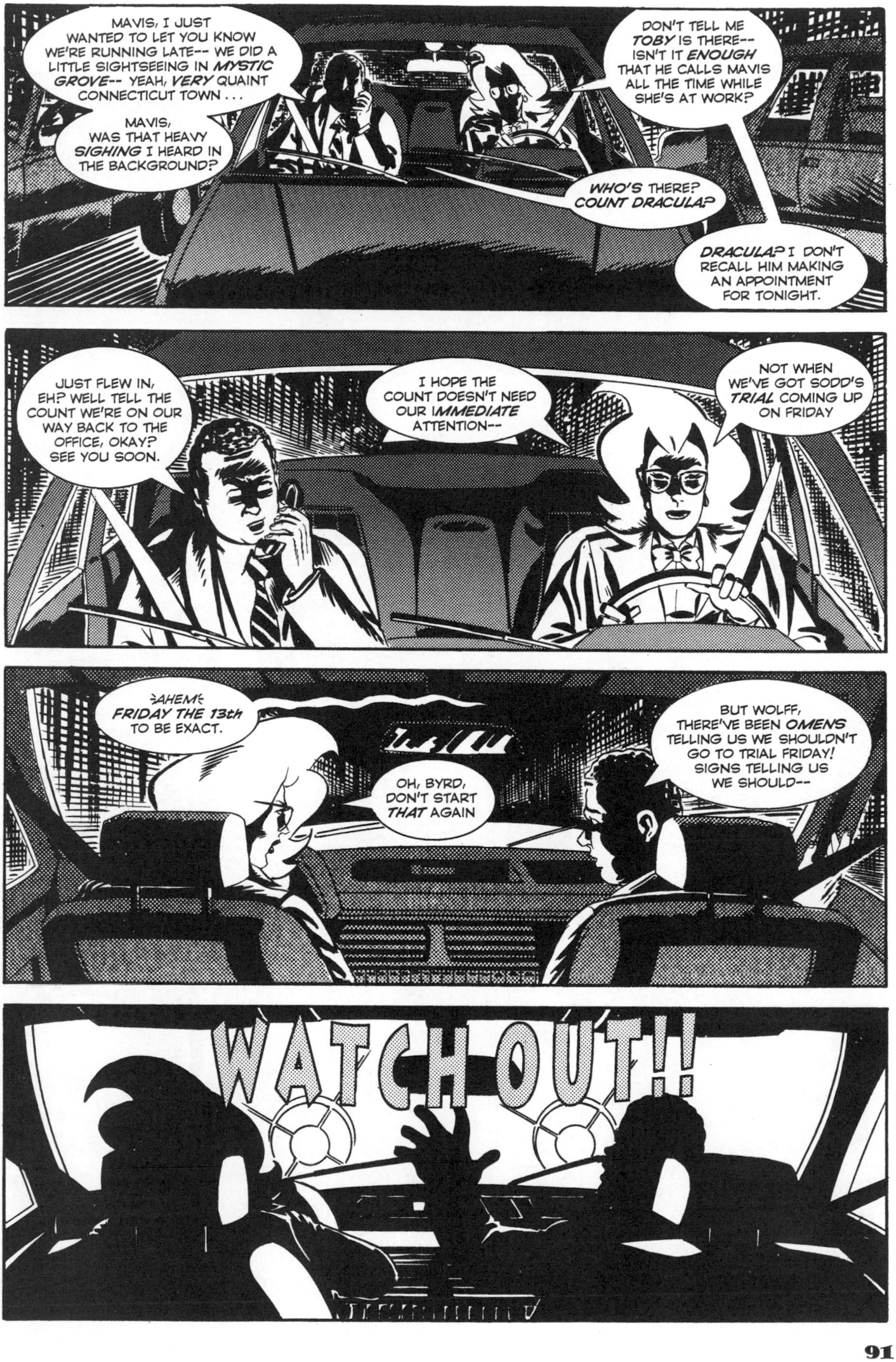
MAVIS, I JUST WANTED TO LET YOU KNOW WE'RE RUNNING LATE-- WE DID A LITTLE SIGHTSEEING IN MYSTIC GROVE-- YEAH, VERY QUAINT CONNECTICUT TOWN . . .
DON'T TELL ME TOBY IS THERE-- ISN'T IT ENOUGH THAT HE CALLS MAVIS ALL THE TIME WHILE SHE'S AT WORK?
MAVIS, WAS THAT HEAVY SIGHING I HEARD IN THE BACKGROUND?
WHO'S THERE? COUNT DRACULA?
DRACULA? I DON'T RECALL HIM MAKING AN APPOINTMENT FOR TONIGHT.
JUST FLEW IN, EH? WELL TELL THE COUNT WE'RE ON OUR WAY BACK TO THE OFFICE, OKAY? SEE YOU SOON.
I HOPE THE COUNT DOESN'T NEED OUR IMMEDIATE ATTENTION--
NOT WHEN WE'VE GOT SODD'S TRIAL COMING UP ON FRIDAY
AHEM FRIDAY THE 13th TO BE EXACT.
BUT WOLFF, THERE'VE BEEN OMENS TELLING US WE SHOULDN'T GO TO TRIAL FRIDAY! SIGNS TELLING US WE SHOULD--
OH, BYRD, DON'T START THAT AGAIN
WATCH OUT!!

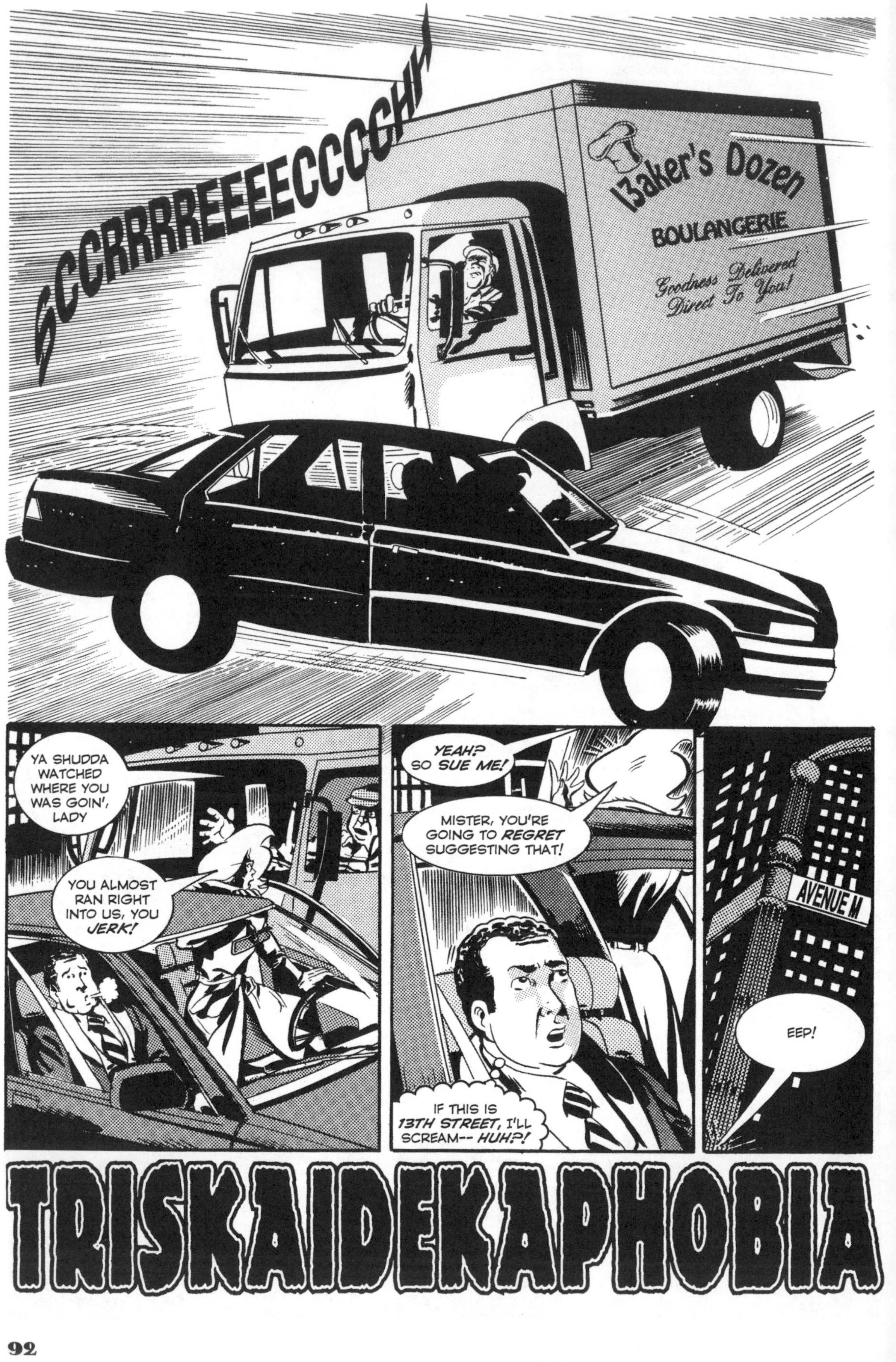
SCCRRRREEEECCCCHH
Baker's Dozen
BOULANGERIE
Goodness Delivered Direct To You!
YA SHUDDA WATCHED WHERE YOU WAS GOIN', LADY
YOU ALMOST RAN RIGHT INTO US, YOU JERK!
YEAH? SO SUE ME!
MISTER, YOU'RE GOING TO REGRET SUGGESTING THAT!
IF THIS IS 13TH STREET, I'LL SCREAM-- HUH?!
AVENUE M
EEP!

TRISKAIDEKAPHOBIA

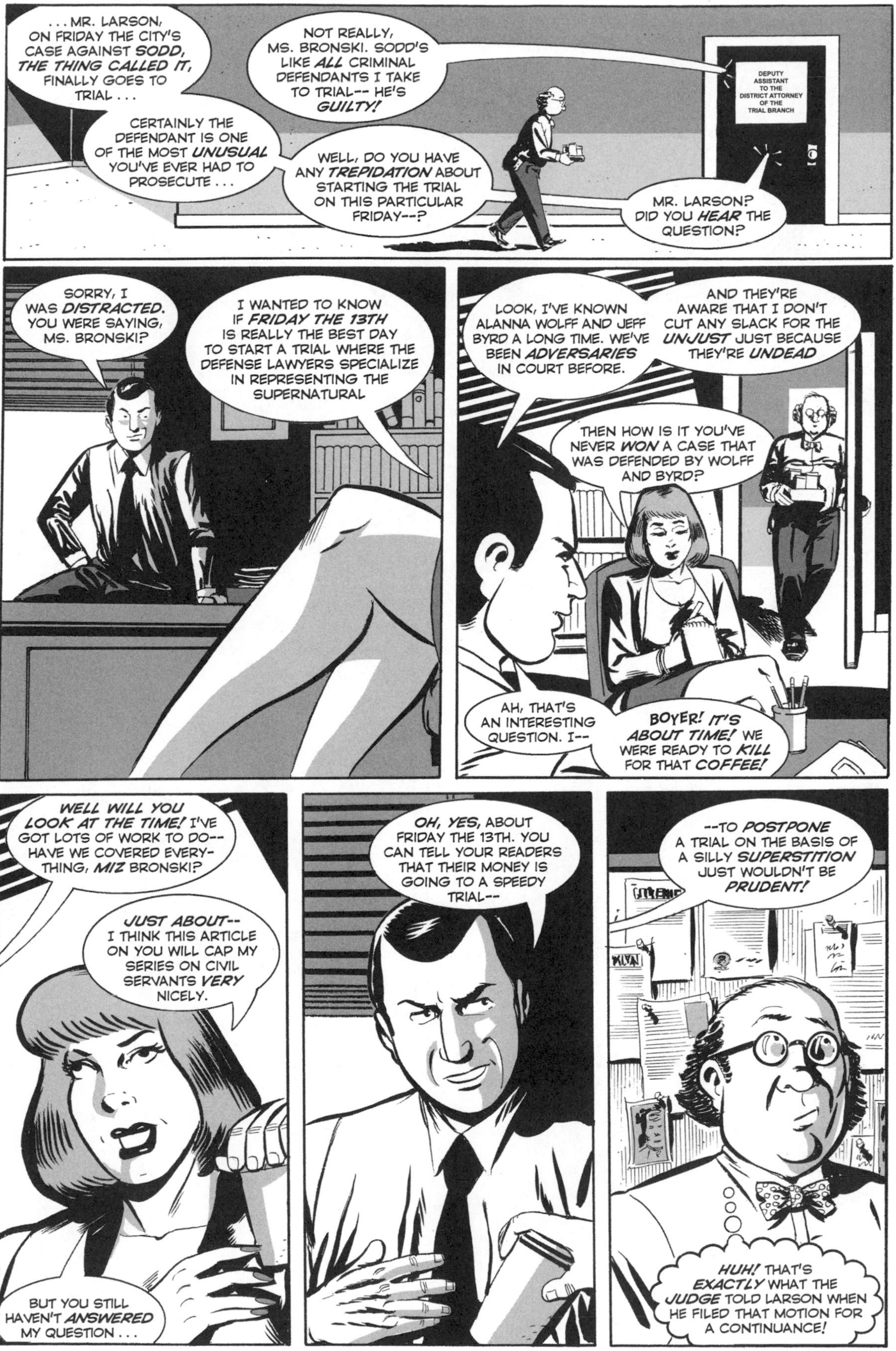
. . . MR. LARSON, ON FRIDAY THE CITY'S CASE AGAINST SODD, THE THING CALLED IT, FINALLY GOES TO TRIAL . . .
CERTAINLY THE DEFENDANT IS ONE OF THE MOST UNUSUAL YOU'VE EVER HAD TO PROSECUTE . . .
NOT REALLY, MS. BRONSKI. SODD'S LIKE ALL CRIMINAL DEFENDANTS I TAKE TO TRIAL-- HE'S GUILTY!
WELL, DO YOU HAVE ANY TREPIDATION ABOUT STARTING THE TRIAL ON THIS PARTICULAR FRIDAY--?
DEPUTY ASSISTANT TO THE DISTRICT ATTORNEY OF THE TRIAL BRANCH
MR. LARSON? DID YOU HEAR THE QUESTION?
SORRY, I WAS DISTRACTED. YOU WERE SAYING, MS. BRONSKI?
I WANTED TO KNOW IF FRIDAY THE 13TH IS REALLY THE BEST DAY TO START A TRIAL WHERE THE DEFENSE LAWYERS SPECIALIZE IN REPRESENTING THE SUPERNATURAL
LOOK, I'VE KNOWN ALANNA WOLFF AND JEFF BYRD A LONG TIME. WE'VE BEEN ADVERSARIES IN COURT BEFORE.
AND THEY'RE AWARE THAT I DON'T CUT ANY SLACK FOR THE UNJUST JUST BECAUSE THEY'RE UNDEAD
THEN HOW IS IT YOU'VE NEVER WON A CASE THAT WAS DEFENDED BY WOLFF AND BYRD?
AH, THAT'S AN INTERESTING QUESTION. I--
BOYER! IT'S ABOUT TIME! WE WERE READY TO KILL FOR THAT COFFEE!
WELL WILL YOU LOOK AT THE TIME! I'VE GOT LOTS OF WORK TO DO-- HAVE WE COVERED EVERY-THING, MIZ BRONSKI?
JUST ABOUT-- I THINK THIS ARTICLE ON YOU WILL CAP MY SERIES ON CIVIL SERVANTS VERY NICELY.
BUT YOU STILL HAVEN'T ANSWERED MY QUESTION . . .
OH, YES, ABOUT FRIDAY THE 13TH. YOU CAN TELL YOUR READERS THAT THEIR MONEY IS GOING TO A SPEEDY TRIAL--
--TO POSTPONE A TRIAL ON THE BASIS OF A SILLY SUPERSTITION JUST WOULDN'T BE PRUDENT!
HUH! THAT'S EXACTLY WHAT THE JUDGE TOLD LARSON WHEN HE FILED THAT MOTION FOR A CONTINUANCE!

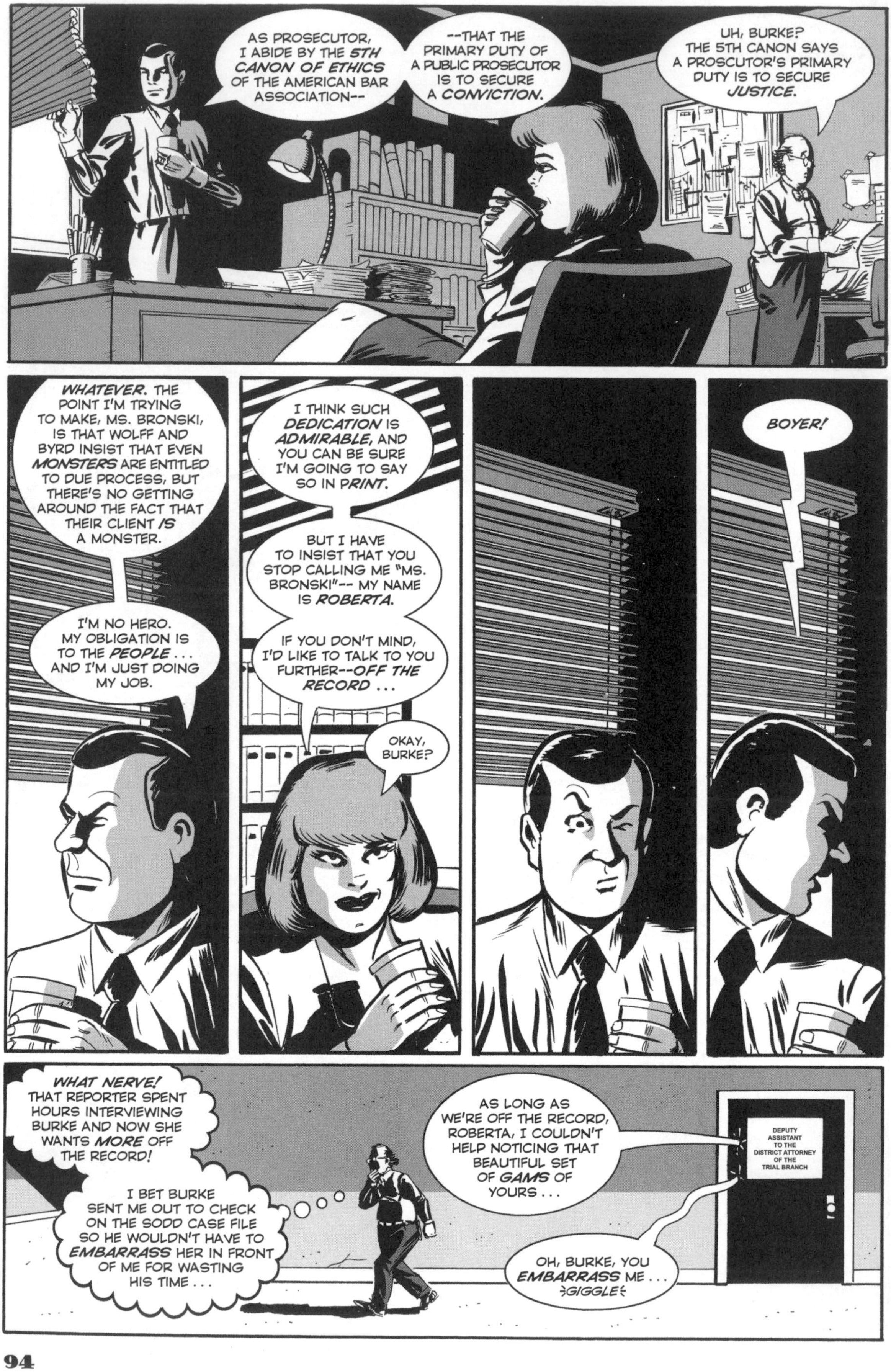
AS PROSECUTOR, I ABIDE BY THE 5TH CANON OF ETHICS OF THE AMERICAN BAR ASSOCIATION--
--THAT THE PRIMARY DUTY OF A PUBLIC PROSECUTOR IS TO SECURE A CONVICTION.
UH, BURKE? THE 5TH CANON SAYS A PROSCUTOR'S PRIMARY DUTY IS TO SECURE JUSTICE.
WHATEVER. THE POINT I'M TRYING TO MAKE, MS. BRONSKI, IS THAT WOLFF AND BYRD INSIST THAT EVEN MONSTERS ARE ENTITLED TO DUE PROCESS, BUT THERE'S NO GETTING AROUND THE FACT THAT THEIR CLIENT IS A MONSTER.
I'M NO HERO. MY OBLIGATION IS TO THE PEOPLE . . . AND I'M JUST DOING MY JOB.
I THINK SUCH DEDICATION IS ADMIRABLE, AND YOU CAN BE SURE I'M GOING TO SAY SO IN PRINT.
BUT I HAVE TO INSIST THAT YOU STOP CALLING ME "MS. BRONSKI"-- MY NAME IS ROBERTA.
IF YOU DON'T MIND, I'D LIKE TO TALK TO YOU FURTHER--OFF THE RECORD . . .
OKAY, BURKE?
BOYER!
WHAT NERVE! THAT REPORTER SPENT HOURS INTERVIEWING BURKE AND NOW SHE WANTS MORE OFF THE RECORD!
I BET BURKE SENT ME OUT TO CHECK ON THE SODD CASE FILE SO HE WOULDN'T HAVE TO EMBARRASS HER IN FRONT OF ME FOR WASTING HIS TIME . . .
AS LONG AS WE'RE OFF THE RECORD, ROBERTA, I COULDN'T HELP NOTICING THAT BEAUTIFUL SET OF GAMS OF YOURS . . .
DEPUTY ASSISTANT TO THE DISTRICT ATTORNEY OF THE TRIAL BRANCH
OH, BURKE, YOU EMBARRASS ME . . .
GIGGLE

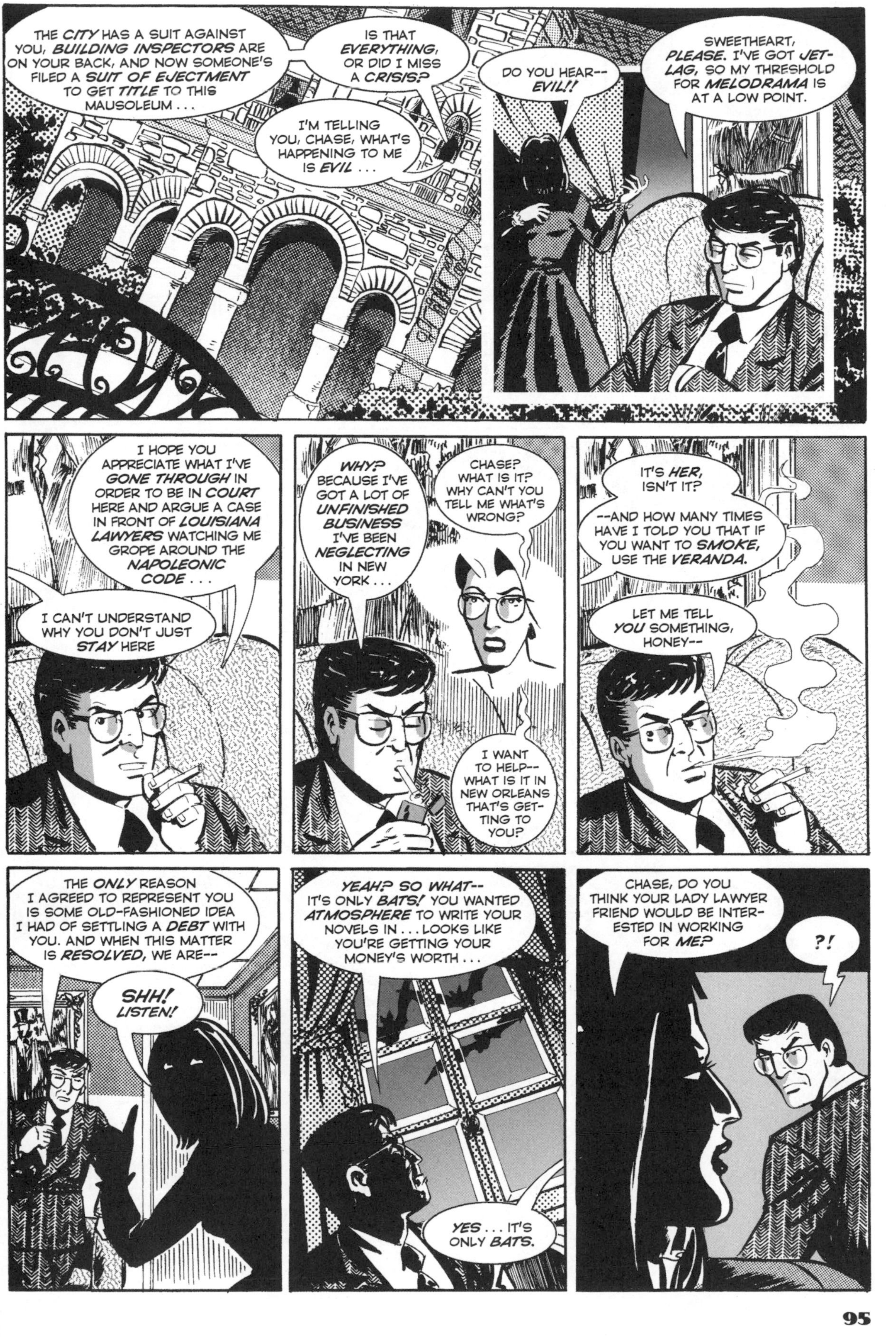
THE CITY HAS A SUIT AGAINST YOU, BUILDING INSPECTORS ARE ON YOUR BACK, AND NOW SOMEONE'S FILED A SUIT OF EJECTMENT TO GET TITLE TO THIS MAUSOLEUM . . .
IS THAT EVERYTHING, OR DID I MISS A CRISIS?
I'M TELLING YOU, CHASE, WHAT'S HAPPENING TO ME IS EVIL . . .
DO YOU HEAR-- EVIL!!
SWEETHEART, PLEASE. I'VE GOT JET-LAG, SO MY THRESHOLD FOR MELODRAMA IS AT A LOW POINT.
I HOPE YOU APPRECIATE WHAT I'VE GONE THROUGH IN ORDER TO BE IN COURT HERE AND ARGUE A CASE IN FRONT OF LOUISIANA LAWYERS WATCHING ME GROPE AROUND THE NAPOLEONIC CODE . . .
I CAN'T UNDERSTAND WHY YOU DON'T JUST STAY HERE
WHY? BECAUSE I'VE GOT A LOT OF UNFINISHED BUSINESS I'VE BEEN NEGLECTING IN NEW YORK . . .
CHASE? WHAT IS IT? WHY CAN'T YOU TELL ME WHAT'S WRONG?
I WANT TO HELP-- WHAT IS IT IN NEW ORLEANS THAT'S GETTING TO YOU?
IT'S HER, ISN'T IT?
--AND HOW MANY TIMES HAVE I TOLD YOU THAT IF YOU WANT TO SMOKE, USE THE VERANDA.
LET ME TELL YOU SOMETHING, HONEY--
THE ONLY REASON I AGREED TO REPRESENT YOU IS SOME OLD-FASHIONED IDEA I HAD OF SETTLING A DEBT WITH YOU. AND WHEN THIS MATTER IS RESOLVED, WE ARE--
SHH! LISTEN!
YEAH? SO WHAT-- IT'S ONLY BATS! YOU WANTED ATMOSPHERE TO WRITE YOUR NOVELS IN . . . LOOKS LIKE YOU'RE GETTING YOUR MONEY'S WORTH . . .
YES . . . IT'S ONLY BATS.
CHASE, DO YOU THINK YOUR LADY LAWYER FRIEND WOULD BE INTERESTED IN WORKING FOR ME?
?!

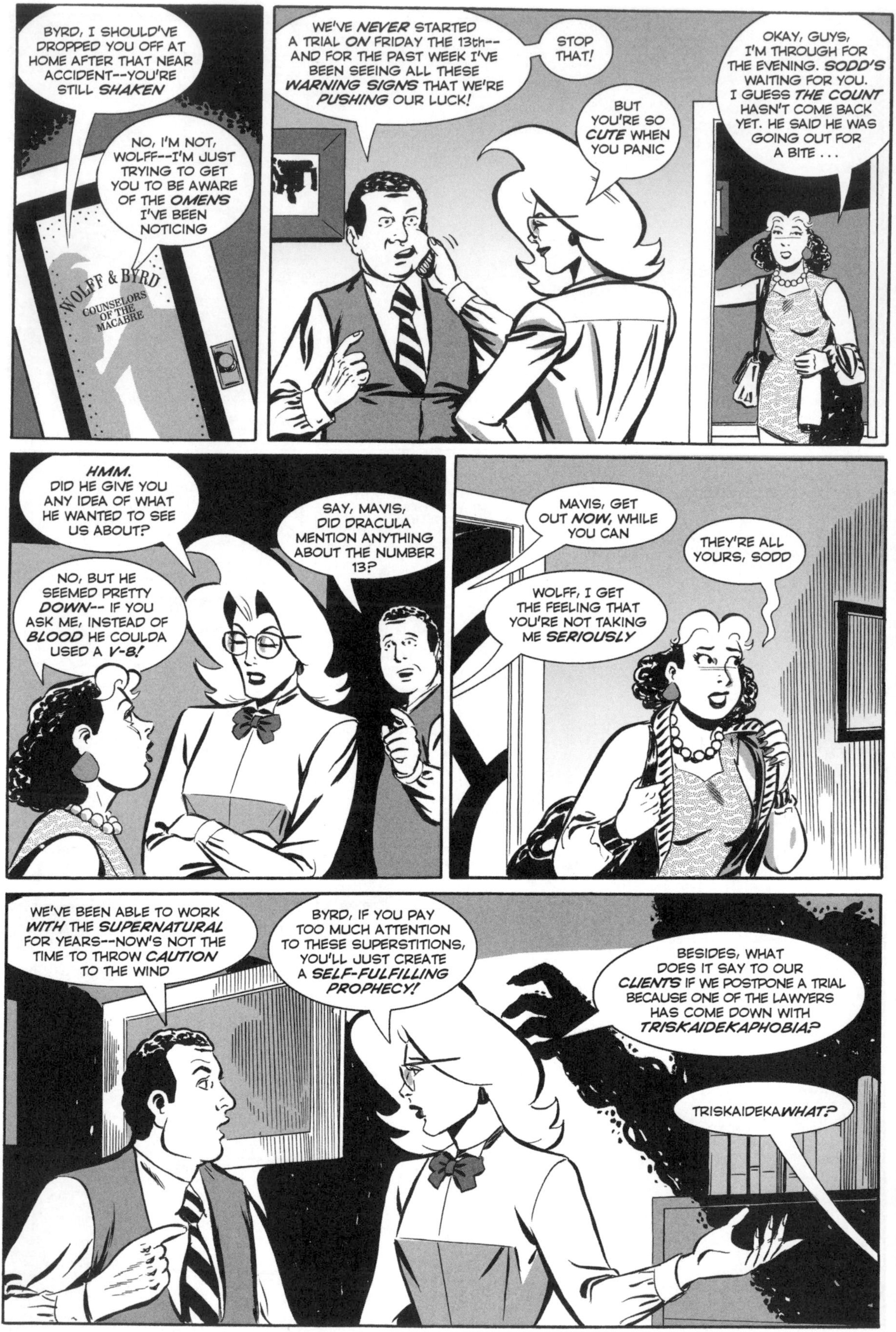
BYRD, I SHOULD'VE DROPPED YOU OFF AT HOME AFTER THAT NEAR ACCIDENT--YOU'RE STILL SHAKEN
NO, I'M NOT, WOLFF--I'M JUST TRYING TO GET YOU TO BE AWARE OF THE OMENS I'VE BEEN NOTICING
WOLFF & BYRD
COUNSELORS OF THE MACABRE
WE'VE NEVER STARTED A TRIAL ON FRIDAY THE 13th-- AND FOR THE PAST WEEK I'VE BEEN SEEING ALL THESE WARNING SIGNS THAT WE'RE PUSHING OUR LUCK!
STOP THAT!
BUT YOU'RE SO CUTE WHEN YOU PANIC
OKAY, GUYS, I'M THROUGH FOR THE EVENING. SODD'S WAITING FOR YOU. I GUESS THE COUNT HASN'T COME BACK YET. HE SAID HE WAS GOING OUT FOR A BITE . . .
HMM. DID HE GIVE YOU ANY IDEA OF WHAT HE WANTED TO SEE US ABOUT?
NO, BUT HE SEEMED PRETTY DOWN-- IF YOU ASK ME, INSTEAD OF BLOOD HE COULDA USED A V-8!
SAY, MAVIS, DID DRACULA MENTION ANYTHING ABOUT THE NUMBER 13?
MAVIS, GET OUT NOW, WHILE YOU CAN
THEY'RE ALL YOURS, SODD
WOLFF, I GET THE FEELING THAT YOU'RE NOT TAKING ME SERIOUSLY
WE'VE BEEN ABLE TO WORK WITH THE SUPERNATURAL FOR YEARS--NOW'S NOT THE TIME TO THROW CAUTION TO THE WIND
BYRD, IF YOU PAY TOO MUCH ATTENTION TO THESE SUPERSTITIONS, YOU'LL JUST CREATE A SELF-FULFILLING PROPHECY!
BESIDES, WHAT DOES IT SAY TO OUR CLIENTS IF WE POSTPONE A TRIAL BECAUSE ONE OF THE LAWYERS HAS COME DOWN WITH TRISKAIDEKAPHOBIA?
TRISKAIDEKAWHAT?

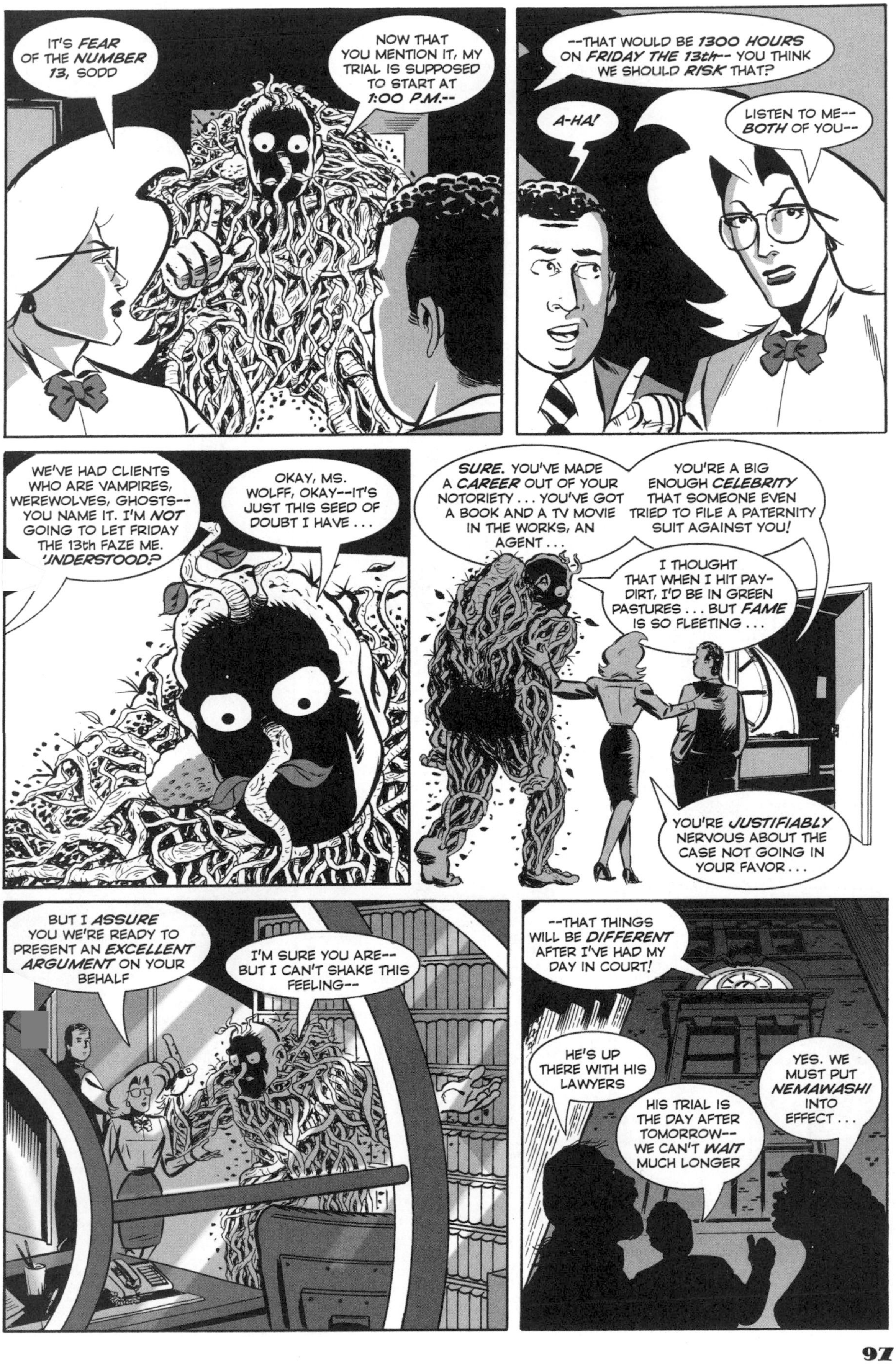
IT'S FEAR OF THE NUMBER 13, SODD
NOW THAT YOU MENTION IT, MY TRIAL IS SUPPOSED TO START AT 1:00 P.M.--
--THAT WOULD BE 1300 HOURS ON FRIDAY THE 13th-- YOU THINK WE SHOULD RISK THAT?
A-HA!
LISTEN TO ME-- BOTH OF YOU--
WE'VE HAD CLIENTS WHO ARE VAMPIRES, WEREWOLVES, GHOSTS-- YOU NAME IT. I'M NOT GOING TO LET FRIDAY THE 13th FAZE ME. UNDERSTOOD?
OKAY, MS. WOLFF, OKAY--IT'S JUST THIS SEED OF DOUBT I HAVE . . .
SURE. YOU'VE MADE A CAREER OUT OF YOUR NOTORIETY . . . YOU'VE GOT A BOOK AND A TV MOVIE IN THE WORKS, AN AGENT . . .
YOU'RE A BIG ENOUGH CELEBRITY THAT SOMEONE EVEN TRIED TO FILE A PATERNITY SUIT AGAINST YOU!
I THOUGHT THAT WHEN I HIT PAY-DIRT, I'D BE IN GREEN PASTURES . . . BUT FAME IS SO FLEETING . . .
YOU'RE JUSTIFIABLY NERVOUS ABOUT THE CASE NOT GOING IN YOUR FAVOR . . .
BUT I ASSURE YOU WE'RE READY TO PRESENT AN EXCELLENT ARGUMENT ON YOUR BEHALF
I'M SURE YOU ARE-- BUT I CAN'T SHAKE THIS FEELING--
--THAT THINGS WILL BE DIFFERENT AFTER I'VE HAD MY DAY IN COURT!
HE'S UP THERE WITH HIS LAWYERS
HIS TRIAL IS THE DAY AFTER TOMORROW-- WE CAN'T WAIT MUCH LONGER
YES. WE MUST PUT NEMAWASHI INTO EFFECT . . .

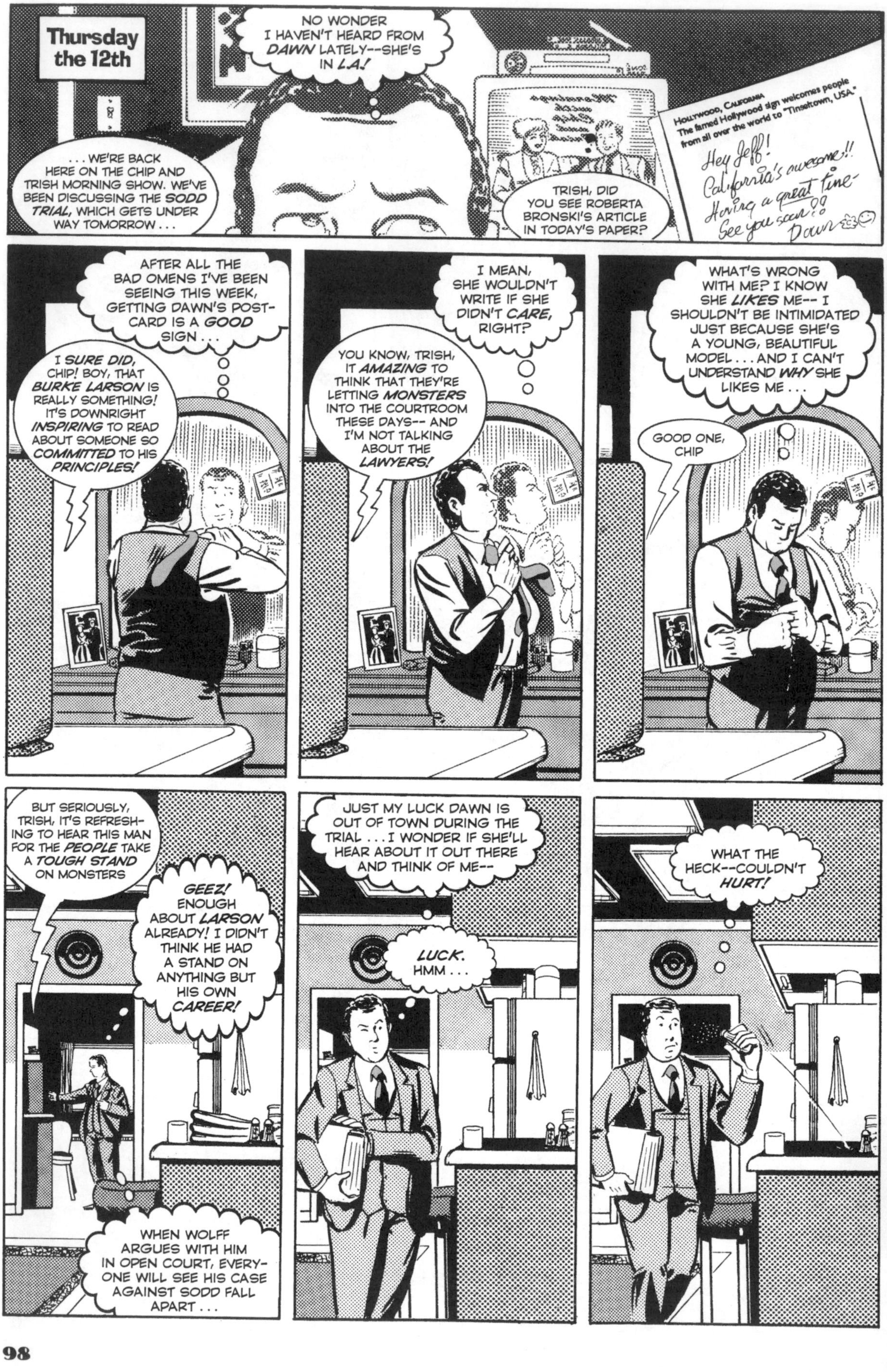
Thursday the 12th
NO WONDER I HAVEN'T HEARD FROM DAWN LATELY--SHE'S IN L.A.!
. . . WE'RE BACK HERE ON THE CHIP AND TRISH MORNING SHOW. WE'VE BEEN DISCUSSING THE SODD TRIAL, WHICH GETS UNDER WAY TOMORROW . . .
TRISH, DID YOU SEE ROBERTA BRONSKI'S ARTICLE IN TODAY'S PAPER?
HOLLYWOOD, CALIFORNIA The famed Hollywood sign welcomes people from all over the world to "Tinseltown, USA."
Hey Jeff! California's awesome!! Having a great time- See you soon!! Dawn
AFTER ALL THE BAD OMENS I'VE BEEN SEEING THIS WEEK, GETTING DAWN'S POST-CARD IS A GOOD SIGN . . .
I SURE DID, CHIP! BOY, THAT BURKE LARSON IS REALLY SOMETHING! IT'S DOWNRIGHT INSPIRING TO READ ABOUT SOMEONE SO COMMITTED TO HIS PRINCIPLES!
I MEAN, SHE WOULDN'T WRITE IF SHE DIDN'T CARE, RIGHT?
YOU KNOW, TRISH, IT AMAZING TO THINK THAT THEY'RE LETTING MONSTERS INTO THE COURTROOM THESE DAYS-- AND I'M NOT TALKING ABOUT THE LAWYERS!
WHAT'S WRONG WITH ME? I KNOW SHE LIKES ME-- I SHOULDN'T BE INTIMIDATED JUST BECAUSE SHE'S A YOUNG, BEAUTIFUL MODEL . . . AND I CAN'T UNDERSTAND WHY SHE LIKES ME . . .
GOOD ONE, CHIP
BUT SERIOUSLY, TRISH, IT'S REFRESH-ING TO HEAR THIS MAN FOR THE PEOPLE TAKE A TOUGH STAND ON MONSTERS
GEEZ! ENOUGH ABOUT LARSON ALREADY! I DIDN'T THINK HE HAD A STAND ON ANYTHING BUT HIS OWN CAREER!
WHEN WOLFF ARGUES WITH HIM IN OPEN COURT, EVERY-ONE WILL SEE HIS CASE AGAINST SODD FALL APART . . .
JUST MY LUCK DAWN IS OUT OF TOWN DURING THE TRIAL . . . I WONDER IF SHE'LL HEAR ABOUT IT OUT THERE AND THINK OF ME--
LUCK. HMM . . .
WHAT THE HECK--COULDN'T HURT!

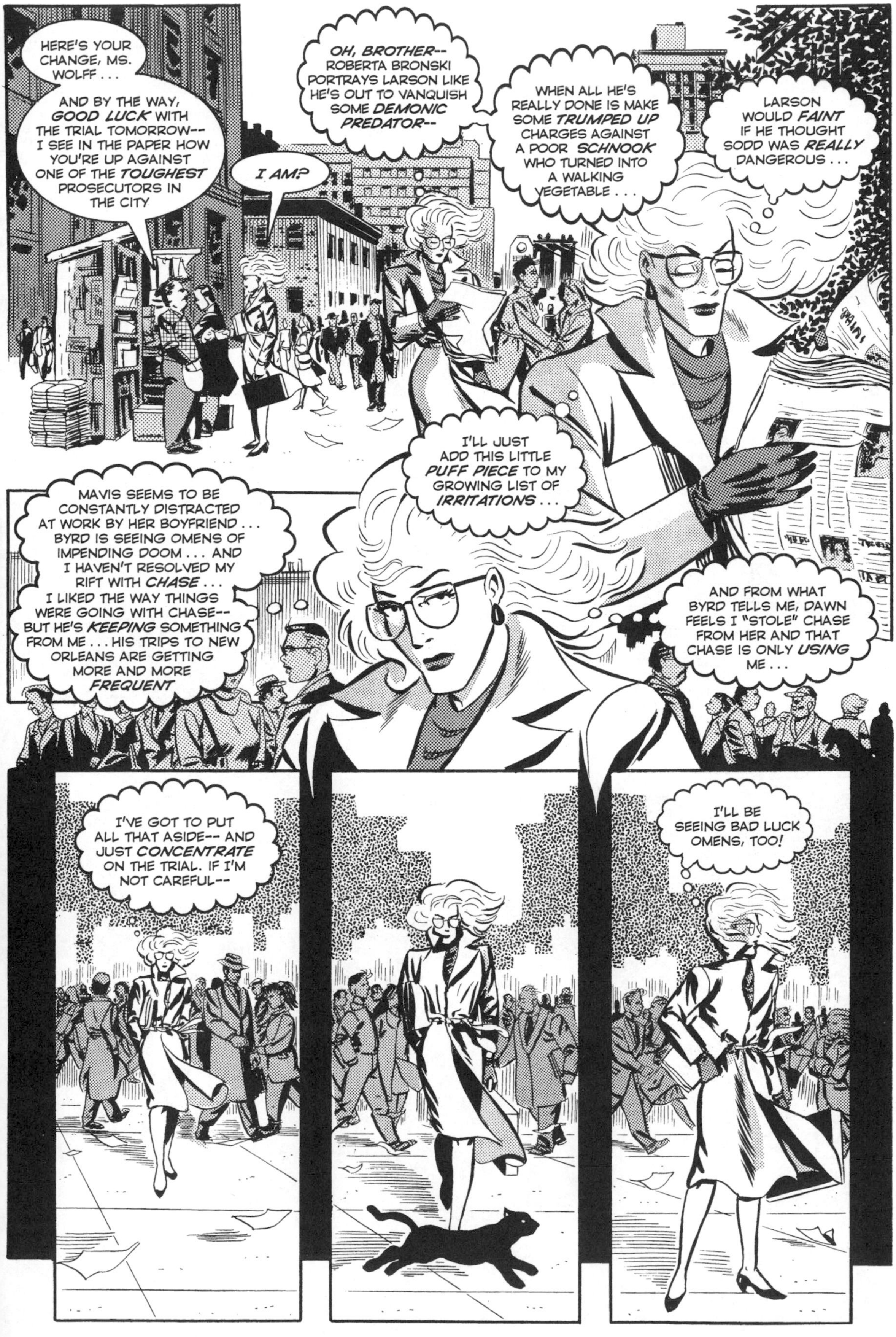
HERE'S YOUR CHANGE, MS. WOLFF . . .
AND BY THE WAY, GOOD LUCK WITH THE TRIAL TOMORROW-- I SEE IN THE PAPER HOW YOU'RE UP AGAINST ONE OF THE TOUGHEST PROSECUTORS IN THE CITY
I AM?
OH, BROTHER-- ROBERTA BRONSKI PORTRAYS LARSON LIKE HE'S OUT TO VANQUISH SOME DEMONIC PREDATOR--
WHEN ALL HE'S REALLY DONE IS MAKE SOME TRUMPED UP CHARGES AGAINST A POOR SCHNOOK WHO TURNED INTO A WALKING VEGETABLE . . .
LARSON WOULD FAINT IF HE THOUGHT SODD WAS REALLY DANGEROUS . . .
I'LL JUST ADD THIS LITTLE PUFF PIECE TO MY GROWING LIST OF IRRITATIONS . . .
MAVIS SEEMS TO BE CONSTANTLY DISTRACTED AT WORK BY HER BOYFRIEND . . . BYRD IS SEEING OMENS OF IMPENDING DOOM . . . AND I HAVEN'T RESOLVED MY RIFT WITH CHASE . . . I LIKED THE WAY THINGS WERE GOING WITH CHASE-- BUT HE'S KEEPING SOMETHING FROM ME . . . HIS TRIPS TO NEW ORLEANS ARE GETTING MORE AND MORE FREQUENT . . .
AND FROM WHAT BYRD TELLS ME, DAWN FEELS I "STOLE" CHASE FROM HER AND THAT CHASE IS ONLY USING ME . . .
I'VE GOT TO PUT ALL THAT ASIDE-- AND JUST CONCENTRATE ON THE TRIAL. IF I'M NOT CAREFUL--
I'LL BE SEEING BAD LUCK OMENS, TOO!

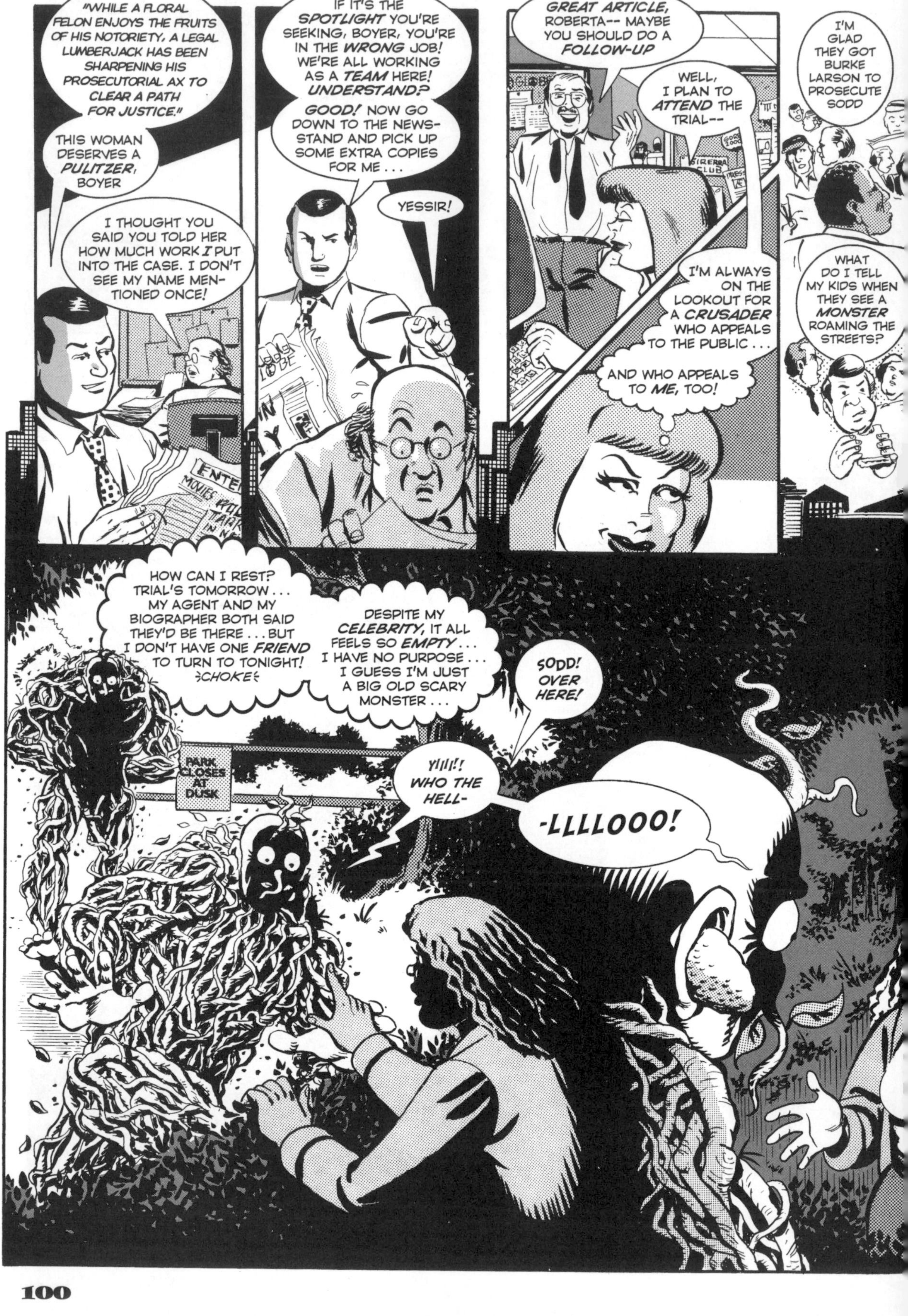
"WHILE A FLORAL FELON ENJOYS THE FRUITS OF HIS NOTORIETY, A LEGAL LUMBERJACK HAS BEEN SHARPENING HIS PROSECUTORIAL AX TO CLEAR A PATH FOR JUSTICE."
THIS WOMAN DESERVES A PULITZER, BOYER
I THOUGHT YOU SAID YOU TOLD HER HOW MUCH WORK I PUT INTO THE CASE. I DON'T SEE MY NAME MENTIONED ONCE!
IF IT'S THE SPOTLIGHT YOU'RE SEEKING, BOYER, YOU'RE IN THE WRONG JOB! WE'RE ALL WORKING AS A TEAM HERE! UNDERSTAND?
GOOD! NOW GO DOWN TO THE NEWS-STAND AND PICK UP SOME EXTRA COPIES FOR ME . . .
YESSIR!
GREAT ARTICLE, ROBERTA-- MAYBE YOU SHOULD DO A FOLLOW-UP
WELL, I PLAN TO ATTEND THE TRIAL--
I'M ALWAYS ON THE LOOKOUT FOR A CRUSADER WHO APPEALS TO THE PUBLIC . . .
AND WHO APPEALS TO ME, TOO!
I'M GLAD THEY GOT BURKE LARSON TO PROSECUTE SODD
WHAT DO I TELL MY KIDS WHEN THEY SEE A MONSTER ROAMING THE STREETS?
HOW CAN I REST? TRIAL'S TOMORROW . . . MY AGENT AND MY BIOGRAPHER BOTH SAID THEY'D BE THERE . . . BUT I DON'T HAVE ONE FRIEND TO TURN TO TONIGHT! *CHOKE*
DESPITE MY CELEBRITY, IT ALL FEELS SO EMPTY . . . I HAVE NO PURPOSE . . . I GUESS I'M JUST A BIG OLD SCARY MONSTER . . .
SODD! OVER HERE!
PARK CLOSES AT DUSK
YIII!! WHO THE HELL-
-LLLOOO!

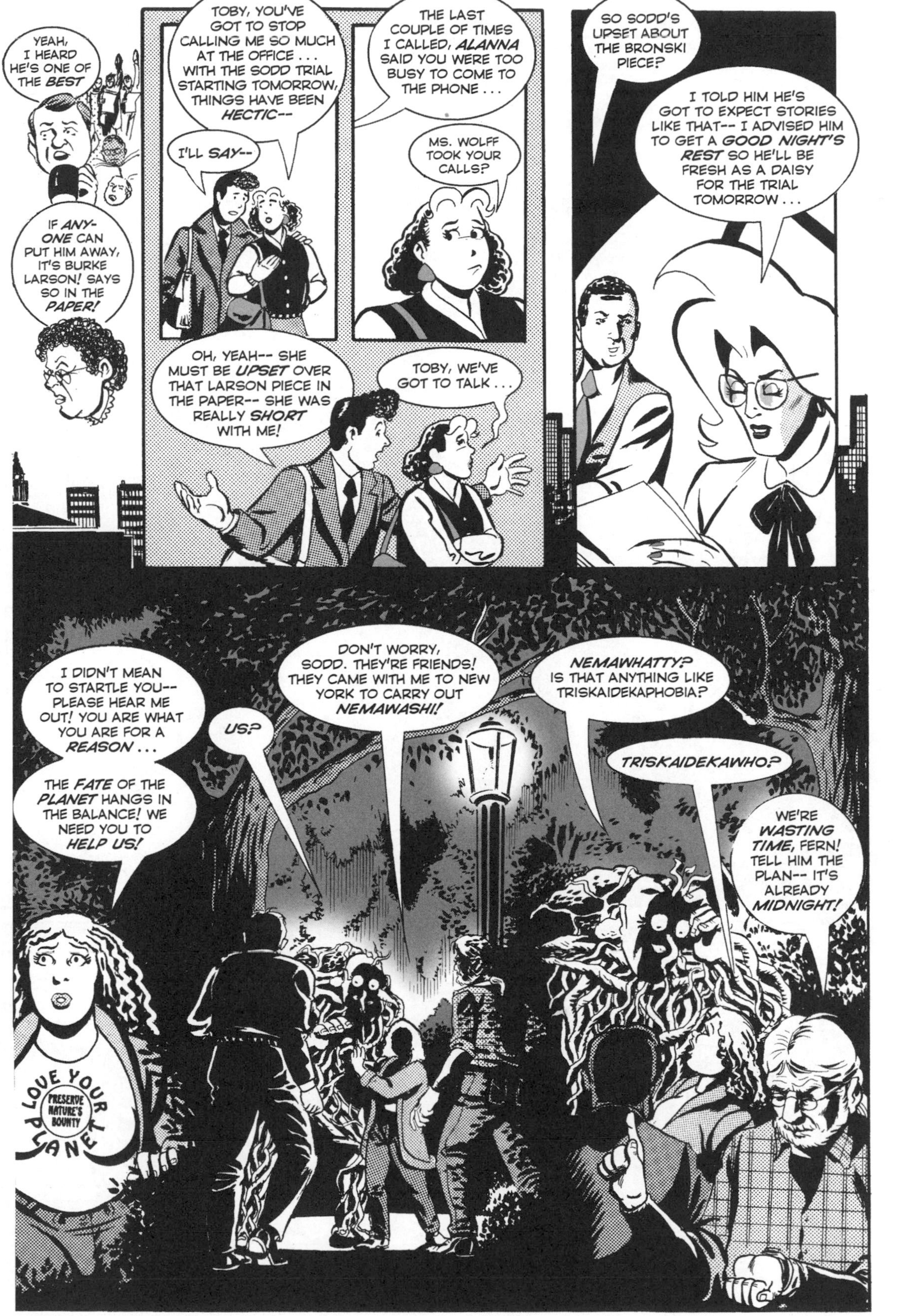
YEAH, I HEARD HE'S ONE OF THE BEST
IF ANYONE CAN PUT HIM AWAY, IT'S BURKE LARSON! SAYS SO IN THE PAPER!
TOBY, YOU'VE GOT TO STOP CALLING ME SO MUCH AT THE OFFICE . . . WITH THE SODD TRIAL STARTING TOMORROW, THINGS HAVE BEEN HECTIC--
I'LL SAY--
THE LAST COUPLE OF TIMES I CALLED, ALANNA SAID YOU WERE TOO BUSY TO COME TO THE PHONE . . .
MS. WOLFF TOOK YOUR CALLS?
OH, YEAH-- SHE MUST BE UPSET OVER THAT LARSON PIECE IN THE PAPER-- SHE WAS REALLY SHORT WITH ME!
TOBY, WE'VE GOT TO TALK . . .
SO SODD'S UPSET ABOUT THE BRONSKI PIECE?
I TOLD HIM HE'S GOT TO EXPECT STORIES LIKE THAT-- I ADVISED HIM TO GET A GOOD NIGHT'S REST SO HE'LL BE FRESH AS A DAISY FOR THE TRIAL TOMORROW . . .
I DIDN'T MEAN TO STARTLE YOU-- PLEASE HEAR ME OUT! YOU ARE WHAT YOU ARE FOR A REASON . . .
THE FATE OF THE PLANET HANGS IN THE BALANCE! WE NEED YOU TO HELP US!
US?
DON'T WORRY, SODD. THEY'RE FRIENDS! THEY CAME WITH ME TO NEW YORK TO CARRY OUT NEMAWASHI!
NEMAWHATTY? IS THAT ANYTHING LIKE TRISKAIDEKAPHOBIA?
TRISKAIDEKAWHO?
WE'RE WASTING TIME, FERN! TELL HIM THE PLAN-- IT'S ALREADY MIDNIGHT!
LOVE YOUR PLANET
PRESERVE NATURE'S BOUNTY

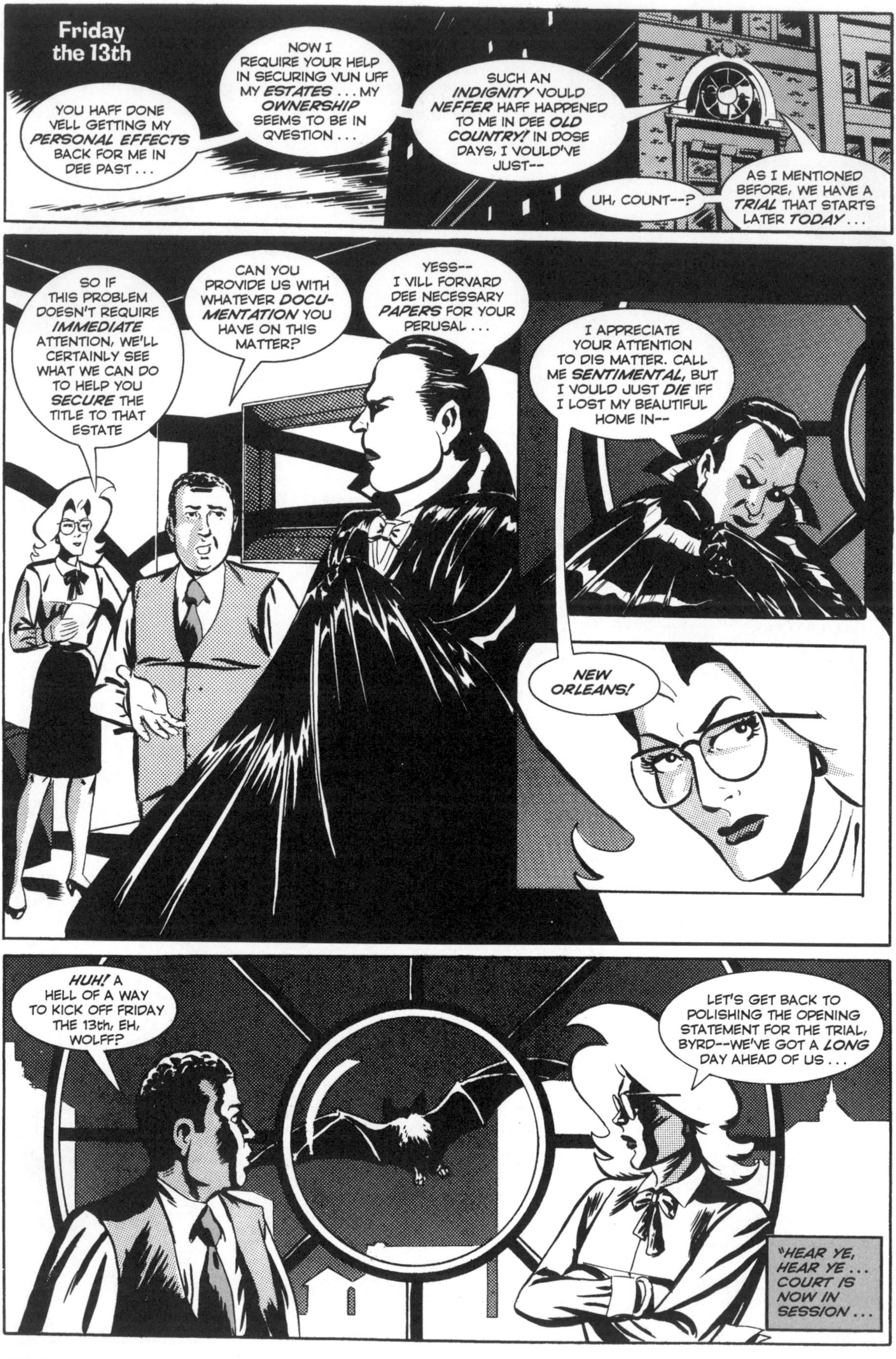
Friday the 13th
YOU HAFF DONE VELL GETTING MY PERSONAL EFFECTS BACK FOR ME IN DEE PAST . . .
NOW I REQUIRE YOUR HELP IN SECURING VUN UFF MY ESTATES . . . MY OWNERSHIP SEEMS TO BE IN QVESTION . . .
SUCH AN INDIGNITY VOULD NEFFER HAFF HAPPENED TO ME IN DEE OLD COUNTRY! IN DOSE DAYS, I VOULD'VE JUST--
UH, COUNT--?
AS I MENTIONED BEFORE, WE HAVE A TRIAL THAT STARTS LATER TODAY . . .
SO IF THIS PROBLEM DOESN'T REQUIRE IMMEDIATE ATTENTION, WE'LL CERTAINLY SEE WHAT WE CAN DO TO HELP YOU SECURE THE TITLE TO THAT ESTATE
CAN YOU PROVIDE US WITH WHATEVER DOCU-MENTATION YOU HAVE ON THIS MATTER?
YESS-- I VILL FORVARD DEE NECESSARY PAPERS FOR YOUR PERUSAL . . .
I APPRECIATE YOUR ATTENTION TO DIS MATTER. CALL ME SENTIMENTAL, BUT I VOULD JUST DIE IFF I LOST MY BEAUTIFUL HOME IN--
NEW ORLEANS!
HUH! A HELL OF A WAY TO KICK OFF FRIDAY THE 13th, EH, WOLFF?
LET'S GET BACK TO POLISHING THE OPENING STATEMENT FOR THE TRIAL, BYRD--WE'VE GOT A LONG DAY AHEAD OF US . . .
"HEAR YE, HEAR YE . . . COURT IS NOW IN SESSION . . .

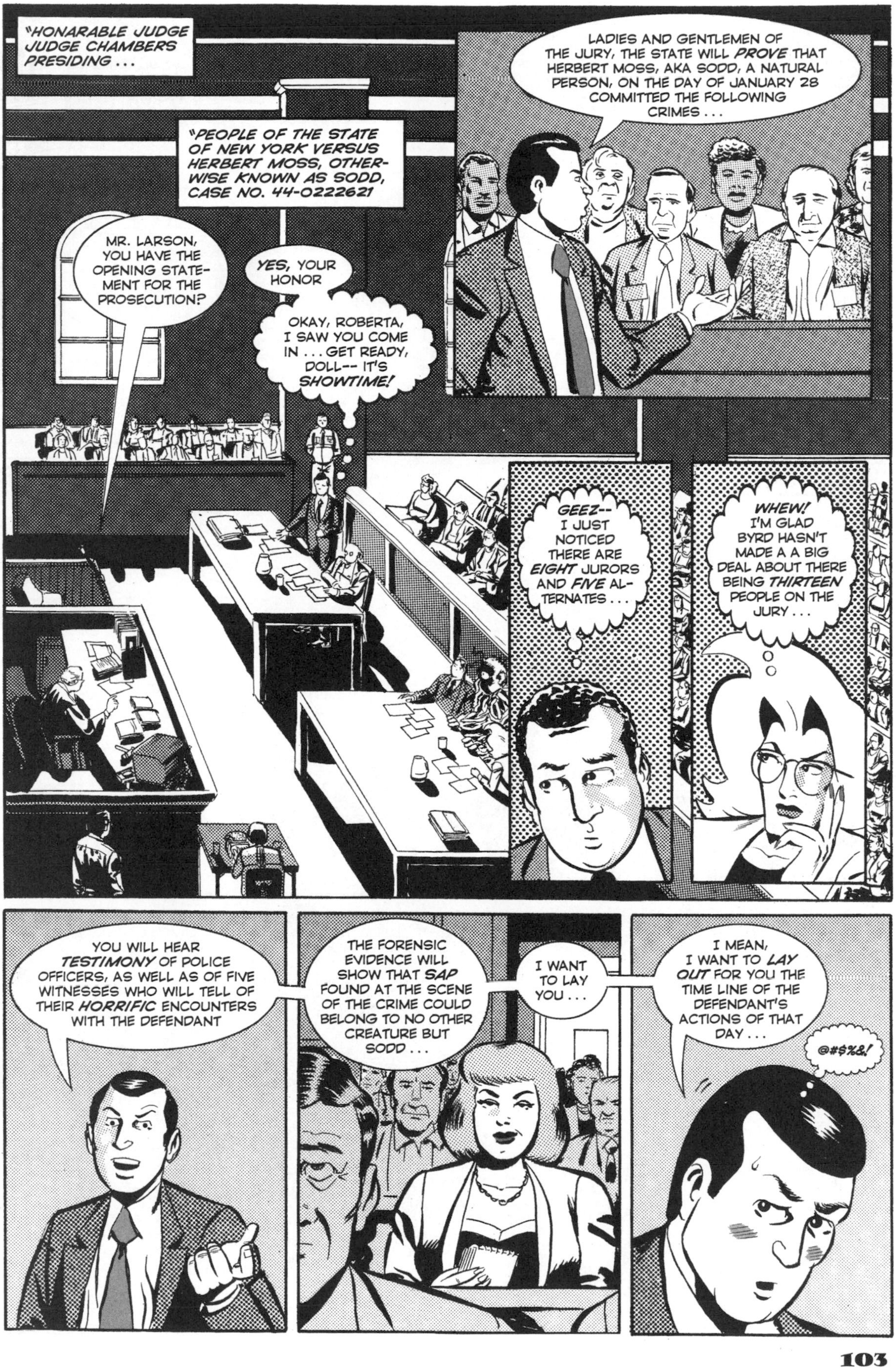
"HONARABLE JUDGE JUDGE CHAMBERS PRESIDING . . .
"PEOPLE OF THE STATE OF NEW YORK VERSUS HERBERT MOSS, OTHERWISE KNOWN AS SODD, CASE NO. 44-0222621
MR. LARSON, YOU HAVE THE OPENING STATEMENT FOR THE PROSECUTION?
YES, YOUR HONOR
OKAY, ROBERTA, I SAW YOU COME IN . . . GET READY, DOLL-- IT'S SHOWTIME!
LADIES AND GENTLEMEN OF THE JURY, THE STATE WILL PROVE THAT HERBERT MOSS, AKA SODD, A NATURAL PERSON, ON THE DAY OF JANUARY 28 COMMITTED THE FOLLOWING CRIMES . . .
GEEZ-- I JUST NOTICED THERE ARE EIGHT JURORS AND FIVE ALTERNATES . . .
WHEW! I'M GLAD BYRD HASN'T MADE A A BIG DEAL ABOUT THERE BEING THIRTEEN PEOPLE ON THE JURY . . .
YOU WILL HEAR TESTIMONY OF POLICE OFFICERS, AS WELL AS OF FIVE WITNESSES WHO WILL TELL OF THEIR HORRIFIC ENCOUNTERS WITH THE DEFENDANT
THE FORENSIC EVIDENCE WILL SHOW THAT SAP FOUND AT THE SCENE OF THE CRIME COULD BELONG TO NO OTHER CREATURE BUT SODD . . .
I WANT TO LAY YOU . . .
I MEAN, I WANT TO LAY OUT FOR YOU THE TIME LINE OF THE DEFENDANT'S ACTIONS OF THAT DAY . . .
@#$%&!

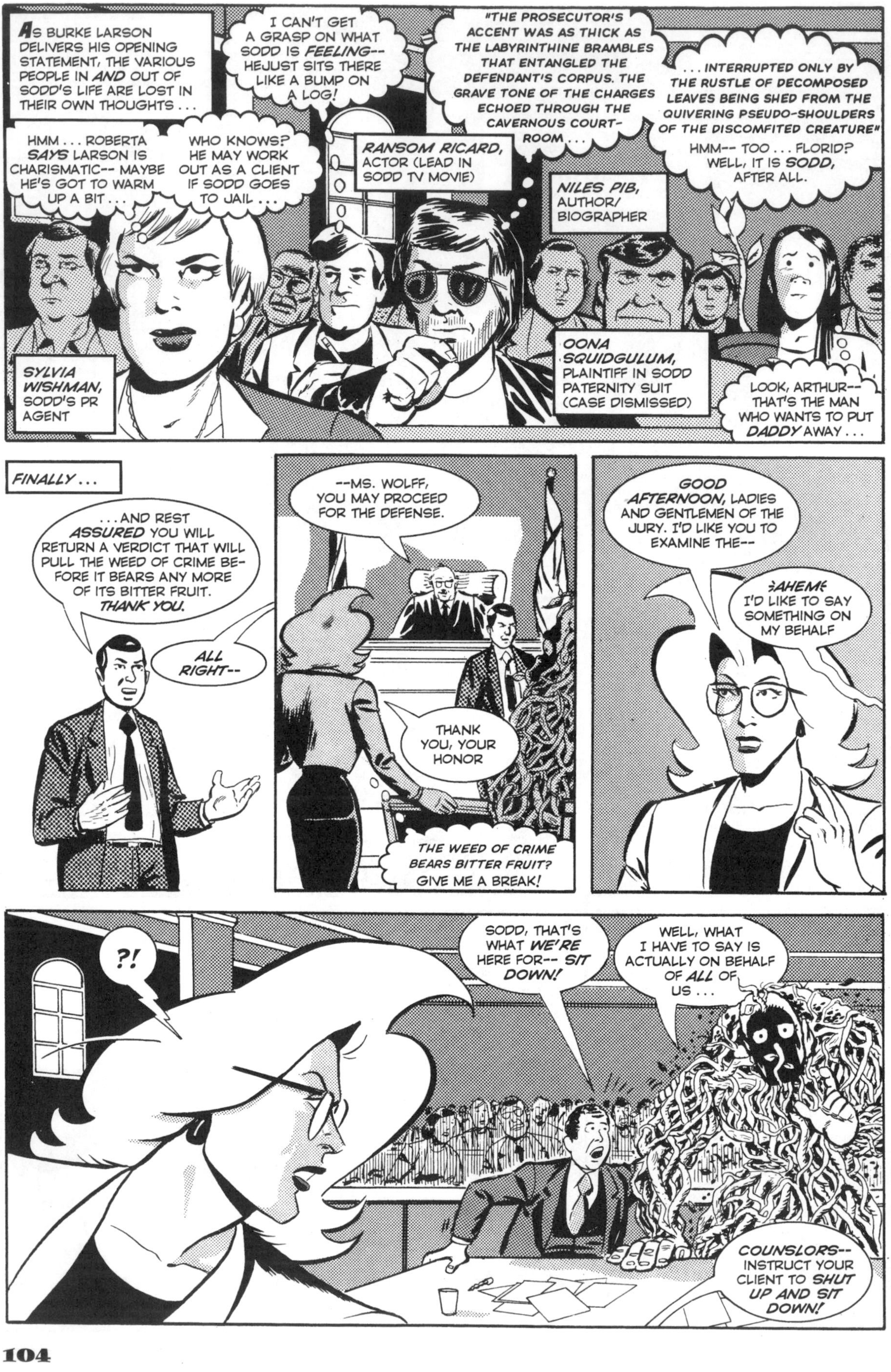

AS BURKE LARSON DELIVERS HIS OPENING STATEMENT, THE VARIOUS PEOPLE IN AND OUT OF SODD'S LIFE ARE LOST IN THEIR OWN THOUGHTS . . .
I CAN'T GET A GRASP ON WHAT SODD IS FEELING-- HEJUST SITS THERE LIKE A BUMP ON A LOG!
"THE PROSECUTOR'S ACCENT WAS AS THICK AS THE LABYRINTHINE BRAMBLES THAT ENTANGLED THE DEFENDANT'S CORPUS. THE GRAVE TONE OF THE CHARGES ECHOED THROUGH THE CAVERNOUS COURT-ROOM . . .
. . . INTERRUPTED ONLY BY THE RUSTLE OF DECOMPOSED LEAVES BEING SHED FROM THE QUIVERING PSEUDO-SHOULDERS OF THE DISCOMFITED CREATURE"
HMM-- TOO . . . FLORID? WELL, IT IS SODD, AFTER ALL.
HMM . . . ROBERTA SAYS LARSON IS CHARISMATIC-- MAYBE HE'S GOT TO WARM UP A BIT . . .
WHO KNOWS? HE MAY WORK OUT AS A CLIENT IF SODD GOES TO JAIL . . .
RANSOM RICARD, ACTOR (LEAD IN SODD TV MOVIE)
NILES PIB, AUTHOR/ BIOGRAPHER
SYLVIA WISHMAN, SODD'S PR AGENT
OONA SQUIDGULUM, PLAINTIFF IN SODD PATERNITY SUIT (CASE DISMISSED)
LOOK, ARTHUR-- THAT'S THE MAN WHO WANTS TO PUT DADDY AWAY . . .
FINALLY . . .
. . . AND REST ASSURED YOU WILL RETURN A VERDICT THAT WILL PULL THE WEED OF CRIME BEFORE IT BEARS ANY MORE OF ITS BITTER FRUIT. THANK YOU.
ALL RIGHT--
--MS. WOLFF, YOU MAY PROCEED FOR THE DEFENSE.
THANK YOU, YOUR HONOR
THE WEED OF CRIME BEARS BITTER FRUIT? GIVE ME A BREAK!
GOOD AFTERNOON, LADIES AND GENTLEMEN OF THE JURY. I'D LIKE YOU TO EXAMINE THE--
AHEM I'D LIKE TO SAY SOMETHING ON MY BEHALF
?!
SODD, THAT'S WHAT WE'RE HERE FOR-- SIT DOWN!
WELL, WHAT I HAVE TO SAY IS ACTUALLY ON BEHALF OF ALL OF US . . .
COUNSLORS-- INSTRUCT YOUR CLIENT TO SHUT UP AND SIT DOWN!

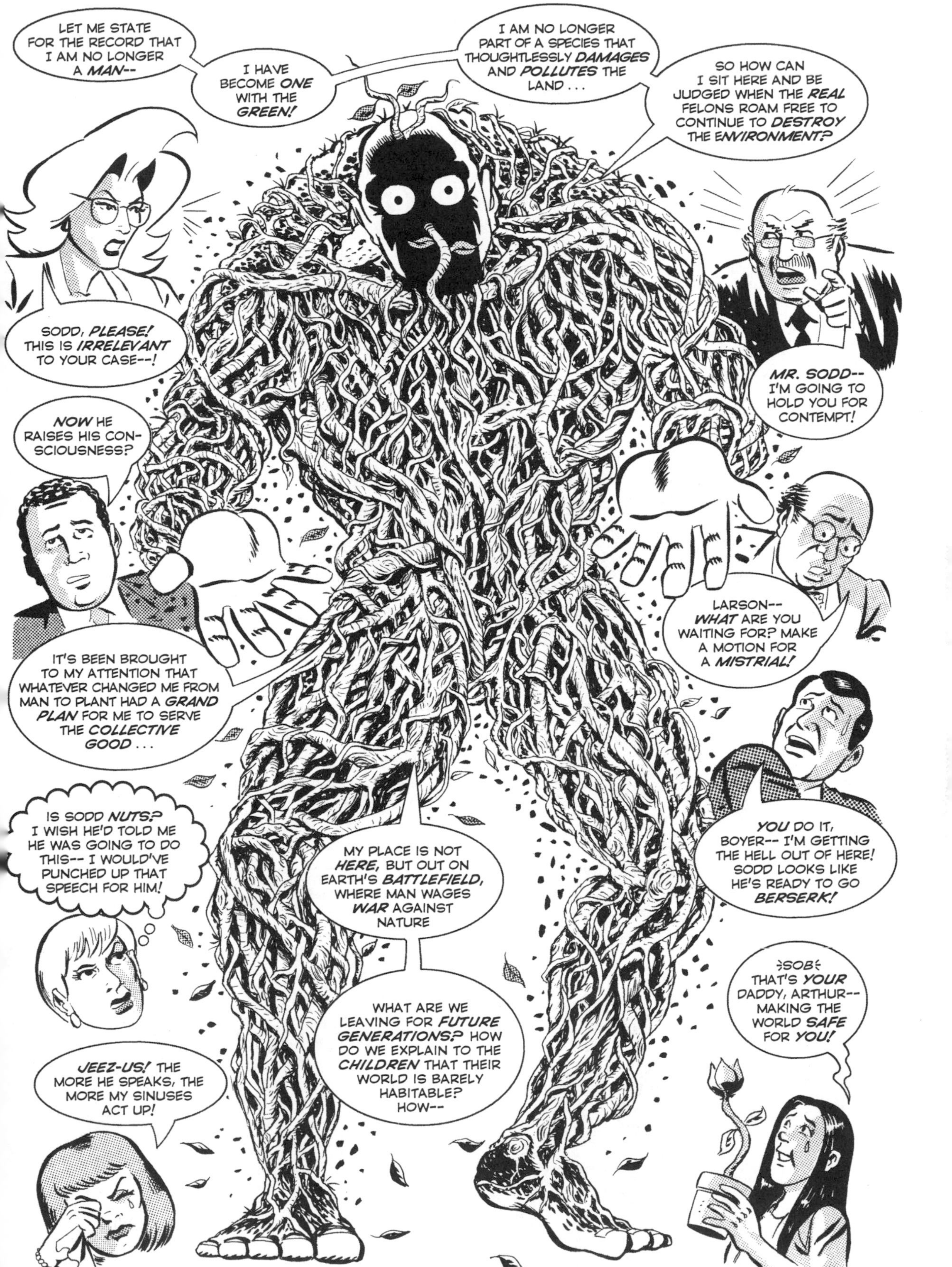
LET ME STATE FOR THE RECORD THAT I AM NO LONGER A MAN--
I HAVE BECOME ONE WITH THE GREEN!
I AM NO LONGER PART OF A SPECIES THAT THOUGHTLESSLY DAMAGES AND POLLUTES THE LAND . . .
SO HOW CAN I SIT HERE AND BE JUDGED WHEN THE REAL FELONS ROAM FREE TO CONTINUE TO DESTROY THE ENVIRONMENT?
SODD, PLEASE! THIS IS IRRELEVANT TO YOUR CASE--!
MR. SODD-- I'M GOING TO HOLD YOU FOR CONTEMPT!
NOW HE RAISES HIS CON-SCIOUSNESS?
LARSON-- WHAT ARE YOU WAITING FOR? MAKE A MOTION FOR A MISTRIAL!
IT'S BEEN BROUGHT TO MY ATTENTION THAT WHATEVER CHANGED ME FROM MAN TO PLANT HAD A GRAND PLAN FOR ME TO SERVE THE COLLECTIVE GOOD . . .
IS SODD NUTS? I WISH HE'D TOLD ME HE WAS GOING TO DO THIS-- I WOULD'VE PUNCHED UP THAT SPEECH FOR HIM!
MY PLACE IS NOT HERE, BUT OUT ON EARTH'S BATTLEFIELD, WHERE MAN WAGES WAR AGAINST NATURE
YOU DO IT, BOYER-- I'M GETTING THE HELL OUT OF HERE! SODD LOOKS LIKE HE'S READY TO GO BERSERK!
WHAT ARE WE LEAVING FOR FUTURE GENERATIONS? HOW DO WE EXPLAIN TO THE CHILDREN THAT THEIR WORLD IS BARELY HABITABLE? HOW--
SOB THAT'S YOUR DADDY, ARTHUR-- MAKING THE WORLD SAFE FOR YOU!
JEEZ-US! THE MORE HE SPEAKS, THE MORE MY SINUSES ACT UP!

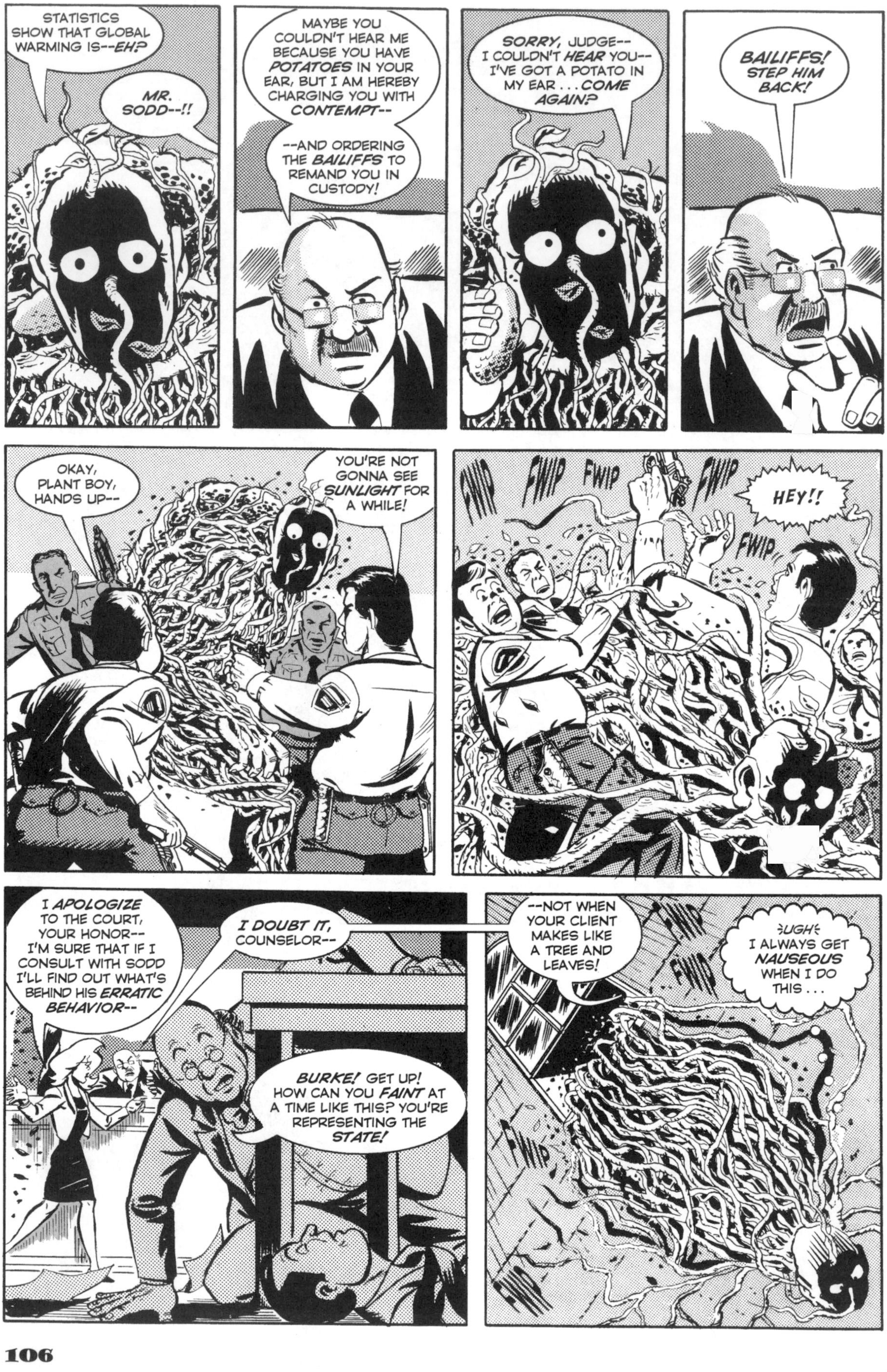
STATISTICS SHOW THAT GLOBAL WARMING IS--EH?
MR. SODD--!!
MAYBE YOU COULDN'T HEAR ME BECAUSE YOU HAVE POTATOES IN YOUR EAR, BUT I AM HEREBY CHARGING YOU WITH CONTEMPT--
--AND ORDERING THE BAILIFFS TO REMAND YOU IN CUSTODY!
SORRY, JUDGE-- I COULDN'T HEAR YOU-- I'VE GOT A POTATO IN MY EAR . . . COME AGAIN?
BAILIFFS! STEP HIM BACK!
OKAY, PLANT BOY, HANDS UP--
YOU'RE NOT GONNA SEE SUNLIGHT FOR A WHILE!
FWIP FWIP FWIP FWIP
HEY!!
FWIP
I APOLOGIZE TO THE COURT, YOUR HONOR-- I'M SURE THAT IF I CONSULT WITH SODD I'LL FIND OUT WHAT'S BEHIND HIS ERRATIC BEHAVIOR--
I DOUBT IT, COUNSELOR--
--NOT WHEN YOUR CLIENT MAKES LIKE A TREE AND LEAVES!
BURKE! GET UP! HOW CAN YOU FAINT AT A TIME LIKE THIS? YOU'RE REPRESENTING THE STATE!
UGH I ALWAYS GET NAUSEOUS WHEN I DO THIS . . .
FWIP FWIP FWIP

"ALTHOUGH *NO* CAMERAS WERE ALLOWED IN THE COURTROOM, OUR *ACTION REMOTE UNIT* CAUGHT SODD AS HE WAS *ESCAPING* DOWN THE OUTSIDE COURTHOUSE WALL. SODD TOOK FLIGHT MOMENTS AFTER HE *DRAMATICALLY* INTERRUPTED HIS OWN DEFENSE LAWYER'S OPENING STATEMENT TO GIVE AN *IMPASSIONED* PLEA TO SAVE THE ENVIRONMENT. SODD'S WHEREABOUTS ARE *UNKNOWN* . . . POLICE ARE COMBING THE LANDSCAPE FOR ANYONE FITTING SODD'S DESCRIPTION . . .

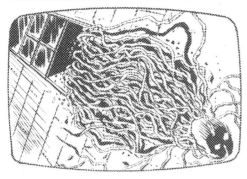

"HOURS AFTER SODD'S ESCAPE, THE STATION RECEIVED A CALL FROM A RADICAL ENVIRONMENTAL GROUP CALLING THEMSELVES *TERRA-ISTS*. THEY CLAIM THEY SUCCESSFULLY PERFORMED A *"SPIRITUAL"* NEMAWASHI ON SODD. *"NEMAWASHI"* IS A TERM FOR CUTTING AROUND THE ROOTS OF A PLANT BEFORE IT IS TO BE *TRANSPLANTED*. HERE IS A PARTIAL TRANSCRIPT OF THE TERRA-ISTS' CALL . . .

TERRA-ISTS CALL

"WITH SODD JOINING THE RANKS OF THE TERRA-ISTS, WE RENEW OUR VOW TO FIGHT VIGOROUSLY FOR THE RIGHTS OF THE EARTH AND ITS LIVING INHABITANTS . . . NEVER TO COMPROMISE THE STRUGGLE TO PRESERVE THE NATURAL BEAUTY OF OUR PLANET, WHICH HAS BEEN RAVAGED BY MAN'S DESTRUCTIVE OBSESSION WITH TECHNOLOGY . . .

"SODD'S *ATTORNEYS* STATED THEY HAD *NO* KNOWLEDGE OF THE ACTION THEIR CLIENT WAS GOING TO TAKE AND WERE *UNAWARE* OF HIS AFFILIATION WITH THE TERRA-ISTS. ALANNA WOLFF AND JEFF BYRD, THE SO-CALLED *COUNSELORS OF THE MACABRE*, *DECLINED* TO COMMENT ANY FURTHER.

"COLUMNIST *ROBERTA BRONSKI* WAS IN THE COURTROOM AT THE TIME OF THE EVENT. ROBERTA, WHAT WAS *YOUR* OBSERVATION OF THE *MENTAL CONDITION* OF THIS CREATURE?

WELL, KEN, IT'S HARD TO ARGUE *WITH* THE *MESSAGE* SODD SO *PASSIONATELY* PRESENTED . . .

"I FOUND MYSELF WITH *TEARS* IN MY EYES WHEN SODD SPOKE IN COURT TODAY. WE *ARE* DESTROYING OUR PLANET. WE ARE LEAVING A *TOXIC LEGACY* TO OUR MOST CHERISHED NATURAL RESOURCE— *THE CHILDREN!* THE CRIMES FOR WHICH SODD WAS STANDING TRIAL SEEM SO *INCONSEQUENTIAL* GIVEN THE BIG PICTURE . . . PERHAPS THE PROSECUTOR SHOULD LOOK BEYOND SODD'S PECCADILLOS . . . AND THINK HARD ON WHAT THIS *PRINCIPLED* FUGITIVE HAD TO SAY . . .

YOU DID THE RIGHT THING, SODD!

GEE, FERN, I NEVER REALIZED WHAT *BAD* SHAPE THE ENVIRONMENT WAS IN UNTIL ♥YOU♥ TOLD ME

SODD! GET UNDER THE CANVAS! YOU WANT SOMEONE TO *SPOT* YOU? WE'RE STILL *MILES* AWAY FROM OUR CAMP! WE'RE NOT OUT OF THE WOODS YET . . .

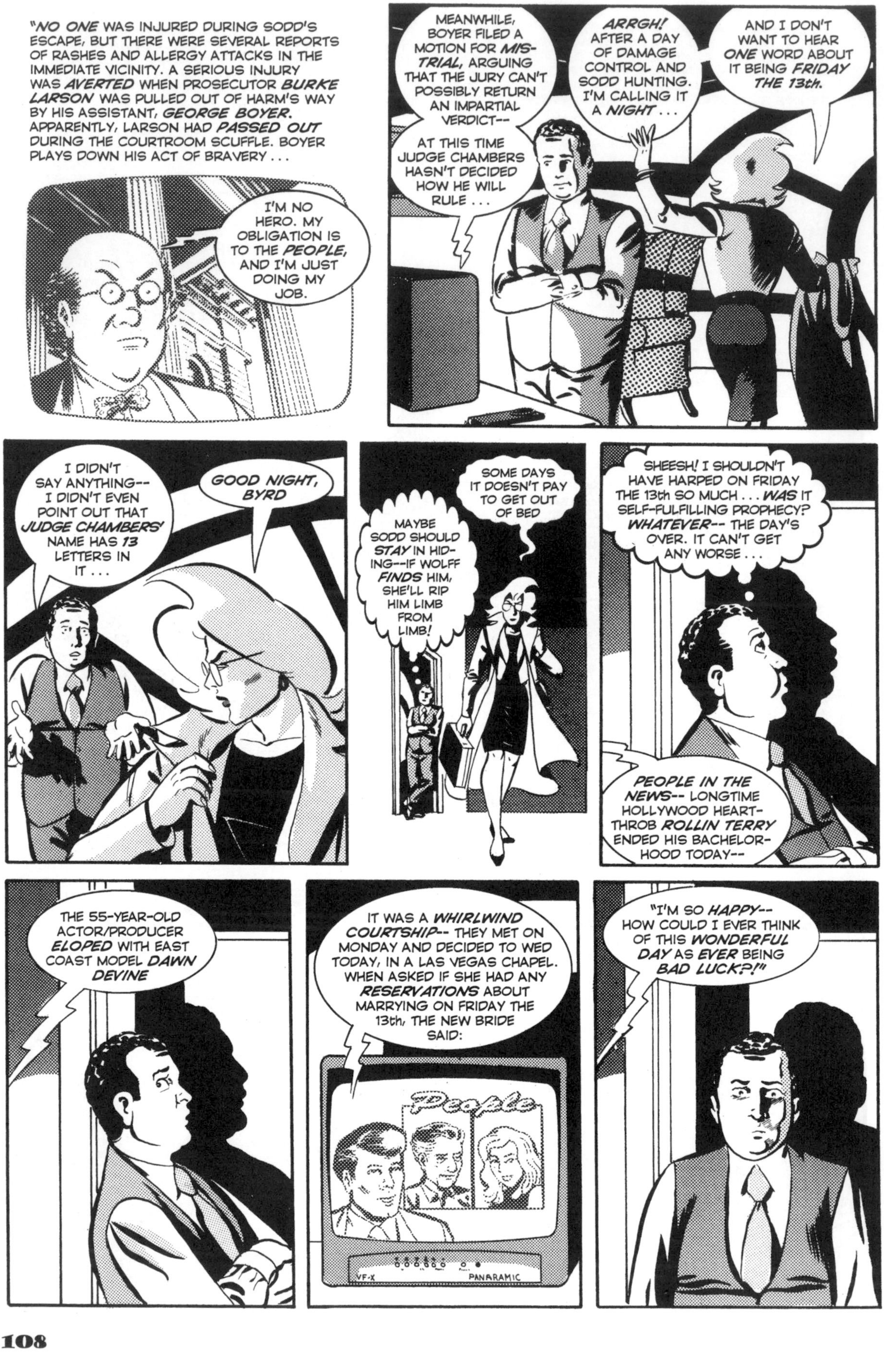
"NO ONE WAS INJURED DURING SODD'S ESCAPE, BUT THERE WERE SEVERAL REPORTS OF RASHES AND ALLERGY ATTACKS IN THE IMMEDIATE VICINITY. A SERIOUS INJURY WAS AVERTED WHEN PROSECUTOR BURKE LARSON WAS PULLED OUT OF HARM'S WAY BY HIS ASSISTANT, GEORGE BOYER. APPARENTLY, LARSON HAD PASSED OUT DURING THE COURTROOM SCUFFLE. BOYER PLAYS DOWN HIS ACT OF BRAVERY . . .
I'M NO HERO. MY OBLIGATION IS TO THE PEOPLE, AND I'M JUST DOING MY JOB.
MEANWHILE, BOYER FILED A MOTION FOR MIS-TRIAL, ARGUING THAT THE JURY CAN'T POSSIBLY RETURN AN IMPARTIAL VERDICT--
AT THIS TIME JUDGE CHAMBERS HASN'T DECIDED HOW HE WILL RULE . . .
ARRGH! AFTER A DAY OF DAMAGE CONTROL AND SODD HUNTING. I'M CALLING IT A NIGHT . . .
AND I DON'T WANT TO HEAR ONE WORD ABOUT IT BEING FRIDAY THE 13th.
I DIDN'T SAY ANYTHING-- I DIDN'T EVEN POINT OUT THAT JUDGE CHAMBERS' NAME HAS 13 LETTERS IN IT . . .
GOOD NIGHT, BYRD
SOME DAYS IT DOESN'T PAY TO GET OUT OF BED
MAYBE SODD SHOULD STAY IN HID-ING--IF WOLFF FINDS HIM, SHE'LL RIP HIM LIMB FROM LIMB!
SHEESH! I SHOULDN'T HAVE HARPED ON FRIDAY THE 13th SO MUCH . . . WAS IT SELF-FULFILLING PROPHECY? WHATEVER-- THE DAY'S OVER. IT CAN'T GET ANY WORSE . . .
PEOPLE IN THE NEWS-- LONGTIME HOLLYWOOD HEART-THROB ROLLIN TERRY ENDED HIS BACHELOR-HOOD TODAY--
THE 55-YEAR-OLD ACTOR/PRODUCER ELOPED WITH EAST COAST MODEL DAWN DEVINE
IT WAS A WHIRLWIND COURTSHIP-- THEY MET ON MONDAY AND DECIDED TO WED TODAY, IN A LAS VEGAS CHAPEL. WHEN ASKED IF SHE HAD ANY RESERVATIONS ABOUT MARRYING ON FRIDAY THE 13th, THE NEW BRIDE SAID:
People
VF-X
PANARAMIC
"I'M SO HAPPY-- HOW COULD I EVER THINK OF THIS WONDERFUL DAY AS EVER BEING BAD LUCK?!"

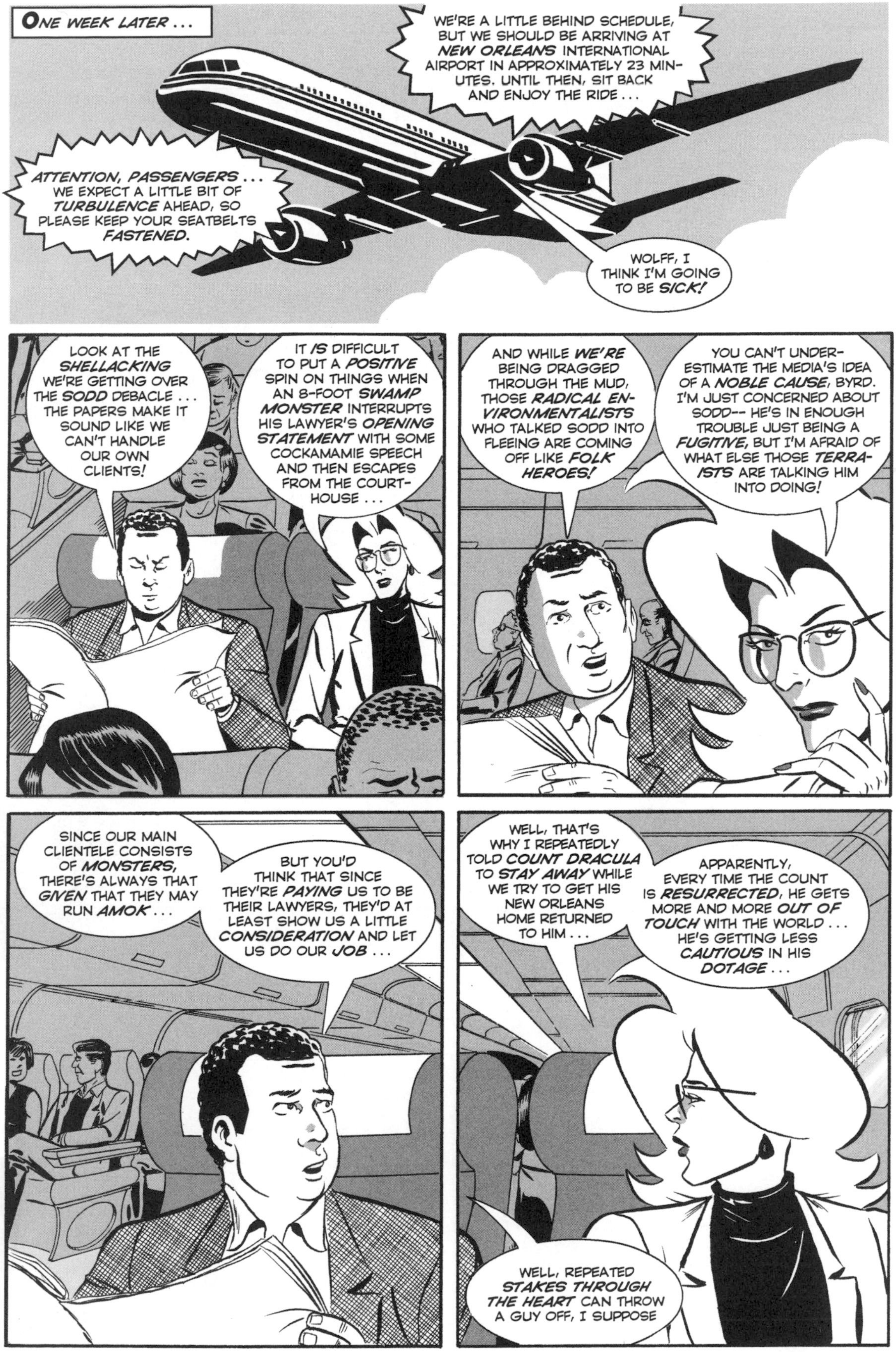
ONE WEEK LATER . . .
WE'RE A LITTLE BEHIND SCHEDULE, BUT WE SHOULD BE ARRIVING AT NEW ORLEANS INTERNATIONAL AIRPORT IN APPROXIMATELY 23 MINUTES. UNTIL THEN, SIT BACK AND ENJOY THE RIDE . . .
ATTENTION, PASSENGERS . . . WE EXPECT A LITTLE BIT OF TURBULENCE AHEAD, SO PLEASE KEEP YOUR SEATBELTS FASTENED.
WOLFF, I THINK I'M GOING TO BE SICK!
LOOK AT THE SHELLACKING WE'RE GETTING OVER THE SODD DEBACLE . . . THE PAPERS MAKE IT SOUND LIKE WE CAN'T HANDLE OUR OWN CLIENTS!
IT IS DIFFICULT TO PUT A POSITIVE SPIN ON THINGS WHEN AN 8-FOOT SWAMP MONSTER INTERRUPTS HIS LAWYER'S OPENING STATEMENT WITH SOME COCKAMAMIE SPEECH AND THEN ESCAPES FROM THE COURTHOUSE . . .
AND WHILE WE'RE BEING DRAGGED THROUGH THE MUD, THOSE RADICAL ENVIRONMENTALISTS WHO TALKED SODD INTO FLEEING ARE COMING OFF LIKE FOLK HEROES!
YOU CAN'T UNDERESTIMATE THE MEDIA'S IDEA OF A NOBLE CAUSE, BYRD. I'M JUST CONCERNED ABOUT SODD-- HE'S IN ENOUGH TROUBLE JUST BEING A FUGITIVE, BUT I'M AFRAID OF WHAT ELSE THOSE TERRA-ISTS ARE TALKING HIM INTO DOING!
SINCE OUR MAIN CLIENTELE CONSISTS OF MONSTERS, THERE'S ALWAYS THAT GIVEN THAT THEY MAY RUN AMOK . . .
BUT YOU'D THINK THAT SINCE THEY'RE PAYING US TO BE THEIR LAWYERS, THEY'D AT LEAST SHOW US A LITTLE CONSIDERATION AND LET US DO OUR JOB . . .
WELL, THAT'S WHY I REPEATEDLY TOLD COUNT DRACULA TO STAY AWAY WHILE WE TRY TO GET HIS NEW ORLEANS HOME RETURNED TO HIM . . .
APPARENTLY, EVERY TIME THE COUNT IS RESURRECTED, HE GETS MORE AND MORE OUT OF TOUCH WITH THE WORLD . . . HE'S GETTING LESS CAUTIOUS IN HIS DOTAGE . . .
WELL, REPEATED STAKES THROUGH THE HEART CAN THROW A GUY OFF, I SUPPOSE

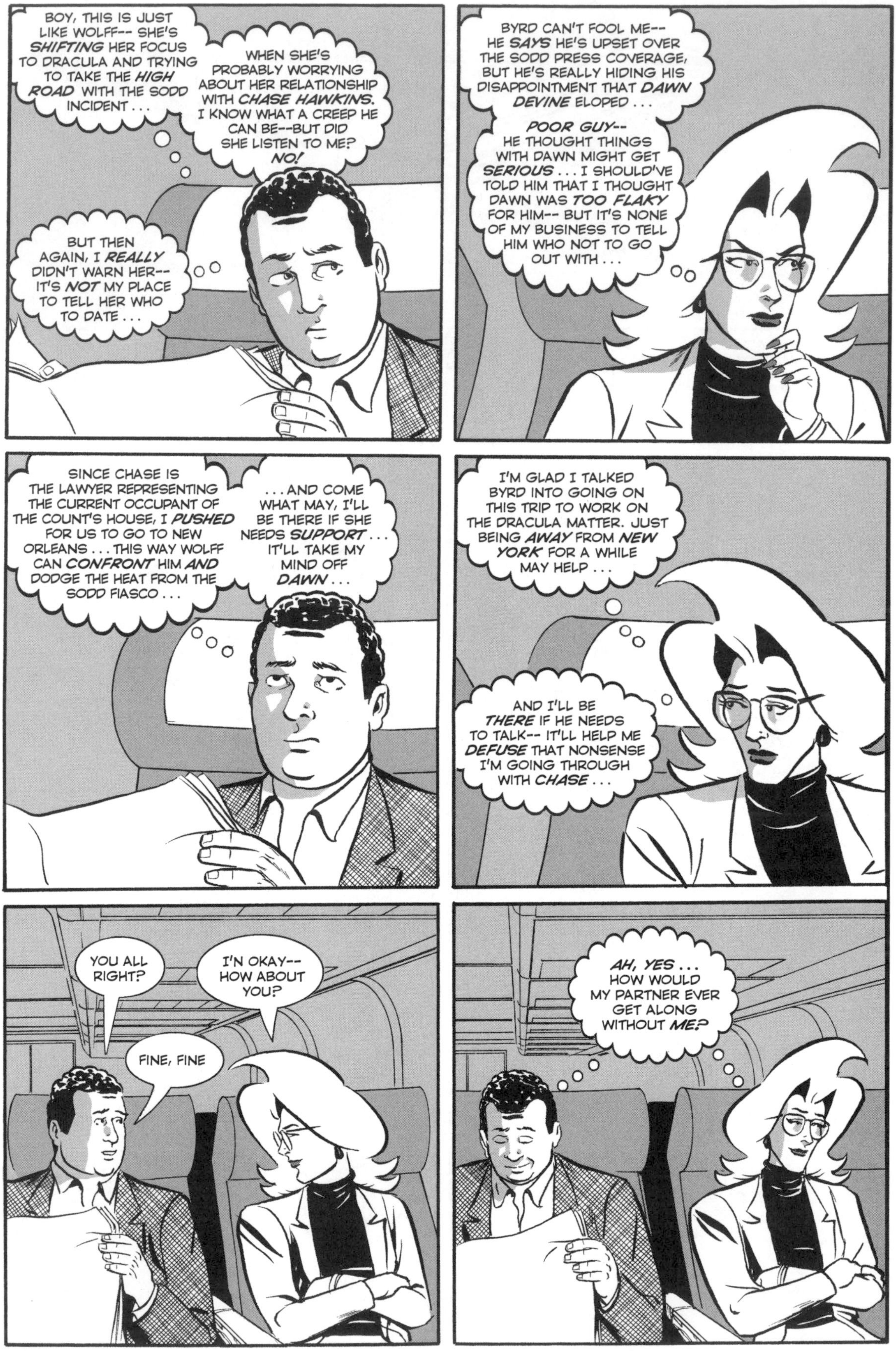
BOY, THIS IS JUST LIKE WOLFF-- SHE'S SHIFTING HER FOCUS TO DRACULA AND TRYING TO TAKE THE HIGH ROAD WITH THE SODD INCIDENT . . .
WHEN SHE'S PROBABLY WORRYING ABOUT HER RELATIONSHIP WITH CHASE HAWKINS. I KNOW WHAT A CREEP HE CAN BE--BUT DID SHE LISTEN TO ME? NO!
BUT THEN AGAIN, I REALLY DIDN'T WARN HER-- IT'S NOT MY PLACE TO TELL HER WHO TO DATE . . .
BYRD CAN'T FOOL ME-- HE SAYS HE'S UPSET OVER THE SODD PRESS COVERAGE, BUT HE'S REALLY HIDING HIS DISAPPOINTMENT THAT DAWN DEVINE ELOPED . . .
POOR GUY-- HE THOUGHT THINGS WITH DAWN MIGHT GET SERIOUS . . . I SHOULD'VE TOLD HIM THAT I THOUGHT DAWN WAS TOO FLAKY FOR HIM-- BUT IT'S NONE OF MY BUSINESS TO TELL HIM WHO NOT TO GO OUT WITH . . .
SINCE CHASE IS THE LAWYER REPRESENTING THE CURRENT OCCUPANT OF THE COUNT'S HOUSE, I PUSHED FOR US TO GO TO NEW ORLEANS . . . THIS WAY WOLFF CAN CONFRONT HIM AND DODGE THE HEAT FROM THE SODD FIASCO . . .
. . . AND COME WHAT MAY, I'LL BE THERE IF SHE NEEDS SUPPORT . . . IT'LL TAKE MY MIND OFF DAWN . . .
I'M GLAD I TALKED BYRD INTO GOING ON THIS TRIP TO WORK ON THE DRACULA MATTER. JUST BEING AWAY FROM NEW YORK FOR A WHILE MAY HELP . . .
AND I'LL BE THERE IF HE NEEDS TO TALK-- IT'LL HELP ME DEFUSE THAT NONSENSE I'M GOING THROUGH WITH CHASE . . .
YOU ALL RIGHT?
I'N OKAY-- HOW ABOUT YOU?
FINE, FINE
AH, YES . . . HOW WOULD MY PARTNER EVER GET ALONG WITHOUT ME?

Bad Blood

I feel my final destination at hand. Soon, I will rise and greet those who have come to pay tribute.

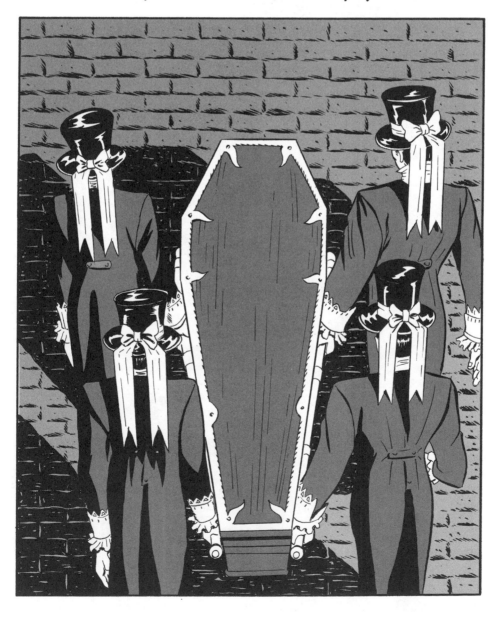

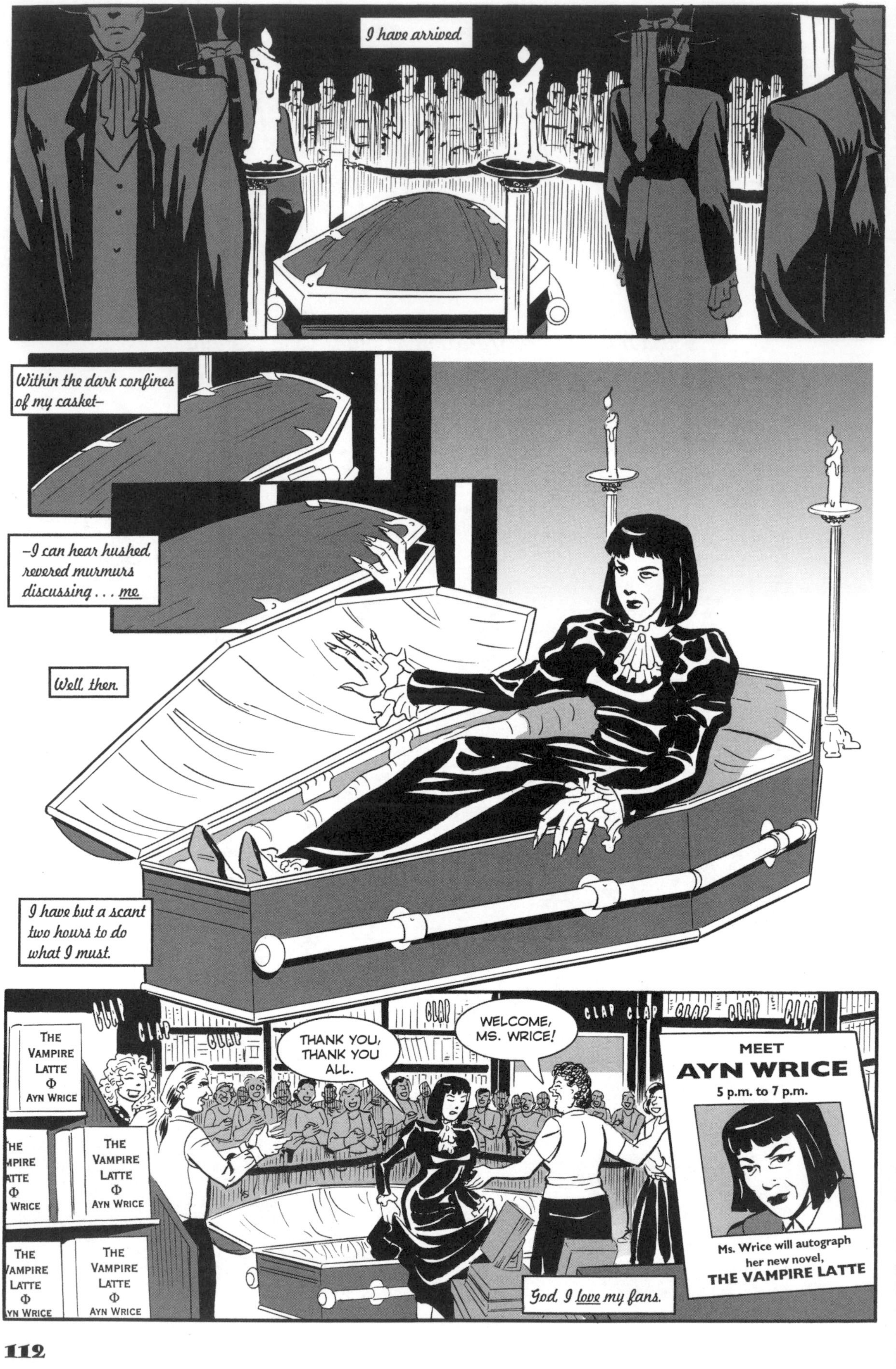

I have arrived.
Within the dark confines of my casket—
—I can hear hushed revered murmurs discussing . . . me.
Well, then.
I have but a scant two hours to do what I must.
CLAP CLAP CLAP CLAP CLAP CLAP CLAP CLAP
THE VAMPIRE LATTE Φ AYN WRICE
THANK YOU, THANK YOU ALL.
WELCOME, MS. WRICE!
MEET AYN WRICE 5 p.m. to 7 p.m.
Ms. Wrice will autograph her new novel, THE VAMPIRE LATTE
God, I love my fans.

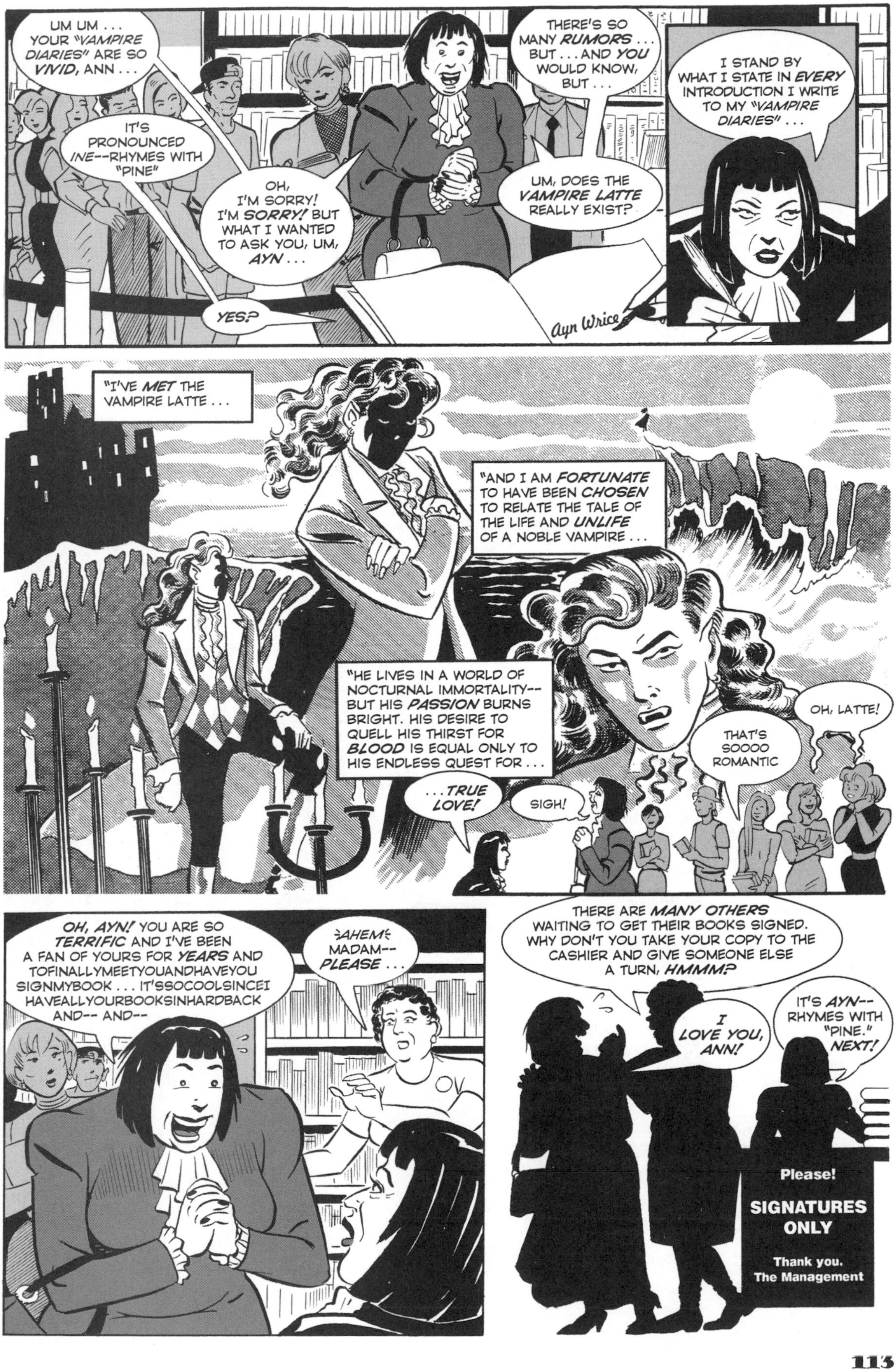
UM UM . . . YOUR "VAMPIRE DIARIES" ARE SO VIVID, ANN . . .
IT'S PRONOUNCED INE--RHYMES WITH "PINE"
OH, I'M SORRY! I'M SORRY! BUT WHAT I WANTED TO ASK YOU, UM, AYN . . .
YES?
THERE'S SO MANY RUMORS . . . BUT . . . AND YOU WOULD KNOW, BUT . . .
UM, DOES THE VAMPIRE LATTE REALLY EXIST?
Ayn Wrice
I STAND BY WHAT I STATE IN EVERY INTRODUCTION I WRITE TO MY "VAMPIRE DIARIES" . . .
"I'VE MET THE VAMPIRE LATTE . . .
"AND I AM FORTUNATE TO HAVE BEEN CHOSEN TO RELATE THE TALE OF THE LIFE AND UNLIFE OF A NOBLE VAMPIRE . . .
"HE LIVES IN A WORLD OF NOCTURNAL IMMORTALITY-- BUT HIS PASSION BURNS BRIGHT. HIS DESIRE TO QUELL HIS THIRST FOR BLOOD IS EQUAL ONLY TO HIS ENDLESS QUEST FOR . . .
. . . TRUE LOVE!
SIGH!
THAT'S SOOOO ROMANTIC
OH, LATTE!
OH, AYN! YOU ARE SO TERRIFIC AND I'VE BEEN A FAN OF YOURS FOR YEARS AND TOFINALLYMEETYOUANDHAVEYOU SIGNMYBOOK . . . IT'SSOCOOLSINCEI HAVEALLYOURBOOKSINHARDBACK AND-- AND--
AHEM MADAM-- PLEASE . . .
THERE ARE MANY OTHERS WAITING TO GET THEIR BOOKS SIGNED. WHY DON'T YOU TAKE YOUR COPY TO THE CASHIER AND GIVE SOMEONE ELSE A TURN, HMMM?
I LOVE YOU, ANN!
IT'S AYN-- RHYMES WITH "PINE." NEXT!
Please!
SIGNATURES ONLY
Thank you.
The Management

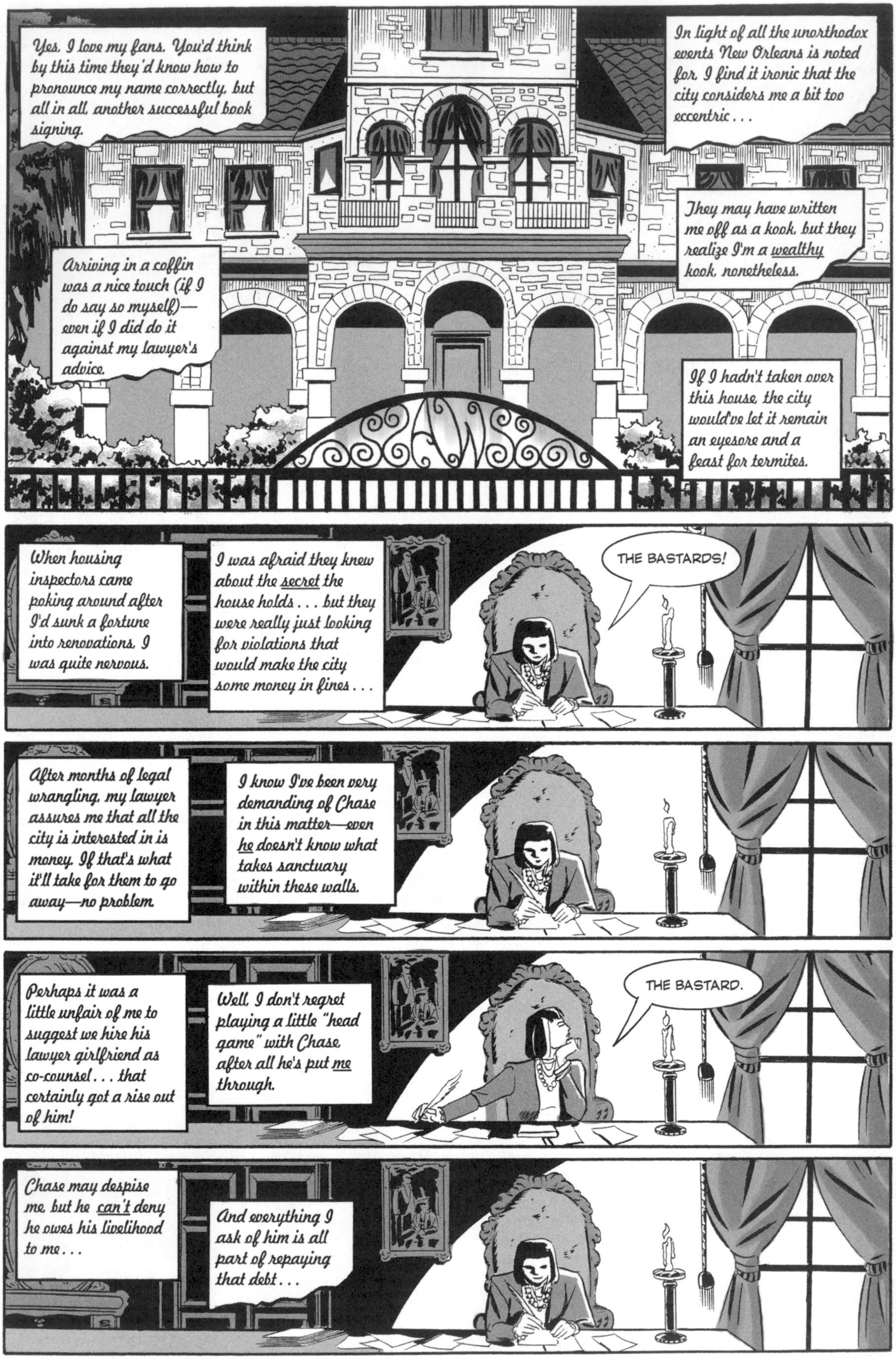
Yes, I love my fans. You'd think by this time they'd know how to pronounce my name correctly, but all in all, another successful book signing.
In light of all the unorthodox events New Orleans is noted for, I find it ironic that the city considers me a bit too eccentric . . .
They may have written me off as a kook, but they realize I'm a wealthy kook, nonetheless.
Arriving in a coffin was a nice touch (if I do say so myself)—even if I did do it against my lawyer's advice.
If I hadn't taken over this house, the city would've let it remain an eyesore and a feast for termites.
When housing inspectors came poking around after I'd sunk a fortune into renovations, I was quite nervous.
I was afraid they knew about the secret the house holds . . . but they were really just looking for violations that would make the city some money in fines . . .
THE BASTARDS!
After months of legal wrangling, my lawyer assures me that all the city is interested in is money. If that's what it'll take for them to go away—no problem.
I know I've been very demanding of Chase in this matter—even he doesn't know what takes sanctuary within these walls.
Perhaps it was a little unfair of me to suggest we hire his lawyer girlfriend as co-counsel . . . that certainly got a rise out of him!
Well, I don't regret playing a little "head game" with Chase, after all he's put me through.
THE BASTARD.
Chase may despise me, but he can't deny he owes his livelihood to me . . .
And everything I ask of him is all part of repaying that debt . . .

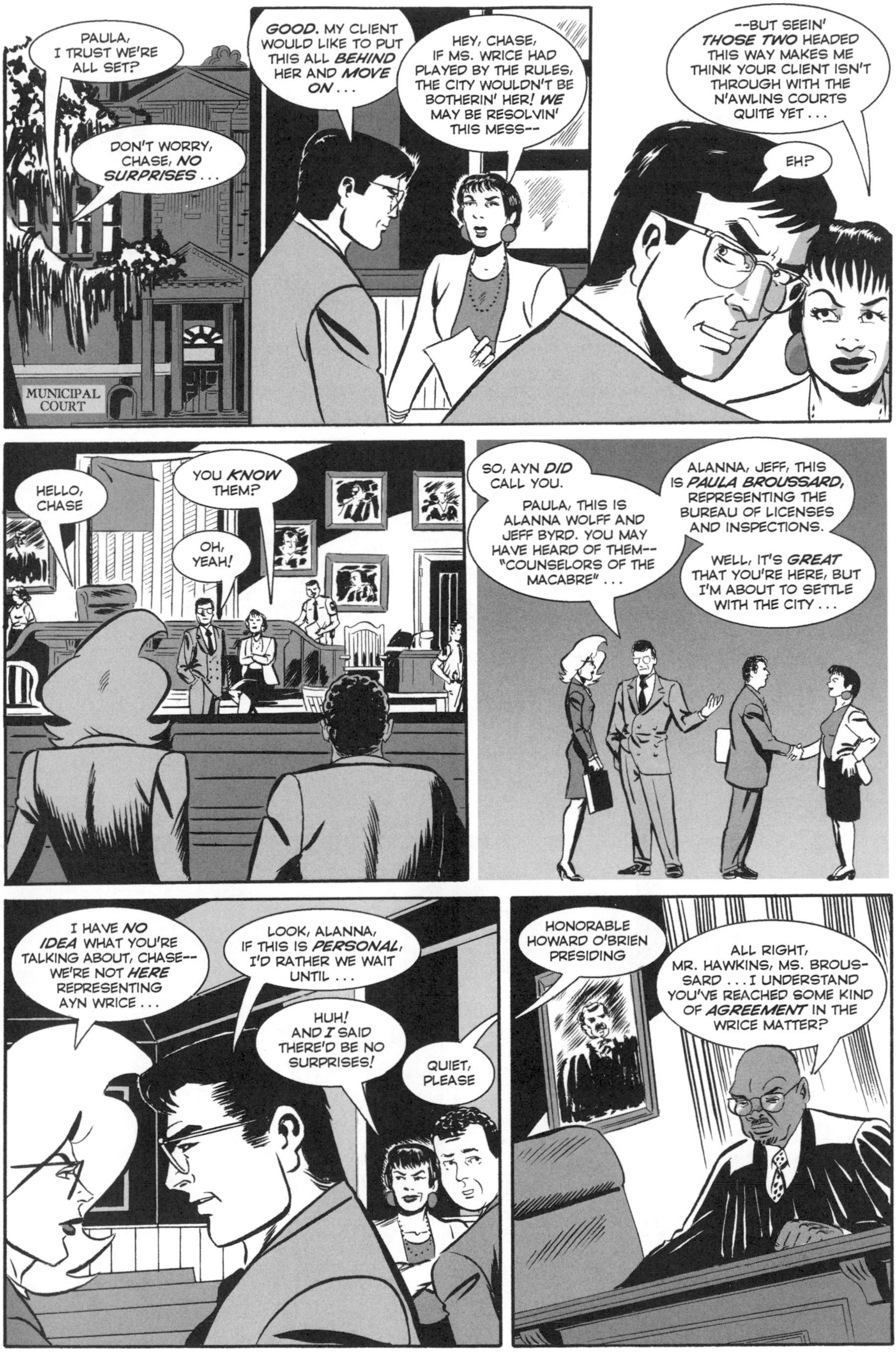
MUNICIPAL COURT
PAULA, I TRUST WE'RE ALL SET?
DON'T WORRY, CHASE, NO SURPRISES . . .
GOOD. MY CLIENT WOULD LIKE TO PUT THIS ALL BEHIND HER AND MOVE ON . . .
HEY, CHASE, IF MS. WRICE HAD PLAYED BY THE RULES, THE CITY WOULDN'T BE BOTHERIN' HER! WE MAY BE RESOLVIN' THIS MESS--
--BUT SEEIN' THOSE TWO HEADED THIS WAY MAKES ME THINK YOUR CLIENT ISN'T THROUGH WITH THE N'AWLINS COURTS QUITE YET . . .
EH?
HELLO, CHASE
YOU KNOW THEM?
OH, YEAH!
SO, AYN DID CALL YOU.
PAULA, THIS IS ALANNA WOLFF AND JEFF BYRD. YOU MAY HAVE HEARD OF THEM-- "COUNSELORS OF THE MACABRE" . . .
ALANNA, JEFF, THIS IS PAULA BROUSSARD, REPRESENTING THE BUREAU OF LICENSES AND INSPECTIONS.
WELL, IT'S GREAT THAT YOU'RE HERE, BUT I'M ABOUT TO SETTLE WITH THE CITY . . .
I HAVE NO IDEA WHAT YOU'RE TALKING ABOUT, CHASE-- WE'RE NOT HERE REPRESENTING AYN WRICE . . .
LOOK, ALANNA, IF THIS IS PERSONAL, I'D RATHER WE WAIT UNTIL . . .
HUH! AND I SAID THERE'D BE NO SURPRISES!
QUIET, PLEASE
HONORABLE HOWARD O'BRIEN PRESIDING
ALL RIGHT, MR. HAWKINS, MS. BROUSSARD . . . I UNDERSTAND YOU'VE REACHED SOME KIND OF AGREEMENT IN THE WRICE MATTER?

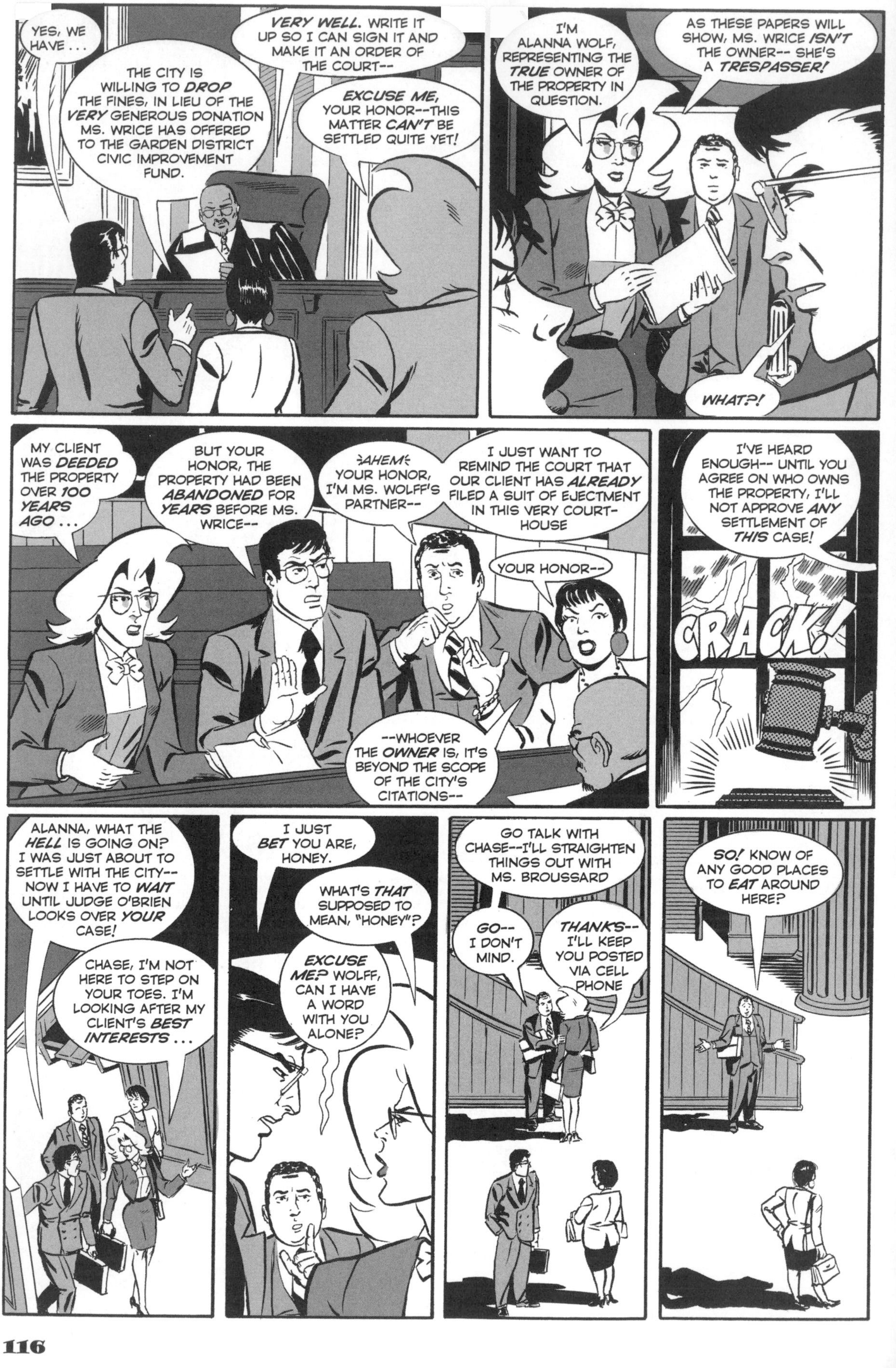

YES, WE HAVE . . .
THE CITY IS WILLING TO DROP THE FINES, IN LIEU OF THE VERY GENEROUS DONATION MS. WRICE HAS OFFERED TO THE GARDEN DISTRICT CIVIC IMPROVEMENT FUND.
VERY WELL. WRITE IT UP SO I CAN SIGN IT AND MAKE IT AN ORDER OF THE COURT--
EXCUSE ME, YOUR HONOR--THIS MATTER CAN'T BE SETTLED QUITE YET!
I'M ALANNA WOLF, REPRESENTING THE TRUE OWNER OF THE PROPERTY IN QUESTION.
AS THESE PAPERS WILL SHOW, MS. WRICE ISN'T THE OWNER-- SHE'S A TRESPASSER!
WHAT?!
MY CLIENT WAS DEEDED THE PROPERTY OVER 100 YEARS AGO . . .
BUT YOUR HONOR, THE PROPERTY HAD BEEN ABANDONED FOR YEARS BEFORE MS. WRICE--
AHEM YOUR HONOR, I'M MS. WOLFF'S PARTNER--
I JUST WANT TO REMIND THE COURT THAT OUR CLIENT HAS ALREADY FILED A SUIT OF EJECTMENT IN THIS VERY COURT-HOUSE
YOUR HONOR--
--WHOEVER THE OWNER IS, IT'S BEYOND THE SCOPE OF THE CITY'S CITATIONS--
I'VE HEARD ENOUGH-- UNTIL YOU AGREE ON WHO OWNS THE PROPERTY, I'LL NOT APPROVE ANY SETTLEMENT OF THIS CASE!
CRACK!
ALANNA, WHAT THE HELL IS GOING ON? I WAS JUST ABOUT TO SETTLE WITH THE CITY-- NOW I HAVE TO WAIT UNTIL JUDGE O'BRIEN LOOKS OVER YOUR CASE!
CHASE, I'M NOT HERE TO STEP ON YOUR TOES. I'M LOOKING AFTER MY CLIENT'S BEST INTERESTS . . .
I JUST BET YOU ARE, HONEY.
WHAT'S THAT SUPPOSED TO MEAN, "HONEY"?
EXCUSE ME? WOLFF, CAN I HAVE A WORD WITH YOU ALONE?
GO TALK WITH CHASE--I'LL STRAIGHTEN THINGS OUT WITH MS. BROUSSARD
GO-- I DON'T MIND.
THANKS-- I'LL KEEP YOU POSTED VIA CELL PHONE
SO! KNOW OF ANY GOOD PLACES TO EAT AROUND HERE?

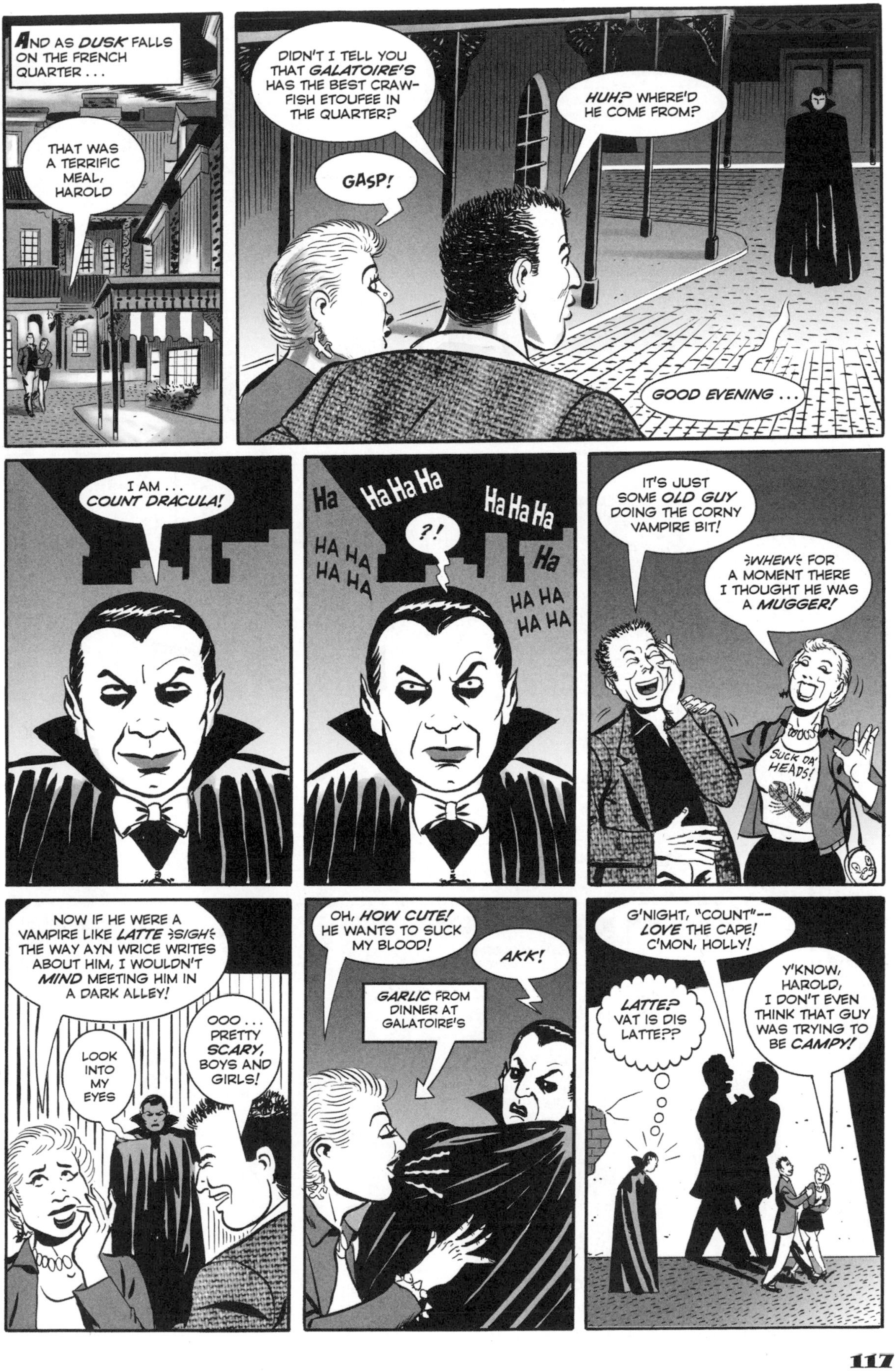
AND AS DUSK FALLS ON THE FRENCH QUARTER . . .
THAT WAS A TERRIFIC MEAL, HAROLD
DIDN'T I TELL YOU THAT GALATOIRE'S HAS THE BEST CRAW-FISH ETOUFEE IN THE QUARTER?
GASP!
HUH? WHERE'D HE COME FROM?
GOOD EVENING . . .
I AM . . . COUNT DRACULA!
Ha HaHaHa HaHaHa
HA HA HA HA
?!
Ha
HA HA HA HA
IT'S JUST SOME OLD GUY DOING THE CORNY VAMPIRE BIT!
WHEW FOR A MOMENT THERE I THOUGHT HE WAS A MUGGER!
SUCK DA' HEADS!
NOW IF HE WERE A VAMPIRE LIKE LATTE SIGH THE WAY AYN WRICE WRITES ABOUT HIM, I WOULDN'T MIND MEETING HIM IN A DARK ALLEY!
LOOK INTO MY EYES
OOO . . . PRETTY SCARY, BOYS AND GIRLS!
OH, HOW CUTE! HE WANTS TO SUCK MY BLOOD!
AKK!
GARLIC FROM DINNER AT GALATOIRE'S
G'NIGHT, "COUNT"-- LOVE THE CAPE! C'MON, HOLLY!
LATTE? VAT IS DIS LATTE??
Y'KNOW, HAROLD, I DON'T EVEN THINK THAT GUY WAS TRYING TO BE CAMPY!

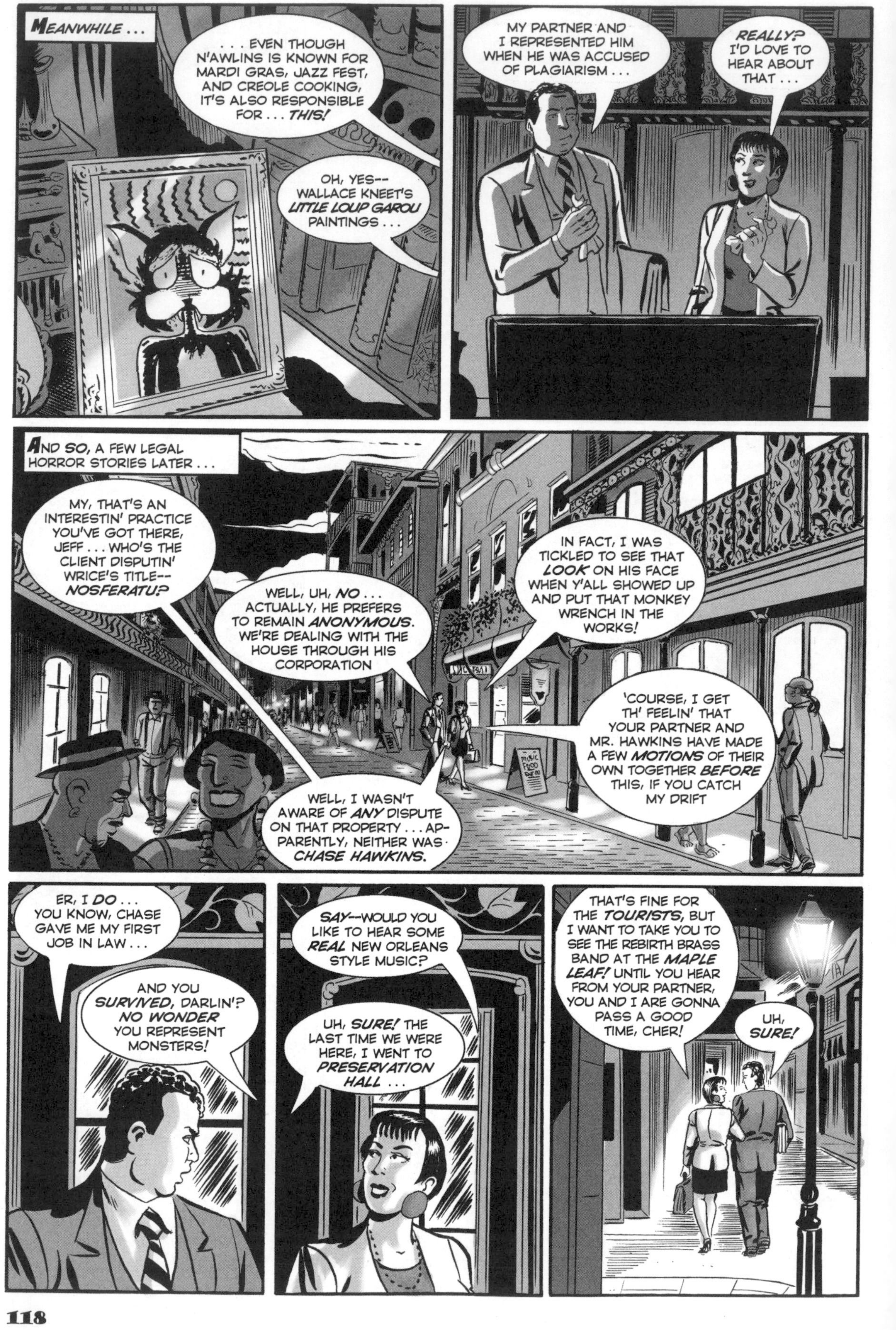
MEANWHILE . . .
. . . EVEN THOUGH N'AWLINS IS KNOWN FOR MARDI GRAS, JAZZ FEST, AND CREOLE COOKING, IT'S ALSO RESPONSIBLE FOR . . . THIS!
OH, YES-- WALLACE KNEET'S LITTLE LOUP GAROU PAINTINGS . . .
MY PARTNER AND I REPRESENTED HIM WHEN HE WAS ACCUSED OF PLAGIARISM . . .
REALLY? I'D LOVE TO HEAR ABOUT THAT . . .
AND SO, A FEW LEGAL HORROR STORIES LATER . . .
MY, THAT'S AN INTERESTIN' PRACTICE YOU'VE GOT THERE, JEFF . . . WHO'S THE CLIENT DISPUTIN' WRICE'S TITLE-- NOSFERATU?
WELL, UH, NO . . . ACTUALLY, HE PREFERS TO REMAIN ANONYMOUS. WE'RE DEALING WITH THE HOUSE THROUGH HIS CORPORATION
WELL, I WASN'T AWARE OF ANY DISPUTE ON THAT PROPERTY . . . APPARENTLY, NEITHER WAS CHASE HAWKINS.
IN FACT, I WAS TICKLED TO SEE THAT LOOK ON HIS FACE WHEN Y'ALL SHOWED UP AND PUT THAT MONKEY WRENCH IN THE WORKS!
'COURSE, I GET TH' FEELIN' THAT YOUR PARTNER AND MR. HAWKINS HAVE MADE A FEW MOTIONS OF THEIR OWN TOGETHER BEFORE THIS, IF YOU CATCH MY DRIFT
ER, I DO . . . YOU KNOW, CHASE GAVE ME MY FIRST JOB IN LAW . . .
AND YOU SURVIVED, DARLIN'? NO WONDER YOU REPRESENT MONSTERS!
SAY--WOULD YOU LIKE TO HEAR SOME REAL NEW ORLEANS STYLE MUSIC?
UH, SURE! THE LAST TIME WE WERE HERE, I WENT TO PRESERVATION HALL . . .
THAT'S FINE FOR THE TOURISTS, BUT I WANT TO TAKE YOU TO SEE THE REBIRTH BRASS BAND AT THE MAPLE LEAF! UNTIL YOU HEAR FROM YOUR PARTNER, YOU AND I ARE GONNA PASS A GOOD TIME, CHER!
UH, SURE!

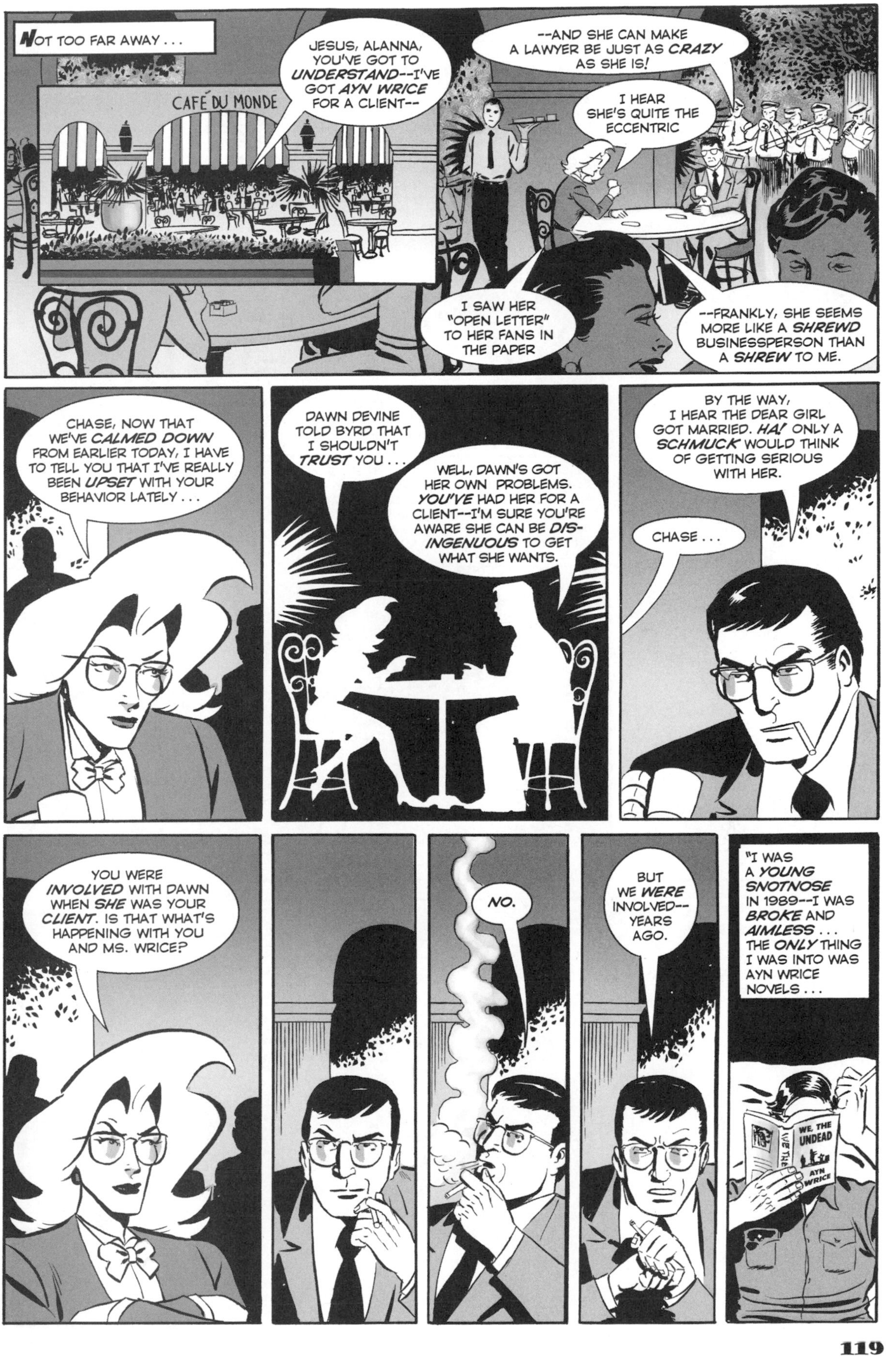
NOT TOO FAR AWAY . . .
CAFÉ DU MONDE
JESUS, ALANNA, YOU'VE GOT TO UNDERSTAND--I'VE GOT AYN WRICE FOR A CLIENT--
--AND SHE CAN MAKE A LAWYER BE JUST AS CRAZY AS SHE IS!
I HEAR SHE'S QUITE THE ECCENTRIC
I SAW HER "OPEN LETTER" TO HER FANS IN THE PAPER
--FRANKLY, SHE SEEMS MORE LIKE A SHREWD BUSINESSPERSON THAN A SHREW TO ME.
CHASE, NOW THAT WE'VE CALMED DOWN FROM EARLIER TODAY, I HAVE TO TELL YOU THAT I'VE REALLY BEEN UPSET WITH YOUR BEHAVIOR LATELY . . .
DAWN DEVINE TOLD BYRD THAT I SHOULDN'T TRUST YOU . . .
WELL, DAWN'S GOT HER OWN PROBLEMS. YOU'VE HAD HER FOR A CLIENT--I'M SURE YOU'RE AWARE SHE CAN BE DIS-INGENUOUS TO GET WHAT SHE WANTS.
BY THE WAY, I HEAR THE DEAR GIRL GOT MARRIED. HA! ONLY A SCHMUCK WOULD THINK OF GETTING SERIOUS WITH HER.
CHASE . . .
YOU WERE INVOLVED WITH DAWN WHEN SHE WAS YOUR CLIENT. IS THAT WHAT'S HAPPENING WITH YOU AND MS. WRICE?
NO.
BUT WE WERE INVOLVED-- YEARS AGO.
"I WAS A YOUNG SNOTNOSE IN 1989--I WAS BROKE AND AIMLESS . . . THE ONLY THING I WAS INTO WAS AYN WRICE NOVELS . . .
WE, THE UNDEAD
AYN WRICE

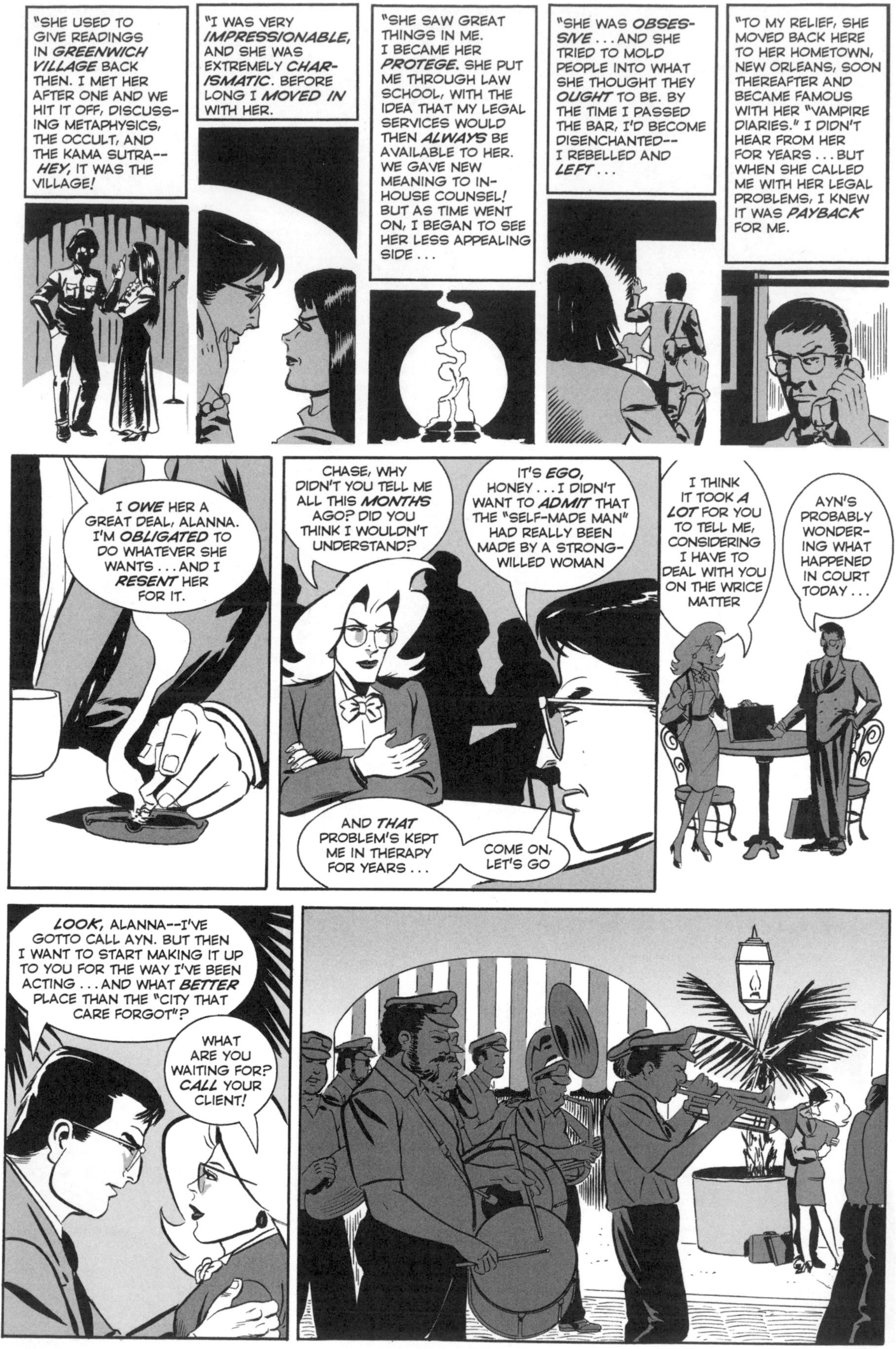

"SHE USED TO GIVE READINGS IN GREENWICH VILLAGE BACK THEN. I MET HER AFTER ONE AND WE HIT IT OFF, DISCUSSING METAPHYSICS, THE OCCULT, AND THE KAMA SUTRA-- HEY, IT WAS THE VILLAGE!
"I WAS VERY IMPRESSIONABLE, AND SHE WAS EXTREMELY CHARISMATIC. BEFORE LONG I MOVED IN WITH HER.
"SHE SAW GREAT THINGS IN ME. I BECAME HER PROTEGE. SHE PUT ME THROUGH LAW SCHOOL, WITH THE IDEA THAT MY LEGAL SERVICES WOULD THEN ALWAYS BE AVAILABLE TO HER. WE GAVE NEW MEANING TO IN-HOUSE COUNSEL! BUT AS TIME WENT ON, I BEGAN TO SEE HER LESS APPEALING SIDE . . .
"SHE WAS OBSESSIVE . . . AND SHE TRIED TO MOLD PEOPLE INTO WHAT SHE THOUGHT THEY OUGHT TO BE. BY THE TIME I PASSED THE BAR, I'D BECOME DISENCHANTED-- I REBELLED AND LEFT . . .
"TO MY RELIEF, SHE MOVED BACK HERE TO HER HOMETOWN, NEW ORLEANS, SOON THEREAFTER AND BECAME FAMOUS WITH HER "VAMPIRE DIARIES." I DIDN'T HEAR FROM HER FOR YEARS . . . BUT WHEN SHE CALLED ME WITH HER LEGAL PROBLEMS, I KNEW IT WAS PAYBACK FOR ME.
I OWE HER A GREAT DEAL, ALANNA. I'M OBLIGATED TO DO WHATEVER SHE WANTS . . . AND I RESENT HER FOR IT.
CHASE, WHY DIDN'T YOU TELL ME ALL THIS MONTHS AGO? DID YOU THINK I WOULDN'T UNDERSTAND?
IT'S EGO, HONEY . . . I DIDN'T WANT TO ADMIT THAT THE "SELF-MADE MAN" HAD REALLY BEEN MADE BY A STRONG-WILLED WOMAN
AND THAT PROBLEM'S KEPT ME IN THERAPY FOR YEARS . . .
COME ON, LET'S GO
I THINK IT TOOK A LOT FOR YOU TO TELL ME, CONSIDERING I HAVE TO DEAL WITH YOU ON THE WRICE MATTER
AYN'S PROBABLY WONDERING WHAT HAPPENED IN COURT TODAY . . .
LOOK, ALANNA--I'VE GOTTO CALL AYN. BUT THEN I WANT TO START MAKING IT UP TO YOU FOR THE WAY I'VE BEEN ACTING . . . AND WHAT BETTER PLACE THAN THE "CITY THAT CARE FORGOT"?
WHAT ARE YOU WAITING FOR? CALL YOUR CLIENT!

AND, AT THAT MOMENT...

LATTE!

HAS DE VORLD SO SOON FORGOTTEN DRACULA? BECAUSE UFF DIS *LATTE?!*

VAT HAS DIS WRICE VOMAN BEEN WRITING ABOUT VAMPIRES? FIRST, SHE TAKES MY *HOME*, AND NOW MY *REPUTATION?*

I *MUST* SEE VAT SHE HAS BEEN WRITING--!

ST. ANN

TRASH!

FRENCH QUARTER BOOKS

DIS IS VAT DE POPULACE REGARDS AS A GOOD VAMPIRE STORY? *BAH!* NOW, *STOKER*-- DERE VAS A WRITER...

IF YOU'RE INTERESTED, SIR, WE STILL HAVE *AUTOGRAPHED* COPIES OF AYN WRICE'S NEW BOOK...

I MUST SAY, THAT'S A *BEAUTIFUL* CAPE! ARE YOU A MEMBER OF A MARDI GRAS KREWE?

BATTONER

THE BITCHING HOUR — AYN WRICE

QUEEN OF THE DARNED — AYN WRICE

Laissez Les Bon Temps Roulez!

TATTLES

LE OF BAWDY THIEF — AYN WRICE

ENOUGH! A PRICE MUST BE PAID FOR SUCH HERESY... *LOOK INTO MY EYES...*

YES, SIR...

WILL THAT BE CASH OR CREDIT CARD?

AKK!

BE NICE TO ME • I GAVE BLOOD

MY *LAWYERS* BE *DAMNED*...

AYN WRICE, IT IS TIME VEE *MET...!*

WELL! THAT OLD FELLA SURE FLEW OUTTA HERE LIKE A BAT OUTTA HELL!

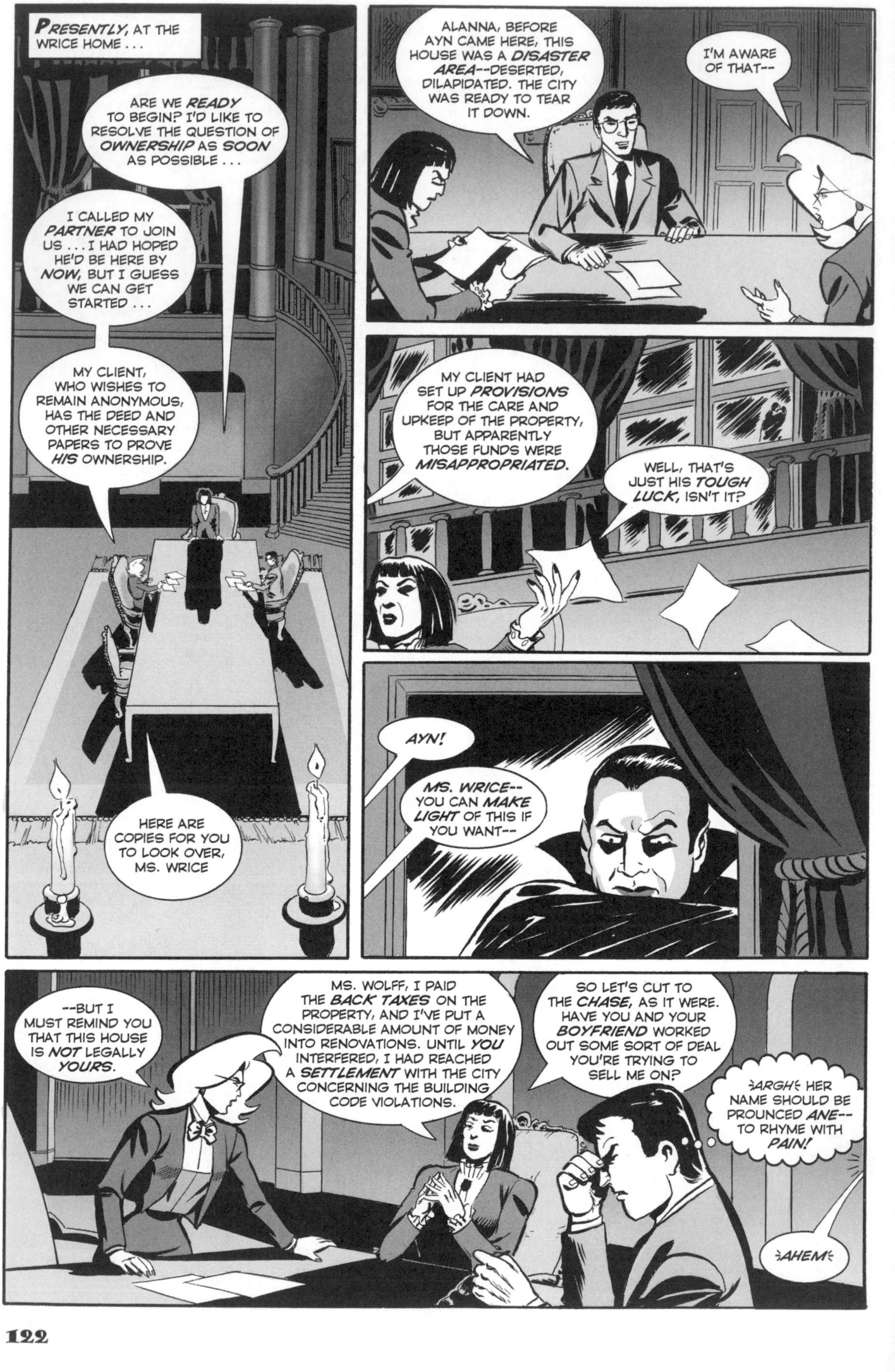
PRESENTLY, AT THE WRICE HOME . . .
ARE WE READY TO BEGIN? I'D LIKE TO RESOLVE THE QUESTION OF OWNERSHIP AS SOON AS POSSIBLE . . .
I CALLED MY PARTNER TO JOIN US . . . I HAD HOPED HE'D BE HERE BY NOW, BUT I GUESS WE CAN GET STARTED . . .
MY CLIENT, WHO WISHES TO REMAIN ANONYMOUS, HAS THE DEED AND OTHER NECESSARY PAPERS TO PROVE HIS OWNERSHIP.
HERE ARE COPIES FOR YOU TO LOOK OVER, MS. WRICE
ALANNA, BEFORE AYN CAME HERE, THIS HOUSE WAS A DISASTER AREA--DESERTED, DILAPIDATED. THE CITY WAS READY TO TEAR IT DOWN.
I'M AWARE OF THAT--
MY CLIENT HAD SET UP PROVISIONS FOR THE CARE AND UPKEEP OF THE PROPERTY, BUT APPARENTLY THOSE FUNDS WERE MISAPPROPRIATED.
WELL, THAT'S JUST HIS TOUGH LUCK, ISN'T IT?
AYN!
MS. WRICE-- YOU CAN MAKE LIGHT OF THIS IF YOU WANT--
--BUT I MUST REMIND YOU THAT THIS HOUSE IS NOT LEGALLY YOURS.
MS. WOLFF, I PAID THE BACK TAXES ON THE PROPERTY, AND I'VE PUT A CONSIDERABLE AMOUNT OF MONEY INTO RENOVATIONS. UNTIL YOU INTERFERED, I HAD REACHED A SETTLEMENT WITH THE CITY CONCERNING THE BUILDING CODE VIOLATIONS.
SO LET'S CUT TO THE CHASE, AS IT WERE. HAVE YOU AND YOUR BOYFRIEND WORKED OUT SOME SORT OF DEAL YOU'RE TRYING TO SELL ME ON?
ARGH HER NAME SHOULD BE PROUNCED ANE-- TO RHYME WITH PAIN!
AHEM

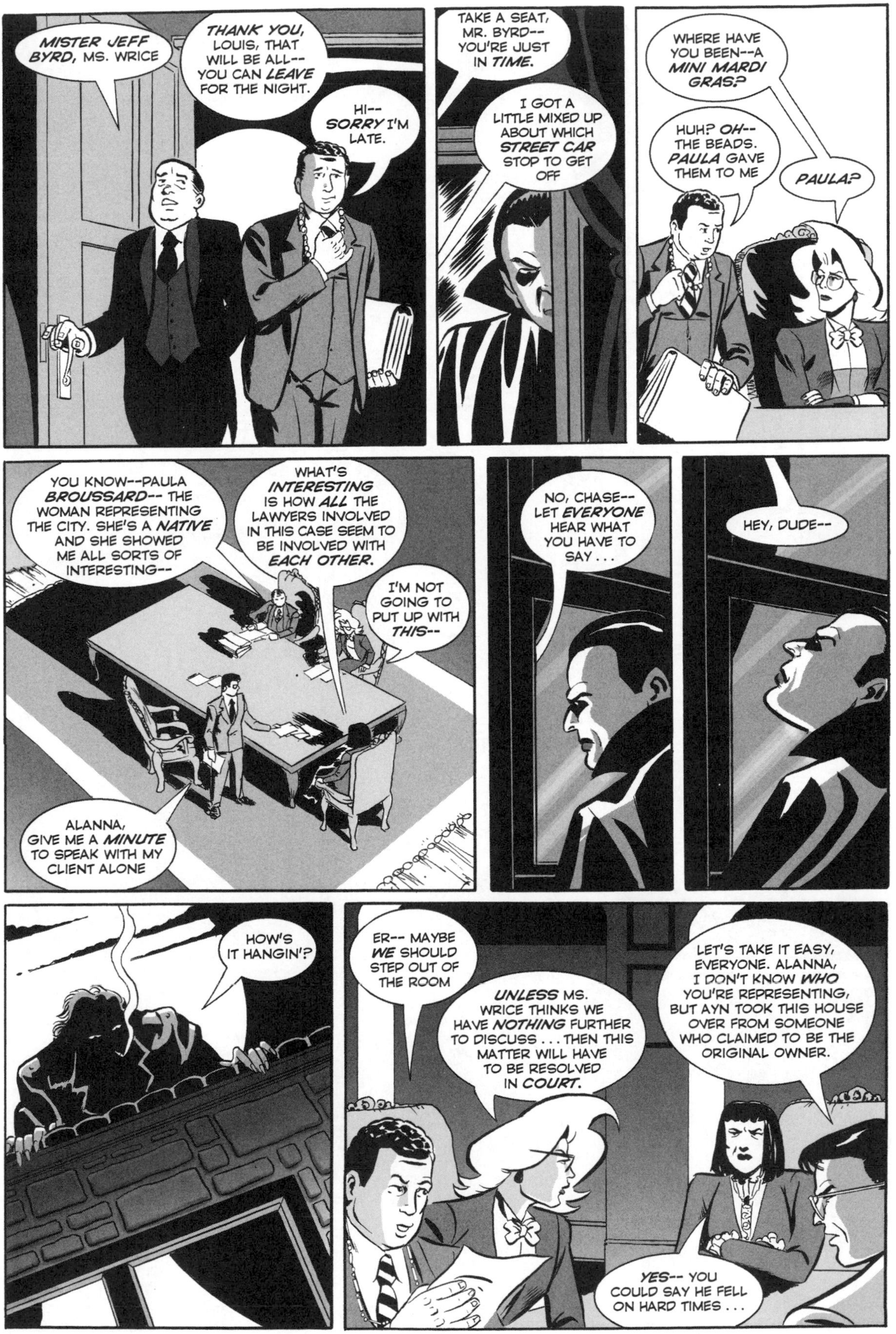
MISTER JEFF BYRD, MS. WRICE
THANK YOU, LOUIS, THAT WILL BE ALL-- YOU CAN LEAVE FOR THE NIGHT.
HI-- SORRY I'M LATE.
TAKE A SEAT, MR. BYRD-- YOU'RE JUST IN TIME.
I GOT A LITTLE MIXED UP ABOUT WHICH STREET CAR STOP TO GET OFF
WHERE HAVE YOU BEEN--A MINI MARDI GRAS?
HUH? OH-- THE BEADS. PAULA GAVE THEM TO ME
PAULA?
YOU KNOW--PAULA BROUSSARD-- THE WOMAN REPRESENTING THE CITY. SHE'S A NATIVE AND SHE SHOWED ME ALL SORTS OF INTERESTING--
WHAT'S INTERESTING IS HOW ALL THE LAWYERS INVOLVED IN THIS CASE SEEM TO BE INVOLVED WITH EACH OTHER.
I'M NOT GOING TO PUT UP WITH THIS--
ALANNA, GIVE ME A MINUTE TO SPEAK WITH MY CLIENT ALONE
NO, CHASE-- LET EVERYONE HEAR WHAT YOU HAVE TO SAY . . .
HEY, DUDE--
HOW'S IT HANGIN'?
ER-- MAYBE WE SHOULD STEP OUT OF THE ROOM
UNLESS MS. WRICE THINKS WE HAVE NOTHING FURTHER TO DISCUSS . . . THEN THIS MATTER WILL HAVE TO BE RESOLVED IN COURT.
LET'S TAKE IT EASY, EVERYONE. ALANNA, I DON'T KNOW WHO YOU'RE REPRESENTING, BUT AYN TOOK THIS HOUSE OVER FROM SOMEONE WHO CLAIMED TO BE THE ORIGINAL OWNER.
YES-- YOU COULD SAY HE FELL ON HARD TIMES . . .

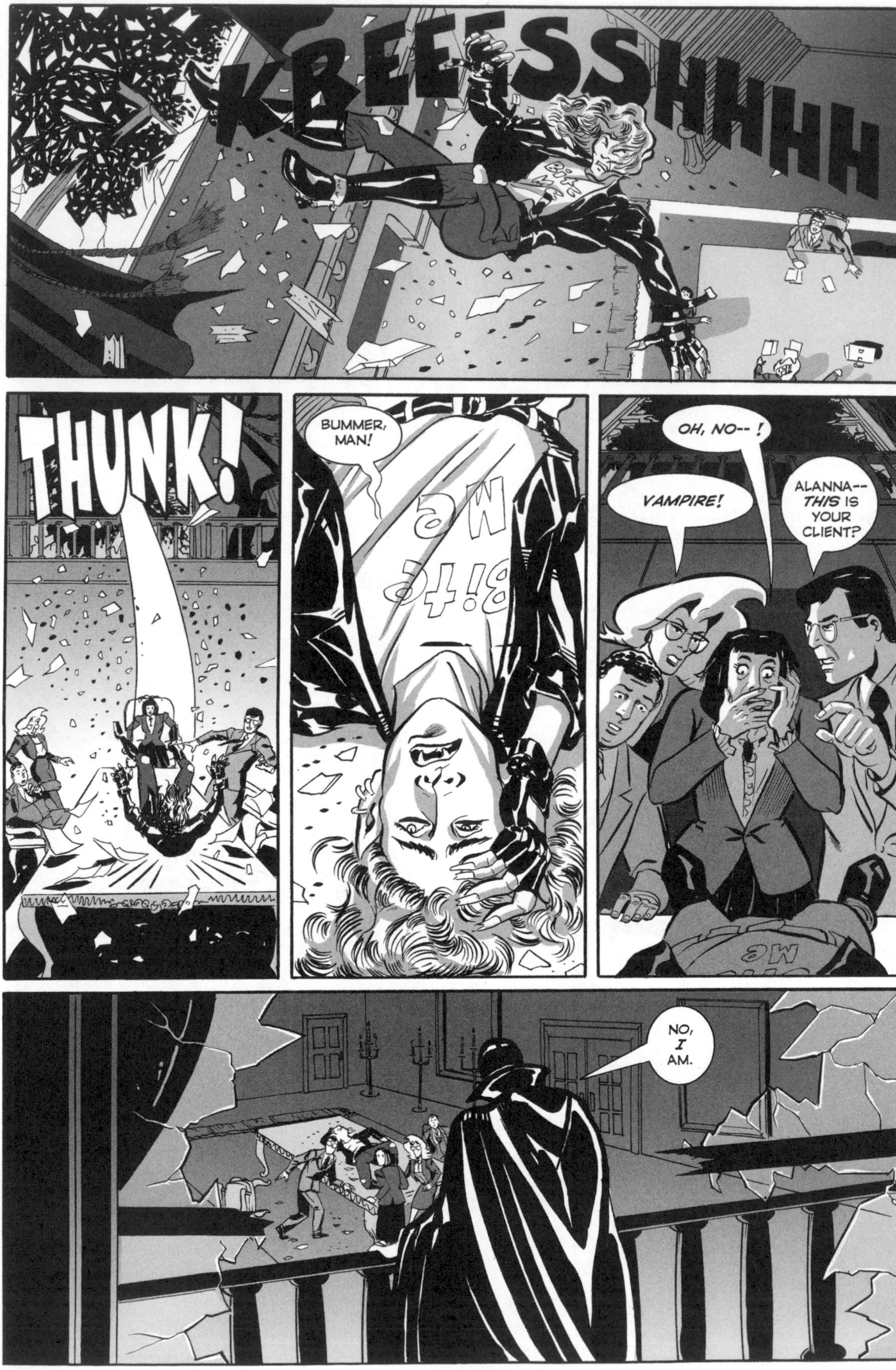
KREEESSHHHHH
THUNK!
BUMMER, MAN!
VAMPIRE!
OH, NO-- !
ALANNA-- THIS IS YOUR CLIENT?
NO, I AM.

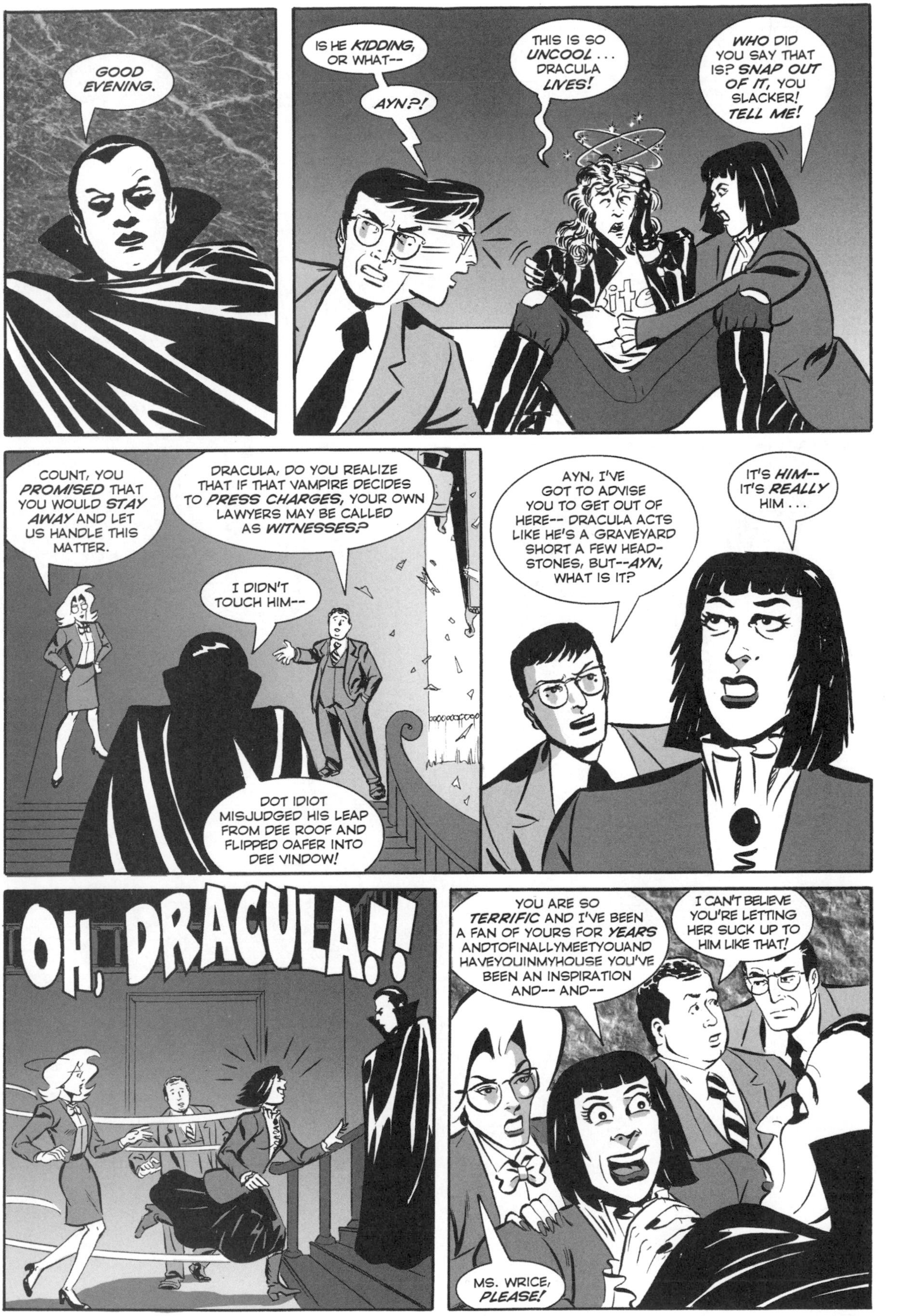
GOOD EVENING.
IS HE KIDDING, OR WHAT--
AYN?!
THIS IS SO UNCOOL . . . DRACULA LIVES!
WHO DID YOU SAY THAT IS? SNAP OUT OF IT, YOU SLACKER! TELL ME!
COUNT, YOU PROMISED THAT YOU WOULD STAY AWAY AND LET US HANDLE THIS MATTER.
DRACULA, DO YOU REALIZE THAT IF THAT VAMPIRE DECIDES TO PRESS CHARGES, YOUR OWN LAWYERS MAY BE CALLED AS WITNESSES?
I DIDN'T TOUCH HIM--
DOT IDIOT MISJUDGED HIS LEAP FROM DEE ROOF AND FLIPPED OAFER INTO DEE VINDOW!
AYN, I'VE GOT TO ADVISE YOU TO GET OUT OF HERE-- DRACULA ACTS LIKE HE'S A GRAVEYARD SHORT A FEW HEAD-STONES, BUT--AYN, WHAT IS IT?
IT'S HIM-- IT'S REALLY HIM . . .
OH, DRACULA!!
YOU ARE SO TERRIFIC AND I'VE BEEN A FAN OF YOURS FOR YEARS ANDTOFINALLYMEETYOUAND HAVEYOUINMYHOUSE YOU'VE BEEN AN INSPIRATION AND-- AND--
I CAN'T BELIEVE YOU'RE LETTING HER SUCK UP TO HIM LIKE THAT!
MS. WRICE, PLEASE!

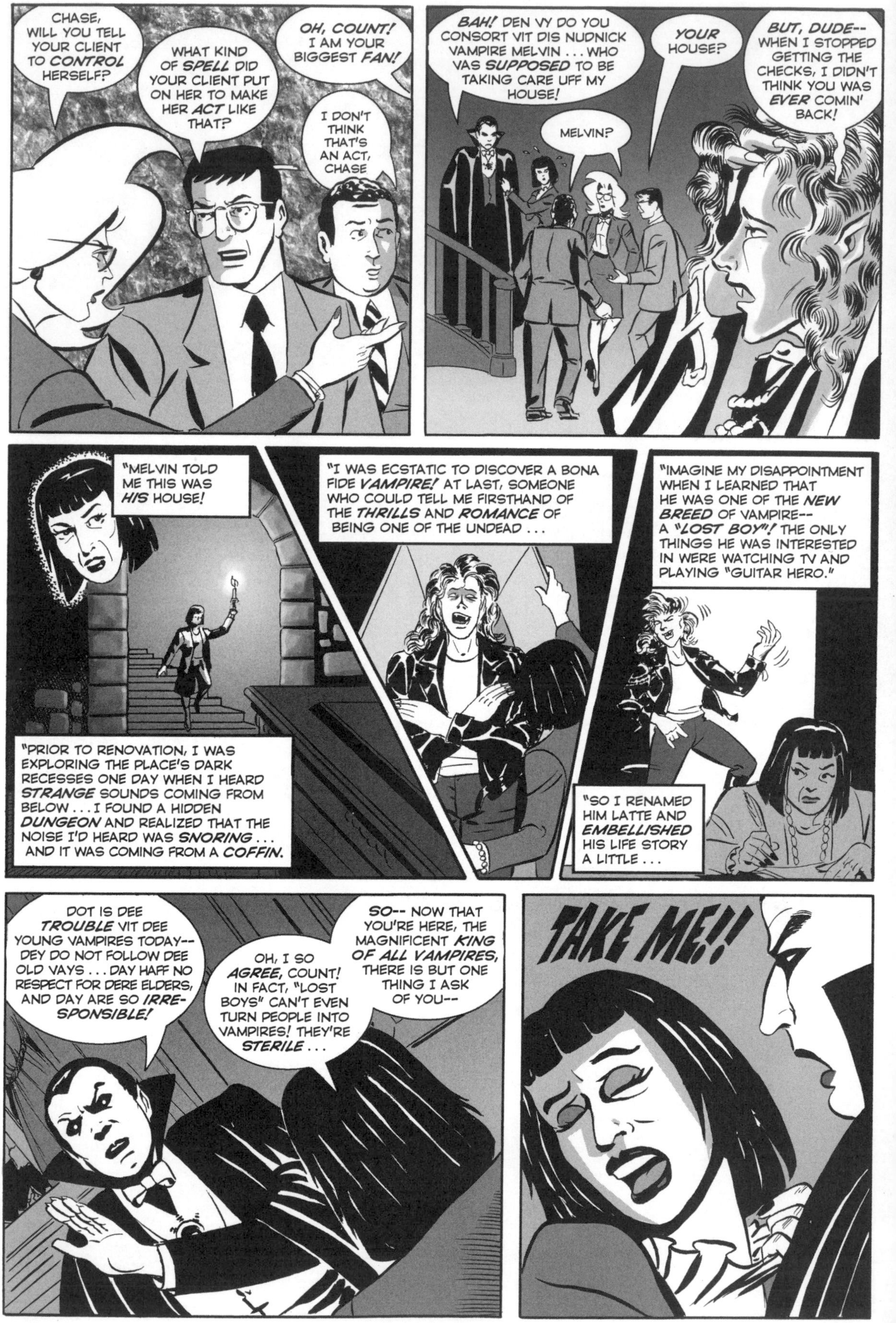
CHASE, WILL YOU TELL YOUR CLIENT TO CONTROL HERSELF?
WHAT KIND OF SPELL DID YOUR CLIENT PUT ON HER TO MAKE HER ACT LIKE THAT?
OH, COUNT! I AM YOUR BIGGEST FAN!
I DON'T THINK THAT'S AN ACT, CHASE
BAH! DEN VY DO YOU CONSORT VIT DIS NUDNICK VAMPIRE MELVIN . . . WHO VAS SUPPOSED TO BE TAKING CARE UFF MY HOUSE!
YOUR HOUSE?
MELVIN?
BUT, DUDE-- WHEN I STOPPED GETTING THE CHECKS, I DIDN'T THINK YOU WAS EVER COMIN' BACK!
"MELVIN TOLD ME THIS WAS HIS HOUSE!
"PRIOR TO RENOVATION, I WAS EXPLORING THE PLACE'S DARK RECESSES ONE DAY WHEN I HEARD STRANGE SOUNDS COMING FROM BELOW . . . I FOUND A HIDDEN DUNGEON AND REALIZED THAT THE NOISE I'D HEARD WAS SNORING . . . AND IT WAS COMING FROM A COFFIN.
"I WAS ECSTATIC TO DISCOVER A BONA FIDE VAMPIRE! AT LAST, SOMEONE WHO COULD TELL ME FIRSTHAND OF THE THRILLS AND ROMANCE OF BEING ONE OF THE UNDEAD . . .
"IMAGINE MY DISAPPOINTMENT WHEN I LEARNED THAT HE WAS ONE OF THE NEW BREED OF VAMPIRE-- A "LOST BOY"! THE ONLY THINGS HE WAS INTERESTED IN WERE WATCHING TV AND PLAYING "GUITAR HERO."
"SO I RENAMED HIM LATTE AND EMBELLISHED HIS LIFE STORY A LITTLE . . .
DOT IS DEE TROUBLE VIT DEE YOUNG VAMPIRES TODAY-- DEY DO NOT FOLLOW DEE OLD VAYS . . . DAY HAFF NO RESPECT FOR DERE ELDERS, AND DAY ARE SO IRRE-SPONSIBLE!
OH, I SO AGREE, COUNT! IN FACT, "LOST BOYS" CAN'T EVEN TURN PEOPLE INTO VAMPIRES! THEY'RE STERILE . . .
SO-- NOW THAT YOU'RE HERE, THE MAGNIFICENT KING OF ALL VAMPIRES, THERE IS BUT ONE THING I ASK OF YOU--
TAKE ME!!

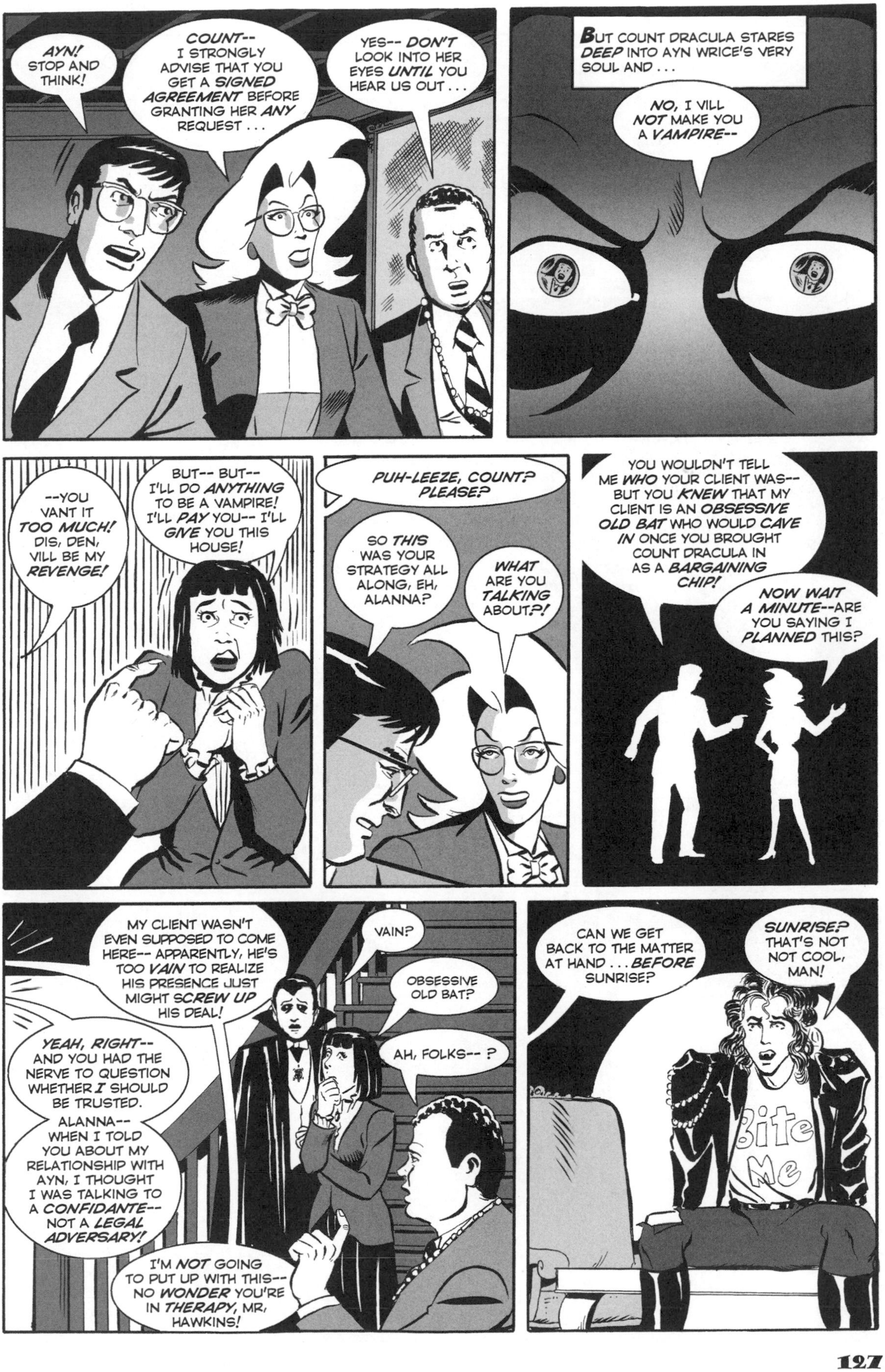
AYN! STOP AND THINK!
COUNT-- I STRONGLY ADVISE THAT YOU GET A SIGNED AGREEMENT BEFORE GRANTING HER ANY REQUEST . . .
YES-- DON'T LOOK INTO HER EYES UNTIL YOU HEAR US OUT . . .
BUT COUNT DRACULA STARES DEEP INTO AYN WRICE'S VERY SOUL AND . . .
NO, I VILL NOT MAKE YOU A VAMPIRE--
--YOU VANT IT TOO MUCH! DIS, DEN, VILL BE MY REVENGE!
BUT-- BUT-- I'LL DO ANYTHING TO BE A VAMPIRE! I'LL PAY YOU-- I'LL GIVE YOU THIS HOUSE!
PUH-LEEZE, COUNT? PLEASE?
SO THIS WAS YOUR STRATEGY ALL ALONG, EH, ALANNA?
WHAT ARE YOU TALKING ABOUT?!
YOU WOULDN'T TELL ME WHO YOUR CLIENT WAS-- BUT YOU KNEW THAT MY CLIENT IS AN OBSESSIVE OLD BAT WHO WOULD CAVE IN ONCE YOU BROUGHT COUNT DRACULA IN AS A BARGAINING CHIP!
NOW WAIT A MINUTE--ARE YOU SAYING I PLANNED THIS?
MY CLIENT WASN'T EVEN SUPPOSED TO COME HERE-- APPARENTLY, HE'S TOO VAIN TO REALIZE HIS PRESENCE JUST MIGHT SCREW UP HIS DEAL!
VAIN?
OBSESSIVE OLD BAT?
AH, FOLKS-- ?
YEAH, RIGHT-- AND YOU HAD THE NERVE TO QUESTION WHETHER I SHOULD BE TRUSTED.
ALANNA-- WHEN I TOLD YOU ABOUT MY RELATIONSHIP WITH AYN, I THOUGHT I WAS TALKING TO A CONFIDANTE-- NOT A LEGAL ADVERSARY!
I'M NOT GOING TO PUT UP WITH THIS-- NO WONDER YOU'RE IN THERAPY, MR. HAWKINS!
CAN WE GET BACK TO THE MATTER AT HAND . . . BEFORE SUNRISE?
SUNRISE? THAT'S NOT NOT COOL, MAN!
Bite Me

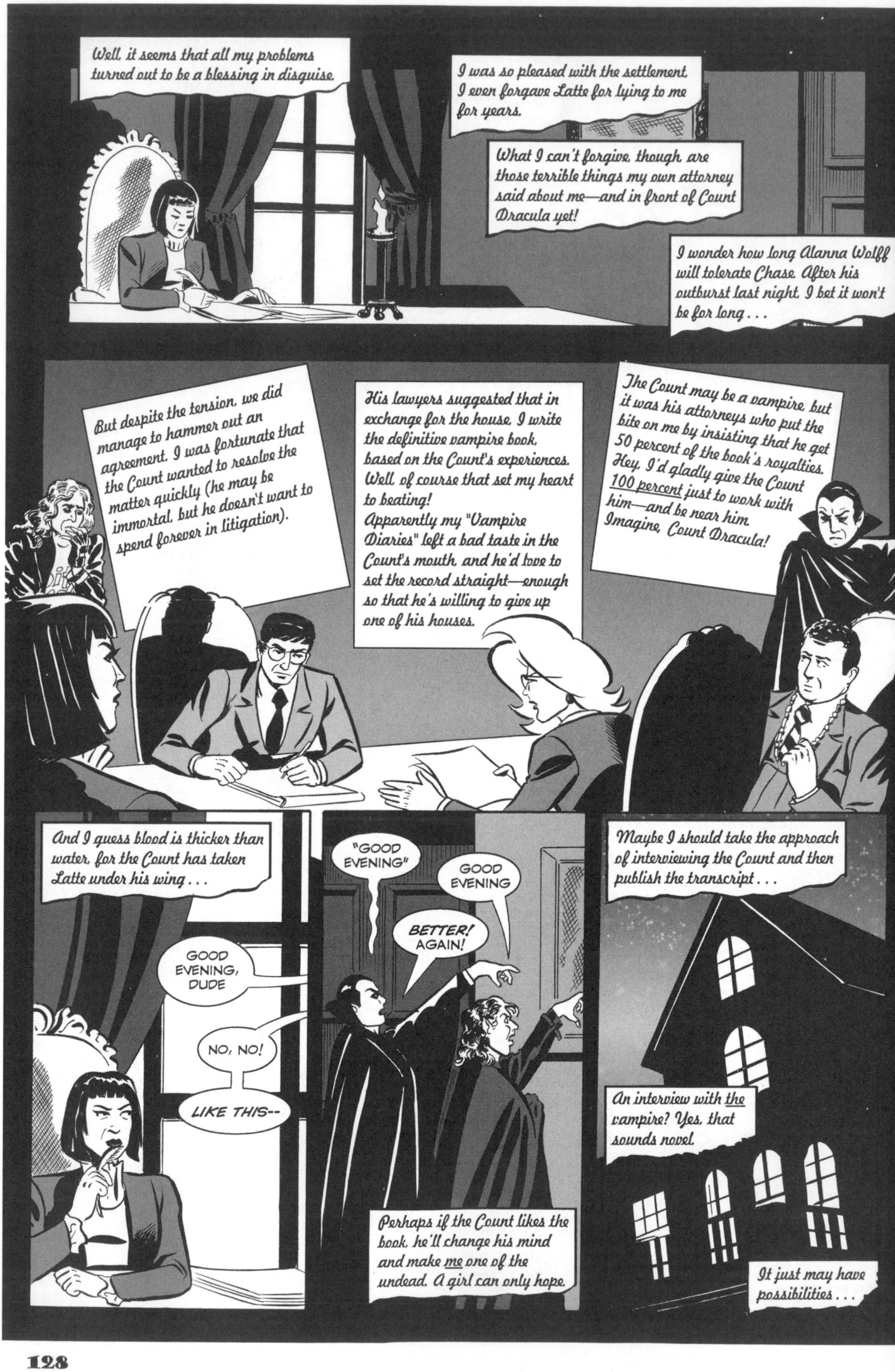
Well, it seems that all my problems turned out to be a blessing in disguise.
I was so pleased with the settlement, I even forgave Latte for lying to me for years.
What I can't forgive, though, are those terrible things my own attorney said about me—and in front of Count Dracula yet!
I wonder how long Alanna Wolff will tolerate Chase. After his outburst last night, I bet it won't be for long . . .
But despite the tension, we did manage to hammer out an agreement. I was fortunate that the Count wanted to resolve the matter quickly (he may be immortal, but he doesn't want to spend forever in litigation).
His lawyers suggested that in exchange for the house, I write the definitive vampire book, based on the Count's experiences. Well, of course that set my heart to beating!
Apparently my "Vampire Diaries" left a bad taste in the Count's mouth, and he'd love to set the record straight—enough so that he's willing to give up one of his houses.
The Count may be a vampire, but it was his attorneys who put the bite on me by insisting that he get 50 percent of the book's royalties. Hey, I'd gladly give the Count 100 percent just to work with him—and be near him. Imagine, Count Dracula!
And I guess blood is thicker than water, for the Count has taken Latte under his wing . . .
"GOOD EVENING"
GOOD EVENING
BETTER! AGAIN!
GOOD EVENING, DUDE
NO, NO!
LIKE THIS--
Perhaps if the Count likes the book, he'll change his mind and make me one of the undead. A girl can only hope.
Maybe I should take the approach of interviewing the Count and then publish the transcript . . .
An interview with the vampire? Yes, that sounds novel.
It just may have possibilities . . .

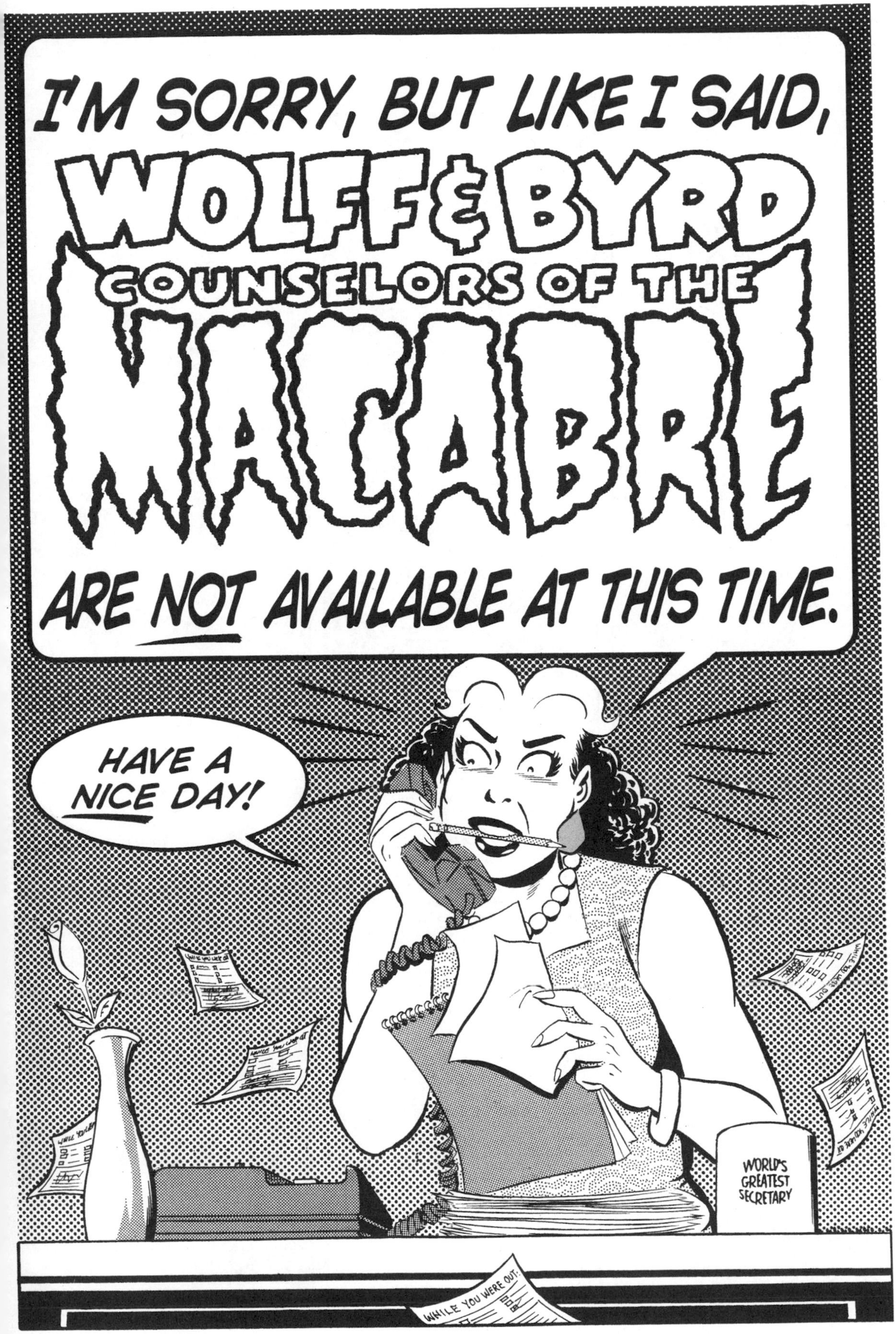
I'M SORRY, BUT LIKE I SAID,
WOLFF & BYRD
COUNSELORS OF THE
MACABRE
ARE NOT AVAILABLE AT THIS TIME.
HAVE A NICE DAY!
WORLD'S GREATEST SECRETARY
WHILE YOU WERE OUT

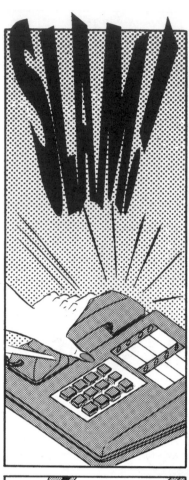

DID I EVER TELL YOU I *HATE* REPORTERS, TOBY?

NOT ONLY DO THEY *KEEP CALLING* TO ASK ABOUT THE *SODD* INCIDENT--

--BUT THEY WANT TO KNOW WHAT *OTHER* SUPERNATURAL CLIENTS WOLFF AND BYRD REPRESENT! HAVEN'T THEY EVERY HEARD OF *CONFIDENTIALITY?*

PRIVILEGED INFORMATION?

MINDING YOUR OWN BUSINESS?

THE MEDIA IS ONLY DOING THEIR *JOB*, MAVIS

WHEN AN EIGHT-FOOT-TALL WALKING *PLANT* IS AT LARGE AFTER FLEEING FROM HIS OWN *TRIAL*, THEY WANT TO *ALERT* THE PUBLIC TO WHAT ELSE THEY MIGHT EXPECT...

ALERT OR *PANIC?* IN ALL THE TIME I'VE WORKED HERE, I'VE NEVER SEEN SUCH A *FLAP* OVER ONE OF OUR CLIENTS.

I THOUGHT THE *ROGER RIZZOLI* CASE WOULD BE *PAGE ONE* MATERIAL, BUT IT WAS *BURIED* IN THE BACK OF THE PAPER...

WHAT WAS THE BIG DEAL ABOUT ROGER RIZZOLI-- *YEOW!* WHAT THE HECK IS THIS *THING?!*

LOOK AT MY *MAIL*, WHY DON'T YOU!

AW, IT'S ONLY A *POSTCARD*-- POSTMARKED *NEW ORLEANS*...

YEAH, MY BOSSES ARE ON THEIR WAY BACK FROM THERE-- *FINALLY!* YOU KNOW THEY'VE BEEN GONE *TOO LONG* WHEN THE POSTCARD BEATS THEM HOME.

BY THE WAY, THERE'S A *STORY* BEHIND THAT *THING* ON THE POSTCARD--I'LL TELL YOU IF YOU'RE INTERESTED...

LOOK, I'M *SWAMPED* HERE. INSTEAD OF GOING TO LUNCH, LET'S ORDER IN, AND IF YOU EAT *ALL* YOUR VEGETABLES, I'LL TELL YOU ABOUT *ROGER RIZZOLI*, TOO-- AND SEE IF YOU CAN KEEP YOUR LUNCH DOWN!

HEY, GORY I CAN TAKE! IT'S THE *PATHETIC LOVESICK LOSERS* I CAN'T *STOMACH!* WHY, I REMEMBER MEETING YOUR BOSSES WHEN I'D JUST STARTED AS IN-HOUSE COUNSEL AT THE *BLACKWOOD MUSEUM*, AND THEY HAD THIS CLIENT...

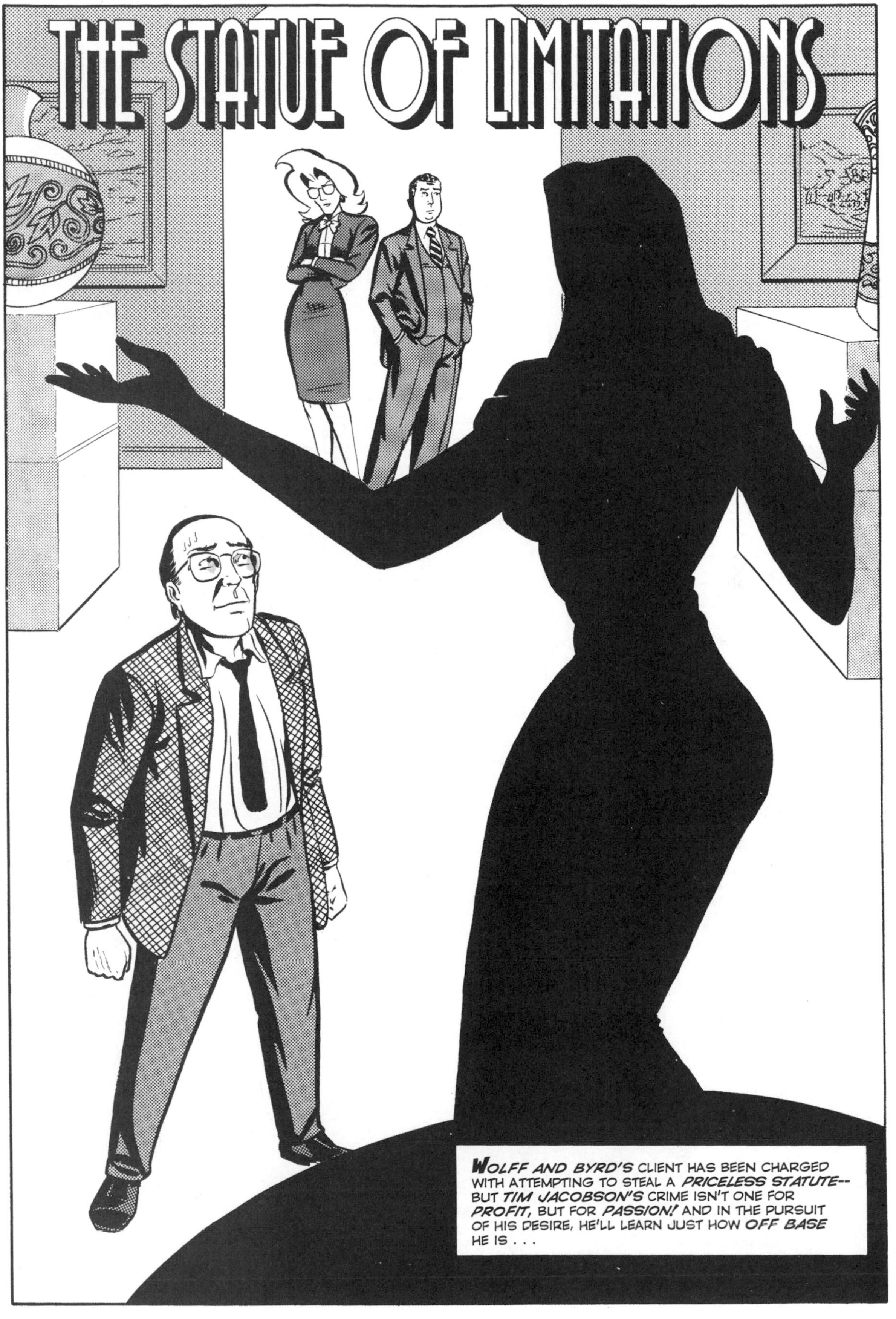
THE STATUE OF LIMITATIONS
WOLFF AND BYRD'S CLIENT HAS BEEN CHARGED WITH ATTEMPTING TO STEAL A PRICELESS STATUTE-- BUT TIM JACOBSON'S CRIME ISN'T ONE FOR PROFIT, BUT FOR PASSION! AND IN THE PURSUIT OF HIS DESIRE, HE'LL LEARN JUST HOW OFF BASE HE IS . . .

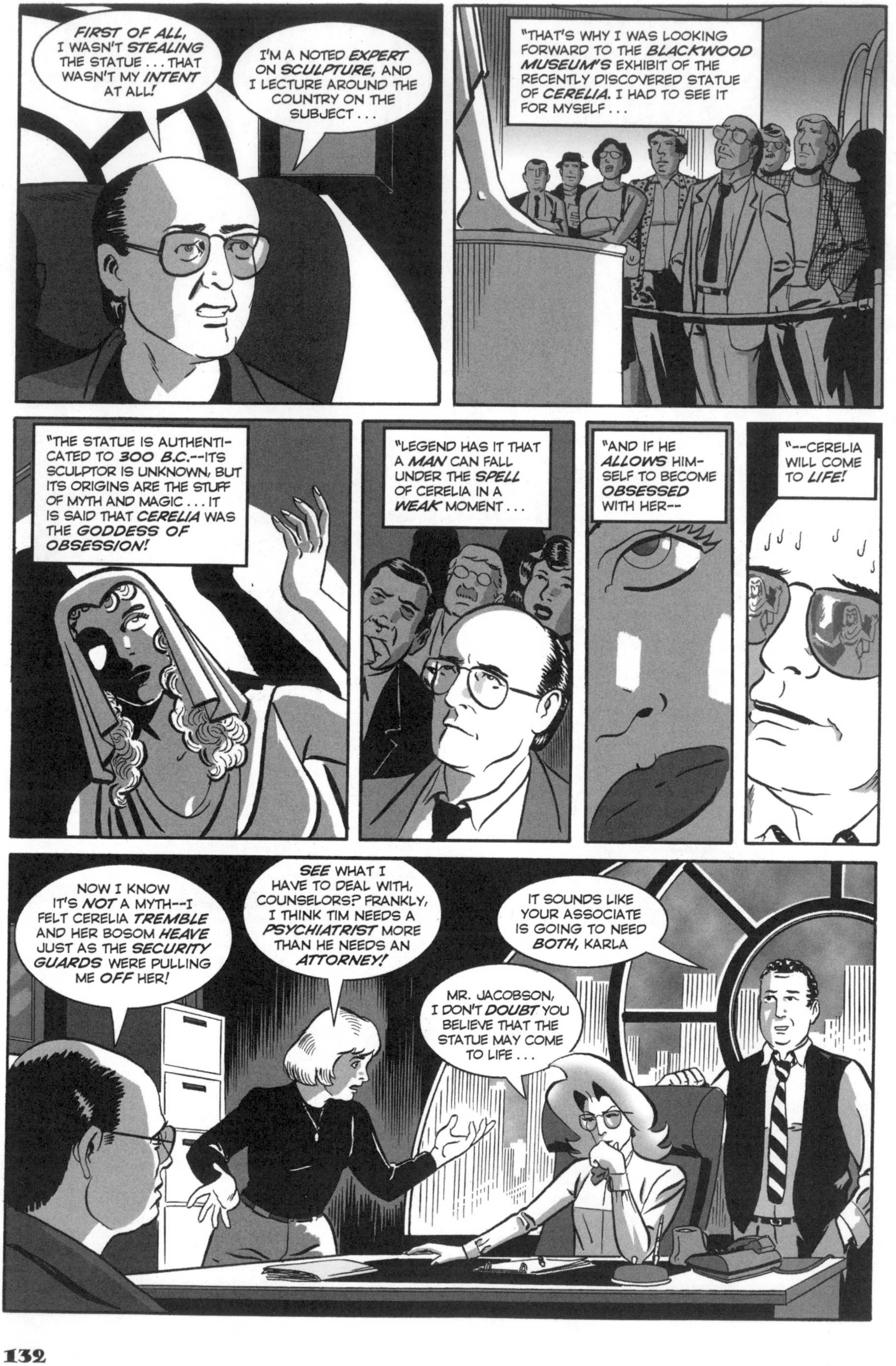
FIRST OF ALL, I WASN'T STEALING THE STATUE . . . THAT WASN'T MY INTENT AT ALL!
I'M A NOTED EXPERT ON SCULPTURE, AND I LECTURE AROUND THE COUNTRY ON THE SUBJECT . . .
"THAT'S WHY I WAS LOOKING FORWARD TO THE BLACKWOOD MUSEUM'S EXHIBIT OF THE RECENTLY DISCOVERED STATUE OF CERELIA. I HAD TO SEE IT FOR MYSELF . . .
"THE STATUE IS AUTHENTICATED TO 300 B.C.--ITS SCULPTOR IS UNKNOWN, BUT ITS ORIGINS ARE THE STUFF OF MYTH AND MAGIC . . . IT IS SAID THAT CERELIA WAS THE GODDESS OF OBSESSION!
"LEGEND HAS IT THAT A MAN CAN FALL UNDER THE SPELL OF CERELIA IN A WEAK MOMENT . . .
"AND IF HE ALLOWS HIMSELF TO BECOME OBSESSED WITH HER--
"--CERELIA WILL COME TO LIFE!
NOW I KNOW IT'S NOT A MYTH--I FELT CERELIA TREMBLE AND HER BOSOM HEAVE JUST AS THE SECURITY GUARDS WERE PULLING ME OFF HER!
SEE WHAT I HAVE TO DEAL WITH, COUNSELORS? FRANKLY, I THINK TIM NEEDS A PSYCHIATRIST MORE THAN HE NEEDS AN ATTORNEY!
IT SOUNDS LIKE YOUR ASSOCIATE IS GOING TO NEED BOTH, KARLA
MR. JACOBSON, I DON'T DOUBT YOU BELIEVE THAT THE STATUE MAY COME TO LIFE . . .

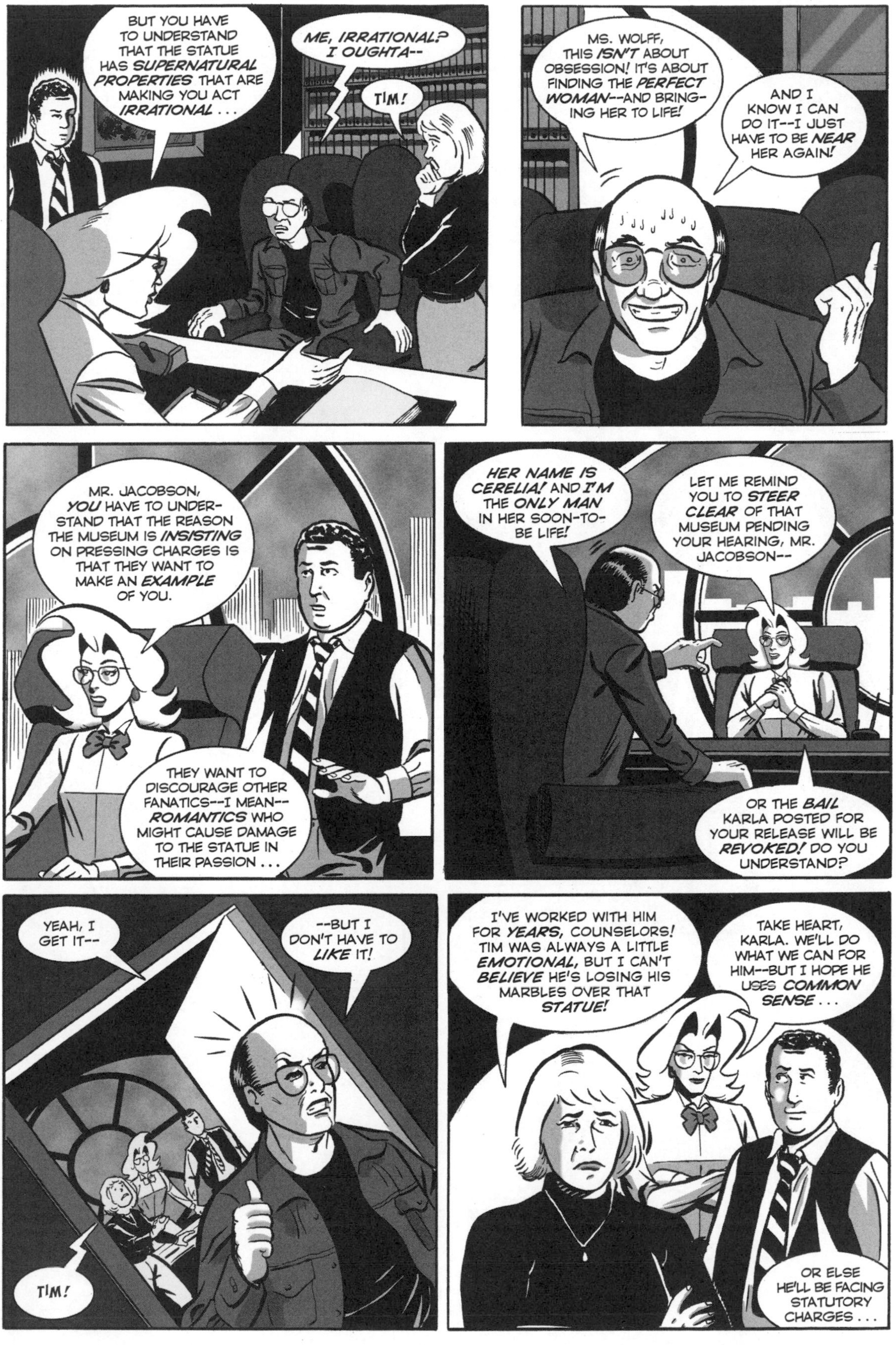
BUT YOU HAVE TO UNDERSTAND THAT THE STATUE HAS SUPERNATURAL PROPERTIES THAT ARE MAKING YOU ACT IRRATIONAL . . .
ME, IRRATIONAL? I OUGHTA--
TIM!
MS. WOLFF, THIS ISN'T ABOUT OBSESSION! IT'S ABOUT FINDING THE PERFECT WOMAN--AND BRINGING HER TO LIFE!
AND I KNOW I CAN DO IT--I JUST HAVE TO BE NEAR HER AGAIN!
MR. JACOBSON, YOU HAVE TO UNDERSTAND THAT THE REASON THE MUSEUM IS INSISTING ON PRESSING CHARGES IS THAT THEY WANT TO MAKE AN EXAMPLE OF YOU.
THEY WANT TO DISCOURAGE OTHER FANATICS--I MEAN--ROMANTICS WHO MIGHT CAUSE DAMAGE TO THE STATUE IN THEIR PASSION . . .
HER NAME IS CERELIA! AND I'M THE ONLY MAN IN HER SOON-TO-BE LIFE!
LET ME REMIND YOU TO STEER CLEAR OF THAT MUSEUM PENDING YOUR HEARING, MR. JACOBSON--
OR THE BAIL KARLA POSTED FOR YOUR RELEASE WILL BE REVOKED! DO YOU UNDERSTAND?
YEAH, I GET IT--
--BUT I DON'T HAVE TO LIKE IT!
TIM!
I'VE WORKED WITH HIM FOR YEARS, COUNSELORS! TIM WAS ALWAYS A LITTLE EMOTIONAL, BUT I CAN'T BELIEVE HE'S LOSING HIS MARBLES OVER THAT STATUE!
TAKE HEART, KARLA. WE'LL DO WHAT WE CAN FOR HIM--BUT I HOPE HE USES COMMON SENSE . . .
OR ELSE HE'LL BE FACING STATUTORY CHARGES . . .

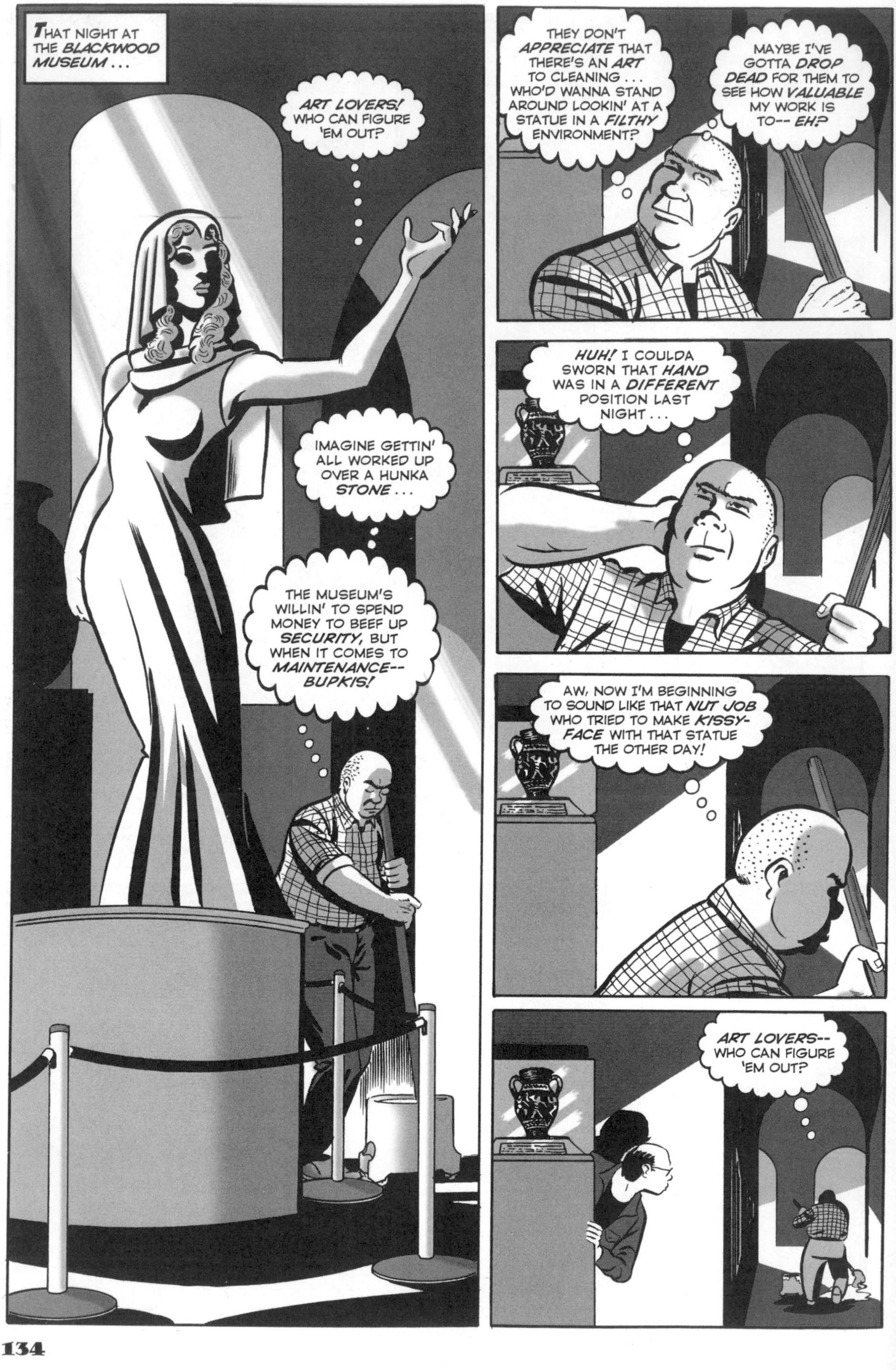
THAT NIGHT AT THE BLACKWOOD MUSEUM . . .
ART LOVERS! WHO CAN FIGURE 'EM OUT?
IMAGINE GETTIN' ALL WORKED UP OVER A HUNKA STONE . . .
THE MUSEUM'S WILLIN' TO SPEND MONEY TO BEEF UP SECURITY, BUT WHEN IT COMES TO MAINTENANCE-- BUPKIS!
THEY DON'T APPRECIATE THAT THERE'S AN ART TO CLEANING . . . WHO'D WANNA STAND AROUND LOOKIN' AT A STATUE IN A FILTHY ENVIRONMENT?
MAYBE I'VE GOTTA DROP DEAD FOR THEM TO SEE HOW VALUABLE MY WORK IS TO-- EH?
HUH! I COULDA SWORN THAT HAND WAS IN A DIFFERENT POSITION LAST NIGHT . . .
AW, NOW I'M BEGINNING TO SOUND LIKE THAT NUT JOB WHO TRIED TO MAKE KISSY-FACE WITH THAT STATUE THE OTHER DAY!
ART LOVERS-- WHO CAN FIGURE 'EM OUT?

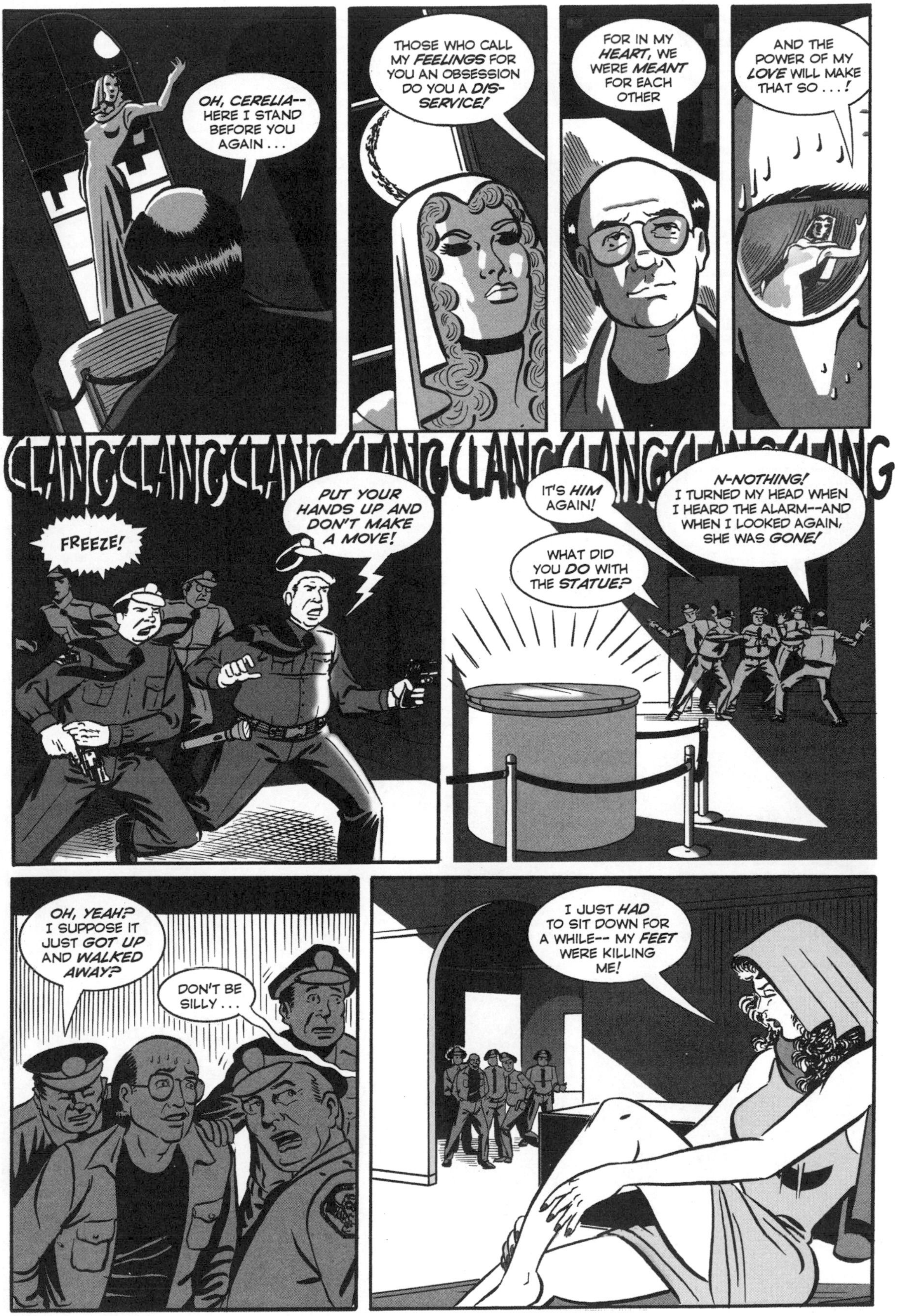
OH, CERELIA-- HERE I STAND BEFORE YOU AGAIN . . .
THOSE WHO CALL MY FEELINGS FOR YOU AN OBSESSION DO YOU A DIS-SERVICE!
FOR IN MY HEART, WE WERE MEANT FOR EACH OTHER
AND THE POWER OF MY LOVE WILL MAKE THAT SO . . . !
CLANG CLANG CLANG CLANG CLANG CLANG CLANG CLANG
FREEZE!
PUT YOUR HANDS UP AND DON'T MAKE A MOVE!
IT'S HIM AGAIN!
WHAT DID YOU DO WITH THE STATUE?
N-NOTHING! I TURNED MY HEAD WHEN I HEARD THE ALARM--AND WHEN I LOOKED AGAIN, SHE WAS GONE!
OH, YEAH? I SUPPOSE IT JUST GOT UP AND WALKED AWAY?
DON'T BE SILLY . . .
I JUST HAD TO SIT DOWN FOR A WHILE-- MY FEET WERE KILLING ME!

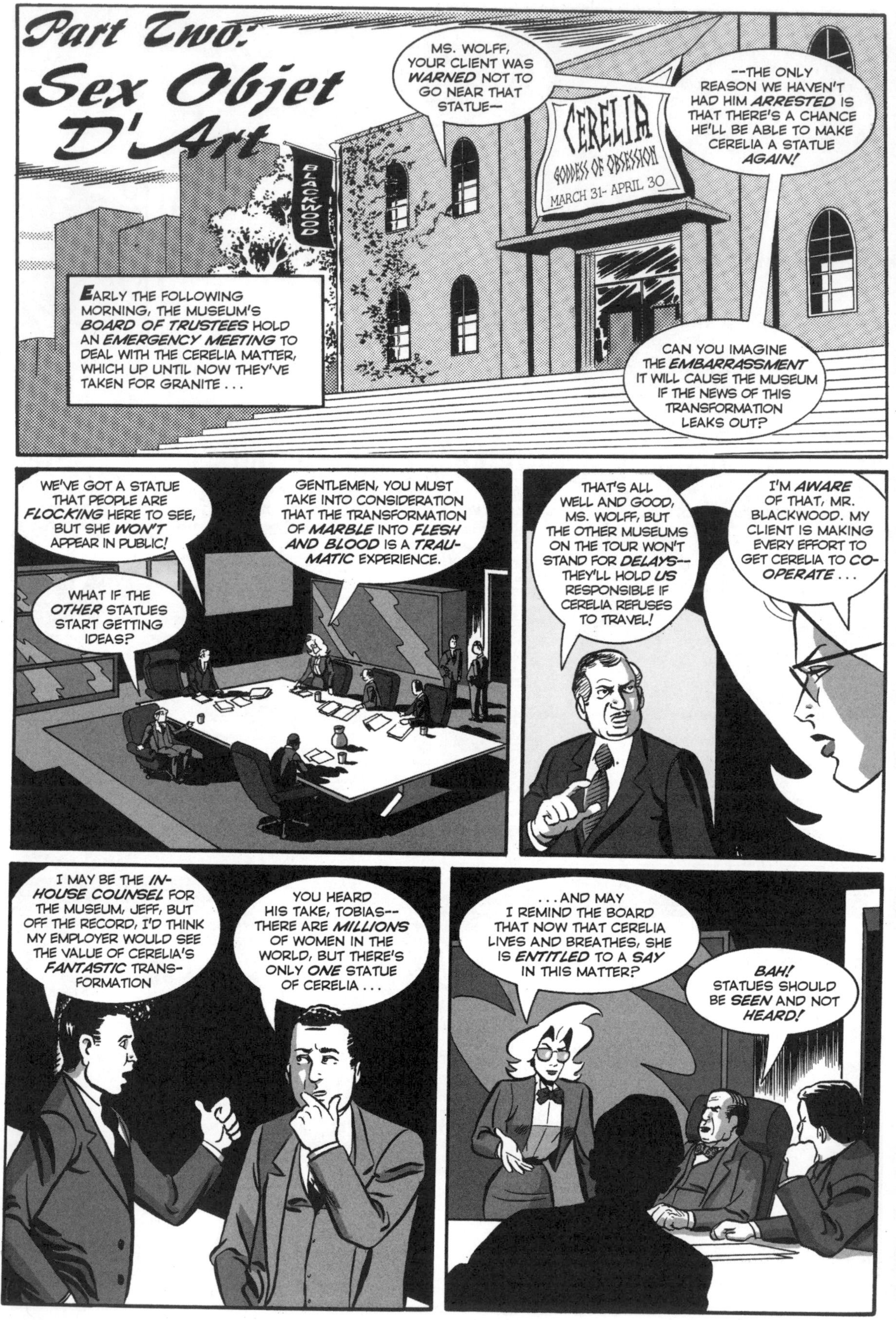
Part Two: Sex Objet D'Art
BLACKWOOD
CERELIA GODDESS OF OBSESSION MARCH 31- APRIL 30
MS. WOLFF, YOUR CLIENT WAS WARNED NOT TO GO NEAR THAT STATUE--
--THE ONLY REASON WE HAVEN'T HAD HIM ARRESTED IS THAT THERE'S A CHANCE HE'LL BE ABLE TO MAKE CERELIA A STATUE AGAIN!
EARLY THE FOLLOWING MORNING, THE MUSEUM'S BOARD OF TRUSTEES HOLD AN EMERGENCY MEETING TO DEAL WITH THE CERELIA MATTER, WHICH UP UNTIL NOW THEY'VE TAKEN FOR GRANITE . . .
CAN YOU IMAGINE THE EMBARRASSMENT IT WILL CAUSE THE MUSEUM IF THE NEWS OF THIS TRANSFORMATION LEAKS OUT?
WE'VE GOT A STATUE THAT PEOPLE ARE FLOCKING HERE TO SEE, BUT SHE WON'T APPEAR IN PUBLIC!
WHAT IF THE OTHER STATUES START GETTING IDEAS?
GENTLEMEN, YOU MUST TAKE INTO CONSIDERATION THAT THE TRANSFORMATION OF MARBLE INTO FLESH AND BLOOD IS A TRAUMATIC EXPERIENCE.
THAT'S ALL WELL AND GOOD, MS. WOLFF, BUT THE OTHER MUSEUMS ON THE TOUR WON'T STAND FOR DELAYS-- THEY'LL HOLD US RESPONSIBLE IF CERELIA REFUSES TO TRAVEL!
I'M AWARE OF THAT, MR. BLACKWOOD. MY CLIENT IS MAKING EVERY EFFORT TO GET CERELIA TO CO-OPERATE . . .
I MAY BE THE IN-HOUSE COUNSEL FOR THE MUSEUM, JEFF, BUT OFF THE RECORD, I'D THINK MY EMPLOYER WOULD SEE THE VALUE OF CERELIA'S FANTASTIC TRANSFORMATION
YOU HEARD HIS TAKE, TOBIAS-- THERE ARE MILLIONS OF WOMEN IN THE WORLD, BUT THERE'S ONLY ONE STATUE OF CERELIA . . .
. . . AND MAY I REMIND THE BOARD THAT NOW THAT CERELIA LIVES AND BREATHES, SHE IS ENTITLED TO A SAY IN THIS MATTER?
BAH! STATUES SHOULD BE SEEN AND NOT HEARD!

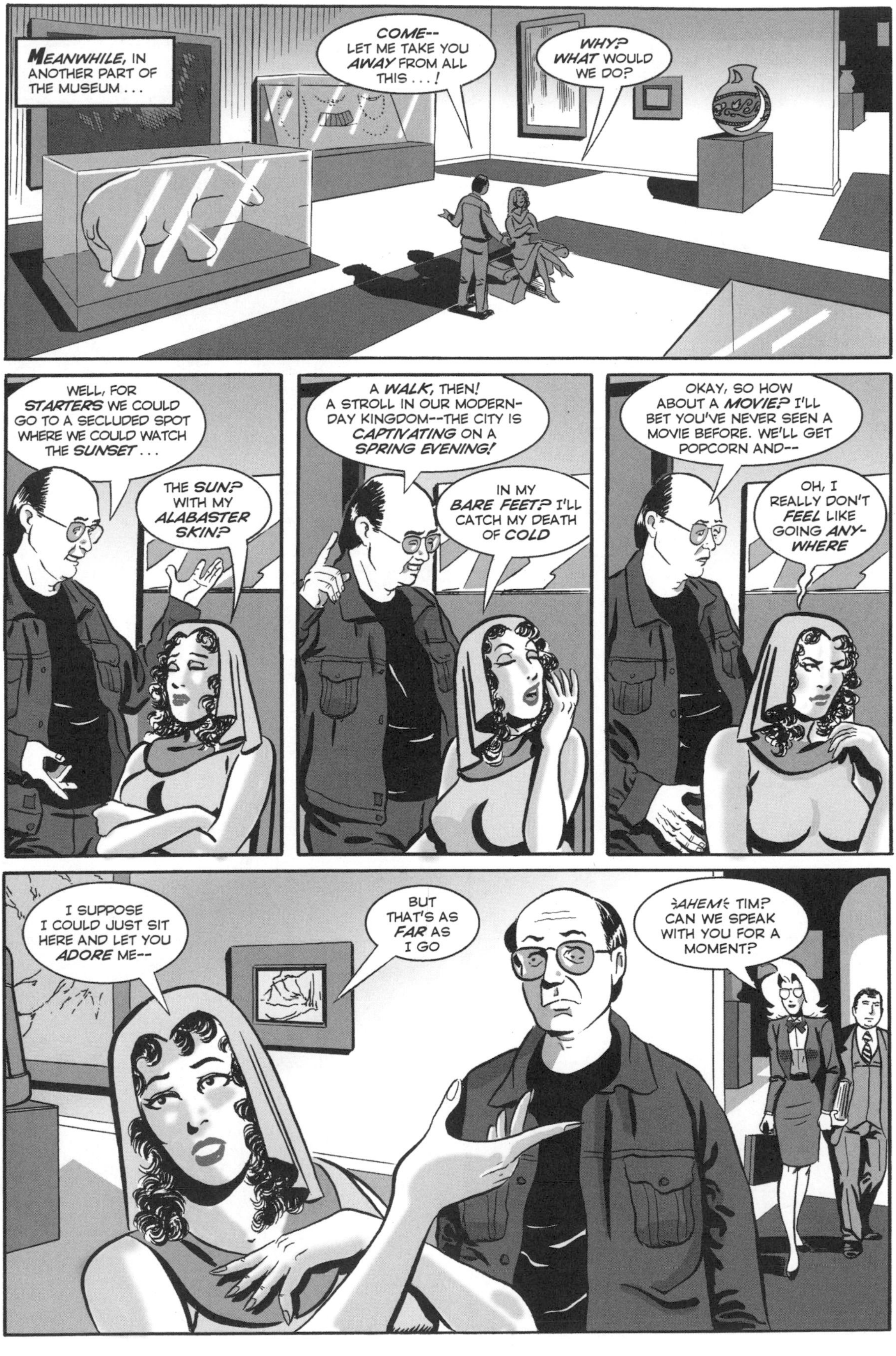
MEANWHILE, IN ANOTHER PART OF THE MUSEUM . . .
COME-- LET ME TAKE YOU AWAY FROM ALL THIS . . . !
WHY? WHAT WOULD WE DO?
WELL, FOR STARTERS WE COULD GO TO A SECLUDED SPOT WHERE WE COULD WATCH THE SUNSET . . .
THE SUN? WITH MY ALABASTER SKIN?
A WALK, THEN! A STROLL IN OUR MODERN-DAY KINGDOM--THE CITY IS CAPTIVATING ON A SPRING EVENING!
IN MY BARE FEET? I'LL CATCH MY DEATH OF COLD
OKAY, SO HOW ABOUT A MOVIE? I'LL BET YOU'VE NEVER SEEN A MOVIE BEFORE. WE'LL GET POPCORN AND--
OH, I REALLY DON'T FEEL LIKE GOING ANY-WHERE
I SUPPOSE I COULD JUST SIT HERE AND LET YOU ADORE ME--
BUT THAT'S AS FAR AS I GO
AHEM TIM? CAN WE SPEAK WITH YOU FOR A MOMENT?

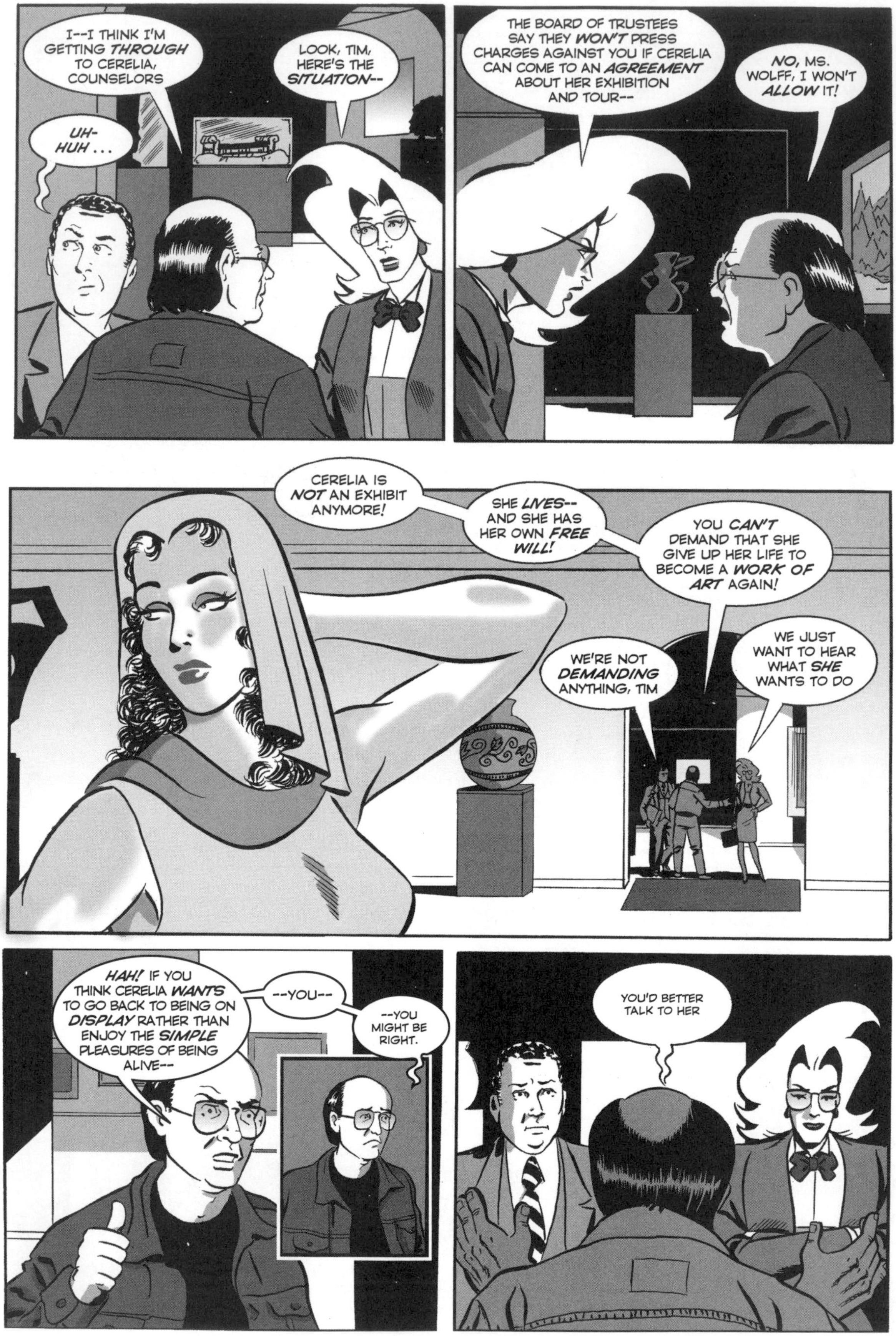
I--I THINK I'M GETTING THROUGH TO CERELIA, COUNSELORS
UH-HUH . . .
LOOK, TIM, HERE'S THE SITUATION--
THE BOARD OF TRUSTEES SAY THEY WON'T PRESS CHARGES AGAINST YOU IF CERELIA CAN COME TO AN AGREEMENT ABOUT HER EXHIBITION AND TOUR--
NO, MS. WOLFF; I WON'T ALLOW IT!
CERELIA IS NOT AN EXHIBIT ANYMORE!
SHE LIVES-- AND SHE HAS HER OWN FREE WILL!
YOU CAN'T DEMAND THAT SHE GIVE UP HER LIFE TO BECOME A WORK OF ART AGAIN!
WE'RE NOT DEMANDING ANYTHING, TIM
WE JUST WANT TO HEAR WHAT SHE WANTS TO DO
HAH! IF YOU THINK CERELIA WANTS TO GO BACK TO BEING ON DISPLAY RATHER THAN ENJOY THE SIMPLE PLEASURES OF BEING ALIVE--
--YOU--
--YOU MIGHT BE RIGHT.
YOU'D BETTER TALK TO HER

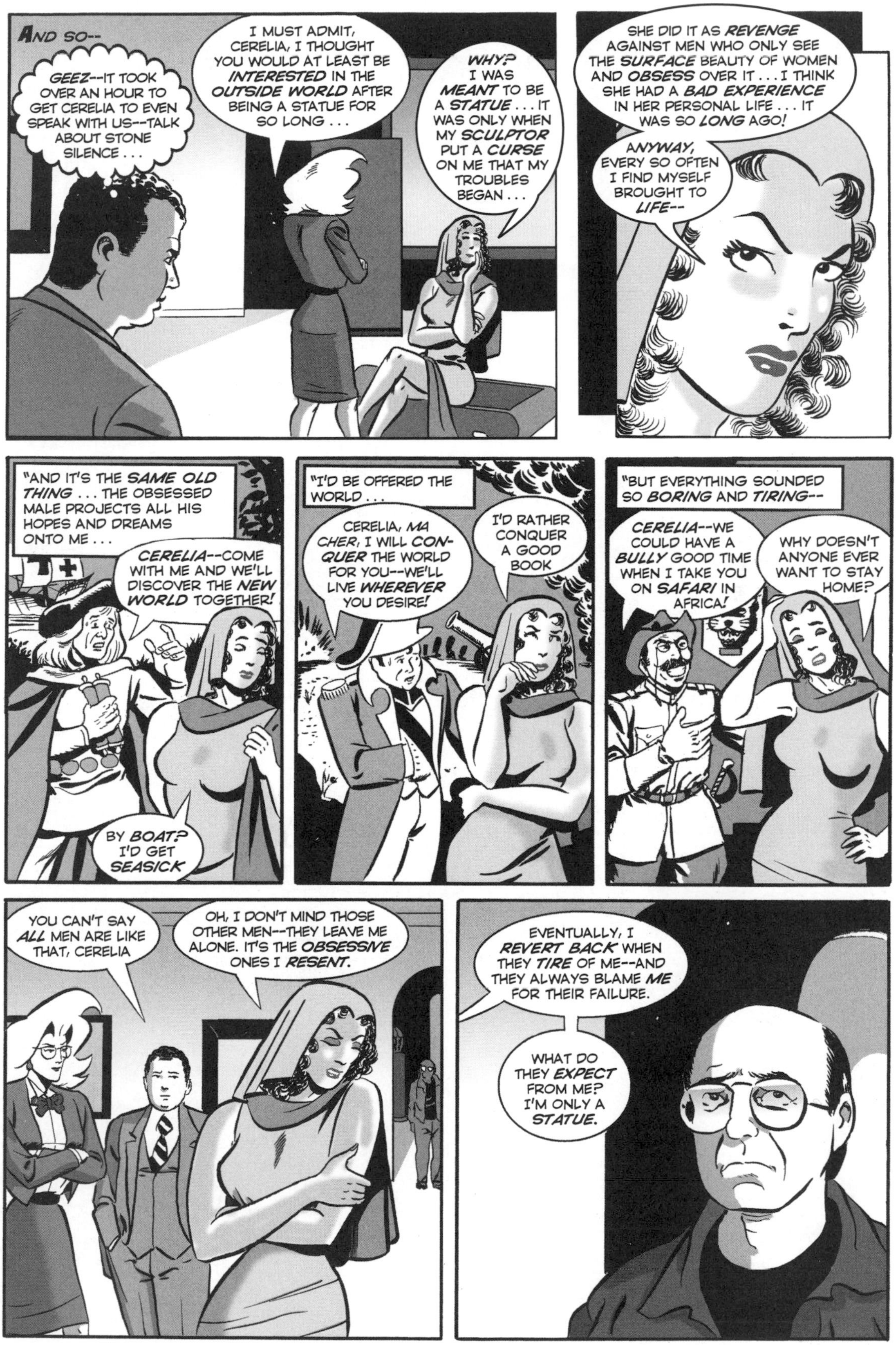
AND SO--
GEEZ--IT TOOK OVER AN HOUR TO GET CERELIA TO EVEN SPEAK WITH US--TALK ABOUT STONE SILENCE . . .
I MUST ADMIT, CERELIA, I THOUGHT YOU WOULD AT LEAST BE INTERESTED IN THE OUTSIDE WORLD AFTER BEING A STATUE FOR SO LONG . . .
WHY? I WAS MEANT TO BE A STATUE . . . IT WAS ONLY WHEN MY SCULPTOR PUT A CURSE ON ME THAT MY TROUBLES BEGAN . . .
SHE DID IT AS REVENGE AGAINST MEN WHO ONLY SEE THE SURFACE BEAUTY OF WOMEN AND OBSESS OVER IT . . . I THINK SHE HAD A BAD EXPERIENCE IN HER PERSONAL LIFE . . . IT WAS SO LONG AGO!
ANYWAY, EVERY SO OFTEN I FIND MYSELF BROUGHT TO LIFE--
"AND IT'S THE SAME OLD THING . . . THE OBSESSED MALE PROJECTS ALL HIS HOPES AND DREAMS ONTO ME . . .
CERELIA--COME WITH ME AND WE'LL DISCOVER THE NEW WORLD TOGETHER!
BY BOAT? I'D GET SEASICK
"I'D BE OFFERED THE WORLD . . .
CERELIA, MA CHER, I WILL CONQUER THE WORLD FOR YOU--WE'LL LIVE WHEREVER YOU DESIRE!
I'D RATHER CONQUER A GOOD BOOK
"BUT EVERYTHING SOUNDED SO BORING AND TIRING--
CERELIA--WE COULD HAVE A BULLY GOOD TIME WHEN I TAKE YOU ON SAFARI IN AFRICA!
WHY DOESN'T ANYONE EVER WANT TO STAY HOME?
YOU CAN'T SAY ALL MEN ARE LIKE THAT, CERELIA
OH, I DON'T MIND THOSE OTHER MEN--THEY LEAVE ME ALONE. IT'S THE OBSESSIVE ONES I RESENT.
EVENTUALLY, I REVERT BACK WHEN THEY TIRE OF ME--AND THEY ALWAYS BLAME ME FOR THEIR FAILURE.
WHAT DO THEY EXPECT FROM ME? I'M ONLY A STATUE.

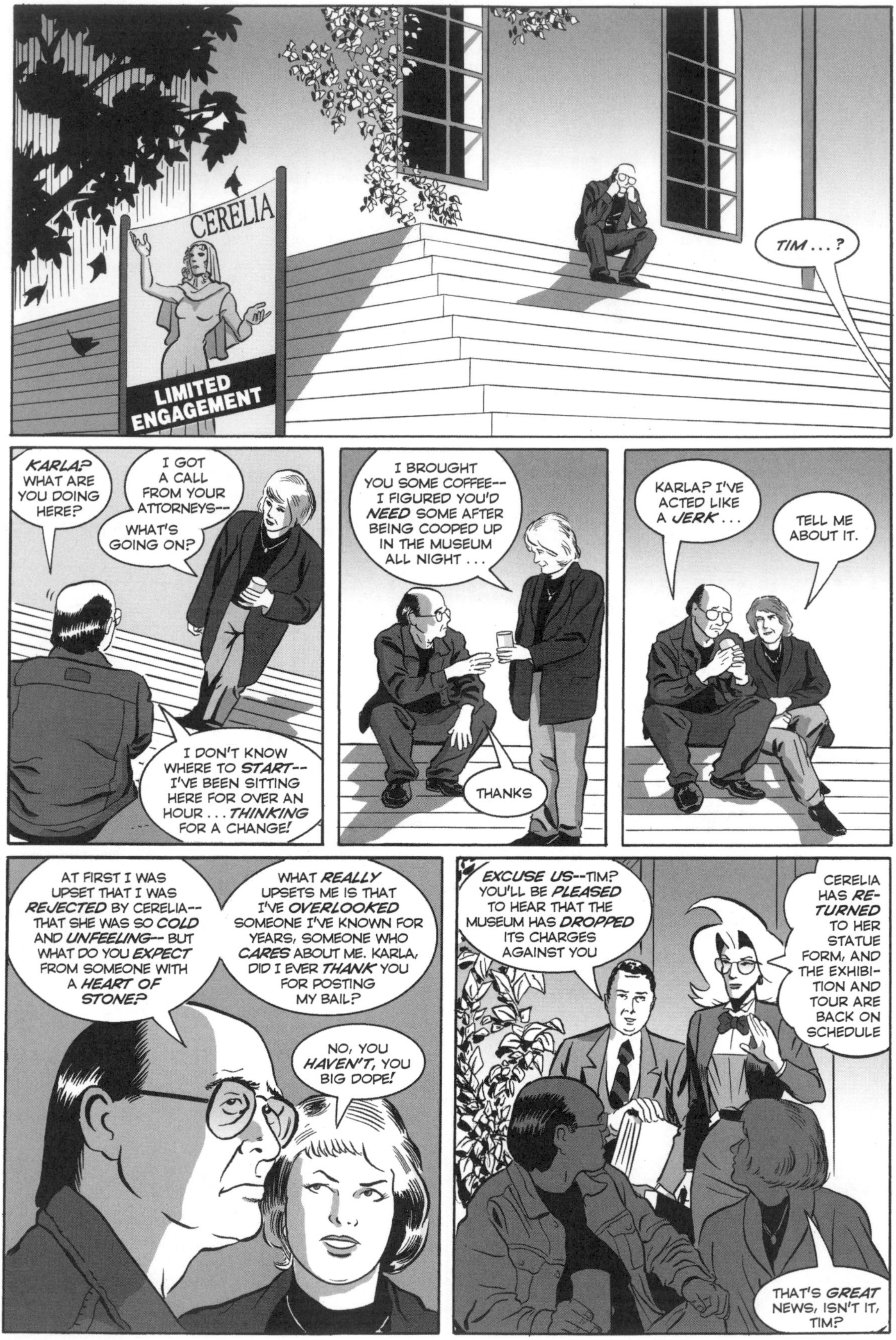
CERELIA
LIMITED ENGAGEMENT
TIM . . . ?
KARLA? WHAT ARE YOU DOING HERE?
I GOT A CALL FROM YOUR ATTORNEYS--
WHAT'S GOING ON?
I DON'T KNOW WHERE TO START-- I'VE BEEN SITTING HERE FOR OVER AN HOUR . . . THINKING FOR A CHANGE!
I BROUGHT YOU SOME COFFEE-- I FIGURED YOU'D NEED SOME AFTER BEING COOPED UP IN THE MUSEUM ALL NIGHT . . .
THANKS
KARLA? I'VE ACTED LIKE A JERK . . .
TELL ME ABOUT IT.
AT FIRST I WAS UPSET THAT I WAS REJECTED BY CERELIA-- THAT SHE WAS SO COLD AND UNFEELING-- BUT WHAT DO YOU EXPECT FROM SOMEONE WITH A HEART OF STONE?
WHAT REALLY UPSETS ME IS THAT I'VE OVERLOOKED SOMEONE I'VE KNOWN FOR YEARS, SOMEONE WHO CARES ABOUT ME. KARLA, DID I EVER THANK YOU FOR POSTING MY BAIL?
NO, YOU HAVEN'T, YOU BIG DOPE!
EXCUSE US--TIM? YOU'LL BE PLEASED TO HEAR THAT THE MUSEUM HAS DROPPED ITS CHARGES AGAINST YOU
CERELIA HAS RE-TURNED TO HER STATUE FORM, AND THE EXHIBI-TION AND TOUR ARE BACK ON SCHEDULE
THAT'S GREAT NEWS, ISN'T IT, TIM?

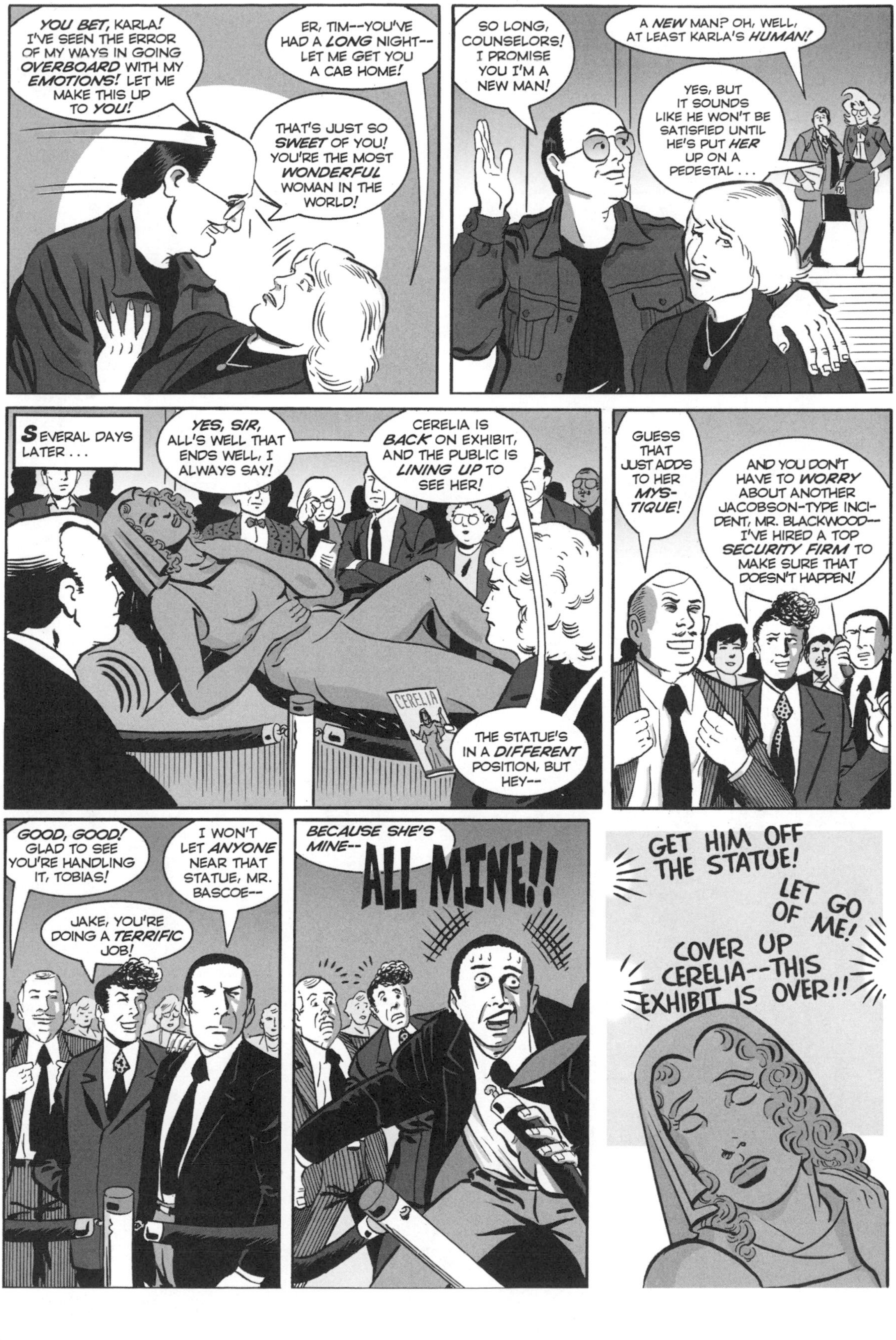
YOU BET, KARLA! I'VE SEEN THE ERROR OF MY WAYS IN GOING OVERBOARD WITH MY EMOTIONS! LET ME MAKE THIS UP TO YOU!
ER, TIM--YOU'VE HAD A LONG NIGHT-- LET ME GET YOU A CAB HOME!
THAT'S JUST SO SWEET OF YOU! YOU'RE THE MOST WONDERFUL WOMAN IN THE WORLD!
SO LONG, COUNSELORS! I PROMISE YOU I'M A NEW MAN!
A NEW MAN? OH, WELL, AT LEAST KARLA'S HUMAN!
YES, BUT IT SOUNDS LIKE HE WON'T BE SATISFIED UNTIL HE'S PUT HER UP ON A PEDESTAL . . .
SEVERAL DAYS LATER . . .
YES, SIR, ALL'S WELL THAT ENDS WELL, I ALWAYS SAY!
CERELIA IS BACK ON EXHIBIT, AND THE PUBLIC IS LINING UP TO SEE HER!
CERELIA
THE STATUE'S IN A DIFFERENT POSITION, BUT HEY--
GUESS THAT JUST ADDS TO HER MYS-TIQUE!
AND YOU DON'T HAVE TO WORRY ABOUT ANOTHER JACOBSON-TYPE INCI-DENT, MR. BLACKWOOD-- I'VE HIRED A TOP SECURITY FIRM TO MAKE SURE THAT DOESN'T HAPPEN!
GOOD, GOOD! GLAD TO SEE YOU'RE HANDLING IT, TOBIAS!
I WON'T LET ANYONE NEAR THAT STATUE, MR. BASCOE--
JAKE, YOU'RE DOING A TERRIFIC JOB!
BECAUSE SHE'S MINE--
ALL MINE!!
GET HIM OFF THE STATUE!
LET GO OF ME!
COVER UP CERELIA--THIS EXHIBIT IS OVER!!

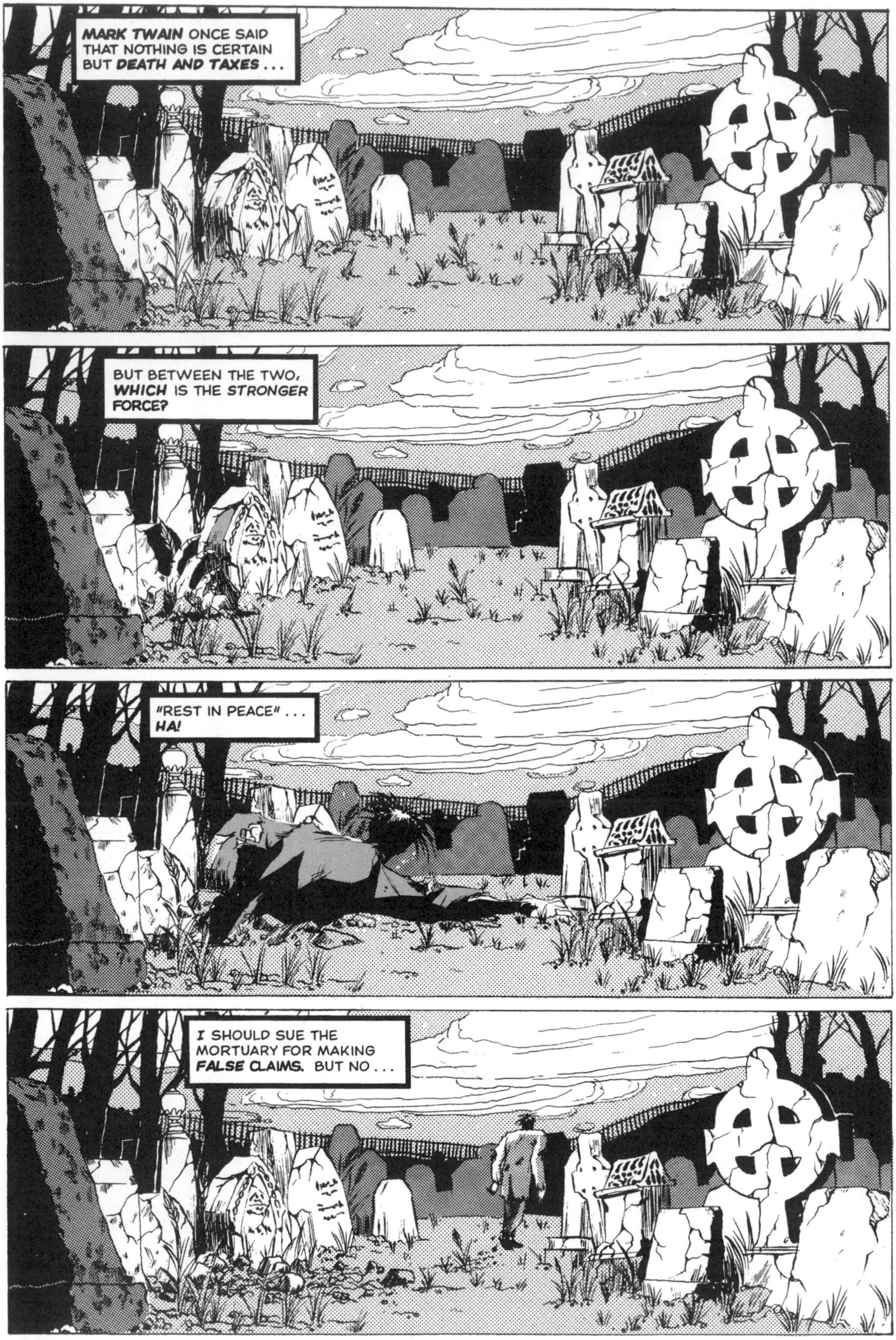
MARK TWAIN ONCE SAID THAT NOTHING IS CERTAIN BUT DEATH AND TAXES . . .
BUT BETWEEN THE TWO, WHICH IS THE STRONGER FORCE?
"REST IN PEACE" . . . HA!
I SHOULD SUE THE MORTUARY FOR MAKING FALSE CLAIMS. BUT NO . . .

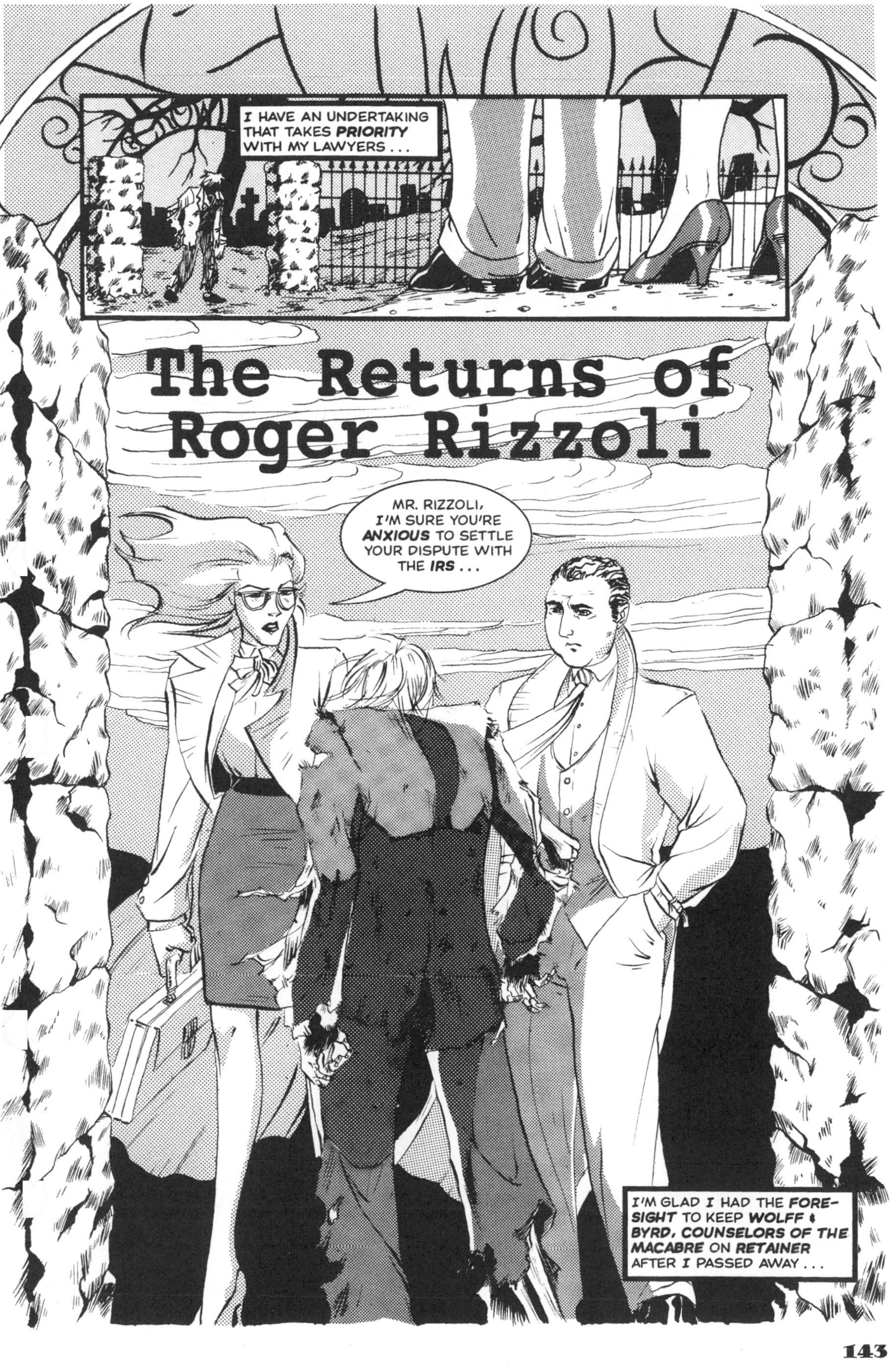
I HAVE AN UNDERTAKING THAT TAKES PRIORITY WITH MY LAWYERS . . .
The Returns of Roger Rizzoli
MR. RIZZOLI, I'M SURE YOU'RE ANXIOUS TO SETTLE YOUR DISPUTE WITH THE IRS . . .
I'M GLAD I HAD THE FORESIGHT TO KEEP WOLFF & BYRD, COUNSELORS OF THE MACABRE ON RETAINER AFTER I PASSED AWAY . . .

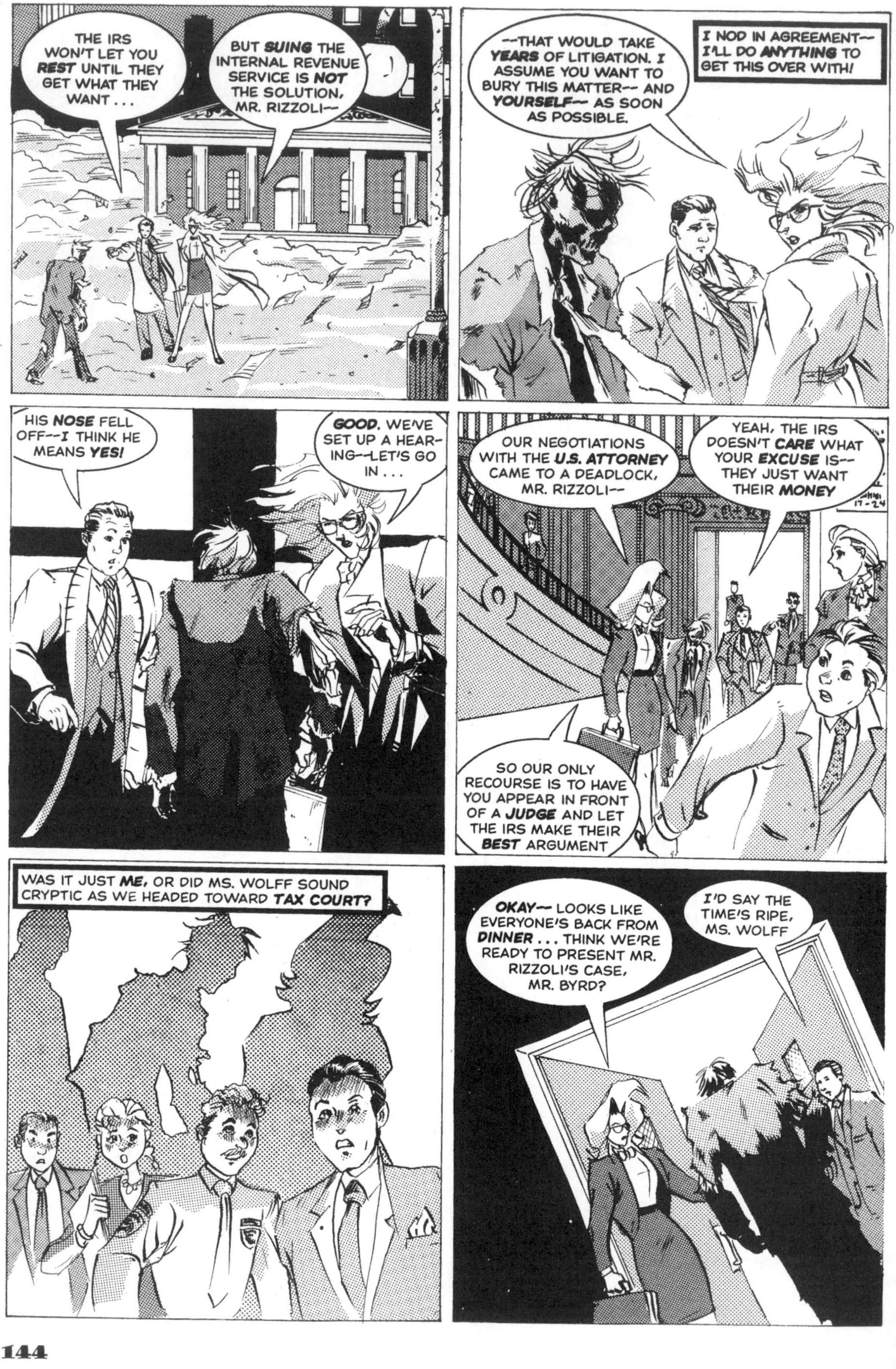
THE IRS WON'T LET YOU **REST** UNTIL THEY GET WHAT THEY WANT . . .
BUT **SUING** THE INTERNAL REVENUE SERVICE IS **NOT** THE SOLUTION, MR. RIZZOLI--
--THAT WOULD TAKE **YEARS** OF LITIGATION. *I* ASSUME YOU WANT TO BURY THIS MATTER-- AND **YOURSELF**-- AS SOON AS POSSIBLE.
I NOD IN AGREEMENT-- I'LL DO ***ANYTHING*** *TO GET THIS OVER WITH!*
HIS **NOSE** FELL OFF--*I* THINK HE MEANS ***YES!***
GOOD. WE'VE SET UP A HEARING--LET'S GO IN . . .
OUR NEGOTIATIONS WITH THE ***U.S. ATTORNEY*** CAME TO A DEADLOCK, MR. RIZZOLI--
YEAH, THE IRS DOESN'T **CARE** WHAT YOUR **EXCUSE** IS-- THEY JUST WANT THEIR **MONEY**
SO OUR ONLY RECOURSE IS TO HAVE YOU APPEAR IN FRONT OF A ***JUDGE*** AND LET THE IRS MAKE THEIR ***BEST*** ARGUMENT
WAS IT JUST ***ME,*** OR DID MS. WOLFF SOUND CRYPTIC AS WE HEADED TOWARD ***TAX COURT?***
OKAY-- LOOKS LIKE EVERYONE'S BACK FROM ***DINNER*** . . . THINK WE'RE READY TO PRESENT MR. RIZZOLI'S CASE, MR. BYRD?
I'D SAY THE TIME'S RIPE, MS. WOLFF

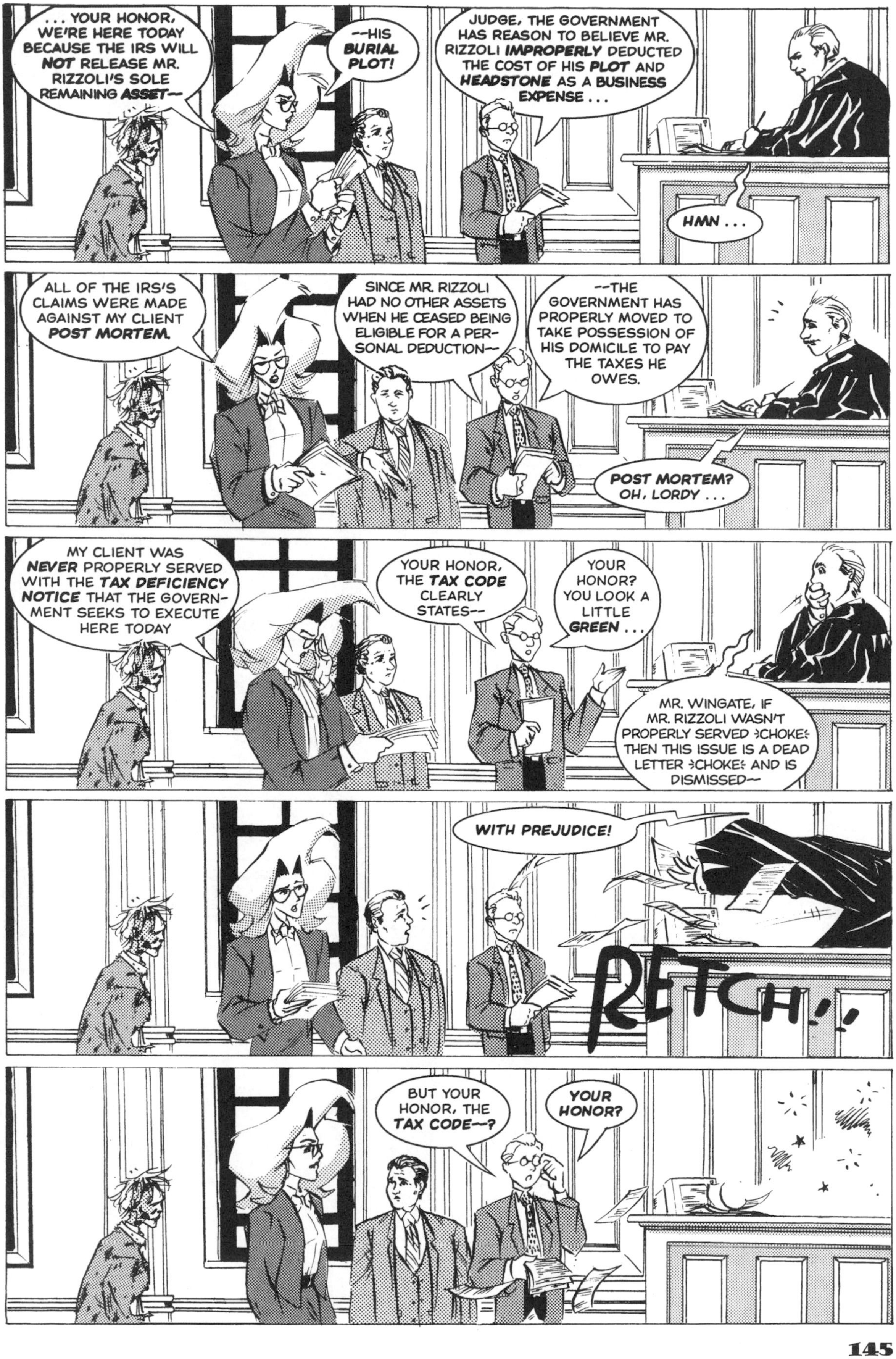
. . . YOUR HONOR, WE'RE HERE TODAY BECAUSE THE IRS WILL **NOT** RELEASE MR. RIZZOLI'S SOLE REMAINING **ASSET**--
--HIS **BURIAL PLOT!**
JUDGE, THE GOVERNMENT HAS REASON TO BELIEVE MR. RIZZOLI **IMPROPERLY** DEDUCTED THE COST OF HIS **PLOT** AND **HEADSTONE** AS A **BUSINESS EXPENSE** . . .
HMN . . .
ALL OF THE IRS'S CLAIMS WERE MADE AGAINST MY CLIENT **POST MORTEM.**
SINCE MR. RIZZOLI HAD NO OTHER ASSETS WHEN HE CEASED BEING ELIGIBLE FOR A PERSONAL DEDUCTION--
--THE GOVERNMENT HAS PROPERLY MOVED TO TAKE POSSESSION OF HIS DOMICILE TO PAY THE TAXES HE OWES.
POST MORTEM? OH, LORDY . . .
MY CLIENT WAS **NEVER** PROPERLY SERVED WITH THE **TAX DEFICIENCY NOTICE** THAT THE GOVERNMENT SEEKS TO EXECUTE HERE TODAY
YOUR HONOR, THE **TAX CODE** CLEARLY STATES--
YOUR HONOR? YOU LOOK A LITTLE **GREEN** . . .
MR. WINGATE, IF MR. RIZZOLI WASN'T PROPERLY SERVED ⫶CHOKE⫶ THEN THIS ISSUE IS A DEAD LETTER ⫶CHOKE⫶ AND IS DISMISSED--
WITH PREJUDICE!
RETCH!!
BUT YOUR HONOR, THE **TAX CODE**--?
YOUR HONOR?

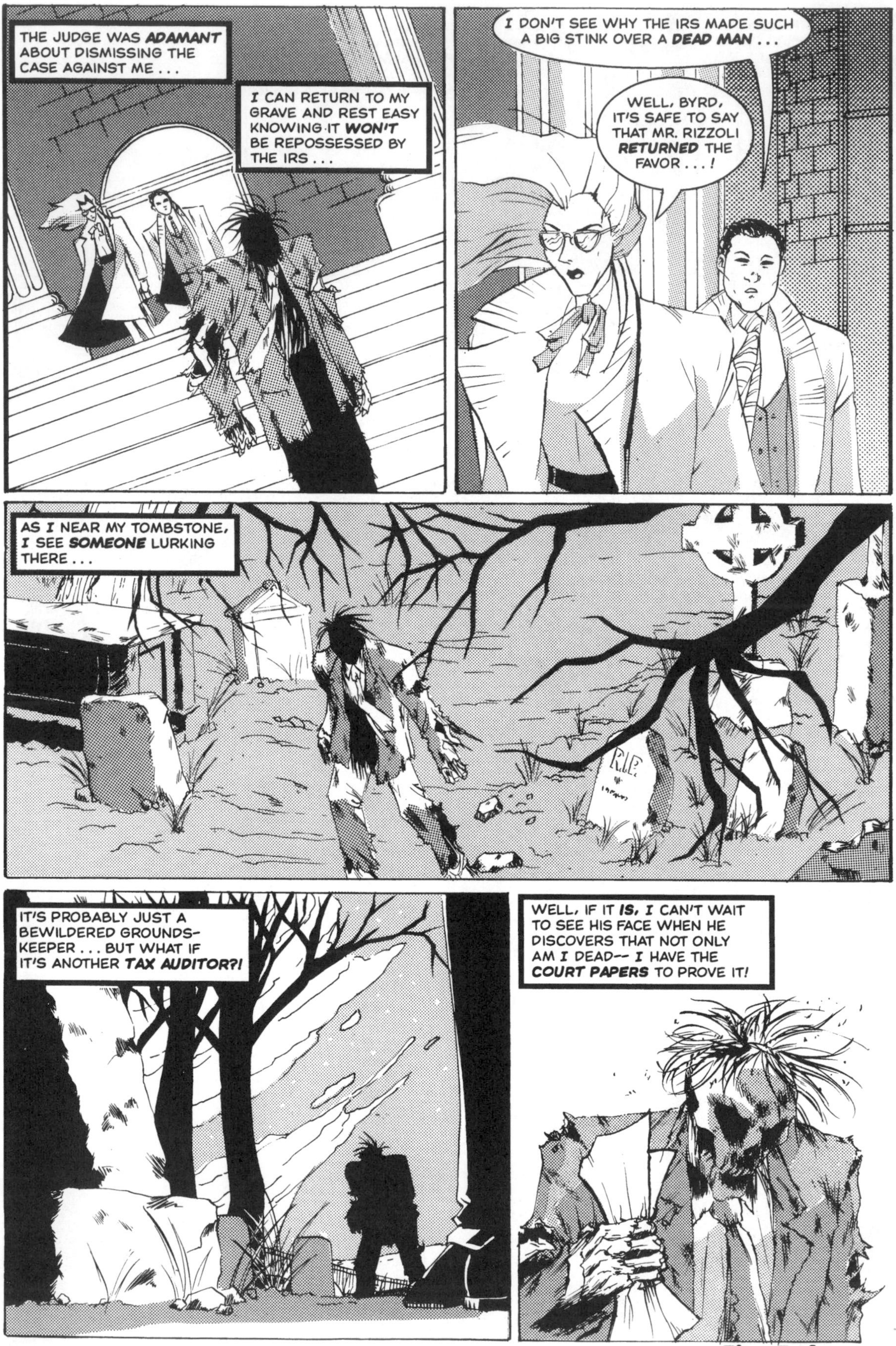
THE JUDGE WAS ADAMANT ABOUT DISMISSING THE CASE AGAINST ME . . .
I CAN RETURN TO MY GRAVE AND REST EASY KNOWING IT WON'T BE REPOSSESSED BY THE IRS . . .
I DON'T SEE WHY THE IRS MADE SUCH A BIG STINK OVER A DEAD MAN . . .
WELL, BYRD, IT'S SAFE TO SAY THAT MR. RIZZOLI RETURNED THE FAVOR . . . !
AS I NEAR MY TOMBSTONE, I SEE SOMEONE LURKING THERE . . .
R.I.P.
IT'S PROBABLY JUST A BEWILDERED GROUNDS-KEEPER . . . BUT WHAT IF IT'S ANOTHER TAX AUDITOR?!
WELL, IF IT IS, I CAN'T WAIT TO SEE HIS FACE WHEN HE DISCOVERS THAT NOT ONLY AM I DEAD-- I HAVE THE COURT PAPERS TO PROVE IT!

The End . . .

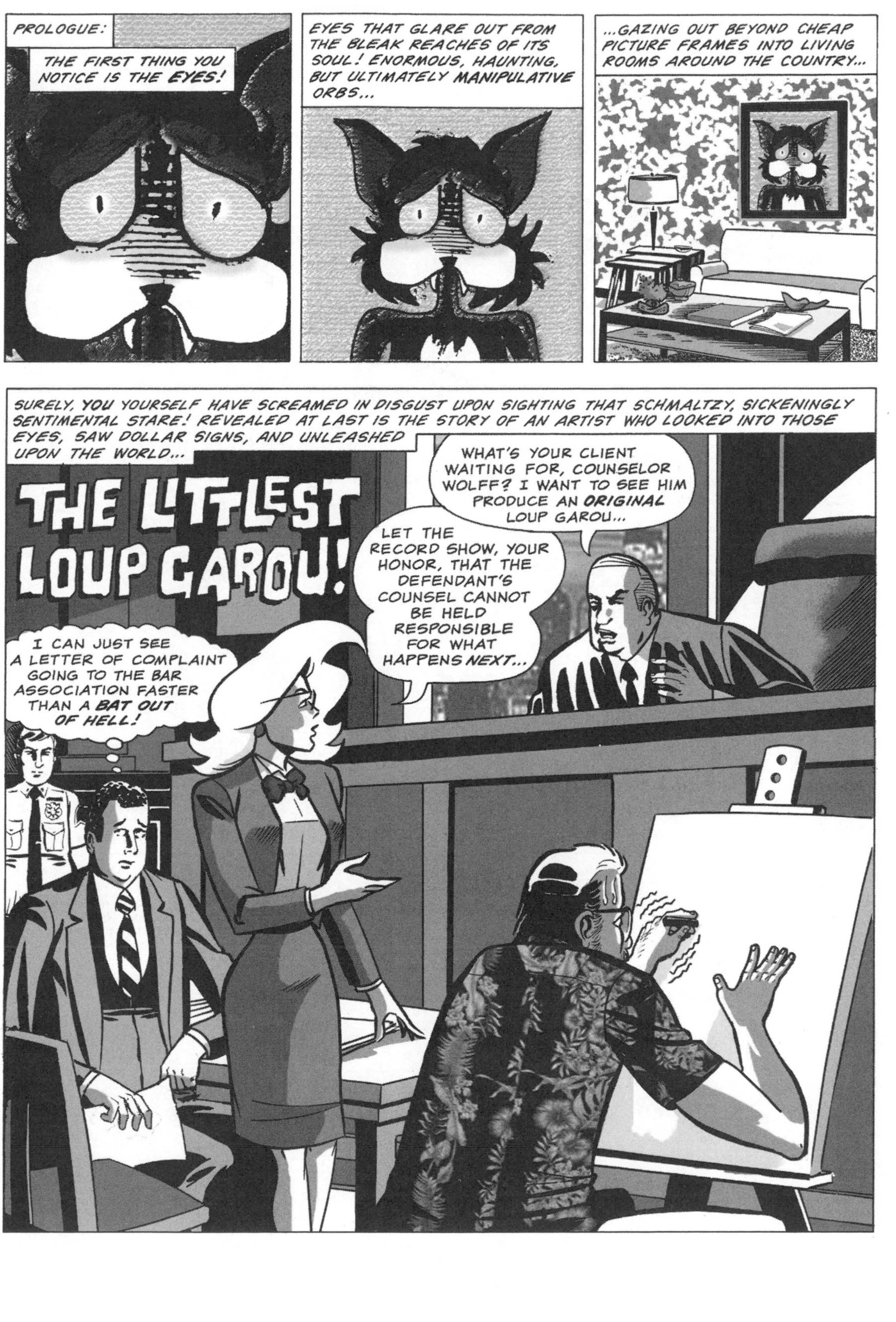
PROLOGUE:
THE FIRST THING YOU NOTICE IS THE EYES!
EYES THAT GLARE OUT FROM THE BLEAK REACHES OF ITS SOUL! ENORMOUS, HAUNTING, BUT ULTIMATELY MANIPULATIVE ORBS...
...GAZING OUT BEYOND CHEAP PICTURE FRAMES INTO LIVING ROOMS AROUND THE COUNTRY...
SURELY, YOU YOURSELF HAVE SCREAMED IN DISGUST UPON SIGHTING THAT SCHMALTZY, SICKENINGLY SENTIMENTAL STARE! REVEALED AT LAST IS THE STORY OF AN ARTIST WHO LOOKED INTO THOSE EYES, SAW DOLLAR SIGNS, AND UNLEASHED UPON THE WORLD...
THE LITTLEST LOUP GAROU!
WHAT'S YOUR CLIENT WAITING FOR, COUNSELOR WOLFF? I WANT TO SEE HIM PRODUCE AN ORIGINAL LOUP GAROU...
LET THE RECORD SHOW, YOUR HONOR, THAT THE DEFENDANT'S COUNSEL CANNOT BE HELD RESPONSIBLE FOR WHAT HAPPENS NEXT...
I CAN JUST SEE A LETTER OF COMPLAINT GOING TO THE BAR ASSOCIATION FASTER THAN A BAT OUT OF HELL!

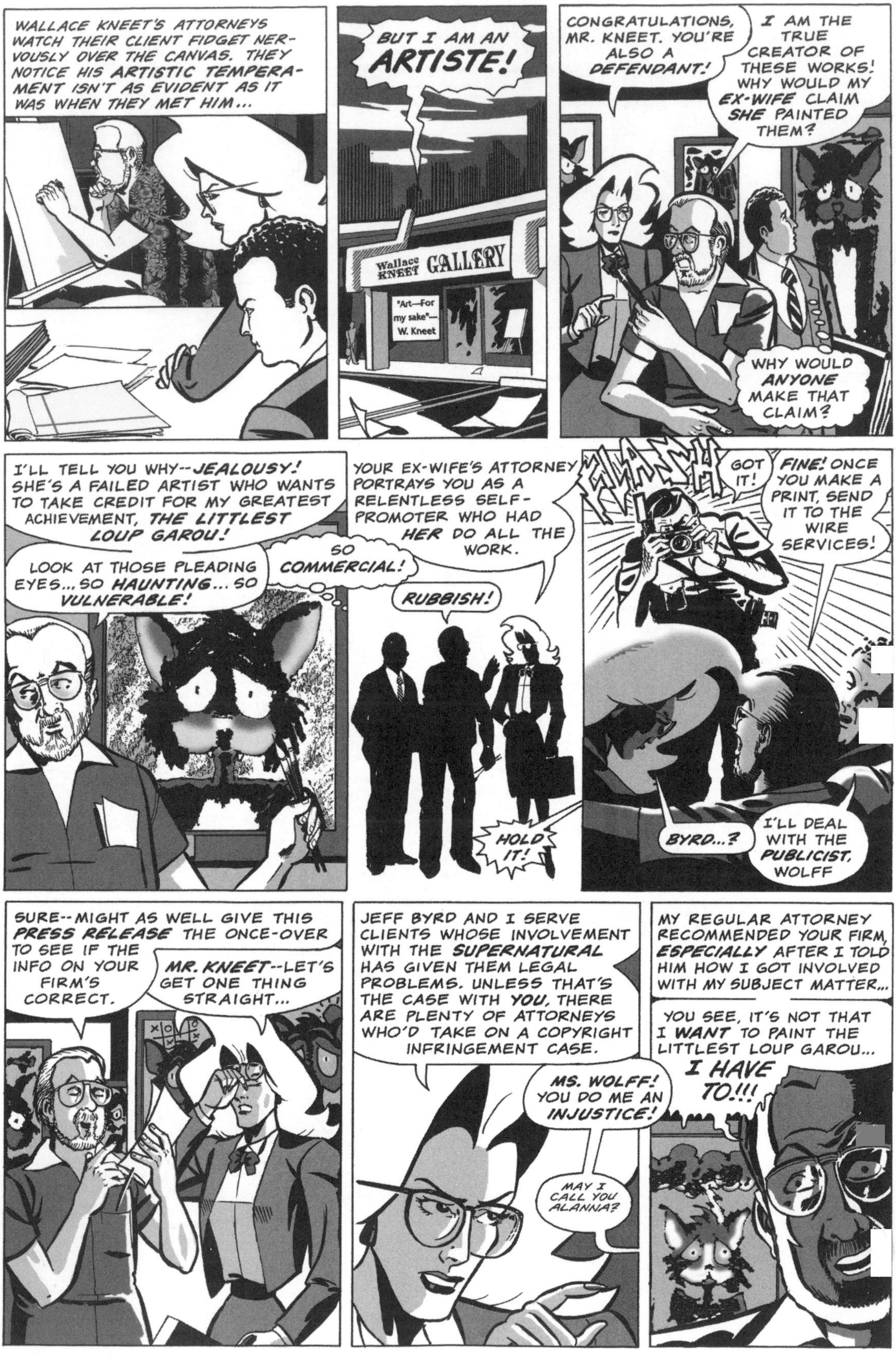
WALLACE KNEET'S ATTORNEYS WATCH THEIR CLIENT FIDGET NERVOUSLY OVER THE CANVAS. THEY NOTICE HIS ARTISTIC TEMPERAMENT ISN'T AS EVIDENT AS IT WAS WHEN THEY MET HIM...
BUT I AM AN ARTISTE!
Wallace KNEET GALLERY
"Art—For my sake"— W. Kneet
CONGRATULATIONS, MR. KNEET. YOU'RE ALSO A DEFENDANT!
I AM THE TRUE CREATOR OF THESE WORKS! WHY WOULD MY EX-WIFE CLAIM SHE PAINTED THEM?
WHY WOULD ANYONE MAKE THAT CLAIM?
I'LL TELL YOU WHY--JEALOUSY! SHE'S A FAILED ARTIST WHO WANTS TO TAKE CREDIT FOR MY GREATEST ACHIEVEMENT, THE LITTLEST LOUP GAROU!
LOOK AT THOSE PLEADING EYES... SO HAUNTING... SO VULNERABLE!
SO COMMERCIAL!
YOUR EX-WIFE'S ATTORNEY PORTRAYS YOU AS A RELENTLESS SELF-PROMOTER WHO HAD HER DO ALL THE WORK.
RUBBISH!
HOLD IT!
FLASH
GOT IT!
FINE! ONCE YOU MAKE A PRINT, SEND IT TO THE WIRE SERVICES!
BYRD...?
I'LL DEAL WITH THE PUBLICIST, WOLFF
SURE--MIGHT AS WELL GIVE THIS PRESS RELEASE THE ONCE-OVER TO SEE IF THE INFO ON YOUR FIRM'S CORRECT.
MR. KNEET--LET'S GET ONE THING STRAIGHT...
JEFF BYRD AND I SERVE CLIENTS WHOSE INVOLVEMENT WITH THE SUPERNATURAL HAS GIVEN THEM LEGAL PROBLEMS. UNLESS THAT'S THE CASE WITH YOU, THERE ARE PLENTY OF ATTORNEYS WHO'D TAKE ON A COPYRIGHT INFRINGEMENT CASE.
MS. WOLFF! YOU DO ME AN INJUSTICE!
MAY I CALL YOU ALANNA?
MY REGULAR ATTORNEY RECOMMENDED YOUR FIRM, ESPECIALLY AFTER I TOLD HIM HOW I GOT INVOLVED WITH MY SUBJECT MATTER...
YOU SEE, IT'S NOT THAT I WANT TO PAINT THE LITTLEST LOUP GAROU...
I HAVE TO!!!

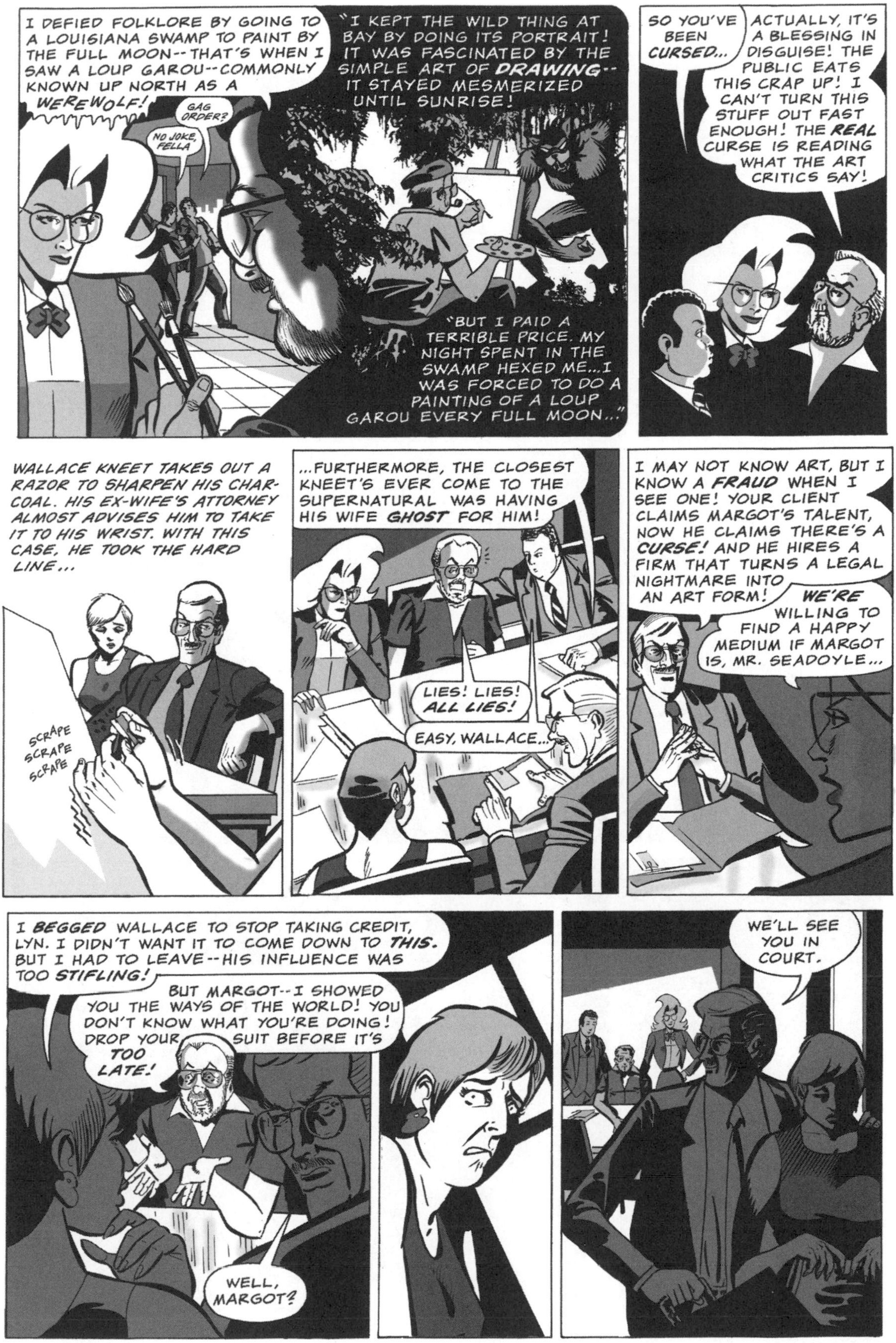

I DEFIED FOLKLORE BY GOING TO A LOUISIANA SWAMP TO PAINT BY THE FULL MOON--THAT'S WHEN I SAW A LOUP GAROU--COMMONLY KNOWN UP NORTH AS A WEREWOLF!
GAG ORDER?
NO JOKE, FELLA
"I KEPT THE WILD THING AT BAY BY DOING ITS PORTRAIT! IT WAS FASCINATED BY THE SIMPLE ART OF DRAWING--IT STAYED MESMERIZED UNTIL SUNRISE!
"BUT I PAID A TERRIBLE PRICE. MY NIGHT SPENT IN THE SWAMP HEXED ME...I WAS FORCED TO DO A PAINTING OF A LOUP GAROU EVERY FULL MOON..."
SO YOU'VE BEEN CURSED...
ACTUALLY, IT'S A BLESSING IN DISGUISE! THE PUBLIC EATS THIS CRAP UP! I CAN'T TURN THIS STUFF OUT FAST ENOUGH! THE REAL CURSE IS READING WHAT THE ART CRITICS SAY!
WALLACE KNEET TAKES OUT A RAZOR TO SHARPEN HIS CHARCOAL. HIS EX-WIFE'S ATTORNEY ALMOST ADVISES HIM TO TAKE IT TO HIS WRIST. WITH THIS CASE, HE TOOK THE HARD LINE...
SCRAPE SCRAPE SCRAPE
...FURTHERMORE, THE CLOSEST KNEET'S EVER COME TO THE SUPERNATURAL WAS HAVING HIS WIFE GHOST FOR HIM!
LIES! LIES! ALL LIES!
EASY, WALLACE...
I MAY NOT KNOW ART, BUT I KNOW A FRAUD WHEN I SEE ONE! YOUR CLIENT CLAIMS MARGOT'S TALENT, NOW HE CLAIMS THERE'S A CURSE! AND HE HIRES A FIRM THAT TURNS A LEGAL NIGHTMARE INTO AN ART FORM!
WE'RE WILLING TO FIND A HAPPY MEDIUM IF MARGOT IS, MR. SEADOYLE...
I BEGGED WALLACE TO STOP TAKING CREDIT, LYN. I DIDN'T WANT IT TO COME DOWN TO THIS. BUT I HAD TO LEAVE--HIS INFLUENCE WAS TOO STIFLING!
BUT MARGOT--I SHOWED YOU THE WAYS OF THE WORLD! YOU DON'T KNOW WHAT YOU'RE DOING! DROP YOUR SUIT BEFORE IT'S TOO LATE!
WELL, MARGOT?
WE'LL SEE YOU IN COURT.

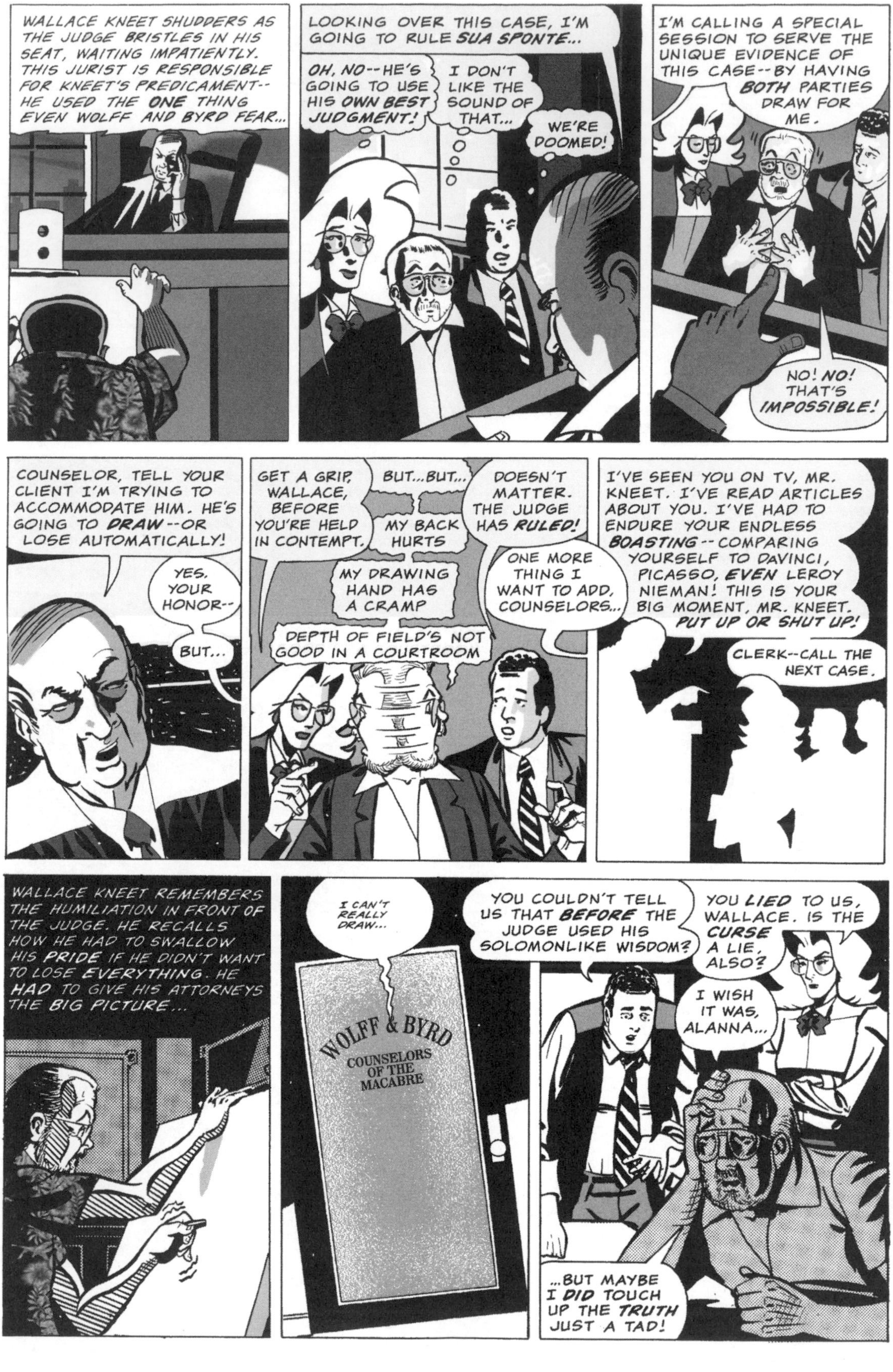
WALLACE KNEET SHUDDERS AS THE JUDGE BRISTLES IN HIS SEAT, WAITING IMPATIENTLY. THIS JURIST IS RESPONSIBLE FOR KNEET'S PREDICAMENT-- HE USED THE ONE THING EVEN WOLFF AND BYRD FEAR...
LOOKING OVER THIS CASE, I'M GOING TO RULE SUA SPONTE...
OH, NO--HE'S GOING TO USE HIS OWN BEST JUDGMENT!
I DON'T LIKE THE SOUND OF THAT...
WE'RE DOOMED!
I'M CALLING A SPECIAL SESSION TO SERVE THE UNIQUE EVIDENCE OF THIS CASE--BY HAVING BOTH PARTIES DRAW FOR ME.
NO! NO! THAT'S IMPOSSIBLE!
COUNSELOR, TELL YOUR CLIENT I'M TRYING TO ACCOMMODATE HIM. HE'S GOING TO DRAW--OR LOSE AUTOMATICALLY!
YES, YOUR HONOR--
BUT...
GET A GRIP, WALLACE, BEFORE YOU'RE HELD IN CONTEMPT.
BUT...BUT...
MY BACK HURTS
MY DRAWING HAND HAS A CRAMP
DEPTH OF FIELD'S NOT GOOD IN A COURTROOM
DOESN'T MATTER. THE JUDGE HAS RULED!
ONE MORE THING I WANT TO ADD, COUNSELORS...
I'VE SEEN YOU ON TV, MR. KNEET. I'VE READ ARTICLES ABOUT YOU. I'VE HAD TO ENDURE YOUR ENDLESS BOASTING--COMPARING YOURSELF TO DAVINCI, PICASSO, EVEN LEROY NIEMAN! THIS IS YOUR BIG MOMENT, MR. KNEET. PUT UP OR SHUT UP!
CLERK--CALL THE NEXT CASE.
WALLACE KNEET REMEMBERS THE HUMILIATION IN FRONT OF THE JUDGE. HE RECALLS HOW HE HAD TO SWALLOW HIS PRIDE IF HE DIDN'T WANT TO LOSE EVERYTHING. HE HAD TO GIVE HIS ATTORNEYS THE BIG PICTURE...
I CAN'T REALLY DRAW...
WOLFF & BYRD
COUNSELORS OF THE MACABRE
YOU COULDN'T TELL US THAT BEFORE THE JUDGE USED HIS SOLOMONLIKE WISDOM?
YOU LIED TO US, WALLACE. IS THE CURSE A LIE, ALSO?
I WISH IT WAS, ALANNA...
...BUT MAYBE I DID TOUCH UP THE TRUTH JUST A TAD!

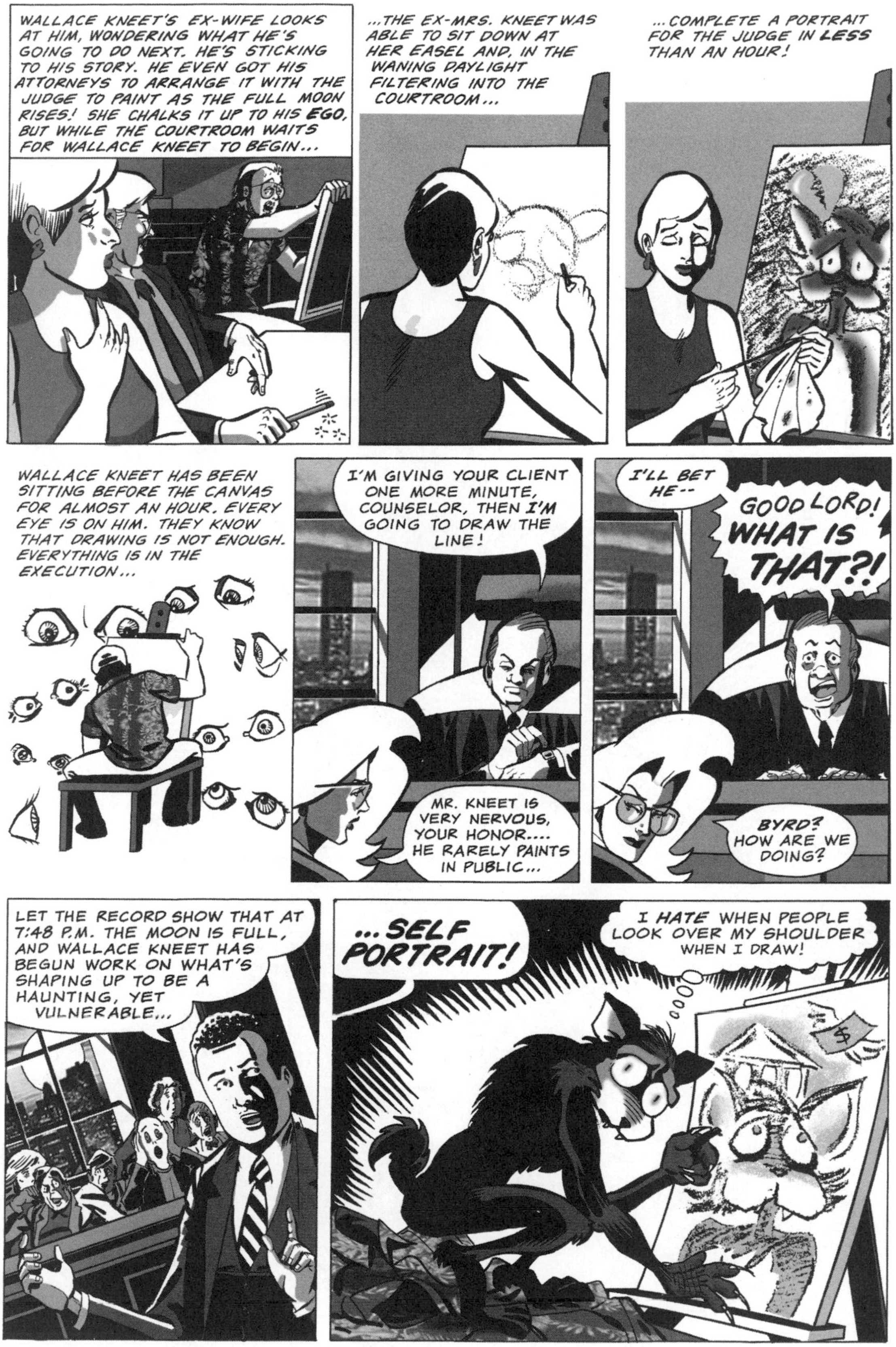
WALLACE KNEET'S EX-WIFE LOOKS AT HIM, WONDERING WHAT HE'S GOING TO DO NEXT. HE'S STICKING TO HIS STORY. HE EVEN GOT HIS ATTORNEYS TO ARRANGE IT WITH THE JUDGE TO PAINT AS THE FULL MOON RISES! SHE CHALKS IT UP TO HIS EGO, BUT WHILE THE COURTROOM WAITS FOR WALLACE KNEET TO BEGIN...
...THE EX-MRS. KNEET WAS ABLE TO SIT DOWN AT HER EASEL AND, IN THE WANING DAYLIGHT FILTERING INTO THE COURTROOM...
...COMPLETE A PORTRAIT FOR THE JUDGE IN LESS THAN AN HOUR!
WALLACE KNEET HAS BEEN SITTING BEFORE THE CANVAS FOR ALMOST AN HOUR. EVERY EYE IS ON HIM. THEY KNOW THAT DRAWING IS NOT ENOUGH. EVERYTHING IS IN THE EXECUTION...
I'M GIVING YOUR CLIENT ONE MORE MINUTE, COUNSELOR, THEN I'M GOING TO DRAW THE LINE!
MR. KNEET IS VERY NERVOUS, YOUR HONOR.... HE RARELY PAINTS IN PUBLIC...
I'LL BET HE--
GOOD LORD! WHAT IS THAT?!
BYRD? HOW ARE WE DOING?
LET THE RECORD SHOW THAT AT 7:48 P.M. THE MOON IS FULL, AND WALLACE KNEET HAS BEGUN WORK ON WHAT'S SHAPING UP TO BE A HAUNTING, YET VULNERABLE...
...SELF PORTRAIT!
I HATE WHEN PEOPLE LOOK OVER MY SHOULDER WHEN I DRAW!

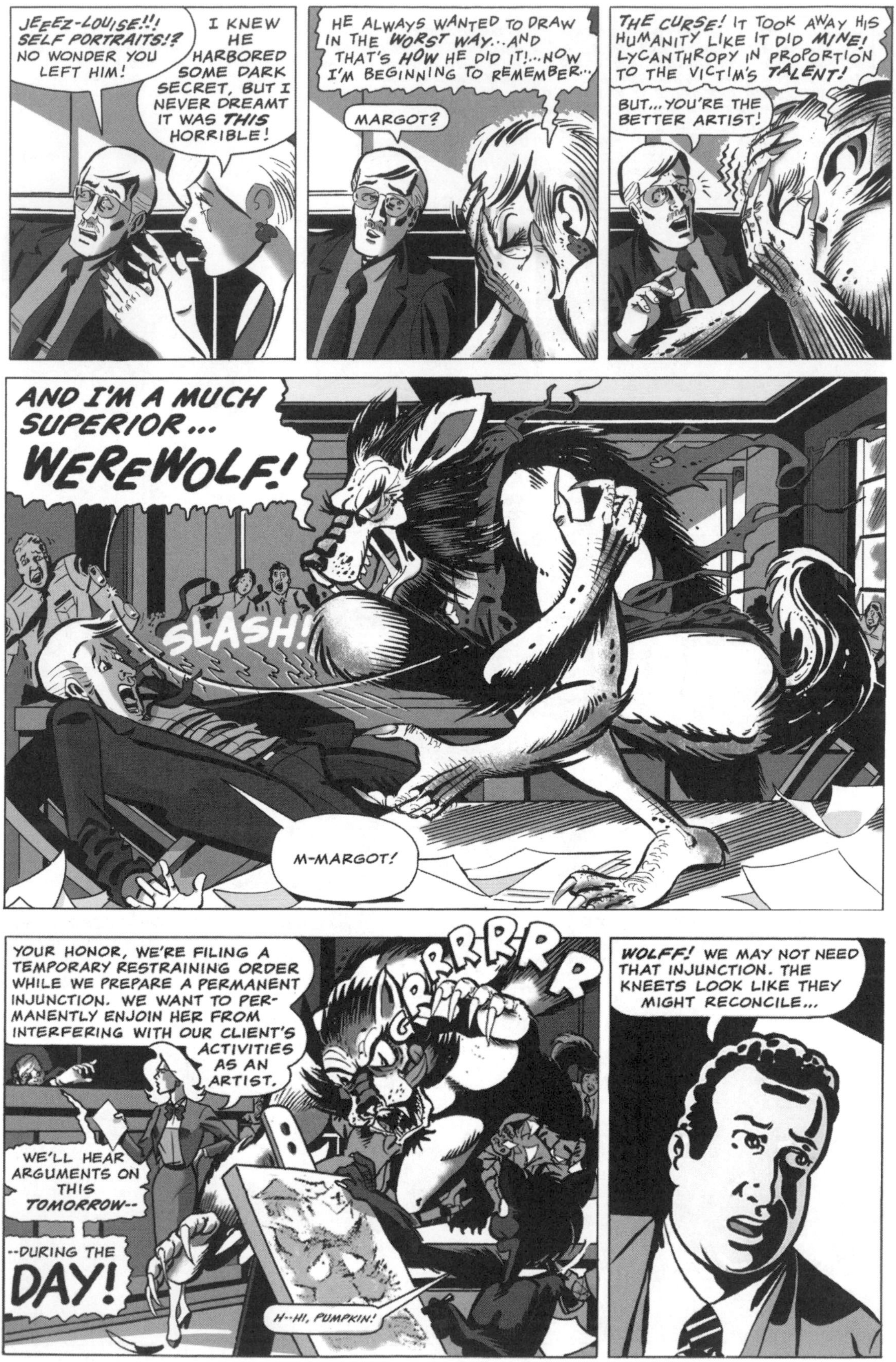
JEEEZ-LOUISE!!! SELF PORTRAITS!? NO WONDER YOU LEFT HIM!
I KNEW HE HARBORED SOME DARK SECRET, BUT I NEVER DREAMT IT WAS THIS HORRIBLE!
HE ALWAYS WANTED TO DRAW IN THE WORST WAY... AND THAT'S HOW HE DID IT!... NOW I'M BEGINNING TO REMEMBER...
MARGOT?
THE CURSE! IT TOOK AWAY HIS HUMANITY LIKE IT DID MINE! LYCANTHROPY IN PROPORTION TO THE VICTIM'S TALENT!
BUT... YOU'RE THE BETTER ARTIST!
AND I'M A MUCH SUPERIOR... WEREWOLF!
SLASH!
M-MARGOT!
YOUR HONOR, WE'RE FILING A TEMPORARY RESTRAINING ORDER WHILE WE PREPARE A PERMANENT INJUNCTION. WE WANT TO PERMANENTLY ENJOIN HER FROM INTERFERING WITH OUR CLIENT'S ACTIVITIES AS AN ARTIST.
GRRRRRR
WE'LL HEAR ARGUMENTS ON THIS TOMORROW--
--DURING THE DAY!
H--HI, PUMPKIN!
WOLFF! WE MAY NOT NEED THAT INJUNCTION. THE KNEETS LOOK LIKE THEY MIGHT RECONCILE...

...IN HELL!!

YOU *BEAST!* HOW DARE YOU TAKE CREDIT FOR MY WORK?

WAK! WAK! WAK!

BUT BUSINESS IS BUSINESS!

YEOUCH!

SUPPLY AND DEMAND!

YOUCH!

WORK FOR HIRE!

YOUCH!

KE-RASSHH!

WALLACE KNEET WAS AN AWFUL ARTIST, BUT A GOOD *TEACHER*...

BUT YER HONOR! WE DON'T HAVE THE BUDGET FOR SILVER BULLETS!

@*#⊙!!

"THE WEREWOLF KNEET CAME ACROSS IN THE SWAMP WAS MARGOT. TO MAKE THE *MOST* OUT OF THEIR CURSE, HE TOOK HER IN AS AN ASSISTANT.

"SHE WAS A NATURAL ARTIST, WHILE HE WAS ONLY A SUPERNATURAL ONE. SHE'D CRANK OUT LOUP GAROU PAINTINGS EVERY DAY OF THE MONTH, WHILE HE HAD TO RELY ON A FULL MOON."

WHILE TURNING INTO A WEREWOLF MEANT TURNING A PROFIT FOR KNEET, HIS WIFE BLOCKED IT OUT OF HER MIND... EVENTUALLY, SHE REBELLED TO SHOW HER INDEPENDENCE!

ACTUALLY, IT'S KIND OF ROMANTIC, IN A SICK, TWISTED WAY!

COUNSELOR WOLFF, COUNSELOR BYRD! I WANT TO SEE YOU IN MY CHAMBERS...NOW!

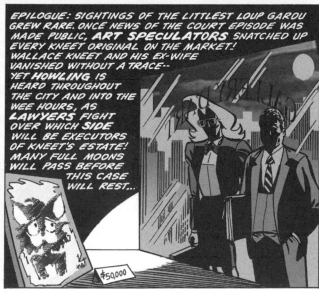

EPILOGUE: SIGHTINGS OF THE LITTLEST LOUP GAROU GREW RARE. ONCE NEWS OF THE COURT EPISODE WAS MADE PUBLIC, **ART SPECULATORS** SNATCHED UP EVERY KNEET ORIGINAL ON THE MARKET! WALLACE KNEET AND HIS EX-WIFE VANISHED WITHOUT A TRACE-- YET *HOWLING* IS HEARD THROUGHOUT THE CITY AND INTO THE WEE HOURS, AS *LAWYERS* FIGHT OVER WHICH *SIDE* WILL BE EXECUTORS OF KNEET'S ESTATE! MANY FULL MOONS WILL PASS BEFORE THIS CASE WILL REST...

$50,000

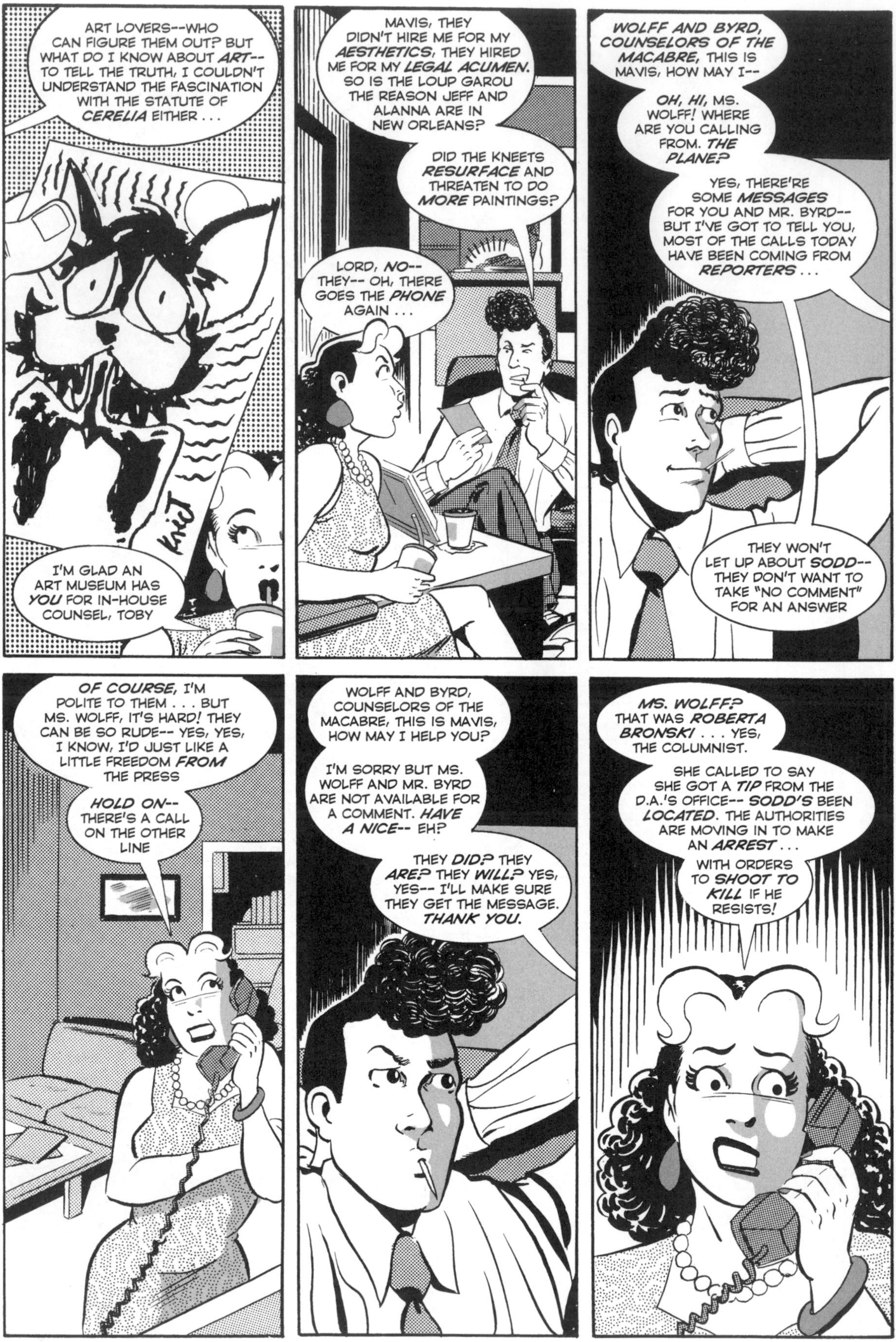
ART LOVERS--WHO CAN FIGURE THEM OUT? BUT WHAT DO I KNOW ABOUT ART-- TO TELL THE TRUTH, I COULDN'T UNDERSTAND THE FASCINATION WITH THE STATUTE OF CERELIA EITHER . . .
I'M GLAD AN ART MUSEUM HAS YOU FOR IN-HOUSE COUNSEL, TOBY
MAVIS, THEY DIDN'T HIRE ME FOR MY AESTHETICS, THEY HIRED ME FOR MY LEGAL ACUMEN. SO IS THE LOUP GAROU THE REASON JEFF AND ALANNA ARE IN NEW ORLEANS?
DID THE KNEETS RESURFACE AND THREATEN TO DO MORE PAINTINGS?
LORD, NO-- THEY-- OH, THERE GOES THE PHONE AGAIN . . .
WOLFF AND BYRD, COUNSELORS OF THE MACABRE, THIS IS MAVIS, HOW MAY I--
OH, HI, MS. WOLFF! WHERE ARE YOU CALLING FROM. THE PLANE?
YES, THERE'RE SOME MESSAGES FOR YOU AND MR. BYRD-- BUT I'VE GOT TO TELL YOU, MOST OF THE CALLS TODAY HAVE BEEN COMING FROM REPORTERS . . .
THEY WON'T LET UP ABOUT SODD-- THEY DON'T WANT TO TAKE "NO COMMENT" FOR AN ANSWER
OF COURSE, I'M POLITE TO THEM . . . BUT MS. WOLFF, IT'S HARD! THEY CAN BE SO RUDE-- YES, YES, I KNOW, I'D JUST LIKE A LITTLE FREEDOM FROM THE PRESS
HOLD ON-- THERE'S A CALL ON THE OTHER LINE
WOLFF AND BYRD, COUNSELORS OF THE MACABRE, THIS IS MAVIS, HOW MAY I HELP YOU?
I'M SORRY BUT MS. WOLFF AND MR. BYRD ARE NOT AVAILABLE FOR A COMMENT. HAVE A NICE-- EH?
THEY DID? THEY ARE? THEY WILL? YES, YES-- I'LL MAKE SURE THEY GET THE MESSAGE. THANK YOU.
MS. WOLFF? THAT WAS ROBERTA BRONSKI . . . YES, THE COLUMNIST.
SHE CALLED TO SAY SHE GOT A TIP FROM THE D.A.'S OFFICE-- SODD'S BEEN LOCATED. THE AUTHORITIES ARE MOVING IN TO MAKE AN ARREST . . .
WITH ORDERS TO SHOOT TO KILL IF HE RESISTS!

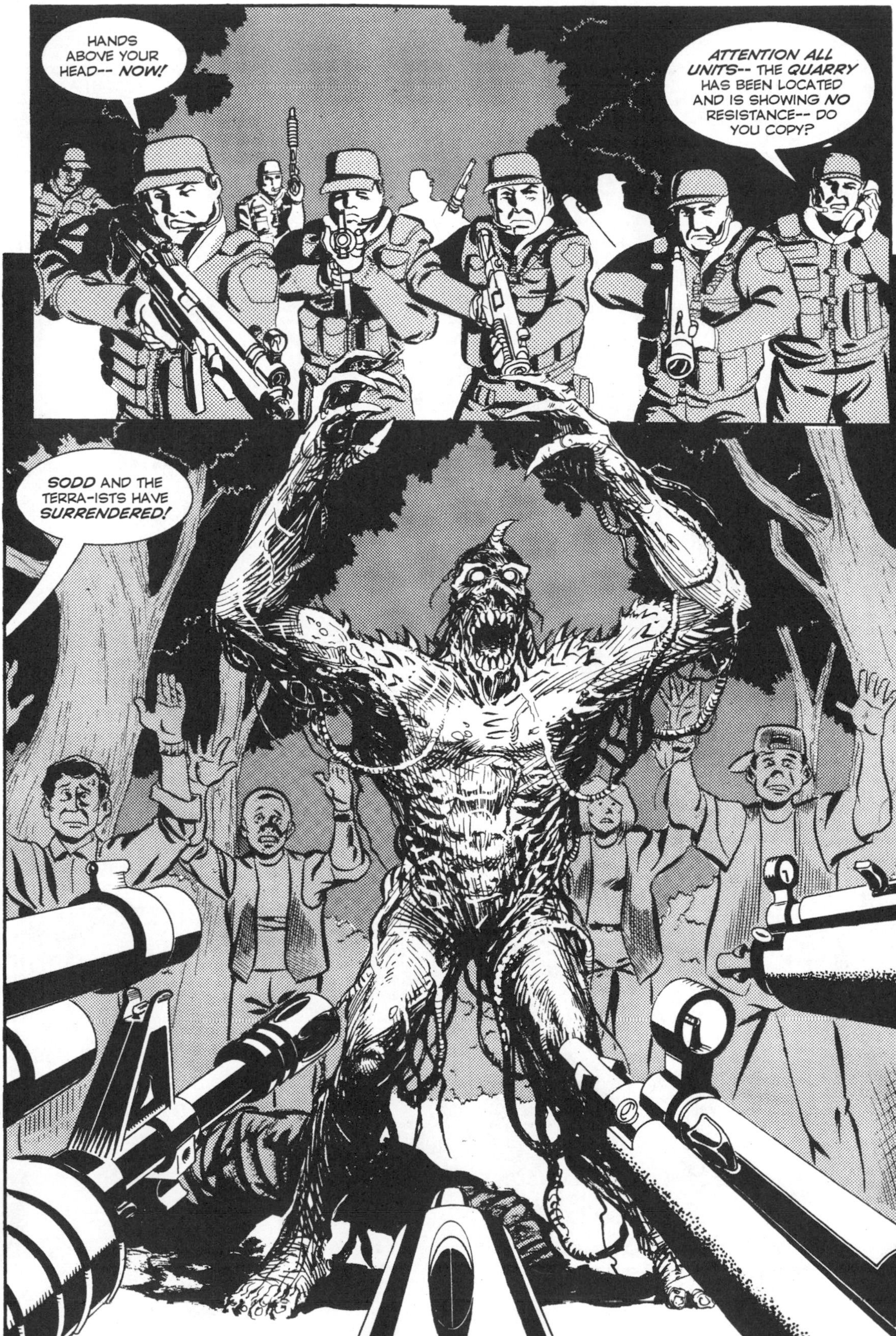
HANDS ABOVE YOUR HEAD-- NOW!
ATTENTION ALL UNITS-- THE QUARRY HAS BEEN LOCATED AND IS SHOWING NO RESISTANCE-- DO YOU COPY?
SODD AND THE TERRA-ISTS HAVE SURRENDERED!

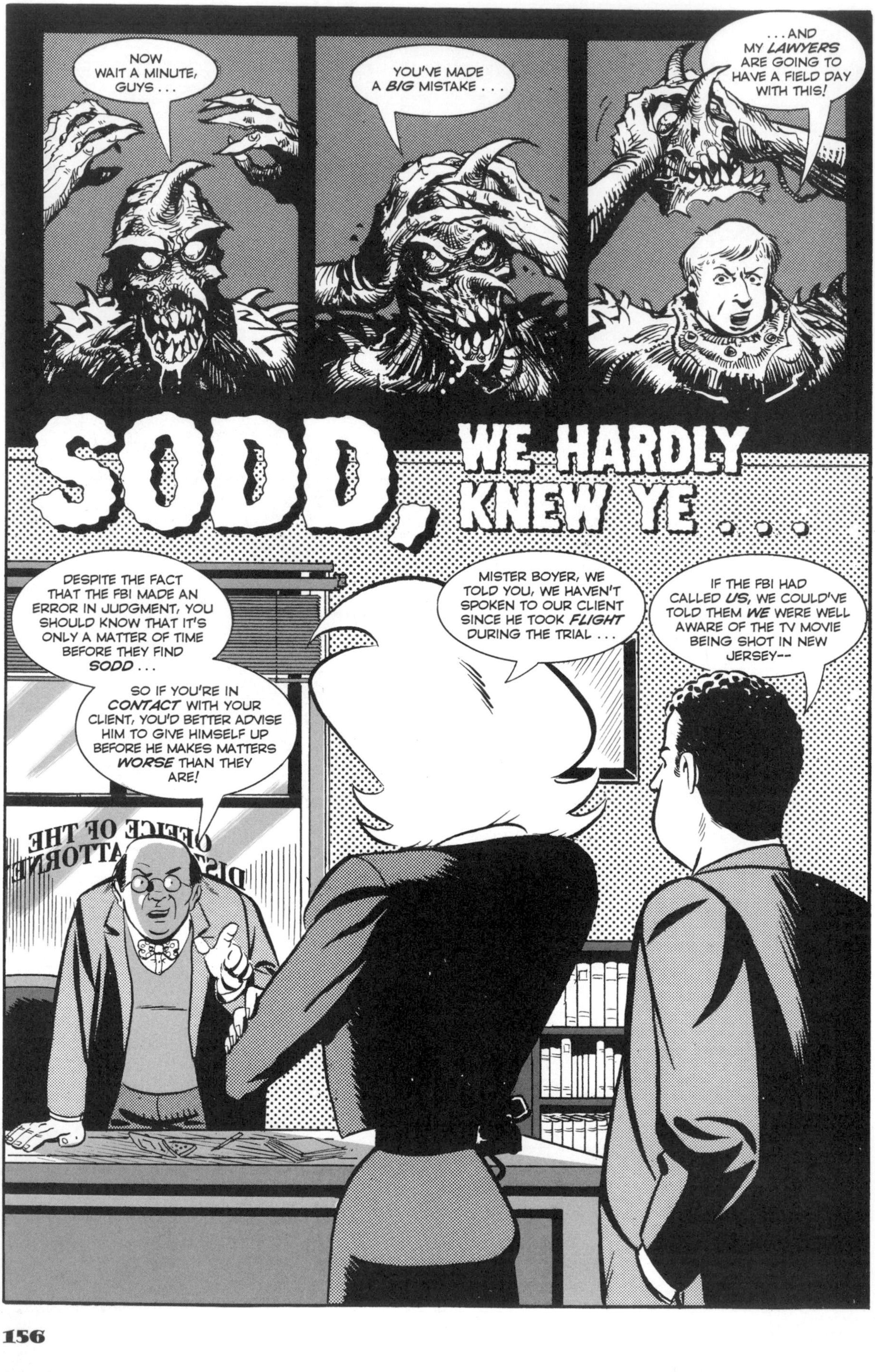
NOW WAIT A MINUTE, GUYS . . .
YOU'VE MADE A BIG MISTAKE . . .
. . . AND MY LAWYERS ARE GOING TO HAVE A FIELD DAY WITH THIS!
SODD, WE HARDLY KNEW YE . . .
DESPITE THE FACT THAT THE FBI MADE AN ERROR IN JUDGMENT, YOU SHOULD KNOW THAT IT'S ONLY A MATTER OF TIME BEFORE THEY FIND SODD . . .
SO IF YOU'RE IN CONTACT WITH YOUR CLIENT, YOU'D BETTER ADVISE HIM TO GIVE HIMSELF UP BEFORE HE MAKES MATTERS WORSE THAN THEY ARE!
MISTER BOYER, WE TOLD YOU, WE HAVEN'T SPOKEN TO OUR CLIENT SINCE HE TOOK FLIGHT DURING THE TRIAL . . .
IF THE FBI HAD CALLED US, WE COULD'VE TOLD THEM WE WERE WELL AWARE OF THE TV MOVIE BEING SHOT IN NEW JERSEY--

--SINCE WE'RE TRYING TO SHUT THAT PRODUCTION DOWN!
SO THAT'S WHY YOUR OFFICE SUBPOENAED OUR PHONE RECORDS-- YOU THOUGHT IT WOULD LEAD YOU TO OUR CLIENT.
MS. WOLFF, SINCE I'VE BEEN ASSIGNED AS PROSECUTOR IN THE SODD CASE, I CAN'T AFFORD TO LEAVE ANY STONE UNTURNED
. . .AND A ROLLING STONE GATHERS NO MOSS WHEN IT COMES TO SODD
YUK
DID YOU SAY SOMETHING, LARSON?
JUST A LITTLE, AH, JOKE . . .
I'LL FINISH UP THESE INTER-OGATORIES
SIR!
NOW, AS I WAS SAYING . . . YOU AND MR. BYRD ARE UNDER SUSPICION OF AIDING AND ABETTING YOUR CLIENT AS A FUGITIVE. AND I'LL USE ANY MEANS POSSIBLE TO . . .
MISTER BOYER-- I ASSURE YOU WE DON'T KNOW WHERE SODD IS . . .
. . .AND IF YOU POINT THAT STUBBY LITTLE FINGER OF YOURS AT ME ONE MORE TIME, I'LL MAKE SURE YOU REGRET IT!
M-MS. WOLFF . . . LET'S STAY WITH THE SUBJECT AT HAND . . .
I DON'T TAKE TH-THREATS LIGHTLY
AND I DON'T TAKE ACCUSATIONS LIGHTLY, MR. BOYER
IF ONLY SODD WOULD COME OUT OF HIDING . . . I WANT THE SATISFACTION OF SEEING ALANNA WOLFF TEAR THAT POWER-MAD TWERP BOYER APART IN OPEN COURT!

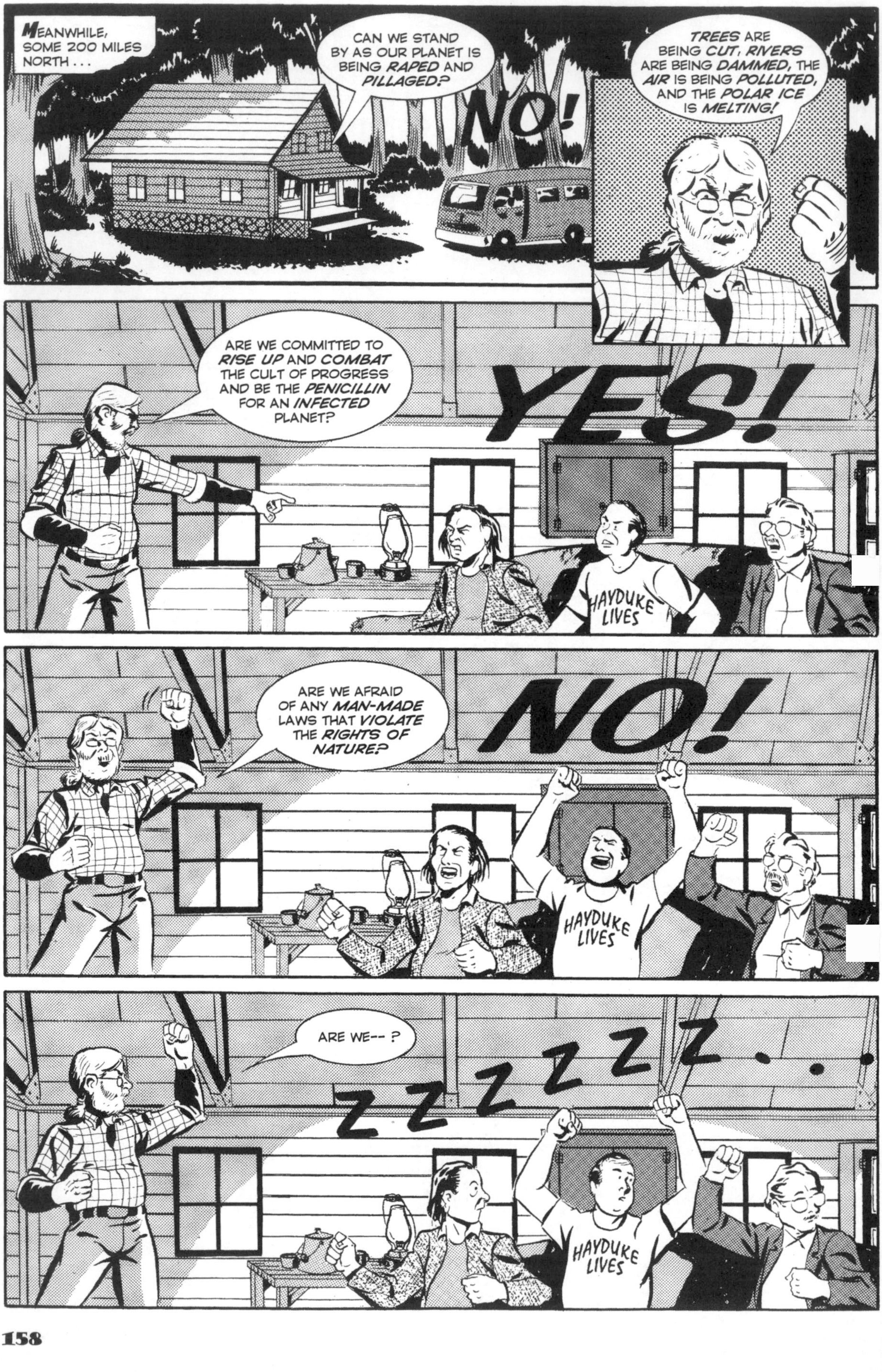
MEANWHILE, SOME 200 MILES NORTH . . .
CAN WE STAND BY AS OUR PLANET IS BEING RAPED AND PILLAGED?
NO!
TREES ARE BEING CUT, RIVERS ARE BEING DAMMED, THE AIR IS BEING POLLUTED, AND THE POLAR ICE IS MELTING!
ARE WE COMMITTED TO RISE UP AND COMBAT THE CULT OF PROGRESS AND BE THE PENICILLIN FOR AN INFECTED PLANET?
YES!
HAYDUKE LIVES
ARE WE AFRAID OF ANY MAN-MADE LAWS THAT VIOLATE THE RIGHTS OF NATURE?
NO!
HAYDUKE LIVES
ARE WE-- ?
Z Z Z Z Z Z Z Z . . .
HAYDUKE LIVES

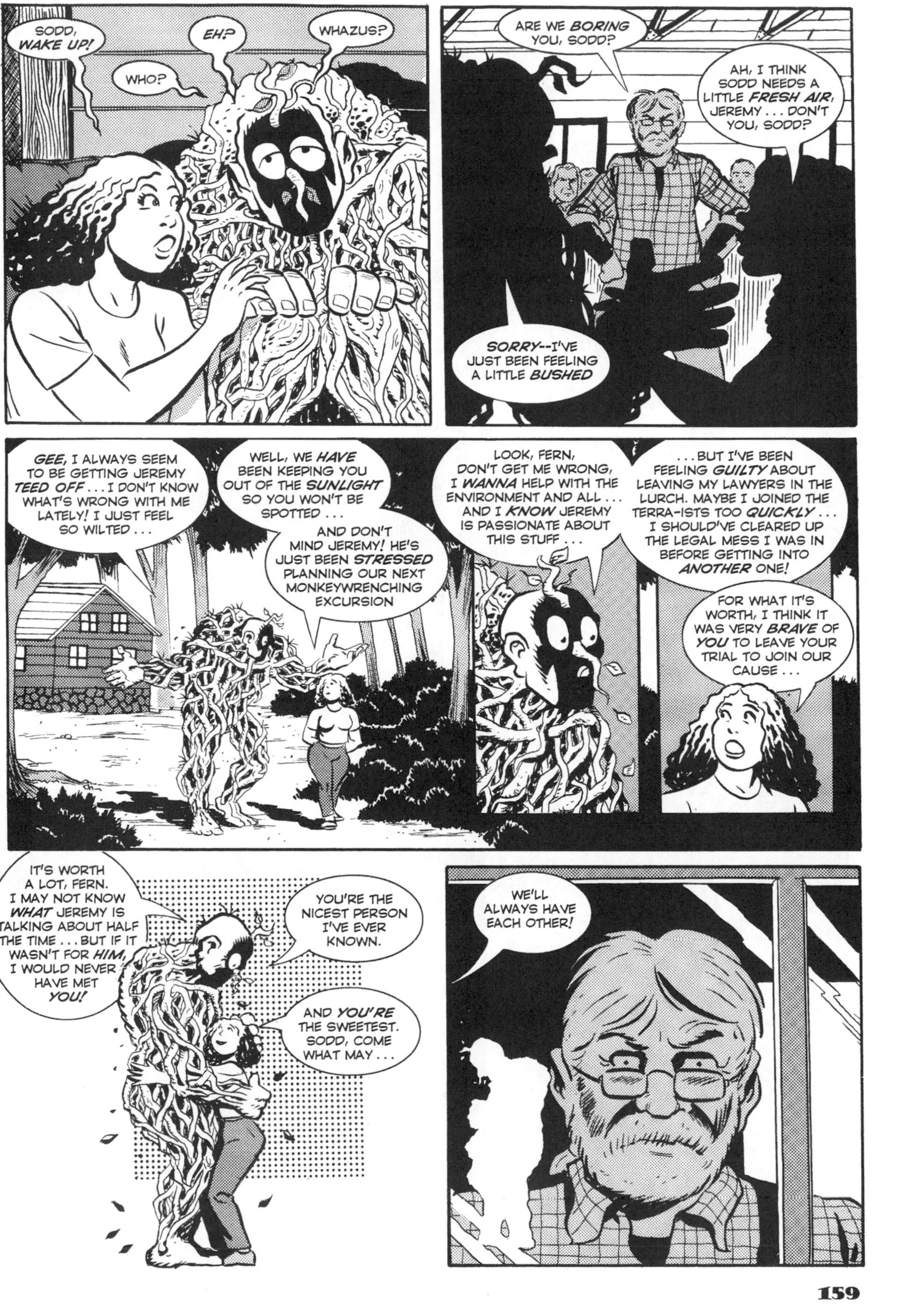
SODD, WAKE UP!
WHO?
EH?
WHAZUS?
ARE WE BORING YOU, SODD?
AH, I THINK SODD NEEDS A LITTLE FRESH AIR, JEREMY . . . DON'T YOU, SODD?
SORRY--I'VE JUST BEEN FEELING A LITTLE BUSHED
GEE, I ALWAYS SEEM TO BE GETTING JEREMY TEED OFF . . . I DON'T KNOW WHAT'S WRONG WITH ME LATELY! I JUST FEEL SO WILTED . . .
WELL, WE HAVE BEEN KEEPING YOU OUT OF THE SUNLIGHT SO YOU WON'T BE SPOTTED . . .
AND DON'T MIND JEREMY! HE'S JUST BEEN STRESSED PLANNING OUR NEXT MONKEYWRENCHING EXCURSION
LOOK, FERN, DON'T GET ME WRONG, I WANNA HELP WITH THE ENVIRONMENT AND ALL . . . AND I KNOW JEREMY IS PASSIONATE ABOUT THIS STUFF . . .
. . . BUT I'VE BEEN FEELING GUILTY ABOUT LEAVING MY LAWYERS IN THE LURCH. MAYBE I JOINED THE TERRA-ISTS TOO QUICKLY . . . I SHOULD'VE CLEARED UP THE LEGAL MESS I WAS IN BEFORE GETTING INTO ANOTHER ONE!
FOR WHAT IT'S WORTH, I THINK IT WAS VERY BRAVE OF YOU TO LEAVE YOUR TRIAL TO JOIN OUR CAUSE . . .
IT'S WORTH A LOT, FERN. I MAY NOT KNOW WHAT JEREMY IS TALKING ABOUT HALF THE TIME . . . BUT IF IT WASN'T FOR HIM, I WOULD NEVER HAVE MET YOU!
YOU'RE THE NICEST PERSON I'VE EVER KNOWN.
AND YOU'RE THE SWEETEST. SODD, COME WHAT MAY . . .
WE'LL ALWAYS HAVE EACH OTHER!

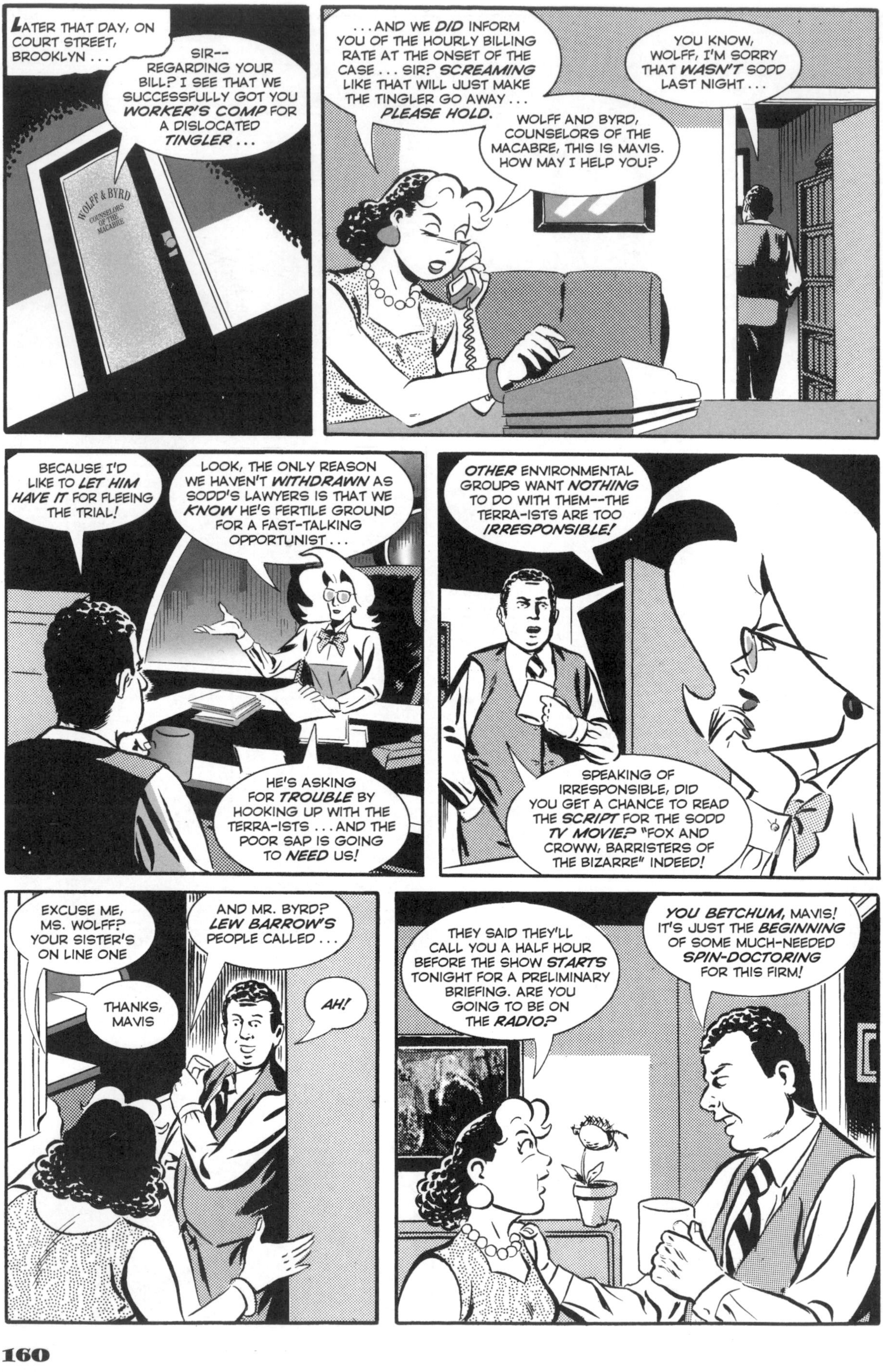
LATER THAT DAY, ON COURT STREET, BROOKLYN . . .
SIR-- REGARDING YOUR BILL? I SEE THAT WE SUCCESSFULLY GOT YOU WORKER'S COMP FOR A DISLOCATED TINGLER . . .
WOLFF & BYRD COUNSELORS OF THE MACABRE
. . . AND WE DID INFORM YOU OF THE HOURLY BILLING RATE AT THE ONSET OF THE CASE . . . SIR? SCREAMING LIKE THAT WILL JUST MAKE THE TINGLER GO AWAY . . . PLEASE HOLD.
WOLFF AND BYRD, COUNSELORS OF THE MACABRE, THIS IS MAVIS. HOW MAY I HELP YOU?
YOU KNOW, WOLFF, I'M SORRY THAT WASN'T SODD LAST NIGHT . . .
BECAUSE I'D LIKE TO LET HIM HAVE IT FOR FLEEING THE TRIAL!
LOOK, THE ONLY REASON WE HAVEN'T WITHDRAWN AS SODD'S LAWYERS IS THAT WE KNOW HE'S FERTILE GROUND FOR A FAST-TALKING OPPORTUNIST . . .
HE'S ASKING FOR TROUBLE BY HOOKING UP WITH THE TERRA-ISTS . . . AND THE POOR SAP IS GOING TO NEED US!
OTHER ENVIRONMENTAL GROUPS WANT NOTHING TO DO WITH THEM--THE TERRA-ISTS ARE TOO IRRESPONSIBLE!
SPEAKING OF IRRESPONSIBLE, DID YOU GET A CHANCE TO READ THE SCRIPT FOR THE SODD TV MOVIE? "FOX AND CROWW, BARRISTERS OF THE BIZARRE" INDEED!
EXCUSE ME, MS. WOLFF? YOUR SISTER'S ON LINE ONE
THANKS, MAVIS
AND MR. BYRD? LEW BARROW'S PEOPLE CALLED . . .
AH!
THEY SAID THEY'LL CALL YOU A HALF HOUR BEFORE THE SHOW STARTS TONIGHT FOR A PRELIMINARY BRIEFING. ARE YOU GOING TO BE ON THE RADIO?
YOU BETCHUM, MAVIS! IT'S JUST THE BEGINNING OF SOME MUCH-NEEDED SPIN-DOCTORING FOR THIS FIRM!

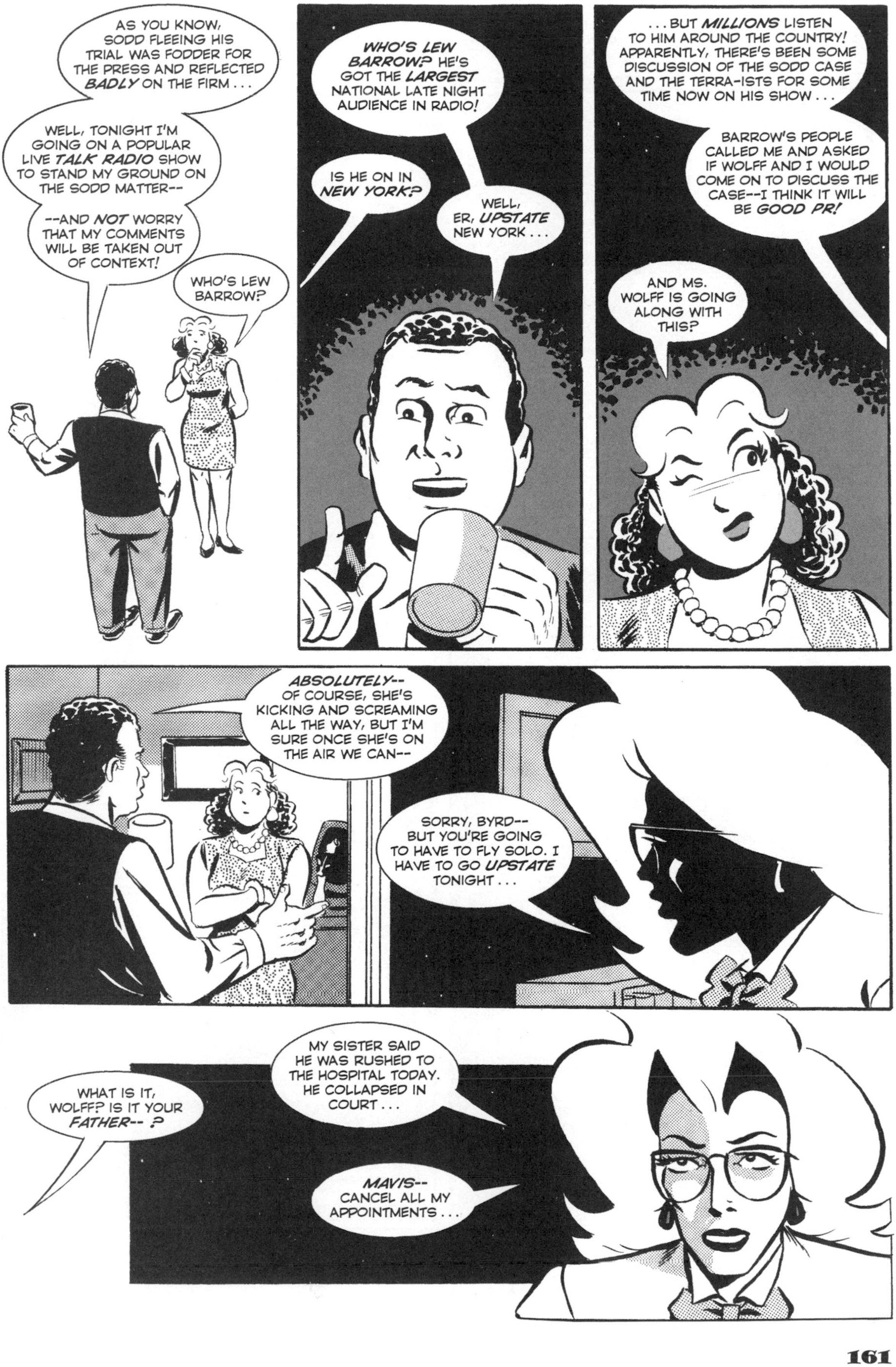
AS YOU KNOW, SODD FLEEING HIS TRIAL WAS FODDER FOR THE PRESS AND REFLECTED *BADLY* ON THE FIRM . . .
WELL, TONIGHT I'M GOING ON A POPULAR LIVE *TALK RADIO* SHOW TO STAND MY GROUND ON THE SODD MATTER--
--AND *NOT* WORRY THAT MY COMMENTS WILL BE TAKEN OUT OF CONTEXT!
WHO'S LEW BARROW?
WHO'S LEW BARROW? HE'S GOT THE *LARGEST* NATIONAL LATE NIGHT AUDIENCE IN RADIO!
IS HE ON IN *NEW YORK?*
WELL, ER, *UPSTATE* NEW YORK . . .
. . . BUT *MILLIONS* LISTEN TO HIM AROUND THE COUNTRY! APPARENTLY, THERE'S BEEN SOME DISCUSSION OF THE SODD CASE AND THE TERRA-ISTS FOR SOME TIME NOW ON HIS SHOW . . .
BARROW'S PEOPLE CALLED ME AND ASKED IF WOLFF AND I WOULD COME ON TO DISCUSS THE CASE--I THINK IT WILL BE *GOOD PR!*
AND MS. WOLFF IS GOING ALONG WITH THIS?
ABSOLUTELY-- OF COURSE, SHE'S KICKING AND SCREAMING ALL THE WAY, BUT I'M SURE ONCE SHE'S ON THE AIR WE CAN--
SORRY, BYRD-- BUT YOU'RE GOING TO HAVE TO FLY SOLO. I HAVE TO GO *UPSTATE* TONIGHT . . .
WHAT IS IT, WOLFF? IS IT YOUR *FATHER-- ?*
MY SISTER SAID HE WAS RUSHED TO THE HOSPITAL TODAY. HE COLLAPSED IN COURT . . .
MAVIS-- CANCEL ALL MY APPOINTMENTS . . .

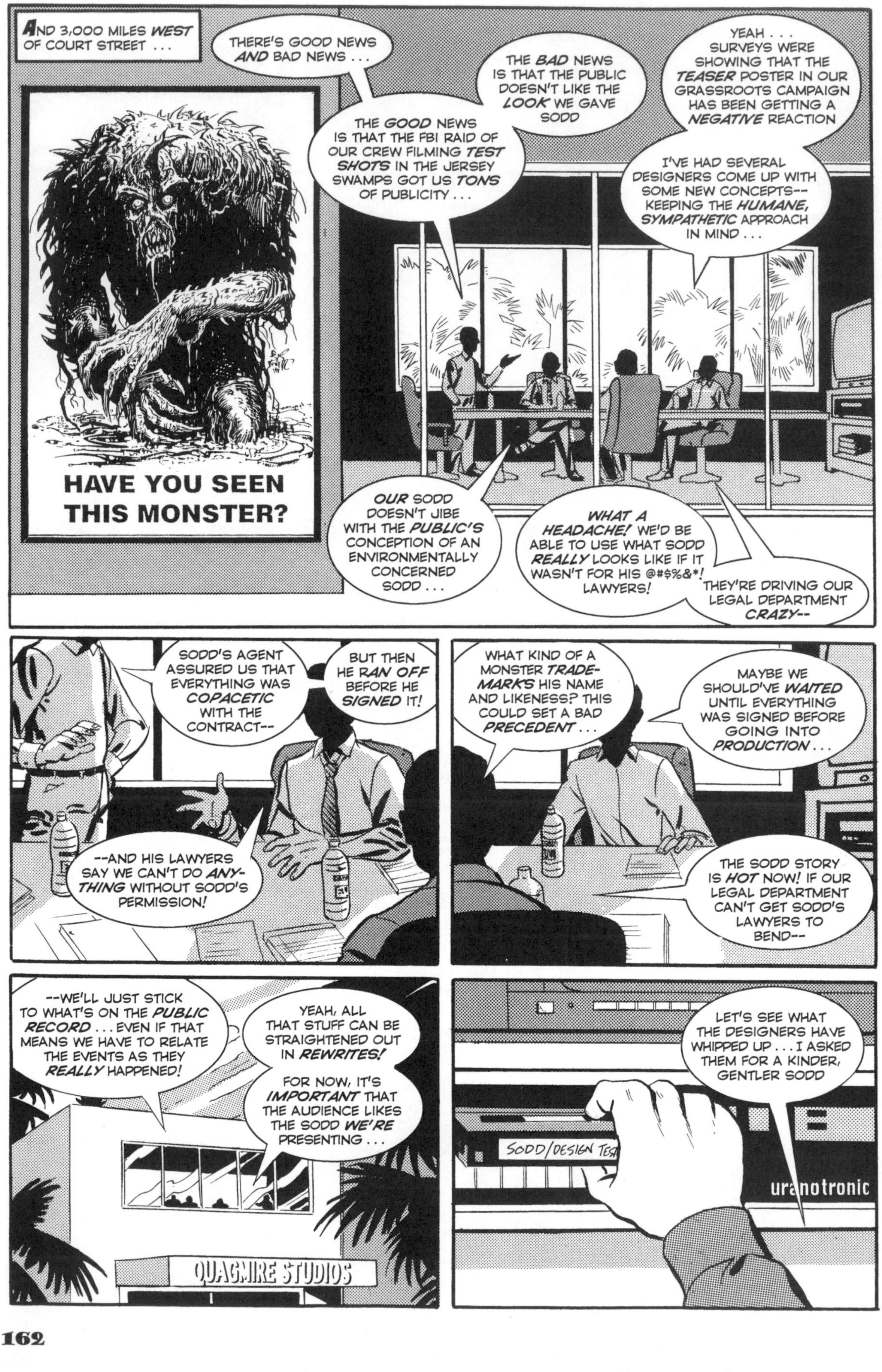
AND 3,000 MILES WEST OF COURT STREET . . .
THERE'S GOOD NEWS AND BAD NEWS . . .
THE GOOD NEWS IS THAT THE FBI RAID OF OUR CREW FILMING TEST SHOTS IN THE JERSEY SWAMPS GOT US TONS OF PUBLICITY . . .
THE BAD NEWS IS THAT THE PUBLIC DOESN'T LIKE THE LOOK WE GAVE SODD
YEAH . . . SURVEYS WERE SHOWING THAT THE TEASER POSTER IN OUR GRASSROOTS CAMPAIGN HAS BEEN GETTING A NEGATIVE REACTION
I'VE HAD SEVERAL DESIGNERS COME UP WITH SOME NEW CONCEPTS-- KEEPING THE HUMANE, SYMPATHETIC APPROACH IN MIND . . .
HAVE YOU SEEN THIS MONSTER?
OUR SODD DOESN'T JIBE WITH THE PUBLIC'S CONCEPTION OF AN ENVIRONMENTALLY CONCERNED SODD . . .
WHAT A HEADACHE! WE'D BE ABLE TO USE WHAT SODD REALLY LOOKS LIKE IF IT WASN'T FOR HIS @#$%&*! LAWYERS!
THEY'RE DRIVING OUR LEGAL DEPARTMENT CRAZY--
SODD'S AGENT ASSURED US THAT EVERYTHING WAS COPACETIC WITH THE CONTRACT--
BUT THEN HE RAN OFF BEFORE HE SIGNED IT!
--AND HIS LAWYERS SAY WE CAN'T DO ANYTHING WITHOUT SODD'S PERMISSION!
WHAT KIND OF A MONSTER TRADEMARKS HIS NAME AND LIKENESS? THIS COULD SET A BAD PRECEDENT . . .
MAYBE WE SHOULD'VE WAITED UNTIL EVERYTHING WAS SIGNED BEFORE GOING INTO PRODUCTION . . .
THE SODD STORY IS HOT NOW! IF OUR LEGAL DEPARTMENT CAN'T GET SODD'S LAWYERS TO BEND--
--WE'LL JUST STICK TO WHAT'S ON THE PUBLIC RECORD . . . EVEN IF THAT MEANS WE HAVE TO RELATE THE EVENTS AS THEY REALLY HAPPENED!
YEAH, ALL THAT STUFF CAN BE STRAIGHTENED OUT IN REWRITES!
FOR NOW, IT'S IMPORTANT THAT THE AUDIENCE LIKES THE SODD WE'RE PRESENTING . . .
QUAGMIRE STUDIOS
LET'S SEE WHAT THE DESIGNERS HAVE WHIPPED UP . . . I ASKED THEM FOR A KINDER, GENTLER SODD
SODD/DESIGN TEST
uranotronic

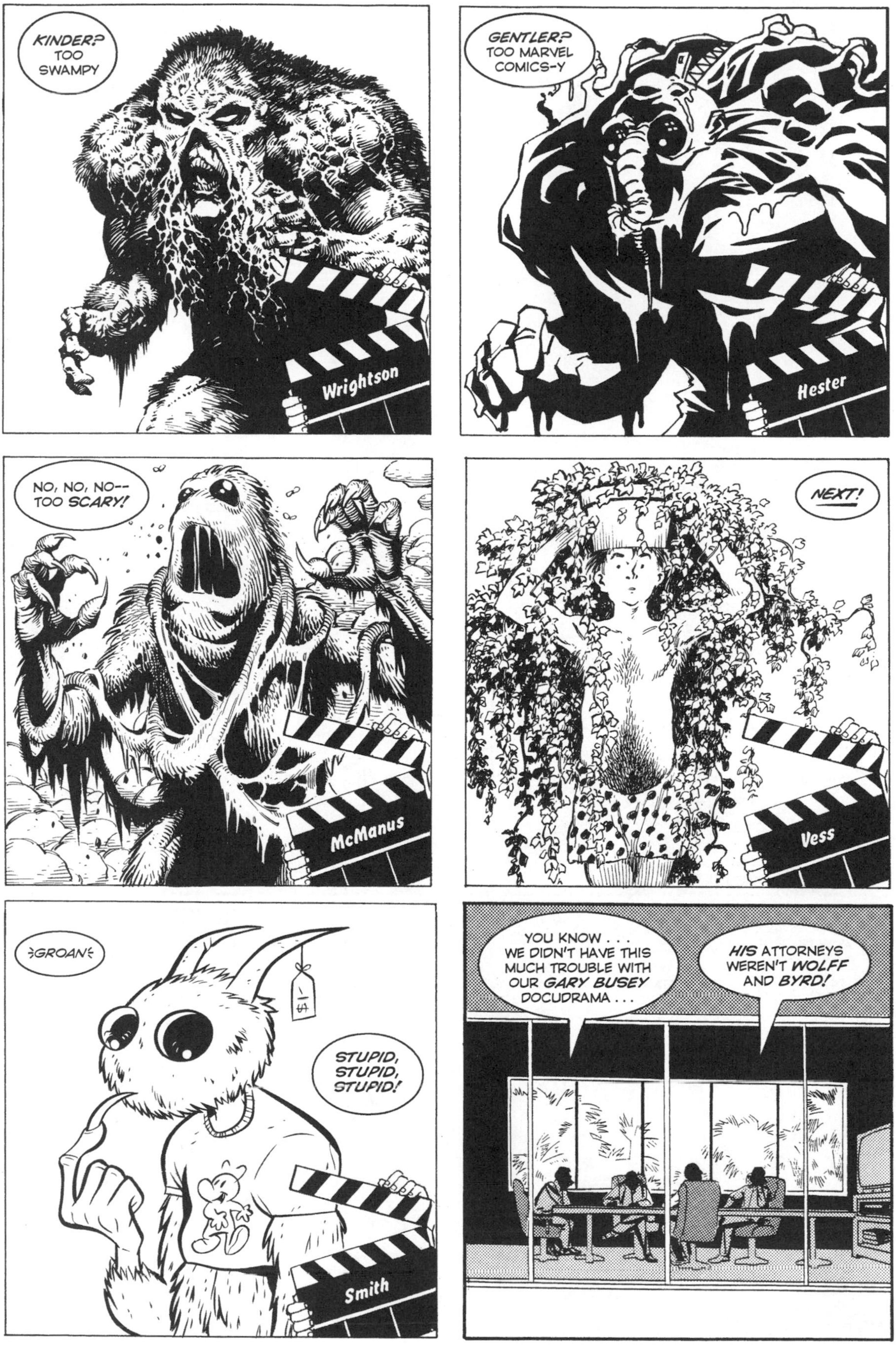
KINDER? TOO SWAMPY
Wrightson
GENTLER? TOO MARVEL COMICS-Y
Hester
NO, NO, NO-- TOO SCARY!
McManus
NEXT!
Vess
GROAN
STUPID, STUPID, STUPID!
Smith
YOU KNOW . . . WE DIDN'T HAVE THIS MUCH TROUBLE WITH OUR GARY BUSEY DOCUDRAMA . . .
HIS ATTORNEYS WEREN'T WOLFF AND BYRD!

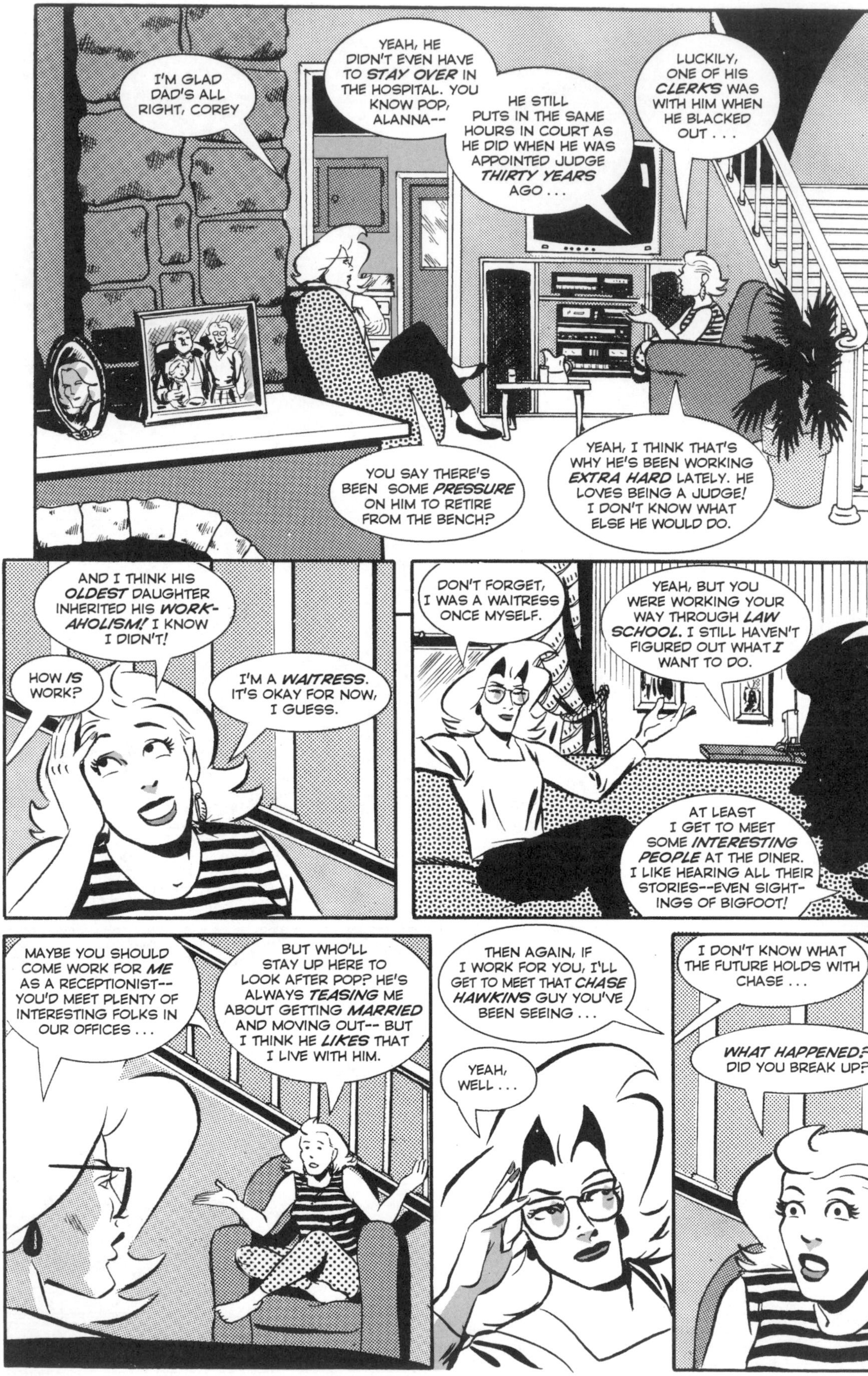
I'M GLAD DAD'S ALL RIGHT, COREY
YEAH, HE DIDN'T EVEN HAVE TO STAY OVER IN THE HOSPITAL. YOU KNOW POP, ALANNA--
HE STILL PUTS IN THE SAME HOURS IN COURT AS HE DID WHEN HE WAS APPOINTED JUDGE THIRTY YEARS AGO . . .
LUCKILY, ONE OF HIS CLERKS WAS WITH HIM WHEN HE BLACKED OUT . . .
YOU SAY THERE'S BEEN SOME PRESSURE ON HIM TO RETIRE FROM THE BENCH?
YEAH, I THINK THAT'S WHY HE'S BEEN WORKING EXTRA HARD LATELY. HE LOVES BEING A JUDGE! I DON'T KNOW WHAT ELSE HE WOULD DO.
AND I THINK HIS OLDEST DAUGHTER INHERITED HIS WORK-AHOLISM! I KNOW I DIDN'T!
HOW IS WORK?
I'M A WAITRESS. IT'S OKAY FOR NOW, I GUESS.
DON'T FORGET, I WAS A WAITRESS ONCE MYSELF.
YEAH, BUT YOU WERE WORKING YOUR WAY THROUGH LAW SCHOOL. I STILL HAVEN'T FIGURED OUT WHAT I WANT TO DO.
AT LEAST I GET TO MEET SOME INTERESTING PEOPLE AT THE DINER. I LIKE HEARING ALL THEIR STORIES--EVEN SIGHT-INGS OF BIGFOOT!
MAYBE YOU SHOULD COME WORK FOR ME AS A RECEPTIONIST--YOU'D MEET PLENTY OF INTERESTING FOLKS IN OUR OFFICES . . .
BUT WHO'LL STAY UP HERE TO LOOK AFTER POP? HE'S ALWAYS TEASING ME ABOUT GETTING MARRIED AND MOVING OUT-- BUT I THINK HE LIKES THAT I LIVE WITH HIM.
THEN AGAIN, IF I WORK FOR YOU, I'LL GET TO MEET THAT CHASE HAWKINS GUY YOU'VE BEEN SEEING . . .
YEAH, WELL . . .
I DON'T KNOW WHAT THE FUTURE HOLDS WITH CHASE . . .
WHAT HAPPENED? DID YOU BREAK UP?

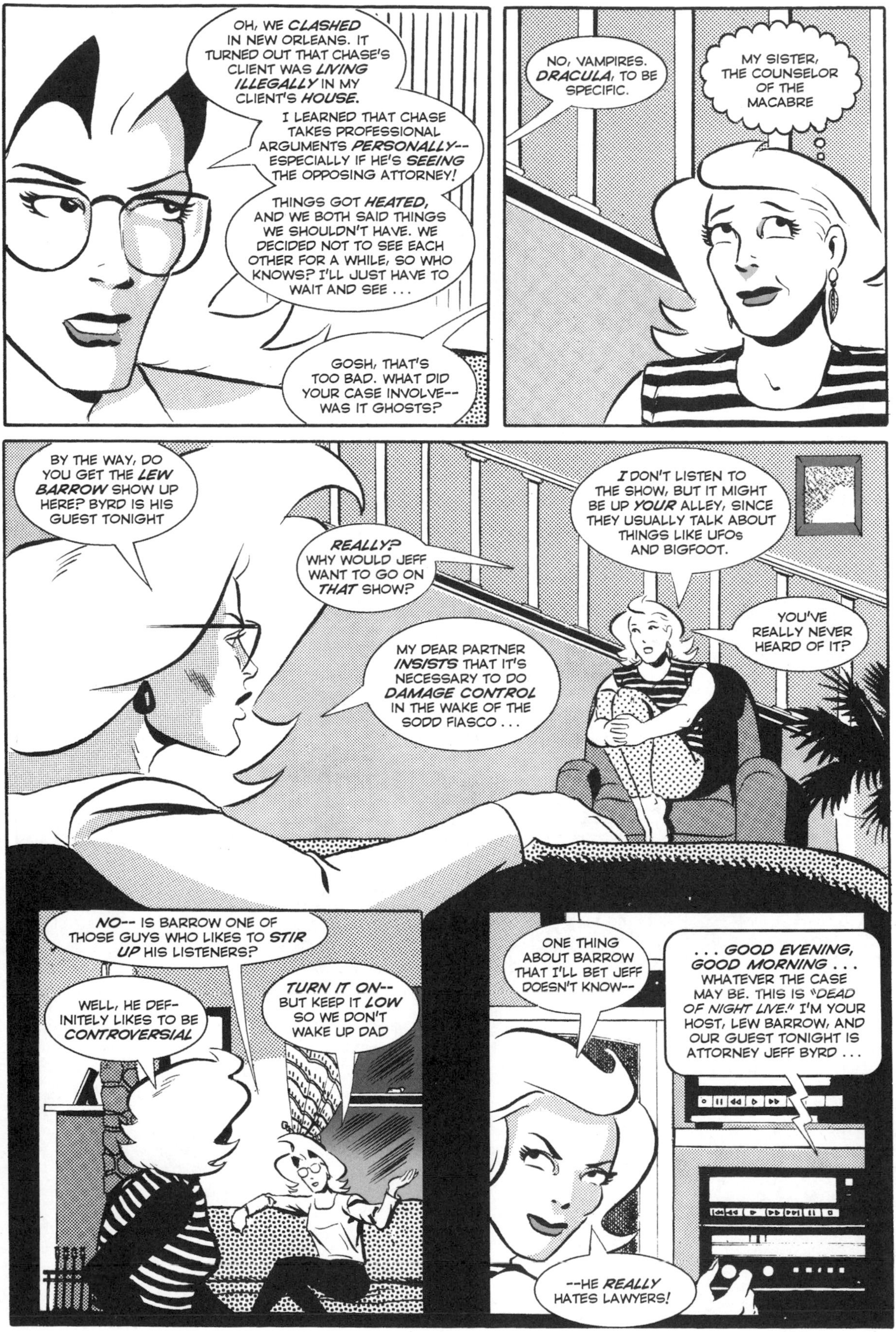

OH, WE CLASHED IN NEW ORLEANS. IT TURNED OUT THAT CHASE'S CLIENT WAS LIVING ILLEGALLY IN MY CLIENT'S HOUSE.
I LEARNED THAT CHASE TAKES PROFESSIONAL ARGUMENTS PERSONALLY-- ESPECIALLY IF HE'S SEEING THE OPPOSING ATTORNEY!
THINGS GOT HEATED, AND WE BOTH SAID THINGS WE SHOULDN'T HAVE. WE DECIDED NOT TO SEE EACH OTHER FOR A WHILE, SO WHO KNOWS? I'LL JUST HAVE TO WAIT AND SEE . . .
GOSH, THAT'S TOO BAD. WHAT DID YOUR CASE INVOLVE-- WAS IT GHOSTS?
NO, VAMPIRES. DRACULA, TO BE SPECIFIC.
MY SISTER, THE COUNSELOR OF THE MACABRE
BY THE WAY, DO YOU GET THE LEW BARROW SHOW UP HERE? BYRD IS HIS GUEST TONIGHT
REALLY? WHY WOULD JEFF WANT TO GO ON THAT SHOW?
MY DEAR PARTNER INSISTS THAT IT'S NECESSARY TO DO DAMAGE CONTROL IN THE WAKE OF THE SODD FIASCO . . .
I DON'T LISTEN TO THE SHOW, BUT IT MIGHT BE UP YOUR ALLEY, SINCE THEY USUALLY TALK ABOUT THINGS LIKE UFOs AND BIGFOOT.
YOU'VE REALLY NEVER HEARD OF IT?
NO-- IS BARROW ONE OF THOSE GUYS WHO LIKES TO STIR UP HIS LISTENERS?
WELL, HE DEF- INITELY LIKES TO BE CONTROVERSIAL
TURN IT ON-- BUT KEEP IT LOW SO WE DON'T WAKE UP DAD
ONE THING ABOUT BARROW THAT I'LL BET JEFF DOESN'T KNOW--
. . . GOOD EVENING, GOOD MORNING . . . WHATEVER THE CASE MAY BE. THIS IS "DEAD OF NIGHT LIVE." I'M YOUR HOST, LEW BARROW, AND OUR GUEST TONIGHT IS ATTORNEY JEFF BYRD . . .
--HE REALLY HATES LAWYERS!

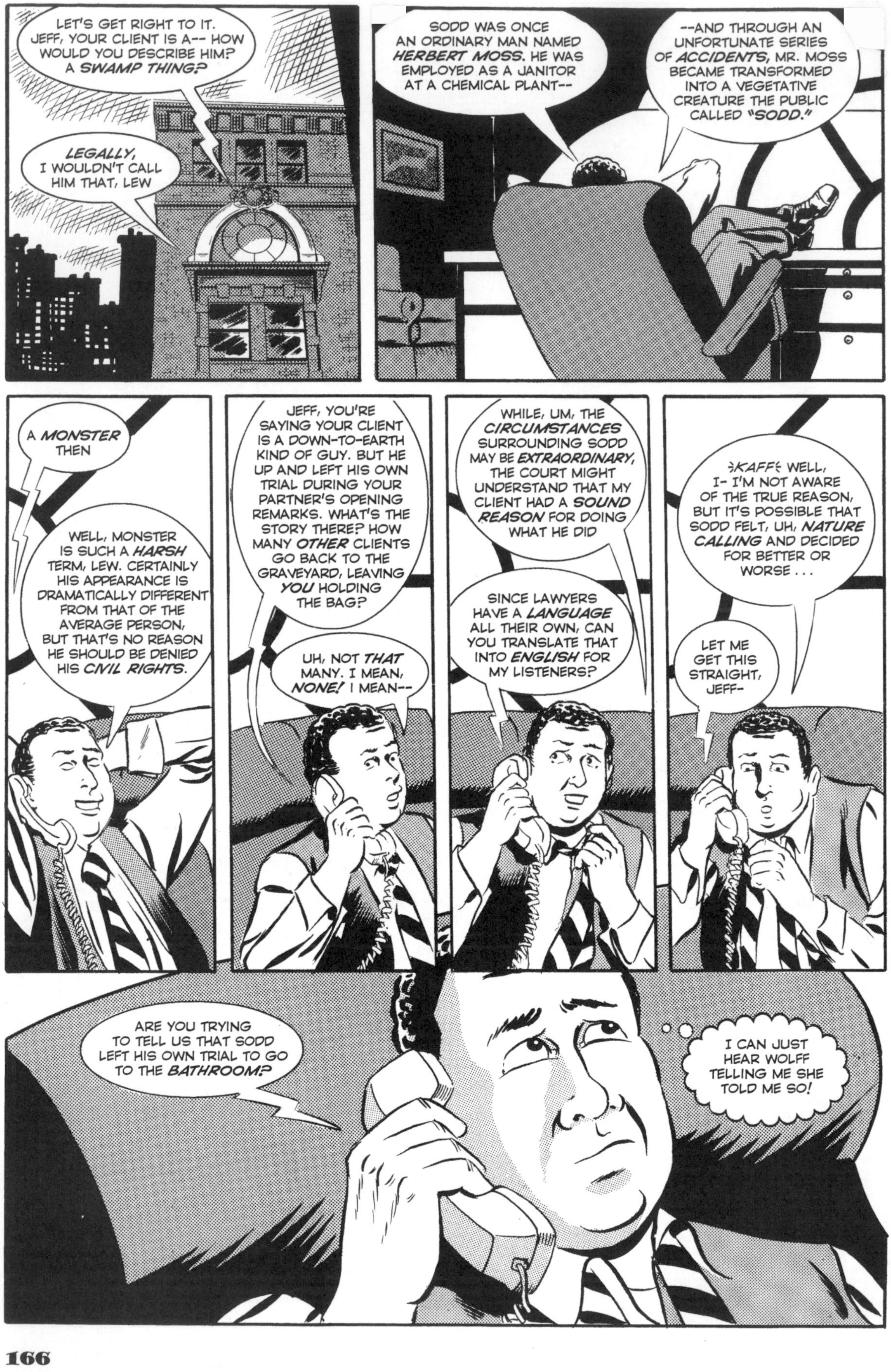
LET'S GET RIGHT TO IT. JEFF, YOUR CLIENT IS A-- HOW WOULD YOU DESCRIBE HIM? A SWAMP THING?
LEGALLY, I WOULDN'T CALL HIM THAT, LEW
SODD WAS ONCE AN ORDINARY MAN NAMED HERBERT MOSS. HE WAS EMPLOYED AS A JANITOR AT A CHEMICAL PLANT--
--AND THROUGH AN UNFORTUNATE SERIES OF ACCIDENTS, MR. MOSS BECAME TRANSFORMED INTO A VEGETATIVE CREATURE THE PUBLIC CALLED "SODD."
A MONSTER THEN
WELL, MONSTER IS SUCH A HARSH TERM, LEW. CERTAINLY HIS APPEARANCE IS DRAMATICALLY DIFFERENT FROM THAT OF THE AVERAGE PERSON, BUT THAT'S NO REASON HE SHOULD BE DENIED HIS CIVIL RIGHTS.
JEFF, YOU'RE SAYING YOUR CLIENT IS A DOWN-TO-EARTH KIND OF GUY. BUT HE UP AND LEFT HIS OWN TRIAL DURING YOUR PARTNER'S OPENING REMARKS. WHAT'S THE STORY THERE? HOW MANY OTHER CLIENTS GO BACK TO THE GRAVEYARD, LEAVING YOU HOLDING THE BAG?
UH, NOT THAT MANY. I MEAN, NONE! I MEAN--
WHILE, UM, THE CIRCUMSTANCES SURROUNDING SODD MAY BE EXTRAORDINARY, THE COURT MIGHT UNDERSTAND THAT MY CLIENT HAD A SOUND REASON FOR DOING WHAT HE DID
SINCE LAWYERS HAVE A LANGUAGE ALL THEIR OWN, CAN YOU TRANSLATE THAT INTO ENGLISH FOR MY LISTENERS?
KAFF WELL, I- I'M NOT AWARE OF THE TRUE REASON, BUT IT'S POSSIBLE THAT SODD FELT, UH, NATURE CALLING AND DECIDED FOR BETTER OR WORSE . . .
LET ME GET THIS STRAIGHT, JEFF-
ARE YOU TRYING TO TELL US THAT SODD LEFT HIS OWN TRIAL TO GO TO THE BATHROOM?
I CAN JUST HEAR WOLFF TELLING ME SHE TOLD ME SO!

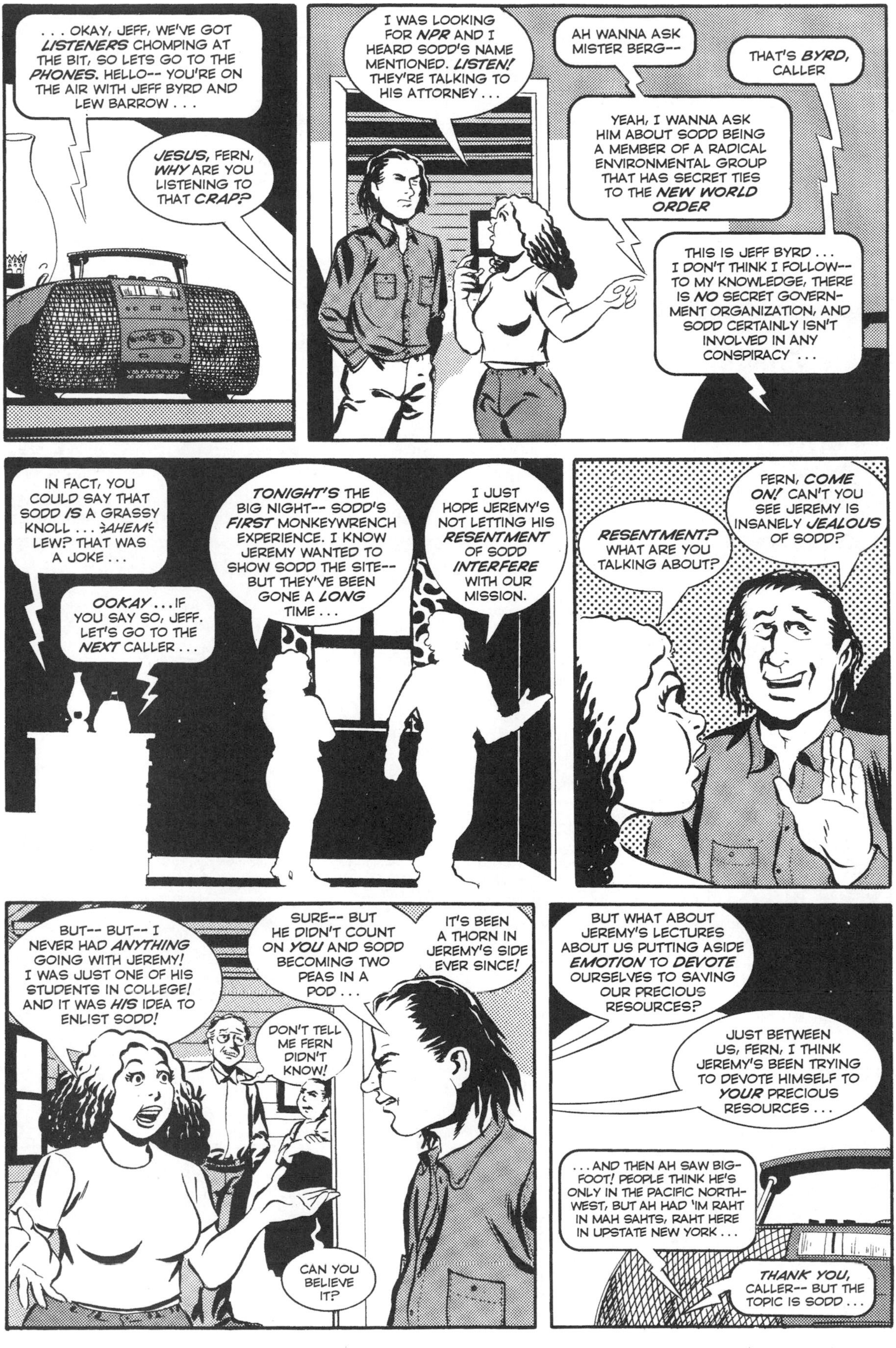

. . . OKAY, JEFF, WE'VE GOT LISTENERS CHOMPING AT THE BIT, SO LETS GO TO THE PHONES. HELLO-- YOU'RE ON THE AIR WITH JEFF BYRD AND LEW BARROW . . .
JESUS, FERN, WHY ARE YOU LISTENING TO THAT CRAP?
I WAS LOOKING FOR NPR AND I HEARD SODD'S NAME MENTIONED. LISTEN! THEY'RE TALKING TO HIS ATTORNEY . . .
AH WANNA ASK MISTER BERG--
THAT'S BYRD, CALLER
YEAH, I WANNA ASK HIM ABOUT SODD BEING A MEMBER OF A RADICAL ENVIRONMENTAL GROUP THAT HAS SECRET TIES TO THE NEW WORLD ORDER
THIS IS JEFF BYRD . . . I DON'T THINK I FOLLOW-- TO MY KNOWLEDGE, THERE IS NO SECRET GOVERNMENT ORGANIZATION, AND SODD CERTAINLY ISN'T INVOLVED IN ANY CONSPIRACY . . .
IN FACT, YOU COULD SAY THAT SODD IS A GRASSY KNOLL . . . AHEM LEW? THAT WAS A JOKE . . .
OOKAY . . . IF YOU SAY SO, JEFF. LET'S GO TO THE NEXT CALLER . . .
TONIGHT'S THE BIG NIGHT-- SODD'S FIRST MONKEYWRENCH EXPERIENCE. I KNOW JEREMY WANTED TO SHOW SODD THE SITE-- BUT THEY'VE BEEN GONE A LONG TIME . . .
I JUST HOPE JEREMY'S NOT LETTING HIS RESENTMENT OF SODD INTERFERE WITH OUR MISSION.
RESENTMENT? WHAT ARE YOU TALKING ABOUT?
FERN, COME ON! CAN'T YOU SEE JEREMY IS INSANELY JEALOUS OF SODD?
BUT-- BUT-- I NEVER HAD ANYTHING GOING WITH JEREMY! I WAS JUST ONE OF HIS STUDENTS IN COLLEGE! AND IT WAS HIS IDEA TO ENLIST SODD!
SURE-- BUT HE DIDN'T COUNT ON YOU AND SODD BECOMING TWO PEAS IN A POD . . .
IT'S BEEN A THORN IN JEREMY'S SIDE EVER SINCE!
DON'T TELL ME FERN DIDN'T KNOW!
CAN YOU BELIEVE IT?
BUT WHAT ABOUT JEREMY'S LECTURES ABOUT US PUTTING ASIDE EMOTION TO DEVOTE OURSELVES TO SAVING OUR PRECIOUS RESOURCES?
JUST BETWEEN US, FERN, I THINK JEREMY'S BEEN TRYING TO DEVOTE HIMSELF TO YOUR PRECIOUS RESOURCES . . .
. . . AND THEN AH SAW BIG-FOOT! PEOPLE THINK HE'S ONLY IN THE PACIFIC NORTH-WEST, BUT AH HAD 'IM RAHT IN MAH SAHTS, RAHT HERE IN UPSTATE NEW YORK . . .
THANK YOU, CALLER-- BUT THE TOPIC IS SODD . . .

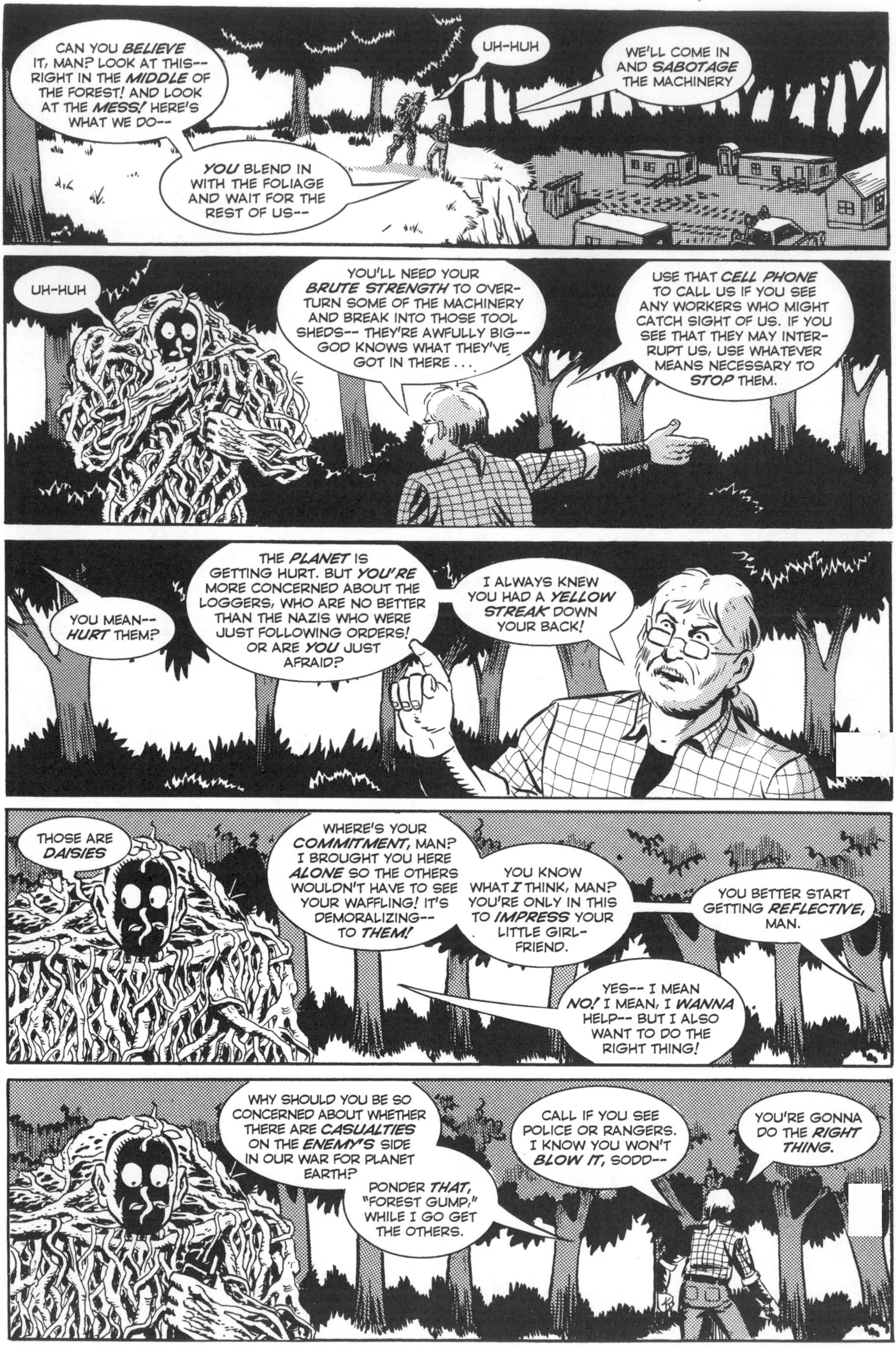
CAN YOU BELIEVE IT, MAN? LOOK AT THIS-- RIGHT IN THE MIDDLE OF THE FOREST! AND LOOK AT THE MESS! HERE'S WHAT WE DO--
UH-HUH
WE'LL COME IN AND SABOTAGE THE MACHINERY
YOU BLEND IN WITH THE FOLIAGE AND WAIT FOR THE REST OF US--
UH-HUH
YOU'LL NEED YOUR BRUTE STRENGTH TO OVER-TURN SOME OF THE MACHINERY AND BREAK INTO THOSE TOOL SHEDS-- THEY'RE AWFULLY BIG-- GOD KNOWS WHAT THEY'VE GOT IN THERE . . .
USE THAT CELL PHONE TO CALL US IF YOU SEE ANY WORKERS WHO MIGHT CATCH SIGHT OF US. IF YOU SEE THAT THEY MAY INTER-RUPT US, USE WHATEVER MEANS NECESSARY TO STOP THEM.
YOU MEAN-- HURT THEM?
THE PLANET IS GETTING HURT. BUT YOU'RE MORE CONCERNED ABOUT THE LOGGERS, WHO ARE NO BETTER THAN THE NAZIS WHO WERE JUST FOLLOWING ORDERS! OR ARE YOU JUST AFRAID?
I ALWAYS KNEW YOU HAD A YELLOW STREAK DOWN YOUR BACK!
THOSE ARE DAISIES
WHERE'S YOUR COMMITMENT, MAN? I BROUGHT YOU HERE ALONE SO THE OTHERS WOULDN'T HAVE TO SEE YOUR WAFFLING! IT'S DEMORALIZING-- TO THEM!
YOU KNOW WHAT I THINK, MAN? YOU'RE ONLY IN THIS TO IMPRESS YOUR LITTLE GIRL-FRIEND.
YOU BETTER START GETTING REFLECTIVE, MAN.
YES-- I MEAN NO! I MEAN, I WANNA HELP-- BUT I ALSO WANT TO DO THE RIGHT THING!
WHY SHOULD YOU BE SO CONCERNED ABOUT WHETHER THERE ARE CASUALTIES ON THE ENEMY'S SIDE IN OUR WAR FOR PLANET EARTH?
PONDER THAT, "FOREST GUMP," WHILE I GO GET THE OTHERS.
CALL IF YOU SEE POLICE OR RANGERS. I KNOW YOU WON'T BLOW IT, SODD--
YOU'RE GONNA DO THE RIGHT THING.

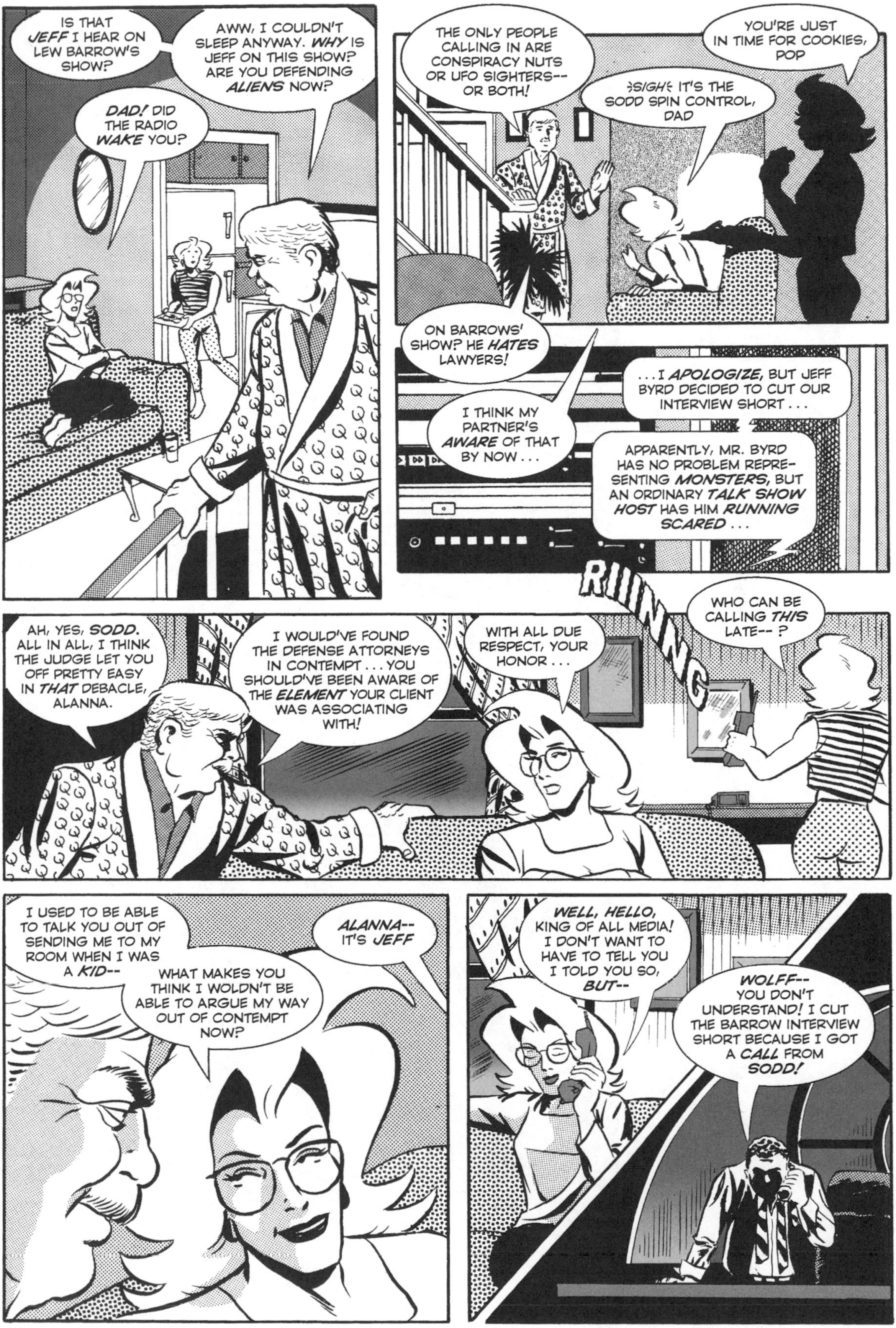
IS THAT JEFF I HEAR ON LEW BARROW'S SHOW?
DAD! DID THE RADIO WAKE YOU?
AWW, I COULDN'T SLEEP ANYWAY. WHY IS JEFF ON THIS SHOW? ARE YOU DEFENDING ALIENS NOW?
THE ONLY PEOPLE CALLING IN ARE CONSPIRACY NUTS OR UFO SIGHTERS-- OR BOTH!
YOU'RE JUST IN TIME FOR COOKIES, POP
SIGH IT'S THE SODD SPIN CONTROL, DAD
ON BARROWS' SHOW? HE HATES LAWYERS!
I THINK MY PARTNER'S AWARE OF THAT BY NOW . . .
. . . I APOLOGIZE, BUT JEFF BYRD DECIDED TO CUT OUR INTERVIEW SHORT . . .
APPARENTLY, MR. BYRD HAS NO PROBLEM REPRESENTING MONSTERS, BUT AN ORDINARY TALK SHOW HOST HAS HIM RUNNING SCARED . . .
RIIINNG
AH, YES, SODD. ALL IN ALL, I THINK THE JUDGE LET YOU OFF PRETTY EASY IN THAT DEBACLE, ALANNA.
I WOULD'VE FOUND THE DEFENSE ATTORNEYS IN CONTEMPT . . . YOU SHOULD'VE BEEN AWARE OF THE ELEMENT YOUR CLIENT WAS ASSOCIATING WITH!
WITH ALL DUE RESPECT, YOUR HONOR . . .
WHO CAN BE CALLING THIS LATE-- ?
I USED TO BE ABLE TO TALK YOU OUT OF SENDING ME TO MY ROOM WHEN I WAS A KID--
WHAT MAKES YOU THINK I WOLDN'T BE ABLE TO ARGUE MY WAY OUT OF CONTEMPT NOW?
ALANNA-- IT'S JEFF
WELL, HELLO, KING OF ALL MEDIA! I DON'T WANT TO HAVE TO TELL YOU I TOLD YOU SO, BUT--
WOLFF-- YOU DON'T UNDERSTAND! I CUT THE BARROW INTERVIEW SHORT BECAUSE I GOT A CALL FROM SODD!

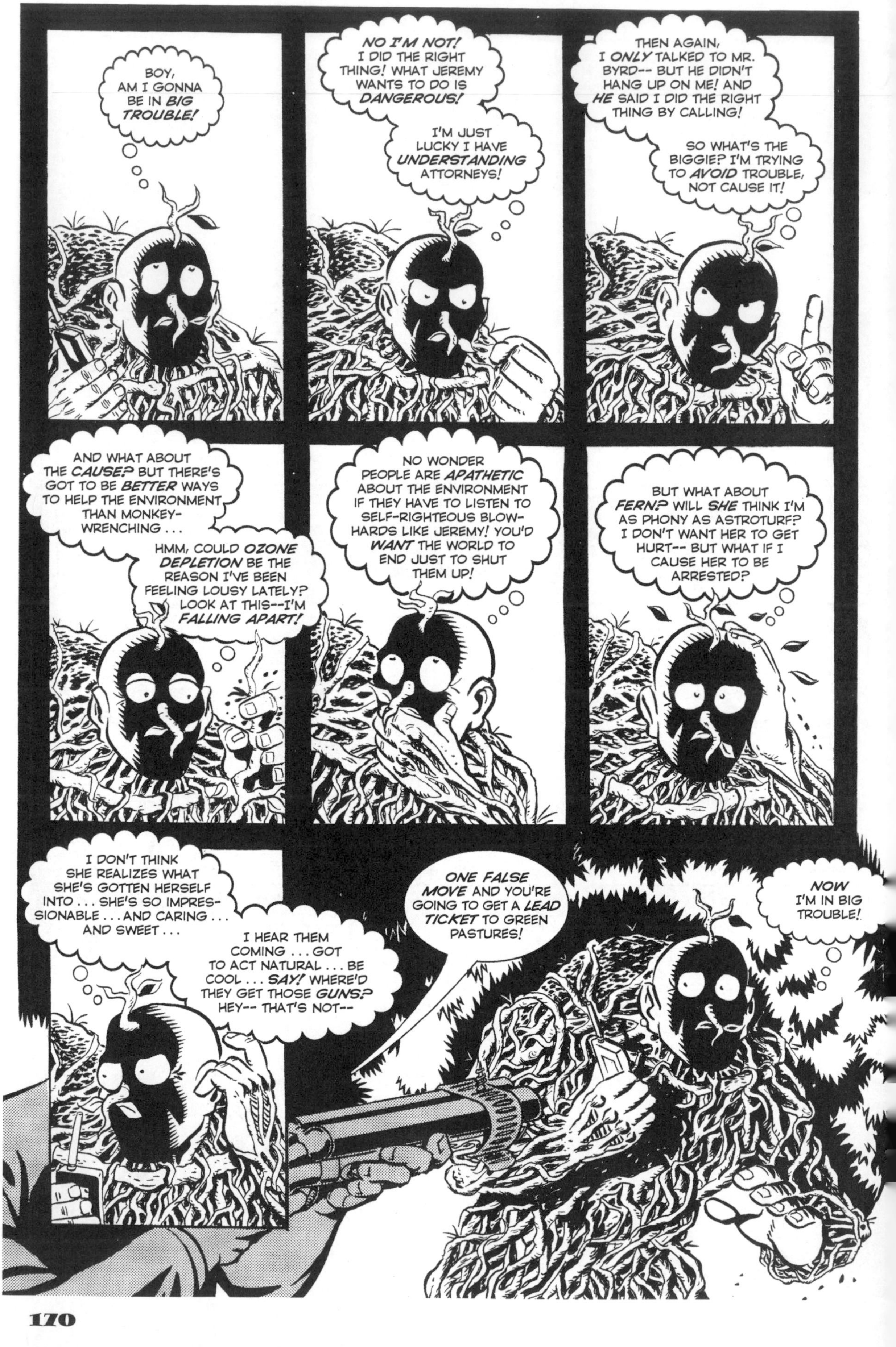
BOY, AM I GONNA BE IN BIG TROUBLE!
NO I'M NOT! I DID THE RIGHT THING! WHAT JEREMY WANTS TO DO IS DANGEROUS!
I'M JUST LUCKY I HAVE UNDERSTANDING ATTORNEYS!
THEN AGAIN, I ONLY TALKED TO MR. BYRD-- BUT HE DIDN'T HANG UP ON ME! AND HE SAID I DID THE RIGHT THING BY CALLING!
SO WHAT'S THE BIGGIE? I'M TRYING TO AVOID TROUBLE, NOT CAUSE IT!
AND WHAT ABOUT THE CAUSE? BUT THERE'S GOT TO BE BETTER WAYS TO HELP THE ENVIRONMENT THAN MONKEY-WRENCHING . . .
HMM, COULD OZONE DEPLETION BE THE REASON I'VE BEEN FEELING LOUSY LATELY? LOOK AT THIS--I'M FALLING APART!
NO WONDER PEOPLE ARE APATHETIC ABOUT THE ENVIRONMENT IF THEY HAVE TO LISTEN TO SELF-RIGHTEOUS BLOW-HARDS LIKE JEREMY! YOU'D WANT THE WORLD TO END JUST TO SHUT THEM UP!
BUT WHAT ABOUT FERN? WILL SHE THINK I'M AS PHONY AS ASTROTURF? I DON'T WANT HER TO GET HURT-- BUT WHAT IF I CAUSE HER TO BE ARRESTED?
I DON'T THINK SHE REALIZES WHAT SHE'S GOTTEN HERSELF INTO . . . SHE'S SO IMPRES-SIONABLE . . . AND CARING . . . AND SWEET . . .
I HEAR THEM COMING . . . GOT TO ACT NATURAL . . . BE COOL . . . SAY! WHERE'D THEY GET THOSE GUNS? HEY-- THAT'S NOT--
ONE FALSE MOVE AND YOU'RE GOING TO GET A LEAD TICKET TO GREEN PASTURES!
NOW I'M IN BIG TROUBLE!

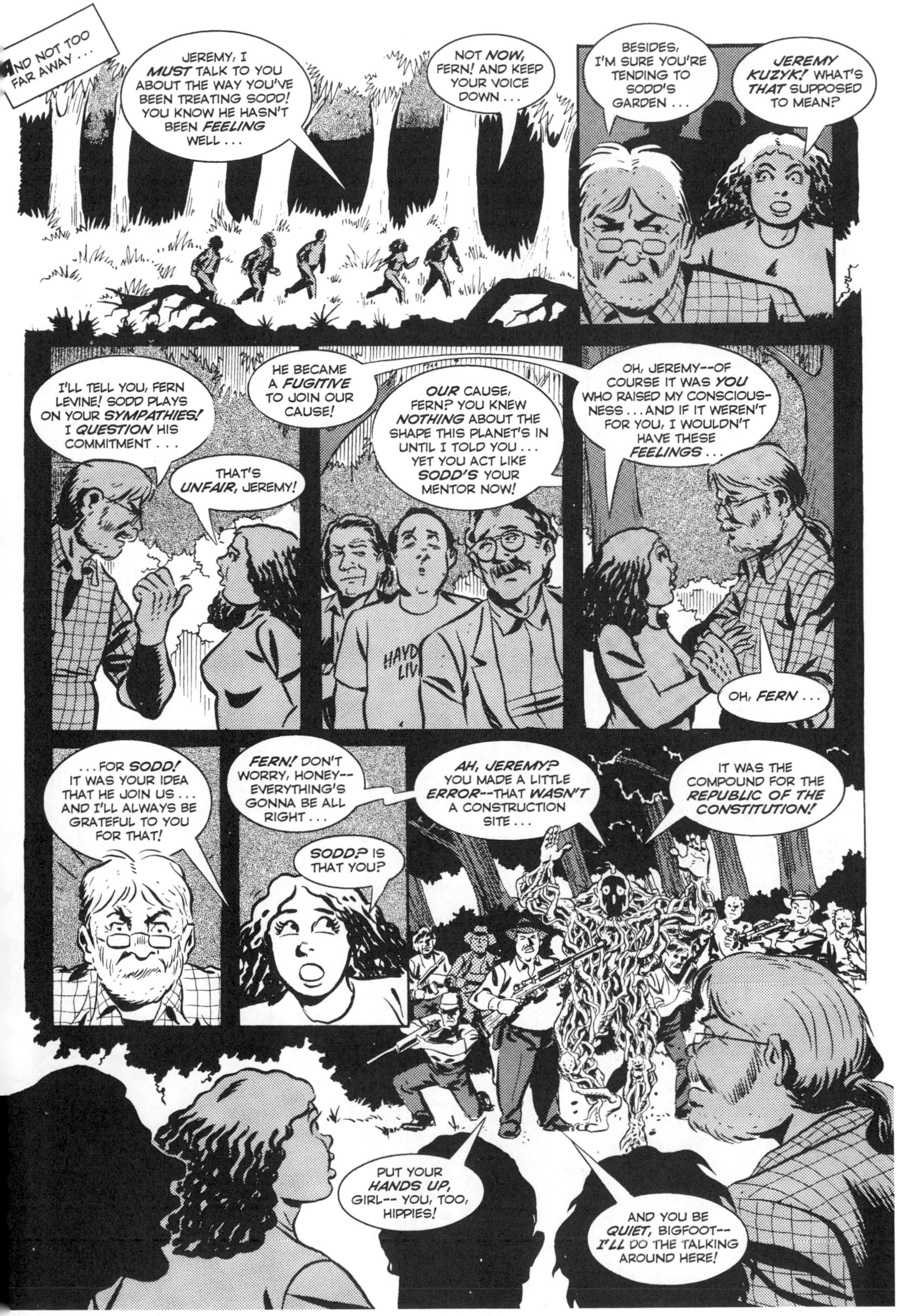

AND NOT TOO FAR AWAY . . .
JEREMY, I MUST TALK TO YOU ABOUT THE WAY YOU'VE BEEN TREATING SODD! YOU KNOW HE HASN'T BEEN FEELING WELL . . .
NOT NOW, FERN! AND KEEP YOUR VOICE DOWN . . .
BESIDES, I'M SURE YOU'RE TENDING TO SODD'S GARDEN . . .
JEREMY KUZYK! WHAT'S THAT SUPPOSED TO MEAN?
I'LL TELL YOU, FERN LEVINE! SODD PLAYS ON YOUR SYMPATHIES! I QUESTION HIS COMMITMENT . . .
THAT'S UNFAIR, JEREMY!
HE BECAME A FUGITIVE TO JOIN OUR CAUSE!
OUR CAUSE, FERN? YOU KNEW NOTHING ABOUT THE SHAPE THIS PLANET'S IN UNTIL I TOLD YOU . . . YET YOU ACT LIKE SODD'S YOUR MENTOR NOW!
OH, JEREMY--OF COURSE IT WAS YOU WHO RAISED MY CONSCIOUSNESS . . . AND IF IT WEREN'T FOR YOU, I WOULDN'T HAVE THESE FEELINGS . . .
OH, FERN . . .
. . . FOR SODD! IT WAS YOUR IDEA THAT HE JOIN US . . . AND I'LL ALWAYS BE GRATEFUL TO YOU FOR THAT!
FERN! DON'T WORRY, HONEY-- EVERYTHING'S GONNA BE ALL RIGHT . . .
SODD? IS THAT YOU?
AH, JEREMY? YOU MADE A LITTLE ERROR--THAT WASN'T A CONSTRUCTION SITE . . .
IT WAS THE COMPOUND FOR THE REPUBLIC OF THE CONSTITUTION!
PUT YOUR HANDS UP, GIRL-- YOU, TOO, HIPPIES!
AND YOU BE QUIET, BIGFOOT-- I'LL DO THE TALKING AROUND HERE!

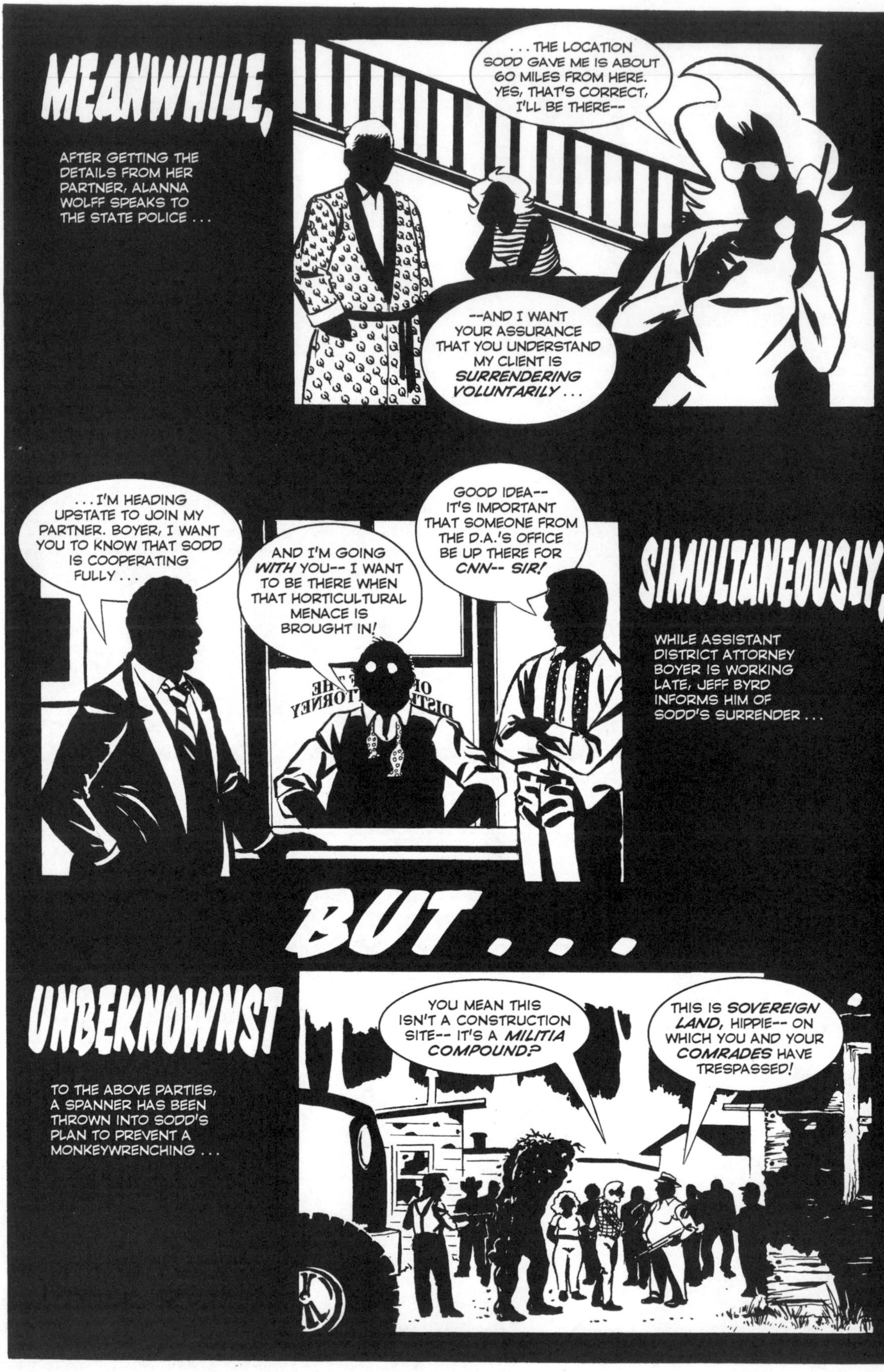
MEANWHILE,
AFTER GETTING THE DETAILS FROM HER PARTNER, ALANNA WOLFF SPEAKS TO THE STATE POLICE . . .
. . . THE LOCATION SODD GAVE ME IS ABOUT 60 MILES FROM HERE. YES, THAT'S CORRECT, I'LL BE THERE--
--AND I WANT YOUR ASSURANCE THAT YOU UNDERSTAND MY CLIENT IS SURRENDERING VOLUNTARILY . . .
SIMULTANEOUSLY,
WHILE ASSISTANT DISTRICT ATTORNEY BOYER IS WORKING LATE, JEFF BYRD INFORMS HIM OF SODD'S SURRENDER . . .
. . . I'M HEADING UPSTATE TO JOIN MY PARTNER. BOYER, I WANT YOU TO KNOW THAT SODD IS COOPERATING FULLY . . .
AND I'M GOING WITH YOU-- I WANT TO BE THERE WHEN THAT HORTICULTURAL MENACE IS BROUGHT IN!
GOOD IDEA-- IT'S IMPORTANT THAT SOMEONE FROM THE D.A.'S OFFICE BE UP THERE FOR CNN-- SIR!
BUT . . .
UNBEKNOWNST
TO THE ABOVE PARTIES, A SPANNER HAS BEEN THROWN INTO SODD'S PLAN TO PREVENT A MONKEYWRENCHING . . .
YOU MEAN THIS ISN'T A CONSTRUCTION SITE-- IT'S A MILITIA COMPOUND?
THIS IS SOVEREIGN LAND, HIPPIE-- ON WHICH YOU AND YOUR COMRADES HAVE TRESPASSED!

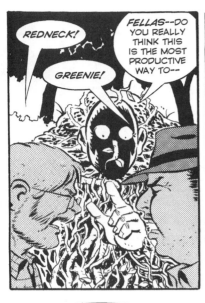

REDNECK!

GREENIE!

FELLAS--DO YOU REALLY THINK THIS IS THE MOST PRODUCTIVE WAY TO--

SHUT UP!

WHOEVER WOULD'VE THOUGHT THAT *BIGFOOT* WOULD BE SUCH A BIG MOUTH?

I'M TELLING YOU, MAN-- THAT'S *NOT* BIGFOOT!

DON'T PLAY YOUR ECO-WARRIOR HEAD GAMES WITH ME, MISTER! OBVIOUSLY, YOU'VE TRESPASSED ON *MY* PROPERTY BECAUSE YOU THINK MY PLATOON'S BEEN *HUNTING* FOR SASQUATCHES! BUT SEEKING THAT PRIMATE IS *NOT* ON OUR AGENDA ...

THEN LET US *GO!*

I *CAN'T* DO THAT, YOUNG LADY. IN FACT, I MUST DETAIN ALL OF YOU *UNTIL* THE REPUBLIC OF THE CONSTITUTION STRIKES A *BLOW* FOR FREEDOM.

WHAT THE HELL ARE YOU TALKING ABOUT?

I OWN THIS PROPERTY, BUT THE *GOVERN-MENT* WANTS TO PUT A ROAD THROUGH IT. THEY THINK THEY CAN JUST *TRAMPLE* ON *GOD'S GREEN EARTH* AND *MAN'S INALIENABLE RIGHTS.*

THEY'RE READY TO *PLOW* RIGHT THROUGH HERE. BUT I DON'T AIM TO LET THAT HAPPEN. AND *NOW* WITH YOU HERE, MAYBE THE GOVERNMENT WILL *LISTEN* TO ME--THINK OF YOU AND YOUR FRIENDS AS *PRISONERS OF WAR.*

HUH! YOU KNOW, SOME OF THESE TREES HAVE BEEN HERE FOR *CENTURIES* ...

THAT'S *RIGHT!* THE GOVERNMENT RAILROADED THROUGH SOME BOGUS ENVIRONMENTAL IMPACT STATE-MENT SO THEY COULD PUT IN THE ROAD-- BUT WHAT THEY'RE REALLY DOING IS *DESTROYING* OUR PRECIOUS WILDERNESS!

I HEAR YOU, MAN

IT'S NOT JUST *OUR* LAND BEING *VIOLATED* ...

NO, IT ISN'T ...

--IT'S THE *CHILDREN'S* ...

SHEESH!

173

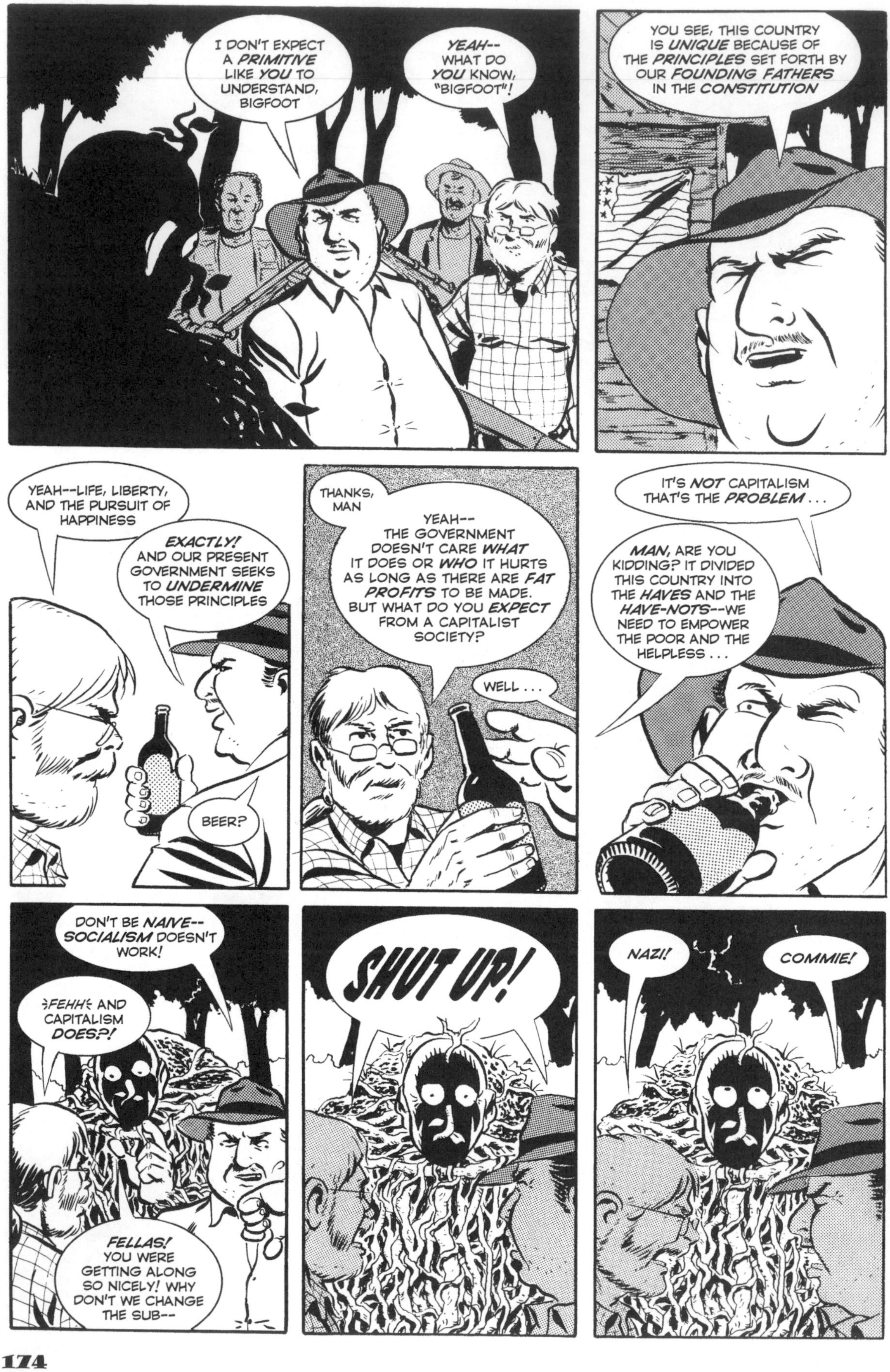

I DON'T EXPECT A PRIMITIVE LIKE YOU TO UNDERSTAND, BIGFOOT
YEAH-- WHAT DO YOU KNOW, "BIGFOOT"!
YOU SEE, THIS COUNTRY IS UNIQUE BECAUSE OF THE PRINCIPLES SET FORTH BY OUR FOUNDING FATHERS IN THE CONSTITUTION
YEAH--LIFE, LIBERTY, AND THE PURSUIT OF HAPPINESS
EXACTLY! AND OUR PRESENT GOVERNMENT SEEKS TO UNDERMINE THOSE PRINCIPLES
BEER?
THANKS, MAN
YEAH-- THE GOVERNMENT DOESN'T CARE WHAT IT DOES OR WHO IT HURTS AS LONG AS THERE ARE FAT PROFITS TO BE MADE. BUT WHAT DO YOU EXPECT FROM A CAPITALIST SOCIETY?
WELL . . .
IT'S NOT CAPITALISM THAT'S THE PROBLEM . . .
MAN, ARE YOU KIDDING? IT DIVIDED THIS COUNTRY INTO THE HAVES AND THE HAVE-NOTS--WE NEED TO EMPOWER THE POOR AND THE HELPLESS . . .
DON'T BE NAIVE-- SOCIALISM DOESN'T WORK!
FEHH AND CAPITALISM DOES?!
FELLAS! YOU WERE GETTING ALONG SO NICELY! WHY DON'T WE CHANGE THE SUB--
SHUT UP!
NAZI!
COMMIE!

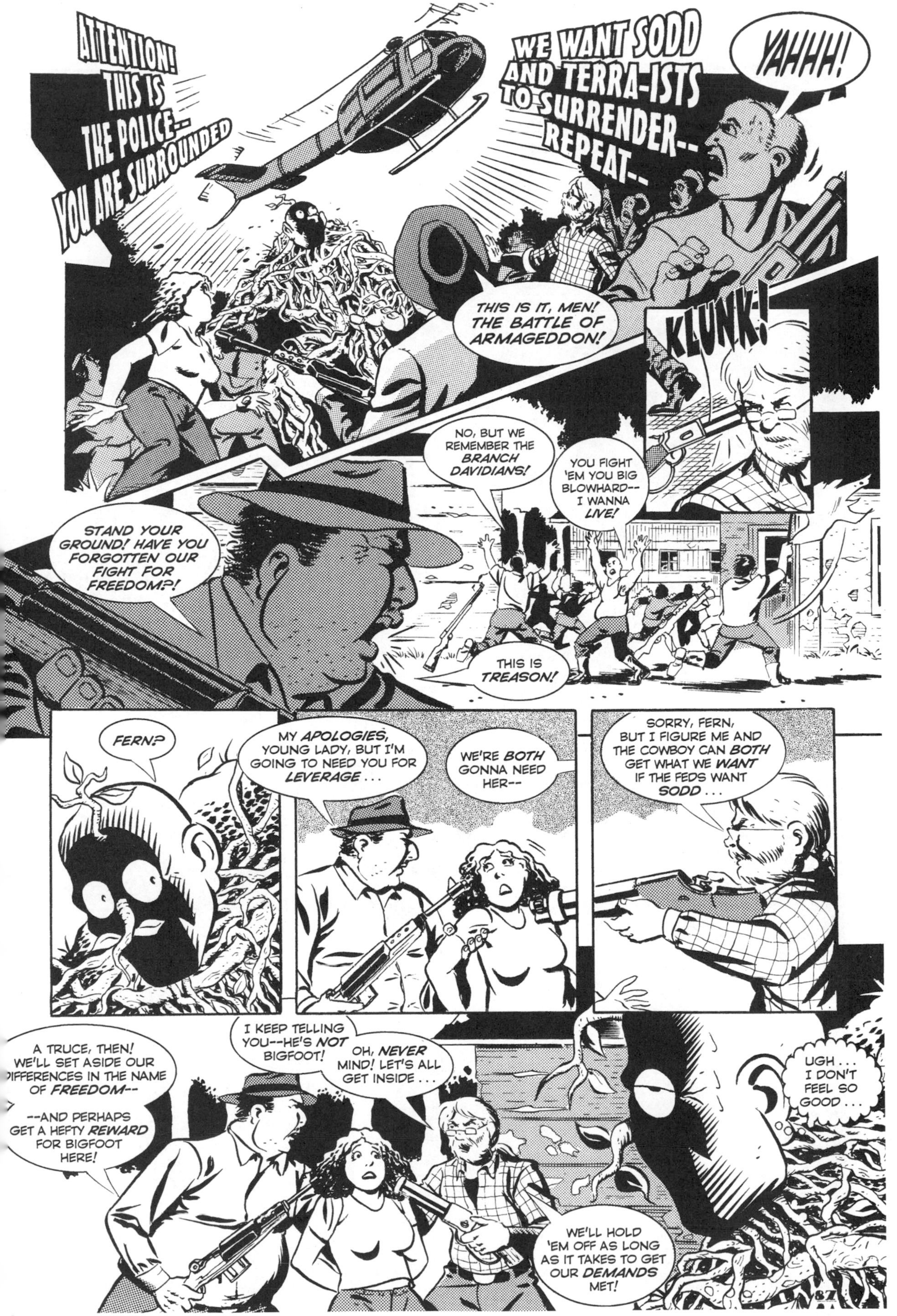
ATTENTION! THIS IS THE POLICE-- YOU ARE SURROUNDED
WE WANT SODD AND TERRA-ISTS TO SURRENDER-- REPEAT--
YAHHH!
THIS IS IT, MEN! THE BATTLE OF ARMAGEDDON!
KLUNK!
STAND YOUR GROUND! HAVE YOU FORGOTTEN OUR FIGHT FOR FREEDOM?!
NO, BUT WE REMEMBER THE BRANCH DAVIDIANS!
YOU FIGHT 'EM YOU BIG BLOWHARD-- I WANNA LIVE!
THIS IS TREASON!
FERN?
MY APOLOGIES, YOUNG LADY, BUT I'M GOING TO NEED YOU FOR LEVERAGE . . .
WE'RE BOTH GONNA NEED HER--
SORRY, FERN, BUT I FIGURE ME AND THE COWBOY CAN BOTH GET WHAT WE WANT IF THE FEDS WANT SODD . . .
A TRUCE, THEN! WE'LL SET ASIDE OUR DIFFERENCES IN THE NAME OF FREEDOM--
--AND PERHAPS GET A HEFTY REWARD FOR BIGFOOT HERE!
I KEEP TELLING YOU--HE'S NOT BIGFOOT!
OH, NEVER MIND! LET'S ALL GET INSIDE . . .
UGH . . . I DON'T FEEL SO GOOD . . .
WE'LL HOLD 'EM OFF AS LONG AS IT TAKES TO GET OUR DEMANDS MET!
87

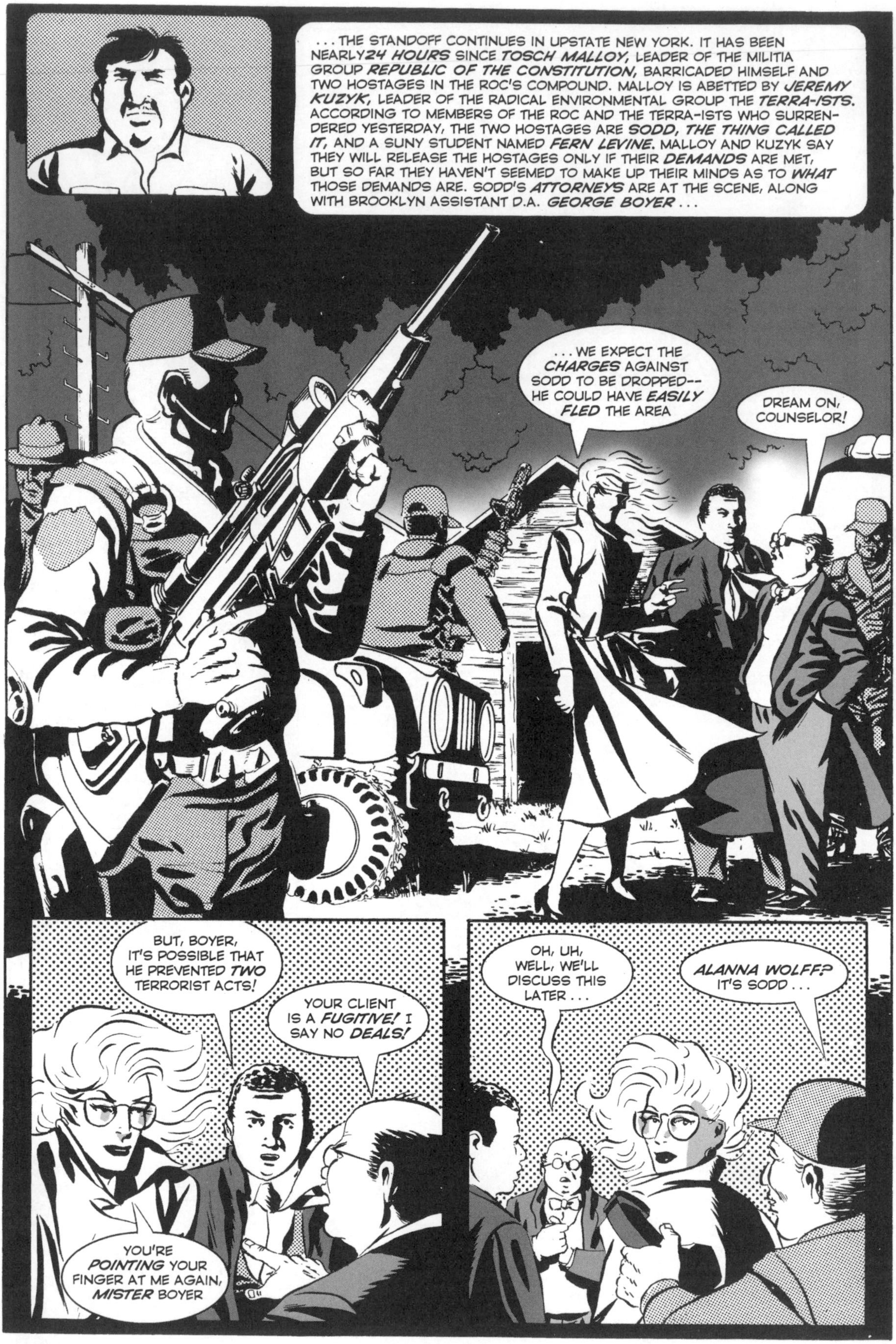
. . . THE STANDOFF CONTINUES IN UPSTATE NEW YORK. IT HAS BEEN NEARLY 24 HOURS SINCE TOSCH MALLOY, LEADER OF THE MILITIA GROUP REPUBLIC OF THE CONSTITUTION, BARRICADED HIMSELF AND TWO HOSTAGES IN THE ROC'S COMPOUND. MALLOY IS ABETTED BY JEREMY KUZYK, LEADER OF THE RADICAL ENVIRONMENTAL GROUP THE TERRA-ISTS. ACCORDING TO MEMBERS OF THE ROC AND THE TERRA-ISTS WHO SURRENDERED YESTERDAY, THE TWO HOSTAGES ARE SODD, THE THING CALLED IT, AND A SUNY STUDENT NAMED FERN LEVINE. MALLOY AND KUZYK SAY THEY WILL RELEASE THE HOSTAGES ONLY IF THEIR DEMANDS ARE MET, BUT SO FAR THEY HAVEN'T SEEMED TO MAKE UP THEIR MINDS AS TO WHAT THOSE DEMANDS ARE. SODD'S ATTORNEYS ARE AT THE SCENE, ALONG WITH BROOKLYN ASSISTANT D.A. GEORGE BOYER . . .
. . . WE EXPECT THE CHARGES AGAINST SODD TO BE DROPPED-- HE COULD HAVE EASILY FLED THE AREA
DREAM ON, COUNSELOR!
BUT, BOYER, IT'S POSSIBLE THAT HE PREVENTED TWO TERRORIST ACTS!
YOUR CLIENT IS A FUGITIVE! I SAY NO DEALS!
YOU'RE POINTING YOUR FINGER AT ME AGAIN, MISTER BOYER
OH, UH, WELL, WE'LL DISCUSS THIS LATER . . .
ALANNA WOLFF? IT'S SODD . . .

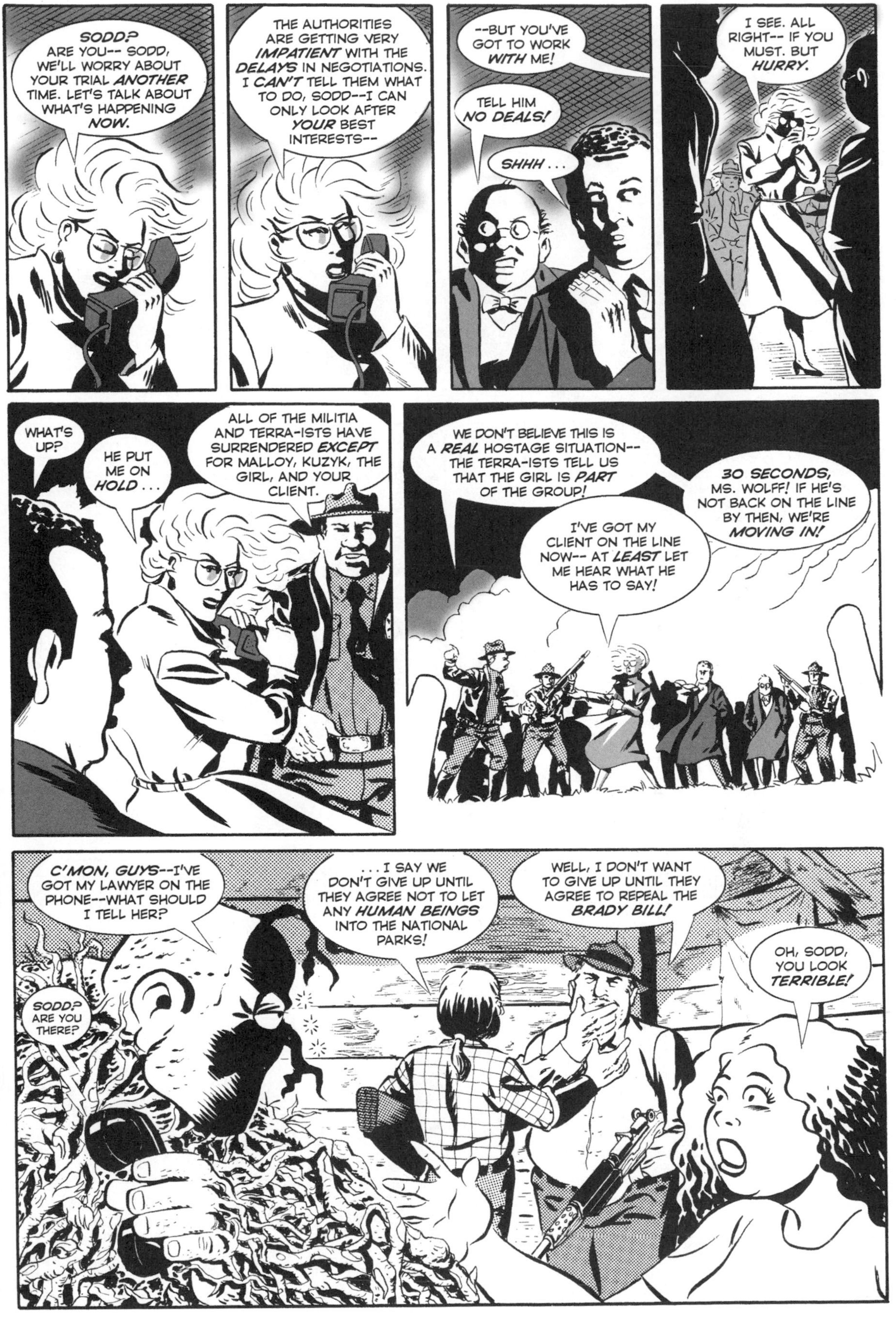
SODD? ARE YOU-- SODD, WE'LL WORRY ABOUT YOUR TRIAL ANOTHER TIME. LET'S TALK ABOUT WHAT'S HAPPENING NOW.
THE AUTHORITIES ARE GETTING VERY IMPATIENT WITH THE DELAYS IN NEGOTIATIONS. I CAN'T TELL THEM WHAT TO DO, SODD--I CAN ONLY LOOK AFTER YOUR BEST INTERESTS--
--BUT YOU'VE GOT TO WORK WITH ME!
TELL HIM NO DEALS!
SHHH . . .
I SEE. ALL RIGHT-- IF YOU MUST. BUT HURRY.
WHAT'S UP?
HE PUT ME ON HOLD . . .
ALL OF THE MILITIA AND TERRA-ISTS HAVE SURRENDERED EXCEPT FOR MALLOY, KUZYK, THE GIRL, AND YOUR CLIENT.
WE DON'T BELIEVE THIS IS A REAL HOSTAGE SITUATION-- THE TERRA-ISTS TELL US THAT THE GIRL IS PART OF THE GROUP!
30 SECONDS, MS. WOLFF! IF HE'S NOT BACK ON THE LINE BY THEN, WE'RE MOVING IN!
I'VE GOT MY CLIENT ON THE LINE NOW-- AT LEAST LET ME HEAR WHAT HE HAS TO SAY!
C'MON, GUYS--I'VE GOT MY LAWYER ON THE PHONE--WHAT SHOULD I TELL HER?
SODD? ARE YOU THERE?
. . . I SAY WE DON'T GIVE UP UNTIL THEY AGREE NOT TO LET ANY HUMAN BEINGS INTO THE NATIONAL PARKS!
WELL, I DON'T WANT TO GIVE UP UNTIL THEY AGREE TO REPEAL THE BRADY BILL!
OH, SODD, YOU LOOK TERRIBLE!

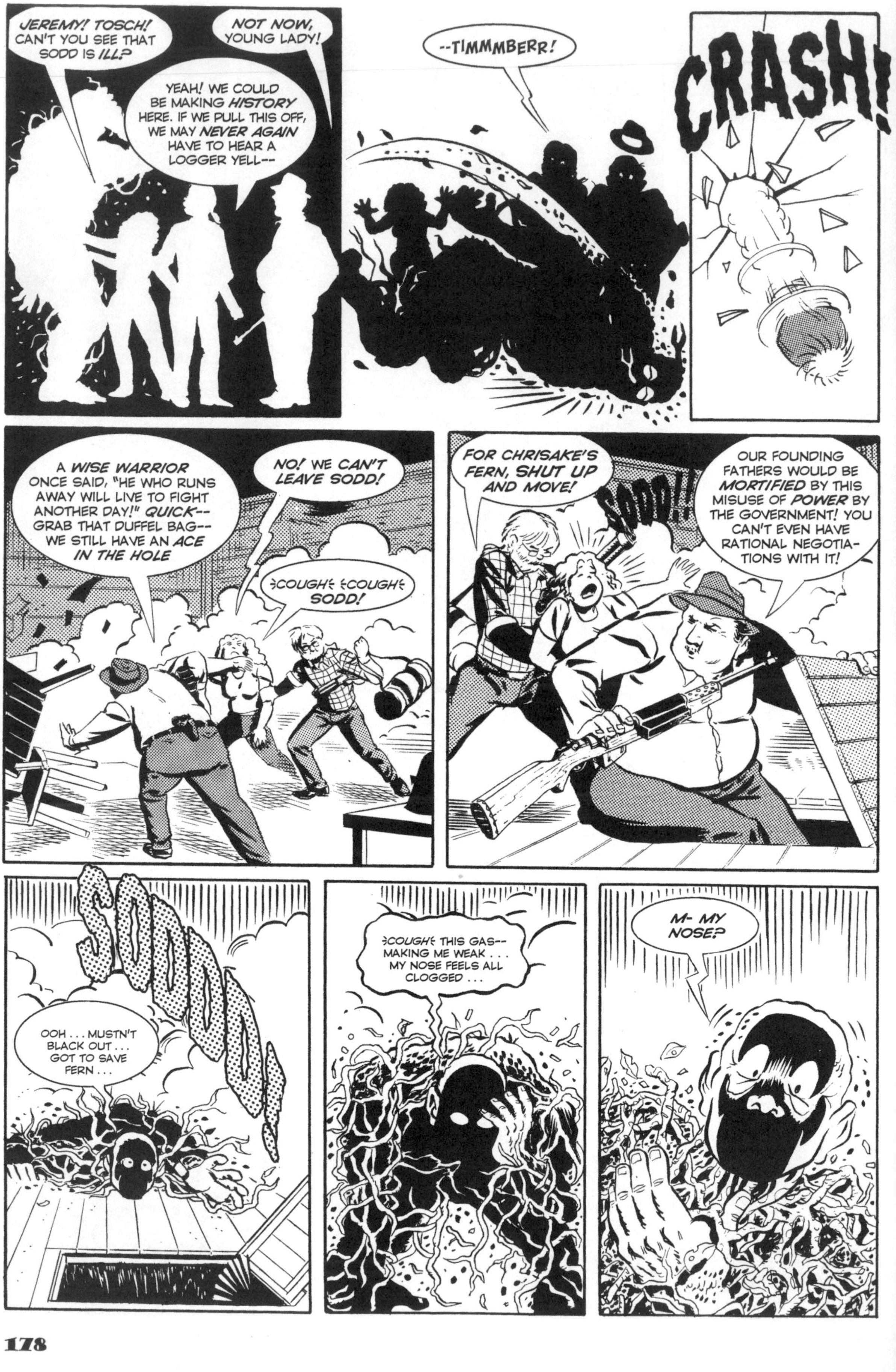

JEREMY! TOSCH! CAN'T YOU SEE THAT SODD IS ILL?
NOT NOW, YOUNG LADY!
YEAH! WE COULD BE MAKING HISTORY HERE. IF WE PULL THIS OFF, WE MAY NEVER AGAIN HAVE TO HEAR A LOGGER YELL--
--TIMMMBERR!
CRASH!
A WISE WARRIOR ONCE SAID, "HE WHO RUNS AWAY WILL LIVE TO FIGHT ANOTHER DAY!" QUICK-- GRAB THAT DUFFEL BAG-- WE STILL HAVE AN ACE IN THE HOLE
NO! WE CAN'T LEAVE SODD!
COUGH COUGH SODD!
FOR CHRISAKE'S FERN, SHUT UP AND MOVE!
OUR FOUNDING FATHERS WOULD BE MORTIFIED BY THIS MISUSE OF POWER BY THE GOVERNMENT! YOU CAN'T EVEN HAVE RATIONAL NEGOTIATIONS WITH IT!
SODDD!!
OOH . . . MUSTN'T BLACK OUT . . . GOT TO SAVE FERN . . .
COUGH THIS GAS-- MAKING ME WEAK . . . MY NOSE FEELS ALL CLOGGED . . .
M- MY NOSE?

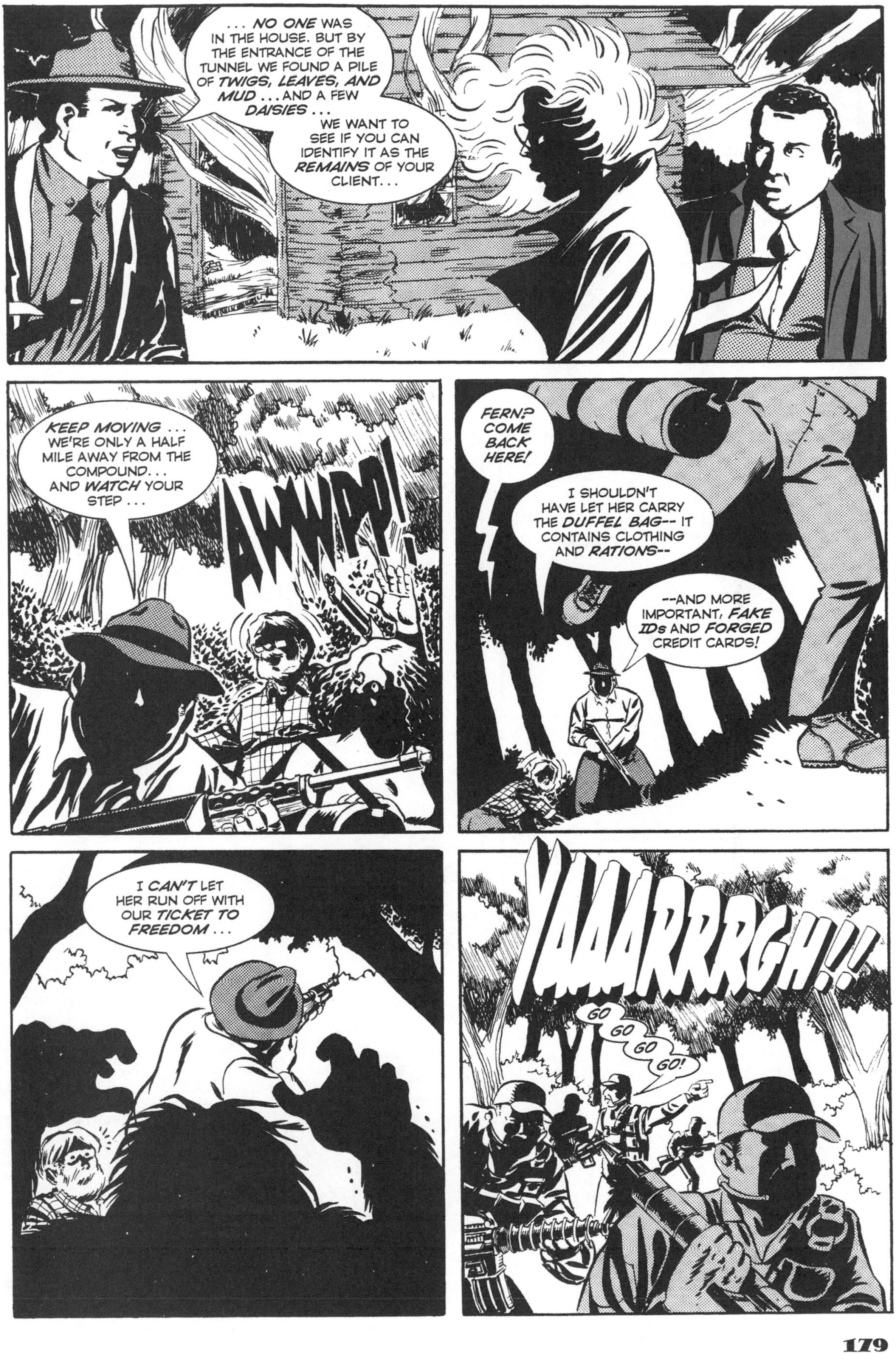
... NO ONE WAS IN THE HOUSE. BUT BY THE ENTRANCE OF THE TUNNEL WE FOUND A PILE OF TWIGS, LEAVES, AND MUD ... AND A FEW DAISIES ...
WE WANT TO SEE IF YOU CAN IDENTIFY IT AS THE REMAINS OF YOUR CLIENT...
KEEP MOVING ... WE'RE ONLY A HALF MILE AWAY FROM THE COMPOUND... AND WATCH YOUR STEP ...
AWWPP!
FERN? COME BACK HERE!
I SHOULDN'T HAVE LET HER CARRY THE DUFFEL BAG-- IT CONTAINS CLOTHING AND RATIONS--
--AND MORE IMPORTANT, FAKE IDs AND FORGED CREDIT CARDS!
I CAN'T LET HER RUN OFF WITH OUR TICKET TO FREEDOM ...
YAAARRRGH!!!
GO GO GO GO!

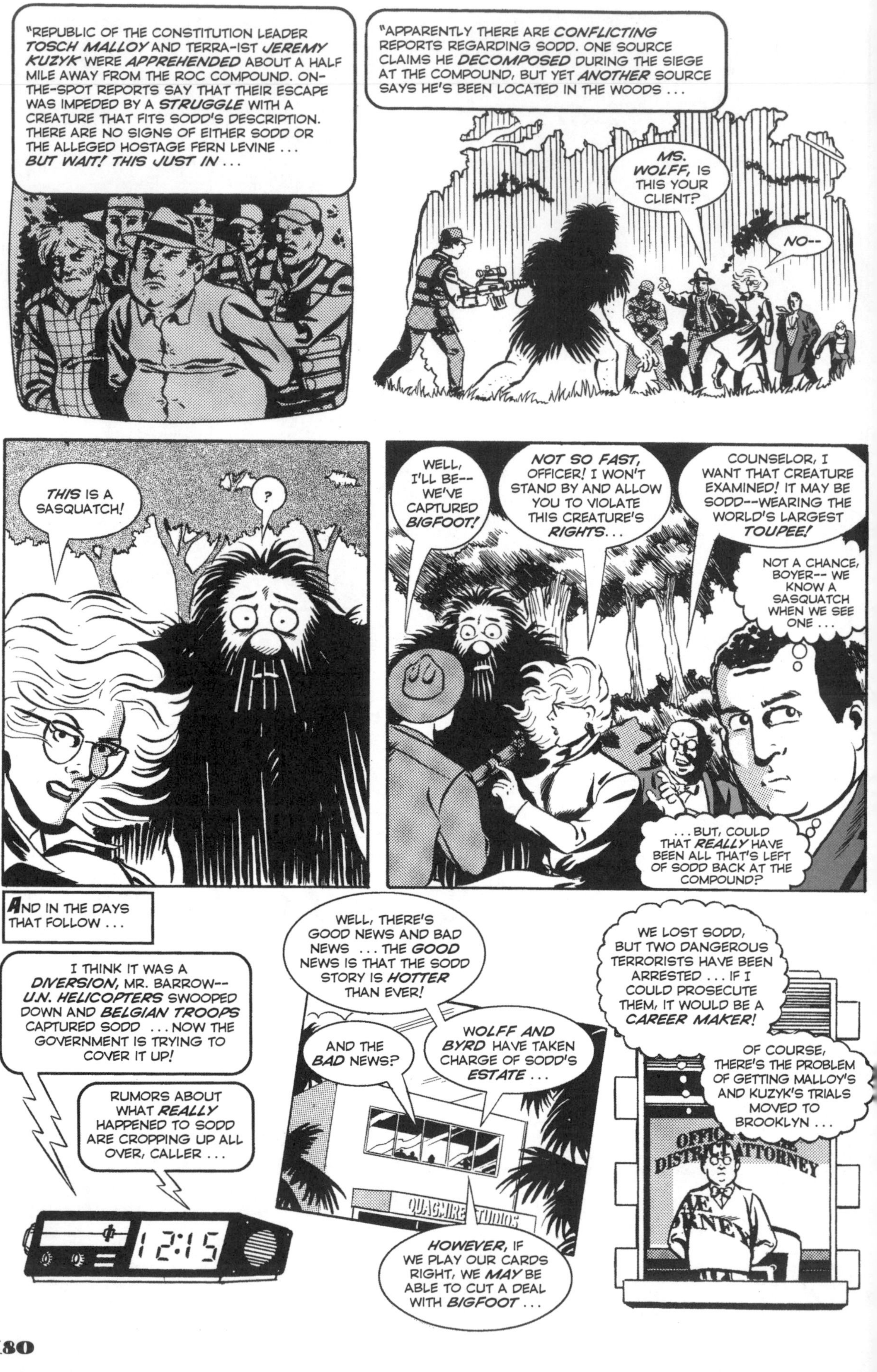
"REPUBLIC OF THE CONSTITUTION LEADER TOSCH MALLOY AND TERRA-IST JEREMY KUZYK WERE APPREHENDED ABOUT A HALF MILE AWAY FROM THE ROC COMPOUND. ON-THE-SPOT REPORTS SAY THAT THEIR ESCAPE WAS IMPEDED BY A STRUGGLE WITH A CREATURE THAT FITS SODD'S DESCRIPTION. THERE ARE NO SIGNS OF EITHER SODD OR THE ALLEGED HOSTAGE FERN LEVINE ... BUT WAIT! THIS JUST IN ...
"APPARENTLY THERE ARE CONFLICTING REPORTS REGARDING SODD. ONE SOURCE CLAIMS HE DECOMPOSED DURING THE SIEGE AT THE COMPOUND, BUT YET ANOTHER SOURCE SAYS HE'S BEEN LOCATED IN THE WOODS ...
MS. WOLFF, IS THIS YOUR CLIENT?
NO--
THIS IS A SASQUATCH!
?
WELL, I'LL BE-- WE'VE CAPTURED BIGFOOT!
NOT SO FAST, OFFICER! I WON'T STAND BY AND ALLOW YOU TO VIOLATE THIS CREATURE'S RIGHTS...
COUNSELOR, I WANT THAT CREATURE EXAMINED! IT MAY BE SODD--WEARING THE WORLD'S LARGEST TOUPEE!
NOT A CHANCE, BOYER-- WE KNOW A SASQUATCH WHEN WE SEE ONE ...
... BUT, COULD THAT REALLY HAVE BEEN ALL THAT'S LEFT OF SODD BACK AT THE COMPOUND?
AND IN THE DAYS THAT FOLLOW ...
I THINK IT WAS A DIVERSION, MR. BARROW-- U.N. HELICOPTERS SWOOPED DOWN AND BELGIAN TROOPS CAPTURED SODD ... NOW THE GOVERNMENT IS TRYING TO COVER IT UP!
RUMORS ABOUT WHAT REALLY HAPPENED TO SODD ARE CROPPING UP ALL OVER, CALLER ...
12:15
WELL, THERE'S GOOD NEWS AND BAD NEWS ... THE GOOD NEWS IS THAT THE SODD STORY IS HOTTER THAN EVER!
AND THE BAD NEWS?
WOLFF AND BYRD HAVE TAKEN CHARGE OF SODD'S ESTATE ...
HOWEVER, IF WE PLAY OUR CARDS RIGHT, WE MAY BE ABLE TO CUT A DEAL WITH BIGFOOT ...
QUAGMIRE STUDIOS
WE LOST SODD, BUT TWO DANGEROUS TERRORISTS HAVE BEEN ARRESTED ... IF I COULD PROSECUTE THEM, IT WOULD BE A CAREER MAKER!
OF COURSE, THERE'S THE PROBLEM OF GETTING MALLOY'S AND KUZYK'S TRIALS MOVED TO BROOKLYN ...

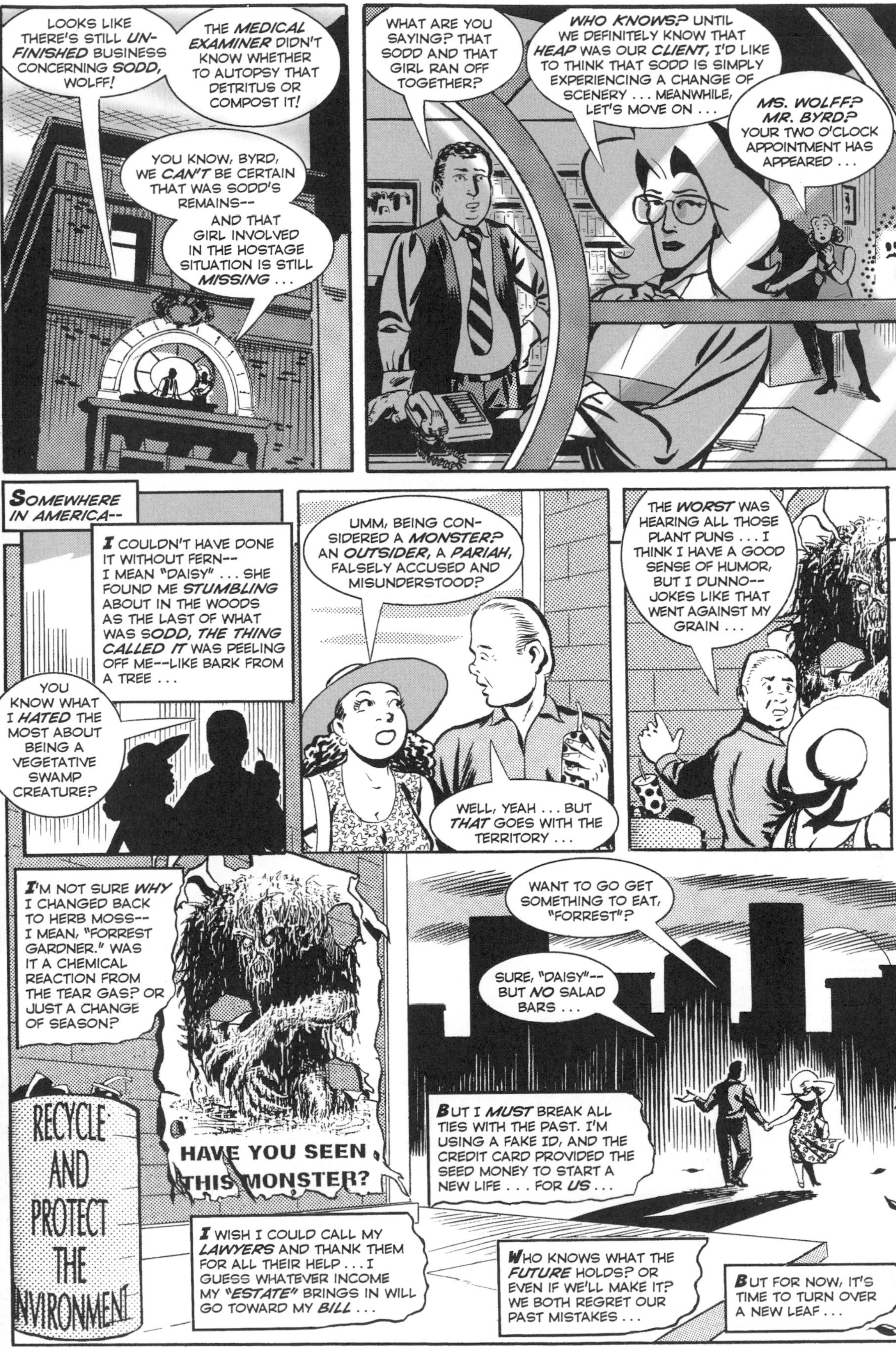
LOOKS LIKE THERE'S STILL UN-FINISHED BUSINESS CONCERNING SODD, WOLFF!
THE MEDICAL EXAMINER DIDN'T KNOW WHETHER TO AUTOPSY THAT DETRITUS OR COMPOST IT!
YOU KNOW, BYRD, WE CAN'T BE CERTAIN THAT WAS SODD'S REMAINS--
AND THAT GIRL INVOLVED IN THE HOSTAGE SITUATION IS STILL MISSING . . .
WHAT ARE YOU SAYING? THAT SODD AND THAT GIRL RAN OFF TOGETHER?
WHO KNOWS? UNTIL WE DEFINITELY KNOW THAT HEAP WAS OUR CLIENT, I'D LIKE TO THINK THAT SODD IS SIMPLY EXPERIENCING A CHANGE OF SCENERY . . . MEANWHILE, LET'S MOVE ON . . .
MS. WOLFF? MR. BYRD? YOUR TWO O'CLOCK APPOINTMENT HAS APPEARED . . .
SOMEWHERE IN AMERICA--
I COULDN'T HAVE DONE IT WITHOUT FERN-- I MEAN "DAISY" . . . SHE FOUND ME STUMBLING ABOUT IN THE WOODS AS THE LAST OF WHAT WAS SODD, THE THING CALLED IT WAS PEELING OFF ME--LIKE BARK FROM A TREE . . .
YOU KNOW WHAT I HATED THE MOST ABOUT BEING A VEGETATIVE SWAMP CREATURE?
UMM, BEING CON-SIDERED A MONSTER? AN OUTSIDER, A PARIAH, FALSELY ACCUSED AND MISUNDERSTOOD?
WELL, YEAH . . . BUT THAT GOES WITH THE TERRITORY . . .
THE WORST WAS HEARING ALL THOSE PLANT PUNS . . . I THINK I HAVE A GOOD SENSE OF HUMOR, BUT I DUNNO-- JOKES LIKE THAT WENT AGAINST MY GRAIN . . .
I'M NOT SURE WHY I CHANGED BACK TO HERB MOSS-- I MEAN, "FORREST GARDNER." WAS IT A CHEMICAL REACTION FROM THE TEAR GAS? OR JUST A CHANGE OF SEASON?
HAVE YOU SEEN THIS MONSTER?
RECYCLE AND PROTECT THE ENVIRONMENT
WANT TO GO GET SOMETHING TO EAT, "FORREST"?
SURE, "DAISY"-- BUT NO SALAD BARS . . .
BUT I MUST BREAK ALL TIES WITH THE PAST. I'M USING A FAKE ID, AND THE CREDIT CARD PROVIDED THE SEED MONEY TO START A NEW LIFE . . . FOR US . . .
I WISH I COULD CALL MY LAWYERS AND THANK THEM FOR ALL THEIR HELP . . . I GUESS WHATEVER INCOME MY "ESTATE" BRINGS IN WILL GO TOWARD MY BILL . . .
WHO KNOWS WHAT THE FUTURE HOLDS? OR EVEN IF WE'LL MAKE IT? WE BOTH REGRET OUR PAST MISTAKES . . .
BUT FOR NOW, IT'S TIME TO TURN OVER A NEW LEAF . . .

About the Author

Cartoonist **Batton Lash,** the creator of the humor/horror series *Supernatural Law* (aka *Wolff & Byrd, Counselors of the Macabre*), studied cartooning and graphic arts at the School of Visual Arts in New York, where his instructors included Will Eisner and Harvey Kurtzman.

After graduating he took on various art-related jobs, including copywriting and art for an ad agency and drawings for a variety of magazines, books, and other clients.

In 1979 one of those clients, Brooklyn Paper Publications, asked Lash to create a comic strip, and he came up with "Wolff & Byrd, Counselors of the Macabre," which ran weekly in *The Brooklyn Paper* until 1996 and in *The National Law Journal* from 1983 to 1997.

Since May 1994, Wolff & Byrd have held court in their own comic book series from Exhibit A Press, which Lash established with his wife, Jackie Estrada. Exhibit A has published several trade paperback collections of the comic book issues (see the next page) and two collections of the weekly comic strips, as well as five specials featuring Mavis, W&B's intrepid secretary.

Lash's non-W&B work has included writing *Archie Meets The Punisher*, the 1994 crossover between Archie Comics and Marvel Comics; the 2008 "Archie: Freshman Year" miniseries; and the *Radioactive Man* series and stories for Bongo Comics. Comic-Con International: San Diego, the premiere event of the comics industry, presented Batton with its Inkpot Award in 2004 for his contributions to comic arts.

Batton is aided and abetted by his wife and Exhibit A co-publisher, **Jackie Estrada**. A professional book editor for over 35 years, Jackie has been involved in the comics industry in various capacities since the 1970s, including having edited the Souvenir Book and onsite Events Guide for Comic-Con International numerous times. Since 1990 she has served as administrator of the Will Eisner Comic Industry Awards (the "Oscars" of the industry). She is particularly proud of having edited Mike Richardson and Steve Duin's *Comics: Between the Panels*, a 500-page four-color hardbound coffeetable book published by Dark Horse Books. In addition to editing all of Exhibit A's publications, Jackie handles the lettering chores.

Want *More* Tales of Supernatural Law?

Here's what some other graphic novelists have had to say about the series:

"*Supernatural Law* gets me laughing out loud every time!"—Frank Miller, *Sin City*

"The finest funny supernatural fiction ever created."—Neil Gaiman, *The Sandman, Neverwhere, Stardust*

"Batton's keen sense of humor is what makes his work so good and so enduring."—Will Eisner, dean of graphic novelists

"When I read *Supernatural Law*, I laugh my ass off!"—Jeff Smith, *Bone*

192 pages $16.95

And here's where to begin:

Tales of Supernatural Law collects the first eight issues in the comic book series.

In this collection you will encounter:

- A couple who has wished badly on "The Monkey's Paw"
- A house that becomes haunted every full moon
- A horror host accused of exposing children to violence
- Dawn DeVine, a supermodel with a terrible secret

- A sideshow manager who claims to have the "real" Dracula and Frankenstein's monster on display
- The first appearance of Sodd, the Thing Called It
- Zombies, werewolves, inter-dimensional creatures, and plenty of things that go bump in the night!

Exhibit A Press   www.exhibitapress.com   mail@exhibitapress.com